W9-BER-102

MCSE Guide to Microsoft® Windows® 2000 Professional Certification Edition

MCSE Guide to
Microsoft® Windows® 2000
Professional
Certification Edition

Ed Tittel
James Michael Stewart
David Johnson

THOMSON
COURSE TECHNOLOGY

Australia • Canada • Mexico • Singapore • Spain • United Kingdom • United States

MCSE Guide to Microsoft® Windows® 2000 Professional Certification Edition is published by Course Technology.

Associate Publisher	Kristen Duerr
Senior Acquisitions Editor	Stephen Solomon
Product Manager	David George
Production Editor	Jennifer Goguen
Developmental Editor	Deb Kaufmann
Quality Assurance Manager	John Bosco
Technical Reviewers	Marcus Goncalves, Floyd Winters, Scott Davis
Associate Product Manager	Laura Hildebrand
Marketing Manager	Susan Ogar
Text Designer	GEX Publishing Services
Composition House	GEX Publishing Services
Cover Designer	Efrat Reis

© 2003 by Course Technology, a division of Thomson Learning.

Thomson Learning is a trademark used herein under license.

All rights reserved. No part of this work may be reproduced, transcribed, or used in any form or by any means—graphic, electronic, or mechanical, including photocopying, recording, taping, Web distribution, or information storage and retrieval systems—without prior written permission of the publisher.

Disclaimer

Course Technology reserves the right to revise this publication and make changes from time to time in its content without notice.

The Web addresses in this book are subject to change from time to time as necessary without notice.

For more information, contact Course Technology, 25 Thomson Place, Boston, Massachusetts, 02210;

or find us on the World Wide Web at *www.course.com*.

For permission to use material from this text or product, contact us by

- Web: www.thomsonrights.com
- Phone: 1-800-730-2214
- Fax: 1-800-730-2215

ISBN 0-619-18682-8

Printed in Canada

1 2 3 4 5 6 7 8 9 WC 07 06 05 04 03

Brief Contents

TABLE OF CONTENTS

CHAPTER FOUR
Managing Windows 2000 File Systems and Storage   113

CHAPTER ELEVEN
Performance Tuning

CHAPTER TWELVE
Windows 2000 Application Support

CHAPTER THIRTEEN
Working with the Windows   447

APPENDIX A
Exam Objectives Tracking for Exam # 70-210: Installing, Configuring, and Administering Microsoft Windows 2000 Professional

APPENDIX B
Active Directory Overview

GLOSSARY

INDEX

COURSEPREP EXAMGUIDE

Preface

Welcome to the *MCSE Guide to Windows 2000 Professional Certification Edition!* This book offers you real-world examples, interactive activities, and hundreds of hands-on projects that reinforce key concepts and help you prepare for the Microsoft certification exam #70-210: *Installing, Configuring, and Administering Microsoft Windows 2000 Professional.* This book will also help prepare you for MCSA certification. This book also features troubleshooting tips for solutions to common problems that you will encounter in the realm of Windows 2000 Professional administration.

This book offers in-depth study of all the salient functions and features of installing, configuring, and maintaining Windows 2000 Professional as a client operating system. Throughout the book, we provide pointed review questions to reinforce the concepts introduced in each chapter and to help prepare you for the Microsoft certification exam. In addition to the review questions, we provide detailed hands-on projects that let you experience firsthand the processes involved in Windows 2000 Professional configuration and management. Finally, to put a real-world slant on the concepts introduced in each chapter, we provide case studies to prepare you for situations that must be managed in a live networking environment.

THE INTENDED AUDIENCE

This book is intended to serve the needs of those individuals and information systems professionals who are interested in learning more about Microsoft Windows 2000 Professional, as well as individuals who are interested in obtaining Microsoft certification on this topic. These materials have been specifically designed to help individuals prepare for this certification exam.

Chapter 1, "A First Look at Windows 2000 Professional," introduces the Windows 2000 networking family and describes the major features of the Windows 2000 environment. In addition, it explores the architecture of Windows 2000. Finally, it defines the minimal system requirements for Windows 2000 Professional and introduces the two major networking models under which Windows 2000 can be used.

In **Chapter 2**, "Installing Windows 2000 Professional," we discuss how to decide whether to perform an upgrade or a fresh installation of Windows 2000 Professional. We also explore how to boot using multiple operating systems. In addition, we examine installation options such as unattended installations; whether to install using Windows 2000 setup disks, CD-ROM, or across the network; and, finally, we describe the various Setup and advanced installation options.

Chapter 3, "Using the MMC, Task Scheduler, and Control Panel," examines the tools used to manage Windows 2000 Professional, namely, the Microsoft Management Console (MMC), Task Scheduler, and Control Panel applets. These tools are used to install and configure new hardware, create hardware profiles for changing system configurations, as well as configure PC cards and multiple displays.

In **Chapter 4**, "Managing Windows 2000 File Systems and Storage," we explore the differences between basic and dynamic storage and discuss the drive configurations supported by Windows 2000. This chapter also introduces file systems supported by Windows 2000 Professional: FAT, FAT32, and NTFS. Additionally, we describe permissions, sharing, and other security issues related to file systems. From an administrative standpoint, we also discuss drive, volume, and partition maintenance and administration under Windows 2000.

We introduce you to the concepts of users, groups, profiles, and policies in **Chapter 5**, "Users, Groups, Profiles, and Policies." This discussion includes setting up, naming, and managing local users and groups and default user and group accounts. From there, we examine the Windows 2000 Professional logon authentication process. This chapter concludes with in-depth coverage of the creation and management of user accounts, profiles, and local security policies.

Chapter 6, "Windows 2000 Security and Access Controls," teaches you about the Windows 2000 security model and the key role of logon authentication. We show you how to customize the logon process, discuss domain security concepts, and provide additional instructions for setting up the local computer policy. This chapter also shows you how to enable and use auditing. We conclude this discussion on security with details on encrypting NTFS files, folders, or drives using the encrypting file system (EFS).

We enter the world of networking in **Chapter 7**, "Network Protocols." Here, you'll explore the protocols supported by Windows 2000. In addition, we detail the intricacies of configuring and managing TCP/IP.

Chapter 8, "Internetworking with Novell NetWare," explores the features included with Windows 2000 Professional to interact with Novell networks. This chapter discusses connecting Windows 2000 Professional computers to NetWare servers. In addition, we examine the steps necessary to install and configure NWLink and the Client Service for NetWare (CSNW).

We examine remote access to Windows 2000 Professional in **Chapter 9**, "Remote Access Service." You'll learn how to use remote access under Windows 2000, configure various RAS connection types, and troubleshoot RAS connection problems.

In **Chapter 10**, "Printing," we discuss Windows 2000 print terminology and architecture, and examine the special features of the Windows 2000 print system. We provide hands-on instruction for creating and managing printers and printer permissions. This chapter concludes with a discussion on troubleshooting printing problems.

Chapter 11, "Performance Tuning," gives you the information you need to understand the performance and monitoring tools of Windows 2000. You'll learn how to create a Counter log for historical analysis, configure Alert events to warn of performance problems, and establish a baseline of normal system operation against which to measure Windows 2000 Professional performance. Finally, we discuss how to detect and eliminate bottlenecks to keep your system running as efficiently as possible.

In **Chapter 12**, "Windows 2000 Application Support," we discuss how to deploy DOS, Win16, OS/2, and POSIX applications. Finally, we explore how to fine-tune the application environment for DOS and Win16.

Chapter 13, "Working with the Windows 2000 Registry," discusses the function and structure of the Registry, which is the underlying database that stores system configuration information in Windows 2000. This chapter describes the purpose of each of the five Registry keys, how to use the Registry editing tools, defines the fault-tolerant mechanisms for the Registry, and provides information on how to back up and restore the Registry.

In **Chapter 14**, "Booting Windows 2000," we explain the steps taken by Windows 2000 Professional during the boot process. This discussion includes the operation of the key Windows 2000 startup files, the boot options offered via the Advanced Options Menu, and how to troubleshoot system restoration by using Safe Mode. In addition, we explore how to edit the Boot.ini file to manipulate the boot process, and how multiboot configurations are created and function.

We introduce you to disaster protection and recovery concepts in **Chapter 15**, "Windows 2000 Professional Disaster Protection and Recovery." Here, you'll learn how to back up data and settings on Windows 2000 Professional and recover a Windows 2000 Professional client's applications and data. Additionally, we introduce IntelliMirror technology and describe its key features, as well as remote operating system installation, and how it can be used with IntelliMirror to recover a PC remotely. Finally, we show you how to create and use an Emergency Repair Disk, the Recovery Console, and the Safe Mode options for starting Windows 2000 Professional.

This book concludes with **Chapter 16**, " Troubleshooting Windows 2000 Professional." Here, we examine how to collect documentation about your systems to aid in troubleshooting and preventing problems, and review common sense approaches to troubleshooting. In addition, we discuss how to troubleshoot general problems with Windows 2000 and use some of the troubleshooting tools of Windows 2000 Professional.

FEATURES

Many features in this book are designed to improve its pedagogical value and aid you in fully understanding Windows 2000 Professional concepts.

- ♦ **Chapter Objectives.** Each chapter begins with a detailed list of the concepts to be mastered within that chapter. This list provides you with a quick reference to the contents of the chapter as well as a useful study guide.

- ♦ **Illustrations and Tables.** Numerous illustrations of screens and components help you visualize common setups, theories, and architectures. In addition, tables provide details and comparisons of both practical and theoretical information.

- ♦ **Chapter Summaries.** The text of each chapter concludes with a summary of the concepts it has introduced. These summaries provide a helpful way to recap and revisit the ideas covered in each chapter.

- ♦ **Key Terms.** Following the Chapter Summary, a list of key Windows 2000 terms and their definitions encourages proper understanding of the chapter's key concepts and provides a useful reference.

- ♦ **Review Questions.** End-of-chapter assessments begin with a set of review questions that reinforce the ideas introduced in each chapter. These questions not only show you whether you have mastered the concepts, but also are written to help prepare you for the Microsoft certification examination.

- ♦ **Hands-on Projects.** Although it is important to understand the theory behind technology, nothing can improve upon real-world experience. Each chapter provides a series of exercises aimed at giving students hands-on implementation experience.

- ♦ **Case Projects.** Finally, each chapter closes with a section that proposes certain situations. You are asked to evaluate the situations and decide upon the course of action to be taken to remedy the problems described. This valuable tool will help you sharpen your decision-making and troubleshooting skills, which are important aspects of network administration.

- ♦ **CoursePrep ExamGuide.** Provides the information you need to master each exam objective. The ExamGuide devotes an entire two-page spread to each certification objective for the exam. In addition, there are several practice test questions for each objective on the right-hand page.

- ♦ **On the CD-ROM.** On the CD-ROM, you will find **CoursePrep®** exam preparation software, which provides 50 sample MCSE exam questions mirroring the look and feel of the MCSE exams.

TEXT AND GRAPHIC CONVENTIONS

Wherever appropriate, additional information has been added to this book to help you better understand what is being discussed in the chapter. Icons throughout the text alert you to additional materials. The icons used in this book are described here:

 Tips give extra information on how to attack a problem, time-saving shortcuts, or what to do in certain real-world situations.

 Important information about potential mistakes or hazards is highlighted with a Caution icon.

 Each step-by-step Hands-on Project is marked by the Hands-on Project icon.

 Case Project icons mark scenario-based assignments in which you are asked to implement independently the information you have learned.

INSTRUCTOR'S MATERIALS

The following supplemental materials are available when this book is used in a classroom setting. All of the supplements available with this book are provided to the instructor on a single CD-ROM.

Electronic Instructor's Manual. The Instructor's Manual that accompanies this textbook includes:

♦ Additional instructional material to assist in class preparation, including suggestions for lecture topics, suggested lab activities, tips on setting up a lab for the hands-on assignments, and alternative lab setup ideas in situations where lab resources are limited.

♦ Solutions to all end-of-chapter materials, including the Review Questions, Hands-on Projects, and Case Projects.

Course Test Manager 1.3. Accompanying this book is a powerful assessment tool known as the Course Test Manager. Designed by Course Technology, this cutting-edge Windows-based testing software helps instructors design and administer tests and pre-tests. In addition to being able to generate tests that can be printed and administered, this full-featured program also has an online testing component that allows students to take tests at the computer and have their exams automatically graded.

PowerPoint presentations. This book comes with Microsoft PowerPoint slides for each chapter. These are included as a teaching aid for classroom presentation, to make available to students on the network for chapter review, or to be printed for classroom distribution. Instructors, please feel at liberty to add your own slides for additional topics you introduce to the class.

STUDENT'S MATERIALS

Student case assignment files. The instructor's CD-ROM comes with student case assignment files for each chapter. These files contain the end-of-chapter Case assignments in electronic format so that students can enter their answers and submit them through e-mail, to a shared network folder, or print them for submission to the instructor.

Electronic glossary. An electronic glossary with hyperlinks is provided on the instructor's CD-ROM for distribution to each student, such as through a Web page or a shared network folder.

WHERE SHOULD YOU START?

This book is intended to be read in sequence, from beginning to end. Each chapter builds upon those that precede it, to provide a solid understanding of Windows 2000 Professional. After completing the chapters, you may find it useful to go back through the book and use the review questions and projects to prepare for the Microsoft certification test for Windows 2000 Professional. Readers are also encouraged to investigate the many pointers to online and printed sources of additional information that are cited throughout this book.

ACKNOWLEDGMENTS

Ed Tittel: I would like to thank my co-author, James Michael Stewart, for shouldering the burden of this book, and for helping us to meet an aggressive schedule. Your work continues to improve, Michael—please keep it up! I'd also like to thank Dawn Rader for her tireless efforts in coordinating this project on the LANWrights side. I'd also like to thank my family and friends for their continued support for my oh-so-interesting career, especially Mom, Kat, Robert, Blackie, and the Big Babboo.

Michael Stewart: Thanks to my boss and co-author, Ed Tittel, for including me in this book series. To my parents, Dave and Sue, thanks for your love and consistent support. To Mark, it seems that the stars are stacked against us, our plans to hang always seem to get foiled! To HERbert, why is it that only an hour after I clip your nails they are sharp as needles again!?!? And finally, as always, to Elvis—I recently was blessed with a sighting of your holy visage, wait a sec, that was just Earlvis, darn.

Collectively: Both of us would like to thank the crew at Course Technology for making this book possible, including Stephen Solomon, our acquisitions editor; Dave George, our project editor; Deb Kaufmann, our developmental editor; Jennifer Goguen, our production editor; and all the other people at Course Technology who helped with the book. We'd also like to thank Carole McClendon, our agent at Waterside Productions, for helping us to cement a business relationship that has proved so worthwhile to everyone. Thanks to one and all!

MICROSOFT WINDOWS 2000 PROFESSIONAL HARDWARE REQUIREMENTS

Following are the Microsoft defined minimum requirements to install and run Windows 2000 Professional:

- 166-MHz Pentium or higher microprocessor (P5 or equivalent compatible clone) or a Compaq Alpha processor with the latest firmware version installed (except for DECpc 150 AXP, DEC 2000-500, Multia, and AXPpci 33 processors)
- 32 MB of RAM for Intel (64 MB or more recommended; 4 GB maximum) or 48 MB of RAM for Alpha (96 MB or more recommended; 8 GB maximum)
- 2 GB hard disk with a minimum of 650 MB of free space
- VGA or higher resolution monitor
- Keyboard
- Microsoft Mouse or compatible pointing device
- A CD-ROM drive (12X or faster recommended)
- A high-density 3.5-inch disk drive
- A Windows 2000 compatible network adapter card and related cable

1

A First Look at Windows 2000 Professional

After reading this chapter and completing the exercises, you will be able to:

♦ Describe the Windows 2000 product family

♦ Describe the major features of the Windows 2000 environment

♦ Understand the architecture of Windows 2000

♦ Define the minimum system requirements for Windows 2000 Professional

♦ Understand the two major networking models under which Windows 2000 can be used

The technological achievements in the computing world are advancing faster than ever before. Consumers can purchase computer systems with power and capabilities that were mere fantasies just a few years ago, and do so at a lower cost. Microsoft has endeavored to maintain a competitive edge on these new powerful systems by continuing to evolve its operating system products. The latest manifestation of the Microsoft operating system product line is Windows 2000, which is a network and desktop operating system designed to take advantage of new hardware and the Internet to produce unsurpassed performance for network activities and application execution.

THE MICROSOFT NETWORKING FAMILY

The Microsoft networking family is a collection of **operating systems** from Microsoft that offers the capability to participate in a network as either a **server** or **client**. This family includes operating systems currently in production as well as older products. Products in production include Windows 2000 and **Windows 98**; older family members include **Windows NT**, **Windows 95**, and **Windows for Workgroups**.

Windows 2000 Family

The Windows 2000 product family, the latest from Microsoft, brings together the best of Windows NT and Windows 95/98 with advanced Internet, security, and connectivity technologies. The result is a network and desktop operating system that offers unsurpassed functionality, security, resource management, and versatility. Windows 2000 consists of four products: **Windows 2000 Server**, **Windows 2000 Advanced Server**, **Windows 2000 Professional**, and **Windows 2000 Datacenter Server**.

Windows 2000 Server

Windows 2000 Server is the successor to Windows NT 4.0 Server and is the core component in a client/server network environment. It establishes and maintains a **domain** in which other servers and thousands of clients can easily and productively participate. One of the most significant improvements to Windows 2000 Server as compared to Windows NT 4.0 Server is the introduction of **Active Directory**. Active Directory is a mechanism to centralize network resource and security management, administration, and control. Active Directory combines previously separate organizational structures into a single manageable whole that includes users, groups, security, services, network resources, and more.

In addition to improved security and resource management, Windows 2000 Server offers many other improvements for networks. These include Web and Internet services that enable improved access to existing resources and that simplify and strengthen the ability to host services and resources over intranets and the Internet. Windows 2000 Server is ideal for supporting network applications on small to medium-sized domains. Windows 2000 Server supports up to four processors out of the box and up to 4 GB of RAM.

Windows 2000 Advanced Server and Datacenter Server

Windows 2000 Advanced Server is an enhanced version of Windows 2000 Server focused on the high-end use of multiple processors and/or clustered processors. Advanced Server was developed to host high-end network applications, such as distributed databases, and to provide unparalleled performance in which instant access, wide availability, scalability, and fault tolerance are required.

Windows 2000 Datacenter Server offers even greater power and capabilities. It is designed for data warehousing, complex mathematical analysis, three-dimensional rendering, real-time transaction processing, and enterprise Internet Service Provider (ISP) Web site hosting.

Windows 2000 Advanced Server supports up to eight processors out of the box and up to 8 GB of RAM. Special Datacenter Server versions supporting up to 32 processors and 64 GB of RAM are available.

Windows 2000 Professional

Windows 2000 Professional is the standalone or client version of Windows 2000. Designed for speed and reliability, Windows 2000 Professional brings a solid computing environment to desktop and mobile computers. Windows 2000 Professional is the ideal client operating system for connecting to and interacting with a Windows 2000 domain. The majority of this book focuses on this product.

Windows 98

Windows 98 is the latest home computer operating system from Microsoft. In the second quarter of 1999, Microsoft released an updated version of the product, called Windows 98 SE (Second Edition). It contained several code patches and several new utilities and related software products.

 All of the most important Windows 98 update items are available for download from the Windows 98 Web area (*www.microsoft.com/Windows*), but the new bells and whistles are available only when you purchase the upgrade.

Windows 98 offers home users an easy-to-use computing environment for work productivity, Internet access, education, and entertainment. Windows 98 focuses on ease of use and a wide range of hardware support. It lacks security features and fault tolerance. Windows 98 does not have as stringent minimal system requirements as Windows NT or Windows 2000 Professional and is thus often the preferred operating system for older or less powerful computer systems.

 Microsoft has plans to develop a home user version of Windows 2000, to be released in 2001 or 2002.

Earlier Windows Operating Systems

As Microsoft releases updated and improved products to keep up with technological advances, its previous releases are pushed to the side. In that context, Windows 2000 has recently pushed Windows NT aside. Many products that are still modestly supported by Microsoft but are no longer actively developed are still widely used in networks.

Microsoft would like users to upgrade to the latest product releases as soon as possible to bring networks into compliance with current technologies. However, the expense of new products is often prohibitive for companies and individuals. Generally, you should upgrade only when technical support for your existing platform is no longer cost-effective and when the needs of your work tasks exceed the capabilities of your current system.

Windows NT, like Windows 2000, is a family of network operating systems: Windows NT Workstation, Windows NT Server, and Windows NT Enterprise Edition. These three versions serve functions similar to those of the Windows 2000 variants. If you would like more information on Windows NT, see the Windows NT Web area at *http://www.microsoft.com/windows/* or *Guide to Windows NT Workstation 4.0*, by Ed Tittel, Christa Anderson, and David Johnson (Course Technology, 1998, ISBN 0-7600-5098-8).

THE WINDOWS 2000 ENVIRONMENT

The Windows 2000 operating environment is a hybrid of Windows NT and Windows 98. The combination of the Windows NT core reliability and security with the Windows 98 **Plug and Play** capability and connectivity results in an operating system that is unsurpassed in function and features. The following sections highlight many of the characteristics of the Windows 2000 environment.

Portability

Windows 2000 can be installed on Pentium class (or higher, or equivalent compatible clones) x86 CPUs.

 Windows NT 4.0 did support PowerPC and MIPS R4x00 CPUs. However, in January 1997, Microsoft announced the termination of continued support for these CPU types. Thus, these systems hosting Windows NT 4.0 cannot be upgraded to Windows 2000. Originally, Microsoft planned Windows 2000 support for the Compaq Alpha platform. Unfortunately, all Alpha platform develpment was cancelled after Compaq decided to discontinue Windows NT/2000 development on the Alpha.

Multitasking

One of the great features of Windows 2000 is **multitasking**—a mode of CPU operation in which a computer processes more than one task at a time. Windows 2000 supports two types of multitasking—preemptive and cooperative. **Preemptive multitasking** defines a processor scheduling regime in which the OS maintains strict control over how long any execution thread (a single task within a multithreaded application, or an entire single-threaded application) may take possession of the CPU. The reason this scheduling regime is called preemptive is because the operating system can decide at any time to swap out the currently executing thread should another, higher-priority thread make a bid for execution (the termination of the lower-priority thread is called preemption). Windows 2000 supports multiple threads, and allows multiple duties to be spread among multiple processors. Most native Windows 2000 applications are written to take advantage of threads, but older applications may not be as well equipped.

Cooperative multitasking defines a processor scheduling regime wherein individual applications take control over the CPU for as long as they like (because this means that applications must be well-behaved, this approach is sometimes called "good guy" scheduling). Unfortunately, this type of multitasking can lead to stalled or hung systems, should any application fail to release its control over the CPU. **Windows 3.x** is one of the best examples of this type of environment because it runs on top of **MS-DOS**, a single-threaded operating system. In contrast, native 32-bit Windows 2000 applications are not hindered by such limitations. The default for Windows 2000 is that all 16-bit Windows applications run within a single virtual machine, which is granted only preemptive CPU access. This guarantees that other processes active on a Windows 2000 machine will not be stymied by an ill-behaved Windows 3.x application.

Multithreading

Multithreading refers to a code design in which individual tasks within a single process space can operate more or less independently as separate, lightweight execution modules, called **threads**. (Threads are called lightweight execution modules because switching among or between threads within the context of a single process involves very little overhead, and is therefore extremely quick.) A thread represents the minimal unit of code in an application or system that can be scheduled for execution.

Within a process, all threads share the same memory and system resources. A **process**, on the other hand, is a collection of one or more threads that share a common application or system activity focus. Processes are called heavyweight execution modules because switching among processes involves a great deal of overhead, including copying large amounts of data from RAM to disk for outbound processes, and repeating that process to copy large amounts of data from disk to RAM for inbound ones. Under Windows 2000, it normally takes more than 100 times longer to switch among processes than it does to switch among threads.

Multithreading allows an operating system to execute multiple threads from a single application concurrently. If the computer on which such threads run includes multiple CPUs, threads can even execute simultaneously, each on a different CPU. Even on single-CPU computers, threaded implementations speed up applications and create an environment in which multiple tasks can be active between the foreground (what's showing on the screen) and the background (what's not on screen). Windows 2000 is unusually adept and efficient at multithreading.

File Systems

Windows 2000 supports three file systems:

- *FAT (file allocation table)*: The file system originally used by DOS (actually, the Windows 2000 implementation is an extension of Virtual FAT, or VFAT, which includes support for long filenames and 4 GB files and volumes). Windows 2000 FAT is also known as FAT16.

- *FAT32*: An enhancement of the FAT16 file system developed for Windows 95 OSR2 and included in Windows 98. Windows 2000 includes support for FAT32 primarily to gain the 32 GB file and volume size improvement over FAT16. FAT32 volumes created by Windows 95 OSR2 or Windows 98 can be mounted under Windows 2000.

- *New Technology File System (NTFS)*: A high-performance, secure, and object-oriented file system introduced in Windows NT. This is the preferred file system for Windows 2000.

 TIP Versions of Windows NT up through 3.51 (that is, not including 4.0) supported the HPFS (High Performance File System), originally present in OS/2 and LAN Manager. Windows 2000 does not support HPFS.

Active Directory

Active Directory is a new control and administration mechanism of Windows 2000. Active Directory is supported by Windows 2000 Server and Advanced Server to create, sustain, and administer a domain or group of related domains. Active Directory combines the various aspects of a network—namely users, groups, hosts, clients, security settings, resources, network links, and transactions—into a manageable hierarchical organizational structure. Active Directory simplifies network administration by combining several previously distinct activities, including security, user account management, and resource access, into a single interface.

Windows 2000 Professional does not include support utilities for installing or managing Active Directory. However, by joining a domain, Windows 2000 Professional will interact with the Active Directory for all resource- and security-related communications.

Security

Windows 2000 incorporates a variety of security features, all of which share a common aim: to enable efficient, reliable control of access to all resources and assets on a network. To that end, the Windows 2000 security features begin with a protected, mandatory logon system. These features extend to include memory protection, system auditing over all kinds of events and activities, precise controls on file and directory access, and all kinds of network access limitations.

Windows 2000 is an operating environment developed to address the following business security needs:

- Enterprise isolation
- Multilevel security
- Auditing and resource tracking
- Isolation of hardware-dependent code

Also, numerous third-party companies offer security enhancements or extensions to Windows 2000 that cover everything from biometric authentication add-ons (so fingerprints or retinal scans can be used to control system access) to firewalls and proxy servers to isolate Windows 2000-based networks from the Internet or other publicly accessible networks.

One of the more popular enhancements to the Windows 2000 security system is the inclusion of the **Kerberos** v5 authentication protocol. Basically, Kerberos is used to authenticate a client to a server (that is, to ensure that they are both valid members of a domain) before communication between them is permitted.

Multiple Clients

Windows 2000 Server supports a wide variety of potential client platforms that can interact with resources on a Windows 2000-based network. Please note that the following list of clients includes two third-party operating systems, as well as a broad range of Microsoft products.

- Windows 95 and Windows 98
- Windows 3.x and Windows for Workgroups
- MS-DOS
- Macintosh
- OS/2
- Windows NT Workstation
- Windows 2000 Professional

 TIP   If TCP/IP (Transmission Control Protocol/Internet Protocol) is used on a Windows 2000-based network, any computer that supports this protocol can function as a client, even if with only limited capabilities. Because nearly all versions of Unix include built-in support for TCP/IP, this extends the reach of Windows 2000-based networks considerably.

Multiple Processors

Windows 2000 supports true **multiprocessing**—support for up to two CPUs is included in every standard version of Windows 2000 Professional. Only Windows 2000 Server and Advanced Server have options for more than four CPUs, and then only in specialized versions.

On multiple-CPU systems, as many processes or threads as there are CPUs can execute simultaneously. This means that multiple applications can execute at the same time, each on a different processor. The network administrator can adjust the priority levels for different processors, to make sure that preferred applications get a bigger slice of the CPUs that are available.

Compatibility

Windows 2000 supports a wide range of applications. This is accomplished through application subsystems that emulate the native environment of each application type. In other words, a virtual machine is created for applications in such a way that they are fooled into seeing themselves as the sole inhabitant of a computer system that matches their execution needs. Windows 2000 supports the following application types:

- DOS 16-bit
- Native 32-bit (**Win32**)

- **OS/2** 1.x character-based
- POSIX.1–compliant (**POSIX** is a platform-independent OS specification based on Unix; 1.1 represents the lowest level of recognized POSIX compliance.)
- Windows 3.1 and Windows for Workgroups 16-bit (**Win16**)

 Windows 2000 Professional supports most Windows 95/98-based programs, in particular Windows 32-bit business programs. It also supports MS-DOS-based programs, except for those that access the hardware directly.

Storage

Windows 2000 Professional supports huge amounts of hard disk and memory space:

- *RAM*: ↯ GB Intel (*Note*: Only half of the maximum RAM is available to any single process, including the OS kernel itself.)
- *Hard disk space*: 2 TB (terabytes) for NTFS volumes, 32 GB for FAT32 volumes, and 4 GB for FAT16 volumes

Connectivity

Windows 2000 supports a wide variety of networking protocols. The following protocols are included in the core OS:

- *AppleTalk*: The protocol suite developed by Apple for use with Macintosh computers. *Note*: Windows 2000 Professional can use AppleTalk to communicate with Apple printers and similar devices, but (unlike Server) it does not support client services for Macintosh users. In addition, AppleTalk remote access is supported by the AppleTalk Remote Access Protocol (ARAP) and the AppleTalk Control Protocol (ATCP).
- *Data Link Control (DLC)*: The protocol used to connect to IBM mainframes and network-attached printers
- *NetBIOS Enhanced User Interface (NetBEUI)*: An enhanced set of network and transport protocols built in the late 1980s to carry NetBIOS information, when earlier implementations became too limiting for continued use
- *NWLink*: Microsoft's 32-bit implementation of Novell's NetWare native protocol stack, IPX/SPX (Internetwork Protocol Exchange/Sequenced Packet Exchange)
- *TCP/IP (Transmission Control Protocol/Internet Protocol)*: The set of protocols used on the Internet, which has been embraced by Microsoft as a vital technology

1

Windows 2000 is compatible with many existing network types and environments, and it has native support for the following:

- TCP/IP intranets/Internet
- Integrated remote access networks
- Macintosh networks
- Microsoft networks (MS-DOS, Windows for Workgroups, LAN Manager)
- Enhanced NetWare connectivity

WINDOWS 2000 PROFESSIONAL HARDWARE REQUIREMENTS

Windows 2000 Professional requires a minimum configuration of hardware to function. It is important that your system comply with these minimum requirements. However, in nearly all cases, you should attempt to purchase the fastest, largest, or best device you can afford. The minimum requirements will enable functionality but will not provide optimum performance. Here are the Microsoft-defined minimum requirements:

- 166 MHz Pentium or higher microprocessor (P5 or equivalent compatible clone)
- 32 MB of RAM for Intel (64 MB or more recommended; 4 GB maximum)
- 2 GB hard disk with a minimum of 650 MB of free space
- VGA or higher resolution monitor
- Keyboard
- Microsoft Mouse or compatible pointing device (optional)

If you are installing from a CD-ROM drive, you'll need:

- A CD-ROM drive (12X or faster recommended)
- High-density 3.5-inch disk drive, unless you configured your PC to boot from the CD-ROM drive, and can start the Setup program from a CD, or if you have an existing OS that can access the CD-ROM drive

If you are installing over a network (Intel only), you'll need:

- Windows 2000-compatible network interface card (NIC) and related cable
- Access to the network share that contains the setup files

Hardware Compatibility List (HCL)

When it comes to configuring a Windows 2000 machine, the Microsoft **hardware compatibility list (HCL)** is an essential piece of documentation. The HCL supplies a list of all known Windows 2000-compatible hardware devices at the time of its creation. The HCL also points to each device's driver—which may be native (included as part of the Windows 2000 installation program), on a subdirectory on the Windows 2000 CD, or available only from the device's vendor. Because Windows 2000 works properly only if a system's hardware is Windows 2000-compatible, it's always a good idea to use the HCL as your primary reference when evaluating a prospective Windows 2000 system, or when selecting components for such a system.

Finding the HCL

Finding the HCL is not always easy. The easiest place to look is on your Windows 2000 CD-ROM, where it resides in the Support folder as a text and a Help file. But the HCL is not a static document—Microsoft's Quality Labs are constantly updating this file. The version of the HCL on the Windows 2000 CD-ROM will quickly become outdated because lots of new drivers and devices are introduced on a regular basis.

It's a good idea to look for the most current version of the HCL, especially when you'll be working with brand-new hardware. The most recent version of the HCL is available for online viewing on Microsoft's Web site at: *http://www.microsoft.com/hcl/default.asp*. On the other hand, if you have access to a copy of the TechNet CD, a new copy is published each time it changes, so the most recent CD is guaranteed to be less than four months old.

Why the HCL Is So Important

Windows 2000 controls hardware directly; unlike other operating systems, it does not require access to a PC's BIOS (basic input/output system) as is the case with Windows 95/98 and earlier versions of DOS and Windows. Although this gives Windows 2000 a much finer degree of control over hardware, it also means that Windows 2000 works only with devices with drivers written specifically for its use. This is especially true for SCSI adapters, video cards, and network interface cards.

Don't be misled into thinking that because a device works with Windows 95 or Windows 98, or even with Windows NT, that it will work as well (or at all) with Windows 2000. There's no substitute for systematically checking every hardware device on a system against the HCL to determine conclusively whether it will work with Windows 2000.

In addition, it is important to note that Microsoft's technical support policy is that any hardware that is not on the HCL is not supported for Windows 2000. If you ask Microsoft for support on a system that contains elements not listed in the HCL, they may blame all problems on the incompatible hardware, and not provide any support at all.

Fortunately, Windows 2000 automatically investigates your hardware and determines whether the minimum requirements are met and if any known incompatibilities or possible device conflicts are present in the system. So, if you check out the major components manually on the HCL, you can probably get away with letting the installation routinely check the rest of the system. If you *really* want to be sure your components are compatible, you can employ the Windows 2000 Hardware Compatibility Tool to detect your hardware and declare it compatible or not. This tool can be ordered online at: *http://www.microsoft.com/hwtest/default.asp*.

Preparing a Computer to Meet Upgrade Requirements

To upgrade a computer from a previous operating system to Windows 2000, you must first verify that the components of the computer match or supercede the minimum system requirements. Preparing a computer to meet upgrade requirements simply means you need to verify that each of the main system components (CPU, memory, storage space, video, keyboard, mouse, etc.) meet the requirements defined by Microsoft. To perform this activity, follow these steps:

1. Open the computer case.

2. Make a list of all present components including model and maufacturer.

3. For each of the hardware requirements of Windows 2000, verify that the component in your computer meets or exceeds the requirements.

4. For each additional component found in the computer, verify that it is listed on the HCL.

5. Remove any non-HCL compliant devices and replace them with HCL-compliant devices.

6. Proceed with your system installation.

FEATURES OF WINDOWS 2000 PROFESSIONAL

Windows 2000 combines Windows NT and Windows 98 features and capabilities with newly developed technologies. This section highlights some of the more outstanding features of Windows 2000 Professional.

Ease of Use

Building on the intuitive interface of Windows NT 4.0 and Windows 98, Windows 2000 offers even more features to simplify computer interaction, including:

- The Start menu automatically displays only the most commonly accessed items, making it easier to locate often-accessed tools.

- Dialog boxes for opening and saving files provide more detailed information (see Figure 1-1).

- Error messages are more detailed and context driven to aid in problem resolution.

- New Control Panel wizards simplify hardware installation and configuration (see Figure 1-2).

- AutoComplete remembers previously used text strings, allowing for quick reaccess.

- Customized toolbars and personalized menus are available in most native utilities.

- Improved network connections simplify the establishment and tuning of network connections of all types (including RAS/DUN, VPN, LAN, WAN, and direct connections).

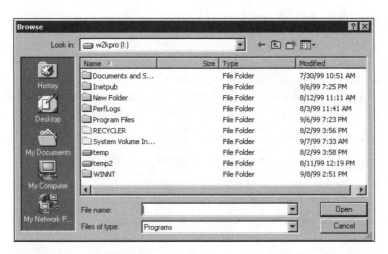

Figure 1-1   Dialog boxes now contain more detailed information

Figure 1-2   The Windows 2000 Professional Control Panel

Storage Improvements

Windows 2000 offers several storage-related improvements. Support for the popular Windows 98 (and Windows 95 OSR2) file system FAT32 is included. NTFS has been improved with support for EFS (Encrypting File System), enhanced content indexing to speed searches, and improved file object properties for identifying and grouping file objects. A disk defragmentation tool (see Figure 1-3) and a disk cleaning tool (which locates and removes orphaned files) have been added to the disk tool arsenal.

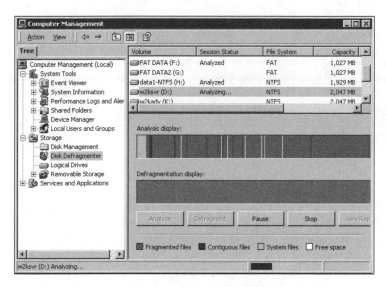

Figure 1-3   The Windows 2000 defragmentation tool

Internet Access

Interacting with the Internet has also been enhanced. AutoComplete allows quick reaccess to previously typed URLs or when filling out Web-based forms. A search assistant (see Figure 1-4) can help locate resources more efficiently. Printing to URLs, browser-based print queue status, and Internet downloadable printer drivers are all new features of the Windows 2000 Internet capabilities.

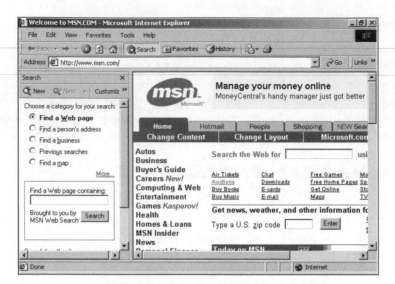

Figure 1-4   The Search tool

Security

Windows 2000 builds on the existing security structure of Windows NT and provides several enhancements. The most publicized enhancement is the use of the Kerberos authentication protocol to verify the server and client before communication over a LAN or WAN link is permitted. EFS, an extension of NTFS, allows files and volumes to be encrypted using a public-key scheme to prevent unauthorized access to confidential files. VPN (virtual private network) security is improved by the addition of the IPSec and L2TP protocols (for PPTP). Windows 2000 also includes support for smart cards—credit-card-sized devices that store information about the user who carries them, which is authenticated using a personal identification number—and other physical authentication methods.

NETWORKING MODELS

There are two networking models to which a Windows 2000 Professional computer can belong: a **workgroup** or a domain.

Workgroup Model

Microsoft's **workgroup model** for networking distributes resources, administration, and security throughout a network. Each computer in a workgroup may be either a server or a client, or both. All computers in a workgroup are equal in stature and responsibility, and are therefore called peers. That's why a workgroup model network is also known as a **peer-to-peer** network.

In a workgroup, each computer also maintains its own unique set of resources, accounts, and security information. Workgroups are quite useful for groups of less than 10 computers, and may be used with groups as large as 25 to 50 machines (with increasing difficulty). Table 1-1 lists the pros and cons of workgroup networking.

Table 1-1 Pros and Cons of Workgroup Networks

Advantages	Disadvantages
Easy-to-share resources	No centralized control of resources
Resources are distributed across all machines	No centralized account management
Little administrative overhead	No centralized administration
Simple to design	No centralized security management
Easy to implement	Inefficient for more than 20 workstations
Convenient for small groups in close proximity	Requires user accounts on each peer
Less expensive, does not require a central server	Increased training to operate as both client and server

Domain Model

By requiring one or more servers to be dedicated to the job of controlling a domain, the **domain model** adds a layer of complexity to networking. But the domain model also centralizes all shared resources, and creates a single point of administrative and security control. In a domain, it is recommended that any member of the domain act exclusively either as a client or as a server. In a domain environment, servers control and manage resources, whereas clients are user computers that may request access to whatever resources are controlled by servers.

Its centralized organization makes the domain model simpler to manage from an administrative and security standpoint, because any changes made to the domain accounts database will automatically proliferate across the entire network. According to Microsoft, domains are useful for groups of 10 or more computers. Microsoft estimates that the maximum practical size of a single domain is somewhere around 25,000 computers, but also describes other multidomain models that it claims can grow to almost arbitrary sizes. In real-world application, 3000 computers is believed to represent a reasonable upper boundary on the number of machines in a single domain.

No matter how many computers it contains, any Windows 2000 domain requires at least one **domain controller (DC)**. The domain controller maintains the domain's Active Directory, which stores all information and relationships about users, groups, policies, computers, and resources. More than one domain controller can exist in a domain. In fact, it is recommended that you deploy a domain controller for every 300 to 400 clients. Unlike domain controllers in a Windows NT 4.0 network, all Windows 2000 domain controllers are peers. All other servers and clients on a domain-based network interact with a domain controller to handle resource requests. Table 1-2 summarizes the pros and cons of the domain model.

Table 1-2   Pros and Cons of Domain Networks

Advantages	Disadvantages
Centralized resource sharing	Significant administrative effort and overhead
Centralized resource controls	Complicated, convoluted designs
Centralized account management	Requires one or more powerful, expensive servers
Centralized security management	Bulletproof security is hard to achieve
Efficient for virtually unlimited workstations	Expense for domain controllers and access lags increases with network size
Users only need to be trained to use clients	Some understanding of domain networks remains necessary
Not restricted to close proximity	Larger scope requires more user documentation and training

WINDOWS 2000 ARCHITECTURE

The Windows 2000 internal organization and **architecture** deeply influence its capabilities and behavior. The following sections explain the Windows 2000 operating system components and its two major operating modes in detail.

Windows 2000 is a modular operating system. In other words, Windows 2000 is not built as a single, large program; instead, it is composed of numerous small software elements, or modules, that cooperate to provide the system's networking and computing capabilities. Each unique function, code segment, and system control resides in a distinct module, so that no two modules share any code. This method of construction allows Windows 2000 to be easily amended, expanded, or patched as needed. Furthermore, the Windows 2000 components communicate with one another through well-defined interfaces. Therefore, even if a module's internals change (or a new version replaces an old one), as long as the interface is not altered, other components need not be aware of any such changes (except perhaps to take advantage of new functionality that was hitherto unavailable).

All Windows 2000 processes operate in one of two modes: **user mode** or **kernel mode**. A **mode** represents a certain level of system and hardware access, and is distinguished by its programming, the kinds of services and functions it is permitted to request, and the controls that are applied to its requests for system resources. Each mode contains only whatever specific components and capabilities might be needed to perform the set of operations that is legal within that mode. The details of what's inherent to user mode and kernel mode are explained further in the following sections. The use of modes in Windows 2000 is very similar to their use in Unix and VMS, and provides further proof of the modularity and built-in security mechanisms in Windows 2000.

1

 Windows 2000 is an object-oriented operating system; in user mode, any request for a system resource ultimately becomes a request for a particular **object**. An object is a collection of attributes with associated data values, plus a set of related services that can be performed on that object. Files, folders, printers, and processes are examples of objects. Because objects may be shared or referenced by one or more processes, they have an existence independent of any particular process in the Windows 2000 environment. Objects are identified by type (which defines what attributes and services they support) and by instance (which defines a particular entity of a certain type—for example, there may be many objects of type "file," but only one object can have a particular unique combination of directory specification and filename). Windows 2000 can control access to individual objects, and it can even control which users or groups are permitted to perform particular services related to such objects.

User Mode

All user interaction with a Windows 2000 system occurs through one user mode process. User mode is an isolated portion of the system environment in which user applications execute. User mode is permitted only mediated access to Windows 2000 system resources. In other words, any user mode requests for objects or services must pass through the Executive Services components in the kernel mode to obtain access. In addition to supporting native 32-bit Windows **APIs (application programming interfaces)**, a variety of user mode subsystems enable Windows 2000 to emulate Win16 and DOS environments, and even permit OS/2 character mode and POSIX.1-compliant software to be executed.

Windows 2000 supports three core environment subsystems:

- *Win32*: Supports Windows 2000, Windows NT, Windows 95, and Windows 98 32-bit applications directly, and, through emulation of virtual DOS machines (VDMs), supports both Windows 16-bit and DOS applications

- *POSIX*: Supports POSIX.1 applications, but these have only limited functionality; third-party solutions (most notably, those from SoftWay Systems) offer considerably more powerful and capable POSIX implementations for Windows 2000

- *OS/2*: Supports character-mode OS/2 1.1 applications (unfortunately, this makes most modern GUI-based OS/2 applications unusable in this environment; here, adds-ons to extend this functionality are available from Microsoft and third parties)

Each subsystem is built around an API that enables suitable Win16, DOS, OS/2, or POSIX applications to run by emulating their native operating systems. But even though other subsystems may be involved in some applications, the Win32 subsystem controls the Windows 2000 user interface and mediates all input/output requests for all other subsystems. In that sense, it is the core interface subsystem for applications in user mode.

As part of the Windows 2000 user mode, the security subsystem is solely responsible for the logon process. The security subsystem works directly with key elements in the kernel mode to verify the username and password for any logon attempt, and permits only valid combinations to obtain access to a system. Here's how: When a logon attempt occurs, the security subsystem creates an authentication package that contains the username and password provided in the Windows 2000 Security logon window. This authentication package is then turned over to the kernel mode, where a module called the security reference monitor (SRM)—the portion of the security subsystem that verifies usernames and passwords against the security accounts database—examines the package and compares its contents to a security accounts database. If the logon request is invalid, an incorrect logon message is returned to the user mode. For valid requests, the SRM constructs an access token, which contains a summary of the logged-on user's security access rights. The token is then returned to the Security subsystem used to launch the shell process in user mode.

 To gain access to the logon interface of Windows 2000, the user must enter a special key combination called the Windows 2000 attention sequence. This is done by pressing Ctrl+Alt+Delete simultaneously. The attention sequence invokes the Windows 2000 logon process; because this key sequence cannot be faked remotely, it guarantees that this process (which also resides in a protected memory area) is not subject to manipulation by would-be crackers.

Kernel Mode

The kernel mode, which is a highly privileged processing mode, defines the inner workings, or **kernel**, of Windows 2000. All components in kernel mode take execution priority over user mode subsystems and processes. In fact, some key elements within the kernel mode remain resident in memory at all times, and cannot be swapped to disk by the Virtual Memory Manager. This is the part of the operating system that handles process priority and scheduling (it's what provides the ability to preempt executing processes and schedule new processes, which is at the heart of any preemptive multitasking operating system, such as Windows 2000).

The kernel insulates hardware and core system services from direct access by user applications. That's why user applications must request any accesses to hardware or low-level resources from the kernel mode. If the request is permitted to proceed—and this mediated approach always gives Windows 2000 a chance to check any request against the access permitted by the access token associated with the requester—the kernel handles the request and returns any related results to the requesting user mode process. This mediated approach also helps maintain reliable control over the entire computer and protects the system from ill-behaved applications. At a greater level of detail, the kernel mode may be divided into three primary subsystems. These are the Executive Services, the kernel, and the hardware abstraction layer (HAL), each of which is discussed in the following subsections.

Executive Services

The **Executive Services** define the interfaces that permit kernel and user mode subsystems to communicate. The Windows 2000 Executive Services consist of several modules:

- I/O Manager
- Security Reference Monitor (SRM)
- Internal Procedure Call (IPC) Manager
- Virtual Memory Manager (VMM)

- Process Manager
- Plug and Play Manager
- Power Manager
- Windows Manager
- File Systems Manager
- Object Manager
- Graphics device drivers

The I/O Manager handles all operating system input and output. The I/O Manager receives requests for I/O services from applications, determines what driver is needed, and requests that driver for the application. The I/O Manager is composed of the following components:

- *Cache Manager*: Handles disk caching for all file systems. This service works with the Virtual Memory Manager to maintain performance. It also works with the file system drivers to maintain file integrity.

- *Network drivers*: Actually a subarchitecture in and of itself, network drivers are the software components that enable communication on the network.

- *Device drivers*: Minidrivers that are 32-bit and multiprocessor-compatible that enable communication with devices.

The Security Reference Monitor compares the access rights of a user (as encoded in an access token) with the access control list (ACL) associated with an individual object. If the user has sufficient rights to honor an access request after the access token and ACL are reconciled, the requested access will be granted. Whenever a user launches a process, that process runs within the user's security context, and inherits a copy of the user's security token. This means that under most circumstances, any process launched by a Windows 2000 user cannot obtain broader access rights than those associated with the account that launched it.

The Internal Procedure Call (IPC) Manager controls application communication with server processes such as the Win32 subsystem—the set of application services provided by the 32-bit version of Microsoft Windows. This makes applications behave as if **dynamic link library (DLL)** calls are handled directly, and helps to explain the outstanding ability of Windows 2000 to emulate 16-bit DOS and Windows run-time environments.

The **Virtual Memory Manager (VMM)** keeps track of the addressable memory space in the Windows 2000 environment. This includes both physical RAM and one or more paging files on disk, which are called **virtual memory** when used in concert. The operation of the VMM will be discussed in more detail later in this chapter.

The Process Manager primarily tracks two kernel-dispatched objects: processes and threads. It is responsible for creating and tracking processes and threads, and then for deleting them (and cleaning up) after they're no longer needed.

The Plug and Play Manager handles the loading, unloading, and configuration of device drivers for Plug and Play hardware. This manager allows the hot-swapping of devices and on-the-fly reconfiguration. Additionally, if a non–Plug-and–Play device uses a Plug-and–Play supporting device driver, it can be controlled through this manager.

The Power Manager is used to monitor and control the use of power. Typically, the services offered by the Power Manager are employed on notebook computers running on batteries or in other environments in which power is an issue. Some of the power-saving features offered include hard drive and CD-ROM drive power down, video/monitor shutdown, and peripheral disconnection.

The Windows Manager introduces a method of network-based centralized control to Windows 2000. It can be used to distribute software, manage systems remotely, and provide a programming interface for third-party management software.

The File System Manager is responsible for maintaining access and control over the file systems of the Windows 2000 environment. The File System manager controls file I/O transfers for all the file systems. Each 32-bit, protected-mode redirector is implemented as a file system driver.

The Object Manager manages all system objects by maintaining object naming and security functions. It allocates system objects, monitors their use, and removes them when they are no longer needed. The Object Manager maintains the following system objects:

- Directory objects
- ObjectType objects
- Link objects
- Event objects
- Process and Thread objects
- Port objects
- File objects

The Kernel

All processes in Windows 2000 consist of one or more threads coordinated and scheduled by the kernel. Executive Services use the kernel to communicate with each other concerning the processes that they share. The kernel runs in privileged mode along with the HAL and the other Executive Services. This means that the kernel is allowed direct access to all system resources. It cannot be paged to disk, meaning that it must run in real memory. A misbehaved kernel process can stall or crash the operating system—a primary reason why direct access to this level of system operation is not available to user mode applications.

The Hardware Abstraction Layer (HAL)

The **hardware abstraction layer (HAL)** ultimately controls all direct access to hardware. This is the only module written entirely in low-level, hardware-dependent code. Its goal is to isolate any hardware-dependent code in order to prevent direct access to hardware. It is the HAL that helps to make Windows 2000 scaleable across multiple processors.

1

Memory Architecture

The memory architecture of Windows 2000 helps make this operating system robust, reliable, and powerful. As noted earlier, Windows 2000 Professional can manage as much as 4 GB of RAM.

Windows 2000 uses a flat (non-multidimensional) 32-bit memory model. It is based on a virtual memory, **demand paging** method that is a flat, linear address space of up to 2 GB allocated to each 32-bit application. Non-32-bit Windows applications, such as Win16, MS-DOS, and OS/2, are managed similarly except that all subsystem components, including the actual application, run within a single 2 GB address space.

 The unit of memory that the Virtual Memory Manager manipulates is called a **page**. A page is 4 KB in size. Pages are stored to and retrieved from disk-based files called page files or paging files. These files are also used for memory reindexing and mapping to avoid allocating memory between unused contiguous space or to prevent fragmentation of physical memory.

The Windows 2000 memory model is a flat model that grows according to the demand for memory, as opposed to every section of memory having a fixed role (as in the problematic Conventional, Expanded, HMA, and Extended Memory architecture present in MS-DOS and Windows 3.x).

CHAPTER SUMMARY

❏ This chapter introduced you to the features and architecture of Windows 2000. Windows 2000 is a product family with at least four members: Professional, Server, Advanced Server, and Datacenter Server. Windows 2000 offers a distinct operating environment, which boasts portability, multitasking, multithreading, multiple file systems (FAT, FAT32, NTFS), Active Directory, robust security, multiple clients, multiple processors, wide application support, large RAM and storage capacity, and a wide range of network connectivity options. Windows 2000 is an inherently networkable operating system with built-in connectivity solutions for NetWare, Macintosh, and TCP/IP. This allows easy implementation on multivendor networks.

❏ Windows 2000 has specific minimum hardware requirements for the Intel platform. Additionally, the hardware compatibility list (HCL) lists all devices known to be compatible with Windows 2000.

❏ Windows 2000 can participate in either of two networking models—workgroup or domain.

❏ Windows 2000 is based on a modular programming technique. Its main processing mechanism is divided into two modes. User mode hosts all user processes and accesses resources via the Executive Services. The kernel mode hosts all system processes and mediates all resource access. The separation of modes provides for a more stable and secure computing environment. User mode supports the application subsystems that enable Windows 2000 to execute DOS, WIN16, WIN32, POSIX, and OS/2 software. Kernel mode's Executive Services manage all operations, including I/O, security, IPC, memory, processes, Plug and Play support, power, distributed control, file systems, objects, and graphical devices.

❑ The Windows 2000 virtual memory model combines the use of both physical RAM and paging files into a demand paging mechanism to maximize memory use and efficiency. Windows 2000 is easy to use, offers new storage capabilities, provides improved Internet access, and maintains strict security.

KEY TERMS

Active Directory — A centralized resource and security management, administration, and control mechanism used to support and maintain a Windows 2000 domain. The Active Directory is hosted by domain controllers.

AppleTalk — The network protocol stack used predominantly in Apple Macintosh networks; this protocol is bundled with Windows 2000.

application programming interface (API) — A set of software routines referenced by an application to access underlying application services.

architecture — The layout of operating system components and their relationships to one another.

client — A computer used to access network resources.

cooperative multitasking — A computing environment in which the individual application maintains control over the duration that its threads use operating time on the CPU.

Data Link Control (DLC) — A low-level network protocol designed for IBM connectivity, remote booting, and network printing.

demand paging — The act of requesting free pages of memory from RAM for an active application.

domain — A centralized enterprise model used in Microsoft networks.

domain controller (DC) — A computer that maintains the domain's Active Directory, which stores all information and relationships about users, groups, policies, computers, and resources.

domain model — The networking setup in which there is centralized administrative and security control. One or more servers are dedicated to the task of controlling the domain, providing access and authentication for shared domain resources to member computers.

dynamic link library (DLL) — A Microsoft Windows executable code module that is loaded on demand. Each DLL performs a unique function or small set of functions requested by applications.

Executive Services — The collection of kernel mode components designed for operating system management.

FAT (file allocation table) or **FAT16** — The file system used in versions of MS–DOS. Supported in Windows 2000 in its VFAT form, which adds long filenames and 4 GB file and volume sizes.

FAT32 — The 32-bit enhanced version of FAT introduced by Windows 95 OSR2, and which expands the file and volume size of FAT to 32 GB. FAT32 is supported by Windows 2000.

hardware abstraction layer (HAL) — One of the few components of the Windows 2000 architecture that is written in hardware-dependent code. It is designed to protect hardware resources.

hardware compatibility list (HCL) — Microsoft's updated list of supported hardware for Windows 2000.

Kerberos — An encryption authentication scheme employed by Windows 2000 to verify the identity of a server and a client before actual data is transferred.

kernel — The core of the Microsoft Windows 2000 operating system. It is designed to facilitate all activity within the Executive Services.

kernel mode — The level where objects can only be manipulated by threads directly from an application subsystem.

mode — A programming and operational separation of components, functions, and services.

MS–DOS — One of the most popular character-based operating systems for personal computers. Many DOS concepts are still in use by modern operating systems.

multiprocessing — The ability to distribute threads among multiple CPUs on the same system.

multitasking — The ability to run more than one program at the same time.

multithreading — The ability of an operating system and hardware to execute multiple pieces of code (or threads) from a single application simultaneously.

New Technology File System (NTFS) — The high-performance file system supported by Windows 2000, which offers file-level security, encryption, compression, auditing, and more. Supports volumes up to 16 Exabytes theoretically, but Microsoft recommends volumes not exceed 2 Terabytes.

NWLink — Microsoft's implementation of Novell's IPX/SPX protocol, used for Microsoft Networking or for facilitating connectivity with Novell networks.

object — A collection of data and/or abilities of a service that can be shared and used by one or more processes.

operating system — Software designed to work directly with hardware to provide a computing environment within which production and entertainment software can execute, and which creates a user interface to allow human interaction with the computer.

OS/2 — An operating system developed by IBM. Windows 2000 offers some OS/2 application support.

page — An individual unit of memory that the Virtual Memory Manager manipulates (moves from RAM to paging file and vice versa).

peer-to-peer — A type of networking in which each computer can be a client to other computers, and act as a server as well.

Plug and Play — The ability of Windows 2000 to recognize hardware, automatically install drivers, and perform configuration changes on the fly.

POSIX — A subsystem that is sanctioned by the IEEE for maintaining consistency between Windows 2000 and various flavors of Unix.

preemptive multitasking — A computing environment in which the operating system maintains control over the duration of operating time any thread (a single process of an application) is granted on the CPU.

process — A collection of one or more threads.

server — The networked computer that responds to client requests for network resources.

TCP/IP (Transmission Control Protocol/Internet Protocol) — A suite of protocols evolved from the Department of Defense's ARPANet. It is used for connectivity in LANs as well as the Internet.

thread — The most basic unit of programming code that can be scheduled for execution.

user mode — The area in which private user applications and their respective subsystems lie.

virtual memory — A Windows 2000 kernel service that stores memory pages that are not currently in use by the system in a paging file. This frees up memory for other uses. Virtual memory also hides the swapping of memory from applications and higher-level services.

Virtual Memory Manager (VMM) — The part of the operating system that handles process priority and scheduling, providing the ability to preempt executing processes and schedule new processes.

Win16 — The subsystem in Windows 2000 that allows for the support of 16-bit Windows applications.

Win32 — The main 32-bit subsystem used by Win32 applications and other application subsystems.

Windows 2000 Advanced Server — The new Microsoft network operating system (NOS) version designed to function as a high-end resource on a network.

Windows 2000 Datacenter Server — An enhanced version of Windows 2000 Server developed to host high-end applications, as well as support data warehousing, real-time transaction processing, and enterprise Web site hosting.

Windows 2000 Professional — The new Microsoft NOS version designed to function as a client/workstation on a network.

Windows 2000 Server — The new Microsoft NOS version designed to function as a resource host on a network.

Windows 3.x — An older, 16-bit version of Windows. Windows 2000 supports backward compatibility with most Windows 3.x applications.

Windows 95 — The 32-bit version of Windows that can operate as a standalone system or in a networked environment.

Windows 98 — An updated version of Windows 95 with improved Internet and network connectivity.

Windows for Workgroups — A version of Windows 3.x that includes minimal network support to allow the software to act as a network client.

Windows NT — The Microsoft network operating system that was the predecessor to Windows 2000.

workgroup — A networking scheme in which resources, administration, and security are distributed throughout the network.

workgroup model — The networking setup in which users are managed jointly through the use of workgroups to which users are assigned.

REVIEW QUESTIONS

1. Which of the following application environments does Windows 2000 support at least minimally?

   a. PICK

   b. SunOS

   c. OS/2

   d. X-Windows

2. Windows 2000 supports _____ of memory and _____ of disk space.

3. Which of the following are kernel mode components in Windows 2000? (Choose all that apply.)

   a. Virtual DOS machines

   b. Security Reference Monitor

   c. hardware abstraction layer

   d. Win16 subsystem

4. Windows 2000 supports only cooperative multitasking. True or False?

5. Windows 2000 supports the HPFS file system. True or False?

6. Windows 2000 has inherent support for facilitating connectivity to which of the following? (Choose all that apply.)

   a. Novell NetWare

   b. Macintosh printers

   c. Linux

   d. TCP/IP networks

7. Memory pages are stored in units of:

    a. 2 KB

    b. 4 KB

    c. 16 KB

    d. 64 KB

8. Which of the following operating systems can be used as a client on a Windows 2000 network? (Choose all that apply.)

    a. Windows for Workgroups

    b. Windows NT 4.0 Workstation

    c. MS-DOS

    d. Windows 98

9. If you want users to share resources, but have no concern for local security on the system, which operating system would be your best choice?

    a. Windows 98

    b. Windows NT Workstation

    c. Windows 2000 Professional

    d. Windows 2000 Advanced Server

10. Which of these configuration specifications will allow for the installation of Windows 2000 Professional? (Choose all that apply.)

    a. Intel 166 MHz Pentium, 32 MB of RAM, 2 GB disk space

    b. Compaq Alpha, 48 MB of RAM, 2 GB disk space

    c. Intel 486DX/66, 16 MB of RAM, 800 MB disk space

    d. Intel 133 MHz Pentium, 24 MB of RAM, 2 GB disk space

11. A dual-boot computer hosts both Windows 98 and Windows 2000 Professional. You need to download an 8 GB datafile, which will be used by both OSs. What file system should you use to format the host volume?

    a. FAT

    b. FAT32

    c. NTFS

12. You are setting up a computer for the purpose of sharing files. Each user connecting will need to have specific levels of access based on their identity. You also want the security system to employ encryption authentication to verify the identity of both the server and client before data transfer can occur. Which operating system would be the most effective solution?

    a. Windows 98

    b. Windows 2000 Professional

    c. Windows NT Workstation

    d. Windows 2000 Server

13. The two networking models supported in Windows 2000 are ___Workgroup___ and ___domain___.

14. The three file systems supported in Windows 2000 are ___Fat___, ___Fat 32___, and ___NTFS___.

15. When a user presses the Ctrl+Alt+Delete key combination in Windows 2000 after booting, what happens?

    a. The computer reboots.

    b. The logon screen appears.

    c. A "blue screen of death" occurs.

    d. A command prompt appears.

16. Windows 2000 runs on top of DOS. True or False?

17. Which of the following are required to install Windows 2000 on Intel-based computers?

    a. an SCSI CD-ROM drive

    b. a tape backup device

    c. a network interface card

    d. none of the above

18. Windows 2000 was designed by Microsoft to replace what other operating system?

    a. Windows 98

    b. Windows NT

    c. Windows for Workgroups

    d. Windows CE

19. Administrators desiring a centralized model of resource management should consider the _____ network model.

    a. workgroup

    b. domain

20. All direct access to hardware is mediated by which component?

    a. kernel

    b. Win32 subsystem

    c. hardware abstraction layer

    d. Executive Services

21. Windows 2000 Professional natively supports _____ processors.

    a. 1

    b. 2

    c. 4

    d. 32

22. Windows 2000 includes native support for what types of security hardware?

    a. voice recognition

    b. smart cards

    c. retinal scanners

    d. body heat imaging

23. Windows NT Professional clients can print to Macintosh printers using the AppleTalk protocol. True or False?

24. When a DOS application that is used to manipulate files on a hard drive is launched on a Windows 2000 Professional system, in what mode does the process execute?

    a. user

    b. kernel

    c. protected

    d. IPC

25. What supported platforms allow the installation of Windows 2000 to occur over a network? (Choose all that apply.)

    a. Intel

    b. PowerPC

    c. Compaq Alpha

    d. MIPS

HANDS-ON PROJECTS

Project 1-1

To explore the desktop:

1. Boot and log on to a Windows 2000 Professional system by pressing **Ctrl+Alt+Delete**.

2. Notice the icons on the desktop (see Figure 1-5).

3. Double-click **My Documents**. This reveals the default storage location for your personal documents, faxes, and pictures.

4. Click the **File** menu, then click **Close**.

5. Double-click **My Computer**. This reveals a list of all drives present on the system, plus a link to the Control Panel.

6. Click the **File** menu, then click **Close**.

7. Double-click **My Network Places**. This reveals the interface used to add new network connections, a link to the entire network, and a list of any recently accessed shares from the network.

8. Click the **File** menu, then click **Close**.

Figure 1-5   Windows 2000 Professional desktop

9. Double–click the **Recycle Bin**. This reveals all items that have been deleted but are still recoverable.

10. Click the **File** menu, then click **Close**.

Project 1-2

To explore the Start menu:

1. Click the **Start** button on the taskbar (see Figure 1-6).

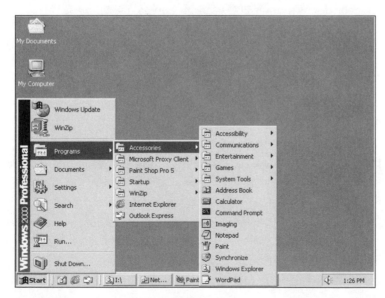

Figure 1-6   Start button items

2. Notice the items that occur in the Start menu by default: Windows Update, Programs, Documents, Settings, Search, Help, Run, and Shut Down.

3. Click **Shut Down**. This reveals a dialog box with a list where you can select to log off the current user account, restart, or shut down the system.

4. Click **Cancel**.

5. Click **Start**, then click **Run**. This reveals the Run dialog box, where you can enter a path and filename to launch.

6. Click **Cancel**.

7. Click **Start**, then click **Help**. This opens the Windows Help system. Explore this interface.

8. Close the Help system by clicking the Close button ⊠ in the upper-right corner of the dialog box.

9. Click **Start**, then point to **Search**. This opens a menu with three selections: For Files or Folders, On the Internet, and For People. Each of these is an interface used to locate file objects, Internet objects, or people, respectively.

10. Click **Start**, then point to **Settings**. This opens a menu with four items: Control Panel, Network and Dial-up Connections, Printers, and Taskbar & Start menu.

11. Click **Start**, then point to **Documents**. This opens a menu that lists fifteen of the most recently accessed documents or files.

12. Click **Start**, then point to **Programs**. This opens the first of several levels of menus in which all of the applications, tools, and utilities of the system are organized for easy access. Explore this multilevel menu.

13. Look at but don't select Windows Update. When launched, Windows Update attempts to connect to the Microsoft Web site. From the special update site, new files and updated components for Windows 2000 can be downloaded.

Project 1-3

To view the Windows 2000 administration tools:

1. Click **Start**, point to **Settings**, then point to **Control Panel**. This opens the Control Panel window (see Figure 1-7).

2. Notice the tools and utilities in the Control Panel.

3. Double-click the **Date/Time** applet. This reveals the Date/Time interface, where the current time and date can be changed.

4. Click **Cancel**.

5. Double-click the **Fonts** applet. This reveals a list of all the fonts currently present on the system.

6. Click **Back** in the button bar to return to the Control Panel.

7. Double-click **Administrative Tools**. This reveals all of the administrative tools for Windows 2000.

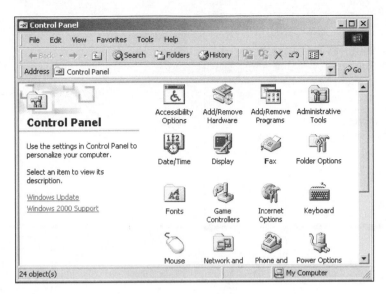

Figure 1-7   Control Panel tools

8. Double-click **Computer Management**. This opens an MMC console, where you can access information on a wide range of components. Explore this interface but be careful not to make any changes.

9. Close Computer Management by clicking ⌧ in the upper-right corner of the window.

10. Click the **File** menu, then click **Close**.

Project 1-4

To explore Task Manager:

1. Right-click over a blank area of the taskbar. This reveals a menu. Select **Task Manager** from the menu.

2. Click the **Applications** tab of Task Manager (see Figure 1-8). This lists all applications currently active in user mode.

3. Click the **Processes** tab of Task Manager. This lists all processes currently active. It also lists details about each process such as its process ID, its CPU usage percentage per second, and its total CPU execution time.

4. Click the **Performance** tab of Task Manager. This tab shows graphs detailing the current and historical use of the CPU and memory. This tab also lists details about memory consumption, threads, and handles.

5. Click the **View** menu, then click **Show Kernel Times**. This alters the graphs so activities of the kernel mode are shown in red and activities of the user mode are shown in green.

6. After watching this interface for a while, close it by selecting **File**, **Exit Task Manager** from the menu.

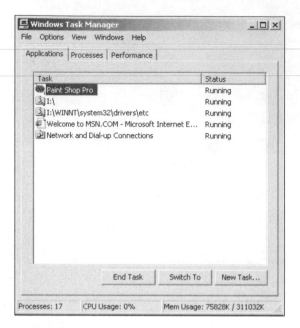

Figure 1-8   Task Manager, Applications tab

Project 1-5

To customize the Taskbar and Start menu:

1. Click **Start**, point to **Settings**, then click **Taskbar & Start Menu**.

2. On the **General** tab of the Taskbar & Start menu properties, notice the check boxes and their current selections.

3. Select the **Auto Hide** item. This causes the taskbar to slide off the screen when not in use. When you place the insertion point near the bottom of the screen, it will reappear.

4. Click the **Advanced** tab.

5. Click the **Clear** button to empty the Documents folder. This clears the list of recently accessed documents from the folder.

6. In the list of Start menu settings, select **Display Administrative Tools**, and **Expand Control Panel**.

7. Click **OK**.

8. Explore your changes. First, move the insertion point to the middle of the screen and click. Notice that the taskbar disappears. Move the insertion point near the bottom of the screen to watch the taskbar reappear.

9. Click **Start**, point to **Settings**, then point to **Control Panel**. Notice that a menu with all of the Control Panel contents is now present.

10. Click **Start**, point to **Programs**, then point to **Administrative Tools**. You may need to expand the menu by clicking the down arrows. This reveals a menu with the same contents as the Administrative Tools icon of the Control Panel.

11. Click a blank portion of the desktop to close the Administrative Tools menu.

Project 1-6

To customize the desktop:

1. Right-click a blank area of the desktop.

2. Select **New**, then **Shortcut** from the menu.

3. Click **Browse** in the window that appears.

4. Locate and select **Notepad.exe** in the main Windows 2000 directory (WINNT). Click **OK**.

5. Click **Next**.

6. Click **Finish**. A shortcut to Notepad now appears on the desktop.

7. Right-click over a blank area of the desktop.

8. Select **Arrange Icons**, then **Auto Arrange**.

9. Notice that the icons on the desktop have repositioned themselves in a uniform pattern.

10. **Right-click** over a blank area of the desktop.

11. Select **Properties**.

12. On the **Background** tab, take note of the current selection, then select an item from the list of background images.

13. Click **OK**.

14. To restore the desktop to its original settings, repeat steps 10–13 but use the original setting. Delete the shortcut you created by selecting it and pressing the **Delete** key, and then confirm the deletion.

CASE PROJECTS

1. You are planning a network in which users need to have a centralized location, where discretionary access control is a necessity. This will be an environment in which consistency is a must.

   Required Result

   ❑ All users must be able to access the server from any computer within the network through a single logon.

   Optional Desired Results

   ❑ Users must also be required to log on before accessing anything on their local machine.

❑ Users will have the exact same desktop GUI.

Proposed Solution

❑ Install Windows 2000 Server as the server platform. Establish a Windows 2000 domain. On half of the users' desktops, install Windows 98, and on the other half, install Windows 2000 Professional. Have all computers configured as part of the Windows 2000 domain.

Which results does the proposed solution produce? Why?

a. The proposed solution produces the required result and produces both of the optional desired results.

b. The proposed solution produces the required result, but only one of the optional desired results.

c. The proposed solution produces the required result, but neither of the optional desired results.

d. The proposed solution does not produce the required result.

2. You have been instructed to evaluate the status of the network environment at Site A. Your goal is to evaluate the current network and determine, first of all, whether upgrading is necessary. If so, then the next step is to determine which operating system will be the migration choice: Windows 2000 Professional or Windows 98. Finally, determine what steps need to occur before the migration can proceed.

Site A has 220 computers currently running Windows 3.1. They are running all 16-bit applications from the DOS and Windows environments. They plan on migrating to Microsoft Office 2000. Each computer has the following hardware configuration:

❑ Intel 486 DX4/100

❑ 8 MB of RAM

❑ 540 MB hard drive

❑ NIC (network interface card)

❑ VGA monitor

Users will not be allowed to share files at the desktop. They will not roam from computer to computer, so all of their files can be stored locally on their own computers.

Which migration path makes the most sense? Why?

a. No migration

b. Windows 2000 Professional

c. Windows 98

If migration to Windows 2000 Professional is necessary, what steps are necessary to establish optimum but cost-effective performance?

2

INSTALLING WINDOWS 2000 PROFESSIONAL

After reading this chapter and completing the exercises, you will be able to:

♦ Decide whether to perform an upgrade or a fresh installation of Windows 2000 Professional

♦ Boot multiple operating systems

♦ Plan an installation or upgrade

♦ Perform an unattended installation

♦ Install Windows 2000 using disks, the CD-ROM, or the network

♦ Describe the various Setup and advanced installation options

There are a number of issues that must be considered when installing any operating system, and Windows 2000 Professional is no exception. This chapter details the various steps that must be taken to get Windows 2000 up and running. It also examines such issues as whether to perform a fresh installation or to upgrade from an earlier version. It covers the various methods used to install Windows 2000 (floppies, CD-ROM, or network-based), as well as a few things to watch out for along the way.

Although the interfaces are similar, Windows 2000 has more capabilities and more features than Windows 98, Windows 95, and even Windows NT 4.0, and also has greater hardware requirements. Before installing Windows 2000 Professional, you must first ensure that your computer meets the minimum requirements (and, preferably, the recommended requirements), as detailed in Chapter 1, and that all hardware to be used with Windows 2000 is listed on the hardware compatibility list (HCL).

UPGRADING VERSUS INSTALLING

When installing Windows 2000 Professional, you have a choice between upgrading an existing installation or performing a completely fresh installation. Upgrading is an option when you have a version of Windows 95/98, or Windows NT 4.0 Workstation or Server already installed, and want to preserve some of the settings and information from the previous installation, including password files, desktop settings, and general configuration. A fresh installation installs a completely new version of Windows 2000 Professional, without regard to any existing files on the system.

Windows 2000 Professional can be installed as a dual-boot OS with an existing installation of:

- Windows 95 (all releases)
- Windows 98 (all releases)
- Windows NT 3.51 Workstation (including service packs)
- Windows NT 4.0 Workstation (including service packs)

Typically, an upgrade installation is selected when you want to retain your existing desktop and network configuration. If you are having problems with your existing operating system and the environmental settings are not that important, a fresh installation may be a better option. A fresh or complete installation can be performed on a system with a blank hard drive, over an existing operating system, or in such a way as to create a **multiboot system** (that is, a system that can boot multiple operating systems).

Upgrading to Windows 2000 from Windows NT or Windows 98 is fairly straightforward. The process attempts to retain as many of the existing configuration and software settings as possible. The only items that will not be retained are system utilities or drivers specific to the existing operating system that are updated or removed from Windows 2000. To upgrade, launch Winnt32 from the distribution CD, and when prompted select the "Upgrade to Windows 2000" option (see Figure 2-1). (Try Hands-on Project 2-6 to practice upgrading.)

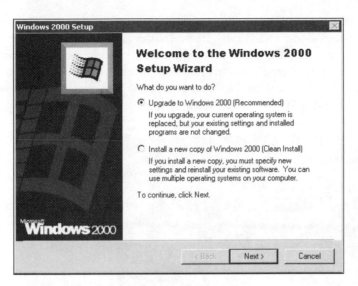

Figure 2-1   Choosing the upgrade option

BOOTING MULTIPLE OPERATING SYSTEMS

It is possible to install more than one operating system (OS) on the same computer, allowing you to determine which OS will be used at boot time. Unless you deliberately overwrite or **format** the **partition** (a space set aside on a disk and assigned a drive letter, which can take up all or part of the space on a disk) where another operating system is located, installing Windows 2000 Professional will not affect the other operating system.

Windows 2000 can be **dual-booted** easily (that is, it does not require third-party utilities) with the following operating systems:

- DOS (and Windows 3.x and Windows for Workgroups 3.x because they exist "on top of" DOS)
- Windows 95 or Windows 98
- Windows NT Workstation and Server 3.50, 3.51, and 4.0
- OS/2

Other operating systems, such as Linux, can be dual-booted with Windows 2000. However, to do so, Windows 2000 requires third-party boot and partition managers such as Partition Magic from PowerQuest (*http://www.powerquest.com*) or System Commander from V Communications (*http://www.v-com.com*).

TIP   In most cases (when third-party boot and partition software is not used), if you want a dual-boot system, you should install Windows 2000 on a system with an existing OS, rather than installing Windows 2000 first and then the other OS.

Installing Windows 2000 second enables the setup routine of Windows 2000 to properly configure the boot loader automatically. The **boot loader** is the software that shows all operating systems currently available and permits the user to choose which one should be booted, through a menu. At boot time, you can choose the operating system you want to run, as shown in Figure 2-2. Note that if you are dual-booting with a non–Windows operating system, the other OS is listed as "Previous Operating System on C:".

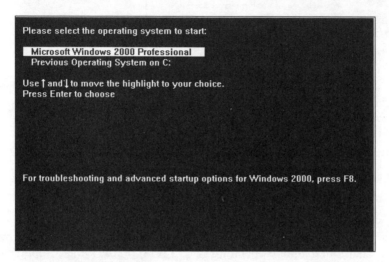

Figure 2-2   The Windows 2000 Professional boot menu

 Just as in Windows NT, Boot.ini is a text file (see Figure 2-3) that creates the Windows 2000 boot loader's menu. To remove an operating system from the boot loader or edit its entry in the boot loader menu, you have to edit the file Boot.ini manually. Take note that by default, this file is read-only. In order to make changes to the file, you must first clear the read-only attribute (to do this, right-click the file in Windows Explorer, select Properties, and deselect the Read-only check box); otherwise, you won't be able to save your work. Plus, before you make changes, it's always a good idea to create a backup of the original (copy Boot.ini and rename it Boot.bak or something similar) just in case your changes cause an error.

If you plan to use more than one operating system, it's important to consider which **file system** to use and whether data must be accessible to more than one OS on the same machine. Windows 2000 may be installed on a FAT, FAT32, or NTFS partition (FAT, FAT32, and NTFS are covered in Chapters 1 and 4). Only NTFS supports the majority of the Windows 2000 file security features, but a partition formatted with NTFS will be invisible to other non–NT operating systems. If you want to share data between operating systems on the same computer, you must create a FAT or FAT32 volume for that purpose.

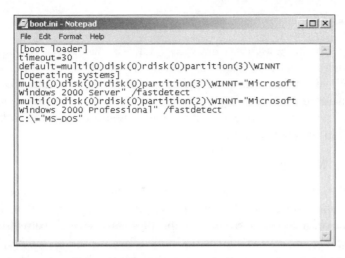

2

Figure 2-3   A Boot.ini file showing a system set to dual-boot Windows 2000 Server and Professional

PLANNING THE INSTALLATION

Careful planning is essential to the smooth execution of any operating system. The importance of checking hardware against the HCL has already been discussed in Chapter 1, but that's only the beginning. It's also important to consider the following:

- The type of installation you want to perform, such as manual or unattended

- The partition on which the OS files will be stored and how that partition is to be formatted

Your computer system must meet Microsoft's minimum hardware requirements before you attempt an installation. Otherwise, you'll be unable to install the operating system properly and will waste a significant amount of time. To review the hardware requirements, refer to Chapter 1.

TIP   Windows 2000 Professional can be installed onto a multiprocessor system that hosts two CPUs. The installation routine will automatically configure the system to use multiple CPUs if they are present on the system. However, if you install Windows 2000 Professional with a single CPU and later add a second CPU, you must reinstall Windows 2000 or perform an upgrade installation when you add the second CPU. This is necessary to update the hardware-specific (motherboard, CPU, and so on) HAL (see Chapter 1) for multiprocessor support.

Types of Installations

For manual installations, you have a choice between a CD-ROM installation (covered in detail later in the chapter) and a network installation (covered in the next section). (Unattended installations are covered in a later section.) Installing from the CD is quite straightforward. If you have an existing OS, you may be able to avoid the **setup boot disks** (or floppies) that come with Windows 2000. A network installation requires a bit more preparation, as discussed in the next section.

Installing over the Network

To install Windows 2000 Professional over the network, you must have access to the Windows 2000 Professional distribution files via a network share (whether that share is a shared CD-ROM drive on a server or a copy of the files on a server's hard drive). The subdirectory containing the installation files varies depending on the architecture of the computer on which you're installing Windows 2000 Professional. For example, **x86**-based systems (386 and later CPUs, including the Pentium-based Intel chip architecture) require the files found in the \i386 folder on the Windows 2000 Professional CD-ROM. You'll want to set the general access permissions (that is, for the Domain Users group) on this shared folder to read-only. (Permissions are covered in Chapter 4, "Managing Windows 2000 File Systems and Storage.") Hands-on Project 2-1 gives step-by-step instructions for installing Windows 2000 Professional over the network.

Installing with or Without Floppy Disks

The Windows 2000 Professional installation CD-ROM comes with four setup boot disks, but these disks are necessary only if you're installing on a drive that is not presently bootable (that is, one that has not yet been formatted). If the setup boot floppies don't include drivers for your CD-ROM drive (this is sometimes the case with off-brand SCSI and IDE drives), you must perform a floppyless installation.

A floppyless installation requires that an existing operating system be present on the computer, or that bootable CD-ROMs are supported. This could be just DOS or anything more advanced. The existing OS must have access to the CD-ROM drive to launch the installation program. Plus, you'll need at least 650 MB of free hard drive space for the files that are copied during installation.

Creating Setup Boot Floppies

If the Windows 2000 setup boot floppies aren't available for some reason, you can create new ones. You'll need four blank floppy disks and a computer system running DOS or Windows. Execute Makeboot (16-bit OSs) or Makebt32 (32-bit OSs) in the \Bootdisk directory on the CD. This will launch the setup boot disk creation utility. Just follow the prompts and insert the blank floppies when instructed. The steps to create floppy setup disks are given in Hands-on Project 2-2.

Partitioning the Hard Disk

You may want to partition your hard disk before installing Windows 2000 Professional. Many people create a DOS boot partition that's accessible when booting from a floppy, so they can run diagnostic software and utilities that only run under DOS, but store data in an NTFS partition that is more secure and is inaccessible unless the system is booted to Windows 2000 or the other OS uses a third-party partitioning tool that supports NTFS partitions. Although it's possible to install Windows 2000 onto a FAT or FAT32 partition, neither version of FAT provides the advanced security features of NTFS, so you must determine which file system (or which combination of them) is more appropriate for your needs. Chapter 4 discusses in detail the capabilities and implications of the file systems supported by Windows 2000 and the criteria for choosing a file system. For now, it is sufficient to say that FAT/FAT32 partitions provide no security; so, if you require the assignment of rights to system resources, NTFS is the file system to use. There are other deciding factors as well, covered in detail in Chapter 4. Partition selection is covered in more detail under the "Text-only Portion of Setup" section of this chapter. Right now, it's important to know that the **active partition** is the partition that houses the Windows 2000 boot files. This is very important: if a computer doesn't know where to look for the boot files, it can't start. You can use the DOS **FDISK** utility to partition the hard disk before installation, or you can use the partitioning interface encountered during setup. Hands-on Project 2-3 walks you through the process of breaking a single large partition into two partitions.

 The DOS FDISK utility can be used to create and delete partitions. However, it has limited capabilities with NTFS. FDISK can only recognize and delete primary NTFS partitions. FDISK cannot recognize or delete NTFS-formatted logical drives in an extended partition. (See the section entitled, "Destroying Partitions" to remove NTFS partitions.)

UNATTENDED INSTALLATIONS

It's possible to configure an **unattended installation** so that you don't have to respond to installation prompts, but instead provide a script containing the appropriate answers. Although it can take a little time and practice to set up an unattended installation, this type of installation can save time if you have to install Windows 2000 Professional on several machines. To run an unattended installation, run **Winnt** (DOS or Windows 3.x) with the /U and /S options from the command line (see the section "Winnt and Winnt32 Advanced Setup Options" later in the chapter) or **Winnt32** (Windows 95, 98, NT) with the /UNATTEND and /S options, to instruct Setup to perform an unattended installation using the files stored in the location you specify with the /S switch. To further customize an unattended installation, you can create an **answer file** in combination with a **uniqueness database file (UDF)**, which makes changes to an answer file that varies from one machine to another. The answer file is a text file that provides answers to installation prompts for unattended installations, the default sample of which is called Unattend.txt. The UDF, in conjunction with the answer file, allows you to create a unique answer set for each Windows 2000 Professional setup. For example, the UDF might contain a username or workstation name that varies from installation to installation. To use the UDF in an unattended installation, specify /UDF:id on the Winnt or Winnt32 command line (the ":id" portion tells setup which UDF to use).

If you're preparing an answer file for an unattended installation on an x86–based system, you'll use the copy of Unattend.txt that's found in the \i386 directory. If you must install several instances of Windows 2000 Professional that vary slightly (for example, the username differs), then you can use a UDF to supplement the answer file and override its parameters, as appropriate. The creation of answer files and UDFs is discussed shortly.

The Unattend.txt file included with Windows 2000 Professional contains default settings for a typical installation. Its contents are as follows:

```
; Microsoft Windows 2000 Professional, Server, Advanced
  Server and Datacenter Server
; (c) 1994 - 1999 Microsoft Corporation. All rights reserved.
;
; Sample Unattended Setup Answer File
;
; This file contains information about how to automate the
  installation
; or upgrade of Windows 2000 Professional and Windows 2000
  Server so the
; Setup program runs without requiring user input.
;

[Unattended]
Unattendmode = FullUnattended
OemPreinstall = NO
TargetPath = WINNT
Filesystem = LeaveAlone

[UserData]
FullName = "Your User Name"
OrgName = "Your Organization Name"
ComputerName = "COMPUTER_NAME"

[GuiUnattended]
; Sets the Timezone to the Pacific Northwest
; Sets the Admin Password to NULL
; Turn AutoLogon ON and login once
TimeZone = "004"
AdminPassword = *
AutoLogon = Yes
AutoLogonCount = 1

;For Server installs
[LicenseFilePrintData]
AutoMode = "PerServer"
```

```
AutoUsers = "5"

[GuiRunOnce]
; List the programs that you want to launch when the machine
  is logged into for the first time

[Display]
BitsPerPel = 8
XResolution = 800
YResolution = 600
VRefresh = 70

[Networking]
; When set to YES, setup will install default networking
  components. The components to be set are
; TCP/IP, File and Print Sharing, and the Client for Microsoft
  Networks.
InstallDefaultComponents = YES

[Identification]
JoinWorkgroup = Workgroup
```

This file can be modified either manually (with a text editor) or with the **Setup Manager**. The Windows 2000 Support Tools includes this wizard for creating or editing your own fully customized Unattend.txt files, along with complete details on how to edit this file and all of the possible syntax combinations. (Hands-on Project 2-4 shows you how to install the Support Tools, and Project 2-5 shows you how to create an answer file with the Setup Manager.) The Setup Manager Wizard is found in the \Program Files\Support Tools\ folder (if the defaults are used to install the Support Tools). Launching its executable file, Setupmgr.exe, will present you with the Windows 2000 Setup Manager Wizard. This wizard can be used to create a variety of installation scripts to perform the following functions:

- Duplicate the current system's configuration, edit an existing Unattend.txt file, or create a new file from scratch

- Create an installation script for Windows 2000 Professional, Server, and Advanced Server

- Run a script that is fully automated (no user interaction), read-only (user can view settings on each page but not make changes), and GUI (graphical user interface; text portion is automated), provide defaults (recommended settings are defined, but user can change during setup), or hide some configuration setup pages

Hands-on Projects 2-4 and 2-5 give examples of how to create an answer file using this wizard.

Creating the UDF

Multiple duplicate installations can be streamlined with the uniqueness database file (UDF). As mentioned, the UDF works in conjunction with the answer file, allowing you to override some settings in the answer file. Rather than having to create a new answer file for every change to the installation, you can just specify a separate UDF. Most information will be covered in the answer file, but if a setting exists in both the specified UDF and the answer file, the UDF takes precedence.

You can create a UDF in a text editor such as EDIT or Notepad. This file provides unique answers for user ID, full name, computer name, time zone, and domain settings. It should look something like the following:

```
[UniqueIDs]
    UserID1 = Userdata,GuiUnattended,Network
    UserID2 = Userdata,GuiUnattended,Network

[UserID1:UserData]
FullName = "Horst Delbruck"
ComputerName = "Monster"

[UserID1:GuiUnattended]
TimeZone = " (GMT+01:00) Prague, Warsaw, Budapest)"

[UserID1:Network]
JoinDomain = "LabTechs"

[UserID2:UserData]
FullName = "Francis N. Stein"
ComputerName = "Doctor"

[UserID2:GuiUnattended]
TimeZone = "(GMT-06:00) Central Time (US & Canada)"

[UserID2:Network]
JoinDomain = "MadScientists"
```

When you've finished the UDF, save it as a text file and store it on disk. It's often helpful to name UDFs for the people using them, as they're likely to be customized for individuals.

 A UDF can also be created using the Setup Manager Wizard from the Windows 2000 Support Tools. The Setup Manager Wizard is easy to use and offers lots of help. It walks you through every combination and option available to you in the setup procedure. More information about UDFs and details about the Setup Manager Wizard can be found in the Windows 2000 Support Tools.

USING THE SYSDIFF UTILITY

If you have a customized Windows 2000 Professional installation that you'd like to copy to other machines on your network, you can use the **Sysdiff** tool (available in the Windows 2000 Support Tools) to record the differences between a basic Windows 2000 Professional installation and the one you've altered.

To use Sysdiff to customize an installation, follow these steps:

1. If you haven't already done so, install Windows 2000 Professional. (See the section titled "Windows 2000 Professional Setup: Step by Step" later in this chapter for detailed instructions on how to do this.)

2. Type **SYSDIFF /SNAP** *<snapfile>* at a command prompt on that computer to create a snapshot of this installation in the filename you specify. (*<snapfile>* is the name of the snapshot file you wish to create.)

3. Install any software applications you'd like and make the system configuration changes you wish to record.

4. Type **SYSDIFF /DIFF** *snapfile* *<diffname>* on that computer to record the differences between the original installation and the new version in the file whose name you specify. (*<diffname>* is the name of the difference file you wish to create.)

5. Install Windows 2000 Professional on each of the destination computers.

 The drive configuration and system root directory name must be identical to those of the original system.

6. Run **SYSDIFF /APPLY** *diffname* on each destination computer to add the files, naming the file created in /DIFF mode.

Those are the basic steps for performing a Sysdiff operation. (The switches that may be used with each of these commands are explained in detail in the Windows 2000 Support Tools.) You use Sysdiff in combination with an unattended installation. Table 2-1 shows what's actually happening when you use each of those commands.

Table 2-1   Sysdiff Switches

Mode	Function
Snap	When used with the Snap argument, Sysdiff takes a snapshot of the current Registry and the file system and directories. This information is recorded in a snapshot file.
Diff	The Diff argument records the differences between the view of the system as recorded with Diff and its state when Sysdiff is run again on the same system. The differences are recorded in a difference file.
Apply	Applies the data in the difference file to the Windows 2000 installation on which it's being run. Any differences in the operating system will be made, and any applications added to the installation.
Inf	Used to apply differences to installations across the network
Dump	Creates a text file listing the changes between the original installation and the amended one

ALTERNATE AUTOMATION OPTIONS

Microsoft has developed two other options for automating the installation of Windows 2000 Professional: the Remote Installation Services (RIS) and the System Preparation tool (Sysprep). RIS is a feature of Windows 2000 Server that can be employed to install any version of Windows 2000, including Professional. RIS takes advantage of DHCP to perform system installations over the network without requiring the installer to visit the destination system. RIS requires that DHCP, DNS, and the Active Directory be present and active on a domain. To employ RIS, you must follow these general steps:

1. Verify that all systems comply with hardware requirements.

2. Install Windows 2000 Server as a standalone/member server system. Install Remote Installation Services as an Optional Component during the installation or after initial installation is complete.

3. If DNS is not already present in the domain, install it.

4. Promote the Windows 2000 Server to a domain controller.

5. If DHCP is not already present in the domain, install it.

6. Initiate the configuration procedure for RIS by launching Risetup.exe from the Run command. Using the wizard, configure RIS for your requirements and network design.

7. Authorize RIS with the Active Directory via the DHCP Manager.

8. Use the Directory Management snap-in to further configure RIS and define remote installation parameters.

As you can see, employing RIS is not a simple task. The Windows 2000 Support Tools and several Technical Notes (specifically Remote Installation Walkthroughs) provide extensive details on using RIS to install Windows 2000 Server and Professional. You can access the Technical Notes through the TechNet CD or online at *http://www.microsoft.com/TechNet/?RLD=87*.

The **System Preparation tool (Sysprep.exe)** is used to prepare a system for disk imaging duplication. This tool allows Windows 2000 and installed applications to be quickly deployed on multiple computers with the exact same hardware components. Sysprep must be used with a third-party disk imaging product because it only prepares a system for duplication, it does not perform the duplication. Basically, Sysprep removes the configurable settings of a system which are defined in a typical Unattend.txt file and prepares the system to redetect all Plug and Play devices upon next reboot. Upon reboot of the source computer or any duplicated computers, a new security ID (SID; see Chapter 6) is created, a setup wizard is launched to prompt you for local system-specific data, such as computer name, product ID, and user name (the wizard can be managed through scripts to fully automate the process), and a full Plug and Play redetection of hardware occurs.

2

The basic process of using Sysprep is as follows:

1. Install Windows 2000.

2. Install any additional applications, services, or drivers.

3. Customize and configure the applications and services.

4. Run Sysprep to prepare the system for duplication. After Sysprep completes, it will shut down the system.

5. Use a disk imaging or duplication product to duplicate the disk.

6. Upon the next reboot of the original system or any duplicated drive, Windows 2000 will redetect Plug and Play devices and prompt you for any information not currently present in the system.

Sysprep can be used with a Sysprep.inf file, which contains the same information and uses the same structure and syntax as the Unattend.txt file created by the Setup Manager. Additional details on Sysprep can be found in the Windows 2000 Support Tools.

 The Setup Manager Wizard from the Windows 2000 Support Tools includes the ability to create automated scripts for both Remote Installation Services and the System Preparation tool. These scripts can be easily employed to automatically install various versions of Windows 2000 onto a host or destination computer.

BEGINNING THE WINDOWS 2000 PROFESSIONAL INSTALLATION

Windows 2000 Professional offers numerous methods to launch, or start, the installation process. This section takes a look at them. You'll see that each has its own unique benefits and requirements.

CD-ROM Installation Launched from Setup Boot Floppies

The most common installation method is using the four setup boot disks to initiate the installation from a local CD-ROM drive. This is the preferred method if you must manually install storage drivers, when an existing OS is not present, or when network access is not available. To initiate this process, simply place the Windows 2000 Professional CD-ROM into an HCL-compliant CD-ROM drive, place the first of the setup boot floppies in the floppy drive, then reboot the system.

Bootable CD-ROM

The Windows 2000 Professional CD-ROM is self-booting. Thus, if your computer hardware supports this feature, you can bypass the four setup floppies by allowing the computer to boot from the CD-ROM. This method is a little faster than the floppy launch method. This method can be used regardless of the presence of an OS on the system or network access.

If your system does support bootable CD-ROMs, you'll need to remember to eject all bootable CDs before rebooting your system. This is especially true for the Windows 2000 CD itself. In most cases, to protect the security of the system, it is a good idea to disable bootable CD-ROMs via your CD-ROM controller's BIOS after you've installed Windows 2000.

CD-ROM Launch from Existing OS

The setup process can be launched from an existing OS or from a boot floppy that contains CD-ROM drivers. Launching the setup requires the execution of the Winnt (DOS or Windows 3.x) or Winnt32 (Windows 95, 98, NT) file from the \i386 directory. See the section later in this chapter on the Winnt and Winnt32 commands.

Network Installation

Performing a network installation simply means launching the setup routine from a network share instead of from a local device. This method requires an existing OS (or a boot floppy) and network access. The network share containing the Windows 2000 Professional distribution files can either be a shared CD-ROM drive on a server or a shared folder to which the files have been copied. In any case, a drive letter on the destination computer must be mapped to the shared drive or folder and then the Winnt or Winnt32 command launched. (See Hands-on Project 2-1.)

 From DOS (and OSs installed over DOS), drive letters are mapped using the command-line syntax of "net use x: \\servername\directory" (where x is the drive letter to which you wish to map the shared network directory, *servername* is the name of the server on which the files are stored, and *directory* is the name of the installation directory). On Windows 95, 98, and NT, drive letters are mapped using the Tools, Map Network Drive command from Windows Explorer.

SETUP OPTIONS

Launching Setup using the various methods mentioned in the previous section can result in one of two setup initializations. If Setup is launched from the setup boot floppies, a bootable CD-ROM drive, or from DOS (including Windows 3.x and Windows for Workgroups 3.x) from either a local CD-ROM or a network share, Setup will launch in a text-only format initially and will later switch into a GUI format. If Setup is launched from Windows 95, 98, or NT from a local CD-ROM drive or from a network share, Setup will open a GUI setup wizard. To make discussion of these two setup initializations a little easier, the former is labeled the DOS setup method and the latter is labeled the Windows setup method.

The DOS setup method is discussed in detail a little later in this chapter. In fact, you will perform a complete, step-by-step walkthrough of this method. The Windows setup method employs an initialization setup wizard to preselect or predefine several setup options. The first

2

option is whether to perform an upgrade installation or to perform a clean installation. As mentioned earlier, an **upgrade installation** retains as much of the existing system as possible. A **clean installation** (also called a **fresh installation**) completely ignores all existing settings. If you select an upgrade installation, the wizard prompts you to read and agree to the license agreement, then it copies the required files to your hard drive before rebooting your system. Once rebooted, Setup runs through the text-only portion without prompting you, then continues into the GUI portion (covered later in this chapter).

If you decide to perform a clean installation, the wizard prompts you to read and agree to the license agreement, then prompts you to change setup options. The setup options are accessed via three buttons: Language Options, Advanced Options, and Accessibility Options. The Language Options button is used to change the base language. Accessibility Options enable the magnifier and narrator options. The Advanced Options button is used to set the following:

- Source path for installation files (default is *<cdrom_drive>*:\i386)

- Systemroot name (that is, where Windows 2000 will be installed—the default is \Winnt)

- Whether to copy all files from CD to a local directory before rebooting (the default is not to copy)

- Whether to allow selection of destination partition (the default is automatic selection)

Next, Setup prompts you to indicate whether you want to format the destination partition with NTFS. If you want to have a secure system, select NTFS. But, if data needs to be accessed from an operating system other than Windows NT (with Service Pack 5 applied) or 2000, select FAT. Finally, Setup copies the required files to your hard drive, then reboots the system. Once rebooted, Setup starts the text-only portion and continues in much the same manner as the DOS setup method. However, those prompts that have been predefined will be skipped.

Winnt and Winnt32 Advanced Setup Options

Earlier in this chapter were a number of references to Winnt and Winnt32 and some of the switches that may be used with each. You might be wondering, however, what the difference is between the two, why you'd use each, and what the complete set of switches is for each command. The function of these two command-line tools has changed from Windows NT. In Windows 2000, they each have a different purpose.

Winnt is the 16-bit setup tool designed to be launched from DOS and operating systems that rely upon DOS (such as Windows 3.x and Windows for Workgroups 3.x). Winnt is designed for standard and automated installations with few additional options. The command-line syntax for the Winnt command is as follows:

 This material is taken from the online Help information on the installation CD in the /i386 directory, obtained by entering the "winnt /?" command at the command prompt.

```
WINNT [/S[:sourcepath]] [/T[:tempdrive]] [/I[:inffile]] [/X]
[/C] [/U[:answer_file]] [/UDF:id[,UDF_file]] [/R[x]:folder]
[/E:command] [/A]
```

- /S[:sourcepath] -- Specifies the source location of the Windows 2000 files. The location must be a full path of the form x:\[path] or \\server\share[\path]. The default is the current folder.

- /T[:tempdrive] -- Directs Setup to place temporary files on the specified drive and to install Windows 2000 on that drive. If you do not specify a location, Setup attempts to locate a drive for you.

- /I[:inffile] -- Specifies the file name (no path) of the Setup information file. The default file name is Dosnet.inf.

- /X -- skips the creation of the Setup startup floppy disks. The Setup startup floppy disks that came with your Windows 2000 software are required after Setup restarts the computer.

- /C -- Skips the free disk space verification of the Setup startup floppy disks.

- /U[:answer_file] -- Performs unattended Setup using an answer file (requires /S). The answer file provides answers to some or all of the prompts you normally respond to during Setup.

- /UDF:id[,UDF_file] -- Indicates an identifier (id) that Setup uses to specify how a uniqueness database file (UDF) modifies an answer file (see /u). The /udf parameter overrides values in the answer file, and the identifier determines which values in the UDF file are used. If no UDF_file is specified, Setup prompts you to insert a disk that contains the $Unique$.udb file.

- /R[:folder] -- Specifies an optional folder to be installed. The folder remains after Setup finishes.

- /Rx[:folder] -- Specifies an optional folder to be copied. The folder is deleted after Setup finishes.

- /E -- Specifies a command to be run at the end of the GUI-mode portion of Setup.

- /A -- Enables accessibility options.

So, for example, if you want Setup to place temporary files on a particular drive, and then install Windows 2000 on that drive with accessibility options, you'd type the following from the command line:

```
WINNT /T[:tempdrive] /A
```

Winnt32 is the 32-bit setup tool designed to be launched from 32-bit operating systems such as Windows 95, 98, and NT. Winnt32 is designed for standard and automated installations, and it also offers several options for source and destination locations as well as debug logging. The command-line syntax for the Winnt32 command is as follows:

 TIP   This material is taken from the online Help information on the installation CD in the /i386 directory, obtained by entering the "winnt32 /?" command at the command prompt.

```
winnt32 [/s:sourcepath] [/tempdrive:drive_letter]
[/unattend[num]:[answer_file]] [/copydir:folder_name]
[/copysource:folder_name] [/cmd:command_line] [/debug[level]:[file-
name]] [/udf:id[,UDF_file]] [/syspart:drive_letter] [/checkup-
gradeonly] [/cmdcons] [/m:folder_name] [/makelocalsource]
[/noreboot]
```

· /s:sourcepath -- Specifies the source location of the Windows2000 files. To simultaneously copy files from multiple servers, specify multiple /s sources. If you use multiple /s switches, the first specified server must be available or Setup will fail.

· /tempdrive:drive_letter -- Directs Setup to place temporary files on the specified partition and to install Windows2000 on that par- tition.

· /unattend -- Upgrades your previous version of Windows2000, WindowsNT3.51—4.0, Windows98, or Windows95 in unattended Setup mode. All user settings are taken from the previous installation, so no user intervention is required during Setup.

· Using the /unattend switch to automate Setup affirms that you have read and accepted the End User License Agreement (EULA) for Windows2000. Before using this switch to install Windows2000 on behalf of an organization other than your own, you must confirm that the end user (whether an individual, or a single entity) has received, read and accepted the terms of the Windows2000 EULA. OEMs may not specify this key on machines being sold to end users.

· /unattend[num]:[answer_file] -- Performs a fresh installation in unattended Setup mode. The answer file provides Setup with your custom specifications.

· Num is the number of seconds between the time that Setup finishes copying the files and when it restarts your computer. You can use num on any computer running WindowsNT or Windows2000.

· Answer_file is the name of the answer file.

· /copydir:folder_name -- Creates an additional folder within the folder in which the Windows2000 files are installed. For example, if the source folder contains a folder called Private_drivers that has modifications just for your site, you can type /copydir:Private_drivers to have Setup copy that folder to your installed Windows2000 folder. So then the new folder location would be C:\Winnt\Private_drivers. You can use /copydir to create as many additional folders as you want.

- /copysource:folder_name -- Creates a temporary additional folder within the folder in which the Windows2000 files are installed. For example, if the source folder contains a folder called Private_drivers that has modifications just for your site, you can type /copysource:Private_drivers to have Setup copy that folder to your installed Windows2000 folder and use its files during Setup. So then the temporary folder location would be C:\Winnt\Private_drivers. Unlike the folders /copydir creates, /copysource folders are deleted after Setup completes.

- /cmd:command_line -- Instructs Setup to carry out a specific command before the final phase of Setup. This would occur after your computer has restarted twice and after Setup has collected the necessary configuration information, but before Setup is complete.

- /debug[level]:[filename] -- Creates a debug log at the level specified, for example, /debug4:C:\Win2000.log. The default log file is C:\%Windir%\Winnt32.log, with the debug level set to 2. The log levels are as follows: 0-severe errors, 1-errors, 2-warnings, 3-information, and 4-detailed information for debugging. Each level includes the levels below it.

- /udf:id[,UDB_file] -- Indicates an identifier (id) that Setup uses to specify how a Uniqueness Database (UDB) file modifies an answer file (see the /unattend entry). The UDB overrides values in the answer file, and the identifier determines which values in the UDB file are used. For example, /udf:RAS_user,Our_company.udb overrides settings specified for the identifier RAS_user in the Our_company.udb file. If no UDB_file is specified, Setup prompts the user to insert a disk that contains the $Unique$.udb file.

- /syspart:drive_letter -- Specifies that you can copy Setup startup files to a hard disk, mark the disk as active, and then install the disk into another computer. When you start that computer, it automatically starts with the next phase of the Setup . You must always use the /tempdrive parameter with the /syspart parameter.

- The /syspart switch for Winnt32.exe only runs from a computer that already has WindowsNT3.51, WindowsNT4.0, or Windows2000 installed on it. It cannot be run from Windows9x.

- /checkupgradeonly -- Checks your computer for upgrade compatibility with Windows2000. For Windows95 or Windows98 upgrades, Setup creates a report named Upgrade.txt in the Windows installation folder. For WindowsNT 3.51 or 4.0 upgrades, it saves the report to the Winnt32.log in the installation folder.

- /cmdcons -- Adds to the operating system selection screen a Recovery Console option for repairing a failed installation. It is only used post-Setup.

- /m:folder_name -- Specifies that Setup copies replacement files from an alternate location. Instructs Setup to look in the alternate location first and if files are present, use them instead of the files from the default location.

- /makelocalsource -- Instructs Setup to copy all installation source files to your local hard disk. Use /makelocalsource when installing from a CD to provide installation files when the CD is not available later in the installation.

> • /noreboot -- Instructs Setup to not restart the computer after
> the file copy phase of winnt32 is completed so that you can execute
> another command.

Advanced Setup Options

Windows 2000 Professional offers several advanced setup options. These options are often used in enterprise network deployments. They require significant preparation work and preconfiguration of systems and setup scripts.

The first advanced option is that of Sysprep. **Sysprep** is a tool used to duplicate an entire hard drive. This tool is useful for installing Windows 2000 onto multiple identical systems that require identical configurations. Basically, you install Windows 2000 onto a single computer and add all applications and make all configuration changes. This system is the master that is duplicated to the other systems. For details on using Sysprep, see the Windows 2000 Support Tools.

Another advanced option is the **Remote Installation Service (RIS)** found on Windows 2000 Server. This service is used to "push" installation of Windows 2000 (Professional or Server) over a network to a client. RIS can install Windows 2000 onto a new client with only a Dynamic Host Configuration Protocol (DHCP) PXE (preboot execution environment)-based remote boot ROM, or an RIS boot disk supported **network adapter**, or a client with an existing OS. In either case, you can completely preconfigure the installation of Windows 2000 so that the only action you need to perform on the client is to power it on.

Microsoft has also added the **Windows Installer Service (WIS)** to Windows 2000 to simplify the deployment of multiple applications onto new clients. Microsoft also plans to offer WIS for Windows 95, 98, and NT. WIS combines the setup procedures for multiple applications into a single administrative action. WIS also centralizes application installations and simplifies the daunting task of maintaining updated software throughout a network.

WINDOWS 2000 PROFESSIONAL SETUP: STEP BY STEP

Installing Windows 2000 Professional is not difficult. In fact, it is a little easier than the process for Windows NT, but not quite as simple as that for Windows 98. In any case, you should be able to perform a typical installation without a hitch. Before we jump into the step-by-step process, we need to detail a few assumptions:

- Your computer's hardware is HCL-compliant, and all required device drivers are found on the distribution CD.

- Your computer does not have any preexisting operating systems installed.

- You have the four setup floppies available.

- You will select the default or typical settings for this installation.

- You will be using a specific IP address. Thus, you need the IP address, subnet mask, and default gateway on hand. If you don't know these yet, you can use 172.16.1.1

for the IP address and 255.255.0.0 for the subnet mask, as working placeholders. You don't need a placeholder for the default gateway.

- You will be a member of an existing domain. You'll need to have the name of this domain and the authentication information for an **Administrator** account (the Administrator account can perform a full array of management functions). If a domain is not available, you can choose to join a workgroup and assign it any name you want.

Text-only Portion of Setup

The first portion of the setup process when you employ a DOS setup method (see the discussion earlier in this chapter) is a text-only interface. This section walks you through every prompt of this portion of Setup.

1. Insert the first Setup boot disk into the floppy drive.

2. Turn on the computer.

3. After the computer starts to boot from the floppy (when the computer begins accessing the floppy drive), place the Windows 2000 Professional CD-ROM into your CD-ROM drive.

4. After data is copied from the first disk, you'll be prompted to insert Disk #2. Remove Disk #1, insert Disk #2, then press Enter. Repeat this for Disks #3 and #4.

5. Next, the setup routine prompt asks whether you wish to set up, repair, or quit:

```
Welcome to Setup.

This portion of the Setup program prepares Microsoft (R)
Windows 2000 (TM) to run on your computer.

* To set up Windows 2000 now, press ENTER.
* To repair a Windows 2000 installation, press R.
* To quit Setup without installing Windows 2000, press F3.
```

Press Enter to continue with the installation.

6. Setup then inspects your hard drives; this should take only a few seconds.

7. Next, you'll be presented with the license agreement. Using the Page Down key, scroll through this document. Once you've read it, press F8 to continue with the installation. If you cannot agree to the terms of the agreement, you should press Esc to end Setup.

8. Next, Setup searches for preexisting operating systems on your computer. If any are found, you'll be prompted to indicate whether to perform a repair or to continue with a clean installation. Because we are assuming you are installing on a new system, if you see this prompt, press Esc to continue with a clean installation.

9. Next, you are prompted for the destination drive and partition where Windows 2000 Professional will be installed. Using the arrow keys, you can select either a preexisting partition or an area of unpartitioned space. Because we assume

you are installing onto a new computer, there should be only unpartitioned space. Select the unpartitioned space on the first (or only) hard drive, then press Enter.

 If you do not wish to make the largest partition possible (for storage reasons), then you can manually create a partition, using the C command. First, select an unpartitioned space, then press C. Then, you'll be prompted for the size of the partition to create (or whether to use the entire drive). Once it is created, you'll be able to select the newly created partition now listed on the original drive and partition list. If you need to delete an existing partition, you can do so by selecting it, then pressing D. You'll need to confirm this process, so be sure to read the next screen and follow its instructions. Once the partition is deleted, the list of drives and partitions will be updated. Be careful when using this interface, because changes are made immediately to the drive's configuration.

10. Next, Setup prompts for the type of file system to use to format the selected destination partition. NTFS is the default selection. We recommend sticking with the default and pressing Enter.

    The list of options includes only FAT and NTFS. NTFS is the recommended file system for Windows 2000. NTFS supports volumes (that is, partitions) up to 16 petabytes, although 2 Terabytes is the Microsoft specified practical limit. FAT can support partitions up to 4 GB. If a partition larger than 2 GB (even though its maximum volume size is 4 GB) is used and FAT is selected, Setup will automatically format the partition with FAT32. FAT32 has the same features as FAT, with the exception of supporting volumes up to 32 GB (its maximum file size is still 4 GB).

11. Next, Setup formats your selected partition. This can take considerable time for larger partitions. Once the format is completed, Setup inspects your hard drive(s), builds a file list, then starts copying files from the CD. This process can take even longer than the formatting.

12. Eventually, the copy process finishes, and the following message will be displayed:

    ```
    The MS-DOS based portion of Setup is complete.
    Setup will now restart your computer. After your computer
    restarts, Windows 2000 Setup will continue.
    If there is a floppy disk in Drive A:, remove it now.
    Press ENTER to restart your computer and continue
    Windows 2000 Setup.
    ```

    Remove Disk #4 from the floppy drive, then press Enter. After the reboot, Setup enters into the GUI portion of the Windows 2000 Professional Setup process. If your computer supports booting from a CD-ROM drive, you must remove the Windows 2000 CD before rebooting.

GUI Portion of Setup

The second part of the installation takes place in GUI mode. This mode takes place in a pseudo-Windows 2000 environment where you provide configuration details.

13. The first screen of the GUI portion of Setup is just a welcome screen. Click Next to continue.

CAUTION

While working through the GUI portion of Setup, use caution when clicking the Next button. Often, the system takes several seconds or even a minute to alter the display, even after you've successfully clicked the Next button. You should click the Next button only once, then wait until the system responds, or at least 5 minutes, before clicking again. Otherwise, you may inadvertently skip a page of the wizard, and in some cases, you'll be unable to use the Back button to access them. If you suspect that you have skipped a wizard page, you can reboot your computer to start the GUI portion of Setup over again.

14. Setup searches for hardware components and attempts to identify Plug and Play components. This may take several minutes. Eventually, you'll be prompted to set your regional and keyboard settings. If you live in the United States, the defaults are correct. Click Next to continue.

15. Next, you are prompted for your name and an organization name. Type these in their respective fields. You can leave the organization field blank. Click Next to continue.

16. Next, you are prompted for a computer name and the password for the Administrator user account. Provide these in their respective fields, then click Next.

17. If a modem is present in your computer and it is properly detected by Setup, you'll be prompted for your area code. Provide this and click Next.

18. Next, Setup prompts you to set and confirm the time, date, and time zone. Set these, then click Next.

19. Setup loads drivers for the networking components it has detected. You'll be prompted to either accept these default settings or change them. If you are using DHCP (a method of automatically assigning IP addresses to client computers), then accepting the typical settings will be sufficient. If you need to specify an IP address, then you must select the custom settings. We assume you are using an assigned IP address, so select Custom Settings, and then click Next.

20. Setup displays the name of the detected NIC near the top of the dialog box. Three network services are listed in a center field: Client for Microsoft Networks, File and Printer Sharing for Microsoft Networks, and Internet Protocol (TCP/IP). You only need to make changes to the protocol, so select TCP/IP and click Properties. This opens the Internet Protocol (TCP/IP) Properties dialog box. Select the "Use the following IP address" radio button, then fill in the fields for IP address (either the one you are assigned or the placeholder 172.16.1.1), subnet mask (either the one you are assigned or the placeholder 255.255.0.0), and default gateway (either the one you are assigned or leave this blank). Click OK when finished. Then click Next to complete the Custom Settings for Networking.

21. Next, you are prompted for the name of the workgroup or domain of which this system will be a member. Select the workgroup or domain name radio button, then provide the appropriate name in the text field. Click Next to continue.

22. If you selected the option to join a domain, you'll be prompted for the name and password of the Administrator account in that domain. This will be used to create a computer account in the domain for your new Windows 2000 Professional system. Provide these details, then click OK.

23. Setup installs and configures numerous core system components, then adjusts the user environment, Start menu, administrative tools, and the Registry. This can take several minutes. Eventually, Setup will indicate that it is complete. Click Finish to reboot the system and boot into Windows 2000 Professional for the first time.

24. Once the system boots, you may see the Network Identification Wizard. If so, Click Next, select "Do not add users at this time," click Next, then click Finish.

25. The logon splash screen is displayed. Press Ctrl+Alt+Delete.

26. Type the password for the Administrator account. Click OK to log on.

27. After several minutes of processing and establishing user profile defaults, the desktop will be displayed. You've successfully logged on and completed the installation of Windows 2000 Professional.

REMOVING WINDOWS 2000 PROFESSIONAL

Windows 2000 does not offer an uninstall utility. In fact, you have to be quite determined to remove Windows 2000. Windows 2000 can be removed from a system in one of two ways. One option is to destroy the partition(s) where Windows 2000 has made its mark (that is, the boot and system partitions), then repartition, format, and install another operating system. The other option is available only if you installed Windows 2000 into a FAT (not FAT32) partition. In this case, you just delete all of the Windows 2000 files and rebuild the **master boot record (MBR)**, which is the first sector on a hard disk and contains executable code and a partition table, which stores information about the disk's primary and extended partitions. The MBR is automatically rebuilt every time a system is rebooted.

Destroying Partitions

In our opinion, the easiest method of removing Windows 2000 is to destroy the Windows 2000 partition and start fresh with some other operating system. The first step to this process is to back up any data that you consider important. Removing a partition may destroy your data (especially on the boot or system partitions). The steps for the removal are as follows:

1. Back up any data or files on the Windows 2000 file system that you want to preserve.

2. Boot the computer, using the four setup boot floppies in the same manner as if you were installing Windows 2000.

3. Continue through the same setup steps described earlier in this chapter.

4. Once you reach Step 10, where you are prompted for the destination drive and partition, you'll want to use this interface to delete all partitions (or at least all NTFS partitions). Use the arrow keys to select each partition, press D to delete, then L to confirm. Once all partitions are deleted, press F3 to exit. You'll have to confirm aborting the setup process by pressing F3 again.

5. At this point, your computer's hard drive is not partitioned. Use a DOS disk or a Windows 95/98/NT installation boot disk to start the installation process for another operating system.

Removing Windows 2000 from FAT

If you installed Windows 2000 into a FAT partition less than 2 GB in size, then you may be able to remove it from your computer without performing the method described in the previous section. You still need to back up all important data. Also, this method works only if you have not used NTFS partitions at all. Otherwise, you'll have to use the destroy method to remove those partitions in addition to the FAT uninstallation.

Before you get started, you'll need to obtain a DOS boot disk with the FDISK, FORMAT, DELTREE, and SYS utilities on it. In most cases, the first disk of the MS-DOS installation disk set will suffice. For the following steps, we assume you installed Windows 2000 into the default directory \Winnt on drive C. If not, you'll need to replace the path details with yours in the following process. The process for removing Windows 2000 from a FAT partition is as follows:

1. The simplest method is to create a batch file to perform all of the file and directory deletions for you. Open a text editor and enter the following:

```
@echo off
   a:
   SYS C:
   DELTREE /Y C:\WINNT
   DELTREE /Y C:\PROGRA~1\WINDOW~1
   DEL C:\PAGEFILE.SYS
   A:\ATTRIB -S -H -R C:\BOOT.INI
   DEL C:\BOOT.INI
   A:\ATTRIB -S -H -R C:\NTDETECT.COM
   DEL C:\NTDETECT.COM
   A:\ATTRIB -S -H -R C:\NTLDR.
   DEL NTLDR.
   A:\ATTRIB -S -H -R C:\BOOTSECT.DOS
   DEL C:\BOOTSECT.DOS
```

2. Save the batch file to a boot floppy or just to drive C, and then give it a name such as "Delw2k.bat".

3. Boot to DOS using your boot disk.

4. Execute the Delw2k.bat file.

5. Remove the DOS boot disk and reboot.

Your system should boot to DOS or to your previous operating system. Although this method does function, we still think that destroying partitions and starting over is a better solution.

2

CHAPTER SUMMARY

- ❑ This chapter taught you how to install and uninstall Windows 2000 Professional, including the tools and information you need to make this possible. At this point, you should understand how to choose hardware for a successful installation, how to install Windows 2000 both locally and across the network, how to use the switches that come with Winnt and Winnt32, and how to run Setup.

- ❑ In addition, this chapter discussed the items you must understand to decide whether to perform an upgrade or a fresh installation of Windows 2000 Professional, as well as provided an understanding of booting multiple operating systems with Windows 2000.

- ❑ This chapter also examined the main points involved in planning an installation of Windows 2000 or an upgrade from an existing version of Windows.

- ❑ Windows 2000 has a number of setup and advanced installation options, including using disks, the CD-ROM, or the network for installation.

- ❑ Finally, this chapter explored the steps necessary for an unattended installation of Windows 2000, using an answer file and a uniqueness database file (UDF) to deploy installations of Windows 2000 Professional across the network without requiring human intervention.

KEY TERMS

active partition — The partition that the computer uses to boot.

Administrator — The Windows 2000 account designed to perform a full array of management functions.

answer file — A text file that contains a complete set of instructions for installing Windows 2000.

boot loader — The software that shows all operating systems currently available and, via a menu, permits the user to choose which one should be booted.

Boot.ini — The text file that creates the Windows 2000 boot loader's menu.

clean installation — See fresh installation.

dual-boot system — A multiboot system with only two operating systems.

FDISK — A DOS utility used to partition a hard disk. The DOS FDISK tool can only see and manipulate primary NTFS partitions; it cannot even view logical drives in an extended partition formatted with NTFS.

file system — The method used to arrange files on disk and read and write them. Windows 2000 supports NTFS, FAT, and FAT32 disk file systems.

format — Rewriting the track and sector information on a disk. This process removes all data previously on the disk.

fresh installation — The installation method in which an operating system is installed without regard to preexisting operating systems. In other words, all settings and configurations are set to the OS's defaults.

master boot record (MBR) — The first sector on a hard disk, which contains executable code and a partition table, which stores information about the disk's primary and extended partitions.

multiboot system — A computer that hosts two or more operating systems that can be booted by selecting one from a boot menu or boot manager during each power on.

network adapter — Another name for network interface card (NIC), the piece of hardware that enables communication between the computer and the network.

partition — A space set aside on a disk and assigned a drive letter. A partition may take up all or part of the space on a disk. You create partitions when installing an operating system or when adding new drives.

Remote Installation Service (RIS) — A service used to "push" an installation of Windows 2000 (Professional or Server) over a network to a client.

setup boot disks (or floppies) — The four disks used by Windows 2000 to initiate the installation process on computer systems that do not have an existing OS, do not have a CD-ROM that supports bootable CDs, or that do not have network access to a Windows 2000 distribution file share. These disks can be created by running the Makeboot file from the Bootdisk directory on the distribution CD.

Setup Manager — The Windows 2000 tool that provides you with a GUI interface for creating an answer file.

Sysdiff — The Windows 2000 utility used to take a snapshot of a basic installation and, after changes have been made, record the changes and then apply them to another installation.

System Preparation tool (Sysprep) — A tool used to duplicate an entire hard drive. This tool is useful when installing Windows 2000 onto multiple identical systems that require identical configurations.

unattended installation — A Windows 2000 installation that uses a previously made script to install from. Such an installation method does not require user interaction.

uniqueness database file (UDF) — A text file that contains a partial set of instructions for installing Windows 2000, to specify settings for individual users. Used to supplement an answer file, when only minor changes are needed that don't require a new answer file.

upgrade installation — The installation method in which data and configuration settings from the previous operating systems remain intact. The level or amount of retained data varies according to the existing operating system's type.

Windows Installer Service (WIS) — A component of Windows 2000 that manages the installation and removal of applications by applying a set of centrally defined setup rules during the installation process.

Winnt — The 16-bit Windows 2000 installation program.

Winnt32 — The 32-bit Windows 2000 installation program.

x86 — The chip architecture used by Intel and others to create 386 and later CPUs (including the Pentium).

2

REVIEW QUESTIONS

1. Which operating systems other than Windows 2000 can be installed onto a computer system in a multiboot configuration without requiring special third-party software? (Choose all that apply.)

   a. DOS

   b. OS/2

   c. Linux

   d. Windows 95

2. Microsoft will provide support only for problems caused by hardware not on the hardware compatibility list. True or False?

3. Which of the following operating systems may be upgraded to Windows 2000 Professional? (Choose all that apply.)

   a. Windows 3.x

   b. Windows for Workgroups 3.x

   c. Windows 95/98

   d. Windows NT 3.x+

4. Data stored on a partition formatted with FAT32 is only accessible from Windows 2000. True or False?

5. Which of the following is the correct location for the x86 installation files on the installation CD?

   a. the root directory of the CD

   b. \Support\i386

   c. \Install\i86

   d. none of the above

6. When sharing an installation folder across the network, you should assign it _____ permission.

7. Which of the following are situations that allow a floppyless installation? (Choose all that apply.)

   a. The network is not yet functioning.

   b. The hard disk for the computer on which Windows 2000 is being installed is not yet formatted.

   c. No CD drivers are present for the existing operating system.

   d. Windows 95 is already installed on the computer.

8. Windows 2000 can be installed with only the CD-ROM if the computer's hardware is properly configured. True or False?

9. What is the command used to create setup floppy disks?

    a. Winnt32 /ox

    b. Makeboot

    c. Winnt32 /b

    d. Start, Settings, System – Create Boot Disk button

10. What is the DOS utility used to create and delete partitions on a hard disk called? FDisk

11. Windows 2000 must be installed to an NTFS partition. True or False?

12. Which of the following statements is true? (Choose all that apply.)

    a. The entries in a uniqueness database file (UDF) override those in an answer file when the two are used together.

    b. An answer file is used to script text-mode Setup, whereas a UDF scripts GUI-mode Setup.

    c. If you have several installations to complete that differ only in the username, then you can use an answer file to customize the settings in the UDF.

    d. Answer files can be created using the Setup Manager.

13. The maximum volume size for FAT32 partitions is 2 TB. True or False?

14. Which file system can be used on an installation destination directory for Windows 2000 Professional if the partition is 4 GB in size? (Choose all that apply.)

    a. FAT

    b. FAT32

    c. NTFS

15. When removing Windows 2000, all NTFS partitions can be deleted with just FDISK. True or False?

16. Which of the following commands is used to record the original state of a Windows 2000 installation?

    a. Sysdiff /apply

    b. Sysdiff /diff

    c. Sysdiff /inf

    d. Sysdiff /snap

17. Running _Sysdiff /dump_ creates a text record of a Sysdiff difference file.

18. Which command would you use to map a network drive from a DOS computer?

    a. NET START

    b. NET LOGON

    c. NET USE

    d. NET CONNECT

19. The _____/I_____ Winnt switch is used to specify a setup information file other than Dosnet.inf.

20. At what point in the installation do you have the option of converting the file system to NTFS?

    a. after selecting the installation partition

    b. after the hard disk has been examined

    c. at the end of the GUI-mode portion of installation

    d. You must convert the partition after Setup has been completed.

21. The Unattend.txt file included as a sample on the Windows 2000 Professional CD can be used without modification to perform an upgrade of Windows NT Workstation. True or False?

22. Unattended, or automated, installation scripts can be created to perform which of the following functions? (Choose all that apply.)

    a. duplicate an existing system's configuration

    b. create a read-only installation whereby viewers can step through the installation but not make any configuration changes

    c. automate only the GUI portion of Setup

    d. provide custom defaults but allow installer to change settings

23. What is the one action you must perform no matter from which operating system you launch a network installation of Windows 2000?

    a. install TCP/IP

    b. map a network drive to the Windows 2000 share

    c. preformat a 4 GB partition with FAT32

    d. use SYS C: to repair the MBR

24. You're preparing for a network installation of Windows 2000. Which of the following is not a step required to accomplish this? (Choose all that apply.)

    a. Copy the \Support directory from the installation CD to the server supplying the installation files.

    b. Share the installation directory with Read permissions.

    c. Boot the destination client computer onto the network.

    d. Run Winnt32 /n on the network server.

25. You want to change the menu description for Windows 2000 in the boot loader's menu. Which file will you edit to make the change?

    a. Dosnet.inf

    b. Unattend.txt

    c. Boot.ini

    d. Winnt.ini

HANDS-ON PROJECTS

Project 2-1

To make the Windows 2000 Professional x86 installation files available for network installations from a Windows 2000 Server computer:

1. Using an Administrator account, log on to the Windows 2000 Server computer that will be sharing the files.

2. Insert the Windows 2000 Professional installation CD-ROM into the CD-ROM drive on the server. The autorun mechanism should open the CD splash screen (see Figure 2-4). Click **Exit** to close the splash screen.

 If a screen appears asking if you would like to upgrade to Windows 2000, click No and then click Exit to close the splash screen.

3. Launch Windows Explorer (**Start**, **Programs**, **Accessories**, **Windows Explorer**).

4. Select the CD-ROM drive icon in the left pane.

5. Locate the \i386 directory in the right pane. Drag and drop the **i386** directory to the C: drive icon in the left pane (or another hard drive with at least 300 MB of free space).

6. This copies the entire directory to your hard drive. Once the copy process is complete, select the **i386** folder on the hard drive and right-click, then select **Sharing** from the resulting menu.

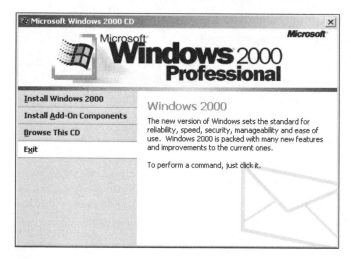

Figure 2-4   The Windows 2000 Professional CD splash screen

7. Select the **Share this folder** radio button. Provide a share name, such as **W2KPRO**.

8. Click **Permissions**, click **Add**. Locate and select the **Everyone** group if necessary, click **Add**, then click **OK**.

9. While the Everyone group is highlighted in the Permissions dialog box, set the access permissions to **Allow Read** (see Figure 2-5). Click **OK** to close the Permissions dialog box. Click **OK** to close the Sharing dialog box. Click OK to close the i386 Properties dialog box.

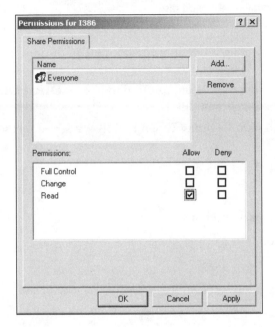

Figure 2-5   Setting permissions for the Everyone group

Project 2-2

To create the four setup boot disks for Windows 2000 Professional:

1. Collect four blank, formatted, high-density floppy disks.

2. Place the Windows 2000 Professional CD into the CD-ROM drive. When the Microsoft Windows 2000 splash screen appears, click **Exit** to close the splash screen.

3. Open the Run command (**Start, Run**).

4. Type **<CD-ROM drive>:\bootdisk\makeboot**, where <CD-ROM drive> is the letter of your CD-ROM drive, then click **OK**.

5. Place the first floppy in the disk drive. Press **A** to indicate the floppy drive letter.

6. Press any key to start the creation process.

7. Once the first disk copy is complete, remove Disk #1, insert Disk #2, and then press any key to copy the next disk.

8. Repeat this process for the remaining disks.

Project 2-3

To use the FDISK utility to partition the hard disk into two partitions:

Back up any data currently on the disk before repartitioning it! FDISK (or any partitioning utility) will permanently destroy any data currently on the hard disk.

1. Boot the computer to DOS by selecting DOS from the boot menu or using a DOS boot disk.

2. Move to the directory containing the FDISK utility. (To find it, type **DIR FDISK.* /s** to search all subdirectories on the current disk.)

3. Type **FDISK** and press **Enter** to start the utility. When FDISK starts, you will see a menu of four options:

   - 1 Create DOS partition or Logical DOS drive
   - 2 Set active partition
   - 3 Delete DOS partition or Logical DOS drive
   - 4 Display partition information

 TIP If your computer has more than one hard disk, you'll see a fifth option: "Change current fixed drive."

4. Type **4** and then press **Enter** to view the partitions currently on the hard disk. In this example, it is assumed that you'll see a single primary DOS partition. After reviewing the information, press **Esc** to return to the main menu.

5. Once at the main menu screen, type **3** and press **Enter** to delete the primary partition. When asked which partition to delete, type **1** and press **Enter**.

6. When prompted, type the volume label (if any) for the partition you're deleting. The label will be listed at the top of the screen with other volume information. If there is no volume label, just press **Enter**.

7. Type **Y** and press **Enter** to confirm the deletion of the selected partition.

8. Press **Esc** to return to the main menu.

9. From the main menu, type **1** and press **Enter** to create a DOS partition.

10. Type **N** and press **Enter** when asked whether you want to use the maximum available space. When prompted, type in the size (in megabytes) of the partition you want to create. For installing Windows 2000, a drive size of about 2 GB is recommended.

11. From the main menu, type **2** and press **Enter** to set the active partition. When prompted, type **1** to choose the partition you just created.

12. Press **Esc** to return to the main menu, then press **Esc** again to exit FDISK.

13. Reboot the computer. You'll need to install an operating system (such as Windows 2000) to format the partition.

 It's unnecessary to partition the remaining space on the drive now, because you can do that while installing Windows 2000.

 ## Project 2-4

To install the Windows 2000 Support Tools:

 You must be logged in with Administrator privileges to complete this project.

1. Insert the Windows 2000 Professional CD into the CD-ROM drive. The Windows 2000 splash screen appears. Click **Exit** to close the splash screen.

2. Open the Run dialog box (**Start**, **Run**).

3. Click the **Browse** button.

4. Locate the CD-ROM drive, find the \Support directory, select **Setup.exe**, and click **Open**.

5. Click **OK** to execute the installation.

6. The Windows 2000 Professional Support Tools installation wizard appears. Click **Next**.

7. Provide your name and organization name (if applicable), and click **Next**.

8. Select the **Typical** installation method (it's the default), and click **Next**.

9. Click **Next** again to start the installation.

10. When copying is complete, click **Finish**.

 ## Project 2-5

To create an answer file for an unattended installation for an x86-based system, using the Setup Manager Wizard from the Windows 2000 Support Tools:

 You must be logged in with Administrator privileges to complete this project.

1. Insert the Windows 2000 Professional CD-ROM into the CD-ROM drive and click **Exit** to close the splash screen.

2. Launch Windows Explorer (**Start, Programs, Accessories, Windows Explorer**) and create a new folder on your hard drive called **SetupMgr**.

3. In Windows Explorer, open the Support\Tools folder on the CD-ROM.

4. Double-click **Deploy.cab**.

5. Copy **Setupmgr.exe** and **Setupmgx.dll** to the folder you created in Step 2.

6. Open the Run command (**Start, Run**).

7. Click **Browse**.

8. Locate and select the **Setupmgr.exe** file in the folder you created in Step 2, and click **Open**.

9. Click **OK** to launch the Setup Manager wizard.

10. The Setup Manager wizard launches. Click **Next**.

11. Select the **Create a new answer file** option (the default) (see Figure 2-6), click **Next**.

12. Select the **Windows 2000 Unattended Installation** option (see Figure 2-7), click **Next**.

13. Select the **Windows 2000 Professional** option, click **Next**.

14. Select the **Fully automated** answer file type (see Figure 2-8), click **Next**.

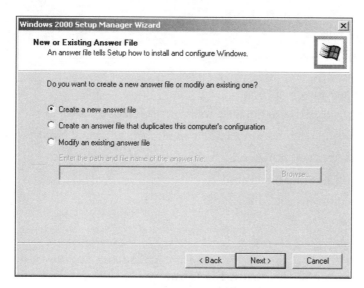

Figure 2-6   Selecting to create a new answer file

2

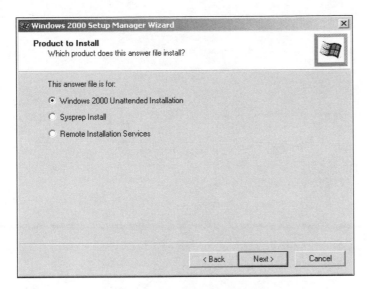

Figure 2-7 Selecting the product to install

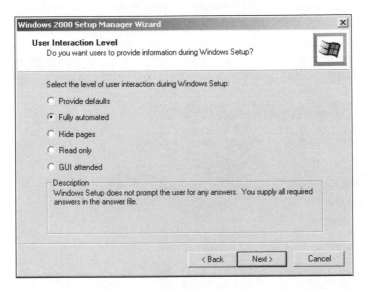

Figure 2-8 Selecting the Fully automated answer file type

15. Click the **I accept the terms of the License Agreement** check box, then click **Next**.

16. Provide a name and organization name for the answer file, then click **Next**.

17. Provide a name for the computer, click **Add**, then click **Next**.

18. Provide the password for the administrator account on this system (see Figure 2-9), then click **Next**.

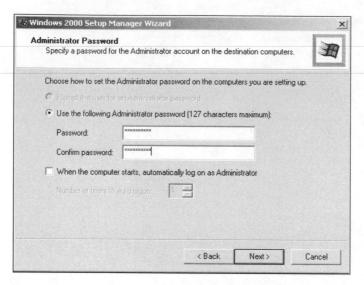

Figure 2-9   Setting the Administrator password

19. Set the **Colors, Screen area**, and **Refresh frequency** based on the destination system's needs. For now, just accept the default setting of **Use Windows default.** Click **Next**.

20. Next, select either typical or custom network configurations. For this project, we'll assume the destination system will use DHCP. So select **Typical settings** (see Figure 2-10) and click **Next**.

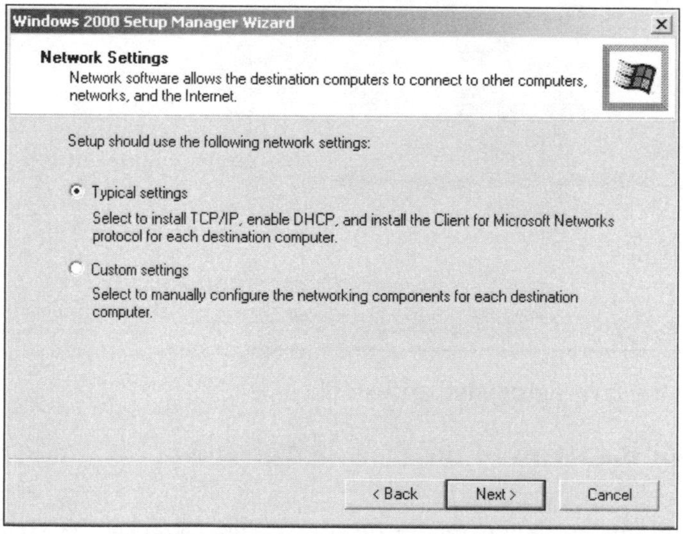

Figure 2-10   Selecting typical network settings

2

21. Select the **Windows Server domain** and provide the name of the domain (see Figure 2-11). Then click the **Create a computer account in the domain** checkbox and provide the name and password (with confirmation) of an administrator account in this domain. Click **Next**.

22. Set the time zone, then click **Next**.

23. Select **No, do not edit additional settings**, then click **Next**.

24. Select **No, this answer file will be used to install from a CD**, then click **Next**.

25. Provide a location and file name for the answer file. Click **Next**.

26. Click **Finish**.

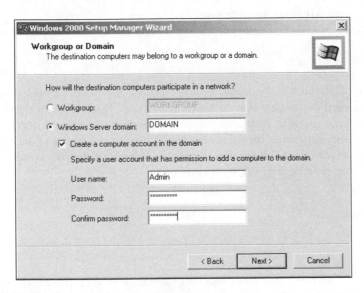

Figure 2-11 Joining a domain

Project 2-6

To upgrade to Windows 2000 Professional from Windows NT or Windows 98:

1. Place the Windows 2000 Professional CD in the cd-rom drive. The autorun mechanism should open the CD splash screen and prompt you whether to upgrade. Click **No**, then click **Exit** to close the splash screen.

2. Open the Run command by selecting **Start, Run**.

3. Click **Browse**.

4. Locate and select **Winnt32.exe** on the Windows 2000 Professional CD using the Browse dialog box.

5. Click **Open**. The path for the Winnt32 file should now appear in the Open field of the Run dialog box.

6. Click **OK**. This launches the installation wizard and you are prompted to choose an installation method.

7. Select the **Upgrade** option (refer to Figure 2-1). Click **Next**.

8. Select the I accept this agreement radio button. Click **Next**.

9. Provide your Product Key from the back of the CD case. Click Next. The Setup wizard will begin the upgrade process, which includes several file copies, system component detection, and reboots. This will take a few minutes.

10. Provide any information or configuration settings required by setup which cannot be obtained from or determined by the previous operating system.

11. The installation will complete and present you with a prompt to press Ctrl+Alt+Delete to log on. Press **Ctrl+Alt+Delete** to log on.

CASE PROJECTS

1. You're in charge of organizing the installation of Windows 2000 Professional onto a number of networked computers that currently host only DOS. Some of these computers will have applications in common, but not all of them, and you'll need to set usernames and computer names for each installation. You've got a lot to take care of, so you'd like the installation to go as quickly as possible. Which of the following will you use? Choose all that apply, and justify your choice(s).

   a. An answer file

   b. A uniqueness database file

   c. Sysdiff

   d. Winnt32

2. Please describe the five types of answer files that can be created by the Setup Manager tool from the Support Tools. Also, describe a scenario for each type of answer file that explains why that type is best suited for the situation.

3

USING THE MMC, TASK SCHEDULER, AND CONTROL PANEL

After reading this chapter and completing the exercises, you will be able to:

♦ Describe the versatility of the Microsoft Management Console (MMC)

♦ Create your own custom MMC consoles

♦ Use the Task Scheduler to automate tasks

♦ Understand and use the Control Panel applets

♦ Install and configure new hardware

♦ Create hardware profiles for changing system configurations

♦ Configure PC Cards and multiple displays

Efficient centralized control is a major theme in Windows 2000. Microsoft has reengineered its administration, configuration, and management interfaces to allow a single computer to be the control point for an entire network. This centralization of control allows complex administrative tasks to be accomplished faster with less effort. There are two main Windows 2000 tools in which this centralized control can be seen, namely, the Microsoft Management Console (MMC) and the Task Scheduler. This chapter explores both of these advanced tools.

The Control Panel is where most of the hardware, device, driver, and service control utilities (applets) reside. Windows 2000 offers a wide range of Control Panel applets, some from Windows NT, some from Windows 98, and others created to support new technologies. This chapter also takes a look at these utilities, and how they can be used to install and configure hardware.

MICROSOFT MANAGEMENT CONSOLE OVERVIEW

The **Microsoft Management Console (MMC)** is a graphical interface shell that provides a structured environment for centralized management through consoles, snap-ins, and extensions. A **console** is like a document window, providing access to a set of administrative controls; one or more consoles can be loaded into the MMC. A **snap-in** is a component that adds control mechanisms to a console to manipulate a service or object. Each console can host one or more snap-ins. Plus, each snap-in can support one or more **extensions** (specialized tools that add functionality to snap-ins). Each snap-in (and its related extensions) is designed to manipulate a specific service or type of object in the Windows 2000 local, remote, domain, or Active Directory environment. The MMC does not provide any management capabilities itself; it merely provides the interface mechanism and environment for system and object controls provided via the snap-ins and extensions.

The MMC was created to simplify administration of the Windows networking environment. Versions of the MMC are included with Internet Information Server (IIS) 4.0 and other products deployed on Windows 98 and Windows NT. However, MMC was not fully realized until the final release of Windows 2000.

The most beneficial feature of MMC is its flexibility. As a control framework that is fully extensible by independent software vendors, its capabilities are unbounded, while it retains ease of use and a common interface. Additionally, multiple snap-ins can be combined into a custom administration layout to suit each administrator's particular needs or responsibilities. No other management tool available offers this wide range of customization.

MMC settings and layout can be stored as an .msc file. This allows custom configurations of snap-ins and extensions to be reused later on the same computer or transferred to another system. The .msc file contains all of the windows currently open in the MMC. You can assign, grant, or restrict access to the .msc files (and the controls they offer) via system policies based on user, group, or computer. Thus, you can selectively and securely assign administrative tasks to nonadministrative users. (Users, groups, and policies are discussed in Chapter 5.)

The Console

The MMC itself is a fairly simple and straightforward interface. To open the MMC without a snap-in, just open the Start, Run window and enter MMC. A blank MMC is displayed (see Figure 3-1). There are really only two parts to the main MMC: the main menu bar and the console window display area. The main menu bar contains the Console, Window, and Help drop-down menus and a movable mini-icon bar with one-click shortcuts to common activities (New, Open, Save, and New Window). The console display area contains the console tree and details pane and functions just like any other Windows application that supports multiple document windows.

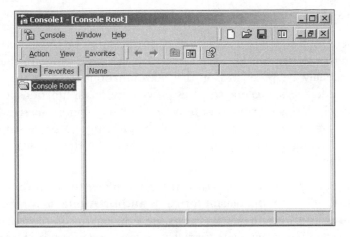

Figure 3-1   The MMC

The console menu bar contains the Action, View, and Favorites menus. The contents of these menus change according to the context of the snap-ins and extensions that are present and active in the console. The console menu bar also contains a mini-icon toolbar of one-click shortcuts to common functions found in the Action and View menus. The console tree is the left pane or division of the console display area (see Figure 3-2). This area lists the loaded snap-ins and extensions along with context selections (such as computers, domains, users, and divisions). The details pane is the right pane or division of the console display area. This area displays the details associated with the active item from the console tree.

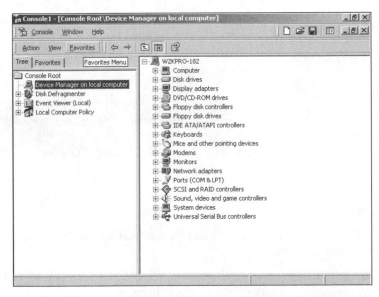

Figure 3-2   The MMC with snap-ins added

Snap-Ins and Extensions

Snap-ins are management tools added to a console to perform actions on services or objects. Microsoft sometimes refers to snap-ins as "standalone snap-ins," to distinguish them from extensions, which are actually a type of snap-in that adds functions to other snap-ins, but does not operate independently. Standalone snap-ins provide the main functions for system administration and control. A single extension can be used on any standalone snap-in with a similar service/object context. Multiple extensions can be present for a single snap-in. For example, the Computer Management snap-in can be extended by the Event Viewer and Device Manager extensions.

Once you've added and configured a console's snap-ins, you can save the console to an .msc file in one of four formats. The first and default format is **author mode**. This mode allows users to add and remove snap-ins, create new windows, view the entire console tree, and save new versions of the console. The other three formats are user mode formats. **User mode** does not allow end users to add or remove snap-ins or resave the console file. The three types of user mode formats are: Full Access, Limited Access/Multiple Windows, and Limited Access/Single Window. Full Access allows users to create new windows and view the entire console tree. The Limited Access formats prevent users from viewing portions of the console tree. Multiple Windows allows users to create new windows but not to close existing windows, and Single Window allows viewing of only one window. The format of the .msc file can be changed by an administrator via the Console, Options menu.

USING THE MMC

Windows 2000 is equipped with several preconfigured consoles designed to offer you administrative control over your system. These tools are found mainly in the Administrative Tools menu (Start, Programs, Administrative Tools, or Start, Settings, Control Panel, Administrative Tools).

 If the Administrative Tools menu does not appear, perform the steps outlined in Hands-on Project 1-5 to make it visible.

The tools found here are:

- *Component Services*: Administers COM applications

- *Computer Management*: Controls disks and contains additional tools that manage local and remote computers

- *Data Sources (ODBC)*: Manages the addition, removal, and configuration of Open Database Connectivity (ODBC) databases and drivers

- *Event Viewer*: Provides an interface for monitoring and troubleshooting messages from Windows and other applications

- *Local Security Policy*: Manages local security policies, such as user rights and audit policies

- *Performance*: Provides graphs of system performance; also sets up data logs and alerts

- *Services*: Provides an interface to stop and start system services

- *Telnet Server Administration*: A DOS-based management interface for Telnet server settings and connections

These predefined consoles are stored in user mode, but the snap-ins used to create them are available to you to create your own custom consoles. (The Windows 2000 Professional pre-defined consoles are explored in the Hands-on Projects at the end of this chapter.) In addition to these predefined consoles, when you install other services or applications they may add other consoles for their custom or unique controls.

> Windows 2000 Professional and Windows 2000 Server have different predefined consoles.

Creating custom consoles is simple. Just launch the MMC via the Start, Run command. Then use the Add/Remove Snap-In command from the Console menu to open the Add/Remove Snap-in dialog box. Click on the Add button to view the Add Standalone Snap-in dialog box (see Figure 3-3). Select the snap-in, and click Add. If the snap-in supports both local and remote operation, you'll be prompted to indicate whether to pull data locally or from a remote system. (Complete instructions for creating a custom console are given in Hands-on Project 3-1.)

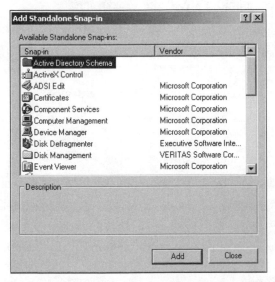

Figure 3-3   The Add Standalone Snap-in dialog box

The snap-ins available by default on a Windows 2000 Professional system are as follows:

- *ActiveX Control*: Allows you to add ActiveX controls to a number of categories, including 3D Direct Transform, Active Scripting Engine, Automation Objects, Document Objects, Embedable Objects, and Internet Explorer Browser Communication Band

- *Certificates*: Manages certificates for yourself, a service, or a computer

- *Component Services*: Points to the Component Services management tool from the Control Panel

- *Computer Management*: Points to the Computer Management tools from the Control Panel

- *Device Manager*: Allows you to view the hardware devices installed on your system and configure their properties

- *Disk Defragmenter*: Points to the Windows 2000 Disk Defragmenter

- *Disk Management*: Points to the Disk Management utility

- *Event Viewer*: Points to the event management utility that displays system event logs

- *Fax Service Management*: Manages faxes and fax devices

- *Folder*: Adds a folder to manage from within the MMC

- *Group Policy*: Manages group policy objects

- *Indexing Service*: Searches files and properties

- *IP Security Policy Management*: Administers Internet Protocol Security (IPSec) policies for secure communications

- *Link to Web Address*: Provides a link to a Web site of your choice

- *Local Users and Groups*: Administers local users and groups

- *Performance Logs and Alerts*: Provides an interface to set up performance logs and alerts

- *Removable Storage Management*: Manages removable storage devices

- *Security Configuration and Analysis*: Manages security configurations for computers using security template files

- *Security Templates*: Edits security template files

- *Services*: Provides an interface for configuring, stopping, and starting system services

- *Shared Folders*: Provides an interface to view information about shared folders, current sessions, and open files

- *System Information*: Provides information about the system for troubleshooting purposes

- *WMI Control*: Manages the Windows Management Instrumentation service

3

Some snap-ins can serve as standalone snap-ins or can be an extension to another snap-in (for example, the Device Manager or Event Viewer both can be either standalone snap-ins or extensions of other snap-ins such as Computer Management). Once you've added one or more snap-ins (that is, they appear in the list on the Add/Remove Snap-In dialog box), you can add or modify extensions by selecting the Extensions tab. Hands-on Project 3-1 explores the Computer Management snap-in extensions.

THE WINDOWS 2000 TASK SCHEDULER

The **Task Scheduler** in Windows 2000 is an updated version of the scheduler service from Windows NT 4.0, used to automate the performance of programs or batch files at a certain time or when a certain system condition occurs. The most obvious change is the presence of the Scheduled Tasks folder in the Control Panel. This folder gives you quick GUI access to all of the features of task scheduling. You don't have to rely on the text-only AT command interface or the WINAT GUI Resource Kit tool, as you did in Windows NT 4.0.

Tasks can be scheduled to run at a specific time, repeat at intervals, and launch with specific user credentials. The Add Scheduled Task Wizard, which appears in the Scheduled Tasks folder, walks you step by step through the scheduling process. (Try using this wizard in Hands-on Project 3-2.) Once a task is defined, you can edit and alter its scheduled properties by right-clicking the item and selecting Properties from the menu. The task Properties dialog box has four tabs. The Task tab (see Figure 3-4) lists the execution path and filename, the start-up directory, user account context, and whether the task is enabled. The Schedule tab (see Figure 3-5) lists the time and date when the task will be launched (once, daily, weekly, monthly, at system startup, at logon, and when idle). The Advanced button on this tab allows you to define a termination period and whether to repeat the task at minute/hour intervals. The Settings tab lists whether to delete the task when complete (default is to retain task), whether to terminate the task if still active after a time period, minimal idle time before launch, and whether to stop the task if the system is running on batteries. The Security tab is used to define the access permissions to this object (that is, who can read or change the task).

 Troubleshooting the Task Scheduler involves verifying the settings of each defined task. Most often, the cause of a task not running when expected is an incorrect time/date setting. You should also check the path for the tool/script/program to be launched as well as any advanced settings dealing with idle time and repeat executions. Double-checking your work is the best method to eliminate programming errors when scheduling tasks.

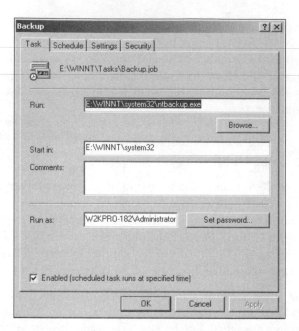

Figure 3-4   The Scheduled Task Properties dialog box, Task tab

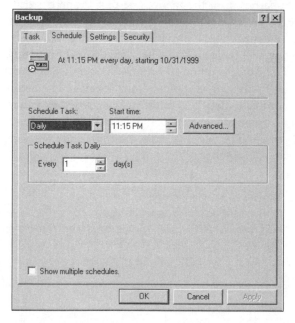

Figure 3-5   The Scheduled Task Properties dialog box, Schedule tab

Scheduled tasks can be moved from system to system. This allows you to define administrative actions or batch files on a single computer, then place them on client systems from a central location.

CONTROL PANEL OVERVIEW

The Windows 2000 **Control Panel** (shown in Figure 3-6) hosts the **applets** (tools or utilities) used to install and configure **devices** (internal or external physical computer components) and software (particularly operating system **services**, such as print spooling, remote access, or user access to network resources). There are several basic applets that appear in the Control Panel, and other applets may be added depending on the services, components, or applications installed with Windows 2000. The common Control Panel applets are discussed in the following sections.

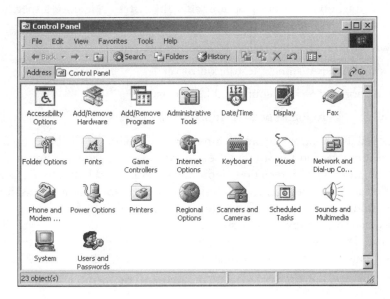

Figure 3-6   The Windows 2000 Control Panel

Accessibility Options

You can enable and fine-tune special interface features for the visually impaired, hearing impaired, or movement impaired in the Accessibility Options applet. There are five tabs in this applet. The Keyboard tab is used to configure the following:

- *StickyKeys*: Enables the use of Ctrl, Shift, and Alt by pressing once instead of requiring the user to hold them down

- *FilterKeys*: Used to ignore quick or repeated keystrokes

- *ToggleKeys*: Plays a tone when Caps Lock, Scroll Lock, or Num Lock keys are pressed

The Sound tab of the Accessibility Options applet is used to configure SoundSentry and ShowSounds. SoundSentry displays visual cues when the system plays a sound, such as flashing a title bar, window, or the desktop. ShowSounds is used to force the display of captions when sounds or speech are played.

The Display tab sets the display to a high contrast color scheme to improve readability. The options include black on white, white on black, or any defined color scheme (via the Display applet's Appearance tab, or via the Settings button on the Display tab of the Accessibility Options applet).

The Mouse tab is used to enable numeric pad control of mouse movements. When enabled, the arrows on the numeric keypad control the direction of mouse insertion point movement. The settings include speed and acceleration of the pointer.

The General tab is used to set the following controls:

- Disable or turn off accessibility options after the system is idle for a specified length of time
- Display a warning when enabling accessibility options
- Play a sound when turning a feature on or off
- Enable support for serially connected key devices
- Apply all settings to logon desktop and/or to new users

Configuring Accessibility Options is simply a matter of enabling or disabling each offered feature on the various tabs and fine-tuning these features by selecting the optional settings that offer you the most help interacting with the system. Troubleshooting Accessibility Options is handled in the same manner as the initial configuration: walk through the tabs and the configuration settings of each feature to make sure the desired settings are selected. If the accessibility option involves a device such as a special keyboard, mouse, etc., check that the driver for that device is up to date, or check with the vendor for additional troubleshooting tips. Sometimes the problem may be with the I/O device and not with the Windows 2000 accessibility options.

Add/Remove Hardware

The Add/Remove Hardware applet is actually a **wizard** (see Figure 3-7). It is used to add a new device, troubleshoot a device that is not functioning properly (these first two functions are part of the same process), or remove an existing device. This wizard is extremely easy to use and very informative. This tool makes adding new devices to Windows 2000 as easy as working with Windows 98.

When adding new hardware, the wizard first searches for **Plug and Play** devices. If any are found, it attempts to locate and install **drivers**. If no new Plug and Play devices are found, it prompts you for the type of device you are installing. This prompt consists of a list of existing devices and drivers that are loaded or known. This list displays an icon by each item. Functioning items have an icon that represents their function (mouse, monitor, NIC, etc.). Nonfunctioning items have either a yellow exclamation point or a stop sign to indicate problems. You can select one of these nonfunctioning items to replace the driver, to attempt a solution (that's the troubleshooting part of this process) or select the Add a new device option to install a driver for a new device. Drivers can be loaded either from the distribution CD, from a manufacturer's CD or floppy disk, or via the Microsoft Update utility.

3

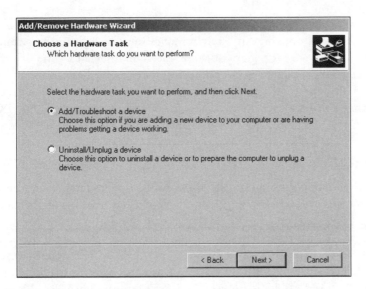

Figure 3-7   The Add/Remove Hardware applet

The Add/Remove Hardware wizard is the best place to start when installing DVD players, CD players, tape devices, scanners, modems, network interface cards, multimedia devices, video devices, smart card readers, cameras, IrDA (Infrared Data Association) devices, wireless devices, and USB devices. As already mentioned, in many cases, Windows 2000 Plug and Play will automatically detect new hardware components and attempt to install drivers for them. However, when devices are not automatically detected or the drivers fail to install, you can employ the Add/Remove Hardware applet to install the drivers for the device.

 TIP   Always check with the vendor, often via their Web site, for the latest drivers for their devices.

Once a device is installed, it can be configured and managed through the Device Manager. This tool is accessed via the Computer Management tool set from the Administrative Tools in the Control Panel. The Device Manager is used to alter device settings, update drivers, add/remove a device from a hardware profile, and to verify functionality of a device. See the "Installing Hardware" section later in this chapter for more information on configuring and managing devices with the Device Manager, and try Hands-on Project 3-8. Troubleshooting any device is a matter of verifying that the proper driver is installed and that the correct settings for the device are made. Both of these items can be verified through the Device Manager. Furthermore, the Device Manager can be used to update, replace, or remove drivers for installed devices. This is accomplished using the Uninstall or Update buttons on the Drivers tab of a device's Properties dialog box from the Device Manager.

To remove a device from your system, you can select one of two removal methods: uninstall or unplug/eject. The uninstall option completely removes the driver from the system. Thus, to regain access to the device later (or after you've physically reinstalled it), the driver for the device must be reinstalled. The unplug/eject option simply temporarily stops the device from being used by the system. This option is often used with removable media drives (such as Jaz or Zip drives), **docking stations** (expansion devices for notebook computers), and PC Cards (formally PCMCIA Cards, discussed later in this chapter).

Add/Remove Programs

The Add/Remove Programs applet is actually three tools in one. First, it can be used to change or remove installed applications. In this mode, it displays installed applications, their drive space usage, and how often the application is actually used. You can select the change option (if the application's own setup routine offers a partial or optional setup method) or remove the application. The second tool (see Figure 3-8) installs new applications from a vendor-supplied distribution floppy disk or CD or from the Microsoft Update site. The third tool (see Figure 3-9) is the Add/Remove Windows Components Wizard. You can add or remove Windows 2000 components through this wizard/tool.

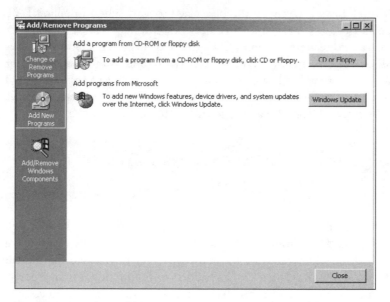

Figure 3-8   The Add/Remove Programs applet, Add New Programs selection

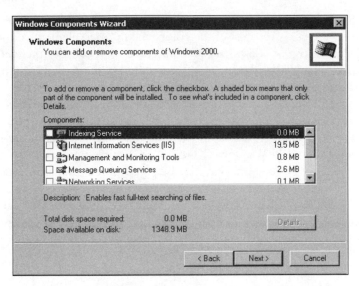

3

Figure 3-9   The Add/Remove Programs applet, Add/Remove Windows Components selection

Administrative Tools

The Administrative Tools item is actually a folder pointing to the same place as the Administrative Tools item in the Start menu. The contents of this menu were briefly discussed in the "Using the MMC" section earlier in this chapter.

Date/Time

The Date/Time applet is used to set the calendar date, clock time, and time zone for the system. On the Date & Time tab, you can set the month and year from pull-down lists and select the day from the displayed month calendar. Time is adjusted by highlighting the hour, minute, second, and AM/PM, and either using the scroll buttons or typing in a new value. When you set the time, the timer clock is set directly on the system's BIOS. The Time Zone tab displays a world map and a pull-down list from which you can select time zones. Time zone information is stored internally as either a negative or a positive offset to Greenwich Mean Time. This also supports automatic updates for daylight-saving time and standard time, in those areas where such seasonal time changes occur.

Display

The Display applet is used to choose from a wide range of interface changes and preference settings. The display properties also can be accessed by right-clicking the mouse button on any blank area of the desktop and selecting Properties from the pop-up menu. There are six tabs to this applet. The Background tab is used to select the wallpaper graphic and indicate whether to center, tile, or stretch the image. The Screen Saver tab is used to set the screen saver, define the idle period before launching the screen saver, and set the energy-saving features of the monitor (the Screen Saver tab links to the Power Options applet, where all power features are configured). The Appearance tab is used to set the color scheme; each element of the display, from fonts to scroll bars to active windows, can be configured to your color preferences. The Web tab is used to enable/disable the display of Web content on the Active Desktop and to define the elements displayed. The Effects tab is used to set the common desktop icons and visual effects, such as menu transition effects, font smoothing, and showing window contents while dragging. The Settings tab is used to set the screen resolution and color depth. There are also buttons to aid in troubleshooting and setting adapter- or monitor-specific settings. The Troubleshoot button leads you to the Windows 2000 Display Troubleshooter. From within this applet, you can answer a series of questions that may help you find a resolution to any problems you may be experiencing. The Advanced button opens the five-tabbed Monitor and Video Adapter dialog box. From this dialog box, you can configure font size, settings for how Windows 2000 responds to setting changes, adapter properties, monitor properties, graphics acceleration, and color management.

Fax

The Fax applet is used to configure the fax capabilities of Windows 2000. Basic fax capabilities supported over a fax/modem allow Windows 2000 users to send and receive faxes. This applet is used to configure user information (see Figure 3-10), define cover pages, set monitor status, and access advanced functions (open the Fax Management Console and add a new fax printer).

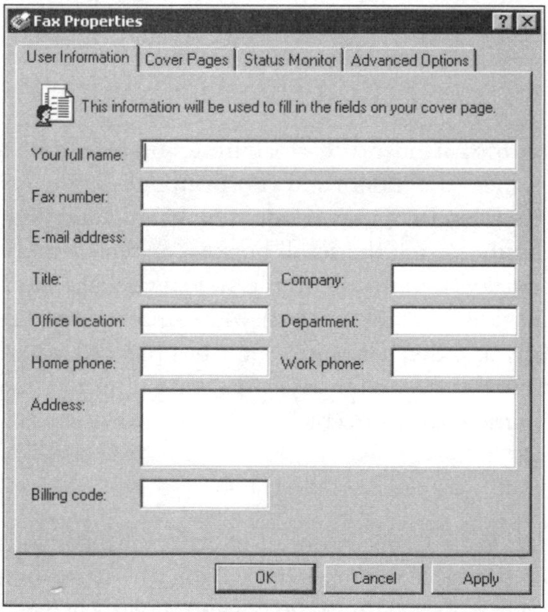

Figure 3-10   The Fax applet

Folder Options

The Folder Options applet accesses the same configuration interface as the Tools, Folder Options command from Windows Explorer. This applet is used to set the functional and visual parameters of the folders on the system. This applet has four tabs. The General tab is used to enable/disable Active Desktop, Web folders view, and open folder in new or current window, and to indicate whether a single- or double-click opens items. The View tab is used to configure advanced settings, such as show hidden files, hide file extensions, and launch folder windows in separate processes. The File Types tab is used to define or associate file extensions with applications. The Offline Files tab is used to enable offline network browsing by caching resources locally.

Fonts

The Fonts applet lists all currently installed fonts used by Windows 2000. Additional fonts can be added and unused fonts can be removed through this interface. Unfortunately, to see a sample of a font's output still requires a word-processing application with print preview capabilities or actually printing a document.

Game Controllers

The Game Controllers applet is used to install and configure the operations of joysticks and other specialized gaming controls that may be attached to sound cards or serial ports. This interface offers access to device-specific properties and troubleshooting aids.

Internet Options

The Internet Options applet (see Figure 3-11) is used to define settings for Internet Explorer and general Internet access. This applet has six tabs. The General tab sets the home page, temporary file cache, URL history, colors, fonts, languages, and accessibility options. The Security tab defines the security level for four Web zones. The security level determines whether software is automatically downloaded, form data is submitted, or cookies (text scripts that a Web browser sends to a server to customize a user's browsing experience) are used. The Content tab is used to configure the Content Advisor (a content-based site blocker), identity certificates, AutoComplete, and your online identity. The Connections tab is used to define how IE (Internet Explorer) and other online tools access the Internet via a network connection or DUN (Dial-Up Networking), often used for home Internet service connections. The Programs tab is used to define which helper applications are used for HTML editing, e-mail, newsgroups, Internet calls, calendar, and contacts. The Advanced tab is used to set advanced features, such as browsing functions, HTTP 1.1, Microsoft VM (virtual memory), multimedia, printing, searching, security, and accessibility.

 For details on configuring Internet Explorer, please consult the IE Help file or the IE Web site at *http://www.microsoft.com/windows/ie/default.htm*.

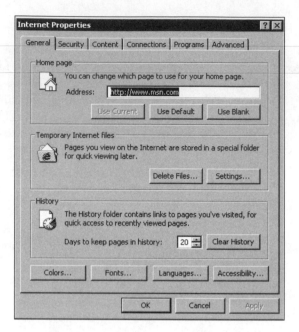

Figure 3-11   The Internet Options applet

Keyboard and Mouse

The Keyboard applet is used to modify how the keyboard functions. Settings include the repeat delay, repeat rate, insertion point blink rate, and language used. The Mouse applet is used to modify how the mouse functions. Settings allow you to switch the functions of left and right buttons, choose single- or double-click to open, indicate how quickly to double-click, choose the graphics used for pointers, indicate how the pointer moves (speed and acceleration), and choose to snap to objects (that is, when the pointer moves to the general vicinity of an object, it selects the object it is near).

Network and Dial-up Connections

The Network and Dial-up Connections applet is used to create and control network settings for both LAN and RAS links.

Phone and Modem Options

The Phone and Modem Options applet is used to define dialing locations, install and configure modems, and configure RAS (Remote Access Service) and TAPI (Telephony Application Programming Interface) drivers and services.

Power Options

The Power Options applet (see Figure 3-12) is used to set the system's power-saving features. Several power schemes are predefined, such as Home/Office Desk, Portable/Laptop, Presentation, Always On, Minimal Power Management, and Max Battery. Each of these schemes is designed with either power or use in mind. You can employ a predefined scheme or create your own. The two primary settings are Turn off monitor and Turn off hard disks after a specified length of time. Other advanced controls include displaying the Power Management icon in the icon tray, enabling hibernation, and indicating whether to enable Advanced Power Management (APM) and uninterruptable power supply (UPS) support.

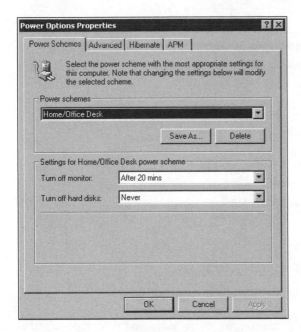

Figure 3-12   The Power Options applet

To configure the Advanced Power Management (APM), you need only select a predefined power scheme through the Power Options applet in the Control Panel. If you want a custom scheme, you can alter the monitor and hard disk timeout values and save those settings as a new power scheme. The four other tabs of the Power Options applet allow you to enable the power icon in the taskbar, allow hibernation, allow APM (an automated feature that reduces battery drain), and to configure a UPS.

Printers

The Printers applet is used to install, share, and configure printers. This applet is used for physical print devices as well as for specialized printers, such as fax machines. Once a printer is in use, this applet also grants access to the print queue for management purposes.

Regional Options

The Regional Options applet is used to define location-specific uses or requirements for numbers, currency, time, dates, and more. You can select a predefined regional scheme based on language or country, then define or customize specifics for numbers, currency (see Figure 3–13), time, and date.

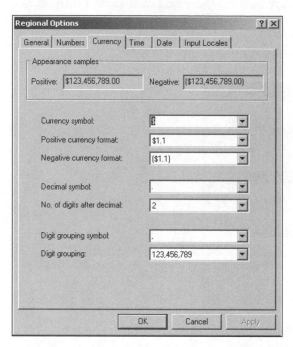

Figure 3-13   The Regional Options applet, Currency tab

To enable and configure multiple language support, you need to decide whether you only want the ability to read and write documents in multiple languages or if you actually need multiple input locales. An input locale is a combination of language and keyboard layout used to define how data is entered into the computer. To enable multiple languages for documents, just select additional languages on the General tab of the Regional Options applet. To enable multiple input locales, add them to the Input Locales tab and define the shortcut key sequence used to switch between them. Once multiple locales are defined, you can also switch between them using the locale indicator that appears in the icon tray of the task bar. (Try Hands-on Projects 3-9 and 3-10.)

The Numbers, Currency, Time, and Date tabs of the Regional Settings applet are used to define the local settings for the computer. These tabs offer controls based on country, region, and language so you can fully customize the interface's handling of these items for your needs or preferences.

Scanners and Cameras

The Scanners and Cameras applet is used to install drivers and configure digital cameras and optical scanners. Once present, these devices can be used with graphics and imaging software to create digital images of real-life or printed materials.

Scheduled Tasks

The Scheduled Tasks applet is used to automate task launching, such as automatic backups. This applet was discussed earlier in this chapter.

Sounds and Multimedia

The Sounds and Multimedia applet (see Figure 3-14) is used to customize the sound scheme (system events that cause sounds, such as program errors, emptying the Recycle Bin, or questions), setting of device preferences, and configuration or troubleshooting of multimedia-related services and drivers.

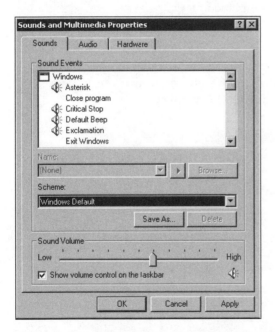

Figure 3-14   The Sounds and Multimedia applet, Sounds tab

System

The System applet (see Figure 3-15) is used to configure or control many system-level or core operational functions of Windows 2000. The System applet has five tabs. The General tab displays system version, registered user, and basic computer information. The Network Identification tab is used to join a domain/workgroup, create local users, and change the computer name. The Hardware tab is used to access the Add/Remove

Hardware Wizard (also an applet), enable/disable driver signing requirements (drivers that have been authenticated by Microsoft), access the Device Manager (Administrative Tools utility), and define hardware profiles. The User Profiles tab is used to create roaming profiles out of local profiles (see Chapter 5). The Advanced tab is used to define performance options (set optimization for applications or background services, and paging file settings), environmental variables, and startup and recovery options.

Driver Signing

Driver signing is used to identify drivers that have successfully passed the Microsoft Windows Hardware Quality Labs evaluations and tests. The configuration of driver signing through the System applet is used to warn users when a non-signed driver is being installed. Pressing the Driver Signing button on the Hardware tab of the System applet reveals the Driver Signing Options dialog box. This dialog box presents three radio buttons:

- *Ignore:* Install all files, regardless of file signature
- *Warn:* Display a message before installing an unsigned file
- *Block:* Prevent installation of unsigned files

Configuring driver signing involves selecting one of these three options. If you are an administrator, you are offered an additional checkbox of "Apply setting as system default" which makes the driver signing setting the same for all users. The only method of troubleshooting driver signing is to return to this dialog box and ensure that the correct item is selected according to your organization's needs or security policy.

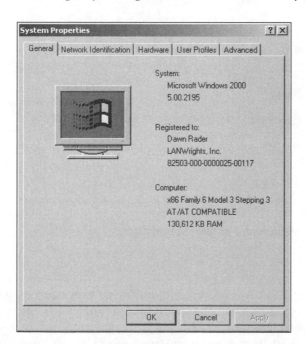

Figure 3-15   The System applet

Virtual Memory

The Virtual Memory dialog box is accessed from the System applet, Advanced tab. Click the Performance button to display the Performance Options dialog box, then press the Change button to display the Virtual Memory dialog box (see Figure 3-16). The Virtual Memory dialog box controls how a Windows 2000 system uses a combination of physical RAM and disk space to create a pool of memory for system and application use when RAM is no longer available.

Virtual memory consists of the machine's actual physical RAM plus one or more **paging files** (Pagefile.sys) that reside on a physical disk attached to the system. The paging file acts like an extension to the system's RAM, which is why it's called virtual memory. Windows 2000 coordinates the swapping of special 4 KB data units between the paging file and RAM, where such units are called **memory pages**, or more simply, **pages**. The combination of memory pages in RAM and on disk creates a collection of pages called virtual memory, that allows a system to run more and larger applications at any given moment than a system's RAM might physically be able to accommodate. Administrators can change the size of the paging file to help optimize system performance. This usually involves increasing the values assigned to the initial and maximum sizes of this file, to give the system more room in which to operate.

The default paging file size for Windows 2000 should equal one and one-half times the amount of physical RAM. Thus, if a system incorporates 128 MB RAM, Setup creates a paging file of 192 MB. Microsoft suggests that if another drive is present on the machine, a paging file should not reside on the same physical disk as the Windows 2000 system files, to decrease disk contention between swapping memory pages and accessing system files. Moving the paging file off the boot partition makes it impossible to perform a memory dump.

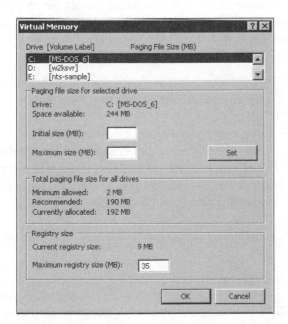

Figure 3-16   The Virtual Memory dialog box

Environmental Variables

The Environment Variables dialog box, which is accessed by clicking the Environment Variables button on the Advanced tab of the System applet, allows environmental variables, such as default operating system, number of processors, and default temp directory to be set. The top pane of the tab controls settings for system-wide environmental variables. The bottom pane controls local user environmental variables. Only a local user who is currently logged on can set variables on this tab. These variables are used to control how Windows 2000 operates, but particularly to control how older 16-bit Windows or DOS programs behave within the Virtual DOS Machines (VDMs) within which they must run in the Windows 2000 environment.

Startup and Recovery Options

The Startup and Recovery Options dialog box, accessed by clicking the Startup and Recovery button on the Advanced tab of the System applet, allows you to define system startup parameters and how STOP errors are handled. Startup controls occur in the region of this window labeled System Startup, and are used to set the default operating system and selection timer for the boot menu. The default is 30 seconds, but is often reduced to 5 or 10 seconds to speed system startup.

In this window, the options in the area labeled Recovery are a bit more esoteric. They provide special controls to deal with an outright Windows 2000 system crash. Normally, when a regular application fails, the application itself generates an error message to the event log, while dumping the contents of its address space to a file. When the whole 2000 system halts due to a STOP error, the entire contents of the computer's virtual memory are dumped to a .dmp file (which resides in the %systemroot% or \Winnt folder, by default). Although this dump file is of little use to ordinary users, and can usually be discarded, this information can be invaluable when you are debugging system or application problems. There are also options for writing an event to the system log, for sending administrative alerts, and for automatic rebooting of the system.

Users and Passwords

The Users and Passwords applet is used to create and manage local user accounts. This applet is also used to manage identity certificates (certificates are electronic documents that verify the identity of a client or server to ensure that sensitive information is not transmitted to an imposter) and group membership, and to determine whether the Ctrl+Alt+Delete keystroke is required to log on. This applet is discussed in detail in Chapter 5.

INSTALLING HARDWARE

Installing hardware under Windows 2000 is fairly straightforward. Upon bootup, the system polls the entire computer, looking for new devices. If they are found, Windows 2000 attempts to identify them. This will be successful for most Plug and Play devices and some non–Plug and Play devices. Windows 2000 will install drivers automatically or prompt you for an alternate source path for drivers. If new hardware is not detected, the Add/Remove Hardware Wizard can be used to manually install vendor-supplied drivers.

In either case, once a device driver is installed, you can verify that it is working properly via the Device Manager. This tool, accessed via the Device Manager button on the Hardware tab of the System applet, lists all installed and known devices and indicates their status. (You can also reach the Device Manager, shown in Figure 3-17, through the Computer Management administration tool by selecting Device Manager from the System Tools console tree.) A yellow exclamation point or a stop sign over a device's icon indicates problems or conflicts. The exclamation point generally indicates a conflict, whereas a stop sign generally indicates that the device is not functioning. By opening the properties of each problem device, you can access information about the nature of the problem, read troubleshooting recommendations, change device settings, or install/upgrade device-related drivers.

 TIP If a new device is not a Plug and Play device, then there is a good possibility that its current settings will conflict with existing hardware. If you want to add a device that isn't Plug and Play, it's always a good idea to find out what hardware resources are available. Then you can use this information to either preset the device (if jumpers and DIP switches are present) or configure the driver.

Figure 3-17   The Device Manager, Devices by Type

The four main areas of hardware resource conflict are:

- *interrupt request (IRQ)*: The IRQ level settings are used to halt CPU operation in favor of the device. Windows 2000 supports 16 interrupts, namely IRQ 0 through 15.

- *I/O port*: The I/O port setting defines the section of memory used by the hardware to communicate with the operating system. When an IRQ is used, the system checks the I/O port memory area for additional information about what function is needed by the device. The I/O port is represented by a hexadecimal number, such as O3F8 – O3FF.

- *direct memory access (DMA)*: DMA is a channel used by a hardware device to access memory directly—that is, bypassing the CPU. Windows 2000 supports 8 DMA channels, numbered 0 through 7.

- *Memory*: This is the area of physical memory hosted by the motherboard that is used by a device to perform its operations. These memory areas are reserved and cannot be used by any other device or process on the system.

You can see the current state of these resources through the Device Manager by selecting Resources By Type (see Figure 3-18) or Resources By Connection from the View menu. Using the data presented, you can configure new hardware so that it does not conflict with any existing devices or drivers. Once a driver is installed, you may be able to alter its resource requirements via the device's Properties dialog box on the Resource tab.

To access this configuration area:

1. Open the **System** applet from the Control Panel.

2. Select the **Hardware** tab.

3. Click the **Device Manager** button.

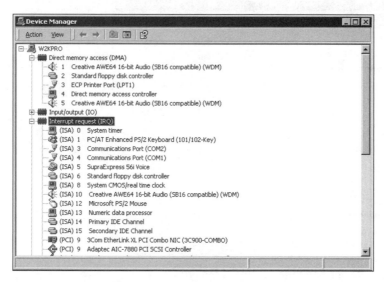

Figure 3-18   The Device Manager, Resources by Type

4. Locate the device in the list and select it.

5. Right-click over the device, and select **Properties** from the resulting menu.

6. Click the **Resources** tab (see Figure 3-19).

7. Click the **Set Configuration Manually** option if the Resource Settings are not displayed.

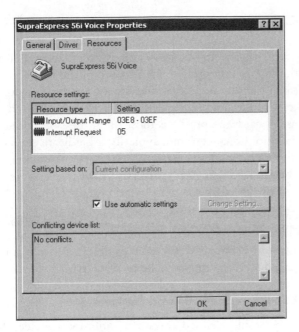

Figure 3-19   A device's Resources tab

REMOVABLE MEDIA

Removable media include any storage device, whether read-only, write-once, or rewriteable, that is installed onto a Windows 2000 system, such as tape devices, DVD and CD-ROM drives, optical drives, Zip or Jaz drives, Bernoulli devices, etc. If a device can be removed or inserted while the computer's power is on ("hot swapped"), then it is a removable device. Removable devices are installed in the same manner as any other device, using either Plug and Play at startup or the Add/Remove Hardware applet.

Once installed, removable media can be configured through the Device Manager. You can also manage the media (tape, disks, CD, DVD, and so on) through the Removable Storage tool found in the Computer Management tool accessed from Administrative Tools in the Control Panel. This tool lists all media present on the system and grants you the ability to create custom sets of media for backup or archival purposes. The Computer Management tool can be used to define the media type for each device, set permissions for the media device, and rename the media device. We recommend you explore the Removable Storage section of the Computer Management tool, especially if you are working with swappable media.

HARDWARE PROFILES

A **hardware profile** is similar to a user profile in that it is a collection of custom settings specific to a particular situation. In the case of user profiles, the situation is the user account used to log on to the system. In the case of hardware profiles, the situation is the conglomeration of hardware that currently makes up the computer (including both internal and external devices and network connections). A hardware profile is most often used on portable computers in which hardware configurations change often. Typically, a hardware profile is used either to enable or disable network support, modems, external monitors, and docking stations. However, hardware profiles can be employed anytime there is a hardware change between bootups, such as with removable media, PC Cards, disconnected peripherals, etc.

In most cases, hardware profiles are not strictly required on Plug and Play compatible systems. But most users find them more convenient and elegant than installing and removing drivers each time the system boots into a new hardware configuration. Basically, a hardware profile is simply a list of all installed devices with selections as to which devices are not enabled for a particular profile. For example, on a notebook computer used away from the office, a hardware profile could be used to disable networking hardware.

On a system with multiple hardware profiles defined, the system attempts to select the hardware profile that matches the discovered hardware (Windows 2000 performs a hardware system check during initial bootup). If a match cannot be determined (that is, an exact match is not found), then you will be prompted as to which hardware profile to use. Furthermore, you can select one profile as the default profile. When the system fails to locate a profile matching existing hardware, after the defined timeout period expires, the default hardware profile will be used.

Hardware profiles are created through the Hardware Profiles dialog box (see Figure 3-20). This dialog box is accessed by clicking the Hardware Profiles button on the Hardware tab of the System applet. Initially, there is only one hardware profile present, the current configuration with all known devices installed and enabled.

To create new profiles:

1. Select an existing hardware profile.

2. Click the **Copy** button.

3. Provide a name for the new profile, then click **OK**.

4. Reboot the computer.

5. While rebooting, select the new hardware profile if prompted.

6. Open the **Device Manager** (System applet, Hardware tab, Device Manager button).

7. For each device you want to remove from this hardware profile, open its **Properties** dialog box (right-click over the device and select **Properties** from the resulting menu).

Figure 3-20   The Hardware Profiles dialog box

8. On the **General** tab of each device's Properties dialog box, change the Device Usage pull-down list to **Do not use this device (disable)**.

9. For each device you want to add back into this hardware profile, open its **Properties** dialog box (right-click over the device and select **Properties** from the pop-up menu).

10. On the **General** tab of each device's Properties dialog box, change the Device Usage pull-down list to **Use this device (enable)**.

11. When you have made all the desired changes, close the Device Manager.

Once you have two or more hardware profiles defined, you need to make two setting changes to the Hardware Profiles dialog box. First, select which profile should be the default. This is done by reordering the profiles so that the most often used or most common profile is at the top of the list. Reordering is accomplished by selecting a profile and using the up and down arrows on the dialog box to alter its position. Second, select whether to wait indefinitely for a hardware profile selection or to use the default if no selection is made after a specified time period. This setting only applies when the system cannot automatically determine which profile to use on the basis of discovered hardware.

PCMCIA or PC Cards

Windows 2000, being a fully Plug and Play compatible operating system, includes support for **PCMCIA (Personal Computer Memory Card International Association)** or **PC Cards**. These are credit-card sized devices that plug into a slot port found on most notebooks and some desktop computers. PC Cards can host many different types of devices, such as memory expansions, SCSI (Small Computer System Interface) cards, NICs (network interface cards), modems, and proprietary peripheral interfaces. Most computers that support PC Cards have two slots, thus allowing up to two additional devices to be added to the system.

Unlike Windows NT and Windows 95/98, Windows 2000 does not have a PC Card (or PCMCIA) applet. Instead, it displays an Unplug Or Eject Hardware icon in the system tray. This tool is used for PC Cards as well as for all removable devices. In most cases, it is a good idea to use this tool to stop the driver of a particular device before unplugging it from the system. This prevents system errors and data loss by allowing the system to elegantly finish using the device, clear all related buffers, and disable the drivers and dependent services.

Card services are installed automatically when Windows 2000 is installed onto a HAL-supported notebook or portable computer (or a desktop computer with a PC Card slot device). Once installed, most of the tasks and processes required to manage and enable PC Card support are handled automatically by Windows 2000. Your primary control is through the "Unplug or Eject Hardware" icon in the system tray. Through this icon (right-click to access a pop-up menu or double-click to open the applet), you can instruct the system to stop using and release control of the PC Card device so it can be removed. Once a new card is inserted, the system will automatically detect and enable it.

VIDEO ADAPTERS

The video or display capabilities of Windows 2000 are often the most visible function of the system. All interaction with the operating system by a user requires some form of visual display to guide the placement of the mouse insertion point or to offer feedback from keyboard use (or visual-to-audio or visual-to-tactile conversion for the visually impaired). The features and functions of the Windows 2000 display mechanism are controlled through the Display applet. The driver for the video adapter is usually installed during system installation via Plug and Play and the Add/Remove Hardware applet. Once a driver is present, it can be reconfigured or updated through the Display applet (that is, by clicking the Advanced button on the Settings tab, then clicking the Properties button on the Adapter tab).

Windows 2000 also supports multiple displays. In fact, you can configure up to nine monitors to display a single extended desktop. There are a few limitations on the multiple display feature:

- Only PCI (Peripheral Component Interconnect) or AGP (Accelerated Graphics Port) devices are supported.

- Video adapters built into the motherboard can be used—but only as secondary adapters—providing that the BIOS (basic input/output system) will allow the on-board adapter to function when an expansion card adapter is present.

- Windows 2000 must be installed with a single adapter first; then other adapters can be physically added, and drivers can be installed and configured.

To configure multiple displays, first install all video adapters and attach monitors. Then, follow these steps:

1. Open the **Display** applet.

2. Select the **Settings** tab.

3. Depending on how many adapters are installed, monitor icons with numbers on them will be displayed. Drag these icons to match your desired display arrangement.

4. Select the primary monitor icon (that is, number 1).

5. Select the display adapter from the pull-down list for this monitor.

6. Set the color depth and display resolution.

7. Select the secondary monitor icon (that is, number 2).

8. Repeat Steps 5 through 7 for each device.

CHAPTER SUMMARY

❑ In this chapter, you learned about the Microsoft Management Console, Task Scheduler, and Control Panel. The MMC is an interface into which consoles, snap-ins, and extensions are loaded to create custom administration tools. The MMC provides an interface to the majority of system tools that you can use to manage Windows 2000, as well as create your own custom consoles to manage applications and services that are specific to your system.

❑ The Task Scheduler is a fully GUI-interactive scheduling service with a wide range of control features for local and remote scheduling. With these two powerful tools, you can effectively manage a local system or an entire network.

❑ The Control Panel contains various applets and tools that are used to manage a Windows 2000 system. This chapter surveyed the most commonly used Control Panel tools.

❑ Finally, this chapter explored the processes of installing hardware, using hardware profiles, dealing with PC Cards, and configuring multiple displays, using the tools introduced in the chapter.

KEY TERMS

applet — A tool or utility found in the Control Panel that typically has a single focused purpose or function.

author mode — The condition of a console that allows users to add and remove snap-ins, create new windows, view the entire console tree, and save new versions of the console.

console — The collection of snap-ins and extensions saved as an .msc file loaded into the MMC that offers administrative controls.

Control Panel — The collection or organization of tools and utilities, called applets, within Windows 2000 (and Windows 95, 98, and Windows NT) where most system- and hardware-level installation and configuration take place.

device — A physical component either internal or external to the computer that is used to perform a specific function. Devices include hard drives, video cards, network inter- face cards, and printers.

direct memory access (DMA) — A channel used by a hardware device to access memory directly, bypassing the CPU. Windows 2000 supports eight DMA channels, numbered 0 through 7.

docking station — An expansion device for notebook computers that allows additional peripherals to be used by the portable computer. Typically, a docking station is used to add a full-sized monitor, keyboard, mouse, CD-ROM drive, tape backup, or printer to a notebook computer.

driver — A software element that is used by an operating system to control a device. Drivers are usually device-specific.

extension — A component that adds additional functions to a snap-in.

hardware profile — A collection of custom device settings used on computers with changing physical components.

I/O port — The section of memory used by the hardware to communicate with the operating system. When an IRQ is used, the system checks the I/O port memory area for additional information about what function is needed by the device. The I/O port is represented by a hexadecimal number.

interrupt request (IRQ) — The interrupt request level that is used to halt CPU operation in favor of the device. Windows 2000 supports 16 interrupts, namely IRQ 0 through 15.

memory page — *See* page.

Microsoft Management Console (MMC) — The standardized interface into which consoles, snap-ins, and extensions are loaded to perform administrative tasks.

page — A 4 KB chunk of data, which is the smallest unit managed by the Virtual Memory Manager. Pages are moved around physical RAM and to and from the paging file.

paging file — A file stored on a hard drive, employed by the Virtual Memory Manager as a temporary storage container for inactive memory pages. Its name is Pagefile.sys.

PC Cards — The modern name of the PCMCIA technology. PC Cards are credit card- sized devices typically used to expand the functionality of notebook or portable computers.

PCMCIA (Personal Computer Memory Card International Association) Cards — The older name for the technology now labeled PC Cards. PCMCIA Cards are credit card-sized devices typically used to expand the functionality of notebook or portable computers.

Plug and Play — A technology that allows an operating system to inspect a device, determine exactly what the device is, install the correct driver, and enable the device— all without user interaction. Plug and play simplifies the addition and removal of hard- ware and can often offer on-the-fly reconfiguration of devices without rebooting.

service — A software element used by the operating system to perform a function. Services include offering resources over the network, accessing resources over the network, print spooling, etc.

snap-in — A component that adds control mechanisms to a console for a specific service or object.

Task Scheduler — The component of Windows 2000 used to automate the execution or launch of programs and batch files on the basis of time and system conditions.

user mode — The condition of a console that prevents adding or removing snap-ins or resaving the console file.

virtual memory — The combination of physical RAM and pagefile space used by the operating system to grant a larger collection of usable memory to processes.

wizard — A tool or utility that has an interactive step-by-step guide to walk you through a complex or detailed configuration process.

REVIEW QUESTIONS

1. Which tool is the primary interface through which most Windows 2000 administrative tasks are performed?

   a. Control Panel

   b. Microsoft Management Console

   c. Task Scheduler

   d. My Computer

2. What are extensions used for in the context of the MMC?

   a. to alter the MMC display

   b. to restrict controls based on user accounts

   c. to add additional functionality to standalone snap-ins

   d. to allow remote administration of services and objects

3. Where do snap-ins originate? (Choose all that apply.)

   a. Windows 2000

   b. other Microsoft software products

   c. Windows 2000 Resource Kits

   d. independent software vendors

4. Using snap-ins, you can create .msc consoles that include only the functionality you need. True or False?

5. Which .msc mode allows users to create new windows but prevents them from viewing some parts of the console tree?

   a. Author mode

   b. User mode: Full Access

   c. User mode: Delegated Access/Multiple Windows

   d. User mode: Delegated Access/Single Window

6. Which of the following are tools found in the Administrative Tools menu? (Choose all that apply.)

   a. Computer Management

   b. My Computer

   c. Event Viewer

   d. Utility Manager

7. What are the methods by which the functions offered by an MMC can be accessed? (Choose all that apply.)

   a. Start, Programs, Administrative Tools

   b. Utility Manager

   c. Control Panel's Administrative Tools icon

   d. Load snap-ins into MMC

8. Which of the following can trigger the launch of an automated event? (Choose all that apply.)

   a. User logon

   b. System idle

   c. Exact time

   d. System startup

9. A scheduled task can function only on the system where it was defined. True or False?

10. A task can be configured so that only specific users can alter its scheduled parameters. True or False?

11. Tasks are automatically deleted after they execute by default. True or False?

12. Which applet is used to configure ToggleKeys and SoundSentry?

    a. Sound and Multimedia

    b. Keyboard

    c. Accessibility Options

    d. System

13. If you want to use the numeric keypad to control the mouse insertion point movement, which applet must you open to configure this option?

    a. Sound and Multimedia

    b. Keyboard

    c. Accessibility Options

    d. System

14. Which of the following actions can the Add/Remove Hardware applet be used to perform? (Choose all that apply.)

    a. troubleshoot an existing device

    b. disable a PC Card driver before it is removed

    c. configure multiple display layout

    d. uninstall a device driver

15. Which applet should you use to add Windows components distributed on the Windows 2000 Professional CD?

    a. System

    b. Add/Remove Programs

    c. Windows 2000 Resource Kit

    d. Regional Settings

16. The Display applet can be used to perform which of the following functions? (Choose all that apply.)

    a. install a new adapter device driver

    b. set the screen saver timeout period

    c. enable Active Desktop

    d. define a custom color scheme

17. Web zones are used to define custom colors, sounds, and icons on the basis of the source of the Web resources. True or False?

18. Where can you define the utilities to handle e-mail, newsgroups, online calls, and contacts?

    a. Folder Options

    b. System

    c. Add/Remove Programs

    d. Internet Options

19. Home/Office Desk, Presentation, and Portable/Laptop are examples of predefined
_____.

    a. Hardware profiles

    b. User profiles

    c. Power Options settings

    d. System profiles

20. Through which applet can you access troubleshooting help for an audio card? (Choose all that apply.)

    a. Add/Remove Hardware

    b. System

    c. Sounds and Multimedia

    d. Accessibility Options

21. Which applet can be used to change domain or workgroup membership?

    a. System

    b. Add/Remove Hardware

    c. Accessibility Options

    d. Workgroup Settings

22. When Windows 2000 is installed, it creates a paging file that is how much larger than the amount of physical RAM present on the system?

    Correct → a. one and one-half times

    b. two times

    c. two and one-half times

    d. three times

23. When a STOP error occurs, what can the system do? (Choose all that apply.)

    a. write an event to the system log

    b. send an administrative alert

    c. write a memory dump file

    d. reboot the system

24. Which tool is used to ensure that a newly installed device is functioning properly?

    a. System

    b. Add/Remove Hardware

    c. Device Manager

    d. Administrative Tools

25. Which of the following are system resources that are often in contention with non-Plug and Play devices? (Choose all that apply.)

    a. Paging file space

    b. I/O Port

    c. Priority CPU cycles

    d. IRQ

HANDS-ON PROJECTS

Project 3-1

To create an MMC console for system management:

1. Select **Start**, then **Run**, type **MMC**, and press **Enter**.

2. Select **Add/Remove Snap-in...** from the Console menu.

3

3. Click **Add**.

4. Locate and select **Computer Management** from the Add Standalone Snap-in dialog box.

5. Click **Add**.

6. Select **Local computer**.

7. Click **Finish**.

8. Click **Close**.

9. Select the **Extensions** tab.

10. Ensure that the **Add All Extensions** check box is selected and examine what each extension does in the Description pane of the dialog box.

11. Click **OK** to return to the MMC. Notice that the Computer Management snap-in is listed in the console tree.

12. Maximize the console root window by double-clicking its title bar.

13. Select the **Save As** command from the Console menu.

14. Change to the directory where you want to store the console file.

15. Give the console file a name, such as **Compmgt.msc**. Click **Save**.

16. Select **Exit** from the Console menu.

Project 3-2

To create an automated task:

1. Open the Control Panel (**Start**, **Settings**, **Control Panel**).

2. Double-click the **Scheduled Task** icon.

3. Launch the Task Scheduler Wizard by double-clicking **Add Scheduled Task**.

4. Click **Next**.

5. Select **Backup** from the list.

6. Click **Next**.

7. Select **Daily**.

8. Click **Next**.

9. Set the time to three minutes from the present.

10. Click **Next**.

11. If you want to launch the task with another user account as the context, provide the username and password. Otherwise, click **Next**.

12. Click **Finish**.

13. Wait the remainder of the three minutes to see Backup launch automatically.

Project 3-3

To add a Windows component:

1. Open the **Control Panel** (**Start**, **Settings**, **Control Panel**).
2. Open the **Add/Remove Programs** applet (double-click the applet's icon).
3. Select **Add/Remove Windows Components**.
4. The Windows Components Wizard appears, showing the list of available components. Locate and select **Other Network File and Print Services**. Click **Next**.
5. Insert the Windows 2000 Professional CD-ROM when prompted, if necessary.
6. Click **Finish**.
7. Close the Add/Remove Programs applet by clicking **Close**.

Project 3-4

To set the calendar date, clock time, and time zone for the system:

1. Open the **Control Panel** (**Start**, **Settings**, **Control Panel**).
2. Open the **Date/Time** applet (double-click the applet's icon).
3. Use the pull-down list to select the correct month.
4. Use the up and down arrows to select the correct year.
5. Select the current day's date from the displayed month calendar.
6. Click the hours in the time field below the analog clock. Use the up and down arrow buttons to adjust the hour to the current time.
7. Select the minutes in the time field. Use the up and down arrow buttons to adjust the minutes to the current time.
8. Select the seconds in the time field. Use the up and down arrow buttons to adjust the seconds to the current time.
9. Select the AM/PM designation in the time field. Use the up and down arrow buttons to adjust the designation to the current time.
10. Select the **Time Zone** tab.
11. Use the pull-down list to select the time zone for your area.
12. Click **OK** to close the Date/Time applet.

Project 3-5

To create a custom sound scheme:

1. Open the **Control Panel** (**Start**, **Settings**, **Control Panel**).
2. Open the **Sounds and Multimedia** applet (double-click the applet's icon).
3. Use the Scheme pull-down list to select **Windows Default**.
4. If prompted to save the previous scheme, click **No**.

5. Select the **Asterisk** item from the list of Sound Events.

6. Use the **Name** pull-down list to select **[None]**.

7. Select the **Exit Windows** item from the list of Sound Events.

8. Use the **Name** pull-down list to select **Windows Logoff Sound**.

9. Click the **Save As** button.

10. Give the sound scheme a name, such as **Windows Example 1**. Click **OK**.

11. Click **OK** to close the Sound and Multimedia applet.

Project 3-6

To configure a Windows 2000 Professional system for standalone home use:

1. Open the **Control Panel** (**Start**, **Settings**, **Control Panel**).

2. Open the **System** applet (double-click the applet's icon).

3. Select the **Network Identification** tab.

4. Click the **Network ID** button.

5. On the Network Identification Wizard, click **Next**.

6. Select **This computer is for home use and is not part of a business network**, then click **Next**.

7. Select **Windows always assumes the following user has logged on to this computer**.

8. Select a username from the pull-down list.

9. Provide the appropriate password in both the Password and Confirm password fields, then click **Next**.

10. Click **Finish**.

11. Click **OK** on the message that states you must reboot for the changes to take effect.

12. Reboot the computer (**Start**, **Shutdown**, **Restart**, **OK**).

Project 3-7

To create a hardware profile for a mobile computer:

1. Open the **Control Panel** (**Start**, **Settings**, **Control Panel**).

2. Open the **System** applet (double-click the applet's icon).

3. Select the **Hardware** tab.

4. Click the **Hardware Profiles** button.

5. Select an existing hardware profile.

6. Click **Copy**, provide a new name, such as **Mobile Profile – no NIC**, click **OK**.

7. Click **OK** to close the Hardware Profiles dialog box.

8. Click **OK** to close the System Properties dialog box.

9. Reboot the system (**Start, Shutdown, Restart, OK**).

10. If prompted, select the new hardware profile, using the arrow keys and pressing **Enter**.

11. Log on to the system (**Ctrl+Alt+Delete**, provide a username and password if applicable).

12. Open the Device Manager (**System** applet, **Hardware** tab, **Device Manager** button).

13. Expand the **Network adapters** item by clicking on the **plus** sign.

14. Select the listed NIC.

15. Right-click the NIC, then select **Properties** from the menu.

16. Change the Device Usage pull-down menu to read **Do not use this device (disable)**.

17. Click **OK**.

18. Close the Device Manager by clicking the **Close** button in the upper-right corner of the title bar.

19. Click **OK** to close the System Properties dialog box.

Now your system has a normal hardware profile and a profile that has the NIC disabled for use when not connected to the network. Upon each reboot you can select the appropriate hardware profile.

Project 3-8

To monitor and manage a device via the Device Manager:

1. Open the Administrative Tools by selecting **Start, Settings, Control Panel**, then double-clicking the **Administrative Tools** icon.

2. Launch the **Computer Management** tool by double-clicking its icon.

3. Select the **Device Manager** of the **System Tools** section of the **Computer Management** tool.

4. Double-click the **DVD/CD-ROM drives** item to expand its contents.

5. Select one of the items that appears.

6. Select **Properties** from the **Action** menu.

7. Notice the Device status message, which should state that the device is working properly. If there was a problem with this device, information about the problem would be listed and you'd be instructed to press the **Troubleshooter** button to access the troubleshooting wizard.

8. Select the **Properties** tab. This is where hardware device-specific settings can be made.

9. Select the **Driver** tab. This is where information about the current driver is presented and where the current driver can be updated, replaced, or removed.

10. Click **OK**.

11. Close the Computer Management tool.

Project 3-9

To enable multiple languages and locales on a computer and use them to compose a document in multiple languages:

1. Open the Control Panel selecting **Start**, **Settings**, **Control Panel**.
2. Open the **Regional Options** applet by double-clicking its icon.
3. Select the **Input Locales** tab.
4. Click **Add**.
5. Under Input Locale select **French (France)**.
6. Under Keyboard layout/IME select **French**.
7. Click **OK**.
8. Click **OK**.
9. Launch **Notepad** by selecting **Start**, **Programs**, **Accessories**, **Notepad**.
10. Type **This is English. 123456789**. Press **Enter**.
11. Click the locale icon in the taskbar, then select **French**.
12. Type **This is French. 123456789**. Notice that number keys appear as special French characters instead of English numerals.
13. Click the **Locale** icon in the taskbar, then select **English**.
14. Close Notepad by selecting **Exit** from the **File** menu. Click **No** when prompted to save changes.

Project 3-10

To change locale settings:

1. Open the Control Panel selecting **Start**, **Settings**, **Control Panel**.
2. Open the **Regional Options** applet by double-clicking its icon.
3. Select the **Numbers** tab.
4. Make any changes you would like for the display of numbers.
5. Select the **Currency** tab.
6. Make any changes you would like for the display of currency.
7. Select the **Time** tab.
8. Make any changes you would like for the display of time.
9. Select the **Date** tab.
10. Make any changes you would like for the display of dates.
11. If necessary, reset the Date, Time, Currency, and Numbers tabs to their original settings.
12. Click **OK**.

CASE PROJECTS

1. You need to delegate administrative tasks to nonadministrative users. However, you are concerned about granting too much power to users. What can you do?

2. You want to participate in the SETI@home project (*http://setiathome.ssl.berkeley.edu/*). However, the utility consumes most of the CPU cycles when it is active. How can you participate in this project but still be able to get other work done on your computer?

3. You have a notebook computer with a docking station. The docking station hosts a 21-inch monitor, a DVD drive, a tape backup, and a color printer. What is the best method to enable your notebook computer to use the devices on the docking station without having problems when not connected to the docking station?

4. You work in a graphics design group. You often have six or seven applications open at one time while editing, creating, or working on design projects. You also flip back and forth between applications very frequently, mainly just to see the graphics displayed. With the capabilities of Windows 2000 and an unlimited budget, what can you do to improve your visual space?

4

MANAGING WINDOWS 2000 FILE SYSTEMS AND STORAGE

After reading this chapter and completing the exercises, you will be able to:

♦ Understand basic and dynamic storage

♦ List the drive configurations supported by Windows 2000

♦ Distinguish the FAT, FAT32, and NTFS file systems

♦ Describe permissions, sharing, and other security issues related to file systems

♦ Understand drive, volume, and partition maintenance and administration under Windows 2000

The Windows 2000 file storage system offers versatile disk management. With the addition of dynamic storage, Windows 2000 is able to support large disk volumes, provide fault tolerance, control access, and offer high performance. By retaining support for previous disk configurations and adding support for FAT32, Windows 2000 is fully capable of operating within a multiboot system. This chapter discusses basic and dynamic storage methods, file systems and drive configurations supported by Windows 2000, and all of the built-in tools used for disk maintenance.

FILE STORAGE BASICS

Windows 2000 supports two types of storage: basic and dynamic. Basic storage is the storage method with which most DOS and Windows NT users are familiar, and centers around partitioning a physical disk. Dynamic storage is a new method supported only by Windows 2000, and is not based around partitions, but is centered on volumes. A **volume** is a portion of one or more hard disks that is combined into a single logical structure, formatted with a single file system, and accessed via a single drive letter or mount point.

Basic Storage

Basic storage is the industry standard or traditional method of dividing a hard drive into partitions. A **partition** is a logical division of the physical space on a hard drive. Each partition can be formatted with a different file system. Partitions must be formatted before they can be used by an operating system.

There are two types of partitions: primary and extended. A single hard drive can host up to four primary partitions or it can host up to three primary partitions and a single extended partition. A **primary partition** is a type of partition on a basic disk that can be marked active, whereas an **extended partition** can be divided into logical drives. Only primary partitions and logical drives can be formatted with a file system. Under Windows 2000 Professional, the total number of formatted partitions cannot exceed 32 on a single physical drive. Thus, a single hard drive can appear as one or more accessible or usable drives (that is, after the partition is properly formatted).

A primary partition can be marked as the **active partition**. This informs the computer's BIOS to look for operating system booting information on that partition. Only primary partitions can be active and only a single partition can be active at a time. The active partition does not have to be the first partition on the drive.

Volumes, in the basic storage type, are 2 to 32 partitions combined into a single logical structure formatted with a single file system. **Volume sets** can be extended simply by adding another partition. However, volume sets can be reduced in size only by breaking the set and creating a new set. The act of breaking the set destroys (or at least makes inaccessible) all data stored on the volume. A volume set can span multiple partitions on one or more physical drives. A volume set is interacted with via the operating system through a single drive letter and provides no fault tolerance. If a single drive or partition in a volume set fails, all data in the set is destroyed.

Typically, you'll want to create partitions or volumes as large as the operating system, hardware, and file system will allow. Under Windows 2000, those file systems and sizes are:

- FAT: 4 GB
- FAT32: 32 GB
- NTFS: 2 TB

Each formatted partition or volume set is assigned a drive letter. The letters A and B are typically reserved for floppy drives, but the letters C through Z can be used for hard-drive-hosted formatted partitions/volumes. Thus, only 24 formatted partitions can be accessed from Windows 2000. In most situations, this limitation does not impose a system restriction.

Basic storage supports a wide range of disk configurations, from single formatted partitions (often called drives or logical drives) to RAID 5 volumes. The main difference between basic storage and dynamic storage is that basic storage disk structures require a system reboot when changed.

Windows 2000 supports this traditional method of storage for backward compatibility with older operating systems. In other words, Windows 2000 can take control of drive configurations (discussed later in this chapter) from previous operating systems (Windows NT, 95, 98, and DOS), if the structure conforms to the current restrictions of the file systems they host and the hosted file system is supported by Windows 2000. Supported file systems include **FAT** (file allocation table, the 16-bit file system originally introduced with DOS), **FAT32** (the 32-bit FAT file system), and **NTFS** (**New Technology File System**, the preferred native file system of Windows 2000). However, Windows 2000 no longer supports the creation of basic storage type drive structures beyond single formatted partitions; it can manage only existing structures.

Windows 2000 can be installed only onto basic storage type partitions. There are two partitions associated with Windows 2000: the system partition and the boot partition. Please take careful note of their descriptions, because, in our opinion, they are counterintuitive. The **system partition** is the active partition where the boot files required to display the boot menu and initiate the booting of Windows 2000 are stored. The **boot partition** hosts the main Windows 2000 system files and is the initial default location for the paging file. The boot partition can be the same partition as the system partition, or it can be any other partition (or logical drive in an extended partition) on any drive hosted by the computer. Neither the system partition nor the boot partition can be a member of a volume set or stripe set. They both can be the source or original partition/drive in a disk mirror or disk duplexing configuration. The drive letters of the system partition and boot partition cannot be changed.

 Once Windows 2000 is installed, the boot partition drive can be transformed into a dynamic storage device, but the system partition host must remain a basic storage device.

Dynamic Storage

Dynamic storage is a new type of storage technique (Microsoft documentation labels it as a new standard) that does not use partitions. Instead, this method views an entire physical hard drive as a single entity, labeled as a volume. This storage method offers drive structures from simple volumes (entire hard drives as a single formatted entity) to fully fault tolerant RAID 5 configurations. The main difference between dynamic storage and basic storage is that dynamic storage structures can be expanded on the fly without rebooting Windows 2000. Furthermore, only Windows 2000 can access data on dynamic storage volumes. No other operating system, including Windows 95, 98, or NT on a multiboot system, can access dynamic volumes.

New drives (including existing drives with all partitions deleted) can be transformed into dynamic storage hosts via a selection wizard. This wizard is launched when you access the **Disk Management** tool (Start, Programs, Administrative Tools, Computer Management, Storage, Disk Management) and a physical hard drive is present with no predefined partitions. This wizard only appears the first time Disk Management is accessed after booting that follows the addition of a new drive or the deletion of all partitions on a drive. You are prompted whether to enable dynamic storage.

Existing drives with partitions can be upgraded to dynamic storage by using the Upgrade to Dynamic Disk command. Windows 2000 Professional supports the following drive configurations:

- *Simple volume*: All or part of a single drive. Does not provide any fault tolerance. NTFS volumes can be extended; FAT and FAT32 volumes cannot be extended.

- *Spanned volume*: Two or more (up to 32) parts of one or more drives or two or more entire drives; the elements of the spanned volume do not have to be equal in size. Data is written to the first drive in the volume until it is full, then data is written to the next drive. This is also called an extended volume and does not provide any fault tolerance. If one partition or drive in the set fails, all data is lost. Spanned volumes cannot be part of a striped volume or a mirrored volume. NTFS spanned volumes can be extended; FAT and FAT32 spanned volumes cannot be extended. The system partition/volume and boot partition/volume cannot be extended. Volume sets can be reduced in size only by breaking the set and creating a new set. The act of breaking the set destroys all data stored on the volume.

- *Striped volume*: Two or more (up to 32) parts of one or more drives or two or more (up to 32) entire drives. Data is written to all drives in equal amounts (in 64 KB units) to spread the workload and improve performance. Each part or drive must be roughly equal in size. This storage scheme does not provide any fault tolerance—if one partition or drive in the set fails, all data is lost. Striped volumes cannot be mirrored or extended.

Windows 2000 Server also supports the following fault tolerant drive configurations:

- *Mirrored volume*: A single volume is duplicated onto another volume on a different hard drive. This storage scheme provides fault tolerance. In Windows NT, a mirror on a drive hosted by a different drive controller was called duplexing, but this distinction no longer is used in Windows 2000.

- *RAID 5 volume*: Three or more (up to 32) parts of one or more drives or three or more (up to 32) entire drives. Data is written to all drives in equal amounts to spread the workload, and parity information is added to the written data to allow for drive failure recovery. This storage scheme provides fault tolerance. If one partition or drive fails in the set, the other members can re-create the missing data on the fly. Once the failed member is replaced or repaired, the data on that drive can be rebuilt and restored. This is also known as disk striping with parity.

Upgrading a drive does not cause data loss or any change in the existing partition structure. Existing drive configurations (mirror, duplex, stripe, and spanned volumes) can be upgraded to dynamic volumes. However, the dynamic disk should be a non-system disk. The drive(s) must have at least 1 MB of unallocated space and you must reboot the computer for the changes to take effect. To upgrade a disk to a dynamic disk:

1. In the Disk Management display, right-click the disk (not volume) you want to upgrade, for example, Disk 1.

2. Choose Upgrade to Dynamic Disk from the menu.

When a drive is converted to dynamic storage, it is labeled as such in Disk Management (see Disk 1 in Figure 4-1).

4

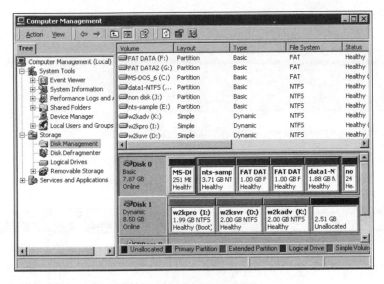

Figure 4-1 The Disk Management tool

After you have a dynamic storage host, the next step is to create a volume. To create a volume on a dynamic disk, follow these steps:

1. Right-click over an unallocated dynamic storage device that is not a system disk, and select **Create Volume** from the resulting menu.

2. This launches the Create Volume Wizard. Click **Next**.

3. You'll be prompted as to what type of volume to create (see Figure 4-2). Select one and click **Next**. (See the "Drive Configurations" section later in this chapter.)

4. Now you must select the available dynamic storage devices and how much of each device to use in the volume being created. Click **Next**.

5. Next, you will be prompted to select a drive letter or a mount point, or to not assign a drive letter at all. Click **Next**. (See the "Drive Letters and Mount Points" section later in this chapter.)

6. Finally, you'll be asked whether to format the volume and with what file system. Click **Next**.

7. Click **Finish** to implement volume creation.

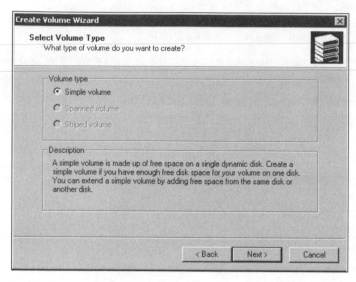

Figure 4-2   Create Volume Wizard, Select Volume Type window

Table 4-1 compares the functions and capabilities of basic and dynamic disks.

Table 4-1   Basic Versus Dynamic Disks

Tasks	Basic Disk	Dynamic Disk
Create and delete primary and extended partitions	X	
Create and delete logical drives within an extended partition	X	
Format and label a partition and mark it active	X	
Delete a volume set	X	
Break a mirror from a mirror set	X	
Repair a mirror set	X	
Repair a stripe set with parity	X	
Upgrade a basic disk to a dynamic disk	X	
Create and delete simple, spanned, striped, mirrored, and RAID 5 volumes	X	X
Extend a volume across one or more disks	X	X
Add a mirror to or remove a mirror from a mirrored volume	X	X
Repair a mirrored volume	X	X
Repair a RAID 5 volume	X	X
Check information about disks, such as capacity, available free space, and current status	X	X
View volume and partition properties such as size	X	X
Make and change drive-letter assignments for hard disk volumes or partitions and CD-ROM devices	X	X
Create volume mount points	X	X
Set or verify disk sharing and access arrangements for a volume or partition	X	X

 Table 4-1 was taken from the *Windows 2000 Server Resource Kit*.

4

Dynamic drives can be returned to basic storage by deleting all volumes and issuing the Revert To Basic Disk command on the drive through the Disk Management snap-in.

CAUTION 🔌

Reverting a disk to basic storage will destroy all data on that drive because you must delete the volumes first.

Removable Storage Devices

The addition of Plug and Play support with Windows 2000 also provides support for **removable storage devices**, such as floppy disks, cartridges, or drives that can be removed between reboots or as a hot swappable device. These removable storage devices or storage media can contain only a single primary partition and cannot participate in dynamic storage. They cannot host extended partitions, nor can they be marked active.

DRIVE CONFIGURATIONS

Windows 2000 supports several drive configurations. Although Windows 2000 can manage configurations using basic storage partitions, it can create new drive configurations only by using dynamic storage devices. There are five drive configurations or structures supported by Windows 2000: simple volumes, spanned volumes, striped volumes, mirrored volumes, and RAID 5 volumes.

 **CAUTION** 🔌

Regardless of what disk configuration you use, always protect your data by using a regularly scheduled backup system.

FILE SYSTEMS

Windows 2000 supports FAT (also known as FAT16), FAT32, and NTFS. FAT is retained by Windows 2000 for backward compatibility with other operating systems. This allows an easy upgrade from another operating system to Windows 2000 and enables multiboot systems to share data drives (when basic storage is used). FAT32 is used to support larger volumes and offers multiboot shared drives with Windows 98 and Windows 95 (OSR2). NTFS is the preferred file system to use with Windows 2000. It offers significantly larger volume support, file-by-file compression, file-by-file security, and more. Windows 2000 NTFS volumes can be accessed by Windows NT 4.0 with Service Pack 4 or higher applied.

FAT and FAT32 are both referred to as FAT in most Microsoft documentation. The separate terms are used only when the differences between FAT and FAT32 are important.

FAT, FAT32, and NTFS all support **long filenames (LFNs)** with lengths up to 256 characters. FAT and FAT32 store equivalents for DOS-style 8.3 filenames (8 characters plus a 3-character extension) for compatibility with DOS-based utilities that do not recognize LFNs.

 To avoid losing file information, it is important to use utilities that support LFNs when performing any disk or file operation involving LFNs.

FAT and FAT32

FAT was originally developed for DOS. It has experienced several revisions and improvements as support for FAT was included in newer operating systems. FAT under Windows 2000 maintains backward compatibility with previous operating systems (DOS, Windows 3.1x, and Windows for Workgroups) while supporting newer features or capabilities. In addition, FAT is most often used to format floppies and other removable media in Windows 2000.

The important features of FAT (under Windows 2000) are:

- Supports volumes up to 4 GB in size
- Most efficient on volumes smaller than 256 MB
- Root directory can contain only 512 entries
- No file-level compression
- No file-level security

FAT32 is simply an enhanced version of FAT that was originally released with Windows 95 OSR2. FAT32's main feature change from FAT is that of volume size. Windows 2000 can support and access FAT32 volumes up to 2 TB in size, but only volumes up to 32 GB can be created. FAT32 volumes have a minimum size of 512 MB.

A FAT volume is divided into clusters. A **cluster** is one or more sectors grouped into a single nondivisible unit. If cluster size is not specified, Windows 2000 configuration will use the default, which varies according to disk size to reduce the amount of space lost and fragmentation in the volume. A **sector** is the smallest division (512 bytes) of a drive's surface. Because of the limitations of the file system, only a maximum number of clusters can be addressed. For FAT16, the maximum number of clusters is 65,536. For FAT32, the maximum number of clusters is 268,435,456 (see Table 4-2).

Table 4-2 FAT16 and FAT32 Cluster Sizes

Drive Size	FAT16 Cluster Size	FAT32 Cluster Size
260 MB–511 MB	8 KB	4 KB
512 MB–1,023 MB	16 KB	4 KB
1,024 MB–2 GB	32 KB	4 KB
2 GB–4 GB	64 KB	4 KB
4 GB–8 GB	Not supported	4 KB
8 GB–16 GB	Not supported	8 KB
16 GB–32 GB	Not supported	16 KB
<\>>32 GB	Not supported	Not supported

Before Windows 95, the maximum volume size of FAT was 2 GB. With the use of 64 KB clusters, this was extended to 4 GB. However, 64 KB clusters can cause problems with some drive utilities. Thus, Windows 2000 will always warn you when you attempt to format a 2 GB to 4 GB partition with FAT16.

NTFS

NTFS is the preferred file system of Windows 2000. The important features of NTFS are:

- Supports volumes up to 2 TB in size (larger sizes are possible, but not recommended by Microsoft)

- Most efficient on volumes larger than 512 MB

- Root directory can contain unlimited entries

- File-level compression

- File-level security

- File-level encryption

- Disk quotas (a **disk quota** is a limitation on the amount of disk space that can be consumed by a user)

- POSIX support

The version of NTFS included with Windows 2000 is different from that of Windows NT 4.0. In fact, you must have Service Pack 4 or higher installed on Windows NT 4.0 to access Windows 2000 NTFS volumes. Microsoft does not recommend a multiboot system with Windows NT and Windows 2000 for this reason.

FAT and FAT32 volumes on a system can be migrated to the Windows 2000 NTFS format without losing data. However, to return to FAT, the volume must be deleted, re-created, formatted, and the data copied back onto the new volume.

NTFS manages clusters more efficiently than FAT32 (see Table 4-3).

Table 4-3   NTFS Default Cluster Sizes

Volume Size	Sectors Per Cluster	Cluster Size
512 MB or less	1	512 bytes
513 MB–1,024 MB	2	1 KB
1,025 MB–2,048 MB	4	2 KB
2,049 MB–4,096 MB	8	4 KB
4,097 MB–8,192 MB	16	4 KB
8,193 MB–16,384 MB	32	4 KB
16,385 MB–32,768 MB	64	4 KB
> 32,768 MB	128	4 KB

File-level compression cannot be used on volumes with a cluster size greater than 4 KB.

POSIX Support via NTFS

Windows 2000 comes with various environmental subsystems. The POSIX subsystem is designed to run POSIX applications and meets the requirements of the POSIX.1 government standard.

POSIX (Portable Operating System Interface for Computing Environments) is a set of standards drafted by the Institute of Electrical and Electronic Engineers (IEEE) that defines various aspects of an operating system, and includes topics such as programming interface, security, networking, and graphical interface. So far, only one of these standards, POSIX.1, has made the transition from draft to final form. It's not widely used, but sufficiently so that POSIX compatibility was necessary for Windows 2000 to be acceptable to the U.S. Department of Defense.

POSIX.1 is based on ideas drawn from the UNIX file system and process model. Because POSIX.1 addresses only API (application programming interface) issues, most applications written to the POSIX.1 API must rely on non-POSIX operating system extensions (in this case, Win32) to provide services such as security and networking.

POSIX applications need certain file system functionality, such as support for case-sensitive filenames (in POSIX, there's a difference between MyFile.doc, MYFILE.DOC, and myfile.doc) and support for files with multiple names (or hard links). NTFS supports these

554

POSIX requirements. Any POSIX application that requires access to file system resources must have access to an NTFS partition, but POSIX applications that do not access file system resources can run on FAT

4

> If you install POSIX utilities or file systems on your Windows 2000 system, be sure to use native POSIX file management utilities to manage them. Just as older DOS utilities will destroy LFN information created by FAT or FAT32, native Windows 2000 file utilities—Windows Explorer, File Manager, and My Computer—will destroy POSIX file structures, especially when the only difference between two or more otherwise identical filenames is their use of uppercase and lowercase characters. For example, POSIX understands very well that MyFile.txt is different from myfile.txt, but NTFS does not (and will actually destroy the folder entry for whichever name appears second in the POSIX-created folder structure).

File Compression

File compression is the ability to compress data on the basis of single files, folders, or entire volumes. File compression offers the benefit of being able to store more data in the same space, but at the cost of some performance. The amount of compression achieved depends on the data stored in the object (that is, text can often be compressed significantly, whereas executable programs can not). Windows 2000 manages compression via the NTFS file system drive. Each time a compressed file is read, it must be uncompressed as it is read. Likewise, saving a compressed file, copying a file into a compressed folder, or creating a new file in a compressed folder requires that the data to be stored is compressed in memory before it is written to the drive.

Configuring and managing file compression involves enabling or disabling the file compression attribute on one or more files or folders. File compression appears as one of the attributes of NTFS file/folder objects on the Advanced Attributes dialog box (see the section entitled "NTFS File Object" later in this chapter; try Hands-on Project 4-11). And, just like all other attributes, file compression can be set on a file-by-file basis or by setting the attribute on a container. When the "Compress contents to save disk space" checkbox is selected, the object(s) are compressed. When this checkbox is cleared, the object(s) are expanded back to their original size.

> Troubleshooting file compression usually involves either recompressing or removing compression from files, or restoring files from backup that were damaged while they were compressed.

Converting Between File Systems

When you first format a drive under Windows 2000, you have the option of selecting FAT, FAT32, or NTFS. If at a later date you decide you need to change the file system, you have only two options: reformat with the new file system or convert from FAT/FAT32 to NTFS.

Before any file system conversion, be sure to back up the drive to ensure you will not lose data.

To reformat, simply employ one of the disk tools, such as Disk Management, and format the volume with a new file system. Remember that all data stored on the drive will be lost, so without a backup you will not be able to recover from a format. To convert from FAT/FAT32 to NTFS, you use the Convert.exe command-line tool (try Hands-on Project 4-14). It has two parameters: /fs:ntfs and /v. The first specifies the conversion should result in the NTFS file system (yes, it is strange to have this parameter because it only supports conversion to NTFS). The second turns on "verbose" mode so all messages regarding the conversion are displayed. When launched, CONVERT will attempt to convert the drive immediately. If the drive is locked (i.e., a process has an open file from the volume to be converted), the conversion will occur during the next bootup of the system.

DISK MANAGEMENT ACTIONS

In addition to creating volumes and transforming devices into dynamic storage, the Disk Management tool offers several other useful features. The All Tasks submenu of the Action menu is context-based, depending on what type of object is selected. The All Tasks submenu is the same menu that pops up when you right-click a drive, partition, or volume object. The commands that appear in this menu are:

- *Add Mirror*—Adds a mirror to duplicate a partition or volume (not available in Windows 2000 Professional)

- *Change Drive Letter and Path*—Changes the drive letter of basic disks and dynamic disks or the mount path of dynamic disks

- *Create Partition*—Creates a partition on a basic disk

- *Create Volume*—Creates a volume on a dynamic disk

- *Delete Partition*—Destroys a partition, returning the space to unallocated status

- *Explore*—Opens the selected volume or partition into a Windows Explorer window

- *Extend Volume*—Adds additional unallocated space to an existing volume

- *Format*—Formats a volume or partition with a file system

- *Help*—Opens the help utility

- *Import Foreign Disks*—Imports a dynamic disk when moved from one Windows 2000 computer to another

- *Mark Partition Active*—Marks a primary partition active

- *Open*—Opens the selected volume or partition into a My Computer window

- *Properties*—Opens the Properties dialog box for the selected object

- *Reactivate Disk*—Brings dynamic disks back online after being powered down, disconnected, or corrupted.

- *Reactivate Volume*—Recovers volumes from a failed status

- *Remove Disk*—Used to deactivate a removable drive

- *Revert to Basic Disk*—Transforms a dynamic disk into a basic disk; requires that all volumes be deleted

- *Upgrade to Dynamic Disk*—Transforms a basic storage device into a dynamic storage device

The Action menu itself has three other non–context-sensitive commands:

- *Refresh*—Updates drive letters, file system, volume, and removable media information and determines which previously unreadable volumes are now readable

- *Rescan Disks*—Updates hardware information by rescanning all attached storage devices (including removable media) for changes in configuration

- *Restore Basic Disk Configuration*—Using a disk configuration file saved from Disk Administrator from Windows NT (4.0 or earlier), restores the state of the physical hard drives to their basic configurations under Windows NT

> Disk Management can be used to manipulate storage devices on remote computers. Simply select the "Computer Management (local)" item in the console tree and issue the "Connect to another computer" command from the Action menu. This opens a list of all known networked systems. Once you've selected another system, you can perform disk management functions as if you were present locally.

The Properties dialog boxes of drives, volumes, and partitions offer lots of details and configuration settings. A drive (disk, not volume or partition) Properties dialog box (see Figure 4-3) will display the following information:

- *Disk*—The ordinal number of the disk, such as Disk 0, Disk 1, etc.

- *Type*—The storage type: basic, dynamic, or removable

- *Status*—The status of the device: online, offline, foreign, or unknown

- *Capacity*—The maximum storage capacity of the drive

- *Unallocated Space*—The amount of space not used in a partition or volume

- *Device Type*—IDE, EIDE, or SCSI, plus type-specific details

- *Hardware Vendor*—Hardware vendor name and disk model

- *Adapter Name*—Type of drive controller to which the drive is attached

- *Volumes contained on this disk*—The volumes and capacity of each volume or partition on the drive

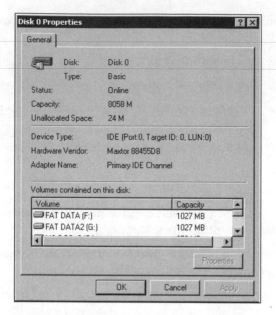

Figure 4-3   A drive Properties dialog box, General tab

The Properties dialog box for a partition or a volume displays the same detailed information. However, an NTFS-formatted partition or volume has two additional tabs that are not present on FAT/FAT32 formatted partitions or volumes. The tabs of the Properties dialog box are: General, Tools, Hardware, Sharing, Security, and Quota (the latter two are NTFS only).

The General tab (see Figure 4-4) displays:

- *Label*—The customizable name of the disk. FAT and FAT 32 drives can be labeled with up to 11 characters, whereas NTFS labels can contain 32 characters.

- *Type*—The type of disk: local, network connection, floppy disk drive, CD-ROM drive, RAM disk, removable drive, or mounted disk

- *File System*—The file system used on the disk: CDFS (for CDs); FAT, FAT32, NTFS, or UDF (Universal Disk Format is common on DVD and compact-discs)

- *Used Space*—The amount of space used by stored files

- *Free Space*—The amount of space still available in the partition

- *Capacity*—The total amount of space in the partition

- *Graph*—A graphical pie chart representation of used and free space

- *Disk Cleanup*—A button to access the Disk Cleanup tool (discussed later in this chapter)

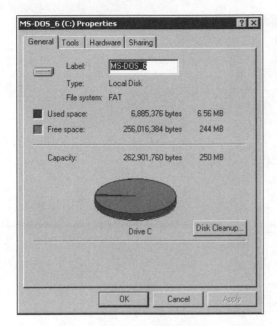

Figure 4-4   A Partition or Volume Properties dialog box, General tab

The Tools tab offers access to:

- *Error-checking:* Accesses the ScanDisk tool to find and repair errors on a drive (discussed later in this chapter)

- *Backup:* Accesses the NT Backup utility to back up files

- *Defragmentation:* Accesses the Defragmentation tool to reduce file fragmentation (discussed later in this chapter)

The Hardware tab lists all physical storage devices and their type. This dialog box accesses the same Troubleshooting and Properties (for drivers) utilities as those accessed through the Device Manager.

The Sharing tab is used to share partitions with the network (discussed later in this chapter).

The Security tab (see Figure 4–5) is used to set the NTFS access permissions on the volume or partition as a whole. Individual users or groups each can be defined with unique permissions of allow or deny for each of the listed object-specific actions (discussed later in this chapter).

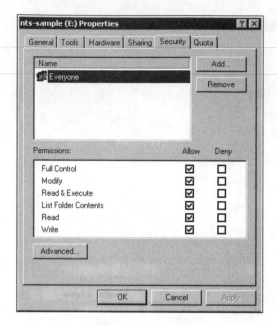

Figure 4-5   An NTFS Partition or Volume Properties dialog box, Security tab

The Quota tab is used to define disk use limitations on NTFS volumes and partitions. The quota can be defined on a general basis and/or fine-tuned for each individual user. Quota tab options include:

- *Enable quota management*—Turns on the quota system

- *Deny disk space to users exceeding quota limit*—Prevents users from gaining more space when in violation of the quota

- *Do not limit disk usage*—Disables system-wide quota level

- *Limit disk space to*—Sets the maximum amount of drive space that can be accessed by a single user

- *Set warning level to*—Sets a threshold that when crossed warns the user about nearing their quota limit

- *Log event when a user exceeds their quota limit*—Adds an item to the Event Viewer (an application that displays event logs)

- *Log event when a user exceeds their warning level*—Adds an item to the Event Viewer

- *Quota Entries*—Opens a dialog box where quota settings for each user can be fine-tuned

Assigning Drive Letters and Mount Points

Windows 2000 uses two methods to access formatted volumes—drive letters and mount points. **Drive letters** are used to grant applications and user interface utilities access to file system resources. Drive letters A and B are typically used for floppies, but in the absence of floppies these letters can be employed as mappings for network shares. (A **share** is a resource—such as an application, file, or printer—that can be accessed or shared over the network.) Drive letters C through Z are used for local hard drives or mappings for network shares. Even without floppies, the first hard drive is always labeled with C. The drive letters of the system and boot partitions/volumes cannot be changed, but all other drive letters can be changed. The "Change Drive Letter and Path" command in the Disk Management console is used to alter a drive letter, apply a mount point path, or remove a drive letter.

A **mount point** or **mounted volume** is an alternative to drive letters. A mount point connects a FAT/FAT32 or NTFS volume or partition to an empty directory on an NTFS volume or partition. This allows more than 24 (or 26, up to 32) hard drives to be present on a single machine. The empty directory becomes the gateway to the linked volume. A mount point is created by following this procedure:

1. Create an empty directory.
2. Open the **Disk Management** tool (**Start**, **Programs**, **Administrative Tools**, **Computer Management**; **Storage**; **Disk Management**).
3. Right-click the volume or partition to be mapped, and then select **Change Drive Letter and Path** from the resulting menu.
4. Click **Add**.
5. Select **Mount in this NTFS folder**.
6. Click **Browse**.
7. Locate and select the empty folder, and then click **OK**.
8. Click **OK**.

 TIP It is possible to create an infinite regression mount point (a pointer that loops back on itself) by mapping a volume to an empty directory that it hosts. Although this is a valid procedure, it can cause system overflows when disk utilities attempt to follow the infinite path.

Freeing Disk Space

Disk Cleanup is a tool used to free up space on hard drives by removing deleted, orphaned, temporary, or downloaded files. This utility can be launched from the General tab of the Properties dialog box from any hard drive, or via Start, Programs, Accessories, System Tools, Disk Cleanup. When launched from a drive's properties dialog box, Disk Cleanup will automatically scan that drive for space that can be freed. When launched from the Start menu, you are prompted to select the hard drive to scan for cleaning. The scanning process can take several minutes, especially on large hard drives with a significant number of files.

When scanning is complete, the Disk Cleanup for (drive:) dialog box is displayed (see Figure 4-6). The Disk Cleanup tab of this dialog box lists the file types that can be removed and how much space they currently use. The View Files button can be used to see the selected file type's details via a My Computer window. Selecting the check box beside a listed file type will cause those files to be deleted (not placed in the Recycle Bin) when you click OK.

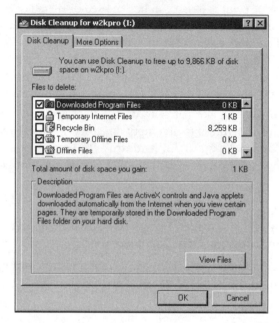

Figure 4-6   Disk Cleanup tab

The More Options tab offers access to the Add/Remove Windows Components utility and the Change or Remove Programs utility. These are the same utilities as those accessed through the Add/Remove Programs applet in the Control Panel.

Using ScanDisk

ScanDisk is a disk integrity inspection utility, accessed from the Start menu, Programs, Accessories, System Tools, ScanDisk. It is used to locate both logical and physical errors on a hard drive. Physical errors are marked and are avoided in all future drive accesses by the operating system. Logical errors are bad pointers in the directory structure of a file system, whether FAT, FAT32, or NTFS and often can be corrected. However, when correction is not possible, ScanDisk saves the data of orphaned fragments to text files in the root directory of the drive and uses incremental filenames of FILE0001, FILE0002, etc.

Once launched, it prompts you whether to "automatically fix file system errors" and whether to "scan for and attempt recovery of bad sectors." ScanDisk usually requires rebooting the system before it scans NTFS volumes so that no files are in use when it performs its check.

Windows 2000 automatically starts ScanDisk when it detects an improper system shutdown or errors in the directory structure of a drive. This usually occurs during booting and the execution process. Results are displayed on the blue screen where the operating system name, version, and build, along with processors and memory size, are detailed.

> The ScanDisk that ships with Windows 2000 is specifically designed to manage the file systems supported by Windows 2000. Do not use ScanDisk from any other operating system to attempt repairs on Windows 2000 hard drives.

Defragmenting Hard Drives

As files are written, altered, deleted, rewritten, etc., the storage device develops gaps between used and unused space. When gaps are used instead of contiguous free space to store files, fragmentation occurs. **Fragmentation** is the division of a file into two or more parts where each part is stored in a different location on the hard drive. As the level of fragmentation on a drive increases, it takes longer for read and write operations to occur. **Defragmentation** is the process of reorganizing files so they are stored contiguously and no gaps are left between files.

The Windows 2000 defragmentation utility is designed for FAT, FAT32, and NTFS volumes. It is accessed either from the Tools tab of a drive's Properties dialog box or via Start, Programs, Accessories, System Tools, Disk Defragmenter.

The Disk Defragmenter (see Figure 4–7) lists all drives in the system. When you select a drive, you can either Analyze the drive for fragmentation or go ahead and defragment the drive. Both processes display a graphical representation of the file storage condition of the drive. When either process is complete, you can view a report that details the findings of the procedure.

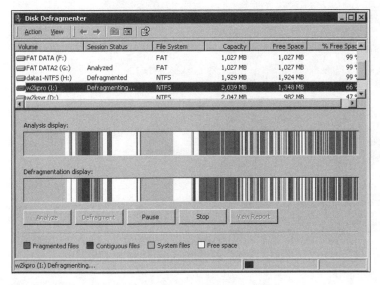

Figure 4-7 Disk Defragmenter

The Disk Defragmenter does not offer a built-in scheduling feature, nor can it be executed from a command line. Thus, you must defragment manually or deploy a third-party utility that automates scheduled defragmentation.

FILE SYSTEM OBJECT-LEVEL CONTROLS

In addition to the drive and volume/partition level controls for storage devices, there are file system controls for folders, files, and mounted volumes. Because folders, files, and mounted volumes are considered objects in Windows 2000, these controls are called object-level controls, and are accessed via the Properties dialog boxes of either a folder or an object. There are minor differences in the dialog boxes depending on whether the file system is FAT/FAT32 or NTFS. There is no difference in file system objects due to having basic or dynamic disks as hosts.

The following sections detail the differences in Properties dialog boxes for each object type. The Sharing and Security tabs of these dialog boxes are discussed in a later section in this chapter.

NTFS Folder Object

An NTFS folder object's Properties dialog box has three tabs: General (see Figure 4-8), Sharing, and Security.

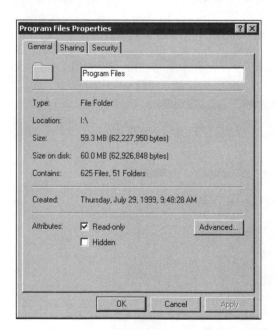

Figure 4-8   An NTFS folder object Properties dialog box, General tab

The General tab offers the following information:

- *Name*—The customizable name of the object

- *Type*—Lists object type: File Folder

- *Location*—The path of the object

- *Size*—The byte size of the object, including its contents

- *Size on disk*—The actual amount of drive space used to store the object

- *Contains*—Lists the number of files and folders the object contains

- *Created*—Lists the object's creation date and time

- *Attributes: Read-only*—A check box used to prevent writing to, changing, or deleting the object

- *Attributes: Hidden*—A check box used to hide the object from view

- *Advanced button: Folder is ready for archiving*—A check box that indicates that this folder, and optionally its contents, is ready for backup (see Figure 4-9)

- *Advanced button: For fast searching, allow Indexing Service to index this folder*—A check box that when selected preindexes the folder, and optionally its contents, for faster searching

- *Advanced button: Compress contents to save disk space*—A check box used to compress the folder, and optionally its contents

- *Advanced button: Encrypt contents to secure data*—A check box used to encrypt the folder, and optionally its contents

Figure 4-9 The Advanced Attributes dialog box of an NTFS object

TIP   When the Properties dialog box for the object is closed, all changes to the settings via the Advanced button will require confirmation by clicking the OK button.

FAT/FAT32 Folder Object

A FAT/FAT32 folder object's Properties dialog box has two tabs: General (see Figure 4-10) and Sharing. The General tab offers the following information:

- *Name*—The customizable name of the object
- *Type*—Lists object type: File Folder
- *Location*—The path of the object
- *Size*—The byte size of the object, including its contents
- *Size on disk*—The actual amount of drive space used to store the object
- *Contains*—Lists the number of files and folders it contains
- *Created*—Lists the object's creation date and time
- *Attributes: Read-only*—A check box used to prevent writing to, changing, or deleting the object
- *Attributes: Hidden*—A check box used to hide the object from view
- *Attributes: Archive*—A check box that indicates that this object should be included in the next backup operation

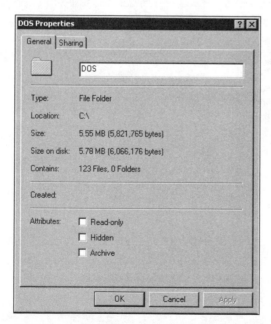

Figure 4-10   A FAT/FAT32 folder object Properties dialog box, General tab

NTFS File Object

An NTFS file object's Properties dialog box has three tabs: General (see Figure 4–11), Security, and Summary.

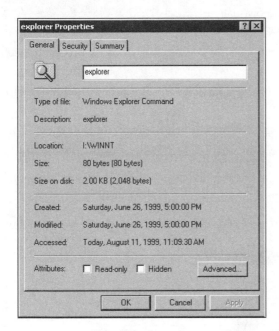

Figure 4-11   An NTFS file object Properties dialog box, General tab

The General tab offers the following information:

- *Name*—The customizable name of the object
- *Type of File*—Names the file type or defines it as a *blank* file where *blank* is the file's extension
- *Description (application files only)*—Names the utility or application
- *Opens with (nonapplication files only)*—Lists the application used to open the file
- *Change (nonapplication files only)*—A button to alter the application used to open the file
- *Location*—The path of the object
- *Size*—The byte size of the object
- *Size on disk*—The actual amount of drive space used to store the object
- *Created*—Lists the creation time and date of the object
- *Modified*—Lists the last time and date of a change to the object
- *Accessed*—Lists the last time and date the object was accessed
- *Attributes: Read-only*—A check box used to prevent writing to, changing, or deleting the object

- *Attributes: Hidden*—A check box used to hide the object from view

- *Advanced button: File is ready for archiving*—A check box that indicates that this file is ready for backup

- *Advanced button: For fast searching, allow Indexing Service to index this file*—A check box that when selected preindexes the object for faster searching

- *Advanced button: Compress contents to save disk space*—A check box used to compress the object

- *Advanced button: Encrypt contents to secure data*—A check box used to encrypt the object

The Summary tab is used to define description and origin details for the object. These details include title, subject, category, keywords, comments, source, author, and revision number. This information can be used to refine searches.

FAT/FAT32 File Object

A FAT/FAT32 file object's Properties dialog box has only the General tab (see Figure 4-12).

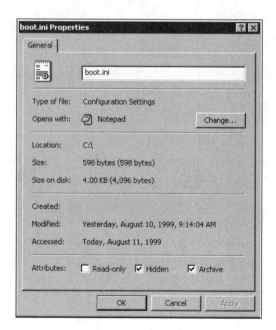

Figure 4-12   A FAT/FAT32 file object Properties dialog box, General tab

The General tab offers the following information:

- *Name*—The customizable name of the object

- *Type of File*—Names the file type or defines it as a *blank* file where *blank* is the file's extension

- *Description (application files only)*—Names the utility or application

- *Opens with (nonapplication files only)*—Lists the application used to open the file

- *Change (nonapplication files only)*—A button for altering the application used to open the file

- *Location*—The path of the object

- *Size*—The byte size of the object

- *Size on disk*—The actual amount of drive space used to store the object

- *Created*—Lists the object's creation date and time

- *Modified*—Lists the last time and date of a change to the object

- *Accessed*—Lists the last time and date the object was accessed

- *Attributes: Read-only*—A check box used to prevent writing to, changing, or deleting the object

- *Attributes: Hidden*—A check box used to hide the object from view

- *Attributes: Archive*—A check box that indicates that this object should be included in the next backup operation

NTFS Mounted Volume Object

An NTFS mounted volume object's Properties dialog box has three tabs: General (see Figure 4-13), Sharing, and Security.

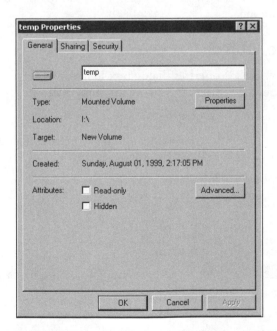

Figure 4-13   An NTFS mounted volume object Properties dialog box, General tab

The General tab offers the following information:

- *Name*—The customizable name of the object
- *Properties*—A button used to access the mounted volume's Properties dialog box, the same dialog box that would be seen via Disk Management
- *Type*—Lists object type: Mounted Volume
- *Location*—The path of the object
- *Target*—Names the mapped volume
- *Created*—Lists the object's creation date and time
- *Attributes: Read-only*—A check box used to prevent writing to, changing, or deleting the object
- *Attributes: Hidden*—A check box used to hide the object from view
- *Advanced button: Folder is ready for archiving*—A check box that indicates that this folder, and optionally its contents, is ready for backup
- *Advanced button: For fast searching, allow Indexing Service to index this folder*—A check box that, when selected, preindexes the folder, and optionally its contents, for faster searching
- *Advanced button: Compress contents to save disk space*—A check box used to compress the folder, and optionally its contents
- *Advanced button: Encrypt contents to secure data*—A check box used to encrypt the folder, and optionally its contents

FAT/FAT32 Mounted Volume Object

A FAT/FAT32 mounted volume object's Properties dialog box has two tabs: General (see Figure 4-14) and Sharing. The General tab offers the following information:

- *Name*—The customizable name of the object
- *Properties*—A button used to access the mounted volume's Properties dialog box, the same dialog box that would be seen via Disk Management
- *Type*—Lists object type: Mounted Volume
- *Location*—The path of the object
- *Target*—Names the mapped volume
- *Created*—Lists the object's creation date and time
- *Attributes: Read-only*—A check box used to prevent writing to, changing, or deleting the object
- *Attributes: Hidden*—A check box used to hide the object from view
- *Attributes: Archive*—A check box that indicates that this object should be included in the next backup operation

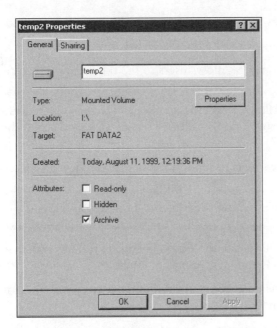

Figure 4-14   A FAT/FAT32 mounted volume object Properties dialog box, General tab

MANAGING NTFS PERMISSIONS

The NTFS file system offers file-level control over access on a user and group basis. The only file system supported by Windows 2000 that offers file level security is NTFS. NTFS security determines what can be done to a file system object and who can perform those actions. There are different permissions for folders and files.

NTFS File and Folder Permissions

NTFS file and folder permissions are nearly identical. The dialog boxes and control interfaces for files and folders are the same. The only differences are: files do not offer child inheritance options (because files are child objects, they do not have child objects themselves) and some obvious permissions apply only to folders or only to files.

> **TIP**   Inheritance is the mechanism by which the contents of a container receive the same settings as the container. Inheritance allows administrators to change a setting on a folder, drive, group, policy, etc., and then force those changes to be applied to all the objects contained within the folder, drive, group, etc.

In some cases, the same permission name has a different meaning for files and folders. In other cases, similar permissions have different names but both names are listed in both dialog box contexts. The NTFS permissions are as follows:

- *Read*—Allows users to view and access the contents of the folder or the file

- *Write (folders)*—Allows users to create new folders and files within the folder

- *Write (files)*—Allows users to overwrite the file and change attributes

- *List Folder Contents (folders only)*—Allows users to see the names of the contents of the folder

- *Read & Execute (folders)*—Allows users to reach files and folders via folders where they do not have access permission; also allows users to view and access the contents of the folder

- *Read & Execute (files)*—Allows users to run applications and to view and access the file

- *Modify (folders)*—Allows users to delete the folder and its contents; also allows users to create new folders and files within the folder and to view and access the contents of the folder

- *Modify (files)*—Allows users to delete the file, to overwrite the file, and change attributes, to run applications and view and access the file

- *Full Control (folders)*—Grants users complete and unrestricted access to all functions of the folder and its contents

- *Full Control (files)*—Grants users complete and unrestricted access to all functions of the file

The NTFS permissions are configured on the Security tab of the object's Properties dialog box (see Figure 4-15). The controls this tab offers are discussed in the following section.

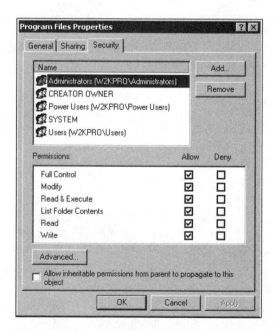

Figure 4-15 An NTFS folder object Properties dialog box, Security tab

To change permissions for a user or group, select that user or group in the Name list. If the user or group is not present, use the Add button to include that user or group in the list. After a user or group is selected, the Permissions field displays the current settings for that specific selection. Selecting or deselecting the Allow or Deny check boxes for each permission level defines the custom permissions for the selected user or group. To remove a user or group, select it in the Name list and click the Remove button. When a user or group is not listed on the Security tab for an object, that user or group has no effective permissions to that object. In other words, the user or group is prevented from accessing the object.

Clicking the Advanced button reveals a three-tabbed dialog box where more detailed access control settings can be defined. The Permissions tab (see Figure 4-16) of the Access Control Settings dialog box is used to define detailed permissions on a per user or per group basis. Similarly to the previous dialog box, users and groups are included in the list via the Add button and deleted with the Remove button. This dialog box also offers two more check boxes. The first check box is the same inheritable permissions as was seen on the previous dialog box—Allow inheritable permissions from parent to propagate to this object. When selected, this check box enables permissions changes to the parent object to affect this object. The second check box appears on folder dialog boxes only and states: "Reset permissions on all child objects and enable propagation of inheritable permissions." This control resets child object inheritance settings to their defaults.

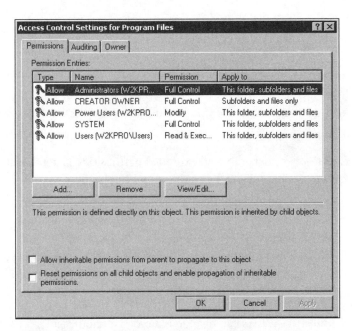

Figure 4-16   The Access Control Settings dialog box, Permissions tab

To edit the permissions of a user or group, select them from the list and click View/Edit. The Permission Entry dialog box (see Figure 4-17) is displayed and shows all of the permissions specific to the user or group. It also has the familiar Allow and Deny check boxes.

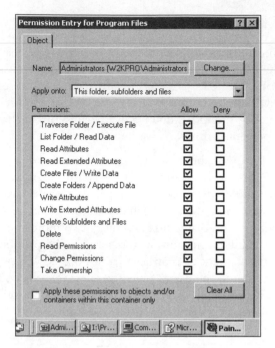

Figure 4-17   The Permission Entry dialog box

The detailed NTFS object permissions are:

- *Traverse Folder/Execute File*—Users can see the directory structure and execute files within that structure.

- *List Folder/Read Data*—Users can view and read folders and the data they contain.

- *Read Attributes*—Users can read data.

- *Read Extended Attributes*—Users can read extended permissions. Extended attributes are defined by programs and may vary from program to program.

- *Create Files/Write Data*—The Create Files portion is a directory level permission that allows new files to be created within a directory. The Write Data permission is for files that allow a user to overwrite the existing file.

- *Create Folders/Append Data*—Users can create folders and append data to the structure.

- *Write Attributes*—Users can write data to files and folders.

- *Write Extended Attributes*—Users can change extended attributes added to objects by programs.

- *Delete Subfolders and Files*—Users can delete subfolders and files.

- *Delete*—Users can delete files and folders.

- *Read Permissions*—Users can read a file.

- *Change Permissions*—Users can change permissions of an object.

- *Take Ownership*—Administrators can acquire ownership of an object.

The Permission Entry dialog box allows you to:

- Change the user or group to which these settings apply (only on objects that do not inherit their permissions)

- (Folders only) set the application of these permissions to: this folder only; this folder, subfolder, and files; this folder and subfolders; this folder and files; subfolders and files only; subfolders only; or files only

- Clear all Allow and Deny check boxes

- Apply these permissions to objects and/or containers within this container only (folders only)

Auditing is recording the occurrence of defined system events or actions. The Auditing tab on the Access Control Settings dialog box (see Figure 4-18) is used to define events that result in an audit detail being written to the Event Viewer's Security log. This tab functions the same way as the Permissions tab. Two check boxes regarding inheritance appear at the bottom, but they apply to audit settings. Users and groups are included or deleted with the Add and Remove buttons. Selected users and groups are edited with the View/Edit button. This button reveals a similar dialog box with all of the detailed permissions. Selecting Allow or Deny on this dialog box indicates that when a user or group performs this action, an audit detail will be written to the Event Viewer Security log.

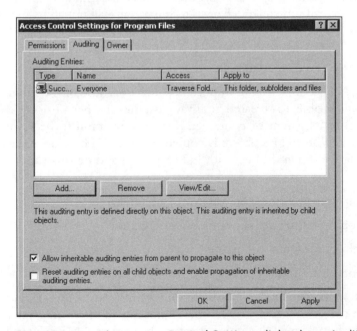

Figure 4-18   The Access Control Settings dialog box, Auditing tab

The Owner tab lists the current owner of the object. To change ownership, select a new owner from the list of possible owners in the center field. The center field lists your user account and group memberships (which have Take Ownership permissions on this object). It also has a check box that can be used to replace the ownership on all child elements with the settings on this object (folders only).

NTFS Permission Rules

There are a few rules to keep in mind when working with NTFS permissions:

- NTFS object permissions *always* apply, regardless of whether the accessing user is local or remote (that is, over a network via a share).

- NTFS object permissions are cumulative. All user-specific permissions are added to all group-specific memberships (assuming the user account is a member of that group). The resulting accumulation of permissions is the access level granted to the user.

- NTFS file permissions override any contradictory settings on the parent or container folder.

- Deny overrides all other specific Allows. That is, if a user is allowed one permission, but is also assigned Deny, then the user is *denied* access regardless of the Allowed access.

- When disabling inheritance for an NTFS object, you will need to select to either Copy the parent's permissions to the current object or Remove permissions assigned from the parent and retain only object-specific settings. In either case, Copy or Remove, all subsequent changes to the parent will not affect the child object.

Copying and Moving NTFS Objects

Copying and moving NTFS objects is an important subject because of the inheritance of permissions. When a new object is created, it always assumes the permissions (and other settings and attributes) of its parent or container. Keep this in mind to help you understand what happens when an NTFS object is copied or moved. There are four different moving/copying scenarios when dealing with NTFS source and destination volumes or partitions:

- Moving an object within the same volume or partition
- Copying an object within the same volume or partition
- Moving an object from one volume or partition to another
- Copying an object from one volume or partition to another

Moving an object within the same volume or partition is actually just a minor change in the location pointer for the object. Thus, its new location is not caused by creating a new file, but just by changing its location address. Such objects retain their original NTFS permissions.

All of the other copy and move situations involve creating a new object. This is obvious for the copy procedure, but when moving from one volume to another, a two-step process is used. First, the system copies the file to the new destination. Second, it deletes the original. The act of creating a new object causes that new object to inherit the NTFS permissions of its new parent or container.

When moving or copying an object from an NTFS volume to a FAT volume, all NTFS settings are lost and the object inherits the FAT attributes and settings of its new container. When moving or copying an object from a FAT volume to an NTFS volume, the object inherits the NTFS settings and permissions of its new container.

4

Managing Shared Folders

The Sharing tab (see Figure 4-19) found on both FAT/FAT32 and NTFS folder Properties dialog boxes is used to enable remote access to the folder. This tab is used to share and configure sharing for this object. Selecting Share this folder or Do not share this folder either offers the resource to the network or removes the share.

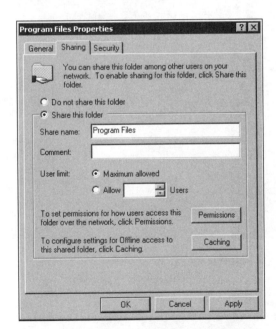

Figure 4-19   A folder's Properties dialog box, Sharing tab

The Sharing tab offers the following controls:

- *Do not share this folder*—Disables sharing for this folder
- *Share this folder*—Enables sharing for this folder
- *Share name*—The name displayed in browse lists and used in UNC (Universal Naming Convention) names to access this share

- *Comment*—A comment about or description of the share

- *User limit*—Used to allow the maximum possible users (as determined by system speed and resources), or to limit simultaneous users to a specified number

- *Permissions button*—Opens the Share Permissions dialog box (see Figure 4-20) where users and groups are granted or denied Full Control, Change, or Read permissions for this folder via the share

- *Caching button*—Opens the Caching Settings dialog box where you can enable or disable caching of resources from this folder and set caching to automatic for documents or programs, or manual for documents. This feature is used in conjunction with the Offline Files settings of Folder Options to cache network resources for use while not connected to the network.

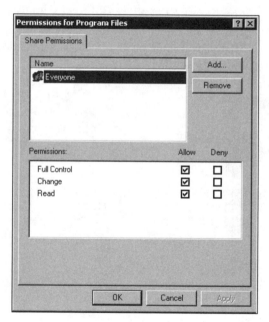

Figure 4-20   The Share Permissions dialog box

The three share permission levels are:

- *Read*—Allows users to access, execute, and open resources via the share

- *Change*—Allows users to create new objects, change and delete existing objects, and to access, execute, and open resources via the share

- *Full Control*—Allows users to perform all actions on resources via the share

There are several important issues to keep in mind when working with shares:

- The three permission levels on a share are the only way to impose security on shared FAT volumes.

- Shares are folders, not individual files.

- Share permissions apply only to the network access point.

- The default permission of a share is Full Control allowed for the Everyone group.

- Multiple share permission levels because of group memberships are cumulative.

- Deny always overrides any other specific Allow.

- The most restrictive permissions of cumulative share and cumulative NTFS apply.

- Share permissions only restrict access for network users, not local users.

- A moved folder is no longer shared.

- A copied folder is not shared, but the original folder retains its shared status.

 Shared folders are easy to recognize because their folder icon has a blue-sleeved hand supporting the folder.

Because the default permission of a share is Full Control allowed for the Everyone group, be sure to set NTFS permissions for shares as they are created to avoid a security breach.

Accessing shared resources on a Microsoft network is handled through several mechanisms. You can map a drive using the Map Network Drive command from Windows Explorer (try Hands-on Project 4-15), My Computer, or My Network Places. You can access shared resources via the My Network Places tool. Most Open and Save dialog boxes offer a link to My Network Places allowing you to open or save files to remote paths. You can also access shares via UNC paths using the Run command. If you use My Network Places, you can use the following access methods:

- *Add Network Place*—A wizard used to map a share to My Network Places (does not assign a drive letter to the mapped share).

- *Computers Near Me*—Lists all computers in your domain or workgroup. Each of these can be accessed to reveal shared resources.

- *Entire Network*—Lists all domains or workgroups seen on the network. Each of these can be accessed to see members of those domains or workgroups. Each of these members can be accessed to reveal shared resources.

 Windows 2000 domains are listed under the Directory heading (for Active Directory). Windows NT/95/98 domains and workgroups and Windows 2000 workgroups are listed under the Microsoft Windows Network heading.

TROUBLESHOOTING PERMISSIONS PROBLEMS

In most cases of access problems, one of two situations exists: either the resource object has the wrong settings, or the user account has the wrong settings. A resource object can have incorrect permissions settings due to inheritance, lack of inheritance, moving/copying, or simple human error (for example, setting the wrong thing). A user account can have the incorrect permissions due to improper group membership, improper permission settings on a valid group, or human error.

To resolve permission or access problems, follow this procedure:

1. Determine what valid access the user should have.

2. Inspect the resource object's permissions based on groups and the specific user and what actions are set to Allow or Deny.

3. Inspect the share's permissions based on groups and the specific user and what actions are set to Allow or Deny.

4. Inspect the user's group memberships.

5. Attempt to access other resources with the user account from the same computer and from a different computer.

6. Attempt to access the problematic resource with the Administrator account from the same computer and from a different computer.

The preceding steps should point you directly to the problem and how to resolve it. Taking the time to make the effort systematic will prevent you from overlooking small details or glaringly obvious problems.

In general, use the following guidelines to lay out or design permission levels to avoid common problems:

- Grant permission only as needed.

- Rely upon NTFS to restrict access.

- Grant Full Control only when necessary, even on shares.

- Change permissions on a folder level, and allow changes to affect all child elements (at least to files, if not subfolders).

- Use multiple folders and subfolders to separate files into groups for different permission levels.

- Do not use the Deny setting unless absolutely necessary.

Optimizing access to files and folders requires a two-part verification. The first verification is to ensure that the share- and direct object-level permissions grant and restrict exactly the activities you want for each user and group. The second verification is to ensure that group memberships do not grant too much access via accumulated rights or prevent necessary access due to a specific right or permission having the Deny box checked. Both of these verification processes must be performed manually.

THE MICROSOFT DISTRIBUTED FILE SYSTEM

The Microsoft **Distributed File System (DFS)** is a Windows 2000 Server hosted service used to manipulate and manage shared resources. DFS combines shared resources from various locations throughout a network into a single hierarchical system. This allows DFS to be a single access or reference point for a logical tree structure without regard to the physical location of the resources. DFS functions by first creating a DFS root on a Windows 2000 Server system. This root looks and acts much like a share. Then shared resources from other systems can be mapped under the DFS root. These are called DFS child nodes. The DFS child nodes appear as subfolders underneath the DFS root.

The benefits of DFS include:

- All network resources are organized in a single tree structure.

- User navigation of resources is simplified because the host computer name is not required.

- Simplified administration. If a server that hosts resources fails, the path to a new alternate location can be defined without affecting the path employed by users to gain access.

- Access permissions are preserved.

- The DFS root is accessed in the same way as a normal share.

- Once inside the DFS root, all other resource accesses are simplified and do not require knowing the name of the host systems.

From a client's perspective, DFS provides simplified access to all resources in an enterprise. Special client software is required to use DFS. Windows 2000 Professional, Windows 95 and 98, Windows for Workgroups, and Windows NT all include this software.

For more information on DFS, see Windows 2000 Server documentation and the *Windows 2000 Server Resource Kit*.

CHAPTER SUMMARY

❑ This chapter discussed dynamic storage, the new Windows 2000 storage mechanism that does not rely upon partitions as does the basic storage method. The divisions of dynamic storage are called volumes. All volumes and partitions can be formatted with FAT, FAT32, or NTFS. Preexisting basic storage drive configurations can be managed by Windows 2000, but only dynamic devices can be used to create new multipart drive configurations. Basic storage devices can be converted to dynamic devices without damaging the data, but to reverse the process requires that all volumes be deleted before converting back to basic storage. The Disk Management snap-in is used to perform all drive-, partition-, and volume-related functions. Windows 2000 supports simple volumes, spanned volumes, striped volumes, mirrored volumes, and RAID 5 volumes.

❏ The FAT and FAT32 file systems are retained by Windows 2000 for backward compatibility with other operating systems on the same multiboot system. FAT does not offer any form of file level security. NTFS is the recommended file system to use under Windows 2000 because it offers file level security, encryption, and disk quotas.

❏ Mount points are a new mapping method in Windows 2000. This method allows volumes or partitions to be mapped to empty directories on NTFS volumes or partitions. With map points, up to 32 drives can be utilized within the limitation of drive letters. There are several disk-related utilities: Disk Cleanup, ScanDisk, and Disk Defragmenter.

❏ All file system objects within Windows 2000 have unique properties and controls. Plus, all NTFS objects offer security, encryption, compression, and auditing. NTFS permissions are used to control access to resources. Shares are used to grant access to local resources across a network.

❏ The Microsoft Distributed File System (DFS) is a service used to manipulate and manage shared resources. DFS can combine shared resources from throughout an enterprise into a single hierarchical system.

KEY TERMS

active partition — A primary partition is marked active when it hosts the necessary files to boot into an operating system.

auditing — The recording of the occurrence of a defined event or action.

basic storage — The drive division method that employs partitions.

boot partition — The partition that hosts the main Windows 2000 system files and is the initial default location for the paging file. The boot partition can be the same partition as the system partition, or it can be any other partition (or logical drive in an extended partition) on any drive hosted by the computer.

cluster — One or more sectors grouped into a single nondivisible unit.

defragmentation — The process of reorganizing files so they are stored contiguously and no gaps are left between files.

Disk Management — The Microsoft Management Console (MMC) snap-in used to manage drives.

disk quota — A limitation on the amount of disk space that can be consumed by a user.

Distributed File System (DFS) — A Windows 2000 Server hosted service used to manipulate and manage shared resources from various locations throughout a network in a single hierarchical system.

drive letter — One of two methods of accessing file system resources on formatted volumes under Windows 2000. A drive letter can be assigned to a partition or volume or a drive configuration of multiple components.

dynamic storage — The drive division method that employs volumes. It is a new standard supported only by Windows 2000.

extended partition — A type of partition on a basic disk that can be divided into logical drives. Only a single extended partition can exist on a physical disk, and when present only three primary partitions can exist.

FAT (FAT16) — The 16-bit file allocation table file system originally introduced with DOS. As supported under Windows 2000, it can be used to format partitions or volumes up to 4 GB.

FAT32 — The 32-bit FAT file system. As supported under Windows 2000, it can be used to format partitions or volumes up to 32 GB.

fragmentation — The division of a file into two or more parts where each part is stored in a different location on the hard drive. As the level of fragmentation on a drive increases, the longer it takes for read and write operations to occur.

long filenames (LFNs) — Filenames up to 256 characters in length, supported by all file systems under Windows 2000.

mirrored volume — A drive configuration of a single volume is duplicated onto another volume on a different hard drive and provides fault tolerance. In Windows NT, a mirror onto a drive hosted by a different drive controller was called duplexing, but this distinction is no longer used in Windows 2000 (Windows 2000 Server only).

mount point or **mounted volume** — A new drive access technique that maps a volume or partition to an empty directory on an NTFS volume or partition.

NTFS (New Technology File System) — The preferred file system of Windows 2000. Supports file level security, encryption, compression, auditing, and more. Supports volumes up to 2 TB.

partition — A logical division of the physical space on a hard drive.

POSIX (Portable Operating System Interface for Computing Environments) — A set of standards drafted by the Institute of Electrical and Electronic Engineers (IEEE) that defines various aspects of an operating system, including topics such as programming interface, security, networking, and graphical interface.

primary partition — A type of partition on a basic disk that can be marked active. Up to four primary partitions can exist on a physical disk, but only one partition can be active.

RAID 5 volume — A drive configuration of three or more (up to 32) parts of one or more drives or three or more (up to 32) entire drives. Data is written to all drives in equal amounts to spread the workload. Parity information is added to the written data to allow for drive failure recovery. Provides fault tolerance. If one partition or drive fails in the set, the other members can re-create the missing data on the fly. When the failed member is replaced or repaired, the data on that drive can be rebuilt and restored. This is also known as disk striping with parity (Windows 2000 Server only).

removable storage device — Any type of floppy, cartridge, or drive that can be either removed between reboots or as a hot swappable device.

sector — The smallest division (512 bytes) of a drive's surface.

share — A resource, such as an application, file, printer, or other device, that can be accessed over the network.

simple volume — A drive configuration of all or part of a single drive. Does not provide any fault tolerance. NTFS volumes can be extended; FAT and FAT32 volumes cannot be extended.

spanned volume — A drive configuration of two or more (up to 32) parts of one or more drives or two or more entire drives; the elements of the spanned volume do not have to be equal in size.

striped volume — A drive configuration of two or more (up to 32) parts of one or more drives or two or more (up to 32) entire drives. Data is written to all drives in equal amounts (in 64 KB units) to spread the workload and improve performance.

system partition — The active partition where the boot files required to display the boot menu and initiate the booting of Windows 2000 are stored.

volume — (1) In basic storage, a collection of 2 to 32 partitions into a single logical structure. (2) In dynamic storage, any division of a physical drive or collection of divisions into a drive configuration.

volume set — A collection of disk partitions that are treated as a logical drive. A volume set may be expanded after it has already been created. To make a volume set smaller, however, you must back up all the data, delete the volume set, define a new (smaller) volume set, and restore the data to that set. If you lose one drive in a volume set, you lose all the data in the entire set, because it offers no fault tolerance.

REVIEW QUESTIONS

1. Which storage method employs primary and extended partitions?
   a. logical drives
   b. basic
   c. dynamic
   d. spanned volumes

2. When logical drives are present on a basic storage device, how many primary partitions can exist?
   a. 1
   b. 2
   c. 3
   d. 4

3. Which of the following statements are true about a volume set, comprised of either partitions or volumes? (Choose all that apply.)
   a. combines two or more volumes/partitions into a single logical storage area
   b. provides fault tolerance
   c. If one element of the set fails, all data in the set is lost.
   d. It can be assigned a single drive letter.

4. A 4 GB partition or volume can be formatted with what file system? (Choose all that apply.)

a. FAT

b. FAT32

c. HPFS

d. NTFS

5. What mechanism(s) of Windows 2000 allow you to access up to 32 volumes on a single system?

a. shares

b. drive letters

c. DFS

d. mounted volumes

6. Under Windows 2000, it is possible to create new RAID 5 volumes on dynamic and basic drives. True or False?

7. Which of the following is the partition that hosts the main Windows 2000 system files and is the initial default location for the paging file?

a. system partition

b. boot partition

c. logical partition

d. dynamic partition

8. The drive configurations supported by Windows 2000 Professional provide fault tolerance. True or False?

9. What is the best file system for a 250 MB volume?

a. FAT

b. FAT32

c. NTFS

10. NTFS volumes created under Windows 2000 cannot be accessed by any other operating system. True or False?

11. Which of the following are true for NTFS under Windows 2000? (Choose all that apply.)

a. supports volumes up to 2 TB in size

b. file level compression, encryption, auditing, and security

c. disk quotas

d. POSIX file system support

e. most efficient on volumes smaller than 512 MB

12. Drives can be converted to and from dynamic storage without damaging the hosted data. True or False?

13. The Properties dialog box for a partition or volume gives you quick access to which drive tools? (Choose all that apply.)

    a. ScanDisk

    b. Defragmentation

    c. Disk Cleanup

    d. Device Manager

    e. Backup

    f. Event Viewer

14. A volume or partition can be attached to a mount point on any other volume or partition. True or False?

15. Quotas can be defined in what manner(s)?

    a. by user

    b. by drive

    c. by group

    d. by volume or partition

16. Disk Cleanup is used to free space on a hard drive by removing orphaned files, cleaning out the Recycle bin, and shrinking the page file. True or False?

17. The built-in defragmentation utility can be scheduled to automatically reorganize local hard drives. True or False?

18. Which of the following are properties of NTFS file or folder objects, but not of FAT file or folder objects? (Choose all that apply.)

    a. Attributes: Read-only

    b. compress contents to save disk space

    c. Attributes: Archive

    d. encrypt contents to secure data

19. What methods can be used to prevent a user from gaining access to an NTFS resource?

    a. Do not include the user account (or its groups) in the list of permissions.

    b. Set the user account's permissions to Deny.

    c. Set the user account's permissions to No Access.

    d. Place the user account in the Guests group.

20. NTFS object permissions are used only when a user is local. True or False?

21. Which of the following are true?

    a. Child objects can inherit the permissions of their parent containers.

    b. Copied files always retain their original settings.

    c. File-level permissions always override contradictory settings on the parent container.

    d. Deny allows overrides of all other specific Allows.

22. Files moved from an NTFS volume to a FAT volume and then to another NTFS volume will reassume their original settings. True or False?

23. Which of the following statements is true about shares? (Choose all that apply.)

    a. offers only three levels of permissions

    b. can be cached on client systems

    c. can restrict simultaneous users

    d. can be individual files or folders

    e. overrides NTFS permissions

    f. The most restrictive permissions of cumulative shares and cumulative NTFS apply.

24. To grant varying levels of access within a share, use NTFS permissions and group files into subfolders. True or False?

25. Which of the following statements is true about the Microsoft Distributed File System? (Choose all that apply.)

    a. All network resources are organized in a single tree structure.

    b. Access permissions are preserved.

    c. A DFS root can be hosted by Windows 2000 Professional.

    d. Once inside the DFS root, all other resource accesses are simplified and do not require knowing the name of the host systems.

HANDS-ON PROJECTS

Project 4-1

To create a partition on a basic drive:

> This hands-on project requires that a basic drive with unallocated space be present in the system. Additionally, the drive must have either only three primary partitions or only two primary partitions if an extended partition is present.

1. Open the **Control Panel** (**Start, Settings, Control Panel**).

2. Open the **Administrative Tools** applet (double-click its icon).

3. Open the **Computer Management** tool (double-click its icon).

4. Expand the **Storage** console node if necessary (click on the plus sign to the left of the node).

5. Select **Disk Management**.

6. Right-click over an unallocated area of a basic drive and select **Create Partition** from the resulting menu.

7. The **Create Partition Wizard** launches. Click **Next**.

8. Select **Primary Partition**. Click **Next**.

9. Select the amount of space to use in this partition. Accept the default of the maximum space available. Click **Next**.

10. Assign a drive letter. Accept the default. Click **Next**.

11. Select the file system to format this partition. Accept the default of **NTFS**. Click **Next**.

12. The wizard displays a list of the actions to be performed in creating this partition. Click **Finish**.

13. The system will create the partition, format the drive, and assign the drive letter. The display of the drive will be updated to reflect the new partition.

Project 4-2

To change a drive letter on a volume or partition:

1. Right–click a partition or volume. Be sure not to select the boot or system partition; select **Change Drive Letter and Path** from the resulting menu.

2. Check that the current drive letter is selected, and then click **Edit**.

3. Select the **Assign a drive letter** radio button if it is not already selected.

4. Use the pull–down list to select a different letter for this drive.

5. Click **OK**.

6. You'll be warned about changing drive letters. Click **Yes**. The Disk Management display will reflect the drive letter change.

Project 4-3

To create a mounted volume:

This hands-on project requires that at least two partitions be present on the system. Partition A must be formatted with NTFS. Partition B can be any partition other than the boot or system partitions.

1. Locate Partition A. Take note of its drive letter: _____

2. Right-click Partition B, select **Change Drive Letter and Path** from the resulting menu.

3. Click **Add**.

4. Make sure the **Mount in this NTFS folder** option is selected.

5. Click **Browse**.

6. Locate Partition A by using its drive letter (see step 1). Select the drive letter.

7. Click **New Folder**.

8. Type in a name for the new folder, such as **MapPartB**, and then press **Enter**.

9. Make sure the newly created folder is highlighted, and then click **OK**.

10. The path to the new folder is now listed in the text field under the **Mount in this NTFS folder** option. Click **OK**.

11. Open **Windows Explorer** (**Start**, **Programs**, **Accessories**, **Windows Explorer**).

12. Expand My Computer.

13. Expand Partition A.

14. Notice that the mounted volume appears as a drive icon with the name of the folder you created. Select the mount point. Notice that the contents of Partition B are displayed in the right pane.

15. Close Windows Explorer.

Project 4-4
To delete a mounted volume:

 This hands-on project requires that Hands-on Project 4-3 be completed.

1. Right-click over Partition B from Hands–on Project 4-3, select **Change Drive Letter and Path** from the resulting menu.

2. Select the mounted volume mapping.

3. Click **Remove**.

4. You'll be asked to confirm the deletion. Click **Yes**.

Project 4-5
To delete a partition from a basic drive:

 This hands-on project requires that Hands-on Project 4-1 be completed.

1. Select the partition you created in Hands-on Project 4-1.

2. Right-click and select **Delete Partition** from the resulting menu.

3. To confirm the deletion, click **Yes**.

Project 4-6

To convert a basic drive to a dynamic drive:

 This hands-on project requires that a second hard drive that is currently a basic drive be present on the system.

1. Select a basic disk in **Disk Management**. The selected disk cannot host the system partition.
2. Right-click and select **Upgrade to Dynamic Disk** from the resulting menu.
3. A list of all hard drives present on the system is displayed. The disk you selected will already be checked. Do not change the status of the check boxes on this list. Click **OK**.
4. Disk Management will display the drive as Dynamic.

Project 4-7

To create a volume on a dynamic drive:

 This hands-on project requires that Hands-on Project 4-6 be completed.

1. Right-click over the unallocated space on a dynamic drive, select **Create Volume** from the resulting menu.
2. This launches the **Create Volume Wizard**. Click **Next**.
3. Select the volume type to create. In this case, select **Simple volume**. Click **Next**.
4. For a simple volume you only need unallocated space from a single drive. Make sure the drive is listed in the Selected dynamic disk field.
5. In the **Size** field, enter the amount of space from the maximum available to use in the volume. Enter an amount of about one-half of that available. Click **Next**.
6. Assign a drive letter. Accept the defaults. Click **Next**.
7. Select the file system to format the new volume. Accept the default of NTFS. Click **Next**.
8. The wizard displays a list of actions to be performed in creating the new volume. Click **Finish**.

Project 4-8

To extend a volume:

> **TIP** This hands-on project requires that Hands-on Project 4-7 be completed.

4

1. Right-click over the volume created in Hands-on Project 4-7, and then select **Extend Volume** from the resulting menu.
2. The Extend Volume Wizard is launched. Click **Next**.
3. Make sure the drive with unallocated space is listed in the Selected dynamic disk field.
4. Change the size of the remaining unallocated space to be added to the existing volume to 80% of the space available (for example, if there are 200 MB remaining, change the number to 180). Click **Next**.
5. The wizard displays a list of actions to perform in extending the volume. Click **Finish**.
6. Disk Management will display the extension with the same drive letter as the original volume.

Project 4-9

To delete a volume:

> **TIP** This hands-on project requires that Hands-on Project 4-7 be completed.

1. Select the volume you created in Hands-on Project 4-7.
2. Right-click and select **Delete Volume** from the resulting menu.
3. Confirm the deletion. Click **Yes**.
4. Disk Management displays the drive as hosting no volumes and consisting only of unallocated space.

Project 4-10

To revert a dynamic drive to a basic drive:

> **TIP** This hands-on project requires that Hands-on Project 4-9 be completed.

1. Select the drive used in Hands-on Projects 4-6 through 4-9.
2. Right-click and select **Revert to Basic Disk** from the resulting menu.
3. Disk Management will display the drive as Basic.

Project 4-11

To compress and decompress a folder:

1. Launch Windows Explorer (**Start, Programs, Accessories, Windows Explorer**).
2. Locate and select any folder on your hard drive, such as C:\Program Files.
3. Right-click the folder, then select **Properties** from the menu.
4. On the **General** tab, take note of the Size and Size on Disk values.
5. On the **General** tab, click the **Advanced** button.
6. Select the **Compress contents to save disk space** checkbox.
7. Click **OK**.
8. Click **OK**.
9. Select the **Apply Changes to this folder, subfolder, and files** radio button.
10. Click **OK**. The system will compress the folder and its contents, this may take several minutes.
11. Right-click the folder, then select **Properties** from the menu.
12. On the **General** tab, take note of the Size and Size on Disk values. The Size on Disk value should be smaller than the original value.
13. On the **General** tab, click the Advanced button.
14. Deselect the **Compress contents to save disk space** checkbox.
15. Click **OK**.
16. Click **OK**.
17. Select the **Apply Changes to this folder, subfolder, and files** radio button. Click **OK**. The system will decompress the folder and its contents, this may take several minutes.

Project 4-12

To optimize folder access:

> **TIP** This hands-on project requires that Windows 2000 be installed and an NTFS partition is present.

4

1. Launch Windows Explorer (**Start, Programs, Accessories, Windows Explorer**).
2. In the left pane, select a drive formatted with NTFS within My Computer.
3. In the right pane, select a file or folder.
4. From the **File** menu, select **Properties**.
5. Select the **Security** tab.
6. Click the **Add** button.
7. Select the **Authenticated Users** group.
8. Click **Add**.
9. Click **OK**.
10. Click the **Authenticated Users** group, which now appears in the list of names on the Security tab for the NTFS object. Take note of the granted permissions.
11. Select the **Sharing** tab.
12. Select the **Share this Folder** radio button.
13. Click **Permissions**.
14. Click **Add**.
15. Select the **Authenticated Users** group.
16. Click **Add**.
17. Click **OK**.
18. Set the Share permissions for the Authenticated Users group as close to the NTFS file level permissions as possible.
19. Click **OK**.
20. Click **OK**.

Project 4-13

To share a folder and remove a share:

> This hands-on project requires that Windows 2000 be installed and an NTFS partition is present.

1. Launch Windows Explorer (**Start, Programs, Accessories, Windows Explorer**).
2. In the left pane, select a drive formatted with NTFS within My Computer.
3. In the right pane, select a file or folder.
4. From the **File** menu, select **Sharing**.
5. Select the **Share this folder** radio button.
6. Click the **Permissions** button.
7. Click **Add**.
8. Select the **Authenticated Users** group.
9. Click **Add**.
10. Click **OK**.
11. Click **OK**. Notice the folder now has a shared hand on its icon.
12. With the folder still selected, select the **Sharing** command from the **File** menu.
13. Select the **Do not share this folder** radio button.
14. Click **OK**. Notice the shared hand on the folder icon disappears.

Project 4-14

To convert a FAT partition to NTFS:

> This hands-on project requires that a FAT volume exist on your Windows 2000 system. This volume will be converted to NTFS. Proceed only if the conversion of this volume will not compromise your system.

1. Launch the Command Prompt by selecting **Start**, **Programs**, **Accessories**, **Command Prompt**.
2. Change to the FAT partition drive, such as by typing **g:**, then press **Enter**.
3. Type **convert g: /fs:ntfs /v** where g: is the drive letter of the FAT volume to convert, press **Enter**.

4. Provide the current label for the drive to be converted, look in **Windows Explorer** to see what the volume name is. Press **Enter** after you have typed in the volume label.

5. You'll be prompted whether to complete the conversion at the next reboot, press **Y**.

6. Reboot the computer. The drive will be converted as part of the startup process.

Project 4-15

To map to a network drive:

 This project requires that the Windows 2000 Professional be a client on a network with at least one shared folder available for mapping.

1. Launch Windows Explorer (**Start, Programs, Accessories, Windows Explorer**).

2. Select the **Map Network Drive** command from the **Tools** menu.

3. Click the **Browse** button.

4. Using the browse list, locate and select a shared folder from the network.

5. Click **OK**.

6. Select a drive letter using the pull-down list next to **Drive:**.

7. Deselect the **Reconnect at logon** checkbox.

8. Click **Finish**.

CASE PROJECTS

1. You must test new media software that plays large multimedia presentations (often 3 MB or larger). The software is being developed for Windows 98, Windows NT, and Windows 2000. Can you configure a multiboot system with all three operating systems in such a way that a single drive can host at least six media presentations which can be accessed from all three OSs? If so, how? If not, what other solution(s) can be used?

2. The security requirements of your organization state that log files of system access must be retained for at least six months on live accessible drives. In the past, these log files have consumed at least 6 GB of drive space per month. However, they are growing larger at an accelerated rate. Because you don't know exactly how much drive space you'll need over the next year or even six months, what options do you have under Windows 2000 to comply with the organization's security requirements?

5

Users, Groups, Profiles, and Policies

After reading this chapter and completing the exercises, you will be able to:

♦ Understand local users and groups

♦ Discuss the Windows 2000 Professional logon authentication

♦ Describe the default user accounts

♦ Establish a naming convention for accounts and groups

♦ Create and manage user accounts and profiles

♦ Understand local security policies

Many computers are used by more than one person, especially in business or educational environments. Each person is identified to the computer and ultimately the network through a unique user account and password. Typically, a **user account** contains details about the user, such as what he or she can and cannot access, and the preferred configuration or environmental settings. To establish such a system where details about each user are maintained, Windows 2000 uses named access accounts that are protected with password security. This chapter discusses these topics in detail.

Windows 2000 Professional User Accounts

Windows 2000 Professional is designed to be used as a network client for a Windows 2000 (and Windows NT) network or as a standalone operating system. From a Windows 2000 Professional system, you are only able to create, configure, and manage **local user accounts**. A local user account exists on a single computer. A local user account cannot be used in any manner with network resources or to gain network access of any kind. A local user account has absolutely no meaning to a domain or network. (A **domain** is an organizational unit used to centralize network users and resources.)

A **domain user account** exists in a domain by virtue of being created on a domain controller (a Windows 2000 Server). A domain user account exists throughout a domain and can be used on any computer that is a member of that domain. A domain user account is used to gain access to network resources. A domain user account can be used to grant access to local resources. Only Windows 2000 Servers can be domain controllers and create domain user accounts.

The information about user accounts and groups discussed in this chapter applies to local user accounts and local groups hosted by a Windows 2000 Professional system. Such local accounts can be maintained whether the host is a standalone desktop computer or a network client. When Windows 2000 Professional is a network client, it can assign access permissions to local resources used by domain groups, but it is unable to create domain groups or alter the membership of domain groups. It will be explicitly stated when material in this chapter applies to both local user accounts and domain user accounts. For more information on domain user accounts, see the Windows 2000 Server online Help, its related documentation, and the *Windows 2000 Server Resource Kit*.

On a Windows 2000 Professional system, whether acting as a client in a domain network or a peer-to-peer workgroup, or even as a standalone desktop system, user accounts are used to govern or control access. A Windows 2000 Professional system can:

- Be a standalone system where all users access local resources through a common user account that automatically logs on to the system upon bootup

- Be a standalone system where each user logs on to the system with a unique user account to gain access to local resources

- Be a network client where each user logs on to the system with a unique domain/network user account to gain access to network and local resources

A user account is used to uniquely identify a user to the system using a named user account and a password. Tied to this user account are numerous details about the user, including security settings and preferences. A Windows 2000 Professional local user account stores details about:

- *Security:* Passwords protect user accounts so only authorized individuals can gain access.

- *Access permissions:* User-specific settings and group memberships define the resources and applications a user has the authority to access and use.

■ *Preferences:* A user's environmental settings and configuration preferences can be stored as a profile. If roaming profiles are enabled, the user's profile will be available from any computer on the network.

In addition to the preceding items, a Windows 2000 Professional system also maintains a wide range of security settings and preferences that affect a user account. These include password policy, account lockout policy, audit policy, user rights assignment, security options, public key policies, IP security policies, and more. Many of these topics are discussed later in this chapter.

Operating systems such as Windows 2000 that can support more than one user are called **multiple-user systems**. Maintaining a separate and distinct user account for each person is the common feature of all multiple-user systems. Windows 2000 implements its multiple-user system through the following:

■ *Groups:* Groups are named collections of users. Each member of a group takes on the access privileges or restrictions defined for that group. Through the use of groups, administrators can manage many users at one time because a group's settings can be defined once and apply to all members of that group. When the group settings are changed or modified, those changes automatically affect every member of that group. Thus, changing each user's account is not necessary. Later in this chapter, you will learn how to create and manage groups.

■ *Resources:* On a network or within a standalone computer, resources are any useful services or objects. This includes printers, shared directories, and software applications. A resource can be accessible by everyone across the network, or be limited to one person on a single machine, or be accessible or limited at any level in between. The range of control over resources within Windows 2000 is astounding. Details on how to manage resources and control who does have and who does not have access are presented later in this chapter.

■ *Policies:* A policy is a set of configuration options that defines aspects of Windows 2000 security. Security policies are used to define password restrictions, account lockouts, user rights, and event auditing. System policies are defined for a user, a computer, or a group to restrict the computing environment. Details on the different types of policies are discussed later in this chapter.

■ *Profiles:* A profile (sometimes called a **user profile**) is a stored snapshot of a user's desktop environment settings, Start menu, and other user-specific details. Profiles can exist on a single computer or can be configured to follow a user around a network, regardless of what workstation is used. User profiles are discussed in detail later in this chapter.

LOGGING ON TO WINDOWS 2000 PROFESSIONAL

Windows 2000 uses **logon authentication** (the requirement that a user provide a name and password to gain access to the computer) for two purposes: first, to maintain security and privacy within a network; and second, to track computer use by user account. Each Windows 2000 user can have a unique user account that identifies that user and contains or references all the system preferences for, access privileges of, and private information about that one user. Thus, Windows 2000 provides security and privacy for all users through the mandatory requirement of logon authentication.

 TIP In the instance of a standalone system where all users access local resources via common user accounts, logon still occurs; it just happens automatically.

Logon authentication is the simple process of entering a valid username and password to gain access to a Windows 2000-based computer. By pressing Ctrl+Alt+Delete at the default splash screen, the Logon Information dialog box appears. This is where users enter logon information—user name, password, and domain (optional)—and then click OK to have the security system validate their information and grant access to the computer. After users have completed their work, they can log off the computer (from Start, Shut Down, Logoff *username*) to make it available for the next user.

DEFAULT USER ACCOUNTS

When Windows 2000 Professional is installed, it automatically creates two default user accounts. These default accounts are Administrator and Guest.

Administrator

The Administrator account is the most powerful user account available in the Windows 2000 environment. This account has unlimited access and unrestricted privileges to every aspect of Windows 2000. The Administrator account also has unrestricted ability to manage all security settings, other users, groups, the operating system environment, printers, shares, and storage devices. Because of these far-reaching privileges, the Administrator account must be protected from misuse. Defining a complicated password for this account is highly recommended. You should also rename this account. This will make it more difficult for hackers to discover a valid user name and password.

The Administrator account has the following characteristics:

- It cannot be deleted.
- It cannot be **locked out** (disabled because of repeated failed logon attempts).
- It cannot be **disabled** (made unusable for logon).
- It cannot be removed from the Administrator's local group.
- It can be renamed.

It's always a good idea to rename the Administrator account to avoid giving away half of the user name/password combination to system attackers. Some administrators even suggest that you set up an account named Administrator, that has no access to the system, but has auditing enabled. By doing this, you not only lock down the most well-known user account, but you also can keep an eye on it in the event someone does try to attack your system using that account.

Guest

The Guest account is one of the least privileged user accounts in Windows 2000. This account has limited access to resources and computer activities. Even so, you should set a new password for the Guest account and it should be used only by authorized one-time users or users with low-security access. Any configuration changes made to the desktop or Start menu are not recorded in the Guest's user profile. If you do allow this account to be used, you should rename it.

The Guest account has the following characteristics:

- It cannot be deleted.
- It can be locked out.
- It can be disabled (it is disabled by default).
- It can have a blank password (it is blank by default).
- It can be renamed.

NAMING CONVENTIONS

Before creating and managing user accounts, you need to understand naming conventions. A **naming convention** is simply a predetermined process for creating names on a network (or a standalone computer). A naming convention should incorporate a scheme for user accounts, computers, directories, network shares, printers, and servers. These names should be descriptive enough so anyone can decipher to which type of object the name corresponds. For example, name computers and resources by department or by use to simplify user access.

 The stipulation of always using a naming convention may seem pointless for small networks, but it is rare for small networks to remain small. In fact, most networks grow at a staggering rate. If you begin naming network objects at random, you'll soon forget to which resource a name corresponds. Even with the excellent management tools of Windows 2000, you will quickly lose track of important resources if you have not established a standard method for naming network resources.

The naming convention on which your organization ultimately settles doesn't matter, as long as it can always provide you with a useful name for each new network object. To give you an idea of a naming scheme, two common rules follow:

- User names are constructed from the first and last name of the user, plus a code identifying his or her job title or department: for example, BobSmithAccounting or SmithBobAccounting.

- Group names are constructed from resource types, department names, location names, project names, and combinations of all four: for example, Accounting01, AustinUsers, BigProject01, etc.

Regardless of what naming convention is deployed, it needs to address the following four elements:

- It must be consistent across all objects.

- It must be easy to use and understand.

- New names should be easily constructed by mimicking the composition of existing names.

- An object's name should clearly identify that object's type.

MANAGING USER ACCOUNTS

Windows 2000 Professional has two user account management tools. The first is the Users and Passwords applet accessed via the Control Panel. The second is the Local Users and Groups MMC snap-in accessed via the Advanced button on the Advanced tab of the Users and Passwords applet. The Users and Passwords applet is used to create a local user account from an existing domain account. The Local Users and Groups snap-in is used to create local user accounts from scratch.

Users and Passwords Applet

The Users and Passwords applet (see Figure 5-1) is used to perform several functions on local user accounts. This applet can be opened only if you are logged on to the Windows 2000 Professional system with the Administrator account, logged on with a user account which is a member of the Administrators group, or by providing the username, password, and domain when you attempt to launch the applet. This applet has two tabs: Users and Advanced. The Users tab displays all user accounts that can be employed to gain local access. This list details the user name, the domain (if the account is part of a domain; the screen differs for standalone computers), and the group memberships of the user account. The term *domain* in this instance refers to the logical environment where the user account originated. All user accounts created on the Windows 2000 Professional system have the local computer name listed as the domain (as in W2KPRO in Figure 5-1). All user accounts from a domain, such as accounts created by Windows 2000 Server, Windows NT Server, or another networking environment, will have the name of that domain listed as its domain (as in LANW in Figure 5-1).

To create new local user accounts, you must decide what type of user account to create. On a Windows 2000 Professional system, there are local user accounts created locally from scratch, and there are local user accounts that are local representations of domain or network user accounts. To create a new local user account from scratch, you need to employ the Local Users and Groups snap-in (see the next section). To create a local representation of an existing domain/network user account, use the Add button on the Users and Passwords applet. (Try Hands-on Project 5-1.)

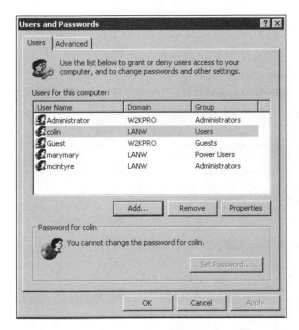

Figure 5-1   Users and Passwords applet

Creating a local representation of an existing domain/network user account grants a network user the ability to access resources hosted by the Windows 2000 Professional system, regardless of whether the system is a member of the domain/network. (This is possible because a workstation can exist on a network as a standalone system or as a workgroup member. Domain users can access resources on nondomain computers by viewing the shared items from the Entire Network via the My Network Places icon. For domain users to access resources, they must have a user account on the nondomain member Windows 2000 Professional system.) These **imported user accounts** cannot be used to log on to a Windows 2000 Professional system, but can be used only to access resources over the network hosted on a Windows 2000 Professional system. Plus, the use of local representations allows the administrator or user of a Windows 2000 Professional system to create a local security configuration of users and groups that does not rely upon the group memberships of the domain/network.

Clicking the Add button reveals the Add New User wizard (see Figure 5-2). If you know the name of the user account and the domain which it is from, you can type them in. You can also click the Browse button to see a list of existing user accounts in a domain. Clicking Next prompts you for the access level to grant the imported user (see Figure 5-3).

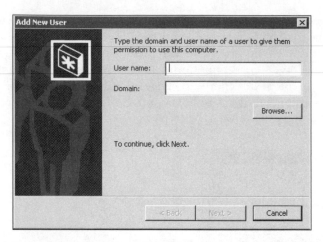

Figure 5-2   Add New User wizard, user account and domain page

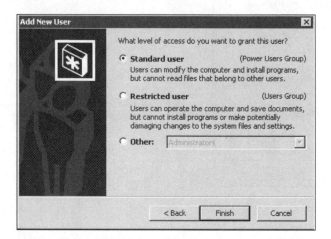

Figure 5-3   Add New User wizard, access level page

The access level to grant the imported user can be chosen from the following:

- *Standard user:* Grants the imported user membership into the Power Users group
- *Restricted user:* Grants the imported user membership into the Users group
- *Other:* Grants the imported user membership into the existing local group selected from the pull-down list

After you click Finish on the wizard, the imported user is added to the list of local users for this computer. To remove an existing user, just select it from the list and click Remove. You'll be prompted to confirm the user account deletion. (Try Hands-on Project 5-3.)

The Properties button on the Users and Passwords dialog box (shown earlier in Figure 5-1) is used to access basic properties for the selected user account. A locally created user account's Properties dialog box has two tabs: General and Group Membership. The General tab is used to change the user name, full name, and description. The Group Membership tab (which looks almost exactly like Figure 5-3) allows you to change a user's group membership. (Try Hands-on Project 5-2.) An imported user account's Properties has only a Group Membership tab, it does not have a General tab. An imported user account can be a member of only a single group. A locally created user account can be a member of more than one group, but the Group Membership tab of the Properties for the user account will allow only a single group to be selected and changed at a time. Adding a user account to multiple groups requires the use of the Local Users and Groups snap-in. Creating groups based on resources, then assigning users to multiple groups, you can create a permission scheme based solely on group permissions. This is advantageous because it is easier to manage group permissions than individual user permissions for every user on the network.

The password for locally created groups can be changed using the Set Password button at the bottom of the Users and Passwords applet (be sure to select the user account first). You will be prompted for the new password and a confirmation of the new password.

Imported user accounts appear in this applet whether or not the Windows 2000 Professional system is logged into the domain from which the accounts are imported. The only requirement is that the applet can communicate with the domain via a network connection. If the Windows 2000 Professional system is physically disconnected from the network media or the domain is not available, then the imported user accounts will not be listed. When the domain of origin returns, the user accounts will reappear.

The Advanced tab of the Users and Password applet grants you access to certificate management, advanced user management, and secure boot settings. Certificate management is used to import and manage certificates that prove your identity as a user and certificate authority (certificate authorities are those organizations that verify your identity and assign you a certificate to use). Advanced user management is discussed in detail in the following section. Secure boot settings is a single check box that determines whether the Ctrl+Alt+Delete key sequence is required before the logon dialog box is displayed.

Local Users and Groups MMC Snap-in

The Local Users and Groups MMC snap-in (see Figure 5-4) is accessed by clicking the Advanced button on the Advanced tab of the Users and Passwords applet, or via a snap-in in the computer management console. This tool is used to create and manage local users only; imported users do not appear in this interface. (Practice creating a new local user account in Hands-on Project 5-4.) The console tree hosts two nodes: Users and Groups, shown as folders on the console screen. The Users folder contains all local user accounts. The Groups folder contains all local group accounts.

Users

Selecting the Users folder displays all existing local user accounts. When Windows 2000 Professional is first installed, only the Administrator and Guest accounts (as seen in Figure 5-4) will be displayed. The details pane on the right lists the name of the user account, the full name of the user, and the description of the account. By selecting a user account and right-clicking, you can access the account's Properties dialog box, which for a local user account has three tabs: General, Member Of, and Profile.

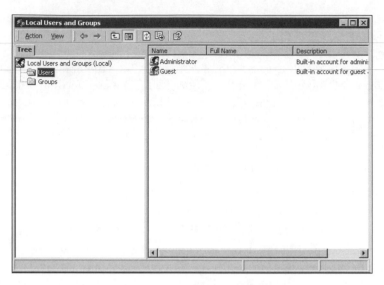

Figure 5-4   Local Users and Groups MMC snap-in

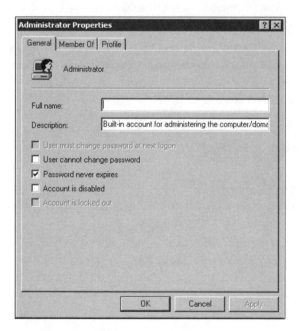

Figure 5-5   A user account's Properties dialog box, General tab

The General tab (see Figure 5-5) of a user account's Properties displays the following:

- *Name of user account*—Not customizable through this dialog box

- *Full Name*—Customizable full name of the person using the account

- *Description*—Customizable text field to describe the purpose or use of the account

- *User must change password at next logon*—A check box used to force a user to change their password the next time they log on to the system

- *User cannot change password*—A check box that prevents the user from altering the current password

- *Password never expires*—A check box that exempts this user from the account policy which defines the maximum lifetime of a password

- *Account is disabled*—A check box used to turn off an account, that prevents the account from being used, but retains it for security auditing purposes

- *Account is locked out*—A check box used by the lockout policy when an account meets the lockout parameters

The Member Of tab (see Figure 5-6) lists the groups of which this user account is currently a member. To add group memberships, click the Add button. This opens the Select Groups dialog box (see Figure 5-7). From this dialog box, you can select existing local groups to add this user account to. Select the group from the list and click Add. Once you've made your selections, click OK. To remove a group membership, select it on the Member Of tab and click Remove. (Try Hands-on Project 5-5 to change group membership for a local user account.)

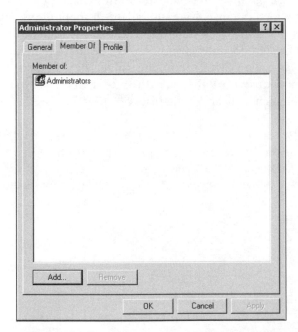

Figure 5-6   A user account's Properties dialog box, Member Of tab

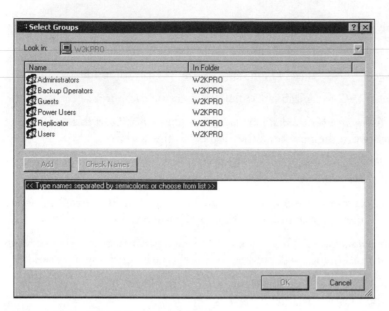

Figure 5-7   Select Groups dialog box

The Profile tab (see Figure 5-8) is used to define the user profile path, logon script, and home folder. The Profile path designation defines the location where a user's profile will be stored. By default, user profiles are stored in partition system root\Documents and Settings\<*username*> where <*username*> is the name of the user to whom the profile belongs or applies. (User profiles are discussed in detail later in this chapter.) Logon script is the local path to a **logon script** which can map drive letters, launch applications, or perform other command-line operations each time the system boots. The home folder is the default location for the storage of user-created documents and files. By default, the home folder is the \Documents and Settings\<*username*>\My Documents folder, but this setting can be used to define an alternate location with either a path statement or with a mapped drive letter to a network share (such as K and \\mainserver\users\steve).

 For a Windows 2000 Professional local user, most of the paths used on the Profile tab should be local (that is, residing on the local computer).

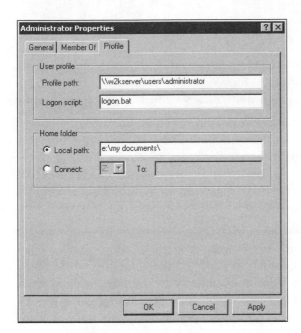

Figure 5-8   A user account's Properties dialog box, Profile tab

When you right-click a local user, the menu shows the Properties command, as well as four major commands:

- *Set Password*—Provide a new password and confirmation; the original password is not required.

- *Delete*—Completely removes a user account from the system; once deleted, it is not recoverable. Re-creating a new account, even with the same name and configuration, will be seen as a different account by the system because its SID (security identifier) will have changed.

- *Rename*—Change the name of the user account.

- *Help*—Access context-sensitive help.

Other local user account settings are defined through the **Local Security Policy** tool. Configuration options on a domain level are available in Windows 2000 Server.

Groups

Selecting the Groups node in the Local Users and Groups interface displays all existing local groups. As mentioned earlier, a group is a named collection of users. All members of a group share the privileges or restrictions of that group. Groups are used to give a specific level of access to multiple users through a single management action. Once a group has access to a resource, users can be added to or removed from that group as needed. The group concept is key to managing large numbers of users and their access to any number of resources. In fact, if you use the group concept effectively, there should be little need to assign access rights to an individual user.

A local user can be a member of multiple groups. Different groups can be assigned different levels of access to the same resources. In most cases, the most permissive of all granted access levels will be used, except when access is specifically denied by one or more groups.

As you plan your network security, user base, and resource allocation, remember to keep in mind how you will manage each of these groups. Think about how groups can be paired with resources to provide you with the greatest range of administrative control. After your resources are in place and all the required groups have been created, most of your administrative tasks will involve adding users to or removing them from these groups. This is mostly a concern when setting up Windows 2000 Server, but you should keep it in mind when planning any part of a network.

To provide the highest degree of control over resources, Windows 2000 uses two types of groups: local and global. **Local groups** exist only on the computer where they are created. **Global groups** exist throughout a domain. Windows 2000 Professional can create and manage local groups. Windows 2000 Professional can add only existing global groups to its local groups to grant access to resources. This distinction is very important, as you'll soon see. Local groups can have members who are users or global groups. Global groups can have only users from the domain in which they reside as members.

One of the differences between Windows 2000 Server and Windows 2000 Professional is that the user account and group tools on a Windows 2000 Professional system can manage local users and local groups. To create and manage groups across domains, you must have a Windows 2000 Server in a client/server environment. The Active Directory Users and Computers interface on Windows 2000 Server is used to create and manage domain users, global groups, and local groups. If a Windows 2000 Professional system is part of a domain, its user tools can add global groups to local groups as members, but that is the only activity it can perform with global groups.

With local and global groups, a complete system of links from resources to users can be established. Each resource is assigned to one or more local groups. Users are assigned to one or more global groups in their domains. Global user groups are assigned to local resource groups. Each local group can be assigned different levels or types of access to the resource. By placing a global group in a local group, you assign all members of that global group the privileges of the local group, that is, access to a resource. In other words, on a domain scale, domain users are members of global groups, which in turn are members of local groups that are assigned access permissions to resources. On a local computer, local users are members of local groups which are assigned access permissions to resources.

 It is important to understand the distinction between local and global groups: local groups can contain members that are users or global groups, whereas global groups can only have users from the domain in which they reside as members. When you assign access permissions to resources, you assign those rights to local groups.

You must plan your group management scheme long before you begin implementation. Planning such a scheme involves applying a naming scheme, dividing users into meaningful groups, and understanding the various levels of access your resources offer. For the group method to be effective, you need to manage all access to resources through groups. Never succumb to the temptation to assign access privileges directly to a user account.

Defining group members is often the most time-consuming process of group management. A group should be formed around a common job position, need of resource, or even geographic location. Some existing groups you can transform into Windows 2000 groups are:

- Organizational functioning units, workgroups, or departments
- Authorized users of network programs and applications
- Events, projects, or special assignments
- Authorized users of network resources
- Location or geography
- Individual function or job description

As stated, local groups exist only on the computer where they are created. On each computer, all local groups must have a unique name. You can duplicate the names of local groups on different computers, but they will be separate and distinct groups. Avoid using the same name twice on any network, even if the architecture allows you to do so.

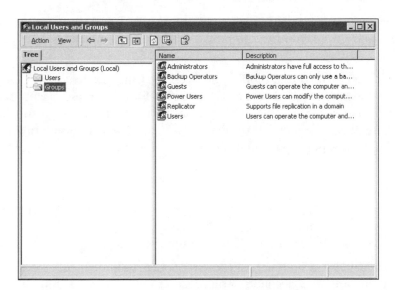

Figure 5-9   Local Users and Groups, Groups folder

Windows 2000 Professional has six default groups. When the Groups node is selected in the Local Users and Groups interface, these default groups (as seen in Figure 5-9) will be displayed:

- *Administrators:* Members of this group have full access to the computer. Default members are the Administrator account and the Domain Admins group if connected to a domain.

- *Backup Operators:* Members of this group can back up and restore all files and folders on a system. It has no default members.

- *Guests:* Members can operate the computer and save files, but cannot install programs or alter system settings. Default member is the Guest account.

- *Power Users:* Members can modify the computer, create user accounts, share resources, and install programs, but cannot access files that belong to other users. It has no default members.

- *Replicator:* This group is used by special user accounts to facilitate file synchronization between systems and domains. It has no default members. For more information about data synchronization, see the *Windows 2000 Resource Kit.*

- *Users:* Members can operate the computer and save files, but cannot install programs, modify user accounts, share resources, or alter system settings. Default members are the Authenticated Users group (a nonconfigurable default group) and the Domain Users group if connected to a domain. By default, Windows 2000 adds all new local user accounts to this group.

New groups are created using the New Group command. (Try Hands-on Project 5-6.) When creating a new group, you need to provide the group name and a description, and add members.

The Properties dialog box for a user group allows you to change its description and alter its membership. You can add members to a group from the list of local user accounts or from the list of domain user accounts. Imported user accounts are not listed in this interface. Groups can also be deleted (see Hands-on Project 5-7) or renamed by selecting the command from the right-click pop-up menu or from the Action menu.

System Groups

Windows 2000 Professional has several built-in system-controlled groups. System groups are preexisting groups that you cannot manage, but which appear in dialog boxes when assigned group membership or access permissions. These groups are:

- *Everyone:* Includes all users accessing the computer, both defined local user accounts and imported accounts. Assign access to the Everyone group with caution because it also includes the Guest account and anonymous logons (such as with Web and FTP servers).

- *Authenticated Users:* Includes all users with a specifically defined local user account, except for the Guest account

- *Creator Owner:* Includes the user account of the current owner of an object

- *Network:* Includes all user accounts accessing the computer over a network connection

- *Interactive:* Includes the user account of the person currently logged into the local system

- *Anonymous Logon:* Any user account that did not go through official authentication by the Windows 2000 security system

- *Dialup:* Includes any user account accessing the computer over a dial-up connection

5

USER PROFILES

A user profile is the collection of desktop and environmental configurations on a Windows 2000 system for a specific user or group of users. By default, each Windows 2000 computer maintains a profile for each user who has logged on to the computer, except for Guest accounts. Each user profile contains information about a particular user's Windows 2000 configuration. Much of this information is about things the user can set, such as color scheme, screen savers, and mouse and keyboard layout. Other information covers settings that are accessible only to a Windows 2000 administrator, such as access rights to common program groups or network printers.

The material stored in a user profile includes:

- *Application Data*—A directory containing user-specific data, such as for Internet Explorer or Outlook

- *Cookies*—A directory containing cookies (cookies are text scripts that a Web browser sends to a server to customize a user's browsing experience) accepted by the user via their browser

- *Desktop*—A directory containing the icons displayed on the user's desktop

- *Favorites*—A directory containing the user's list of URLs from Internet Explorer

- *Local Settings*—A directory containing user-specific history information and temporary files

- *My Documents*—A directory containing user-created data

- *NetHood*—A directory containing user-specific network mappings

- *PrintHood*—A directory containing user-specific printer mappings

- *Recent*—A directory containing user-specific links to the last accessed resources

- *Sent To*—A directory containing user-specific links used in the Sent To command of the right-click pop-up menu

- *Start Menu*—A directory containing the user-specific Start menu layout

- *Templates*—A directory containing user-specific Microsoft Office templates

- *Ntuser.dat*—A file containing user-specific Registry information

- *Ntuser.dat.log*—A transaction log file that ensures the user profile can be re-created in the event of a failure

- *Ntuser.ini*—A file containing profile-related settings, such as what directories should not be uploaded to a roaming profile

Optionally, an administrator can force users to load a so-called **mandatory profile**. Users can adjust this profile while they're logged in, but all changes are lost as soon as they log out.

> A mandatory profile is created by manually renaming the Ntuser.dat file to Ntuser.man. This technique provides a way for administrators to control the look and feel of shared accounts, or to restrict nonpower users from exercising too much influence over their desktops.

User profiles are managed through the User Profiles tab that appears in the System applet. This tab (see Figure 5-10) lists all profiles for users who have logged into the Windows 2000 Professional system under examination. The dialog box displays the name of the user account, along with defining its domain of origin, the disk space consumed by the profile, the profile type, and when it was last changed. Profiles can be two types: local or roaming.

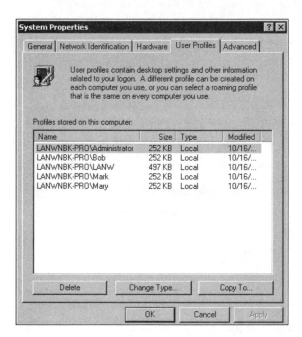

Figure 5-10   System applet, User Profiles tab

Local Profiles

A **local profile** is a set of specifications and preferences for an individual user, stored on a local machine. Windows 2000 provides each user with a folder containing their profile settings. Individual profiles are stored in the system partition root\Documents and Settings folder. A different location for the Profiles folder can be specified through the Local Users and Groups tool.

Local profiles are established by default for each user who logs on to a particular machine, and reside in the %*username*% subfolder beneath the system partition root\Documents and Settings folder. Although it may seem inevitable that an explicit user profile management utility would exist for Windows 2000, user profiles really represent a specialized snapshot of a user's preferences, desktop configuration, and related settings.

There is no single tool that permits all user profile information to be manipulated abstractly. There are only two ways to create a user profile:

- A user logs on and arranges things as needed, and upon logout this information will become that user's local profile (which may then be transformed into a roaming profile as you'll learn later),

- Assign a mandatory profile to a user from an existing definition (but even this must be set up by example, rather than through explicit controls).

Windows 2000 Professional local users (including imported users) have only local profiles. It is not possible to transform a local user's local profile to a roaming profile. However, a domain user account that logs on to a Windows 2000 Professional system will have a local profile created the first time they log on (assuming they do not already have a roaming profile on the network). This local profile for the domain user can be transformed into a roaming profile.

Roaming Profiles

A **roaming profile** resides on a network server to make it broadly accessible. When a user whose profile is designated as roaming logs on to any Windows 2000 system on the network, that profile is automatically downloaded when the user logs on. This avoids having to store a local profile on each workstation that a user uses, but it also has a disadvantage. If a user's roaming profile is large, logging on to the network takes quite a while because that information must be copied across the network each time the user logs in.

The default path designation for a roaming profile is *computername**username*. To create a roaming profile, use the "Copy to" button that appears in the User Profile tab of the System applet on a machine where a local profile for the user already exists. The destination for the copy operation must match the path that defines where the roaming profile resides (as manually defined in the user account). (This is the profile path shown in Figure 5-8.) The Profile path is defined either on the local computer for local accounts, or on a domain controller for domain accounts. The path is the mechanism that tells the startup module where to find a user's roaming profile. Local profiles are always stored in the system partition\Documents and Settings folder and do not require setting a profile path in the user account properties. Roaming profiles, however, require you to specify a path to the network profile share.

Keep in mind that only domain accounts can use roaming profiles. Once a local profile is present on a client, such as a Windows 2000 Professional system, you must use the System applet on that system to copy the profile to a network file server. Then, you must access the Active Directory Users and Computers tool on a Windows 2000 Server machine to alter the profile path for the domain user account.

LOCAL SECURITY POLICY

Windows 2000 has combined several security and access controls into a centralized policy. This centralized policy is called the group policy. A **group policy** is an MMC snap-in that is used to specify users' desktop settings. There are group policies for local computers, groups, and domains, and **organizational units (OUs)**. (An organizational unit is an administrative container object that can contain users, groups, resources, and other OUs).

All group policy types can be managed from a Windows 2000 Server system, but only a local computer group policy can be managed from a Windows 2000 Professional system.

Group policies are applied in the following order:

1. Any existing legacy Windows NT 4.0 Ntconfig.pol file is applied.

2. Any unique local group policy is applied (that is, the group policy for the local machine).

3. Any site group policies are applied.

4. Any domain group policies are applied.

5. Any OU group policies are applied.

The order of application of these policies is important because contradictory settings in later policies will override the settings of the former policies. The cumulative result of this priority application of group policy is known as the **effective policy**. On Windows 2000 Professional systems, the effective policy is either all of these group policies properly combined when logged on with a domain user account, or only the local group policy when logged on with a local user account.

The Local Security Policy tool is used to edit the local group policy on a Windows 2000 Professional system. This tool is accessed from the Administrative Tools applet from the Control Panel. (Try Hands-on Project 5-8.) The local group policy consists of several sub-policies, including: password, account lockout, audit, user rights, security options, public key, and IP security.

Notice in the details section of the MMC snap-in tool that each specific policy item is listed with both its local setting and its effective setting. Local settings apply only when logged in with a local user account. Effective settings apply when logged in with a domain user account. For all policy items, only the local default setting is listed because the effective setting varies based on network configuration.

Password Policy

The **password policy** defines the restrictions on passwords, as shown in Figure 5-11. This policy is used to enforce strong passwords for a more secure environment. By using a password policy, you can assign any of the items listed in Table 5-1 to a user to force the user to use a certain type of password.

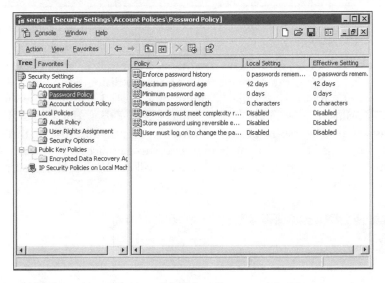

Figure 5-11   Local Security Policy, Password Policy

Table 5-1   Password Policy Items and Their Descriptions

Policy Item: Default Setting	Description
Enforce password history: 0 Passwords	Maintaining a password history prevents reuse of old passwords. A setting of 5 or greater for this item is recommended.
Maximum password age: 42 days	Defines when passwords expire and must be replaced. A setting of 30, 45, or 60 days is recommended.
Minimum password age: 0 days	Defines the least amount of time that can pass between password changes. A setting of 1, 3, or 5 days is recommended.
Minimum password length: 0 characters	Sets the minimum number of characters that must be present in a password. A setting of 6 or more is recommended.
Passwords must meet complexity requirements of installed password filter: Disabled	Determines whether passwords must comply with installed password filters. See the *Windows 2000 Resource Kit* for details.

Table 5-1   Password Policy Items and Their Descriptions (continued)

Policy Item: Default Setting	Description
Store passwords using reversible encryption for all users in the domain: Disabled	Determines whether SPAP (Shiva Password Authentication Protocol) is used to encrypt passwords. Leave this disabled unless required by a client.

Account Lockout Policy

The **account lockout policy** defines the conditions that result in a user account being locked out. Figure 5-12 shows the Account Policy Lockout dialog box, which is accessed from the Local Security Policy tool of the Administration tools. Lockout is used to prevent brute force attacks against user accounts. For example, if a user tries to log on and is unsuccessful more than five (or the specified number) times, it's a good idea to lock that user out. Then the user must get assistance from an administrator to gain access to the system. If the person attempting to gain access is not a valid user, they will not be able to log on to the system using that user name.

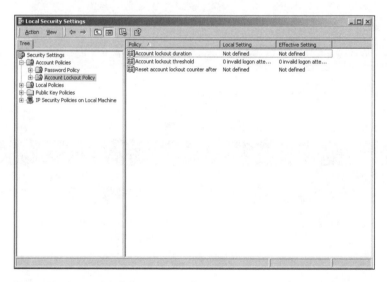

Figure 5-12   Local Security Policy, Account Lockout Policy

The items in this policy are:

- *Account lockout threshold: 0 Invalid logon attempts*—Defines the number of failed logons that must occur before an account is locked out. A setting of 3 to 5 is recommended.

- *Account lockout duration: Not Defined*—Defines the length of time an account will remain locked out. A value of 0 will cause locked out accounts to require administrative action to unlock. A setting of 30 minutes to 2 hours is recommended.

■ *Reset account lockout counter after: Not Defined*—Defines the length of time that must expire before the failed logon attempts counter for a user account is reset. A setting of 15 minutes is recommended.

Audit Policy

The **audit policy** defines the events that are recorded in the Security log of the Event Viewer. The audit policy is configured in the Audit Policy dialog box shown in Figure 5-13. Auditing tracks the use and misuse of resources. Take, for example, the recommendation earlier in this chapter to create a fake Administrator account. If someone were to try to use that account to gain access to the system, you could track those attempts and know when someone was trying to attack your system. You then could take additional preventative measures. Each item in this list can be set to audit the Success and/or Failure of the event.

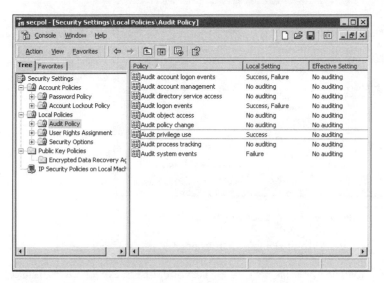

Figure 5-13   Local Security Policy, Audit Policy

The items in this policy are:

■ *Audit account logon events*—Audits the logon and logoff of user accounts

■ *Audit account management*—Audits the changes to user accounts and group memberships

■ *Audit directory service access*—Audits access to network resources

■ *Audit logon events*—Audits nonuser account logon and logoff events

■ *Audit object access*—Audits resource access

■ *Audit policy change*—Audits changes to the security policy

■ *Audit privilege use*—Audits use of special rights or privileges

- *Audit process tracking*—Audits the activity of processes
- *Audit system events*—Audits system-level activities

User Rights Policy

The **User Rights Policy** defines which groups or users can perform specific privileged actions (see Figure 5-14). For example, you may want to give a group, such as Power Users, the right to add a workstation to a domain.

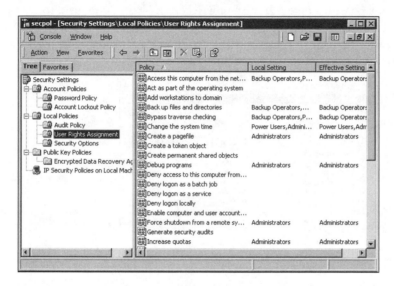

Figure 5-14 Local Security Policy, User Rights Assignment

The items in this policy and their default settings are:

- *Access this computer from the network*—Everyone, Users, Power Users, Backup Operators, Administrators
- *Act as part of the operating system*—none
- *Add workstations to domain*—none
- *Back up files and directories*—Backup Operators, Administrators
- *Bypass traverse checking*—Everyone, Users, Power Users, Backup Operators, Administrators
- *Change the system time*—Power Users, Administrators
- *Create a pagefile*—Administrators
- *Create a token object*—none
- *Create permanent shared objects*—none
- *Debug programs: Administrators*

5

- *Deny access to this computer from the network*—none
- *Deny logon as a batch job*—none
- *Deny logon as a service*—none
- *Deny logon locally*—none
- *Enable computer and user accounts to be trusted for delegation*—none
- *Force shutdown from a remote system*—Administrators
- *Generate security audits*—none
- *Increase quotas*—Administrators
- *Increase scheduling priority*—Administrators
- *Load and unload device drivers*—Administrators
- *Lock pages in memory*—none
- *Log on as a batch job*—none
- *Log on as a service*—none
- *Log on locally*—Guests, Users, Power Users, Backup Operators, Administrators
- *Manage auditing and security log*—Administrators
- *Modify firmware environment values*—Administrators
- *Profile single process*—Power Users, Administrators
- *Profile system performance*—Administrators
- *Remove computer from docking station*—Users, Power Users, Administrators
- *Replace a process-level token*—none
- *Restore files and directories*—Backup Operators, Administrators
- *Shut down the system*—Users, Power Users, Backup Operators, Administrators
- *Synchronize directory service data*—none
- *Take ownership of files or other objects*—Administrators

User Rights are enabled as defined in the previous list by default. You can alter this configuration via the User Rights Assignment section of the Local Security Policy (try Hands-on Project 5-8).

TIP

> Troubleshooting user rights involves testing access to or control of resources, reconfiguring rights as needed, and retesting. If you suspect an action cannot be performed that should be possible, test, reset the associated user right, relog on as that user, and try the action again. Be sure to double-check any file or object permissions associated with the action because it may be blocked by lack of access rather than a user right.

> **TIP**   For more details on these security options, please consult the *Windows 2000 Professional Resource Kit*.

Security Options

The **security options** define and control various security features, functions, and controls of the Windows 2000 environment (see Figure 5-15). For example, you can disable the option to allow the system to be shut down without having to log on to tighten security. The items in this policy and their default settings are described in Table 5-2.

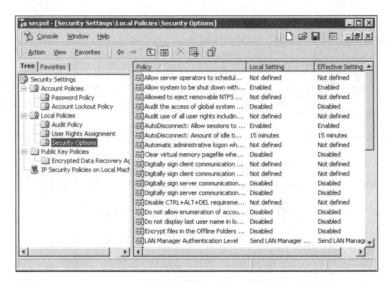

Figure 5-15   Local Security Policy, Security Options

Table 5-2   Security Options and Their Default Settings

Security Option	Default Setting
Additional restrictions for anonymous connections	None. Rely on default permissions
Allow server operators to schedule tasks (domain controllers only)	Not defined
Allow system to be shut down without having to log on	Enabled
Allow to eject removable NTFS media	Administrators
Amount of idle time required before disconnecting session	15 minutes
Audit the access of global system objects	Disabled
Audit use of Backup and Restore privilege	Disabled
Automatically log off users when logon time expires (local)	Enabled
Clear virtual memory pagefile when system shuts down	Disabled

Table 5-2   Security Options and Their Default Settings (continued)

Security Option	Default Setting
Digitally sign client communication (always)	Disabled
Digitally sign client communication (when possible)	Enabled
Digitally sign server communication (always)	Disabled
Digitally sign server communication (when possible)	Disabled
Disable CTRL+ALT+DEL requirement for logon	Not defined
Do not display last user name in logon screen	Disabled
LAN Manager Authentication Level	Send LAN Manager and NTLM responses
Message text for users attempting to log on	blank
Message title for users attempting to log on	blank
Number of previous logons to cache (in case domain controller is not available)	10 logons
Prevent system maintenance of computer account password	Disabled
Prevent users from installing printer drivers	Disabled
Prompt user to change password before expiration	14 days
Recovery Console: Allow automatic administrative logon	Disabled
Recovery Console: Allow floppy copy and access to all drives and all folders	Disabled
Rename administrator account	Not defined
Rename guest account	Not defined
Restrict CD-ROM access to locally logged-on user only	Disabled
Restrict floppy access to locally logged-on user only	Disabled
Secure channel: Digitally encrypt or sign secure channel data (always)	Disabled
Secure channel: Digitally encrypt secure channel data (when possible)	Enabled
Secure channel: Digitally sign secure channel data (when possible)	Enabled
Secure channel: Require strong (Windows 2000 or later) session key	Disabled
Send unencrypted password to connect to third-party SMB servers	Disabled
Shut down system immediately if unable to log security audits	Disabled
Smart card removal behavior	No Action
Strengthen default permissions of global system objects (e.g. Symbolic Links)	Enabled
Unsigned driver installation behavior	Not defined
Unsigned non-driver installation behavior	Not defined

5

TIP For more details on these security options, please consult the *Windows 2000 Professional Resource Kit*.

CHAPTER SUMMARY

- ❑ This chapter discussed local users and groups. Windows 2000 Professional can employ three types of users: locally created users, imported users, and domain users. A user account stores security and preference settings for each person who uses a computer. Each user can have their own profile that retains all of their preferred desktop settings. Users are collected into groups to simplify management and grant access or privileges.

- ❑ Users and groups are managed through the Users and Passwords applet and the Local Users and Groups MMC snap-in. Windows 2000 Professional has two built-in users, Administrator and Guest, and several built-in groups. Some groups allow you to customize their membership whereas others are system-controlled groups whose memberships cannot be customized.

- ❑ User profiles can be local profiles when working with local users or imported users, or they can be roaming when using a domain user account. User profiles store a wide variety of personalized or custom data about a user's environment. A user profile can be mandatory just by changing Ntuser.dat to Ntuser.man.

- ❑ The Local Security Policy is used to manage passwords, account lockouts, audits, user rights, security options, and more. These controls aid in enforcing security and controlling who is able to perform specific actions on the system.

KEY TERMS

account lockout policy — Defines the conditions that result in a user account being locked out.

audit policy — Defines the events which are recorded in the Security log of the Event Viewer.

disabled — The state of a user account which is retained on the system but cannot be used to log on.

domain — An organizational unit used to centralize network users and resources.

domain user account — A user account which can be used throughout a domain.

effective policy — The cumulative result of the priority application of group policies.

global group — A group which exists throughout a domain. A global group can be created only on a Windows 2000 Server system.

group policy — An MMC snap-in that is used to specify desktop settings for group members.

groups — Named collections of users to which you assign permissions. For example, the Administrators group contains all users who require administrative access to network resources and user accounts.

imported user account — A local account created by duplicating the name and password of an existing domain account. An imported account can be used only when the Windows 2000 Professional system is able to communicate with the domain of the original account.

5

local group — A group which exists only on the computer where it was created. A local group can have users and global groups as members.

local profile — A set of specifications and preferences for an individual user stored on a local machine.

Local Security Policy — The centralized control mechanism which governs password, account lockout, audit, user rights, security options, public key, and IP security.

local user account — A user account that exists on a single computer.

locked out — The state of a user account that is disabled because of repeated failed logon attempts.

logon authentication — The requirement to provide a name and password to gain access to the computer.

logon script — A code script that can map drive letters, launch applications, or perform other command-line operations each time the system boots.

mandatory profile — A user profile which does not retain changes after the user logs out. Mandatory profiles are used to maintain a common desktop environment for users.

multiple-user system — An operating system which maintains separate and distinct user accounts for each person.

naming convention — A standardized regular method of creating names for objects, users, computers, groups, etc.

organizational unit (OU) — A container object that is an administrative partition of the Active Directory. OUs can contain users, groups, resources, and other OUs. OUs enable the delegation of administration to distinct subtrees of the directory.

password policy — Defines the restrictions on passwords.

policy — A set of configuration options that defines aspects of Windows 2000 security.

profile — See user profile.

resources — Any useful service or object on a network. This includes printers, shared directories, and software applications. A resource can be accessible by everyone across the network or by only one person on a single machine, and at any level in between.

roaming profile — A profile that resides on a network server to make it broadly accessible. When a user whose profile is designated as roaming logs on to any Windows 2000 system on the network, that profile is automatically downloaded when the user logs on.

security options — Define and control various security features, functions, and controls of the Windows 2000 environment.

user account — A named security element used by a computer system to identify individuals and to record activity, control access, and retain settings.

user profile — A collection of user-specific settings that retain the state of the desktop, start menu, color scheme, and other environmental aspects across logons. By default, user profiles are stored in system partition root\Documents and Settings\<*username*>, where *username* is the name of the user to whom the profile applies.

User Rights Policy — Defines which groups or users can perform the specific privileged action.

REVIEW QUESTIONS

1. What types of user accounts can Windows 2000 Professional create and manage? (Choose all that apply.)

   a. local

   b. domain

   c. imported

   d. global

2. What types of user accounts can be used on a Windows 2000 Professional system? (Choose all that apply.)

   a. local

   b. domain

   c. imported

   d. global

3. When not connected to a network, what types of user accounts can be employed on a Windows 2000 Professional system?

   a. local

   b. domain

   c. imported

   d. global

4. A multiuser system is an operating system that allows more than one user account to log on to a single workstation simultaneously. True or False?

5. Which of the following are true of groups? (Choose all that apply.)

   a. Several default groups are built into Windows 2000.

   b. Groups are named collections of users.

   c. The system groups can be deleted through the Local Users and Groups tool.

   d. Groups used to simplify the assignment of permissions.

6. Why does Windows 2000 require logon authentication? (Choose all that apply.)

   a. to prevent the spread of viruses

   b. to track computer usage by user account

   c. to maintain security

   d. to promote a naming scheme

7. Which of the following are true for both the Administrator account and the Guest account? (Choose all that apply.)

   a. cannot be deleted

   b. can be locked out

   c. cannot be disabled

   d. can be renamed

8. When logged in under the Guest account, a user has the same access as other members of what group?

   a. Authenticated Users

   b. Users

   c. Power Users

   d. Everyone

9. Through what interface are imported user accounts managed?

   a. User Manager for Domains

   b. Users and Passwords

   c. Local Users and Groups

   d. Active Directory Users and Computers

10. Which of the following are true of imported users? (Choose all that apply.)

    a. can be a member of only a single group

    b. you can change their password

    c. exist only when their domain of origin is present online

    d. are used to grant domain users access to the local resources

11. When creating a new user via the Users and Passwords applet, the Restricted user selection makes the new user a member of what group?

    a. Guests

    b. Power Users

    c. Users

    d. Backup Operators

12. To configure more than one group membership for a local user account requires the use of the Users and Passwords applet. True or False?

13. When the control item under Secure boot on the Advanced tab of the Users and Passwords applet is selected, not only is Ctrl+Alt+Delete not required, but the last user account to successfully log on will be automatically reused to log on to the system. True or False?

14. You create several new user accounts. You tell everyone they need to log on and change their password to something other than the dummy "password" you entered to create the account. In the past most users forget or refuse to change the password. What setting can you use to force them to make this change?

    a. user cannot change password

    b. user must change password at next logon

    c. password never expires

    d. account is disabled

15. On a Windows 2000 Professional client, what types of profiles can be used? (Choose all that apply.)

    a. Local

    b. Roaming

    c. Mandatory

    d. Dynamic

16. User profiles are stored by default in a subdirectory named after the user account in what default directory on a Windows 2000 Professional system?

    a. \Winnt\Profiles

    b. \Users

    c. \Profiles

    d. \Documents and Settings

17. The user account Properties dialog box from the Local Users and Groups tool can be used to change the password. True or False?

18. The user tools of Windows 2000 Professional can create and manage both local and global groups. True or False?

19. Local groups can have global groups as members. True or False?

20. Which of the following groups are not configurable? (Choose all that apply.)

    a. Administrators

    b. Interactive

    c. Backup Operators

    d. Creator Owner

    e. Authenticated Users

21. What makes a profile mandatory?

    a. check box setting via the user account's Properties dialog box

    b. storing it locally

    c. renaming a file with the extension .man

    d. not connecting to a network

22. The effective policy is the result of applying all network or domain hosted security policies, then applying the local security policy. True or False?

23. The local security policy is a collection of what individual policies? (Choose all that apply.)

    a. Password

    b. Account lockout

    c. Audit

    d. User rights

    e. Security options

    f. Public key

    g. IP security

24. To prevent malicious users from breaking into your computer system by repeatedly trying to guess a password, what built-in security tool can you use?

    a. Password policy

    b. IP security

    c. Lockout

    d. Encryption

25. What control element in Windows 2000 is used to assign specific privileged actions to users and groups?

    a. Auditing

    b. User rights

    c. Profiles

    d. Security options

5

HANDS-ON PROJECTS

Project 5-1

To import a user account:

 This hands-on project requires that a domain be accessible over a network connection.

1. Open the **Control Panel** (**Start**, **Settings**, **Control Panel**).
2. Open the **Users and Passwords** applet (double-click its icon).
3. Click **Add**.
4. In the **Add New User** wizard, click **Browse**.
5. Select a user account from the list, and then click **OK**.
6. Click **Next**.
7. Select **Standard User** when prompted about the level of access to grant this user, and then click **Finish**.
8. Notice the imported user appears in the list of users on the Users and Passwords applet.
9. Click **OK** to close the applet.

Project 5-2

To change group membership of an imported user:

 This project requires that Hands-on Project 5-1 be completed.

1. In the **Users and Passwords** applet, select the imported user you created in Hands-on Project 5-1.
2. Click **Properties**.
3. Select the **Other** radio button on the **Group Membership** tab.
4. From the pull-down list, select **Power Users**.
5. Click **OK**.

Project 5-3

To delete a user account:

1. In the **Users and Passwords** applet, select the imported user created in Hands–on Project 5-1.
2. Click **Remove**.
3. When asked to confirm, click **Yes**.

Project 5-4

To create a new local user account:

1. Select the **Advanced** tab on the **Users and Passwords** applet.
2. Click the **Advanced** button.
3. Select the **Users** node in the console tree of **Local Users and Groups**.
4. From the Action menu, select **New User**.
5. In the New User dialog box, enter a user name (such as "BobTemp"), full name (such as "Bob Smith"), and description (such as "A temporary account for Bob").
6. Provide a password and a confirmation of that password.
7. Deselect the **User must change password at next logon** option.
8. Click **Create**.
9. Click **Close**.
10. The BobTemp user account will now be listed in the details pane.

Project 5-5

To change group membership for a local user account:

 This project requires that Hands-on Project 5-4 be completed.

1. Select the BobTemp user account you created in Hands-on Project 5-4.
2. Select **Properties** from the Action menu.
3. Select the **Member Of** tab.
4. Click the **Add** button.
5. Select the **Power Users** group.
6. Click **Add**.
7. Click **OK**.
8. Select the **Users** group.

9. Click **Remove**.
10. Click **OK** to close the **Properties** dialog box.

Project 5-6

To create a local group:

  This project requires that Hands-on Project 5-4 be completed.

1. Select the **Groups** node in the console tree.
2. Select the **New Group** command from the Action menu.
3. In the **New Group** dialog box, provide a name (such as "SalesGrp") and a description (such as "members of the sales department").
4. Click **Add**.
5. Select the **BobTemp** user.
6. Click **Add**.
7. Click **OK**.
8. Click **Create**.
9. Click **Close**.

Project 5-7

To delete a group:

  This project requires that Hands-on Project 5-6 be completed.

1. Select the **SalesGrp** you created in Hands-on Project 5-6.
2. Select **Delete** from the **Action** menu.
3. When prompted to confirm, click **Yes**.
4. Close the **Local Users and Groups** tool by clicking the **X** button in the upper-right corner of the title bar.
5. Close the **Users and Passwords** applet by clicking **OK**.

Project 5-8

To change the Local Security Policy:
1. If not already open, open the **Control Panel** (**Start**, **Settings**, **Control Panel**).
2. Open the **Administrative Tools** applet (double-click its icon).

3. Open the **Local Security Policy** applet (double-click its icon).

4. Expand the **Account Policies** node (click the plus sign beside the node).

5. Select the **Password Policy** node.

6. Select **Enforce password history**.

7. Select the **Security** command from the Action menu.

8. In the setting dialog box, set the value to **5**.

9. Click **OK**.

10. Select **Maximum password age**.

11. Select the **Security** command from the Action menu.

12. In the setting dialog box, set the value to **60**.

13. Click **OK**.

14. Select **Minimum password age**.

15. Select the **Security** command from the Action menu.

16. In the setting dialog box, set the value to **2**.

17. Click **OK**.

18. Select **Minimum password length**.

19. Select the **Security** command from the Action menu.

20. In the setting dialog box, set the value to **6**.

21. Click **OK**.

22. Select the **Account Lockout Policy** node.

23. Select **Account lockout threshold**.

24. Select the **Security** command from the Action menu.

25. In the setting dialog box, set the value to **3**.

26. Click **OK**, then click **OK** again.

27. Select **Account lockout duration**.

28. Select the **Security** command from the Action menu.

29. In the setting dialog box, set the value to **30** (if it is not already set to 30).

30. Click **OK**.

31. Select **Reset account lockout counter after**.

32. Select the **Security** command from the Action menu.

33. In the setting dialog box, set the value to **15**.

34. Click **OK**.

35. Expand the **Local Policies** node (click the plus sign beside the node).

36. Select the **Audit Policy** node.

37. Select **Audit logon events**.

5

38. Select the **Security** command from the Action menu.

39. In the setting dialog box, select **Failure**.

40. Click **OK**.

41. Select **Audit system events**.

42. Select the **Security** command from the Action menu.

43. In the setting dialog box, select **Success and Failure**.

44. Click **OK**.

45. Close all open windows.

Project 5-9

To change user rights:

1. Open the Control Panel by selecting **Start**, **Settings**, **Control Panel**.

2. Double-click the **Administrative Tools** icon.

3. Double-click the **Local Security Policy** icon.

4. Double-click the **Local Policies** node.

5. Select **User Rights Assignment**.

6. Double-click **Add workstations to domain**.

7. Click **Add**.

8. Locate and select **Power Users**.

9. Click **Add**.

10. Click OK.

11. Click OK.

12. Close the Local Security Settings dialog box.

CASE PROJECTS

1. Your notebook computer is attached to a docking station whenever you are in the office. Although your Windows 2000 Professional notebook does not become a member of the domain when docked, it does have the ability to communicate with the domain. Your docking station hosts a color slide printer. How can you grant access to the printer to domain users when your notebook is docked?

2. You are concerned about file security. Recently a staff member was reprimanded because he restored files to a FAT partition instead of to an NTFS partition. The user account is a member of the Backup Administrators group and the Power Users group. Because FAT does not have file level security, the settings on the files allowed everyone on the network to view the confidential files. How can you change the Local Security Policy to prevent this from occurring in the future?

6

WINDOWS 2000 SECURITY AND ACCESS CONTROLS

After reading this chapter and completing the exercises, you will be able to:

♦ Describe the Windows 2000 security model, and the key role of logon authentication

♦ Customize the logon process

♦ Discuss domain security concepts

♦ Understand the local computer policy

♦ Enable and use auditing

♦ Encrypt NTFS files, folders, or drives, using the encrypting file system (EFS)

Because Windows 2000 plays a pivotal role on so many networks, the operating system has been constructed to provide a wide range of control over access to its resources. In fact, Windows 2000 Server has been designed to be able to check access permissions for every request before granting access to resources. This chapter will explore the details of the Windows 2000 security model, its logon process, and the ways in which the operating system associates security information with all objects under its control. You will also see that any user's or program's request for system resources is subjected to close scrutiny at blinding speeds.

THE WINDOWS 2000 SECURITY MODEL

Windows 2000 Professional can establish local security when used as a standalone system, or participate in domain security (managed by Windows 2000 Server, Windows NT Server, or some other NOS). Before a user can use any Windows 2000 resource, he or she must log on to a system, a workgroup, or a domain by supplying a valid user ID and **password**. A user who successfully logs on receives an **access token**. The access token includes information about the user's identity, any permissions specifically associated with the user's account name, and a complete list of all the groups to which the user belongs—including custom groups defined for your network and Windows 2000 predefined default groups. A complex string of bits represents the token, which is attached to every **process** that the user initializes until that user logs off. In other words, each time a user runs a program, enters a system command, or accesses a resource, a copy of that user's access token accompanies the request.

Each time a user attempts to access a resource, the user's access token is compared with a list of permissions associated with the resource. This list is called an **access control list (ACL)**. The access control list is one of the more important attributes associated with any Windows 2000 resource. Whenever an object is requested, the ACL and the access token are carefully compared, and a request for the object is granted only when a match is found.

If the system finds a match between the access token and the ACL, the request can proceed. If a Deny permission occurs or if the requested service is not permitted, the request is denied. A match between the access token and the ACL is like a key that fits a particular lock. In fact, many experts explain the access token using the analogy of a ring of keys that you try in a lock one at a time until a match is found or until there are no more keys to try. Matches between an access token and the ACL can be a function of permissions associated with the individual user's account or permissions that derive from the user's membership in a local or global group. Whatever the source of the permissions, the user's request is allowed to proceed unhindered if a match is found.

Windows 2000 domain security is centered around **Active Directory**, the centralized database of security, configuration, and communication information maintained by domain controllers in a Windows 2000 network. Active Directory supports everything from authentication of domain users' accounts to accessing shared resources. Windows 2000 Professional as a standalone desktop system does not use Active Directory, relying instead on the Registry and internal security systems (similar to Windows NT 4.0) to control user access. However, Windows 2000 Professional participates in Active Directory when it is used as a client in a Windows 2000 domain network. All of the information about the domain and all of the resources shared by the network are managed by Active Directory. Windows 2000 Professional uses Active Directory to gain access to the domain network. Both domain and local security use logon authentication, objects, and access control to gain access to Windows 2000 resources.

Because Active Directory is not a Windows 2000 Professional feature or component, it is not discussed in great detail here. However, an overview of Active Directory is included in Appendix B, "Working with Active Directory."

Logon Authentication

Windows 2000 logon is mandatory to gain access to the system and to applications and resources. The logon process has two components: identification and authentication. **Identification** requires that a user supply a valid account name (and in a domain environment, the name of the domain to which that **user account** belongs). **Authentication** means that a user must use some method to verify his or her identity. By default in Windows 2000, possession of the proper password for an account constitutes authentication, although Windows 2000 also supports third-party authentication add-ins, including biometric systems that check fingerprints or perform retinal scans, and smart card systems that require physical possession of a unique electronic keycard to prove a user's identity.

Most typical Windows 2000 systems rely solely on passwords for authentication, so using hard-to-guess passwords is an important aspect of good system security. Good passwords generally include both uppercase and lowercase letters as well as numbers, for example, Ag00dPA55w0Rd. By creating passwords such as this, it becomes impossible for programs that attempt system break-ins to gain access by using dictionary lists to search for valid passwords.

When a user successfully logs on to a Windows 2000 machine, the security subsystem working with Executive layer services creates an access token for that user. The access token includes all security information pertaining to that user, including the user's **security ID (SID)** and SIDs for each of the groups to which the user belongs. Indirectly, through the user rights policy, this collection of SIDs informs the system of the user's rights. An access token includes the following components:

- The unique SID for the account

- A list of groups to which the user belongs

- A list of rights and privileges associated with the user's specific account

Access to the system is allowed only after the user receives the access token. Each access token is created for one-time use during the logon process. Once constructed, the access token is attached to the user's **shell** process, which defines the run-time environment inside which the user executes programs or spawns other processes. (The default shell process for Windows 2000 is Windows Explorer. It defines the desktop, Start menu, taskbar, and other elements of the default user interface. Alternate shells from third parties can be employed, or even the Windows NT 3.51 Program Manager can be used.) As far as Windows 2000 is concerned, a process is a computer program designed for some specific function. A process is a term synonymous with program. Every activity within the user mode and kernel mode is performed by a process. Each process is launched using the access token of its parent—that is, the process that caused it to be launched. When a user launches a process manually, he or she does so through the shell process, usually Windows Explorer, and it is the access token of the shell process that is inherited by the new process.

Objects

In Windows 2000, access to individual resources is controlled at the **object** level. Each object hosts its own access control list (ACL), which defines which users and groups have access permissions and exactly what type of access they are granted (read, write, print, modify, list, etc.). Everything within the Windows 2000 environment is an object; this includes files, folders, processes, user accounts, printers, and computers. Requests for resources, therefore, translate into requests for objects. An individual object is identified by its type, which defines its permitted range of contents and the kinds of operations (called services) that may be performed upon it. Any individual object is an instance of its type and consists of data and a list of services that can be used to create, manipulate, control, and share the data it contains.

Windows 2000 is able not only to control access at the object level, but also to control which services defined for the object's type a particular security token is allowed to perform or request. All objects are logically subdivided into three parts: a type identifier, a list of services or functions, and a list of named attributes, which may or may not have associated data items—called values.

When defining an object, its type describes the kind of entity it is. For example, an object's type may be file, directory, printer, or network share. An object's services define how the object can be manipulated; for example, possible services for a directory object are Read, Write, and Delete. An object's attributes are its named characteristics, such as *filename*, read-only, hidden, file size, and date created for an object whose type is file. The values for these attributes are their content, such as the actual name of the file, selected, not selected, 142,302 bytes, and 10/3/99 04:23:34 PM, respectively.

Remember, access or permission to use to an object is determined on the basis of the entire object and also for each of the services defined for that object. For example, a user can have access to read a file, such as an e-mail program executable file, but not to edit or delete it. Thus, users can have permission to access the object in general, but may have more specific controls about which services they can request in connection with that access.

CAUTION

Keep in mind that Windows 2000 automatically grants the Everyone group Full Control to the object whenever a new object or share is created. Thus, you must implement restrictions on new objects and new shares. In other words, Windows 2000 allows everyone access to new objects by default.

Access Control

The Windows 2000 logon process is initiated through the attention sequence (the Ctrl+Alt+Delete keystroke combination, known to many DOS users as the "three-fingered salute"). This attention sequence initiates a hardware interrupt that cannot be "faked" by a program and brings up a logon procedure dialog box that is stored in a protected area of memory, thus securing the system from attack through an unauthorized remote logon.

This combination of characteristics for the logon authentication procedure is the key to the entire Windows 2000 security scheme, because all other security features are based upon the level of authority granted a user who has successfully logged on. The Windows 2000 security structure requires a user to log on to a computer with a valid username and password. Without this step, nothing more can be accomplished in the Windows 2000 environment.

The Windows 2000 logon procedure provides security through the use of the following:

- *Mandatory logon:* The user must log on to access the computer.

- *Restricted user mode:* Until a successful logon takes place, all user-mode privileges are suspended. Among other things, this means that the user cannot launch applications, access resources, or perform any action or operation on the system.

- *Physical logon:* The structure of the logon sequence ensures that the logon occurs from the local keyboard, rather than from some other internal or external source. This is because the attention sequence initiates a hardware interrupt that accepts input only from the local keyboard.

- *User profiles:* Windows 2000 allows each user who logs on to a particular machine to save user preferences and environment settings, called a **user profile**. Each user can have a set of specific preferences restored at logon or can be supplied with a mandatory or default set, depending on how the system is configured. A user profile that is configured to follow a user throughout a network is called a roaming profile. (Profiles are covered in detail in Chapter 5.)

CUSTOMIZING THE LOGON PROCESS

A system administrator can alter the default logon process appearance and function using WinLogon. The **WinLogon** process produces the logon dialog box in which the username, password, and domain are selected. WinLogon also controls automated logon, warning text, the display of the Shutdown button, and the display of the last user to log on to the system. WinLogon operates in the user mode portion of the Windows 2000 system architecture and communicates with the Security Reference Monitor and SAM database in the kernel's Executive Services to authenticate users and launch their environment shell with an attached user-specific access token. The WinLogon process can be customized to display some or all of the following characteristics:

- Retain or disable the last logon name entered
- Add a logon security warning

- Change the default shell
- Enable/Disable the WinLogon Shutdown button
- Enable automated logon

 TIP Most of these characteristics can be altered through the Local Security Policy, accessed from the Control Panel, Administrative Tools, Local Security Policy (see Chapter 5). All of these characteristics can be controlled through the Registry (see Chapter 13) via the HKEY_LOCAL_MACHINE\SOFTWARE\Microsoft\Windows NT\CurrentVersion\WinLogon key. However, Microsoft recommends using the Local Security Policy interface to alter these items instead of the Registry when possible.

Several possible configuration changes for the Windows 2000 logon process are detailed in the following sections.

Disabling the Default Username

By default, the logon window displays the name of the last user to log on. If the same user consistently logs on to a single machine, displaying the logon name is convenient; however, for shared or public-access machines, this provides a key piece of information that someone could use to break into your system. It is possible to change the default by altering the value of its associated Registry key (DontDisplayLastUserName) or by setting a Local Security Policy value. Another common form of attack is a dictionary attack, which involves supplying the contents of a dictionary, one word at a time, as a logon password. Avoiding such systematic break-in attempts explains why it's a good idea to limit the number of failed logon attempts via the Lockout Policy.

Disabling the default username option presents a blank username field at the logon prompt. Note that the related value and its corresponding assignment do not occur in the Registry by default. The value is named DontDisplayLastUserName, and it is of type "String," where a value assignment of 1 disables the name display and a value of 0 enables it. This control appears by default in the Local Security Policy (as noted, it is recommended that you use the Local Security Policy too to manage this feature rather than edit the Registry). (Try Hands-on Project 6-2 to disable the display of the username of the last successful logon.)

Adding a Security Warning Message

Depending on your organization's security policy, you might be legally obligated to add a warning message that appears before the logon prompt is displayed. U.S. law states that if you want to be able to prosecute individuals for unauthorized entry to or use of a system, you must warn all users that usage is monitored, unauthorized access is forbidden, and that unauthorized users might be liable for prosecution.

Two Registry or Local Security Policy values are involved in this effort:

- *LegalNoticeCaption*: Puts a label on title bar of the legal notice window that appears during logon. This field works best with 30 characters or less of text.

- *LegalNoticeText*: Contains text information that provides the details of the warning to be issued to system users. This field may be up to 65,535 characters long, but most warning messages do not exceed 1000 characters in length.

After this feature has been activated and configured, a warning message appears each time a user enters the Windows 2000 attention sequence. This message requires the user's acknowledgment by pressing OK before the logon window displayed. (Try Hands-on Project 6-3 to add a legal notice to your logon.)

Changing the Shell

The default shell (the application launched by WinLogon after a successful logon) is Windows Explorer. You can change the shell to a custom or third-party application, depending on the needs or security policy of your organization. For example, you could change to the use of the Program Manager familiar to NT 3.51 and Windows 3.x users. To make this change, you change the Shell value in the WinLogon key from Explorer.exe to Progman.exe.

If you change from the Explorer shell to the Program Manager shell, your system will lose its onscreen taskbar, and you will no longer be able to use the Start menu to launch programs from your desktop. For this reason, most organizations use the default shell.

If you use the default shell, remember that one of the options that appears on the WinLogon window is Task Manager. This tool is available any time you enter the attention sequence. From there, you can select the Applications tab, and New Task (Run) from the File menu lets you browse and launch applications from the desktop. (Try Hands-on Project 6-4 to change your default shell.)

Disabling the Shutdown button

By default, the Windows 2000 Professional logon window includes an enabled Shutdown button. However, in an environment in which users have access to the keyboard and mouse on a Windows 2000 machine, this option has the potential for unwanted system shutdowns. Fortunately, this option can be disabled. It should be noted, however, that if the user still has access to the physical power switch on the computer, disabling this option might cause more headaches than it solves. A system that has been shut down or rebooted through the operating system has a much higher chance of coming back up successfully than one that was simply powered off. Note that by default, this button is enabled for Windows 2000 Professional machines, but disabled for Windows 2000 Server machines.

The value named ShutdownWithoutLogon is the one you'll need to edit in either the Registry or the Local Security Policy. It's enabled (set to the value 1) on Windows 2000 Professional machines by default. To disable this button, change its value assignment to 0 (zero); to reenable it, reset its value to 1. When the button is disabled, it still appears in the WinLogon window, but it's grayed-out and unusable.

For laptops or other advanced computers with automatic shutdown capabilities, an additional button labeled "Shutdown and Power Off" appears. Similar machines might also support a sleep mode, in which all processing is suspended and all power turned off, except to the computer's RAM. In that case, Sleep also shows up as a shutdown option. This particular setting permits users to eliminate most of a computer's power consumption, yet be ready to resume activity at the push of a single button or movement of the mouse. If the machine warrants such settings, users will find related Registry values in their WinLogon key settings that help them control how these functions are handled.

Be aware that leaving the Shut Down button enabled means that anyone with access to the keyboard can enter the Windows attention sequence and shut down the local machine.

Automating Logons

Some special- or limited-use Windows 2000 machines (for example, airport kiosks or hotel information stations) may need to be always available and always logged into a low-security account for access to some dedicated application. Although the logon process cannot be bypassed, the values for username and password can be coded into the Registry to automate logons. This normally is of interest only when installing machines for public use, such as for information centers, kiosks, museum guides, or other situations in which a computer is used to provide information to the public. In such cases, it's important to have computer and user policies to prevent Windows-2000-savvy users from attempting to break out of the public application and explore other, less-public aspects of the system (or worse, of the network to which it may be attached).

To set up an automated logon, the following Registry keys must be defined and set:

- *DefaultDomainName:* Defines the name of the domain to log on to (needed only when logging on to a networked machine that's part of a domain)

- *DefaultUserName:* Defines the default logon account name

- *DefaultPassword:* Defines the password associated with the default account name. This value is not present by default. When auto logon is disabled, delete this value, because it stores the password in plain text.

- *AutoAdminLogon:* Instructs the machine to log itself on immediately following each bootup. A value of 1 automatically logs on, using the credentials from the other three values in this list. A value of 0 disables the auto logon feature.

Automated logon creates a situation in which the computer automatically makes itself available to users without requiring an account name or a password. It is essential, therefore, that this capability be exercised *only* when security is not a concern (if a machine hosts only a single application and is not connected to the network) or if access to the equipment is otherwise controlled.

Automatic Account Lockout

Automatic account lockout disables a user account if a predetermined number of failed logon attempts occurs within a specified time limit. This feature is intended to prevent intrusion by unauthorized users attempting to gain access by guessing a password or launching a dictionary attack. The default setting of Windows 2000 is to allow an unlimited number of failed access attempts to a user account without locking out that account. However, this is not recommended when there is even a remote chance that unauthorized people can gain physical access to logon consoles. (The account lockout feature of Windows 2000 is discussed in Chapter 5.)

6

DOMAIN SECURITY CONCEPTS AND SYSTEMS

A **domain** is a collection of computers with centrally managed security and activities. A domain offers increased security, centralized control, and broader access to resources than any other computer system configuration. Security policies are domain-wide controls that specify password requirements, account lockout settings, auditing, user rights, security options, and more.

Domain Security Overview

Domain security is the control of user accounts, group memberships, and resource access for all members of a network instead of for only a single computer. The mechanisms used by Windows 2000 Professional are similar to those employed by domain controllers (that is, Windows 2000 Servers) to manage an entire network's security. All of the information about user accounts, group memberships, group policies, and access controls for resources is contained in Active Directory, a database maintained by one or more domain controllers. A **domain controller** is a Windows 2000 Server system with Active Directory services installed and configured.

Kerberos and Authentication Services

Authentication takes place in a Windows 2000 domain network under two conditions: interactive logon and network authentication. Interactive logon occurs when you press the attention sequence, and then enter your username and password. If you log on to a local system, such as a standalone Windows 2000 Professional system, all authentication is performed by the local security subsystem. If you are logging on to a domain, the local security subsystem communicates with a domain controller using **Kerberos** v5—an authentication encryption protocol—to protect your logon credentials.

A **network authentication** occurs when you attempt to connect to or access resources from some other member of the domain network. Network authentication is used to prove that you are a valid member of the domain, your user account is properly authenticated, and that you have access permissions to perform the requested action. The communications that occur during network authentication are protected by one of several methods, including:

- Kerberos v5

- Secure Sockets Layer/Transport Layer Security (SSL/TLS)

- NTLM (NT LAN Manager) authentication for compatibility with Windows NT 4.0

> **TIP** The authentication protection method is determined by either the communications mechanism (such as IIS or a standard network connection) or the settings in the Local Security Policy. Only one is used, but all can be "active" at one time, so as the client requests or uses one or the other, the server can actively respond. The server responds with the same authentication scheme requested by the client.

Kerberos v5 Authentication

Windows 2000 uses Kerberos v5 as the primary protocol for authentication security. The system uses this protocol to verify the identity of both the client (user) and server (network service or application) upon each resource access. This is known as mutual authentication. It protects the server from unauthorized clients and prevents the user from accessing the wrong or spoofed servers (a spoofed server is one that is programmed to appear to be a particular server when it is another; this is most commonly used on the Internet when an attacker is trying to gain access to credit card information).

The Kerberos authentication system was designed to allow two parties to exchange private information across an open network, such as the Internet. Kerberos assigns a unique key, called a ticket, to each user who logs on to the network. This unique ticket is then embedded in messages to identify the sender of the message to the message's recipient. The Kerberos process is completely invisible to the user. For more information on Kerberos, consult the *Windows 2000 Resource Kit*.

Secure Sockets Layer/Transport Layer Security (SSL/TLS)

Secure Sockets Layer/Transport Layer Security (SSL/TLS) is an authentication scheme often used by Web-based applications and supported in Windows 2000 via IIS (Internet Information Services). SSL functions by issuing an identity **certificate** to both the client and server. A third-party certificate authority that both the client and server have chosen to trust, such as VeriSign (*http://www.verisign.com*), issues these certificates. When a resource request is made, the client sends its certificate to the server. The server verifies the validity of the client certificate, then sends its own certificate to the client along with an encryption key. The client verifies the validity of the server certificate, then uses the encryption key to initiate a communication session with the server. This encrypted communication link is used for all future communications during this session. Once the session is terminated, the link must be rebuilt by starting over with the client sending its certificate to the server.

For more information on SSL, please consult the *Windows 2000 Resource Kit* and the *IIS Resource Kit*.

NTLM

NTLM (NT LAN Manager) authentication is the mechanism used by Windows NT 4.0. Windows 2000 supports this authentication method solely for backward compatibility with Windows NT Server and Windows NT Workstation. NTLM functions by using a static encryption level (40-bit or 128-bit) to encrypt traffic between a client and server.

For more information on NTLM, please consult the *Windows 2000 Resource Kit* or the *Windows NT 4.0 Resource Kit*.

LOCAL COMPUTER POLICY

6

Another security control built into Windows 2000 is the **local computer policy**. This policy is a combination of controls that in Windows NT existed only in the Registry, via system policies, or as Control Panel applets. Sometimes the local computer policy is called a software policy, an environmental policy, or even a Windows 2000 policy. No matter what name is actually used, the local computer policy is simply the group policy (see Chapter 5) of the local system. The effective local computer policy is the result of the combination of all group policies applicable to the system.

In a Windows 2000 domain network environment, the local computer policy is controlled on a domain basis on a Windows 2000 Server domain controller. This control is based on site, domain, and organizational unit group policies. On a Windows 2000 Professional system, you must manually launch the MMC and add the Global Policy snap-in to manage or change the local computer policy. Once the Global Policy snap-in is loaded, it is displayed as Local Computer Policy. You cannot manage domain policies from a Windows 2000 Professional machine.

The contents of the local computer policy are determined during installation and based on system configuration, existing devices, and selected options and components. Custom policies can be created through the use of .adm files, such as those used by the Windows NT 4.0 System Policy Editor. Such files from Windows NT 4.0 can be used with Windows 2000 with some caveats. When you open and edit the local group policy, you are working with the System.adm file. The .adm files used by the Group Policy editor reside in the \Inf subfolder of the main Windows 2000 directory. Third-party software vendors can use custom .adm files to add additional environmental controls based on their software or services. To learn about creating custom .adm files, see the *Windows 2000 Resource Kit*.

The local computer policy is divided into two sections (see Figure 6-1): Computer Configuration and User Configuration. The Computer Configuration section contains controls that focus on the computer, such as hardware and software settings. The User Configuration section contains controls that focus on the user and the user environment, such as permissions and desktop settings.

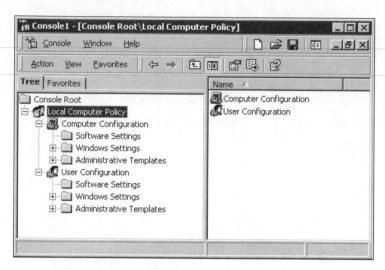

Figure 6-1   The Local Computer Policy snap-in

Because the local computer policy contains over 300 individual controls, you should take the time to peruse the entire collection level by level. (Try Hands-on Project 6-1 to view the local computer policy.)

Computer Configuration

The Computer Configuration section of the local computer policy contains three subfolders: Software Settings, Windows Settings, and Administrative Templates. Software Settings is empty by default; most third-party add-in application settings appear in this folder. The Windows Settings folder contains two items: Scripts and Security Settings. The Scripts item allows you to define one or more scripts to be automatically executed at system startup or shutdown. Security Settings is a container for settings for Account Policies, Local Policies (Audit, User Rights, and Security Options), Public Key Policies, and IP Security Policies. Account Policies and Local Policies were discussed in Chapter 5; Public Key Policies and IP Security Policies are discussed in the following sections. The Administrative Templates folder contains a multilevel collection of computer-related controls (see the "Administrative Templates" section later in this chapter).

Public Key Policies

There are three purposes for using the **public key policies** controls: to offer additional controls over the encrypting file system (EFS), to enable the issuing of certificates, and to allow you to establish trust in a certificate authority. Please consult the *Windows 2000 Resource Kit* for complete details. (Try Hands-on Project 6-5 to encrypt files with EFS.)

IP Security Policies

IP Security (IPSec) is a security measure added to TCP/IP to protect communications between two systems using that protocol. Windows 2000 is one of the first operating systems to include native support for IPSec. IPSec negotiates a secure encrypted communications link between a client and server through the management of public and private encryption keys. IPSec policies govern how a system communicates via TCP/IP based on your defined security needs. Windows 2000 includes three predefined IPSec policies; however, you can create and manage your own custom IPSec policies. None of the predefined IPSec policies are enabled or assigned by default. For information on creating custom IPSec policies, consult the *Windows 2000 Resource Kit*.

The three predefined IPSec policies are Client (Respond Only), Server (Request Security) and Secure Server (Require Security). See Figure 6-2. The Client (Respond Only) policy is for systems that do not require secure communications at all times. This policy initiates a secure communications link only when another system requests it. This policy does not initiate secure communications by default. The Server (Request Security) policy is for systems that need to use secure communications most of the time. This policy always requests that communications be secured, but allows unsecured communications to occur if IPSec is not available on the other system. The Secure Server (Require Security) policy is for systems that require secure communications at all times. This policy allows communications only if the remote system offers IPSec. Each of these policies can be modified via its Properties dialog box. However, Microsoft recommends creating new policies instead of modifying the default policies.

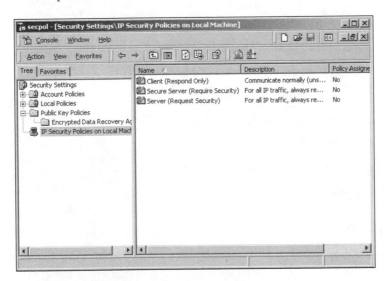

Figure 6-2   Setting IP security policies

Administrative Templates

Administrative templates offer controls on a wide range of environmental functions and features. An administrative template is simply a collection of predefined security and operational controls for Windows 2000. As shown in Figure 6-3, the Administrative Templates folder in the Computer Configuration node of the Local Computer Policy snap-in contains folders and subfolders with specific control items focused on a single aspect of the computer or environmental function.

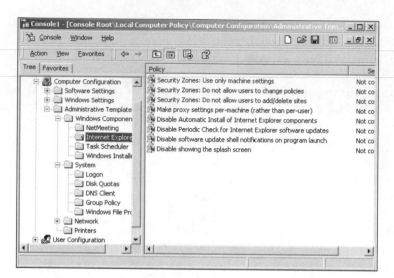

Figure 6-3   The Administrative Templates folder

The controls available through the Administrative Templates folder under computer configurations include:

- Controlling security and software updates for Internet Explorer
- Controlling access and use of the Task Scheduler and Windows Installer
- Controlling logon security features and operations
- Controlling disk quotas
- Managing the way group policies are processed
- Managing system file protection
- Managing offline access of network resources
- Controlling printer use and function

User Configuration

The User Configuration portion of the local computer policy is structured in much the same way as the Computer Configuration portion. The User Configuration folder is also divided into three subfolders: Software Settings, Windows Settings, and Administrative Templates. Software Settings is empty by default. Any user-specific Microsoft or third-party software settings appear in this folder. The Windows Settings folder contains three items: Internet Explorer (IE), Scripts, and Security Settings. The Internet Explorer section is used to control user-specific activities of IE, such as the browser interface appearance, connection methods, links, and security zones. The Scripts item allows you to define one or more scripts to automatically execute at user logon or logoff. Security Settings is initially empty, but can become a container for user-specific (rather than computer-specific) security controls. The Administrative Templates folder contains a multilevel collection of user-specific functional and environmental controls. Keep in mind that these controls are for the local computer only. If the computer is a member of a domain, some of these controls may be overwritten by a group, computer, or organizational unit policy from the domain. The items contained in the User Configuration's Administrative Templates section include:

- Internet Explorer configuration, interface, features, and functions controls

- Management of Windows Explorer (interface, available commands, features)

- Management of the MMC

- Control over the Task Scheduler and Windows Installer

- Control over Start menu and taskbar features

- Management of the desktop environment

- Management of the Control Panel applets

- Control of offline network access

- Management of network connections

- Control over logon and logoff scripts and application of group policy

 TIP For more information on any control in the Local Computer Policy, open its Properties dialog box and view the Explain tab (see Figure 6-4).

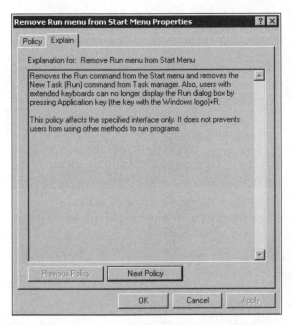

Figure 6-4   The Explain tab of a Local Computer Policy control dialog box

The Policy tab on the Properties dialog box for each control (see Figure 6-5) offers three settings:

- *Not Configured*—The default for all controls; does not change the existing setting of this control
- *Enabled*—Enables the function or restriction of this control
- *Disabled*—Disables the function or restriction of this control

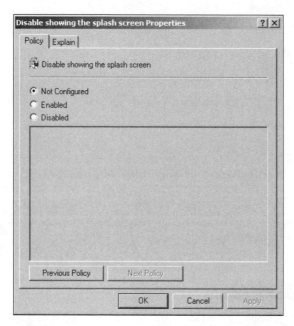

Figure 6-5 The Policy tab on the Properties dialog box

By carefully reading the materials on the Explain tab, you'll be able to understand which of the three settings for each control makes the most sense for the action you wish to enforce or allow. In some cases, selecting the Enable control reveals additional controls, such as selection lists, numerical entry fields, or text entry fields, which provide the additional settings required by some controls. For example, the timeout settings require you not only to enable the control but also to define a time period in minutes or seconds for that timeout period.

AUDITING

Auditing is the security process that records the occurrence of specific operating system **events** in a Security log. Every object in the Windows 2000 system has audit events related to it. These events can be recorded on a success or failure basis and in some cases according to users or groups. For example, logging all failed logon attempts may warn you when an attack attempting to breach your security is occurring; monitoring classified documents for read access can let you know when and who is accessing them. Auditing can provide valuable information about security breaches, resource activity, and user adeptness. Auditing is also useful for investigating performance and planning for expansion.

Auditing is enabled through the Local Security Policy (see Chapter 5). Once enabled, the audited events are recorded in the Security log of the **Event Viewer**. The Event Viewer is accessed via the Administrative Tools (accessed from the Start menu or Control Panel). The Event Viewer maintains logs about application, security, and system events on your computer, enables you to view and manage the logs, to gather information about hardware and software problems, and monitor Windows 2000 security events. To view the items related to auditing, select the Security Log node (see Figure 6-6). Double-clicking an event opens the Event dialog box (see Figure 6-7). This particular audit event records the data about a successful logon of the Administrator account on the workstation named W2KPRO. Audit entries in the Security log contain information about the event, including user logon identification, the computer used, time, date, and the action or event that instigated an audit.

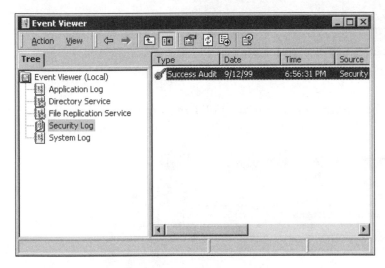

Figure 6-6 An event from the Security Log

If you select the option to audit object access on either a Success or Failure basis, you can define the actions or activities to audit for objects on an object-by-object basis for each possible action, based on that object's type, for specific users and groups. For example, you might audit access to certain network resources, such as files or printers, by different users and/or groups. To set an object's auditing controls:

1. Open the properties dialog box for an NTFS object (such as a file, folder, or printer). Right-click the object, then select **Properties** from the menu.

2. Select the **Security** tab.

3. Click the **Advanced** button.

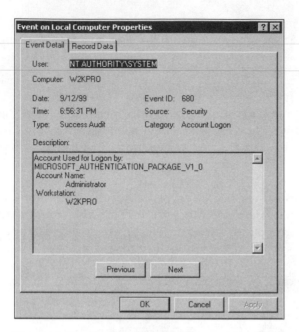

Figure 6-7   The Event dialog box

4. Select the **Auditing** tab as shown in Figure 6–8. This displays all of the currently defined audit events for this object. It is blank by default.

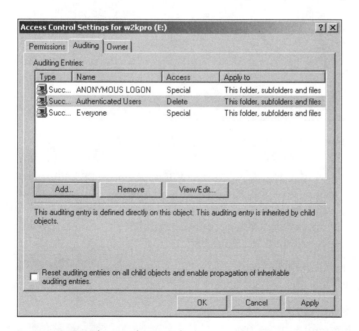

Figure 6-8   The Auditing tab

5. Click the **Add** button.

6. Select a computer, a group, or a user from the Select User, Computer, or Group dialog box.

7. Click **OK**.

8. Select either Successful or Failed for any of the listed actions for this object type. The selections made here are the actions that are recorded in the Security log.

> If you selected the option to record only Failures in the Local Security Policy, selecting Successful actions in this dialog box does not record items in the Security log.

6

9. Click **OK**.

10. Repeat Steps 5 through 9 for all users, computers, or groups you wish to audit.

11. Repeat Steps 1 through 10 for all objects.

12. Click **OK** to exit the Access Control Settings dialog box.

13. Click **OK** to exit the Properties dialog box.

> Auditing access by the Everyone group ensures that all access to a user right, object, etc. is audited.

> Auditing numerous objects or events can result in a large Security log and can slow down network or computer performance.

The Event Viewer can be configured to monitor the size of the Security log and to take action when it reaches a target size. The actions are Overwrite Oldest Entries as Needed, Overwrite Entries a Specified Number of Days Old, or Never Overwrite. If the maximum size is reached and Never Overwrite is selected, an alert appears stating that the log needs to be cleared. To access these controls, select Properties from the menu that appears when you right-click the log in the Event Viewer.

ENCRYPTING FILE SYSTEM (EFS)

Microsoft has extended the native NTFS file system to include encrypted storage. This new security measure, the **encrypting file system (EFS)**, enables you to encrypt data stored on an NTFS drive. When EFS is enabled on a file, folder, or drive, only the enabling user can gain access to the encrypted object. The EFS is enabled through a check box accessed through the Advanced button on the General tab of an object's Properties dialog box (see Figure 6-9).

Figure 6-9   Enabling EFS

EFS employs a public and private key encryption method. The private key is assigned to a single user account. No other user (other than Local Administrators or Domain Administrators who are recovery agents by default), computer, or operating system can gain access to the encrypted files. For the authorized user (that is, the user with the correct private key), access to the encrypted files is unhindered. In fact, the entire encryption process is invisible to the user.

Keep in mind that encryption is just another attribute of NTFS, and you should treat encryption in the same manner as attributes and permissions. Any new file created or copied into an encrypted folder assumes the settings of that folder. Moving an encrypted file to a nonencrypted folder on the same volume allows the file to retain its original settings, but copying the encrypted file causes the file to assume the settings of the destination folder. Because EFS is an additional level of processing required by the operating system to grant access to file-level objects, the performance of the file system can be noticeably impaired. You'll need to perform your own baseline comparison of your storage system's performance to determine exactly how much degradation is caused by EFS.

Windows 2000 includes a command-line tool for batch processing of encryption (that is, encrypting or decrypting large numbers of files or folders via a command-line or batch file). The CIPHER command has the following syntax:

```
CIPHER [/E ,   /D] [/S[:dir]] [/A] [/I] [/F] [/Q] [filename [...]]
```

The following list defines each of the CIPHER command's parameters:

- /E—Encrypts the listed filename(s)
- /D—Decrypts the listed filename(s)
- /S—Performs the action on all subcontents
- /I—Ignores errors and proceeds with processing

- /F—Forces encryption, even on already encrypted files

- /Q—Silences activity except for essential feedback

- *filename*—Specifies a pattern, file, or directory. Wildcards can be used; each pattern must be separated by a space.

When CIPHER is used with only a filename and without parameters, the status of the object is displayed, indicating whether the object is encrypted and whether new files added to a folder will be encrypted.

The primary benefit of EFS is that if your computer is either physically accessed or stolen, the data is protected as long as the malicious user does not gain access to the username and password that holds the private key for the encrypted files. The primary drawback is the increased processing power required to encrypt all writes and decrypt all reads on the fly. This will negatively affect performance to a noticeable extent on many systems.

6

CHAPTER SUMMARY

❑ Windows 2000 has object-level access controls that provide the foundation for all resource access. By comparing the access control lists associated with individual objects to the access tokens that define the rights of any user process, Windows 2000 decides which object access requests to grant and which to deny.

❑ The Windows 2000 logon process (WinLogon) strictly controls how users identify themselves and log on to a Windows 2000 machine. The attention sequence (Ctrl+Alt+Delete) guarantees that an unauthorized user cannot obtain system access. Likewise, WinLogon's protected memory structures prevent this all-important gatekeeper function from being replaced by would-be system crackers. Authentication can take place using various encryption schemes, including Kerberos, SSL, or NTLM.

❑ WinLogon also supports a number of logon controls: handling of a default logon name, providing security notices, changing the default shell, handling system shutdown options, and enabling automatic logon. Key local computer policy settings can be used to block unauthorized break-in attempts.

❑ The local computer policy controls many aspects of the security system as well as enabling or restricting specific functions and features of the operating system. You can use Windows 2000 auditing capabilities to track down errant behavior or detect when system problems may be occurring. Encrypting file system (EFS) protects your data by an encryption system. All in all, Windows 2000 offers a secure operating environment that is designed to help administrators keep their important assets safe from harm and unwanted exposure.

KEY TERMS

access control list (ACL) — A list of security identifiers that are contained by a resource object. Only those processes with the appropriate access token can activate the services of that object.

access token — Objects containing the security identifier of an active process. These tokens determine the security context of the process.

Active Directory — The database that contains information about a domain's user accounts, group memberships, group policies, and access controls for resources.

auditing — The process of tracking events by recording selected types of events in the Security log.

authentication — The process of validating a user's credentials to allow access to certain resources.

certificate — An electronic identity verification mechanism. Certificates are assigned to a client or server by a certificate authority. When communication begins, each side of the transmission can decide to either trust the other party based on its certificate and continue with the communication or not to trust the other party and terminate communication.

domain — A collection of computers with centrally managed security and activities.

domain controller — A specified computer role of a Windows 2000 Server that authenticates domain logons and maintains the security policies and the account database for a domain.

domain security — The control of user accounts, group memberships, and resource access for all members of a network instead of for only a single computer.

encrypting file system (EFS) — A security feature of NTFS under Windows 2000 that allows files, folders, or entire drives to be encrypted. Once encrypted, only the user account that enabled the encryption has the proper private key to decrypt and access the secured objects.

event — Any significant occurrence in the system or in an application that requires users to be notified or a log entry to be added. Types of events include audits, driver failures, user logons, process launchings, and system shutdowns.

Event Viewer — The utility which maintains logs about application, security, and system events on your computer, and enables you to view and manage the event logs, gather information about hardware and software problems, and monitor Windows 2000 security events.

identification — The process of establishing a valid account identity on a Windows 2000 machine by supplying a correct and working domain name (if necessary) and an account name.

IP Security (IPSec) — An encrypted communication mechanism used by TCP/IP to create protected communication sessions. IPSec is a suite of cryptography-based protection services and security protocols.

Kerberos — An authentication encryption protocol employed by Windows 2000 to protect logon credentials.

local computer policy — A Windows 2000 security control feature used to define and regulate security-related features and functions.

local computer security — The control of user accounts, group memberships, and resource access for a single computer.

network authentication — Part of the act of connecting to or accessing resources from some other member of the domain network. Network authentication is used to prove that you are a valid member of the domain, that your user account is properly authenticated, and that you have access permissions to perform the requested action.

NTLM (NT LAN Manager) authentication — The authentication mechanism used on Windows NT that is retained by Windows 2000 for backward compatibility.

object — Everything within the Windows 2000 operating environment is an object. Objects include files, folders, shares, printers, and processes.

password — A unique string of characters that must be provided before a logon or an access is authorized. Passwords are a security measure used to restrict initial access to Windows 2000 resources.

process — The primary unit of execution in the Windows 2000 operating system environment, a process may contain one or more execution threads, all associated with a named user account, SID, and access token. Processes essentially define the container within which individual applications and commands execute under Windows 2000.

public key policy — A security control of Windows 2000 whereby recovery agents for EFS and domain-wide and trusted certificate authorities are defined and configured. These policies can be enforced on a user-by-user basis.

Secure Sockets Layer/Transport Layer Security (SSL/TLS) — A mechanism used primarily over HTTP communications to create an encrypted session link through the exchange of certificates and public encryption keys.

security ID (SID) — A unique name that identifies a logged-on user to the security system. SIDs can identify one user or a group of users.

shell — The default user process that is launched when a valid account name and password combination is authenticated by the WinLogon process for Windows 2000. The default shell of Windows 2000 is Windows Explorer. The default shell process manages the desktop, Start menu, taskbar, and other interface controls. The shell process defines a logged-on user's run-time environment from the point of authentication forward, and supplies all spawned processes or commands with its access token to define their access permissions, until that account logs out.

user account — This entity contains all of the information that defines a user to the Windows 2000 environment.

user profile — A file that saves a user's preferences and environmental settings.

WinLogon — The process used by Windows 2000 to control user authentication and manage the logon process. WinLogon produces the logon dialog box where username, password, and domain are selected, and it controls automated logon, warning text, the display of the shutdown button, and the display of the last user to log onto the system.

6

REVIEW QUESTIONS

1. Which of the following determines which users and groups have access to a particular Windows NT object?

   a. Security Access Manager

   b. local computer policy

   c. Event Viewer

   d. group policy

2. All processes in Windows 2000 require an access token. True or False?

3. A SID is a unique number and is never duplicated. True or False?

4. Permissions that are changed while the user is actively logged on do not take effect until that user logs on to the system again. True or False?

5. The default Windows 2000 authentication method requires the user to supply valid domain and account names, plus a valid password; however, Windows 2000 permits use of alternate authentication techniques. True or False?

6. What is the first thing the security system looks for when it scans an ACL for an object?

   a. a Deny to the object for the requested service, at which point access is immediately denied

   b. any ACL that provides the requested permission

   c. It checks the default, and if access is permitted, it allows the request to proceed.

   d. none of the above

7. Windows 2000 _____ access to new objects by default.

   a. restricts

   b. allows

8. Which of the following is a good reason for adding DontDisplayLastUserName to the Windows 2000 Registry? (Choose all that apply.)

   a. to prevent easy discovery of user account names

   b. to improve security on a shared machine

   c. to reduce burnout on the machine's monitor

   d. to force users to provide a valid username in addition to a password to logon

9. The Windows 2000 authentication process can be automated by adding default user information and the _____ value to the Registry.

   a. DontDisplayLastUsername

   b. AutoAdminLogon

   c. Legal Notice Caption

   d. AutomateLogon

10. Which of the following is the most likely reason to have a security notice appear when users attempt to log on to a Windows 2000 machine at the National Security Agency?

    a. to make sure that outsiders don't try to break into the system

    b. to inform unauthorized users that they are subject to legal action if they obtain unauthorized access to the system

    c. to remind valid system users about Acceptable Use Policies

    d. none of the above

11. The default shell process for Windows 2000 is called the:

    a. Windows Explorer

    b. Program Manager

    c. command shell

    d. C shell

12. The _____ is created by the Windows 2000 security subsystem at logon and identifies the current user to the subsystem.

    a. access ID

    b. security ID

    c. group ID

    d. access token

13. The _____ key sequence initiates the logon process.

    a. Ctrl+Esc

    b. Alt+Tab

    c. Ctrl+Break

    d. Ctrl+Alt+Delete

14. An access token is required to access any Windows 2000 object. True or False?

15. To customize the security structure of your Windows 2000 system, you can change the behavior of the logon process. True or False?

16. What is the primary protocol that Windows 2000 uses for authentication?

    a. NTLM

    b. Secure Sockets Layer

    c. Kerberos

    d. NetBIOS

6

17. Which of the following statements are true about the local computer policy? (Choose all that apply.)

    a. It is used to control aspects of the Windows 2000 security system.

    b. It is used to assign user accounts to groups.

    c. It can be customized by third-party applications.

    d. It can be superceded by a domain's group policy.

18. What is the special-purpose application invoked by the Windows 2000 attention sequence that serves as the logon process?

    a. WinPopup.exe

    b. WinLogon.exe

    c. Usermgr.exe

    d. Explorer.exe

19. What security feature is added to Windows 2000 specifically to protect TCP/IP communications?

    a. Kerberos

    b. IPSec

    c. strong passwords

    d. EFS

20. What is EFS used to protect?

    a. passwords

    b. data files

    c. group policy

    d. communication sessions

21. If the 2000 Explorer shell is replaced with the Program Manager shell, which of the following side effects will occur? (Choose all that apply.)

    a. no access to the Start menu

    b. no taskbar

    c. no access to the Task Manager

    d. no more DOS command prompt

22. Only the user who encrypted a file via EFS can access that file later. True or False?

23. What predefined IPSec policy should you use to employ encryption only when required by a remote system?

    a. Client (Respond Only)

    b. Server (Request Security)

    c. Secure Server (Require Security)

24. Auditing can be defined for an object for specific users and groups for one or more individual services or actions. True or False?

25. Audit events are recorded in the System Log. True or False?

HANDS-ON PROJECTS

Project 6-1

To open the local computer policy:

> **TIP**   This project shows you where security controls are managed.

1. Open the Run command (**Start**, **Run**).
2. Type **mmc**, then click **OK**. This launches the Microsoft Management Console.
3. Select **Add/Remove Snap-in** from the Console menu.
4. Click the **Add** button.
5. Locate and select **Group Policy**.
6. Click **Add**.
7. On the Select Group Policy object dialog box, notice that Local Computer is listed by default. Click **Finish**.
8. Click **Close** on the Add Standalone Snap-in dialog box.
9. Click **OK** on the Add/Remove Snap-in dialog box.
10. The Local Computer Policy node should now appear in the MMC.

Project 6-2

To disable the display of the last username on the logon screen:

> **TIP**   This project requires that you first complete Hands-on Project 6-1.

1. In the Local Computer Policy console, locate the Computer Configuration node. Click its boxed **plus sign** to expand its contents.
2. Locate the Windows Settings node. Click on its boxed **plus sign** to expand its contents.

3. Locate the Security Settings node. Click on its boxed **plus sign** to expand its contents.

4. Locate the Local Policies node. Click on its boxed **plus sign** to expand its contents.

5. Locate and select the **Security Options** node.

6. In the Details pane, locate and select **Do not display last user name in logon screen**.

7. Select the **Action** menu, then click **Security**. The Local Security Policy Setting dialog box for the selected control is displayed.

8. Select the **Enabled** radio button.

9. Click **OK**.

Project 6-3

To display a legal warning message at logon:

 TIP   This project requires that you first complete Hands-on Project 6-1.

1. In the Local Computer Policy console, locate and select the subnode of **Computer Configuration**, **Windows Settings**, **Security Settings**, **Local Policies**, **Security Options**.

2. Locate and select **Message title for users attempting to log on**.

3. Select the **Action** menu, then click **Security**.

4. In the field, type **Warning!** Click **OK**.

5. Select **Message text for users attempting to log on**.

6. Select the **Action** menu, then click **Security**.

7. In the field, type a warning message similar to the following: (*Note:* This excellent security warning message is reproduced from *The Windows NT Security Handbook*, by Tom Sheldon, Osborne/McGraw-Hill: Berkeley, 1997.) **Authorized Users Only! The information on this computer and network is the property of (*name organization here*) and is protected by intellectual property law. You must have legitimate access to an assigned account on this computer to access any information. You are permitted only to access information as defined by the system administrators. Your activities may be monitored. Any unauthorized access will be punished to the full extent of the law.**

8. Click **OK**.

Project 6-4

To change the default shell:

TIP
> Changing the shell will result in a new user interface. The Program Manager does not offer a Start menu, toolbar, Task Manager, and many other interface controls to which you are accustomed from Windows 2000. Employ this Hands-on Project with caution.

1. Open the Run command (**Start**, **Run**).
2. Type **regedit**, then click **OK**.
3. Locate and select the key:
   HKEY_LOCAL_MACHINE\SOFTWARE\Microsoft\ Windows NT\CurrentVersion\Winlogon.
4. Locate and select the **Shell** value.
5. Select **Modify** from the Edit menu.
6. Change the value data from Explorer.exe to **Progman.exe**.
7. Click **OK**.
8. Select **Exit** from the Registry menu. The system is now configured to launch the Windows NT 3.51 Program Manager as the shell.
9. To return the shell to Windows Explorer, either reopen the Registry editor now and change the Shell value back to its original setting (Explorer.exe), or, if you have already logged in with Program Manager as the shell, use the Run command from the File menu of the Program Manager to launch Regedit and make the change.

Project 6-5

To encrypt a folder with EFS:

TIP
> The folder must be on an NTFS file system to complete this exercise.

1. Launch Windows Explorer (**Start**, **Programs**, **Accessories**, **Windows Explorer**).
2. Select the **C** drive in the left column. (If drive C is not formatted with NTFS, select some other drive which is formatted with NTFS.)
3. Select the **File** menu, then **New**, **Folder**.
4. Type a name for the folder (such as **EFStemp**), then press **Enter**.
5. Right-click the new folder, then select **Properties** from the menu.
6. On the General tab, click the **Advanced** button.
7. Click to place a check in the **Encrypt contents to secure data** check box.

8. Click **OK**.

9. Click **OK**.

10. Log off (**Start**, **Shutdown**; select **log off**).

11. Log on to the system with a different user account (Ctrl+Alt+Delete, then provide a different user name and password).

12. Launch Windows Explorer (**Start**, **Programs**, **Accessories**, **Windows Explorer**).

13. Locate and try to access the **EFStemp** folder. Notice that you are unable to gain access.

14. Log off (**Start**, **Shutdown**; select **log off**).

15. Log on with the user account used to encrypt the folder (Ctrl+Alt+Delete, then provide user name and password).

16. Locate and try to access the EFStemp folder. Notice that you are able to gain access.

17. Right-click the EFStemp folder, then select **Properties** from the menu.

18. On the General tab, click the **Advanced** button.

19. Deselect (uncheck) the **Encrypt contents to secure data** check box. Click **OK**.

20. Click **OK**.

21. Click **OK**.

Project 6-6

To explore the local computer policy:

 TIP This project requires that you first complete Hands-on Project 6-1.

1. Expand the **Computer Configuration** node of the Local Computer Policy snap-in.

2. Expand the **Administrative Templates** node.

3. Expand each of the **Windows Components**, **System**, **Network**, and **Printers** subnodes.

4. Select each subnode one by one. Review the control details contained in each.

5. To open the Properties of a control detail, select it, select the **Action** menu, and then click **Properties**.

6. View the Policy and Explain tabs of all control details that interest you.

7. Expand the **User Configuration** node and all of its subnodes.

8. Perform the same expansion and exploration as you did under the Computer Configuration node.

9. Select the **Exit** command from the Console menu of the MMC to close the utility. Click **Cancel** to discard any changes, if prompted.

Project 6-7

To set permissions on a file or folder:

 This hands-on project requires that Windows 2000 be installed and an NTFS partition is present.

1. Launch Windows Explorer (**Start**, **Programs**, **Accessories**, **Windows Explorer**).
2. In the left pane, select a drive formatted with NTFS within My Computer.
3. In the right pane, select a file or folder.
4. From the **File** menu, select **Properties**.
5. Select the **Security** tab.
6. Click the **Add** button.
7. Select the **Authenticated Users** group.
8. Click **Add**.
9. Click **OK**.
10. Click the **Authenticated Users** group which now appears in the list of names on the Security tab for the NTFS object.
11. Select the **Modify** checkbox in the **Allow** column.
12. Select the **Everyone** group. Notice how the defined permissions for these two groups differ.
13. Click **OK**.

Project 6-8

To enable file access auditing:

1. Open the Control Panel by selecting **Start**, **Settings**, **Control Panel**.
2. Double-click the **Administrative Tools** icon.
3. Double-click the **Local Security Policy** icon.
4. Expand the **Local Policies** node by double-clicking it.
5. Select the **Audit** policy.
6. Double-click the **Audit object access** item.
7. Select the **Success** checkbox. Click **OK**.
8. Launch **Windows Explorer**.
9. Locate and select any text document on your computer, such as **%systemroot%\Winnt\setuplog.txt**.
10. Select the **Properties** command from the **File** menu.
11. Select the **Security** tab.

12. Click **Advanced**.

13. Select the **Auditing** tab.

14. Click **Add**.

15. Select **Authenticated Users**.

16. Click **OK**.

17. Select the **List Folder/Read Data** check box under Successful.

18. Click **OK**.

19. Click **OK**.

20. Click **OK**.

21. Double-click the text file to open it.

22. Close Notepad.

23. Return to Administrative Tools by clicking its button on the taskbar.

24. Double-click the **Event Viewer** icon.

25. Select the **Security** log.

26. Double-click one of the event details.

27. Using the arrow buttons, scroll through the most recent event details to locate an event dealing with the successful reading of the text file.

28. Click **OK** to close the Event detail.

29. Close the Event Viewer.

30. Close Administrative Tools.

31. Close Windows Explorer.

32. On the Local Security Settings dialog box, double-click **Audit object access**.

33. Deselect **Success**.

34. Click **OK**.

35. Close Local Security Settings.

Case Projects

1. You've been assigned the task of defining a security policy for your company. You've been given basic guidelines to follow. These include preventing users from installing software, securing the logon process, and enforcing disk quotas. Using the Local Computer Policy snap-in, detail the controls you should configure and what settings you think would work best to accomplish these goals.

2. You've recently inherited the responsibility of administering a Windows 2000 network. The last administrator was rather lax in restricting user access. After working through the data folders to correct the access permissions, you suspect that some users still have access to confidential files. What can you do to determine if this type of access is still occurring? Describe the steps involved in enabling this mechanism and examining the results.

7

NETWORK PROTOCOLS

After reading this chapter and completing the exercises, you will be able to:

♦ Understand the network protocols supported by Windows 2000

♦ Configure TCP/IP

In this chapter, we discuss the networking protocols that Windows 2000 supports, as well as how and when to use them. We also discuss the importance of TCP/IP (Transmission Control Protocol/Internet Protocol) and what is required to configure Windows 2000 to employ this protocol for network communications.

WINDOWS 2000 NETWORK COMPONENTS

Windows 2000 is designed for networking, and includes all the elements necessary for interacting with a network without requiring any additional software. Windows 2000 networking is powerful and efficient, and relatively easy to configure and use, with graphical user interface and wizards for configuration support.

Windows 2000 Professional and Windows 2000 Server (as well as Windows 2000 Advanced Server and Datacenter Server) can function as a network client or as a network server (or both) and can participate in peer-to-peer, client/server, and terminal/host environments. Windows 2000 also has everything needed to access the Internet, including all the necessary protocols and client capabilities, a powerful Web browser (Internet Explorer), and other Internet tools and utilities.

In Windows 2000, numerous components work together to define its networking capabilities. Each component provides one or more individual network functions and defines an interface through which data moves on its way to and from other system components. This allows Windows 2000 to support multiple protocols easily and transparently; applications need only know how to communicate through a standard application programming interface (API), while the modular organization of the operating system shields them from the complex details that can sometimes be involved.

Networking components can be added to or deleted from a Windows 2000 system without affecting the function of other components, except in those cases where such components are bound to other components. (Binding is discussed later in this chapter.) Adding new components brings new services, communications technologies, and other capabilities into existing networks, and allows additional protocols to join the mix at any time.

NETWORK PROTOCOLS

Windows 2000 supports three core network transport protocols. Each of these protocols works best on networks of a particular size, where each such network has its own special performance and access requirements. The major network protocols are NetBEUI, NWLink (IPX/SPX), and TCP/IP. Each of these network transports has specific advantages and drawbacks, as outlined in the sections that follow. The following list sums up the important characteristics of each of the three protocols:

- NetBEUI works best on small networks (10 computers or fewer), single-server, or peer-to-peer networks, where ease of access and use are most important. It is an enhanced version of **NetBIOS (Network Basic Input/Output System)**.

- NWLink works best on networks of medium scope (20 servers or fewer in a single facility). It's also important on networks that include NetWare servers.

- TCP/IP works on a global scale, as demonstrated by its use on the Internet. TCP/IP is a complicated, yet powerful transport that scales well from small networks all the way up to the Internet. It is the most widely used of all networking protocols.

NetBEUI

NetBIOS Enhanced User Interface (NetBEUI) implements the simplest of the three basic Windows 2000 transport protocols. It is also sometimes known as the NetBIOS Frame (NBF) transport protocol. IBM developed NetBEUI in the late 1980s for use with the OS/2 and LAN Manager operating systems.

The developers of NetBEUI did not design the protocol to enable networked PCs to function in a complex networked environment, in which routing support is mandatory. Instead, they built NetBEUI to function best within workgroups ranging in size from 2 to 200 computers. Because of this, NetBEUI is not routable, and unfortunately this limitation restricts NetBEUI to purely local LAN segments that contain either Microsoft or IBM networking clients and servers.

Some networks use bridges to move NetBEUI traffic across multiple LAN segments, but NetBEUI is seldom permitted to transmit across any WAN connections that might otherwise be accessible through network routers. NetBEUI is known as an excessively "chatty" protocol, which makes it unsuitable for WAN use. Microsoft's TCP/IP implementations of NBT (or NetBIOS over TCP/IP) and NetBIOS over IPX, combined with the multiprotocol support offered by Windows 2000, make it possible to use nonbroadcast IP or IPX equivalents to provide usable NetBIOS connectivity across router-managed WAN links that routinely block all broadcast traffic.

NetBEUI Advantages

The two primary advantages of NetBEUI are that it is compact and speedy. Although its chatty characteristics make it unsuitable for WAN use, NetBEUI is by far the fastest of all the **TDI (Transport Driver Interface)** transports in Windows 2000. This makes it ideal on small networks where routing is not required. The most significant features of NetBEUI are:

- It is the fastest of all native Windows 2000 protocols on small networks.
- It supports up to 1023 sessions; earlier implementations supported only 254 sessions.
- It has been optimized to perform well across slow serial links.
- It is easy to install and configure because it relies on NetBIOS naming and delivers automatic addressing.
- It is inherently self-tuning, so no analysis or maintenance of its configuration is necessary.
- It incorporates data integrity checks and retransmission for erroneous or lost packets.
- It incurs the lowest memory overhead of all the major Windows 2000 protocols. For older DOS computers, where RAM space for protocols and drivers is scarce and larger protocols may not fit into available memory, this can make all the difference.

NetBEUI Drawbacks

Unroutability and broadcast overhead make NetBEUI unusable on internetworks or on networks that include WAN as well as LAN links. Because of product specificity, NetBEUI is seldom used except in Microsoft and IBM networks. Possibly because of its insularity, there are few if any diagnostic or troubleshooting utilities for NetBEUI. In short, NetBEUI is not a contender for deployment in large, complex networks. (You can practice installing and removing NetBEUI in Hands-on Project 7-6.)

NWLink

NWLink is the Microsoft implementation of Novell's **Internetwork Packet Exchange/Sequenced Packet Exchange (IPX/SPX) protocol** stack. Rather than supporting the native Novell **Open Datalink Interface (ODI)**, NWLink works with the **NDIS (Network Driver Interface Specification)** driver technology that's native to Windows 2000; NDIS defines parameters for loading more than one protocol on a network adapter. NWLink is sufficiently complete to support the most important IPX/SPX APIs, including:

- *Novell Windows Sockets:* Provides the interface support for existing NetWare applications written to comply with IPX/SPX

- *NetBIOS over IPX:* Links the NetBIOS interface with the NWLink transport protocol. This is actually the NWNBLink (NetWare-NetBIOS Link) that allows Microsoft networks to use the NetBIOS interface for NetWare Connectivity or to facilitate Microsoft networking using the routable **IPX** transport protocol.

 Although IPX/SPX is the default protocol for NetWare prior to version 5, TCP/IP is the default protocol in version 5.

NWLink Advantages

NWLink offers some powerful capabilities that are conspicuously lacking in NetBEUI, including:

- *SPX II:* SPX II is a new version of **SPX** that has been enhanced to support windowing and can set a maximum frame size.

- *Autodetection of frame types:* NWLink automatically detects which IPX frame type is used on a network during initial startup and broadcast advertisement phases. When multiple frame types appear, Windows 2000 defaults to the industry-standard 802.2 frame type.

- *Direct hosting over IPX:* The ability to host ongoing network sessions using IPX transports. Because it eliminates the overhead associated with NetBIOS, direct hosting over IPX can increase network performance by as much as 20% on client computers. This is especially beneficial for client/server applications.

NWLink Drawbacks

On large networks, IPX may not scale well. IPX lacks a built-in facility for centralized address management like the service that DNS provides for TCP/IP. This omission allows address conflicts to occur—especially when previously isolated networks that employed identical defaults or common addressing schemes attempt to interoperate. Novell established an address registry in 1994 (IPX was introduced in 1983), but it is generally neither used nor acknowledged. The Internet Network Information Center (InterNIC) and its subsequent assigns have managed all public IP addresses since 1982. Like its proprietary cousin, NetBEUI, IPX fails to support a comprehensive collection of network management tools. Finally, IPX imposes a greater memory footprint on DOS machines and runs less efficiently than NetBEUI across slow serial connections.

TCP/IP

7

Transmission Control Protocol/Internet Protocol (TCP/IP) represents an all-embracing suite of protocols that cover a wide range of capabilities (more than 100 component protocols that belong to the TCP/IP suite have been standardized).

TCP/IP has also been around for a long time; the original version of TCP/IP emerged from research funded by the Advanced Research Projects Agency (ARPA, a division of the U.S. Department of Defense). Work on this technology began in 1969, continued throughout the 1970s, and became broadly available in 1981 and 1982. Today, TCP/IP is the most common networking protocol in use worldwide, and it is the protocol suite that makes the Internet possible.

TCP/IP has become the platform for a wide variety of network services, including newsgroups (NNTP), electronic mail (SNMP and MIME), file transfer (FTP and ANS), remote printing (lpr, lpd, lpq utilities), remote boot (bootp and **DHCP—Dynamic Host Configuration Protocol**), and the World Wide Web (HTTP—Hypertext Transfer Protocol).

To provide NetBIOS support using TCP/IP transports, Microsoft includes an implementation of NBT (NetBIOS over TCP/IP) with Windows 2000. Microsoft extends the definition of NBT behaviors by adding a new type of NetBIOS network node to the NBT environment, called an "H" node. An H node inverts the normal behavior of the standard NBT "M" (or Mixed) node. It looks first for a NetBIOS name service, such as a **Windows Internet Naming Service (WINS)** server, then sends a broadcast to request local name resolution. An M node broadcasts first, then attempts a directed request for name resolution. This approach reduces the amount of broadcast traffic on most IP-based networks that use NetBIOS names.

TCP/IP Advantages

As network protocols go, TCP/IP is not extremely fast or easy to use. However, TCP/IP supports networking services better than the other Windows 2000 protocols, through its multiple components (see Figure 7-1 and Table 7-1). TCP/IP supports multiple routing protocols that can support large, complex networks. It also incorporates better error detection and handling, and works with more kinds of computers than any other protocol. The following is a list of the elements shown in Figure 7-1:

- *Other:* Any of the nearly 40 other service/application-level protocols defined for TCP/IP

- **File Transfer Protocol (FTP)**: The service protocol and corresponding TCP/IP application that permit network file transfer

- **Telnet**: The service protocol and corresponding TCP/IP applications that support networked terminal emulation services

- **Simple Mail Transfer Protocol (SMTP)**: The most common e-mail service protocol in the TCP/IP environment. (POP3, the Post Office Protocol version 3, and IMAP, the Internet Message Access Protocol, are also involved in a great deal of Internet e-mail traffic.)

- **User Datagram Protocol (UDP)**: A secondary transport protocol on TCP/IP networks, UDP is a lightweight cousin of TCP. It is **connectionless**, has low overhead, and offers best-effort delivery rather than the delivery guarantees offered by TCP. It is used for all kinds of services on TCP networks, including NFS and TFTP.

- **Network File System (NFS)**: A UDP-based networked file system originally developed by Sun Microsystems and widely used on many TCP/IP networks. (Windows 2000 does not include built-in NFS support, but numerous third-party options are available.)

- **Trivial File Transfer Protocol (TFTP)**: A lightweight, UDP-based alternative to FTP designed primarily to permit users running Telnet sessions elsewhere on a network to grab files from remote machines

- **Domain Name Service (DNS)**: An address resolution service for TCP/IP-based networks that translates between numeric IP addresses and symbolic names known formally as fully qualified domain names (FQDNs)

- **Simple Network Management Protocol (SNMP)**: The primary management protocol used on TCP/IP networks, SNMP is used to report management data to management consoles or applications and to interrogate repositories of management data around a network

- **Transmission Control Protocol (TCP)**: The primary transport protocol in TCP/IP, TCP is a robust, reliable, guaranteed delivery, **connection-oriented** transport protocol

- *Routing protocols:* These embrace a number of important IP protocols, including the Routing Internet Protocol (RIP), the Open Shortest Path First (OSPF) protocol, the Border Gateway Protocol (BGP), and others.

- **Address Resolution Protocol (ARP)**: Used to map from a numeric IP address to a MAC-layer address

- *Reverse Address Resolution Protocol (RARP):* Used to map from a MAC-layer address to a numeric IP address

- **Internet Protocol (IP)**: The primary protocol in TCP/IP, IP includes network addressing information that is manipulated when a packet is routed from sender to receiver, along with data integrity and network status information.

- **Internet Control Message Protocol (ICMP)**: The protocol that deals with quality of service, availability, and network behavior information; also supports the **PING (Packet Internet Groper)** utility often used to inquire if an address is reachable on the Internet

- *IEEE 802.X:* Includes the 802.2 networking standard, plus standard networking technologies such as Ethernet (802.3) and Token Ring (802.5), among others

- **Asynchronous Transfer Mode (ATM)**: A cell-oriented, fiber- and copper-based networking technology that supports data rates from 25 Mbps to as high as 2.4 Gbps

- *Fiber Distributed Data Interface (FDDI):* A 100 Mbps fiber-based networking technology.

- *Integrated Services Digital Network (ISDN):* A digital alternative to analog telephony, ISDN links support 2 or more 64-Kbps channels per connection, depending on type.

- *X.25:* An ITU standard for packet-switched networking, X.25 is very common outside the U.S., where its robust data-handling makes it a good match for substandard telephone networks.

- *Ethernet II:* An older version of Ethernet that preceded the 802.3 specification, Ethernet II offers the same 10 Mbps as standard Ethernet, but uses different frame formats.

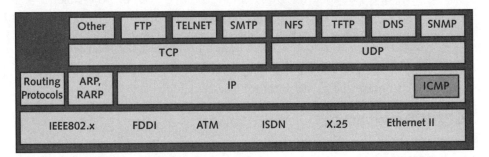

Figure 7-1   TCP/IP protocol stack

Table 7-1   Protocols in the Windows TCP/IP Stack

Protocol	Primary Function
Simple Network Management Protocol (SNMP)	Allows monitoring across host computers
Windows Sockets API	The standard interface between TCP/IP socket applications and protocols
NBT	NetBIOS over TCP/IP: Provides NetBIOS naming services
Transmission Control Protocol (TCP)	Provides connection-oriented services
User Datagram Protocol (UDP)	Provides connectionless services
Address Resolution Protocol (ARP)	Obtains hardware addresses for communication at the Network layer
Internet Protocol (IP)	Provides addressing and routing functions
Internet Control Message Protocol (ICMP)	Reports messages and errors regarding data delivery

In addition to its many services and capabilities, TCP/IP also supports the following:

- Direct Internet access from any TCP/IP-equipped computer with a link to the Internet, by phone, some kind of digital link (ISDN, frame relay, T1, and so forth), or across any network with routed Internet access

- Powerful network management protocols and services, such as SNMP and the Desktop Management Interface (DMI, which supports interrogation of desktop hardware and software configuration data)

- Dynamic Host Configuration Protocol (DHCP), which provides unique IP addresses on demand and automates IP address management

- Microsoft Windows Internet Naming Service (WINS) to enable IP-based NetBIOS name browsing for Microsoft clients and servers, as well as the Domain Name Service (DNS) that is the most common name resolution service used to map FQDNs to numeric IP addresses throughout the Internet

Unlike IPX/SPX, the InterNIC manages all TCP/IP domain names, network numbers, and IP addresses, to make the global Internet work reliably.

TCP/IP Drawbacks

For all the clear advantages of TCP/IP, there are some drawbacks. Configuring and managing a TCP/IP-based network requires a fair degree of expertise, careful planning, and constant maintenance and attention. Each of the many services and protocols that TCP/IP supports brings its own unique installation, configuration, and management chores. In addition, there's a huge mass of information and unforgiving detail work involved in establishing and maintaining a TCP/IP-based network. In short, it's a demanding and unforgiving environment, and should always be approached with great care.

DATA LINK CONTROL

The **Data Link Control (DLC)** transport mechanism is not designed for connectivity between computers, as are the other transport protocols we discuss. Windows 2000 uses DLC to connect to IBM mainframes (via 3270 terminal emulation) or to access network-attached printers such as the HP 4si.

DLC offers only limited functionality as a network transport. It has been supplanted by TCP/IP in most networks because most direct-attached printers available today rely primarily on TCP/IP-based remote printing protocols. TCP/IP supports IBM host access protocols such as Tn3270 and Tn5250; these protocols not only provide better terminal emulation capabilities, but also are inherently routable and do not rely on extensive broadcast traffic, as does DLC.

DLC has the following disadvantages:

- It cannot support higher-level file transfer protocols (that is, it's good only for printing and terminal emulation, and that's all).

- It is not only unroutable, it's also hard to bridge.

- It is a simple, primitive network transport and is entirely unsuited for higher-level services.

INTERPROCESS COMMUNICATION (IPC)

In the Windows 2000 environment, communication among processes is quite important because of the operating system's multitasking, multithreaded architecture. **Interprocess communication (IPC)** defines a way for such processes to exchange information. This mechanism is general-purpose, so it doesn't matter whether such communications occur on the same computer or between networked computers. IPC defines a way for client computers to request services from some servers and permits servers to reply to requests for services. In Figure 7-2, IPC operates directly below the redirector on the client side and the network file system on the server side to provide a standard communications interface for handling requests and replies.

In Windows 2000, IPC mechanisms fall into two categories: programming interfaces and file systems. Programming interfaces permit general, open-ended client/server dialog as mediated by applications or system services. Normally, such dialog is not strictly related to data streams or data files. File systems support file sharing between clients and servers. Where programming interfaces are concerned, individual APIs differ depending on what kinds of client-server dialog they support. Where file systems are concerned, they must behave the same way, no matter how (or where) they employ Windows 2000 networked file systems and services.

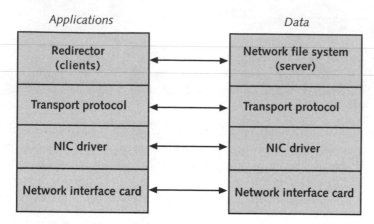

Figure 7-2   Interprocess communication between client and server

IPC File System Mechanisms

Windows 2000 includes two IPC interfaces for file system access: named pipes and mailslots. These mechanisms work through the Windows 2000 redirector, which distinguishes between local and network resource requests. This process permits one simple set of file I/O commands to handle both local and network access to file system data.

Named Pipes

Named pipes support a connection-oriented message-passing service for clients and servers. To be connection-oriented, a message's receiver must acknowledge each message received. Named pipes offer a reliable method for clients and servers to exchange requests, replies, and associated files. Named pipes provide their own methods to ensure reliable data transfer, which makes them a good match for lightweight, unreliable transport protocols such as the User Datagram Protocol. In short, named pipes delivery guarantees make transport-level delivery guarantees less essential.

The Windows 2000 version of named pipes includes a security feature called impersonation, which permits the server side of the named pipes interface to masquerade as a client that requests a service. This allows the interface to check the client's access rights and to make sure that the client's request is legal, before returning any reply to a request for data.

Mailslots File System

Mailslots are like a connectionless version of named pipes; mailslots offer no delivery guarantees, nor do they acknowledge the successful receipt of data. Windows 2000 uses mailslots as an internal method of supporting nonessential system-to-system communications. Such things as registering names for computers, domains, and users across a network, passing messages related to the Windows 2000 browser service, and providing support for broadcasting text messages across the network fall into this category. Except for such lightweight uses, mailslots are used less frequently than named pipes.

IPC Programming Interfaces

For communications to succeed, the client and server sides of an application must share a common programming interface. Windows 2000 offers a number of distinct interfaces to support IPC mechanisms for various kinds of client/server applications. Windows 2000 supports several programming interfaces, including NetBIOS, Windows Sockets, RPC, and NetDDE.

 External applications can support other programming interfaces or implement private interfaces.

NetBIOS

NetBIOS is a widely used but simple PC client/server IPC mechanism. Because it is so easy to program, it has remained quite popular ever since IBM published its definition in 1985. NetBIOS services are required to permit a Microsoft Windows network to operate. Fortunately, NetBIOS works with all TDI-compliant transports, including NetBEUI (NBF), NWLink (NWLink over NetBIOS or NWNBLink), and TCP/IP (NBT).

Windows Sockets (WinSock)

Windows Sockets (WinSock) defines a standardized and broadly deployed interface to network transports such as TCP/IP and IPX. WinSock was created to migrate UNIX applications written to the Berkeley Sockets specification to the Windows environment. WinSock also makes it easier to standardize network communications used on multiple platforms, because one socket interface is much like another, even if one runs on UNIX and the other on some variety of Windows (such as Windows 2000, where WinSock 2.0 is becoming the standard sockets API).

WinSock appears in many programs that originated as UNIX programs, including the majority of Internet utilities, especially the most popular IP utilities, such as Web browsers, e-mail software, and file transfer programs.

Remote Procedure Call (RPC)

Remote Procedure Call (RPC) implements IPC tools that can invoke separate programs on remote computers, supply them with input, and collect whatever results they produce. This permits the distribution of a single processing task among multiple computers, a process that can improve overall performance and help balance the processing load across numerous machines.

RPC is indifferent to where its client and server portions reside. It's possible for both client and server portions of an application to run on a single computer. In that case, they will communicate using local procedure call (LPC) mechanisms. This makes building such applications easy because they can be constructed on one computer, while allowing processing to be distributed on one machine or across many machines, as processing needs dictate. This creates an environment that is both flexible and powerful.

RPC consists of four basic components:

- A remote stub procedure that packages RPC requests for transmission to a server. It's called a stub because it acts as a simple, extremely compact front end to a remote process that may be much larger and more complex elsewhere on the network.

- An RPC run-time system to pass data between local and remote machines or between client and server processes.

- An application stub procedure that receives requests from the run-time RPC system. Upon such receipt, this stub procedure formats requests for the designated target RPC computer and makes the necessary procedure call. This procedure call can be either a local procedure call (if both client and server components are running on the same computer) or a remote procedure call (if client and server components are running on two machines).

- One or more remote procedures, which may be called for service (whether locally or across the network).

NetDDE

Network Dynamic Data Exchange (NetDDE) creates ongoing data streams called exchange pipes (or simply pipes) between two applications across a network. This process works just like Microsoft's local **Dynamic Data Exchange (DDE)**, which creates data exchange pipes between two applications on the same machine. DDE facilitates data sharing, object linking and embedding (OLE), and dynamic updates between linked applications. NetDDE extends local DDE across the network.

NetDDE services are installed by default during the base Windows 2000 installation, but they remain dormant until they are explicitly started. NetDDE services must be started using the Services control in Computer Management, where they appear under the headings Network DDE (the client side of NetDDE) and Network DDE DSDM (DDE Share Database Manager, the server side of NetDDE).

Distributed Component Object Model (DCOM)

DCOM (previously known as "Network OLE") is a protocol that facilitates the communication of application components over a network by providing a reliable, secure, and efficient mechanism for exchanging information. DCOM can operate over most network transport mechanisms, including HTTP. Microsoft based its implementation of DCOM on the Open Software Foundation's DCE-RPC specification, but expanded its capabilities to include Java and ActiveX support.

Windows Network (WNet) Interface

The WNet interface allows applications to take advantage of Windows 2000 networking capabilities through a standardized API. This means that the application does not require specific control data about the network provider or implementation, allowing applications to be network-independent while still able to interact with network-based resources.

Win32 Internet API (WinInet)

The WinInet API is a mechanism that enables applications to take advantage of Internet functionality without requiring extensive proprietary programming. Via WinInet, applications can be designed to include FTP, Web, and Gopher support with a minimum of additional coding. WinInet makes interacting with Internet resources as simple as reading files from a local hard drive, without requiring programming to WinSock or TCP/IP.

REDIRECTORS

A **redirector** examines all requests for system resources and decides whether such requests are local (they can be found on the requesting machine) or remote. The redirector handles transmission of remote requests across the network so that the requests are filled.

Windows 2000 file and print sharing are regarded as the most important functions supplied by any network operating system. Windows 2000 delivers these services through two critical components: the Workstation service and the Server service. Both of these services are essentially file system drivers that operate in unison with other file system drivers that can access local file systems on a Windows 2000 machine. The following components are redirectors that operate at this level:

- Workstation service

- Server service

- Multiple Universal Naming Convention Provider (MUP)

- Multi-Provider Router (MPR)

All of these system components take client requests for service and redirect them to an appropriate network service provider. Redirectors interact and interface directly with user applications. The sections that follow explain more about each of these components and their roles in the Windows 2000 networking environment.

Workstation Service

The **Workstation service** supports client access to network resources and handles functions such as logging in, connecting to network shares (directories and printers), and creating links using the Windows 2000 IPC options. The Workstation service has two elements, the User mode interface and the redirector. The User mode interface determines the particular file system that any User mode file I/O request is referencing. The redirector recognizes and translates requests for remote file and print services and forwards them to lower-level **boundary layers** aimed at network access and delivery.

This service encompasses a redirector file system that handles access to shared directories on networked computers. The file system is used further to satisfy remote access requests, but if any request uses a network name to refer to a local resource, it will pass that request to local file system drivers instead.

The Workstation service requires that at least one TDI-compliant transport and at least one MUP are running. Otherwise, the service cannot function properly because it supports connections with other Windows 2000 machines (through their Server services), LAN Manager, LAN Server, and other MS-Net servers, which require a MUP to be running. The Workstation service, like any other redirector, communicates with transport protocols through the common TDI boundary layer.

Server Service

The Windows 2000 **Server service** handles the creation and management of shared resources and performs security checks against requests for such resources, including directories and printers. The Server service allows a Windows 2000 computer to act as a server on a client/server network, up to the maximum number of licensed clients. This limits to 10 the number of simultaneous connections possible to a Windows 2000 Professional machine, in keeping with its built-in connection limitations.

Just as with the Workstation service, the Server service operates as a file system driver. Therefore, it also uses other file system drivers to satisfy I/O requests. The Server service is also divided into two elements:

- *Server.exe:* Manages client connection requests.
- *Srv.sys:* The redirector file system that operates across the network, and that interacts with other local file system drivers when necessary.

Multiple Universal Naming Convention Provider (MUP)

Windows 2000 supports multiple redirectors that can be active simultaneously. As an example, both the Workstation and Server services and the NetWare redirector built into the Windows 2000 **Client Service for NetWare (CSNW)** can be active at the same time. Like the Server service, the NetWare redirector handles Microsoft Windows network shares, but exposes them to NetWare clients instead of Microsoft network clients. The ability to support multiple clients uniformly is possible because a common provider interface allows Windows 2000 to treat all redirectors the same way.

The **Multiple Universal Naming Convention Provider (MUP)** defines a link between applications that make UNC requests for different redirectors. MUP allows applications to remain oblivious to the number or type of redirectors that might be in use. For incoming requests, the MUP also decides which redirector should handle that request by parsing the UNC share name that appears within the request.

Here's how the MUP works: When the I/O subsystem receives any request that includes a UNC name, it turns that request over to the MUP. The MUP first checks its internal list of recently accessed shares, which it maintains over time. If the MUP recognizes the UNC name, it immediately passes the request to the required redirector. If it doesn't recognize the UNC name, the MUP sends the request to each registered redirector and requests that it service the request.

The MUP chooses redirectors on the basis of the highest registered response time during which the redirector claims it can connect to a UNC name, information that can be cached until no activity occurs for 15 minutes. This can make trying a series of redirectors incredibly time-consuming and helps explain why the binding order of protocols is so important, because that also influences the order in which name resolution requests will be handled.

Universal Naming Convention Names

Universal Naming Convention (UNC) names represent the format used in NetBIOS-oriented name resolution systems. UNC names precede the computer portion of a name with two slashes, followed by a slash that precedes (and separates elements of) the share name and the directory path, followed by the requested filename. Thus the following string:

> \\computername\sharename\dir-path\filename.ext

represents a valid UNC name. In this example the name of the computer is "computername," the name of the share is "sharename," the directory path is "dir-path," and the file is named "filename.ext."

Multi-Provider Router (MPR)

Not all programs use UNC names in the Windows 2000 environment. Programs that call the Win32 API must use a file system service called the **Multi-Provider Router (MPR)** to designate the proper redirector to handle a resource request. The MPR lets applications written to older Microsoft specifications behave as if they were written to conform to UNC naming. The MPR is able to recognize the UNCs that represent drive mappings, so it can decide which redirector can handle a mapped network drive letter (such as X:) and make sure that a request that references that drive can be properly satisfied.

The MPR handles all Win32 network API calls, passing resource requests from that interface to those redirectors that register their presence through special-purpose dynamic link libraries (DLLs). That is, any redirector that wants to support the MPR must provide a DLL that communicates through the common MPR interface. Normally this means that whichever network developer supplies a redirector must also supply this DLL. Microsoft implemented CSNW as a DLL that supports this interface. This allows the NetWare redirector to provide the same kind of transparent file system and network resource access as other Windows 2000 redirectors.

NETWORKING UNDER WINDOWS 2000

The Windows 2000 networking system is controlled by a single multifaceted interface that combines networking access for LAN, Internet, and modem. The interface is called Network and Dial-up Connections (see Figure 7-3). It is accessed through the Settings entry in the Start menu or through the My Computer, Control Panel display.

Adding new network interface cards (NICs) to Windows 2000 Professional is handled in the same fashion as installing any other piece of hardware—physically install it, allow

Windows 2000 Plug and Play to detect it, and install the appropriate driver(s), or use the Add/Remove Hardware applet to manually install the device. Both of these procedures are discussed in Chapter 3. Once a new NIC is installed, Windows 2000 automatically creates a new Local Area Connection icon, which you can use to customize the settings for your networking needs.

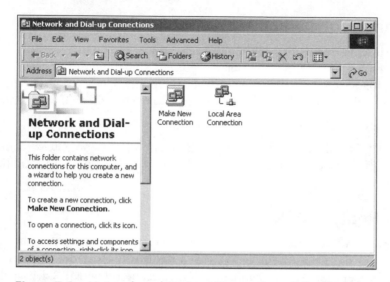

Figure 7-3   Network and Dial-up Connections dialog box

Network and Dial-up Connections is an Internet Explorer-based tool used to create and configure network connections. The Make New Connection icon links to a wizard that takes the user through the process of establishing new network links. The wizard is used for any network links employing modems, virtual private networks (VPNs) over the Internet, or serial, parallel, or infrared ports. Windows 2000 automatically enables all "normal" network links achieved through a network adapter and an attached cable. A Local Area Connection icon is listed in the Network and Dial-up Connections window for each installed adapter. If there are two or more LAN connections, rename the Local Area Connection icons to reflect the domain, network, or purpose of the link. (Try Hands-on Project 7-1 to view the status of a local area connection.)

Existing Local Area Connections can be configured by opening the Properties for that object either via the File menu or the right-click menu. A typical default configuration of a Local Area Connection Properties dialog box is shown in Figure 7-4, listing the adapter in use as well as all installed protocols and services that can function over this interface. The Configure button is used to access the Properties dialog box for the adapter. Each listed service or protocol has a check box. When checked, the protocol or service is bound to the adapter (that is, it can operate over the network link established by the adapter). When unchecked, the protocol of service is not bound to the adapter.

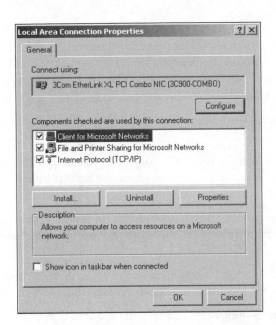

Figure 7-4   A Local Area Connection Properties dialog box

The Install button is used to add new client interfaces, protocols, and services that any of the Connection objects can use. When a new element is added, all possible bindings are enabled by default. The following are the additional networking elements (not including the default elements listed in Figure 7-4) that can be installed in Windows 2000 Professional:

- *Client: Client Service for NetWare*—Used to gain access to NetWare resources (see Chapter 8)

- *Service: QoS Packet Scheduler*—An extension service for WinSock used to reserve bandwidth for communications

- *Service: SAP Agent*—Used by Windows 2000 to participate actively in NetWare networks (see Chapter 8)

- *Protocol: AppleTalk Protocol*—Used to access Macintosh-hosted printers

- *Protocol: DLC Protocol*—Used to access network attached printers or IBM mainframes

- *Protocol: NetBEUI Protocol*—Nonroutable protocol

- *Protocol: Network Monitor Driver*—Driver used to allow full versions of Network Monitor to obtain network activity information from Windows 2000 Professional systems

- *Protocol: NWLink IPX/SPX/NetBIOS Compatible Transport Protocol*—Protocol most often used on NetWare networks (see Chapter 8)

The Uninstall button is used to remove a client, protocol, or service. Once an element is removed, it is removed for all Connection objects. The Properties button opens the Properties dialog box for the selected installed component (client, service, or protocol). (Not all components have configurable options.) This dialog box also offers a check box control to display an icon in the icon tray when the Connection object is in use.

The Network and Dial-up Connections interface File and Advanced drop-down menus include the following functions:

- *File: Disable*—Prevents the selected Connection object from being used to establish a communications link. This command is for automatic connections, such as those for a LAN.

- *File: Enable*—Allows the selected Connection object to be used to establish a communications link. This command is for automatic connections, such as those for a LAN.

- *File: Connect*—Launches the selected Connection object to establish a communications link. This command is for manual connections, such as those over a modem.

- *File: Status*—Displays a Status window for the selected Connection object that lists whether the object is connected, how long the connection has been active, the speed of the connection, and packet counts. This window offers Properties and Disable buttons to perform the same functions as the File menu commands.

- *File: New Connection*—Launches the Make New Connection Wizard

- *File: Create Copy*—Creates a duplicate copy of the selected Connection object

- *File: Create Shortcut*—Creates a shortcut to the selected Connection object

- *File: Delete*—Removes the selected Connection object

- *File: Rename*—Changes the name of the selected Connection object

- *File: Properties*—Opens the Properties dialog box for the selected Connection object

- *File: Close*—Exits the Network and Dial-up Connection interface

- *Advanced: Operator-Assisted Dialing*—Used to manually dial a connection number and then have the computer take control of the line once the remote system answers the call

- *Advanced: Dial-up Preferences*—Opens a dialog box in which RAS-related controls are set (see Chapter 9)

- *Advanced: Network Identification*—Opens the Network Identification tab of the System applet that displays the current computer name and workgroup/domain name. To join a domain and create a local user, click Network ID.

- *Advanced: Advanced Settings*—Opens a dialog box where bindings and provider order can be managed. See the "Managing Bindings" section later in this chapter.

- *Advanced: Optional Networking Components*—Used to add other networking components such as Monitoring and Management Tools, Networking Services, and Other Network File and Print Services

Some of these commands appear only when a specific Connection object type is selected.

 TIP For most networks, the default Local Area Connection that Windows 2000 creates automatically is sufficient for LAN activity. As shown earlier in Figure 7-4, this Connection object is designed to link up with a Microsoft-based network (workgroup or domain), allows file and printer sharing, and employs the TCP/IP protocol.

To change the TCP/IP settings, select the protocol from the list of components in the Properties window of a Local Area Connection, then click Properties. This reveals the Internet Protocol (TCP/IP) Properties dialog box (see Figure 7-5). From here, you can easily enable DHCP for this computer, or define a static IP address, subnet mask, and gateway. You can also define the preferred and alternate DNS servers. The Advanced button brings up a multitabbed dialog box in which multiple IP addresses, additional gateways, DNS and WINS functionality, and TCP/IP service extension properties can be defined.

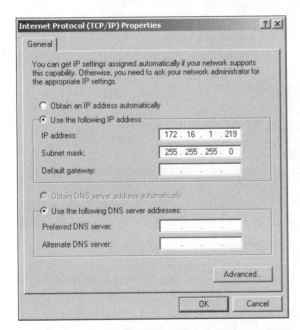

Figure 7-5 The Internet Protocol (TCP/IP) Properties dialog box

MANAGING BINDINGS

Binding refers to the order in which Windows 2000 networking components are linked. These linkages and the order in which multiple components are linked affect how the systems behave and how well they perform. Binding is defined in the Advanced Settings dialog box (see Figure 7-6). This dialog box is reached by clicking the Advanced Settings command from the Advanced menu of the Network and Dial-up Connections window. (You can view network bindings in Hands-on Project 7-5.)

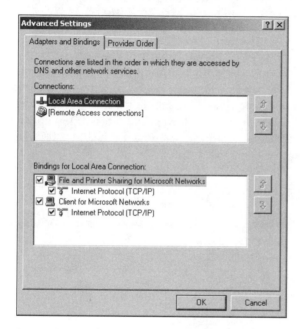

Figure 7-6 The Advanced Settings dialog box, Adapters and Bindings tab

By default, Windows 2000 binds any two components that share a common boundary layer, unless such bindings are explicitly removed. In fact, Windows 2000 binds all components that share a common boundary to the boundary layer they share, unless one or more of these bindings is removed manually.

Because this default is what is called "complete binding"—that is, all possible bindings are created—it can lead to system inefficiencies, especially when bindings are created that will not be used. Such unused bindings might appear higher in the binding order than bindings that are used. This arrangement can build delays into the system because the MUP attempts to satisfy UNC requests for names it does not recognize in the order in which bindings appear, and unused bindings must time out before the next binding in the order is attempted.

Disabling all protocol bindings that are not needed or used improves system performance and decreases the likelihood of communication errors. If remote access with NetBEUI is not required, disable the binding between the NetBEUI transport and the Remote Access WAN

Wrapper (it appears as a "virtual" adapter in the bindings list). It's also important to understand that because clients (in this case Windows 2000 Professional machines) initiate communications with Windows 2000 Servers, changing the binding order of protocols on clients is what matters. Servers respond using whatever protocol requests appear within the transmission, so changing their binding order won't do much to improve performance. Changing a client's binding order, on the other hand, can sometimes deliver dramatic performance improvements.

Binding priority affects network performance because Windows 2000 makes connections according to the order in which protocols are bound. For two machines that use NetBEUI and TCP/IP, Windows 2000 uses whichever protocol appears higher in the services binding list. If both computers run NetBEUI and TCP/IP, and NetBEUI ranks higher than TCP/IP in the binding list, they will establish a faster connection (NetBEUI is faster than TCP/IP) than if the bindings were reversed. To change the priority for any transport protocol, highlight an object on the Adapters and Bindings tab, then use the arrow buttons to increase or decrease its priority level. You can also unbind services and protocols by unselecting the check box in front of the object's name.

The Provider Order tab is used to alter the binding priority of various providers, such as network connectivity or print servers. This is useful only when two or more providers of the same type can be employed by a system. For example, if a computer can participate in NetWare and Windows 2000 networking environments, it can be useful to change the priority of the providers to favor the most often accessed network.

7

TCP/IP ARCHITECTURE

TCP/IP supports easy cross-platform communications and provides the technical foundation for the Internet. TCP/IP is actually a suite of protocols; in this discussion, we break it down into IP and TCP. Under each of these protocols lie many additional protocols that give the TCP/IP suite such a wide range of functionality.

Internet Protocol

The Internet Protocol (IP) provides source and destination addressing and routing in the TCP/IP suite. IP addresses are logical addresses that are 32 bits (4 bytes) long. Each byte, or octet, is represented by a decimal number from 0 to 255 and separated from the others by a period, for example, 183.24.206.18. IP is a connectionless datagram protocol that, like all connectionless protocols, is fast but unreliable. IP assumes that other protocols will be available to ensure reliable delivery of the data.

 TIP Although 8 bits have 256 possible combinations, the numbers 0 and 255 are reserved for special purposes. In the range of 0–255, the zero address is reserved to identify the network, and the 255 address is used for broadcasts that are read by all IP hosts on the network. IP network hosts can use only numbers 1 through 254. "Host" is the IP-specific term that identifies any device on an IP network that is assigned a specific address.

Part of the IP address assigned to a computer designates which network the computer is on, and the remainder of the address represents the host ID of that computer. The 4 bytes that IP uses for addresses can be broken up in multiple ways; in fact, several classes of IP addresses have been defined that use different boundaries for the network part and the host ID part. These are shown in Table 7-2.

Table 7-2   Classes of IP Addresses

Class	Network IDs	Host IDs	Usable Network IDs
A	126	16,777,214	1–126
B	16,328	65,534	128.1–191.255
C	2,097,150	254	192.0.1–223.255.254

In a Class A address, the first octet is used to identify the network, and the three trailing octets are used to identify the hosts. This creates a situation in which a small number of networks (126, to be exact) is possible, but a large number of hosts (over 16 million per network) can be defined on each one. Class B addresses split the octets evenly, so the first two identify the network and the second two identify the host. This permits over 16,000 networks with over 65,000 hosts. Class C addresses use the first three octets for the network portion of an address and the final octet for the host portion. This permits over two million networks, but only a maximum of 254 hosts for each Class C network.

For example, if a computer has an address of 183.24.206.18, this indicates that it is a Class B address because the first two octets fall in the range of 128.1–191.255, as indicated in the fourth column of Table 7-2. Thus, the first two octets represent the network address (183.24), and the host address portion is 206.18. The computer next to it might have the address of 183.24.208.192, which indicates that it's on the same network (183.24) but has a different host address (208.192).

IP uses a special bit mask called a **subnet mask** to determine which part of an address denotes the network and which part the host. The job of the subnet mask is to block out the host section of the address so that only the network ID portion remains significant. For the addresses on the 183.24 network, the subnet mask can be stated as 255.255.0.0. Notice that the two most significant octets are occupied by a binary value that translates into all ones (255 is 11111111 in binary), whereas the host portion is all zeros (0 is the same as 00000000 in binary).

Sometimes IP network administrators use part of what the IP address class considers the host portion of an address to further subdivide a single Class A, B, or C network. You might see the occasional subnet mask that looks like 255.192 for a Class A network, 255.255.192 for a Class B network, and 255.255.255.192 for a Class C network. 192 equals 11000000 in binary, so this extends the network portion two digits into the host ID portion of the address and permits defining two subnets within a single range of host addresses. The top and bottom values (0 and 3, in this case) are reserved to identify the subnetwork and to handle broadcasts, respectively.

Another form of addressing is increasingly used on IP networks, especially when individual networks don't need, or can't use, an entire Class B or Class C address. This technique is called Classless Interdomain Routing (CIDR), pronounced "cider".) CIDR uses the same technique described in the preceding paragraph to let Internet service providers (ISPs) subdivide their available addresses into more numerous subnetworks and make better use of the IP address space that's still available.

All TCP/IP addresses must be unique on the Internet—and in fact, on any IP-based network. If two IP addresses are identical, neither machine with that address will be able to access the network. That's why managing IP addresses is quite important. At present, this responsibility falls under the aegis of the InterNIC. All the Class A addresses were handed out years ago, most Class Bs have been allocated, and Class C addresses are becoming scarce. (When you add all possible networks allowed by all three address classes, you get the maximum number of individual networks on the Internet as 2,113,604). Given the vast number of networks on the Internet and the continuing growth in that arena, it is clear that subnet masking tricks and CIDR merely represent stopgap measures to extend the current address space as much as possible. At the same time, the standards body that governs the Internet (the IAB, or Internet Activities Board) is working to complete a new version of TCP/IP called IPv6 (the current version is IPv4) that will extend the address space significantly. (The address space expands to 128 bits with IPv6, as compared to the current 32 bits; this is enough to support trillions of networks with trillions of nodes per network.)

 All IP-based devices on a single network segment must use the same subnet mask.

Internet Control Message Protocol (ICMP)

Internet Control Message Protocol (ICMP) is used to send control messages (such as error messages, quality of service information, and confirmations) between IP hosts. PING is used to request a response from a remote host. It uses ICMP to return messages regarding this function, such as whether the response was received or timed out, or the host was not reachable. (PING is covered in more detail in a later section.)

Address Resolution Protocol (ARP)

The Address Resolution Protocol (ARP) is used to associate a logical (IP) address to a physical (MAC) address. When a system begins a conversation with a host for which it does not have a physical address, the system sends an ARP broadcast packet requesting a physical address that corresponds to the logical address. Given this information, the packet can be correctly sent across a physical network.

Ethernet is the common form of network in use, and on most networks the MAC address is identical to the Ethernet address. The Ethernet or M address is a 48-bit address normally represented as 12 hexadecimal digits. In other words, on an Ethernet network the physical address or MAC address is the same as the Ethernet address burned into PROM on the network interface card that attaches a computer to a network. On other types of networks, the interfaces also supply unique MAC layer addresses, but their formats vary according to the kind of network in use.

Dynamic Host Configuration Protocol (DHCP)

The Dynamic Host Configuration Protocol (DHCP) is used to automatically configure computers. A DHCP server manages a defined block of IP addresses that can be assigned to computers upon request. Network devices basically take out a lease on an address, and can use that address only so long as the lease remains valid. The DHCP server handles granting, renewing, or canceling such leases. It can also block out reserved IP addresses within a numeric range, permitting certain computers (which may not be able to communicate with the DHCP server) to use static, fixed IP address assignments.

Using DHCP makes it easy for network administrators to manage IP addresses, and makes it more or less automatic for users to gain access to IP-based resources. DHCP has proven to be a real boon for those reasons, and one of the best features of Windows 2000 is that it can be configured for TCP/IP by selecting a single radio button on the IP Protocol Properties dialog box that reads "Obtain an IP address automatically."

Transmission Control Protocol

Transmission Control Protocol (TCP) is the primary Internet transport protocol. It accepts messages of any length and provides transport to a TCP peer on a remote network host. TCP is connection-oriented, so it provides more reliable delivery than connectionless-oriented IP. When a connection is established, a TCP port number is used to determine which process on the designated host is to receive any particular packet. TCP is responsible for message fragmentation and reassembly. It uses a sequencing function to ensure that packets are reassembled in the correct order, and includes mechanisms both to acknowledge successful delivery of correct packets and to request retransmission of damaged or lost packets.

UDP

User Datagram Protocol (UDP) is a connectionless protocol. As a result of its reduced overhead, it is generally faster, although less reliable, than TCP. UDP was designed primarily to transport purely local services, where it is relatively safe to assume network reliability. This is one reason why it's used for distributed file systems like the Network File System (NFS) and for the Trivial File Transfer Protocol (TFTP), where the underlying assumption is that access is either purely local (NFS) or that guaranteed delivery is not required (TFTP).

FTP

File Transfer Protocol (FTP) provides file transfer services, as well as directory and file manipulation services, such as listing directory contents, deleting files, and specifying file formats.

 A command-line version of FTP is available as part of Windows 2000. To learn more about this command, open a Command Prompt window (Start, Programs, Accessories, Command Prompt) and enter *FTP* at the command line, then enter *?*. This produces the Help file for FTP.

Telnet

Telnet is a remote terminal emulation protocol that is primarily used to provide connectivity between dissimilar systems (PC and VAX/VMS, PC and router, UNIX and VMS), where the remote client works on the Telnet host machine as if it were a terminal attached directly to that host. Using Telnet, remote equipment, such as routers and switches, can be monitored and configured, or remote systems can be operated as needed. Despite a primitive, character-oriented interface, Telnet remains one of the most important IP services.

 A 32-bit windowed version of Telnet is available as part of Windows 2000. To learn more about this utility, launch Telnet (execute *Telnet* from a Start, Run command) and access its Help utility.

SMTP

Simple Mail Transfer Protocol (SMTP) is used to provide IP-based messaging services. Although it is not the only e-mail protocol available in the IP environment, most experts regard SMTP as the basis for Internet e-mail.

SNMP

Simple Network Management Protocol (SNMP) is a TCP/IP protocol used for network management. SNMP is an industry-standard protocol supported by most networking equipment manufacturers. SNMP can query collections of management data, called management information bases (MIBs), on networked devices. This permits management applications to use SNMP to poll devices on the network and obtain regular status updates about their operating conditions, network utilization, and quality of service.

In addition, SNMP supports a "trap" mechanism that permits networked devices to send a message to a management application when specific events or error conditions occur. This capability is quite important because it permits networked devices to report potential or actual problems as soon as they're detected, rather than waiting for a management application to poll the device.

 SNMP services are not activated by default on Windows 2000. To enable these services, use the Optional Networking Components command from the Advanced menu of the Network and Dial-up Connections interface.

The Berkeley R Utilities

Among the many enhancements added to the UNIX TCP/IP implementation present in the Berkeley Software Distribution (BSD) in the 1980s was a collection of IP-based network commands collectively known as the "R utilities," where the "R" stands for remote. This includes such commands as **rsh (remote shell)**, which permit a user on one network host to access shell commands on another network host, and **rexec (remote execution)**, which permits a user on one network host to execute a program remotely on another network host. Windows 2000 Professional supports both of these R utilities from the client side (but cannot act as a rsh or rexec server to other machines elsewhere on the network).

 To learn more about rsh and rexec, open a Command Prompt window (Start, Programs, Accessories, Command Prompt) and enter either *rsh ?* or *rexec ?* to access the Help files for these command-line utilities.

PING

Packet Internet Groper (PING) is one of the most colorful acronyms in the TCP/IP utility box. PING is a command-line utility that uses the ICMP protocol to inquire if a designated host is reachable on the network. It also provides information about the round-trip time required to deliver a message to that machine and receive a reply. (Try using PING in Hands-on Project 7-2 at the end of the chapter.)

PING is a very useful utility that permits you to see if your own machine is properly attached to the network. You can PING yourself by entering the command PING 127.0.0.1 or PING loopback; in the latter case, this special address is defined as the loopback address, or the address of your own machine. You can find out if the network itself is working (by PINGing a nearby machine). Finally, you can determine if a particular machine is reachable (by PINGing either its host name or the equivalent numeric IP address). All of this capability comes in handy when you are installing and testing IP on a new machine or when you need to troubleshoot a network connection.

 To learn more about PING, launch a Command Prompt window (Start, Programs, Accessories, Command Prompt) and enter PING (with no arguments) to access its online Help file. Note that PING can supply all kinds of routing and quality of service data, as well as simply test for reachability.

TFTP

Trivial File Transfer Protocol (TFTP) is a lightweight analog of FTP that uses UDP as its transport protocol rather than TCP. TFTP is a more stripped-down version of file transfer services than FTP; it basically supports the ability to communicate with a TFTP server elsewhere on the network and to copy files from the workstation to a remote host, or vice versa. For directory navigation, file grooming, or format translations, FTP is a much better choice.

To learn more about TFTP, open a Command Prompt window (Start, Programs, Accessories, Command Prompt), and enter *TFTP ?* to view its online Help file.

The HOSTS File

The **HOSTS** file is a static file placed on members of a network to provide a resolution mechanism between host names and IP addresses. The HOSTS file was the name resolution mechanism used before DNS was created. HOSTS files are used only on small networks where the deployment of a DNS server is unwarranted or for remote systems to reduce traffic over slow WAN links. Each line of a HOSTS file contains an IP address followed by one or more corresponding host names to that IP address. A system processes the HOSTS file on a line-by-line basis when attempting to resolve a host name. Once the first match is reached, the resolution process terminates and the acquired IP address is used. HOSTS files are only as useful as they are current. Most administrators update their HOSTS file on a regular basis and have a logon script automatically download the HOSTS file from a central location to remote systems each time they log on to the network.

Windows 2000 includes a sample HOSTS file in the %systemroot%\System32\drivers\etc folder. The HOSTS file is a plain text document that can be edited with Notepad or any other text editor. Basic information about editing the HOSTS file is included in its own header text, but for complete information consult the *Windows 2000 Resource Kit.*

DNS

Domain Name Service (DNS) is a critical component of the Internet's ability to span the globe. DNS handles the job of translating a symbolic name such as *lanw02.lanw.com* into a corresponding numeric IP address (172.16.1.7). It can also provide reverse lookup services to detect machines that are masquerading as other hosts. (A reverse lookup obtains the symbolic name that goes with an IP address; if the two do not match, the DNS server may assume that some form of deception is at work.)

DNS is a powerful, highly distributed database that organizes IP names (which for its purposes must take the form of fully qualified domain names) into hierarchical domains. When a name resolution request occurs, all the DNS servers that can identify themselves to each other cooperate very quickly to resolve the related address. DNS servers include sophisticated caching techniques that permit them to store recently requested name-address pairs, so that users can get to a previously accessed address quickly.

Windows 2000 Professional can communicate with DNS servers, but only Windows 2000 Server supports a full-fledged DNS server implementation.

The LMHOSTS File

The **LMHOSTS** file is a static file placed on members of a network to provide a resolution mechanism between NetBIOS names and IP addresses. The LMHOSTS file was the name resolution mechanism used before WINS was created. Now LMHOSTS files are used only on small networks where the deployment of a WINS server is unwarranted or for remote systems to reduce traffic over slow WAN links. Each line of an LMHOSTS file contains an IP address followed by the corresponding NetBIOS name. A system processes the LMHOSTS file on a line-by-line basis when attempting to resolve NetBIOS names. Once the first match is reached, the resolution process terminates and the acquired IP address is used. LMHOSTS files are only as useful as they are current. Thus, most administrators update their LMHOSTS file on a regular basis and have a logon script automatically download the LMHOSTS file from a central location to remote systems each time they log on to the network.

Windows 2000 includes a sample LMHOSTS file in the %systemroot%\System32\drivers\etc folder, which is named Lmhosts.sam. The LMHOSTS file is a plain text document that can be edited with Notepad or any other text editor. (Try Hands-on Project 7-3 to view the LMHOSTS sample file.) Basic information about editing the LMHOSTS file is included in its own header text, but for more information consult the *Windows 2000 Resource Kit*.

WINS

The Windows Internet Naming Service (WINS) is not a true "native" TCP/IP service; it is an extension added by Microsoft. As previously discussed, most of the internal and network communications within a Microsoft network employ NetBIOS. On a TCP/IP network, NetBIOS names must be resolved into IP addresses so packets can be properly delivered to the intended recipient. This process is automated by WINS. WINS dynamically associates NetBIOS names with IP addresses and automatically updates its database of associations as systems enter and leave a network, so it does not require ongoing maintenance. WINS is the dynamic service that is used to replace the static mechanism of the LMHOSTS file.

TCP/IP CONFIGURATION

TCP/IP configuration is performed through the Network and Dial-up Connections interface. When configuring TCP/IP for Windows 2000 Professional, there are many items of information that you need to know. If the machine uses DHCP, the DHCP server handles all these details. If not, here's a list of items that you might need to obtain from a network administrator (or figure out for yourself, if that's your job):

- A unique IP address for the computer
- The subnet mask for the network to which the computer belongs
- The address of the default gateway, the machine that attempts to forward any IP traffic not aimed at the local subnet (which makes it the gateway to other networks)

- The address of one or more DNS servers, to provide IP name resolution services. This is more important on bigger networks than on smaller ones. If you use an ISP for network access, you'll probably need to get this address from them.

- On Windows 2000 or Windows NT networks in particular, and IP-based Microsoft networks in general, you might need to provide an address for a WINS server. This permits NetBIOS name resolution requests to be transported across IP networks (even through routers if necessary).

When TCP/IP is installed, its default settings are to seek out a DHCP server to provide all configuration settings. If a DHCP server is already present on your network, you do not need to configure TCP/IP to be able to access the network.

TCP/IP configuration takes place in the Internet Protocol (TCP/IP) Properties dialog box (refer to Figure 7-5). Access the dialog box by clicking the Properties button after selecting TCP/IP from the list of installed components from the Properties dialog box of a Local Area Connection from the Network and Dial-up Connections interface. On a multihomed system (a computer with more than one network interface card) the configuration for each adapter can be different. Be sure to select the correct Local Area Connection object for the adapter you wish to modify. (You can practice step-by-step configuration of TCP/IP in Hands-on Project 7-4.)

There are two ways to assign an IP address to a computer: manually or via DHCP. As discussed earlier, DHCP is used to automatically configure the TCP/IP settings for a computer. If a DHCP server is available and will be used to configure this computer, select the "Obtain an IP address automatically" option. If there is no DHCP server available or if the configuration is to be handled manually, select the "Use the following IP address" option.

Before you can do this, however, you must obtain a valid IP address from a network administrator or your ISP. If your network does not need to access the Internet directly (or if address translation software mediates Internet access on your behalf), you can assign "private IP" addresses from a number of reserved address ranges that the InterNIC has set aside for this purpose. To learn more about these private address ranges and how to use them, you can download a copy of RFC 1918 from the InterNIC at *ftp://ds.internet.net/rfc/rfc1918.txt.* (As an alternative, you can read a hypertext version of this document at *http://www.cis.ohio-state.edu/rfc/rfc1918.txt.*)

If you select Specify an IP address, the remaining three boxes become active. When you're finished, the IP Address box should display the correct IP address for that computer.

> If you're entering an IP address into an entry box, press the period key to jump from one octet to the next. This comes in handy when an address does not contain a three-digit number in any octet field. You can also use the right arrow key to advance the insertion point, but don't use the Tab key—it advances the insertion point to the next input field and forces you to backtrack to complete the IP address specification.

As described earlier, the subnet mask defines which part of the IP address represents the network and which part represents the host. You must supply this information or your computer will not be able to communicate using TCP/IP.

The default gateway for a computer defines the host, usually a router, to which the computer should send data that is not destined for the computer's subnet. For example, if a computer's address is 156.24.99.10 with a subnet mask of 255.255.255.0, its host address is 10 and its network address is 156.24.99. If this computer had data to send to a computer whose address was 203.15.13.69, it would send the packets to the default gateway for forwarding to the appropriate network. Whenever connectivity to other networks is required, you must provide an IP address for the default gateway on the machine's network segment. If you don't, traffic from your machine will not be able to get to machines that aren't on the same network segment as your computer.

Pressing the Advanced button opens the window shown in Figure 7-7. The IP addresses area allows you to assign multiple addresses to one network adapter, whereas the Default gateways area provides support for multiple router configurations.

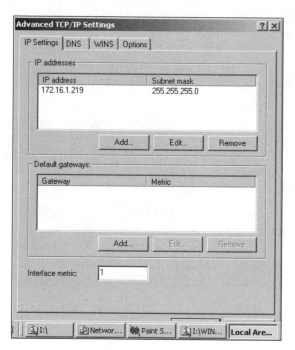

Figure 7-7   The Advanced TCP/IP Settings dialog box, IP Settings tab

By selecting the DNS tab, shown in Figure 7-8, the user is able to configure DNS on his or her computer. Multiple DNS servers can be defined along with setting their use priority. You can also define how incomplete domain names or host names are resolved (for example, by adding suffixes to create a fully qualified domain name).

Use the WINS tab (see Figure 7-9) to configure WINS settings. You can define multiple WINS servers and set their use priority. You can also enable or disable the use of an LMHOSTS file. Furthermore, you can enable, disable, or save the setting to the DHCP server whether or not this system will use NetBIOS over TCP/IP.

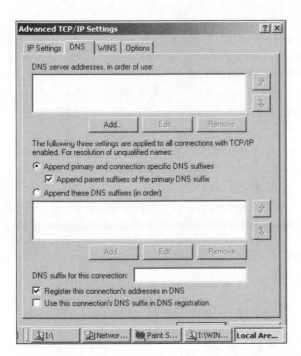

Figure 7-8   The Advanced TCP/IP Settings dialog box, DNS tab

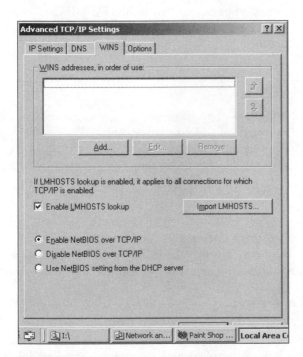

Figure 7-9   The Advanced TCP/IP Settings dialog box, WINS tab

The Options tab lists optional TCP/IP-related services or capabilities. The two default optional items are IP Security and TCP/IP filtering. Selecting a listed item and clicking Properties reveals a service-specific configuration dialog box. For more information about configuring these and other optional items, consult the *Windows 2000 Resource Kit.*

CHAPTER SUMMARY

❑ Windows 2000 supports three core network transport protocols: NetBEUI, NWLink (IPX/SPX), and TCP/IP. Each of these protocols works best on a network of a particular size, where each such network has its own special performance and access requirements.

❑ Windows 2000 Professional provides network access primarily by using TCP/IP. TCP/IP is routable, supports enterprise-level networks, and has been designed to interconnect dissimilar types of computers, which helps to explain why it's the protocol of choice on the Internet. TCP/IP is an industry-standard protocol that provides easy cross-platform communication.

❑ Interprocess communication (IPC) defines communication among the Windows 2000 operating system's threads and tasks. IPC also applies to networked computers; it defines a way for client computers to request services from some servers and permits servers to reply to requests for services. In Windows 2000, IPC mechanisms fall into two categories: programming interfaces and file systems.

❑ Windows 2000 includes a number of applications that utilize TCP/IP and provide Internet connectivity. In spite of TCP/IP's complexity, configuring Windows 2000 to employ this protocol is not difficult.

KEY TERMS

Address Resolution Protocol (ARP) — The IP protocol used to resolve numeric IP addresses into their MAC layer physical address equivalents.

Asynchronous Transfer Mode (ATM) — A cell-oriented, fiber- and copper-based networking technology that supports data rates from 25 Mbps to as high as 2.4 Gbps.

binding — The process of developing a stack by linking network services and protocols. The binding facility allows users to define exactly how network services operate in order to optimize the network performance.

boundary layer — Microsoft term for an interface that separates two classes of network or other system components. Boundary layers make it simpler for developers to build general-purpose applications without requiring them to manage all the details involved in network communications.

Client Service for NetWare (CSNW) — Service included with Windows 2000 Professional that provides easy connection to NetWare servers.

connectionless — A class of network transport protocols that makes only a "best effort" attempt at delivery, and that includes no explicit mechanisms to guarantee delivery or data integrity. Because such protocols need not be particularly reliable, they are often much faster and require less overhead than connection-oriented protocols.

connection-oriented — A class of network transport protocols that includes guaranteed delivery, explicit acknowledgment of data receipt, and a variety of data integrity checks to ensure reliable transmission and reception of data across a network. Although reliable, connection-oriented protocols can be slow because of the overhead and extra communication.

Data Link Control (DLC) — A network transport protocol that allows connectivity to mainframes, printers, and servers running Remote Program Load software.

Domain Name Service (DNS) — TCP/IP service that is used to resolve FQDN names to IP addresses.

Dynamic Data Exchange (DDE) — A method of interprocess communication within the Windows operating system.

Dynamic Host Configuration Protocol (DHCP) — An IP-based address management service that permits clients to obtain IP addresses from a DHCP server. This allows network administrators to control and manage IP addresses centrally, rather than on a per-machine basis.

Ethernet II — An older version of Ethernet that preceded the 802.3 specification, offering the same 10 Mbps as standard Ethernet, but using a different frame format.

Fiber Distributed Data Interface (FDDI) — A 100 Mbps fiber-based networking technology.

File Transfer Protocol (FTP) — The protocol and service that provides TCP/IP-based file transfer to and from remote hosts and confers the ability to navigate and operate within remote file systems.

HOSTS — A static file placed on members of a network to provide name resolution between hosts and IP addresses.

Internet Control Message Protocol (ICMP) — The protocol in the TCP/IP suite that handles communication between devices about network traffic, quality of service, and requests for specific acknowledgments (such as those used in the PING utility).

Internet Protocol (IP) — The protocol that handles routing and addressing information for the TCP/IP protocol suite. IP provides a simple connectionless transmission that relies on higher-layer protocols to establish reliability.

Internetwork Packet Exchange (IPX) — The protocol developed by Novell for its NetWare product. IPX is a routable, connectionless protocol similar to IP but much easier to manage, and with lower communication overhead.

Internetwork Packet Exchange/Sequenced Packet Exchange (IPX/SPX) — The two primary protocols developed by Novell for its NetWare network operating system. IPX/SPX is derived from the XNS protocol stack and leans heavily on XNS architecture and functionality. See also IPX and SPX.

interprocess communication (IPC) — The mechanism that defines a way for internal Windows processes to exchange information.

LMHOSTS — File used in Microsoft networks to provide NetBIOS name-to-address resolution.

7

Multiple Universal Naming Convention Provider (MUP) — A Windows 2000 software component that allows two or more UNC providers (for example, Microsoft networks and NetWare networks) to exist simultaneously. The MUP determines which UNC provider will handle a particular UNC request and forwards the request to that provider.

Multi-Provider Router (MPR) — A file system service that can designate the proper redirector to handle a resource request that does not use UNC naming. The MPR lets applications written to older Microsoft specifications behave as if they used UNC naming. The MPR is able to recognize those UNCs that correspond to defined drive mappings.

NetBIOS Enhanced User Interface (NetBEUI) — A simple transport program developed to support NetBIOS installations. NetBEUI is not routable, so it is not appropriate for larger networks.

Network Basic Input/Output System (NetBIOS) — A client/server interprocess communication service developed by IBM in 1985. NetBIOS presents a relatively primitive mechanism for communication in client/server applications, but allows an easy implementation across various Microsoft Windows computers.

Network Driver Interface Specification (NDIS) — Microsoft specification that defines parameters for loading more than one protocol on a network adapter.

Network Dynamic Data Exchange (NetDDE) — An interprocess communication mechanism developed by Microsoft to support the distribution of DDE applications over a network.

Network File System (NFS) — A UDP-based networked file system originally developed by Sun Microsystems and widely used on many TCP/IP networks. (Windows 2000 does not include built-in NFS support, but numerous third-party options are available.)

NWLink — Microsoft's implementation of Novell's IPX/SPX protocol suite.

Open Datalink Interface (ODI) — A part of the Novell protocol suite that provides the ability to bind more than one protocol to an adapter.

Packet Internet Groper (PING) — An IP-based utility that can be used to check network connectivity or to verify whether a specific host elsewhere on the network can be reached.

redirector — Software that examines all requests for system resources and decides whether such requests are local or remote.

remote execution (rexec) — The IP-based utility that permits a user on one machine to execute a program on another machine elsewhere on the network.

remote shell (rsh) — The IP-based utility that permits a user on one machine to enter a shell command on another machine on the network.

Reverse Address Resolution Protocol (RARP) — Used to map from a MAC-layer address to a numeric IP address.

Sequenced Packet Exchange (SPX) — A connection-oriented protocol used in the NetWare environment when guaranteed delivery is required.

Server service — The Windows 2000 component that handles the creation and management of shared resources and performs security checks against requests for such resources, including directories and printers. The Server service allows a Windows 2000 computer to act as a server on a client/server network, up to the maximum number of licensed clients.

Simple Mail Transfer Protocol (SMTP) — The IP-based messaging protocol and service that supports most Internet e-mail.

Simple Network Management Protocol (SNMP) — The IP-based network management protocol and service that makes it possible for management applications to poll network devices and permits devices to report on error or alert conditions to such applications.

subnet — A portion of a network that might or might not be a physically separate network. A subnet shares a network address with other parts of the network but is distinguished by a subnet number.

subnet mask — The number used to define which part of a computer's IP address denotes the host and which part denotes the network.

Telnet — The TCP/IP-based terminal emulation protocol used on IP-based networks to permit clients on one machine to attach to and operate on another machine on the network as if the other machines were terminals locally attached to a remote host.

Transmission Control Protocol/Internet Protocol (TCP/IP) — A suite of Internet protocols upon which the global Internet is based. TCP/IP is the default protocol for Windows 2000.

Transmission Control Protocol (TCP) — The reliable, connection-oriented, IP-based transport protocol that supports many of the most important IP services, including HTTP, SMTP, and FTP.

Transport Driver Interface (TDI) — The specification to which all Windows transport protocols must be written to be used by higher-layer services, such as programming interfaces, file systems, and interprocess communication mechanisms.

Trivial File Transfer Protocol (TFTP) — A lightweight alternative to FTP that uses UDP to provide only simple get-and-put capabilities for file transfer on IP-based networks.

Universal Naming Convention (UNC) — A multivendor, multiplatform convention for identifying shared resources on a network.

User Datagram Protocol (UDP) — A lightweight, connectionless transport protocol used as an alternative to TCP in IP-based environments to supply faster, lower overhead access, primarily (but not exclusively) to local resources.

Windows Internet Naming Service (WINS) — A service that provides NetBIOS name-to-IP-address resolution.

Workstation service — The Windows component that supports client access to network resources and handles functions such as logging on, connecting to network shares (directories and printers), and creating links using the Windows 2000 IPC options.

X.25 — An ITU standard for packet-switched networking; common outside of the United States where its robust handling makes it a good match for substandard telephone networks.

REVIEW QUESTIONS

1. The _____ enables a system to determine which part of an IP address represents the host, and which part represents the network.

2. _____ is a TCP/IP service used to resolve host or domain names to addresses.

3. The _____ service can be used to automatically assign IP configurations to a computer.

4. The _____ file provides NetBIOS name-to-IP-address resolution.

5. _____ is a TCP/IP protocol that is used for file manipulation.

6. By changing the _____, you alter the order in which services are accessed.

7. _____ is the Microsoft service that provides NetBIOS name-to-IP-address resolution.

8. The _____ examines requests for system resources and decides whether they are local or remote.

9. NDIS allows any number of adapters to be bound to any number of transport protocols. True or False?

10. Of the following protocols, which is the fastest and best suited for small single-segment LANs?

    a. TCP/IP

    b. NWLink

    c. NetBEUI

    d. DLC

11. DLC supports which two of the following network functions? (Choose all correct answers.)

    a. direct connection to IBM mainframes

    b. terminal emulation services

    c. network routing

    d. access to network-attached printers

12. What Windows 2000 networking component allows a system to access shared resources?

    a. TCP/IP

    b. Workstation service

    c. RPC

    d. NetDDE

13. If you are assigned the IP address 172.16.1.1, what full class subnet mask is most likely the correct one to use?

 a. 255.0.0.0

 b. 255.255.0.0

 c. 255.255.255.0

14. What class of IP addresses offers the most flexibility with regard to subnetting by providing for the most number of hosts?

 a. Class A

 b. Class B

 c. Class C

15. What should be placed on remote systems that connect to routed networks over slow WAN links? (Choose all correct answers.)

 a. NetBEUI

 b. LMHOSTS

 c. DNS

 d. HOSTS

 e. WinInet

16. What TCP/IP command can test the presence of a remote system?

 a. Telnet

 b. PING

 c. ARP

 d. Route

17. Which of the following is the static text-based equivalent of the Windows 2000 NetBIOS name-to-IP-address resolution service?

 a. HOSTS

 b. LMHOSTS

 c. DNS

 d. WINS

18. If your network hosts the correct service, you do not need to configure TCP/IP to participate in a network. True or False?

19. Which of the following protocols is used to inquire if an address is reachable on the Internet?

 a. SMTP

 b. UTP

 c. PING

 d. IMAP

7

20. What two IPC interfaces are used by Windows 2000 for file system access? (Choose all correct answers.)

   a. WinSock

   b. named pipes

   c. mailslots

   d. OLE

21. Which protocols can be used on a network where the clients are granted Internet access? (Choose all correct answers.)

   a. NetBEUI

   b. NWLink

   c. TCP/IP

22. The NetBEUI protocol under Windows 2000 can support a maximum of _____ devices on a network.

   a. 16

   b. 64

   c. 254

   d. 1023

23. What is provided by NDIS and ODI?

   a. Dynamic client configuration

   b. Distribution of driver software

   c. Binding of multiple protocols to multiple adapters

   d. Resolution of names to IP addresses

24. Which of the following will reduce broadcasts the most in a TCP/IP environment?

   a. DNS

   b. WINS

   c. NWLink

   d. DLC

25. TCP/IP is the most widely used protocol in the world. True or False?

HANDS-ON PROJECTS

Project 7-1

To view the status and properties of a Local Area Connection:

> TIP   This project assumes that your Windows 2000 Professional system is connected to a network.

1. Open the Network and Dial-up Connections dialog box (click **Start**, select **Settings**, and then click **Network and Dial-up Connections**).
2. Select the **Local Area Connection** object.
3. From the **File** menu, select **Status**.
4. This reveals the Status dialog box. Notice the details provided on this dialog box: connection status, duration, speed, and packets.
5. Click the **Properties** button.
6. This reveals the Properties dialog box for this connection. Notice how this dialog box reveals the NIC involved with this connection and all of the services and protocols associated with this connection.
7. Click **Cancel** to close the Properties dialog box.
8. Click **Close** to close the Status dialog box.
9. Close the Network and Dial-up Communications dialog box.

Project 7-2

To use PING to test TCP/IP communications:

> TIP   This project assumes that you are connected to a TCP/IP network. You must know the IP address or host name or domain name of at least one system on your network (or the Internet if you also have Internet access).

1. Open the Command Prompt by clicking on the **Start** menu, then selecting **Programs**, then selecting **Accessories**, then clicking **Command Prompt**.
2. Type **PING <IP address or name>** where *<IP address or name>* is the IP address of a system on your network, the name of a system on your network, or the domain name of a system on the Internet. Press **Enter**.
3. You should see a statement similar to "Pinging 172.16.1.7 with 32 bytes of data:" followed by four lines listing whether a reply was received or a timeout occurred.
4. Close the Command Prompt by typing **exit** and then pressing **Enter**.

Project 7-3

To view the HOSTS and LMHOSTS sample files:

1. Open Notepad by clicking on the **Start** menu, then selecting **Programs**, then selecting **Accessories**, and then clicking **Notepad**.

2. From the File menu, select **Open**.

3. Use the Open dialog box to locate and select the **\Winnt\System32\drivers\etc** directory. This can be accomplished by using the Up One Level button to move to a parent container or by double-clicking on a displayed drive or folder to move to a child container.

4. Change the Files of type to **All Files** by using the pull-down list.

5. You should see a list of files in this folder. Select **hosts**, then click **Open**.

6. Scroll down through this file, reading the information it provides. Do not make any changes to the file at this time.

7. From the File menu, select **Open**. You should still be viewing the \etc directory.

8. Change the Files of type to **All Files** by using the pull-down list.

9. You should see a list of files in this folder. Select **Lmhosts.sam**, then click **Open**.

10. Scroll down through this file, reading the information it provides. Do not make any changes to the file at this time.

11. From the File menu, select **Exit**.

Project 7-4

To configure TCP/IP:

> **TIP** The IP address of 172.16.1.1 and subnet mask of 255.255.255.0 can be replaced by your own assigned values.

1. Open the Network and Dial-up Connections interface. Click **Start**, select **Settings**, then click **Network and Dial-up Connections**.

2. Select the **Local Area Connection** object.

3. Click the **File** menu, then click **Properties**. This reveals the Properties dialog box for the selected Local Area Connection object.

4. Select the **Internet Protocol (TCP/IP)** in the list of components.

5. Click **Properties**. This reveals the Internet Protocol (TCP/IP) Properties dialog box.

6. Select the **Use the following IP address** radio button.

7. Type the IP address of **172.16.1.1**.

8. Type in the subnet mask of **255.255.255.0**.

9. Click **OK**.

10. Click **OK**.

11. Click the **File** menu, then click **Close**.

12. Restart the system for the changes to take effect.

Project 7-5

To view network bindings:

1. Open the Network and Dial-up Connections interface. Click **Start**, select **Settings**, then click **Network and Dial-up Connections**.

2. Click the **Advanced** menu, then click **Advanced Settings**. This reveals the Advanced Settings dialog box where bindings are managed.

3. Select a connection from the connection box.

4. Notice the contents of the lower field, where installed services and protocols are listed in their binding order.

5. Notice that the items closer to the top of the list are bound in priority to those listed lower on the list.

6. Notice the check box beside each item that allows you to disable that service or protocol.

7. Click **Cancel** to ensure you've made no changes.

8. Click the **File** menu, then click **Close**.

Project 7-6

To install and remove NetBEUI:

1. Open the **Network and Dial-up Connections** interface. Click **Start**, select **Settings**, then click **Network and Dial-up Connections**.

2. Select the **Local Area Connection** object.

3. Click the **File** menu, then click **Properties**. This reveals the Properties dialog box for the selected Local Area Connection object.

4. Click the **Install** button.

5. Select **Protocol** from the list of Network Component Types.

6. Click **Add**.

7. Select **NetBEUI Protocol** from the list of Protocols.

8. Click **OK**.

9. Notice that NetBEUI now appears in the list of network components.

10. Select **NetBEUI Protocol**.

11. Click **Uninstall**.

12. Click **Yes** when asked to confirm the deletion.

7

13. If prompted to reboot, click **Yes**.

14. Close the Properties dialog box.

15. If not prompted to reboot, click the **File** menu, then click **Close**. Then reboot the system by clicking the **Start** menu and then clicking **Shutdown**. Select **Restart**, then click **OK**.

CASE PROJECTS

1. Describe the functions and features of TCP/IP included with Windows 2000.

2. As a network administrator at XYZ Corp., you always hear about it when performance problems arise on the network. In the past two weeks, you've been involved in switching the network over from using NetBEUI exclusively, to a mixture of NetBEUI and TCP/IP. You've installed TCP/IP on all Windows 2000 Server and Professional systems, and made sure that all the machines are properly configured. Because the network is growing, and an additional cable segment has been added, with more planned for the future, you plan to switch entirely from NetBEUI to TCP/IP over time. All of a sudden, your users complain that the network has slowed dramatically. What steps can you take that might improve speed performance? Which machines should you make changes on, and why?

8

INTERNETWORKING WITH NOVELL NETWARE

> **After reading this chapter and completing the exercises, you will be able to:**
>
> ◆ Discuss connecting Windows 2000 Professional computers to NetWare servers
> ◆ Install and configure NWLink
> ◆ Install and configure Client Service for NetWare (CSNW)

Although Microsoft has positioned Windows 2000 as the replacement for other network operating systems, it is necessary to provide connectivity to other systems for compatibility. For this reason, Microsoft provides numerous utilities, applications, and protocols for connecting to various types of computers. In this chapter, you explore connecting Windows 2000 Professional computers to Novell NetWare networks.

NetWare Networks

Novell NetWare is designed for file and printer sharing on a network. Because it was one of the first true network operating systems, NetWare garnered a substantial and loyal following throughout the late 1980s and early 1990s. By the mid-90s, NetWare servers functioned as the backbone for more networks than any other type of server on the market. The most recent iteration of NetWare is NetWare 5. With the growth of PC capabilities and the advent of the Internet, NetWare has adapted and expanded to provide robust services, while maintaining its solid file and printer sharing performance.

Although Windows NT and Windows 2000 servers account for a growing number of network servers, a large number of companies around the world rely on Novell NetWare for their server requirements. For this reason, Microsoft includes interconnectivity enhancements to allow Windows 2000-based computers to connect to and function with NetWare servers. These enhancements include NWLink, Client Service for NetWare, File and Print Services for NetWare, and Gateway Services for NetWare. Of these, only NWLink and Client Service for NetWare are used by Windows 2000 Professional systems. File and Print Services for NetWare and Gateway Services for NetWare are used by Windows 2000 Server computers.

Beginning with version 1.0, NetWare utilized the **bindery**, which is a proprietary database that contains all network resource information, such as user and group names, print server settings, and file server configurations. With NetWare 4.0, Novell introduced **Novell Directory Services (NDS)**. NDS is the hierarchical database used by NetWare 4.0 and higher servers to store network resource object configuration information, comparable to the function of Active Directory in Windows 2000. With this introduction, Novell began the era of object-oriented directory services. In this context, a directory is a dynamic database that contains information for network objects such as printers, applications, and groups. Later sections of this chapter discuss the differences between connecting to bindery (pre-version 4.0) servers and NDS servers.

Windows 2000 Professional and NetWare

Because the Professional edition of Windows 2000 is designed to operate as a network client, it includes features that enable it to connect to a variety of network servers, including NetWare servers. Because both bindery and NDS servers are in use today, Windows 2000 is able to connect to both types. Once connected, the Windows 2000 Professional computer utilizes resources on the NetWare server as if they were actually on a Windows 2000 server. In this manner, all network resources are accessed through the same method, making a heterogeneous network appear seamless to network users.

NETWARE COMPATIBILITY COMPONENTS

There are two main components that facilitate Windows 2000 Professional compatibility with NetWare servers: NWLink and Client Service for NetWare. The next sections discuss installing and configuring these components.

NWLink

Like many network operating systems developed in the 1980s, Novell found that the available protocols were not sufficient to support the demands of its new product. To fit their needs, the developers at Novell produced a protocol suite based on the Xerox Network System (XNS) protocol suite. XNS was developed during the creative networking heyday of the early 1970s at Xerox's Palo Alto Research Center (PARC). PARC is also responsible for many areas that form the foundation of today's computing environment, including client/server architecture, Ethernet, laser printers, the first commercially viable mouse, graphical user interfaces, and HTTP, the protocol of the World Wide Web. PARC is still operating today and is one of the most fascinating stories in computing. For more information on PARC's contributions to computing, visit the PARC Web site at *http://www.parc.xerox.com*.

The developers at Novell determined that, although XNS formed a solid foundation for their network protocol suite, it was not robust enough to accommodate the required communications between networked PCs. Novell modified XNS to create the **Internetwork Packet Exchange/Sequenced Packet Exchange (IPX/SPX)** protocol suite. **IPX** is a connectionless protocol that provides quick network transport for most of the communications on a NetWare network. Because it is connectionless, IPX does not guarantee packet delivery, but it is generally sufficient for network communications. **SPX** is a connection-oriented protocol that provides guaranteed packet delivery. However, because it is connection-oriented, it requires higher overhead and is slower than IPX. For this reason, SPX is used in NetWare communications for only certain applications, such as those that manage the server's console.

NWLink is Microsoft's implementation of the IPX/SPX protocol suite and can communicate with all NetWare implementations. Novell and Microsoft approach networking in a slightly different manner, meaning that the underlying architecture of each company's network communication is different. Novell's specification is called **Open Datalink Interface (ODI)**. Microsoft's architecture is called the **Network Device Interface Specification (NDIS)**. Strictly speaking, IPX/SPX is ODI-compliant, but not NDIS-compliant. NWLink is the NDIS-compliant implementation of IPX/SPX.

Installing NWLink

Like all networking components of Windows 2000, NWLink is installed through the Network and Dial-up Connections applet of the Control Panel. To run this applet, select Settings from the Start menu, then select Control Panel. Once the Control Panel is opened, double-click Network and Dial-up Connections. The same applet can be initiated by right-clicking the My Network Places icon on the Desktop, or directly from the Start, Settings menu. Figure 8-1 shows the Network and Dial-up Connections dialog box.

8

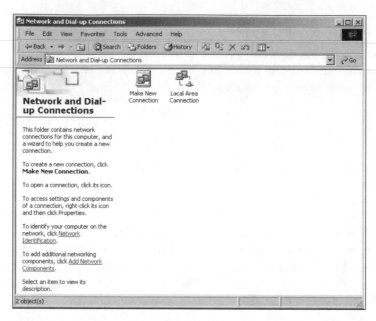

Figure 8-1   The Network and Dial-up Connections dialog box

Displayed in the dialog box are icons for each of the connections currently configured on the computer. On the computer shown in Figure 8-1, only a Local Area Connection has been configured. If a dial-up connection or a secondary network connection had previously been installed on the computer, its icon would be displayed in the dialog box as well. Simply double-clicking the icon for the Local Area Connection displays the Local Area Connection Status dialog box, shown in Figure 8-2. This dialog box provides, at first glance, the number of packets sent and received, as well as the status, speed, and duration of the connection. The Disable button prevents the connection from being used. Double-clicking the outline of the connection reenables the connection.

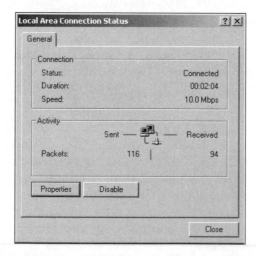

Figure 8-2   The Local Area Connection Status dialog box

Clicking the Properties button brings up the Local Area Connection Properties dialog box. It is through this dialog box that all networking components are added to Windows 2000. If the Typical installation option is selected during the Windows 2000 installation process, Client for Microsoft Networks, File and Printer Sharing for Microsoft Networks, and Internet Protocol (TCP/IP) are loaded by default, as shown in Figure 8-3.

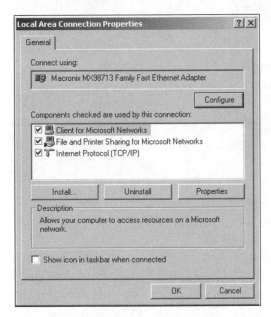

Figure 8-3 The Local Area Connection Properties dialog box

To connect to a NetWare network, the NWLink protocol must be loaded. To add a new net-working component to the Local Area Connection, click the Install button. You are presented with the Select Network Component Type dialog box, which allows you to install a Client, Service, or Protocol. Because NWLink is a protocol suite, select Protocol, and click Add. In the Select Network Protocol dialog box, you are able to select from the available protocols not yet installed on the computer. If TCP/IP is the only protocol installed, the list includes the following: AppleTalk Protocol, DLC Protocol, NetBEUI Protocol, Network Monitor Driver, and NWLink IPX/SPX/NetBIOS Compatible Transport Protocol. The protocols other than NWLink support many different networking devices and are discussed in other chapters. To continue with the installation, select NWLink IPX/SPX/NetBIOS Compatible Transport Protocol from the list and click OK. After a brief moment for configuration, you are again presented with the Local Area Connection Properties dialog box, as shown in Figure 8-4. To complete the installation of NWLink, click Close on the Local Area Connection Properties dialog box. (Complete steps for installing NWLink are given in Hands-on Project 8-1.)

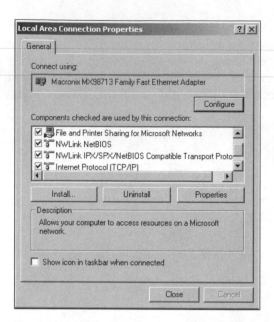

Figure 8-4   The Local Area Connection Properties after adding NWLink

Note that in addition to the NWLink IPX/SPX/NetBIOS Compatible Transport Protocol, the NWLink NetBIOS protocol has been added. Just as Novell's networking model is built on the XNS protocol suite and networking system, Microsoft's networking architecture was built on existing technology. Microsoft's first steps in the networking arena were in a partnership with IBM on the LANManager product. LANManager used the **Network Basic Input/Output System (NetBIOS)** for network naming and transport. As Microsoft developed its own networking strategy, it kept the NetBIOS naming system. All Microsoft networking implementations must be NetBIOS-compliant to provide interconnectivity. Because IPX/SPX is not NetBIOS-compatible, NWLink includes an additional protocol to provide this functionality.

Configuring NWLink: Ethernet Frame Types and IPX Network Numbers

After installation is complete, NWLink has two configuration options available: Ethernet frame types and network numbers. Ethernet can utilize four **frame types** supported by NWLink: Ethernet 802.2, Ethernet 802.3, Ethernet II, and Ethernet SNAP. A packet's frame type defines the structure of the packet and the fields that are included. For example, one frame may put the packet components in order of header, source computer, source network, destination computer, destination network, checksum, and data. A different frame's order may be header, destination network, destination computer, source network, source computer, data, and checksum.

CAUTION

It is very important for all computers communicating on the network to use the same frame type to ensure that communication takes place. If frame types do not match, communication is not possible.

By default, as shown in Figure 8-5, Windows 2000 determines the frame type being used on the network and configures itself accordingly. It does this by accepting the first NWLink packet it receives and using the same frame type. If all computers on the network are set to Auto Detect, the Ethernet 802.2 frame type is used because it is the accepted industry standard.

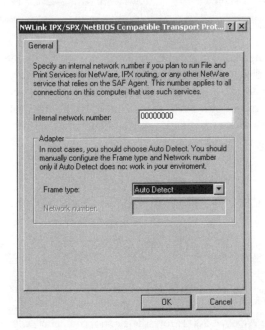

Figure 8-5   The NWLink Properties dialog box

Unless there is a specific reason to use a different frame type, it is best to let Windows 2000 detect the frame type being used on the network. By doing so, potential problems caused by frame type mismatches are eliminated. However, if it is necessary to specify the frame type being used by the computer, select the appropriate frame from the Frame type drop-down list in the NWLink IPX/SPX/NetBIOS Compatible Transport Protocol Properties dialog box. When a frame type other than Auto Detect is selected, you must specify the **network number** (the network and computer identifier) used by the frame type.

Like TCP/IP, NWLink (IPX) makes a distinction between the computer ID and the network ID on which the computer resides. However, unlike TCP/IP, the computer ID and network ID, or network number, are separate fields in IPX. When the computer is configured to automatically detect the frame type used on the network, it is also able to determine the network number from the frames it receives. However, when a specific frame type is selected, you must also specify the network number to which the computer is attached. To ensure that this information is accurate, check with your network administrator before changing the frame type. If the network number does not match the network number used by other computers on the network, your system will not be able to communicate.

 Network numbers on IPX networks are not limited to numerals. Because IPX translates the network numbers from hexadecimal to binary, it is able to support the letters A through F in its network number field. This makes it very easy to ensure unique network numbers on large networks. It also gives the network administrator an opportunity to be creative. For example, a network number 1B0001 could be used to indicate the first network on the first floor of Building B. Then again, a network number of BAD4DAD is both descriptive and fun.

Refer back to Figure 8-5. Note that there is also an option at the top of the dialog box for the Internal network number. Part of the design of IPX utilizes a network number assigned to the internal operations of the computer. Under most circumstances, it is not necessary to change this number. However, if the network number that is assigned to the internal network number is in use elsewhere on the network as a normal network number, communication will be sporadic and very difficult to troubleshoot.

Client Service for NetWare

The **Client Service for NetWare (CSNW)** component of Windows 2000 Professional allows a Windows 2000 computer to access resources on NetWare servers version 2x, 3x, and 4x. CSNW supports full access to NetWare file and print servers, NetWare utilities, bindery connections, and some NDS connections.

The version of CSNW that is included with Windows 2000 Professional is not compatible with all features of the NetWare 5.x version of NDS. CSNW allows authentication to NetWare 5.0 NDS-enabled servers, but to allow full functionality, you must load the client software provided with NetWare.

File and Print Servers

To provide access to NetWare file and print servers, CSNW adds a new NetWare-focused redirector that acts as an extension of the file system, in much the same way that the native redirector supports access to Microsoft Windows 2000 and Windows NT servers. (Redirectors handle transmission of remote requests across the network so that the requests are filled.) The difference is that CSNW implements **NetWare Core Protocol (NCP)** requests for file and print services, whereas the native redirector uses the **Common Internet File System (CIFS)**, an enhanced version of the **Server Message Block (SMB)** protocol. Both NCP and SMB perform the same functions, but provide access to different file systems.

Once CSNW is installed, the Windows 2000 user is able to use a single logon to attach to all resources on the network, regardless of the server hosting the resources. In a NetWare-only environment, only CSNW is active and it provides access to the resources. However, in a mixed NetWare/Windows 2000 or Windows NT environment, the appropriate client software is used, depending on the type of server being accessed. (Installation of CSNW is covered in a later section; complete steps are given in Hands-on Project 8-2.)

Supported NetWare Utilities

To ensure proper desktop integration in a NetWare server environment, CSNW supports most NetWare utilities and functions. It provides access to character-based NetWare administration utilities such as SYSCON and PCONSOLE. Many of the utilities are dependent on the versions of NetWare in use. Versions 3.12 and lower support only character-based applications, whereas versions 4.0 and above utilize mainly GUI-based applications. However, even in NetWare 5, some character-based utilities can be used to manage the server environment.

> By default, NetWare versions before 5.0 do not support the long filenames supported by Microsoft products such as Windows 2000. To ensure that the Windows filenames are not truncated when they are copied to NetWare servers, the servers must load the OS/2 name space. This is done on the NetWare server itself and ensures that all files retain their settings when stored on the server.

NWLink and CSNW also support IPX burst mode, which enhances bulk data transfer over an IPX network. By design, IPX is best suited to handle small to medium-sized packets and many network communications. When tasked with transferring large amounts of data, IPX loses efficiency and creates excessive network traffic. Burst mode allows routed network connections to negotiate the largest possible packet size so that fewer packets must be sent to transmit large data files. This improves bandwidth utilization and reduces overhead on the network.

Bindery and NDS Support

To effectively ensure that client computers can attach to any server on the network, Client Service for NetWare includes support for both bindery and Novell Directory Services servers. As mentioned, versions of NetWare prior to 4.0 utilized the bindery to store their configuration information, including user and group lists, printers, and security settings. When users log on to a bindery-based NetWare server, they access the bindery for logon authentication, confirmation of security authorizations, group memberships, and so forth. One of the primary limitations of bindery-based NetWare is that each server on the network has its own bindery. Users that access resources on multiple servers are required to log on to each server individually.

Beginning with NetWare 4.0, Novell utilized the Novell Directory Services (NDS) database to store and maintain the information previously stored in the bindery. The NDS database is much more dynamic and supports enterprise-wide networks. The NDS database is a hierarchical tree that is stored on many servers on the network to provide single-logon access to resources.

In addition, centralized administration and resource management is possible with NDS—a dramatic improvement over administering earlier versions of NetWare.

Because NDS is a hierarchical database that can be stored on multiple servers on the network, an NDS implementation resembles a tree and is referred to as the **NDS tree**. At the base of the tree is the Root object, which generally represents the largest organization connected to the network, often the entire corporation. Working down through the tree, each department may have a container, then each group within the department may have another container. In NDS, each network resource, whether a user, group, file server, printer, or storage area, is represented as an object. Objects are stored in containers representing their function on the network. A network object's location in the NDS tree is called its **context**. Figure 8-6 is an example of what an NDS tree might look like.

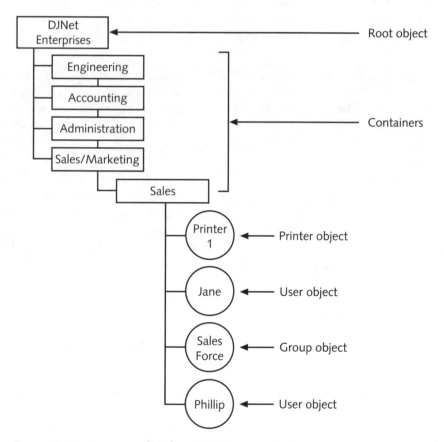

Figure 8-6   An example of an NDS tree structure

In the example shown in Figure 8-6, the Phillip user object is stored in the Sales container, which is in turn stored in the Sales/Marketing container, which resides under the DJNet Enterprises Root object. The context for the Phillip user is DJNet Enterprises.Sales/Marketing.Sales.

Installing and Configuring Client Service for NetWare

Like NWLink, installation of Client Service for NetWare is accomplished through the Local Area Connection Properties dialog box. To begin installation, right-click My Network Places and select Properties. When the Network and Dial-up Connections dialog box opens, right-click the Local Area Connection icon and again select Properties. Click Install; you will be asked to whether to install a Client, Service, or Protocol. As its name implies, Client Service for NetWare is a client component. Select Client and click Add. If the default configuration is installed, the only client available for installation is CSNW. Ensure that Client Service for NetWare is selected and click OK to continue the installation. Once installation is complete, you will be asked to restart your computer. You must do so before CSNW can be used. Click Yes to reboot your computer.

TIP Client Service for NetWare relies on NWLink to operate. If NWLink is not loaded when CSNW is installed, it will be installed automatically.

8

Assigning a Default Tree and Context Using CSNW

After the computer has restarted, you will be presented with the Select NetWare Logon dialog box, shown in Figure 8-7. It is through this dialog box that you assign the default NetWare tree and context on the NDS-enabled NetWare network to which the Windows 2000 Professional computer will be connecting. Unlike most areas of Windows 2000, you are not able to browse for the tree and context. You must have this information available to type into the dialog box. If this information is not available the first time the computer is restarted, you can click Cancel and enter the information later.

Figure 8-7   Use the Select NetWare Logon dialog box to configure the default tree and context

Unlike many networking components, CSNW is not configured through the Local Area Connection Properties dialog box. When CSNW is installed, a separate utility is placed in the Control Panel, and represented by the CSNW icon. If at any point you need to change the default tree and context settings, or any CSNW settings, double-click the CSNW icon to access the Client Service for NetWare configuration dialog box. When accessed by this method, additional configuration options are available, which will be discussed in later sections.

Preferred Server vs. Directory Tree

In the event that you are connecting a Windows 2000 Professional computer to a bindery-based NetWare server, you will need to utilize the Preferred Server configuration options available in the Select NetWare Logon dialog box (refer to Figure 8-7). Unlike the Default Tree and Context settings, where you have to manually type in the tree and context, clicking the down arrow next to the Preferred Server box displays a list of the servers advertising themselves on your network. From the list, select the name of the NetWare server to which you are attaching. You can also directly enter the server's name in the Preferred Server box. If this method is used, be sure the server's name is spelled correctly. If an incorrect server name is entered, the dialog box shown in Figure 8-8 will be displayed, informing you that you could not be authenticated on the selected server because the network path could not be found. Clicking No returns you to the Select NetWare Logon dialog box, whereas clicking Yes accepts the configuration.

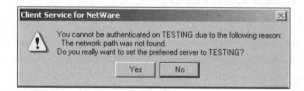

Figure 8-8   A Client Service for NetWare configuration error

Regardless of the configuration changes you make, a dialog box is invoked notifying you that the changes will take effect the next time you log in. Click OK to continue. The computer must be restarted manually, because the configuration program does not automatically restart the computer after the dialog box is closed.

Other Configuration Settings

When the Client Service for NetWare applet is used to configure the networking components, configuration options are available that are not presented when the client is first installed. As shown in Figure 8-9, these options make up the bottom half of the dialog box, in the Print Options and Login Script Options section.

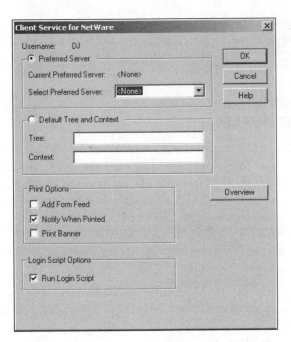

Figure 8-9   Client Service for NetWare configuration options

The settings available in the Print Options section determine whether the computer will send a form feed command to the printer when the print job is finished, send a notification message to the user when the print job is complete, or print a banner before the print job itself. Form feed commands are generally necessary only on older printers, usually those that use tractor-feed paper; most laser and inkjet printers do not require form feed commands after the job. If this option is used on a laser printer, for example, a blank sheet of paper is ejected from the printer after the job. Many users in a networked environment are not within eyesight of the printers they are using. For that reason, the Client Service for NetWare can be configured to send a network notification to the user after the job is complete. If this option is selected, a pop-up box appears on the user's computer when their print job is done. The banner page is also used in many larger networks. A banner page identifies the user that initiated the print job and the name of the job. In this way, users can easily identify their print jobs when they go to pick them up from the printer.

When the Run Login Script option is selected, the computer runs the NetWare logon script specified for the user by the administrator. This preserves the logon scripts that network administrators have developed for their clients and provides easy, centralized administration on all client computers. This is especially important to ensure client standardization, regardless of the client type. However, many of the functions that have been performed by logon scripts are now handled by Windows 2000 functions such as Map Network Drive. As client computers are converted to Windows 2000 Professional, it may no longer be necessary to utilize logon scripts, and this option can be disabled.

TIP   Note that Novell uses the terms "log in" and "login," whereas Microsoft uses "log on" and "logon."

CONNECTING TO NETWARE RESOURCES

Because Client Service for NetWare integrates so closely with Windows 2000, connecting to NetWare resources is accomplished in the same manner as connecting to other resources. Most often, this is accomplished through My Network Places. In an NDS environment, if the resources to which you are connecting are in the same NDS tree, your initial logon provides you access to available resources. However, on bindery-based networks, you must log on to each server to access the resources on that server. Once you have logged on to the appropriate server or directory tree, the NetWare security system determines whether you should be granted access to the requested resources.

Through the Computers Near Me icon in My Network Places, you can connect to resources on servers or trees to which you have already logged on. To search for other servers or NDS trees, double-click the Entire Network icon, and click the *entire contents* link shown in the lower-left corner (see Figure 8-10).

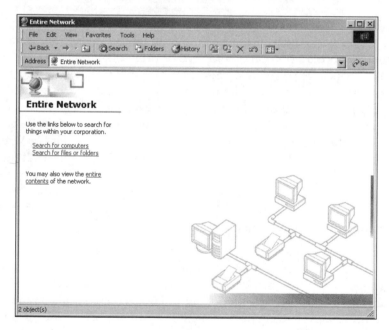

Figure 8-10   Select the <u>entire contents</u> link to search for additional NetWare resources

After clicking on the link, you will be presented with icons for each type of client installed, usually Microsoft Windows Network and NetWare or Compatible Network. To browse for additional NetWare resources, double-click the NetWare or Compatible Network icon.

NetWare-Aware Applications

In many cases, clients utilize network servers strictly for file storage and print functions. However, applications are being designed more and more to operate in conjunction with the network server. These types of applications are true client/server applications, utilizing the processing power of the server for CPU-intensive functions, and performing more simple tasks on the client workstation.

Applications designed to interact in this manner with NetWare servers are referred to as "NetWare-aware." To operate correctly, these applications must function without regard for the underlying operating system. CSNW provides the resources that NetWare-aware applications need to operate.

However, there are some NetWare utilities that are not compatible with CSNW; these are utilities designed for DOS connection to NetWare servers and are not needed in a Windows 2000 environment. For example, a DOS-based workstation uses the *attach* command to initiate a connection to a NetWare server. In Windows 2000, of course, this is done through the My Network Places dialog box. Attach cannot be run through a Command Prompt window because the command prompt is not granted complete access to manage network connections. For the most part, the NetWare utilities used to monitor and manage a NetWare environment function normally on a Windows 2000 client.

NetWare Client for Windows

Client software is available from Novell for connecting computers to its NetWare servers. This software performs the same function as Client Service for NetWare and is installed via the CD-ROM provided with the NetWare operating system. When connecting your Windows 2000 computer to most NetWare servers, it is best to use the Microsoft Client Service for NetWare because of its tight integration with the Windows 2000 operating system. However, as noted earlier, Client Service for NetWare does *not* fully support the NetWare 5.x version of NDS. Therefore, it is necessary to load NetWare Client for Windows provided by Novell if you wish to provide full functionality.

CHAPTER SUMMARY

- ☐ NetWare is designed for file and printer sharing on a network. Because it was one of the first network operating systems, it obtained a large share of the server market and by the mid-1990s functioned as the backbone for more networks than any other type of server.

- ☐ Although Microsoft servers make up a large portion of the servers installed today, many networks still rely on NetWare for their basic file and print services. For this reason, Microsoft includes NWLink, Client Service for NetWare, and other components to ensure compatibility with NetWare systems. This is especially important in the case of Windows 2000 Professional because it's designed to function as a network client, not as a server.

❑ Early versions of NetWare utilized a bindery to store network resource configuration information. With the introduction of NetWare 4.0, Novell moved from storing this information in the bindery to using Novell Directory Services (NDS), a hierarchical enterprise solution for object-oriented storage of network resource information. By using Client Service for NetWare, Windows 2000 Professional is able to connect to both bindery-based and NDS-based NetWare servers. However, Client Service for NetWare does not support the new design of the NetWare 5.x NDS database. To connect to a NetWare 5 server, Novell client software must be installed on the Windows 2000 Professional client.

❑ The two main networking components that facilitate Windows 2000 Professional connectivity to NetWare servers are NWLink and Client Service for NetWare. Novell's primary protocol suite for network communication is IPX/SPX. The Internetwork Packet Exchange (IPX) protocol is a connectionless protocol that provides fast network transport between client and server. The Sequenced Packet Exchange (SPX) protocol is a connection-oriented protocol that provides guaranteed packet delivery but operates more slowly than IPX. NWLink is the Microsoft implementation of the IPX/SPX protocol suite. It is able to function within the NDIS specification to provide communication between computers on the network, including NetWare servers.

❑ After installing NWLink, you can configure the Ethernet frame type and network numbers to be used by the computer. The frame type specifies the structure of the packets being sent on the network. Windows 2000 will automatically detect the frame type currently being used on the network. However, there may be occasion to specify the frame type being used. When this option is selected, it is also necessary to specify the network number for communication. IPX and NWLink use unique network numbers to specify the location of the computers on the network. In addition, an internal network number, which can also be configured through the NWLink properties, is used to further identify the server computer and facilitate communication.

❑ Client Service for NetWare allows Windows 2000 computers to access network resources on NetWare servers. CSNW supports full access to NetWare file and print services, NetWare utilities, and the bindery and some NDS databases. CSNW adds a NetWare-focused redirector that acts as an extension of the file system. CSNW provides access to both character-based and GUI-based NetWare utilities. NetWare versions up to 3.12 utilize only character-based utilities, whereas later versions (4.0–5.x) utilize GUI-based utilities almost exclusively. NWLink and CSNW also support IPX burst mode, which enhances bulk data transfer over the network. CSNW is able to connect to both bindery databases and NDS trees. When users log on to bindery-based servers, they access the bindery database for logon authentication and security information, among other things. The primary limitation of bindery-based NetWare is that each server on the network has its own bindery database with user and group information.

❑ NDS is a hierarchical database that is used to store and maintain the information previously handled by the bindery. Unlike bindery networks, the NDS database is stored on many servers on the network and provides a single logon to users. It also provides centralized administration of network resources, which was not possible with the bindery. An NDS implementation is called an NDS tree because of the hierarchical design of the database. An object's location in the NDS tree is called its context.

❑ Because CSNW integrates closely with Windows 2000, NetWare resources are accessed in the same way as other network resources—through the My Network Places dialog box. CSNW also provides support for NetWare-aware applications and utilities. All of the utilities that are needed by Windows 2000 are supported by CSNW. However, some of the DOS-based NetWare commands and utilities are not. The functionality provided by these commands is provided by other CSNW or Windows 2000 components such as My Network Places.

KEY TERMS

bindery — The database used by versions of NetWare before 4.0 to store network resource configuration information.

Client Service for NetWare (CSNW) — The Windows 2000 networking component that enables communications with NetWare servers.

Common Internet File System (CIFS) — An enhanced version of SMB used for file and print services.

context — The location of an NDS object in the NDS tree.

frame type — One of four available packet structures supported by IPX/SPX and NWLink. The four frame types supported are Ethernet 802.2, Ethernet 802.3, Ethernet II, and Ethernet SNAP.

Internetwork Packet Exchange (IPX) — Novell's connectionless protocol used for most network communication.

IPX/SPX — The protocol suite consisting of IPX and SPX. *See* IPX and SPX for more information.

NDS tree — The hierarchical representation of the Novell Directory Services database on NetWare 4.0 and higher networks.

NetWare Core Protocol (NCP) — The protocol used by CSNW to make file and print services requests of NetWare servers.

Network Basic Input/Output System (NetBIOS) — The method used by LANManager for network naming and transport functions.

Network Device Interface Specification (NDIS) — Microsoft's specification for network device communication with the operating system.

network number — The specific network identifier used by IPX for internal and network communication.

Novell Directory Services (NDS) — The hierarchical database used by NetWare 4.0 and higher servers to store network resource object configuration information.

NWLink — Microsoft's implementation of Novell's IPX/SPX protocol suite.

Open Datalink Interface (ODI) — Novell's specification for network device communication.

8

Sequenced Packet Exchange (SPX) — Novell's connection-oriented, reliable network communications protocol.

Server Message Block (SMB) — The protocol used by Microsoft clients to request file and print services from Microsoft servers such as Windows 2000 Advanced Server.

REVIEW QUESTIONS

1. All versions of NetWare utilize NDS. True or False?

2. Which of the following is configured through its own Control Panel applet?

   a. NWLink

   b. CSNW

   c. TCP/IP

   d. NDIS

3. The Client Service for NetWare is not able to provide full functionality to _____ NDS trees.

4. Which of the following served as the basis for Microsoft's networking model?

   a. IBM LANManager

   b. Banyan Vines

   c. Novell ShareNet

   d. Windows NT

5. In addition to NWLink, _____ is installed to provide communication compatibility with Windows networks.

6. For IPX/SPX communication to succeed on a network, all computers must use the same frame type. True or False?

7. Which of the following Windows 2000 networking components are not available in the Professional edition? (Choose all that apply.)

   a. File and Print Services for NetWare

   b. Client Service for NetWare

   c. NWLink IPX/SPX Compatible Transport

   d. Gateway Service for NetWare

8. Novell's IPX/SPX protocol suite is based on _____ developed at _____.

9. The location of a network resource in an NDS tree is called its _____.

10. Which of the following NetWare protocols provides guaranteed packet delivery?

    a. NWLink

    b. IPX

    c. SPX

    d. NCP

11. In a mixed NetWare and Windows 2000 Server environment, which of the following networking components must be installed on the Windows 2000 Professional computer? (Choose all that apply.)

    a. Client for Microsoft Networks

    b. NWLink

    c. Client Service for NetWare

    d. TCP/IP

12. All NetWare 3.12 command-line utilities are compatible with the Windows 2000 Client Service for NetWare. True or False?

13. Although their functions can be accomplished through Windows 2000 utilities, such as Map Network Drive, CSNW supports NetWare _____.

14. Because IPX/SPX is not compatible with the Windows networking naming system, _____ is installed in conjunction with NWLink.

15. When configuring CSNW, which of the following provides a drop-down list from which you can browse available resources?

    a. default context

    b. frame type

    c. preferred server

    d. default tree

8

HANDS-ON PROJECTS

Project 8-1

To install NWLink:

1. If you have not already done so, log on to your Windows 2000 Professional computer as Administrator.

2. Right-click **My Network Places** and then select **Properties**.

3. Right-click **Local Area Connection** and then select **Properties**.

4. In the Local Area Connection Properties dialog box, click **Install**.

5. Select **Protocol** from the list of available components and then click **Add**.

6. Select **NWLink IPX/SPX/NetBIOS Compatible Transport Protocol** from the list, as shown in Figure 8-11. Click **OK**.

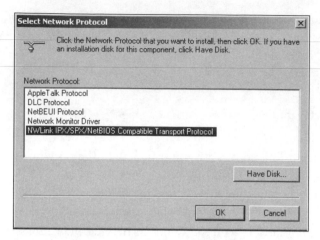

Figure 8-11   Select the NWLink IPX/SPX/NetBIOS Compatible Transport Protocol

7. Click **Close** to complete the installation. Note that you do not need to reboot the computer for this addition to take effect.

8. Right-click again on the **Local Area Connection** icon and select **Properties** to configure NWLink. Note that NWLink NetBIOS has been added to the installed components list.

9. Select **NWLink IPX/SPX/NetBIOS Compatible Transport Protocol** from the list and then click **Properties**.

10. Enter an internal network number for the computer. Use any combination of up to six numbers and letters A–F. For example, 1FAD or 1999A.

11. Click the down arrow for the **Frame type** dropdown list and select a frame. If you are in a classroom environment, select the frame type specified by the instructor.

12. Note that you must specify the network number for the selected frame. Enter a network number in the space provided. If you are in a classroom environment, enter the network number specified by the instructor.

13. Click **OK** twice to complete the configuration. Note that the changes take effect immediately. If you are in a classroom environment, ensure that communications are available to computers with the same frame type and network number.

14. Close the Network and Dial-up Connections window.

Project 8-2

To install and configure Client Service for NetWare:

1. If you have not already done so, log on to your Windows 2000 Professional computer as Administrator.

2. Right-click **My Network Places** and then select **Properties**.

3. Right-click **Local Area Connection** and then select **Properties**.

4. In the Local Area Connection Properties dialog box, click **Install**.

5. Select **Client** from the list of available components and then click **Add**. Note that the only client available to be installed is Client Service for NetWare.

6. Select **Client Service for NetWare** and then click **OK**.

7. When prompted, supply the default tree and context for your computer on the network or the preferred server to which the computer will connect. If you are in a classroom environment, obtain the tree and context information from your instructor.

8. Wait a moment while the configuration changes are made, then when prompted, click **Yes** to restart the computer.

9. Click **OK** to continue.

10. Click **OK** to continue.

11. After the computer has restarted, log on to your Windows 2000 Professional computer as Administrator.

12. Open the Control Panel by selecting **Start**, **Settings**, **Control Panel**. Note that the CSNW icon has been added.

13. Double-click the **CSNW** icon to open the Client Service for NetWare dialog box. Adjust the Print Options and Login Script Options as desired and click **OK**.

14. Note that you receive an information box telling you that the changes will take effect the next time you log in. Click **OK** to continue.

15. Close the Control Panel.

CASE PROJECTS

1. As the network administrator for a mid-sized R&D company, you are responsible for integrating Windows 2000 Professional into your existing network. Because of the engineering requirements for your company, you've decided to upgrade all 35 engineering computers to Windows 2000 Professional. You currently have two Windows NT Servers providing intranet support for your network, and seven NetWare servers, all version 4.0. You are not planning on upgrading the servers at this time, but it may be an option in the future. Discuss the steps you will take to ensure that all users who install Windows 2000 are able to connect to all existing network resources.

2. Using Case 1 as the basis for your design, create a plan to add a NetWare 5 server to the network. What changes will need to be made to the client computers to ensure connectivity to all resources?

9

REMOTE ACCESS SERVICE

After reading this chapter and completing the exercises, you will be able to:

♦ Understand remote access under Windows 2000

♦ Configure various RAS connection types for a Windows 2000 Professional system

♦ Enable offline file access

♦ Troubleshoot RAS problems

When it comes to network access, not all access occurs from computers that are directly attached to the network where the resources and data reside. Especially for roving workers, such as salespeople and field engineers, and increasingly for telecommuters as well, the ability to gain access to a network remotely—that is, from some location other than where the network itself resides—is an important capability. This is an area where Windows 2000 really shines: it is one of the few major network operating systems that includes remote access capabilities with the core software at no additional charge. For Windows 2000 Professional, this means that a single dial-in or dial-out connection that can use a modem, an **ISDN (Integrated Services Digital Network)** line, frame relay, or any of the other, more exotic digital remote link technologies is part of the package. For Windows 2000 Server, a complete multiuser Remote Access Server is included with the core offering, and it can support up to 256 simultaneous dial-in/dial-out connections. Since Windows NT 3.51 became a force to be reckoned with in 1995, remote access services have played a crucial role in its burgeoning popularity and widespread acceptance through the current Windows 2000 release.

REMOTE ACCESS SERVICE (RAS)

You can use the **Remote Access Service (RAS)** to log on to a Windows 2000 system for user or administrative access while you are away from the office. For example, when you are traveling on business, you can access the system from a hotel room.

 RAS initiates and maintains the access information from the client system. A client system is defined as a Windows 2000, Windows NT, or Windows 95/98 system that initiates access to a Windows 2000 system established as a remote access server.

A Windows 2000 RAS configuration includes the following components:

- *Clients:* Windows 2000, Windows NT, Windows 95/98, Windows for Workgroups, MS-DOS (with Microsoft network client software installed), and LAN Manager RAS clients can all connect to a Windows 2000 RAS server. Clients can also be any platform that supports the **Point-to-Point Protocol (PPP)**. PPP provides connectivity over serial or modem lines, and can negotiate any transport protocol used by both systems involved in the link.

- *Protocols:* Windows 2000 RAS servers support the PPP protocol, enabling any PPP client to use the Transmission Control Protocol/Internet Protocol (TCP/IP), NWLink (IPX/SPX), or NetBEUI. Windows 2000 as a dial-up client can also access the installed base of **Serial Line Internet Protocol (SLIP)** remote access servers. SLIP is an implementation of the IP protocol over serial lines; however, SLIP cannot be used to connect to a Windows 2000 RAS system. Windows 2000 RAS can accept inbound calls from AppleTalk clients using AppleTalk Remote Access Protocol (ARAP). Windows 2000 RAS also includes backward-compatible support for the RAS protocol (a.k.a. Asynchronous NetBEUI or AsyBEUI) used by legacy clients, such as Windows NT 3.1, Windows for Workgroups, MS-DOS, and LAN Manager.

- *WAN connectivity:* Clients can dial in using standard telephone lines with a modem or modem pool, employing legacy analog or the new Asymmetric Digital Subscriber Line (ADSL) technology. Faster links are possible using ISDN or T-carrier lines. You can also connect RAS clients to RAS servers by using X.25, Asynchonous Transfer Mode (ATM, discussed in Chapter 7), or an RS-232C null modem. Windows 2000 also supports **Multilink PPP**, which is the ability of RAS to aggregate multiple data streams into one network connection for the purpose of using more than one modem or ISDN channel in a single connection. Windows 2000 also supports cable modems; however, in most cases, proprietary software and drivers from the vendor are used to establish connections over these network adapter-like devices because they don't function quite like a modem.

- *Security:* Windows 2000 logon and domain security, support for security hosts, data encryption, and callback provide secure network access for remote clients. With Windows 2000, you also have the option of separating LAN traffic from RAS traffic with the **Point-to-Point Tunneling Protocol (PPTP)** or the **Layer 2**

Tunneling Protocol (L2TP). PPTP allows users to create secure connections to corporate networks over the Internet, using **virtual private networks (VPNs)**, which are network connections that use encryption to transport private data across public links. L2TP is a VPN protocol developed by Cisco to improve security over Internet links by integrating **IPSec (IP Security)**.

- *Server:* Windows 2000 Server RAS allows up to 256 remote clients to dial in. Windows 2000 Professional allows one remote client to dial in. The RAS server can be configured to provide access to an entire network or to limit access to the RAS server only.

- *LAN protocols:* IP protocol support allows you to access a TCP/IP network, such as the Internet. NWLink (IPX/SPX) protocol support enables remote clients to access NetWare servers and printers. You can also use NetBIOS applications over IPX, TCP/IP, or NetBEUI. Windows Sockets applications over TCP/IP or IPX, named pipes, Remote Procedure Call (RPC), and the LAN Manager API are also supported (see Chapter 7).

 Remote control and RAS are two remote technologies that work in different ways. Remote control employs a remote client as a dumb terminal for the answering system, whereas RAS establishes an actual network connection between a remote client and the answering computer system, using a link device (such as a modem) as a network adapter. RAS keyboard entries and mouse movements occur locally; with remote control, these actions are passed to a host system. Using RAS, computing operations are executed on the client; remote control computing operations are executed on the host with the resultant video signal being sent to the client.

Remote access services and terminal services are also two different mechanisms. Terminal services allow thin clients (that is, basic computers consisting of a display, keyboard, and mouse with only enough intelligence to connect to the terminal server host) to participate in a rich computing environment. Basically, the terminal server host acts as the CPU for the thin client. All operations and calculations are performed on the terminal server host; only the display changes are sent to the client, and only keyboard and mouse information is sent back to the terminal server. Terminal services are often employed in situations in which budget restrictions prevent the purchase of fully capable desktop systems or when complete security is required (that is, not allowing data to exist anywhere but on the secure server). RAS, on the other hand, is a mechanism by which remote computers that exist as independent systems are able to make connections over some type of communications link to a system or standalone machine. This link is used to access data or to gain further access to linked networks.

FEATURES OF RAS IN WINDOWS 2000

RAS is an integral part of Windows 2000. In fact, RAS is a standard component of Windows 2000 and does not require a manual installation to enable remote access, as was required in Windows NT. Some of the impressive features of RAS under Windows 2000 include: Multilink PPP, PPTP, L2TP, restartable file copy, idle disconnect, autodial and logon dial, client and server enhancements, a new look and feel, and callback security, each of which is defined as follows:

- *Multilink PPP RAS:* Multilink PPP allows you to increase overall throughput by combining the bandwidth of two or more physical communications links, such as analog modems, ISDN, and other analog/digital links.

- *Point-to-Point Tunneling Protocol (PPTP):* PPTP is a networking technology that supports multiprotocol VPNs, which allow users to access corporate networks securely via the Internet. Using PPTP, you can shift the burden of hardware support for devices such as modems and ISDN cards from the RAS server to a front-end processor (FEP) located at the Internet service provider (ISP). Clients using PPTP can access a corporate LAN by dialing an ISP or directly through the Internet. In both cases, the PPTP tunnel is encrypted and secure, and works with any protocol.

- *Layer 2 Tunneling Protocol (L2TP):* The Layer 2 Tunneling Protocol (L2TP) is a PPTP alternative that has been developed by Cisco Systems. Similar to PPTP, L2TP encapsulates PPP frames for transport over various networks, including IP, X.25, frame relay, and ATM. L2TP is used in combination with IPSec (a security protocol that secures data at the packet level) to provide a secure encrypted VPN link over public networks.

- **Restartable file copy:** The restartable file copy feature automatically retransmits file transfers that are incomplete because of RAS connectivity interruption. This feature reduces the time it takes to transmit large files over lower-quality connections, cost (because it avoids retransmission of the whole file), and the frustration that accompanies interrupted transfers.

- **Idle disconnect:** The idle disconnect feature breaks off a RAS connection after a specified period of time has gone by with no activity. This feature reduces the costs of remote access, helps you troubleshoot by closing dead connections, and frees up inactive RAS **ports** (any physical communication channel to which a modem, direct cable, or other device can be connected to enable a link between two computers).

- *Autodial and Logon Dial:* You can configure RAS access to automatically connect and retrieve files and applications stored on a remote system. Users do not have to establish an RAS connection each time they want to transfer a remote object; Windows 2000 handles all RAS events, providing quick and efficient access. By maintaining a virtual database of mappings between resources and connection objects, Windows 2000 RAS is able to reestablish links when previously accessed resources are requested.

- *Client and server enhancements:* Windows 2000 RAS includes a number of client and server components that allow third-party vendors to develop RAS and dial-up networking applications.

- *Look and feel:* Windows 2000 RAS is somewhat different from its manifestations in Windows NT or even Windows 95/98. The RAS capabilities have been integrated with the networking components, which results in a multipurpose management interface in which both standard LAN networking links and RAS links are established and configured. The Network and Dial-up Connections interface is a new, centralized control mechanism. Just about everything related to RAS is controlled through this interface. The only exception is that all RAS hardware, such as a modem, is installed through the Add/Remove Hardware applet in the Control Panel.

■ *Callback security:* You can control access to the system from specified phone numbers by using callback security. Selecting the Call Back radio button forces calls to originate from known phone numbers ("Preset to" option), or the remote access client can set the phone number dynamically ("Set by Caller" option). Setting the number dynamically allows users to access the system from different phone numbers even with the callback feature enabled and negates the callback security feature because remote access can be accomplished from any phone number.

WAN CONNECTIVITY

Wide area networks (WANs) link sites that are often a considerable distance apart. Using RAS and Windows 2000 enables you to create a WAN by connecting existing LANs via RAS over telephone, ISDN, or other communications lines. This is an inexpensive and cost-effective solution if you have minimal-to-moderate network traffic between sites. You can improve the performance of RAS-based WANs in one of three ways:

■ Increase the RAS connection bandwidth

■ Link multiple communication links, using Multilink PPP

■ Implement PPTP over the Internet

INTERNET NETWORK ACCESS PROTOCOLS

Windows 2000 RAS supports all standard protocols for remote Internet access as well as Multilink PPP. The RAS protocol that is used to establish and maintain a WAN link is dependent on the client and server operating system and the LAN protocols. Windows-2000-supported RAS protocols are discussed in the following sections.

Point-to-Point Protocol (PPP)

PPP is the current remote access standard. Remote access protocol standards are defined in RFCs (Request for Comments), official standards documents published by the Internet Engineering Task Force (IETF). You can find detailed information on the following RFCs at *http://www.ietf.org/rfc*. The RFCs supported in Windows 2000 RAS are:

■ RFC 1661: The Point-to-Point Protocol (PPP)

■ RFC 1549: PPP in HDLC Framing

- RFC 1552: The PPP Internetwork Packet Exchange Control Protocol (IPXCP)
- RFC 1334: PPP Authentication Protocols
- RFC 1332: The PPP Internet Protocol Control Protocol (IPCP)

Microsoft recommends using PPP because it is flexible and an industry standard, which means continued compatibility with client and server hardware and software in the future. Remote clients connecting to third-party PPP servers may need to use a post-connect terminal script (a script that provides login information to log on to the PPP server). The server will inform users it is switching to PPP framing mode (users must start the terminal to complete logon).

 When using a version of PPP other than Microsoft's to dial into a Windows 2000 Server that is a part of a domain and not a domain controller, the server looks only to its local accounts for the account name and password you specified on dial-in. If the server doesn't find the name and password locally, it doesn't check the domain accounts; it simply denies access. A domain controller does not have local accounts that it can use for verification; it uses the accounts in the domain database to grant or deny access.

Point-to-Point Tunneling Protocol (PPTP)

Point-to-Point Tunneling Protocol (PPTP) is one of the most interesting features of Windows 2000: it allows you to establish a secure RAS pipeline over the public Internet and to "tunnel" IPX, NetBEUI, or TCP/IP traffic inside PPP packets. PPTP can provide real benefits for companies with numerous remote users who already subscribe to a local ISP for e-mail and Internet access, because they can use the same connection to access the corporate LAN. These VPNs can support the IPX, TCP/IP, and NetBEUI LAN protocols and provide private network access from any Internet connection point. PPTP's significant features include:

- *Reduced transmission costs:* PPTP uses the Internet as the primary long-distance connection medium rather than leased lines or long-distance telephone lines, which reduces the cost of establishing and maintaining a RAS connection.

- *Reduced hardware costs:* PPTP requires less hardware by letting you locate modems and ISDN hardware on a network rather than directly attaching them to the RAS server.

- *Less administrative overhead*: PPTP permits centralized management of RAS networks and users.

- *Improved security:* PPTP connections over the Internet are encrypted and secure.

L2TP is a protocol similar to PPTP developed by Cisco for use with IPSec to support secure VPN links. From a user's perspective, it operates in the same manner as PPTP.

Multilink PPP

Multilink PPP combines two or more physical RAS links (modem, ISDN, or X.25 links) into one logical bundle with greater bandwidth. Multilink can combine analog and digital links in the same logical bundle. The only drawback to Multilink is that all connections to be aggregated must be of the same technology type. For example, ISDN and modem links cannot be aggregated, but three ISDN lines can be.

Because only one phone number can be stored in a user account, Multilink will not function with the callback security feature. The only exception to this rule is dual ISDN lines that have the same phone number. In this one instance, callback security will work with multilink.

Microsoft RAS Protocol (Asynchronous NetBEUI)

Microsoft's proprietary RAS protocol supports NetBEUI; any RAS client dialing into a Windows NT 3.1 or Windows for Workgroups system must use this protocol. When a connection has been established, the RAS server will act as a **gateway** for the remote client, providing access to resources via the NetBEUI, TCP/IP, or IPX protocols.

NetBIOS Gateway

Microsoft includes the **NetBIOS gateway** in Windows 2000 to enable backward compatibility for earlier versions of Windows NT, Windows for Workgroups, and LAN Manager. Remote clients connect using NetBEUI, and the RAS server translates packets as necessary between clients and local IPX or TCP/IP resources and servers. The NetBIOS gateway allows client access to LAN resources without local support for IPX or TCP/IP.

Serial Line Internet Protocol (SLIP)

SLIP was one of the first protocols developed specifically for TCP/IP support over dial-up connections. SLIP is not used much anymore because of its limitations as compared to PPP. For example, SLIP does not support the **Dynamic Host Configuration Protocol (DHCP)**, a method of dynamically assigning IP addresses, so a static IP address must be assigned to every SLIP client, which makes IP address administration more difficult. Unlike PPP, SLIP does not support IPX or NetBEUI. However, SLIP's biggest drawback is that it does not support encrypted passwords; its passwords are transmitted as plain text. RAS does not offer a SLIP server. RAS supports SLIP only as a client, which allows Windows 2000 clients to access UNIX servers that support SLIP.

The RFCs supported by RAS SLIP are:

- RFC 1144: Compressing TCP/IP Headers for Low-Speed Serial Links
- RFC 1055: A Nonstandard for Transmission of IP Datagrams over Serial Lines: SLIP

TELEPHONY FEATURES OF RAS

The RAS **Telephony Application Programming Interface (TAPI)** supplies a uniform way of accessing fax, data, and voice. TAPI is part of the Windows Open System Architecture (WOSA), developed to aid third-party vendors in designing powerful, integrated telephony applications. TAPI handles all communication between a TAPI-aware computer and a Private Branch Exchange (PBX), including basic phone functions (call park, hold, transfer, conferencing, and so on). TAPI treats a telephone network as a system resource using standard APIs and device drivers, so once installed, TAPI applications have seamless access to phone features and server-based communications.

Here are some of the benefits of and improvements in TAPI 3.0:

- *Comprehensive support:* TAPI is packaged with Windows 95, Windows 98, and Windows NT 4.0 Server and Workstation, as well as with Windows 2000 Server and Professional.

- *Native 32-bit components:* TAPI 3.0 core components are 32-bit and have additional full support for symmetrical multiprocessing, multithreaded applications, and preemptive multitasking.

- *Portability:* 32-bit TAPI applications designed for one TAPI platform will run without modification on any other, including Windows 95, Windows 98, Windows NT, and Windows 2000.

- *Device sharing capability:* Separate applications for inbound and outbound calls can control a single device, reducing hardware costs and enlarging the communications capacities of small business.

For more information about TAPI 3.0, refer to the IP Telephony with TAPI 3.0 white paper at *http://www.microsoft.com/windows/server/Technical/networking/iptelephony.asp*.

CONFIGURATION OF RAS

Unlike Windows NT, RAS under Windows 2000 is an integrated default component of the operating system. Therefore, no additional service installation is required to take immediate advantage of the communication offered via RAS. RAS is configured and managed from the Network and Dial-up Connections window (see Figure 9-1). (Dial-up connections were discussed in Chapter 7.) This window is accessed by selecting Start, Settings, Network and Dial-up Connections.

You have to create all RAS or remote links. The Make New Connection Wizard is used to establish new connections. You launch this wizard by double-clicking the Make New Connection icon in the Network and Dial-up Connections window. Five remote connection options are offered to you, as you can see in the Network Connection Type window shown in Figure 9-2.

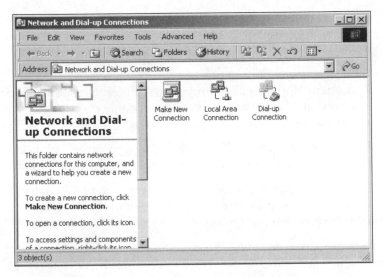

Figure 9-1   The Network and Dial-up Connections window

9

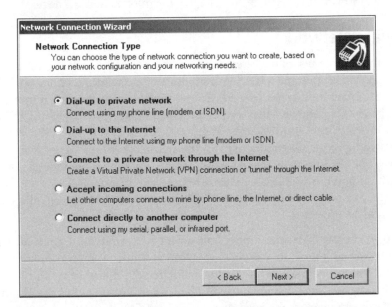

Figure 9-2   The select network connection type page of the Make New Connection Wizard

The options are as follows:

- *Dial-up to private network:* This option is used to create a connection object used to establish communications with a Windows 2000 or Windows NT RAS server.

- *Dial-up to the Internet:* This option is used to create a connection object used to establish communications with an ISP to gain Internet access.

- *Connect to a private network through the Internet:* This option is used to create a connection object used to establish a VPN connection to a remote LAN over a public network (such as the Internet). This connection can employ either PPTP or L2TP.

- *Accept incoming connections:* This option configures the system to accept inbound calls or connections. Windows 2000 Professional can only support a single inbound connection, but that link can be a direct connection, modem/dial-up connection, or a VPN link.

- *Connect directly to another computer:* This option is used to create a connection object used to establish communications over a serial cable, parallel cable, or infrared port.

Establishing RAS connection objects via the wizard is very elegant and quick. In the following sections, you look at the step-by-step process for each of these connection types and the postcreation properties you can manipulate.

All of the following network connection types require that the hardware device used to establish the RAS link be installed and configured before creating the connection object. This includes modems, cable modems, ADSL devices, infrared ports, and so on. See the section titled "Installing RAS Hardware" later in this chapter for information on device installation.

Dial-up to Private Network

Telecommuters and mobile personnel often need to communicate with the office LAN for a wide variety of purposes. Because a RAS link supports all network functions, such as access to files, printers, the Internet, various network services, and security control, remote connections to the LAN are very useful. Many organizations are taking advantage of the distance communication enabled by Windows 2000, Windows NT, and Windows 95/98 to reduce office space costs and increase the productivity of their employees. You can establish telecommuting with ease. The Dial-up to private network connection type is used for all connections over temporary communications lines between a remote client and a RAS server. To create a connection object on a remote client to be used to connect to a RAS server, follow the steps described in Hands-on Project 9-1.

After a Dial-Up to Private Network connection object is created, the Connect dialog box is automatically launched. The Connect dialog box offers four action buttons at the bottom of its display (see Figure 9-3). The Dial button launches the connection and attempts to establish a connection using the defined settings. The Cancel button closes the Connect dialog box and discards any changes made to that dialog box. The Properties button opens the multitabbed Properties dialog box for the connection object. The Help button launches the Windows 2000 Help system in the Network and Dial-up Connections context section.

In most cases, you want to click Dial to test the new object. If the connection is successful, an icon appears in the icon tray of the taskbar. The icon looks like two overlapping monitors. Each time a packet is passed over the connection, the color of the monitor screen flashes and changes from gray to teal. Double-clicking this icon reveals a connection status page, which can be used to access the connection's properties or to disconnect the link. You can also right-click over the tray icon to access dial-up properties or disconnect functions.

Figure 9-3   The Connect dialog box

A private network connection object functions by using the default settings in most cases, but you may want to fine-tune your connection to improve performance or capabilities. The Properties dialog box for a connection object can be accessed through a variety of means:

- Select the connection object in the Network and Dial-up Connections window, then either select Properties from the File menu or right-click the icon and select Properties from the resulting menu.

- If the connection object is already in use, right-click the tray icon and select Properties from the resulting menu.

- If the connection object is already in use, double-click the tray icon, then click the Properties button in the Status dialog box.

No matter how you get there, the Properties dialog box (shown in Figure 9-4) for a private network connection object is used to configure a wide variety of settings that are not offered via the Make New Connection Wizard.

The General tab is used to configure the devices and dial-up numbers. The "Connect using" field lists all installed communications devices. The devices with a marked check box are employed by the connection object in an attempt to establish a connection. The listed devices can be ordered to give priority to the faster or more reliable devices. By default, all devices dial the same phone number. If you deselect the "All devices call the same number" check box, the Phone number area becomes dependent on the selection of a device. The Phone number area includes settings for the area code, phone number, country/region code, and dialing rules. (See the "Phone and Modem Options" section later in this chapter for more information.) You can configure individual devices by clicking the Configure button when a device is selected. This opens a device-specific configuration dialog box in which elements such as communication speed, modem protocols, hardware features, terminal window, logon scripts, and modem speaker are configured. Note that settings in this dialog box apply only to the selected device. The Options tab includes connection object settings for the terminal window and logon scripts. The "Show icon in taskbar when connected" check box enables an icon for this connection to appear in the icon tray. This icon is used for quick access to connected links.

9

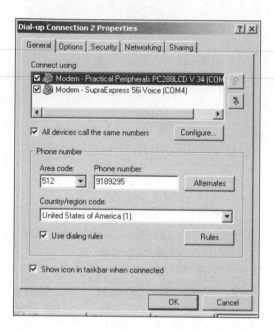

Figure 9-4   The Properties dialog box for a private network connection object, General tab

The Options tab (see Figure 9-5) configures how the connection object behaves while establishing a connection.

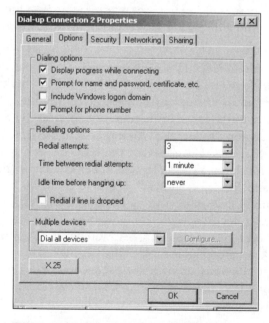

Figure 9-5   The Properties dialog box for a private network connection object, Options tab

The available settings on the Options tab are:

- *Display progress while connecting*—Provides you with a visual status of the connection establishment process. This option is selected by default.

- *Prompt for name and password, certificate, etc.*—Forces you to provide access credentials before launching the Connection object. This option is selected by default.

- *Include Windows logon domain*—Forces the connection to request logon domain information from the RAS server. By default, this option is not selected.

- *Prompt for phone number*—Forces the connection object to always prompt for verification of the phone number before attempting to establish a connection. This option is selected by default.

- *Redial attempts*—Sets the number of retries the system will make when a connection cannot be established with the remote system. The default is three retries.

- *Time between redial attempts*—Sets the time period between redials. The default is 1 minute.

- *Idle time before hanging up*—Sets the inactivity disconnect time period. The default is never.

- *Redial if line is dropped*—Forces the connection object to attempt to reconnect if the link is broken for any reason.

- *Multiple devices*—Used to enable Multilink. This is set to "Dial all devices" by default. Other settings include "Dial only first available device," which only establishes a single link with the remote system, and "Dial devices only as needed," which is used to establish activity-based dialing. Clicking the Configure button for the latter selection opens the Automatic Dialing And Hanging Up dialog box (see Figure 9-6). This dialog box is used to define when additional devices are dialed or disconnected, based on the level and time period of traffic. Defaults are to dial using new devices when current bandwidth has been at 75% utilization for 2 minutes and to disconnect when utilization has been less than 10% for 2 minutes.

- *The X.25 button*—Opens the configuration dialog box for X.25 connections. Through this dialog box you can define the X.25 network type in use, your X.25 address, and the two optional settings of user data and facilities. For more information on X.25, consult the *Windows 2000 Resource Kit*.

9

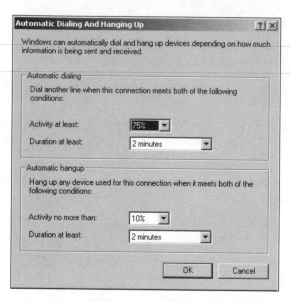

Figure 9-6   Automatic Dialing and Hanging Up dialog box

The Security tab (see Figure 9-7) is used to define the security requirements of the connection object. This tab offers two top-level security settings: "Typical (recommended settings)" and "Advanced (custom settings)." The default setting is "Typical (recommended settings)," which allows for unsecured passwords and has two other options: Require secured password and Use smart card. Two check boxes further define these alternate security options. The "Automatically use my Windows logon name and password (and domain if any)" check box should be used when your local and remote logon credentials are identical. The "Require data encryption (disconnect if none)" option protects not only the authentication process, but also all data transferred over the link.

The second top-level security setting of "Advanced (custom settings)" is used to specify exactly the level of security to use for this connection object. The Settings button reveals the Advanced Security Settings dialog box (see Figure 9-8).

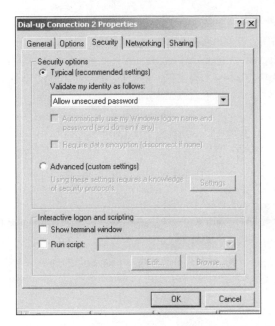

Figure 9-7 The Properties dialog box for a private network connection object, Security tab

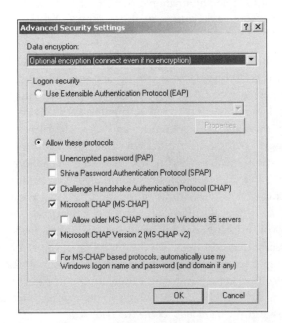

Figure 9-8 Advanced Security Settings dialog box

The Advanced Security Settings dialog box offers the following settings:

- *Data encryption*—Defines the encryption requirements. Selections are "No encryption allowed (server will disconnect if it requires encryption)," "Optional encryption (connect even if no encryption)," and "Require encryption (disconnect if server declines)."

- *Use Extensible Authentication Protocol (EAP)*—Allows you to require the use of smart card or third-party security mechanisms. The Properties button accesses mechanism-specific configuration settings.

- *Allow these protocols*—Select the encryption protocols allowed over this connection object. Options include the Password Authentication Protocol (PAP), the Shiva Password Authentication Protocol (SPAP), the Challenge Handshake Authentication Protocol (CHAP), Microsoft CHAP (MS-CHAP), MS-CHAP for Windows 95 servers, and MS-CHAP v2.

- *Use Windows logon name and password (and domain if any) automatically for MS-CHAP based protocols*—Uses local logon credentials over the connection object.

CAUTION

Defining custom security settings can be a complex and intricate process. We recommend consulting the *Windows 2000 Resource Kit* for more information on custom security settings before you attempt to deploy a custom security scheme on your network or over your RAS connections.

The bottom of the Security tab offers controls over whether to pop up a terminal window and run a script after a connection is established. These settings apply to all devices used by this connection object. To define device-specific items, use the Configure button on the General tab. In most cases, terminal windows and logon scripts are unnecessary; however, depending on the type of server you are connecting to and the security mechanisms employed, you may need to alter these settings. A terminal window allows you to enter keystrokes directly into the authentication mechanism on the remote server. Some systems require multiple passwords, selecting a logon method from a menu, or issuing protocol launch commands. If the logon requirements of a system can be automated, you can create a logon script that will provide these items automatically, without requiring a terminal window and user input each time the connection is established. Dial-up logon scripts can be as complex as necessary, and can include branching decision trees based on data from the remote server. Windows 2000 includes several sample scripts in the %systemroot%\System32\RAS folder that you can customize for your own purposes. For details on creating and modifying logon scripts, please consult the content of the sample scripts (which include useful details in the form of context-specific comments) and the *Windows 2000 Resource Kit*.

The Networking tab (see Figure 9-9) is used to configure the network communication components employed by the connection object. As you can see, this tab is very similar to the Properties window of a local area connection object. Keep in mind that a RAS connection is the same as a local connection, with a difference only in the speed of the connection, so this similarity should not surprise you.

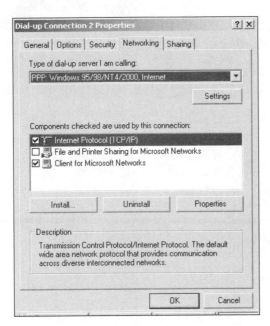

Figure 9-9   The Properties dialog box for a private network
connection object, Networking tab

The most important setting on this tab is the type of dial-up server to which this connection
object is to connect. Your options are PPP and SLIP. Because Windows 2000 and Windows NT
RAS servers can only accept inbound PPP connections, you will most likely select PPP; however, if you are connecting to an older UNIX system, you may need to employ SLIP. If you
don't know which to choose, try PPP first because it is the current standard remote link connection technology. PPP offers two further configuration details via the Settings button:
enabling Link Control Protocol (LCP) extensions and enabling software compression. In most
cases, the default settings are correct, but when connecting to older UNIX (or other) platforms,
the LCP extensions and software compression capabilities of the Windows 2000 version of PPP
may prevent stable communications.

The remaining portion of this tab is used to enable, install, and configure networking components. Enabling and disabling a component applies only to this connection object, but
installing or removing a component applies to all connection objects. By default, only the
Internet Protocol (TCP/IP) and Client for Microsoft Networks components are enabled;
the File and Print Sharing for Microsoft Networks component is disabled. For information
on configuring network components, refer to Chapter 7.

The Sharing tab (see Figure 9-10) is used to configure this connection object as a shared
communications channel. By enabling sharing for a connection object, you allow other
computers on your network to access resources over that external link. This feature, known
as Internet Connection Sharing, can be employed for either standard LAN or Internet connections. Internet Connection Sharing incorporates the Network Address Translation (NAT)
function, a Dynamic Host Configuration Protocol (DHCP) address allocator, and a Domain

Name Service (DNS) proxy. The mechanism hides your internal network configuration (a good idea to keep this information secure), provides automatic assignment of unregistered nonroutable IP addresses to internal clients, and provides a forwarding hand-off procedure for all requests for external services. Basically, Internet Connection Sharing transforms your Windows 2000 system into a limited DHCP proxy server. Try Hands-on Project 9-6 to configure Internet Connection Sharing.

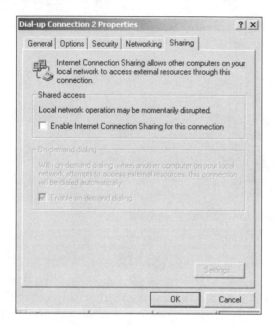

Figure 9-10   The Properties dialog box for a private network connection object, Sharing tab

After Internet Connection Sharing is enabled, you can also select whether to enable on-demand dialing. This feature automatically reestablishes the remote link when a client attempts to access external resources over your system via the currently offline connection object. For further information about the tuning and configuration of the Internet Connection Sharing service, please consult the *Windows 2000 Resource Kit*.

Troubleshooting the Internet Connection Service involves three distinct activities. First, verify that the configuration options for Internet Connection Service are properly defined. This is done through the Settings button on the Sharing tab of a dial-up connection's Properties dialog box. Specifically, the settings for Internet Connection Service allow you to either custom define applications and TCP/UDP ports, or to select from a list of known common services such as FTP, IMAP, SMTP, POP3, and Telnet. Second, verify that the connection is active and functioning. This can usually be accomplished using a Web browser. Finally, verify that communication from other clients can access your system over the network by either PINGing or attempting to access a shared resource from your client.

Dial-up to the Internet

The Internet has quickly become the communication medium of the masses. References to Web sites or e-mail addresses seem to be everywhere: on television, in magazines, in the local paper, and on thousands of products. Microsoft includes Internet access as a standard component of Windows 2000 remote communication. Windows 2000 also includes Internet Explorer and Outlook Express, in addition to the other common TCP/IP utilities often used over the Internet, such as File Transfer Protocol (FTP), Telnet, PING, and Tracert.

The Dial-up to the Internet Wizard can be used to establish a new user account with the MSN (Microsoft Network) dial-up network, move an existing MSN account to this computer, create a non-MSN Internet connection, or connect to the Internet over a network via a proxy server. A **proxy server** is software that sits between network users and the Internet, providing a layer of security to reduce the risk of network break-ins from the Internet. In most cases, you will either be configuring a non-MSN Internet connection or accessing a proxy server; however, if you want to employ MSN as your ISP (for an additional fee), simply select that option when prompted. To create a connection object for Internet access, follow the steps described in Hands-on Project 9-2.

After you have set up your connection object, if your modem is properly configured, your phone line is attached, and the service is not giving you a busy signal, you should have established an Internet connection, and the default homepage should be displayed in Internet Explorer. Close Internet Explorer by selecting Close from the File menu. You may be prompted to terminate your connection, but choose No to keep the connection active for now. Notice the connection icon in your icon tray—it is the one with the two overlapping monitors that blink. Double-clicking this icon opens the Connection Status dialog box (see Figure 9-11). You can terminate your connection at any time by clicking the Disconnect button in this dialog box.

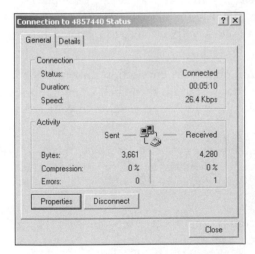

Figure 9-11   The Connection status dialog box

> If you selected the option to employ a proxy server to gain secure Internet access over a LAN, you will not see a connection object in the Network and Dial-up Connections window. Proxy connections are defined via the Internet Options applet (or by selecting the Internet Options command from the Tools menu of Internet Explorer), on the Connection tab, LAN Settings button. Any changes to your proxy settings should be made through the LAN Settings dialog box because a connection object is not created for proxy connections. Also, when you are employing a proxy connection over a LAN, the connection status icon does not appear in the icon tray.

The Connection Status dialog box is the same dialog box that appears for all dial-up connections. The General tab displays connection status, duration, speed, packets, compression, and errors. From this tab, you can access the connection object's properties or disconnect the link. The Details tab lists data such as server type, protocols, and the IP address of server and client.

The Properties dialog box of an Internet connection object is identical to that of a dial-up connection object. The only difference between these two objects is that one focuses on connecting to Windows 2000/Windows NT RAS servers and the other connects to ISPs.

Connect to a Private Network Through the Internet

The VPN is a trend in mobile computing that employs the Internet as a long-distance carrier to enable distant secure LAN connections. The "Connect to a private network through the Internet" option of the connection wizard enables mobile or remote computers to establish a connection with a LAN over a local connection to an ISP. In other words, you can connect to the Internet anywhere in the world via a local access point, then use Windows 2000 VPN technology to link to your LAN. Such a RAS link offers you all of the functionality of a network client—except that the speed of the connection may not be as fast, depending on the communications link used. Furthermore, a Windows 2000 VPN encrypts not only your authentication credentials, but also all of the data transferred, ensuring private, secure, confidential, long-distance computing. To create a VPN connection object, follow the steps described in Hands-on Project 9-3.

After you have created a VPN connection object, the connection launch dialog box for it is displayed. Provide your logon name and password, and then click Connect to test the connection. If all settings are correct, you will have a VPN connection to your RAS server.

> The RAS server to which you are connecting must be preconfigured to accept VPN connections. See the "Accept Incoming Connections" section to learn how to configure a Windows 2000 system to accept inbound connections.

The Properties dialog box for a VPN connection object is very similar to that of a dial-up connection object. The only differences are on the General and Networking tabs. The General tab (see Figure 9-12) offers control over the IP address/domain name of the RAS server and whether or not to employ a dial-up connection object to establish Internet access. The Network tab offers a pull-down list to select Automatic (selects a protocol already in use automatically), PPTP, or L2TP connection types. This selection should be made on the basis of the setting of the RAS server to which you are connecting.

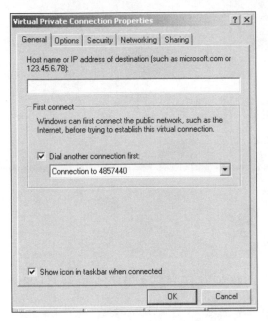

Figure 9-12 The General tab of a VPN Connection object's Properties dialog box

Accept Incoming Connections

Windows 2000 Professional, although designed as a network client, can act as a RAS server for a single inbound connection, which can occur over a modem, an existing Internet/network connection, or a direct access cable. You would probably use this feature only for special-purpose applications, for example, to gain access to your home system while traveling or to simplify technical support help for telecommuters. To configure Windows 2000 to accept an inbound connection, follow the steps described in Hands-on Project 9-4.

First, the incoming connection object is added to the Network and Dial-up Connection window, using the Make New Connection Wizard, as detailed in Hands-on Project 9-4. Opening this object's Properties reveals a dialog box with three tabs. The General tab (see Figure 9-13) is used to change the devices for this object and enable VPN connections. The Users tab is used to select which users can connect to this system over the inbound connection object. Furthermore, you can require that all users have "Require data encryption (disconnect if none)" set on their clients to protect passwords and data and decide whether to allow directly connected devices to connect without providing a password. By opening the Properties for a user, you can change that user's full name and password as well as set the callback options for that user. The Networking tab is where the networking components are configured.

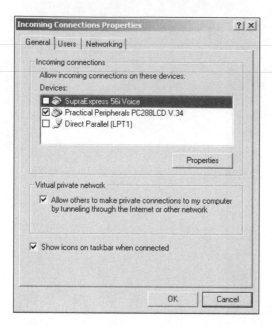

Figure 9-13   The General tab of the Incoming Connections Properties dialog box

Once an incoming connection object is created, the devices selected for that object are placed into answer mode. Therefore, when a call is received by that device, Windows 2000 automatically answers the call and attempts to authenticate the connection. When a device is placed into answer mode, it can only be used by a single process for inbound connections. However, a device in answer mode can be used to establish outbound calls. In other words, creating an incoming connection object for your modem does not prevent you from using that modem to establish a connection with your ISP or office LAN. However, it does prevent you from running two answering processes at the same time, for example, RAS and a fax service.

Connect Directly to Another Computer

All too often, you discover that you need to move several megabytes of data from one system to another, and either one or both of the systems do not have a network interface. In such cases, you have only a few reasonable options: use a tool that allows you to span copies across multiple floppy disks, purchase and install a NIC, or create a direct cable connection. Spanning floppies is often a doomed task, especially when working with more than 3 MB of material. If you do not have a NIC, the best option is to use a direct connect serial or parallel cable between the two computers, either connecting the COM ports or LPT ports (or even infrared ports, if already present on the systems), which you probably already have on hand or can purchase for less than $10.

To employ the direct connection, first attach the cable between the two systems, as mentioned either between COM or LPT ports (or orient the infrared devices). Next, you need to create a direct connection object on both systems—one acts as the host and the other acts as the guest. Just be sure to select the correct link type based on your hardware (that is, serial, parallel, or infrared). To create the direct connection objects, follow the steps described in Hands-on Project 9-5.

 You can create the host connection object through either the "Accept incoming connections" or the "Connect directly to another computer" wizard options. However, you can only create the guest or connect the object via the "Connect directly to another computer" wizard option.

After the link is established, you have a link to the other system just as if both systems were members of the same workgroup connected by network cables.

The Properties dialog box for a host direct connection object is the same as that of an incoming connection object. The Properties dialog box for a guest connection object is the same as that of any dial-up connection object, with the General tab offering control over the connection device.

9

INSTALLING RAS HARDWARE

Before any remote access connection can be established, the hardware required by that connection must be physically present and its drivers properly installed. Under Windows 2000, the process of installing hardware is often simple and requires little user input. Upon startup, Windows 2000 inspects the state of the hardware and attempts to identify any new devices. If a device's identity is recognized, it then attempts to locate and install drivers for that device. In some cases, you are prompted for additional paths to search for drivers. When Windows 2000 is unable to identify a device, you are either prompted to provide a path for the drivers or you need to use the Add/Remove Hardware applet or the Phone and Modem Options applet to install the drivers. For some specialty hardware, such as cable modems and DSL devices, you may need to use a vendor-supplied installation routine to install the correct drivers.

 Because the range of RAS-related devices is so broad, we recommend consulting the device's manual or contacting the vendor for further help with installation. However, this should only be necessary for a few uncommon devices.

PHONE AND MODEM OPTIONS

The primary Control Panel applet related to remote access devices and operations is the Phone and Modem Options applet. This applet is used to control dialing rules, modems, and telephony driver properties. The Dialing Rules tab lists the defined dialing location. A dialing location is a collection of remote access properties used to govern how links are established. The Dialing Rules tab provides you with three buttons: New, which allows you to create new locations, Edit, to alter existing locations, and Delete, to remove a location. Both New and Edit open the same three-tabbed interface in which the default or existing settings of a location can be altered.

The General tab of a new location (see Figure 9-14) is used to define:

- Location name
- Country/region
- Area code
- Number to dial to gain access to an outside line for local calls
- Number to dial to gain access to an outside line for long-distance calls
- Disable call waiting
- Dial using pulse or tone

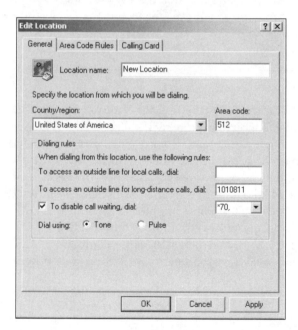

Figure 9-14   General tab of a new location

The Area Code Rules tab is used to define how numbers are dialed that exist within the current area code or outside the current area code. These rules include which prefixes (the first three numbers of a seven-digit phone number) are included in an area code (and thus are local calls), whether to dial 1 first when calling certain prefixes, and whether to include the area code when dialing certain prefixes.

The Calling Card tab is used to define a method to charge long distance calls to a credit card or dialing card. There are dozens of predefined cards that only require you to provide your account number and PIN. In addition, you can define your own calling card billing rule. Please consult the online help and the *Windows 2000 Resource Kit* for details on calling card rule creation.

After you have created an alternate location (that is, set dialing rules), it will appear in a drop-down list on most connection interfaces. Therefore, each time you initiate a remote access link, you can select the location profile to use.

The Modems tab of the Phone and Modem Options applet lists all currently installed modems and their attached ports. New modems are installed by clicking the Add button, and existing modems are deleted using the Remove button. The Properties button is used to access device/driver-specific properties and configuration controls.

The Advanced tab of the Phone and Modem Options applet lists all of the telephony providers present on the system. These are the drivers employed by the remote access system to tie communications devices to the networking components. Telephony providers are the interface between the operating system and the communications device. In most cases, you never interact with this tab. Please consult the *Windows 2000 Resource Kit* or your telephone services provider for configuration information.

WINDOWS 2000 AND THE INTERNET

9

Windows 2000 Professional provides a number of tools used in conjunction with the Internet: Internet Explorer, Outlook Express, FTP client, Telnet client, and Peer Web Services (PWS). The connections created via the Network and Dial-up Connections applet (such as a LAN with a proxy server) point to the Internet or to an Internet access and can be employed to access the vast resources of the Internet. Internet access is a key element in the design of Windows 2000. This is evident in ease of connecting to the Internet as well as the myriad tools included with the operating system.

Internet Explorer

Microsoft Internet Explorer is included with the Windows 2000 operating system. Newer versions of (and updates to) Internet Explorer can be obtained from the Microsoft Web site at *http://www.microsoft.com/ie/*.

In a nutshell, Internet Explorer represents the best that a state-of-the-art Web browser can offer. In addition to being powerful and easy to use as a straightforward Web-surfing tool, Internet Explorer is tightly integrated with other Microsoft applications, so it can invoke Word to open .doc files or Excel to open .xls files across the Web. Internet Explorer also includes advanced support for newsgroups and FTP, and is tightly integrated with Outlook Express (a free version of Outlook 2000 available with Office 2000).

The latest release also includes support for Java and ActiveX controls, which can add powerful interactive features to Web pages. Finally, Internet Explorer includes built-in support for so-called "push" technologies (which allow you to send updated Web page information to registered customers automatically), and you have the option of choosing from numerous incoming channels of information (such as PointCast News, CNN, and other online information services) that can be piped into your browser on an ongoing basis.

Outlook Express

One of the most popular e-mail client utilities is Microsoft Outlook, which is part of the suite of applications known as Office 2000. To tempt you with its impressive features and to offer you a taste of a multifunction e-mail client, Microsoft has included Outlook Express in Windows 2000. Outlook Express is limited only in the types of messaging it supports—specifically, it can only manage Internet e-mail involving POP3, IMAP, and SMTP services. Outlook Express can be used to read and write e-mail, file and sort messages, and more. It can act as a contact management tool, it is integrated with Internet Explorer for easy task switching, and it offers customizable interfaces and rules (actions to be performed on messages automatically).

If free is your highest criterion for an e-mail package, Outlook Express is no slouch. However, if you are willing to spend a few dollars for a worthwhile product, Outlook 2000 is worth the upgrade. For more information on Outlook 2000 and Outlook Express, please visit *http://www.microsoft.com/office/outlook/default.htm*.

FTP Client

FTP is an IP-based protocol that handles file transfer and remote file system access and file manipulation functions. Microsoft includes a command-line implementation of an FTP client as part of the Windows 2000 operating system. This client is installed automatically when TCP/IP is installed.

To learn more about this program, launch a Command Prompt window (Start, Programs, Accessories, Command Prompt), then type *ftp* at the command line. When the ftp> prompt appears, type *help* to read the program's associated list of commands. (Type *help* *<command>* to obtain information about a specific command, and replace "*<command>*" with the name of an actual FTP command—for example, *get* or *put*.)

Even though the command-line version of FTP included with Windows 2000 is perfectly adequate, there are numerous freeware and shareware GUI implementations of FTP that are much easier and friendlier to use. For a complete listing of such utilities, visit either of the following Web sites, select Windows as the platform, and use "FTP" or "FTP client" as your search string:

- *www.shareware.com*
- *www.download.com*

Telnet Client

Telnet is the text-based remote interaction tool commonly used on older UNIX systems to gain access to shell accounts (an account with an ISP that provides a text-only command-line interface to a remote system). Some ISPs still offer shell access to customers. The Telnet client included with Windows 2000 is a simple tool that attempts to establish a Telnet session with a remote system on the basis of domain name or IP address. You can alter the display fonts and record the session for later perusal (remember, it's all text anyway). For more information on Telnet, enter *telnet* from a Command Prompt (Start, Programs, Accessories, Command Prompt), then type *?help* at the Microsoft Telnet prompt.

Peer Web Services

Peer Web Services (PWS) is the Windows 2000 Professional version of Internet Information Services (IIS, a Windows 2000/Windows NT product). This application allows a Windows 2000 Professional system to host Web and FTP services. In most cases, PWS is used for site development and testing before deployment on an IIS system. PWS is limited to the same 10 simultaneous connections as Windows 2000 Professional itself; therefore, it is not a platform designed or intended for public Web/FTP site hosting. (Try Hands-on Project 9-7 to install PWS.)

Perhaps the most important, and in fact most widely recognized, function of PWS is the WWW (World Wide Web) Service, which allows users to publish Hypertext Markup Language (HTML) documents for use on the Web. Web browsers, such as Internet Explorer, use the Hypertext Transfer Protocol (HTTP) to retrieve HTML documents from servers.

Other than the limitation on the number of simultaneous users, and the omission of certain site management tools (such as FrontPage 2000, which is included with IIS 4.0, but not with PWS), the two environments are nearly identical. Certainly, they are more than consistent enough to facilitate development on Windows 2000 Professional and PWS, and deployment on Windows 2000 Server and IIS.

The FTP server installed with PWS is used to transfer files from the server to remote computers. Most installations of FTP on the Internet are used to download drivers and other data or software files.

 TIP The FTP Server code module represents the server side of FTP, whereas the FTP software mentioned earlier in the chapter deals with the client side of FTP. In other words, the FTP Server module allows other machines elsewhere on the network to upload files to a Windows 2000 Professional system, or to download files from that same system. The client-side software only allows the system to perform these activities with other FTP servers elsewhere on the network.

Web server resources are managed in much the same way as any other network resource. You should think of Web and FTP services as a type of share for Internet clients. Troubleshooting access problems for Web resources is performed in the same manner as dealing with the same issues regarding other network resource shares. Thus, you need to manage file permissions on an NTFS file object level and general access to resources via the share (or in this case Web or FTP services). If a user is unable to gain access to a resource via Web or FTP, first check the NTFS file object level permissions on the file/object/resource itself, then on all of its parent containers. Next, check the setting on the Web or FTP service. To access resources over the Web or FTP, the user must have at least Read access granted through the service, and at least Read access on the file or resource based on group memberships. Keep in mind that most Web access is anonymous, whereas most FTP access requires user authentication.

The anonymous user account, IUSR_<computername> is a member of both the Everyone and the Authenticated Users groups. So, be sure to check the permissions for these groups as well.

Try Hands-on Project 9-8 to practice managing resources hosted by a Web server. For more information on PWS, consult the *Windows 2000 Resource Kit*.

USING OFFLINE FILES

One of the biggest problems with mobile computers is granting users access to important files and documents, whether they are connected to the office LAN or the Internet, or disconnected from all network mediums. Additionally, this problem is compounded by the hassle of managing file versions between the remote system and the office LAN or the Internet. To resolve this issue, Microsoft has developed a scheme known as Offline Files. Offline Files is a multipart solution that involves file designation, data transfer, and follow-up synchronization.

From a mobile system, you can enable access for files and folders on a case-by-case basis, even though a direct connection to the network is not established. Simply use My Network Places or Windows Explorer to view a list of shared folders or individual files. Right-click an item you want to be able to access while offline (or not directly connected to the network), then select "Make Available Offline" from the resulting menu. The selected items are transferred to a local storage area. When using this tool, the files and folders made available offline are still accessed in the same manner that they would be if they were not stored locally. Unlike the Briefcase from Windows NT, which makes a copy of the file and then requires you to access the copy via the briefcase container, Offline Files does not change your access methods and maintains the duplicate offline version of the files; all redirections are completely unseen by the user. The Windows 2000 method is much more elegant and logical than previous schemes. When you are not connected to the network, the browse lists of My Network Places and Windows Explorer list only those resources cached locally. When a file or folder is marked for offline access, its icon is altered to display a double-rotating-arrow overlay (you can see this folder symbol in Figure 9-15).

The first time a file is marked for offline availability, Windows 2000 launches a wizard that introduces you to the feature and helps with basic configuration. All of the settings offered through the wizard can be accessed at any time through the Offline Files tab (see Figure 9-15) of the Folder Options command from the Tools menu of Windows Explorer.

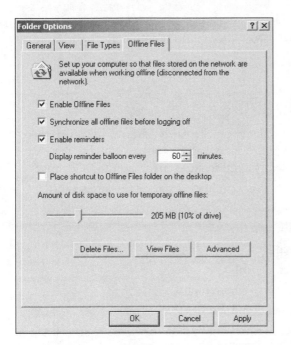

Figure 9-15   Offline Files tab of the Folder Options command
from the Tools menu of Windows Explorer

The controls on this tab are:

- Enable Offline Files

- Synchronize all offline files before logging off

- Enable reminders (to ensure that you are aware that you are working offline, displayed initially and then at defined intervals)

- Place shortcut to Offline Files folder on the desktop

- Amount of disk space to use for temporary offline files (this is a slider)

- Delete Files button

- View Files button

- Advanced button (determines how to deal with computers that go offline)

When the mobile system is reconnected to the network, Windows 2000 automatically synchronizes the offline files with their LAN-based originals. To alter the default, access the Synchronize Files command from the Tools menu of Windows Explorer. This interface lists all offline folders and their last updated status. To disable synchronization, deselect the check box beside a file or folder. To configure more advanced options, click the Setup button. Through this interface, you can define whether objects are synchronized automatically upon logon or logoff, only when idle, or at scheduled times.

Try Hands-on Project 9-9 to create and disable offline files. For more information on Offline Files, consult the *Windows 2000 Resource Kit*. File synchronization is also discussed in Chapter 15.

REMOTE ACCESS TROUBLESHOOTING

Troubleshooting remote access problems can be fairly elusive; however, there are several common-sense steps and several useful Windows 2000 tools to simplify the process. Your first approach to a remote access problem should include checking the following:

- Physical connections, such as phone lines, serial cables, and so on
- Power to external devices
- Properly installed and updated drivers
- Properly configured settings
- Correct authentication credentials
- Similar encryption or security requirements
- Proper protocol requirements and settings

If reviewing these items still fails to uncover the problem, there are several log files you can examine to try to glean more specific information. There are three logs related to remote access events. The first log is a file containing all communications between the operating system and the modem device during connection establishment. This modem log must be enabled via the Diagnostics tab of the modem's Properties on the Modems tab of the Phone and Modem Options applet. Once enabled, a text file named after the modem (in the format "ModemLog_Practical Peripherals PC288LCD V.34.txt") is stored in the main Windows 2000 directory. This file can be viewed with Notepad or simply by clicking View Log next to the enable check box on the Diagnostics tab.

The second log file is the PPP.log file, which records the communications involved in the setup, management, and operation of a PPP connection. The easiest way to enable PPP logging is through the use of a Netsh command. At the command prompt enter the following to enable the PPP logging on the client:

Netsh ras set tracing ppp enabled.

This will cause the creation of a PPP.log in the %systemroot%\Tracing folder. You can then use any text editor to view the log file. If you wish to disable PPP logging on the client enter the following Netsh command at the command prompt:

Netsh ras set tracing ppp disabled.

(For more information on working with the Registry, see Chapter 13.)

The final log is the System log as viewed through the Event Viewer. This log often records events related to remote access connection failures. For more information about using logs and Event Viewer, see Chapter 11.

By combining the data gleaned from these logs, you should be able to determine the cause of your connection problem and easily discover a simple resolution. If you need further remote access troubleshooting help, consult the *Windows 2000 Resource Kit*.

CHAPTER SUMMARY

- ❐ Windows 2000 provides the Remote Access Service (RAS) to create remote WAN connections. This is done through support for various remote access and secure protocols.

- ❐ Windows 2000 simplifies the installation and configuration processes for RAS, and enables you to take full advantage of RAS dial-up networking and security features.

- ❐ The Internet access features built into Windows 2000 allow you to easily gain access to vast public and private resources.

- ❐ Windows 2000 is designed to participate in VPNs by establishing an encrypted link over the Internet between two systems.

- ❐ The Offline Files feature enables mobile computer users to work offline on files and folders used on the network.

- ❐ Finally, there are tools available to help you troubleshoot problems with RAS.

KEY TERMS

Dynamic Host Configuration Protocol (DHCP) — A method of automatically assigning IP addresses to client computers on a network.

gateway — A computer that serves as a router, a format translator, or a security filter for an entire network.

idle disconnect — A feature that breaks off a RAS connection after a specified period of time has gone by with no activity. This feature reduces the costs of remote access, helps you troubleshoot by closing dead connections, and frees up inactive RAS ports.

Integrated Services Digital Network (ISDN) — A direct, digital, dial-up Public Switched Telephone Network (PSTN) Data Link layer connection that operates at 64 KB per channel over regular twisted-pair cable between a subscriber site and a PSTN central office.

Internet Protocol Security (IPSec) — A security protocol that secures data at the packet level.

Layer 2 Tunneling Protocol (L2TP) — A VPN (virtual private network) protocol developed by Cisco to improve security over Internet links by integrating with IPSec (IP Security).

Multilink PPP — The ability of RAS to aggregate multiple data streams into one network connection for the purpose of using more than one modem or ISDN channel in a single connection.

NetBIOS gateway — A service provided by RAS that allows NetBIOS requests to be forwarded independently of transport protocol. For example, NetBEUI can be sent over the network via NWLink.

Point-to-Point Protocol (PPP) — A Network layer transport protocol that provides connectivity over serial or modem lines. PPP can negotiate any transport protocol used by both systems involved in the link and can automatically assign IP, DNS, and gateway addresses when used with TCP/IP.

Point-to-Point Tunneling Protocol (PPTP) — A network protocol that allows users to create secure connections to corporate networks over the Internet, using virtual private networks (VPNs), which use encryption to transport private data across public links.

port — Any physical communications channel to which a modem, direct cable, or other device can be connected to enable a link between two computers.

proxy server — Software that sits between network users and the Internet, providing a layer of security to reduce the risk of network break-ins from the Internet.

restartable file copy — A RAS feature that automatically retransmits file transfers that are incomplete because of a RAS connectivity interruption.

Remote Access Service (RAS) — The service in Windows 2000 that allows users to log on to the system remotely over phone lines.

Serial Line Internet Protocol (SLIP) — An implementation of the IP protocol over serial lines. SLIP has been made obsolete by PPP.

Telephony Application Programming Interface (TAPI) — A Windows feature that supplies a uniform way of accessing fax, data, and voice. TAPI is part of the Windows Open System Architecture (WOSA) developed to aid third-party vendors in designing powerful, integrated telephony applications.

virtual private networks (VPNs) — Network connections that use encryption to transport private data across public links.

REVIEW QUESTIONS

1. You have configured a Windows 2000 Professional client to dial up and establish a connection to a Windows 2000 Server computer. The user adds a dial-up connection object and sets the proper network configuration, and the modem is functioning properly. The user submits the username and password correctly. Unfortunately, the user is unable to be authenticated properly. What might be causing this problem?

   a. The user did not configure the NetBIOS gateway properly.

   b. The user was not granted the appropriate dial-in permissions.

   c. The user was not added to the dial-in users group.

   d. none of the above

2. DHCP is the option for automatically assigning IP configurations to TCP/IP dial-up clients. True or False?

3. Windows 2000 Professional supports PPP logon scripts. True or False?

4. Which of the following RAS-related logs are enabled by default?

   a. PPP.LOG

   b. Modemlog_<*modem name*>.txt

   c. System log

5. Windows 2000 Professional supports which of the following encrypted authentication options through RAS? (Choose all that apply.)

   a. PAP

   b. SPAP

   c. DES-3

   d. MS-CHAP

6. The special protocol _____ allows multiple channels to be aggregated to increase bandwidth.

   a. Multilink PPP

   b. PPTP

   c. PPP

   d. SLIP

7. Where in Windows 2000 Professional do you specify which users have dial-in permissions to the RAS server?

   a. Network and Dial-up Connections

   b. Control Panel

   c. Remote Access Admin Tool

   d. My Computer

8. Which RAS security option also has an additional option to encrypt data?

   a. Require encrypted authentication

   b. Require C2 encrypted authentication

   c. Require B encrypted authentication

   d. Require Microsoft encrypted authentication

9. Which RAS callback option provides the greatest level of security?

   a. Set by caller

   b. Set by server

   c. Preset to

   d. Callback and confirm RAS password

10. Which of the following protocols are supported by both Windows 2000 RAS clients and RAS servers?

   a. SLIP

   b. PPP

   c. none of the above

   d. all of the above

9

11. Which of the following are similar technologies used to establish secured WAN links over the Internet? (Choose all that apply.)

    a. MPPP

    b. PPTP

    c. SLIP

    d. L2TP

12. Which LAN protocols are supported by RAS? (Choose all that apply.)

    a. AppleTalk

    b. TCP/IP

    c. NetBEUI

    d. DLC

    e. IPX

13. Which connection protocol can be used by Windows 2000 Professional to connect to remote systems over standard telephone lines?

    a. SLIP

    b. PPP

    c. DLC

    d. PPTP

14. Which connection protocol is retained by Windows 2000 to provide backward-compatibility with earlier versions of Windows NT, Windows for Workgroups, and LAN Manager?

    a. SLIP

    b. NetBIOS Gateway

    c. DLC

    d. AppleTalk

15. The Make New Connection Wizard from Network and Dial-Up Connections is used to create both RAS connections and LAN connections. True or False?

16. If you only want to connect to servers that offer secured data transmission, which of the following encryption settings should you define for your connection object?

    a. No encryption allowed (server will disconnect if it requires encryption)

    b. Optional encryption (connect even if no encryption)

    c. Require encryption (disconnect if sever declines)

17. Windows 2000 supports direct cable connections under RAS using which of the following? (Choose all that apply.)

    a. RS-232 null modem cables

    b. APC UPS cables

    c. LapLink cables

    d. Printer cables

18. RAS is remote control for Windows 2000. True or False?

19. Which two options from the Make New Connection Wizard are essentially the same, although one is used for calling an ISP whereas the other is used to call a RAS server?

    a. Dial-up to Private Network

    b. Dial-up to the Internet

    c. Connect to a Private Network Through the Internet

    d. Accept Incoming Connections

    e. Connect Directly to Another Computer

20. You can connect to another computer from a RAS client, using resources in the same manner as if you were connected on a LAN. True or False?

21. Dialing rules or dialing locations are used to define the geographic location of a mobile computer so as to prescribe the dialing procedures. True or False?

22. The modem-specific log file is enabled via which utility?

    a. Computer Management

    b. Phone and Modem Options

    c. Network and Dial-up Connections

    d. Server applet

23. Which of the following are Internet utilities included with Windows 2000 Professional? (Choose all that apply.)

    a. Internet Explorer

    b. Internet Information Server

    c. Outlook

    d. Telnet

    e. FTP client

24. The Offline Files mechanism of Windows 2000 is exactly the same as the Briefcase from Windows NT. True or False?

25. Offline Files are cached locally at logoff, are accessed in the same way as the original files, and are automatically synchronized by default. True or False?

9

HANDS-ON PROJECTS

Project 9-1

To create a "Dial-up to Private Network" connection object:

> TIP   This hands-on project assumes that a modem is installed.

1. Launch the Make New Connection Wizard by double-clicking the **Make New Connection** icon displayed in the Network and Dial-up Connections window.

2. The first page of the wizard is a welcome message. Click **Next**.

3. Select the network connection type to create, select **Dial-up to private network**, then click **Next**.

4. Provide the dial-up number for your RAS server.

5. If this RAS client is a mobile computer (notebook, portable, etc.), select the **Use dialing rules** check box, then provide the area code, and select the country/region code.

6. Click **Next**.

7. Set the availability of this connection. Your options are to allow all users of this system access to this connection object or to restrict access to your user account.

8. Click **Next**.

9. Finally, define a name for this connection. The default Dial-up Connection name can be changed to something descriptive, such as the name of the RAS server or the network this object will be used to connect to.

10. If you want this object to appear as a shortcut on the desktop, select the **Add a shortcut to desktop** check box.

11. Click **Finish**.

12. The Make New Connection Wizard completes the connection object creation (that is, it now appears in the Network and Dial-up Connections window); however, instead of returning to the Network and Dial-up Connections window, the new connection object is launched for the first time.

13. The Connect dialog box (see Figure 9-16) displays connection details for this connection object.

Figure 9-16 The Connect dialog box for the newly created
Dial-up to private network connection object

9

14. In the User name field, type the name of the user account you need to employ when connecting to the remote RAS system.

15. In the Password field, type the password for that user account—your keystrokes are echoed with asterisks instead of the actual character you type to prevent over-the-shoulder theft of your password.

16. If you want the system to retain your password, select the **Save password** check box. If you decide not to check this box, you will have to provide the password each time this connection object is used to establish the RAS link.

17. Double-check that the listed phone number in the Dial field is correct. If not, change it to the correct number.

18. If you are working from a mobile system, select the dialing location in the Dialing from field. If your current location is not predefined, click **Dialing Rules** to create a new location profile.

Project 9-2

To create a Dial-up to the Internet connection object:

 This hands-on project assumes that a modem is installed.

1. Launch the Make New Connection Wizard by double-clicking the **Make New Connection** icon displayed in the Network and Dial-up Connection window.

2. The first page of the wizard is a welcome message. Click **Next**.

3. Select the network connection type to create, select **Dial-up to the Internet**, then click **Next**.

4. This launches the Internet Connection Wizard, which prompts you for the type of Internet connection. Your choices are to create a new MSN account, move an existing MSN account, or connect to a non–MSN ISP/network proxy. For our purposes, select the final option that states **I want to set up my Internet connection manually, or I want to connect through a local area network (LAN)**. See Figure 9-17. Then, click **Next**.

Figure 9-17   The Internet Connection Wizard

5. Next, indicate which type of connection you want to establish. The choices are a modem connection or over a LAN. If you are using a modem, select that radio button. If you are using a LAN connection, select that radio button. Modem users click **Next**, then continue to Step 6. LAN users click **Next**, then jump to Step 16.

6. Select the dialing device from the pull-down list of installed modems. Click **Next**.

If there is only one modem or dialog device installed, you will not see the wizard screen in Step 6.

7. Provide the telephone number for the ISP. Verify that the area code and country/region settings are accurate.

8. If your ISP requires advanced settings (most do not), click the **Advanced** button. This reveals a dialog box in which you can select the connection type (PPP, SLIP, or CSLIP), logon procedures (none, manual logon, or logon script), IP address (automatically assigned or static), and DNS server address (automatically provides or primary/alternative static defined). All of these settings can be altered via the properties for this connection object after its initial creation.

9. Click **Next**.

10. Provide the username and password used to log on to the ISP. Click **Next**.

11. Provide a name for this connection object. Click **Next**.

12. Next the Wizard asks if you wish to configure Outlook Express to retrieve your e-mail, if so select **Yes**; otherwise, select **No**. Click **Next**.

13. If you selected **Yes**, you must provide a profile name, the e-mail address, the POP3, IMAP, or HTTP server address for incoming mail, the SMTP server address for outbound mail, and mail system authentication credentials (username and password). Provide the data required and click **Next** to proceed through the E-mail Setup Wizard.

14. The final page of the Internet Connection Wizard has a check box stating: To connect to the Internet immediately, select this box then click Finish. Follow those instructions. This completes the creation of the connection object. The system launches Internet Explorer, attempts to establish an Internet link using the newly created connection object, then loads the MSN homepage.

15. If you are a modem user, skip the remainder of these steps.

16. If you are using a LAN to gain Internet access, you are prompted for the method to obtain proxy configuration information. You can select **Automatic** or provide the URL of the configuration script. Your proxy server documentation informs you of which method to employ. Make a selection, provide the URL if necessary, then click **Next**.

17. If you want to configure Outlook Express, select **Yes**, otherwise select **No**. Click **Next**. Review Step 13 if you selected Yes.

18. The final page of the Internet Connection Wizard has a check box stating: To connect to the Internet immediately, select this box then click Finish. Follow those instructions. This completes the creation of the connection object. The system launches Internet Explorer, attempts to establish an Internet link using the newly created connection object, then loads the MSN homepage.

Project 9-3

To create a Connect to a Private Network Through the Internet connection object:

1. Launch the Make New Connection Wizard by double-clicking the **Make New Connection** icon displayed in the Network and Dial-up Connections window.

2. The first page of the wizard is a welcome message. Click **Next**.

3. Select the network connection type to create, select **Connect to a private network through the Internet**, then click **Next**.

4. The **Network Connection Wizard** prompts you for whether this object will automatically dial an existing ISP connection object or will rely upon you to establish a connection manually before launching this VPN connection object. If you change locations often and require unique access point phone numbers, selecting manual connection is your best choice. However, if you reuse the same access point often, allowing the VPN connection object to make the connection automatically simplifies your connection activities. For now, select automatic and select the ISP connection created previously. Click **Next**.

5. Provide the IP address or fully qualified domain name (FQDN) of the RAS server you want to connect to over the Internet. Click **Next**.

6. Indicate whether this VPN connection object will be available to all users or only to you. Click **Next**.

7. Provide a name for this connection object, then indicate whether to create a desktop icon. Click **Finish**.

Project 9-4

To create an Accept Incoming Connections connection object:

1. Launch the Make New Connection Wizard by double-clicking the **Make New Connection** icon displayed in the Network and Dial-up Connections window.

2. The first page of the wizard is a welcome message, click **Next**.

3. Select the network connection type to create, select **Accept incoming connections**, then click **Next**.

4. The Network Connection Wizard prompts you for the device over which a connection will be answered. This should list all modems and access ports (serial, parallel, and infrared). Mark the check boxes beside one or more devices.

5. If you need to alter the settings of a device, select it from the list, then click **Properties**. This reveals a device-specific settings dialog box.

6. Click **Next**.

7. Select whether to allow VPN connections. (VPN connections require a static IP address.) Click **Next**.

8. Select which users can establish a VPN connection with this system. Mark the check box beside each user to allow them to connect. You can create new users by clicking the **Add** button. Click **Next**.

9. The wizard offers you the ability to configure or alter the networking components to be used over this link. This interface is the same as the one seen when configuring other connection objects, and lists the protocols, services, and clients currently installed. Make any necessary changes, then click **Next**.

10. Provide a name for this Incoming connection. Click **Finish**.

Project 9-5

To create a Connect Directly to Another Computer connection object:

1. Go to the system that will act as the host in the direct connect pair. Typically, the host system has the resource that needs to be transferred or accessed by the guest system.

2. Launch the Make New Connection Wizard by double-clicking the **Make New Connection** icon displayed in the Network and Dial-up Connections window.

3. The first page of the wizard is a welcome message, click **Next**.

4. Select the network connection type to create, **Connect Directly to Another Computer**, then click **Next**.

5. Select the **Host** option. Click **Next**.

6. Select the link device type (serial, parallel, infrared, etc.) from the drop-down list. Click **Next**.

7. Select the user(s) who can connect over this link. Click **Next**.

8. Provide a name for this connection object. Click **Finish**.

9. Go to the system that will act as the guest in the direct connect pair.

10. Launch the Make New Connection Wizard by double-clicking the **Make New Connection** icon displayed in the Network and Dial-up Connections window.

11. The first page of the wizard is a welcome message. Click **Next**.

12. Select the network connection type to create, **Connect Directly to Another Computer**, then click **Next**.

13. Select the **Guest** option. Click **Next**.

14. Select the link device type (serial, parallel, infrared, etc.) from the drop-down list. Click **Next**.

15. Select the option to restrict this object to the current user or to allow all users access. Click **Next**.

16. Provide a name for this connection object. Click **Finish**.

17. The **Connect Direct Connection** dialog box appears. Provide a name and password (for a user account granted access to connect in Step 7). Click **Connect**.

9

Project 9-6

To configure Internet Connection Sharing:

 This hands-on project requires that a dial-up connection already be defined.

1. Open the Network and Dial-Up Connections tool by selecting **Start**, **Settings**, **Network and Dial-Up Connections**.

2. Select the predefined dial-up connection item from the Network and Dial-Up Connections tool.

3. Select **Properties** from the **File** menu.

4. Select the **Sharing** tab.

5. Select the **Enable Internet Connection Sharing for this connection** check box.

6. Click the **Settings** button.

7. Select the **Services** tab.

8. Select the checkbox beside **FTP Server**.

9. Click **OK**.

10. Click **OK**.

Project 9-7

To Install Peer Web Services on a Windows 2000 Professional system:

1. Open the Control Panel by selecting **Start, Settings, Control Panel**.

2. Double-click the **Add/Remove Programs** icon.

3. Select the **Add/Remove Windows Components** item in the left column. This launches the Windows Component Wizard.

4. Select the check box beside **Internet Information Services (IIS)**.

5. Click **Next**.

6. When prompted, provide the path to the Windows 2000 Professional CD. This may involve just inserting the CD into the drive and clicking OK, or using a Browser dialog box to locate the \i386 directory on the CD.

7. The installation wizard will copy files to your system. This will take several minutes. You may be prompted for the path to the CD a second time. Eventually, click **Finish**.

8. Click **Close** to terminate the Add/Remove Programs applet.

9. Close the Control Panel by selecting **Close** from the **File** menu.

Project 9-8

To manage resources hosted by a Web server:

1. Launch the Personal Web Manager from the Administrators. Tools applet in the Control Panel by selecting **Start, Settings, Control Panel**. Double-click **Administrative Tools**, then double-click **Personal Web Manager**.

2. On the Main page, which appears by default, take note of the path for **Your home directory**.

3. Select **Exit** from the **Properties** menu in the Personal Web Manager.

4. Launch Windows Explorer by selecting **Start, Programs, Accessories, Windows Explorer**.

5. Locate the folder as indicated by the path on the Main page of the Personal Web Manager and select it in the left pane of Windows Explorer.

6. In the right pane of Windows Explorer, right-click over an empty area, select **New** from the pop-up menu, then select **Text Document** from the resulting menu.

7. Type **default.htm** as the filename, then press **Enter**. If prompted about whether to change the filename extension, click **Yes**.

8. Open Notepad by selecting **Start**, **Programs**, **Accessories**, **Notepad**.

9. Select **Open** from the **File** menu.

10. Change the **Files of type** pull-down list to **All Files**.

11. Locate and select the **default.htm** document.

12. Click **Open**.

13. Type the following into the body of this document: **<HTML><BODY>This is the default document.<P></BODY></HTML>**.

14. Select **Save** from the **File** menu.

15. Select **Exit** from the **File** menu.

16. Double-click the **Internet Explorer** icon on the desktop.

17. Select the **Open** command from the **File** menu.

18. Type **localhost** and click **OK**.

19. The Web browser should display the default document you created by showing a line stating **This is the default document**.

20. Select **Close** from the **File** menu of Internet Explorer.

Project 9-9

To create and disable offline files:

> TIP This hands-on project requires that Windows 2000 Professional be a client in a Windows network and that some online resources are available via a share.

1. Open Windows Explorer selecting **Start**, **Programs**, **Accessories**, **Windows Explorer**.

2. Expand the **My Network Places** area of Windows Explorer, then expand **Entire Network** and expand **Microsoft Windows Network**.

3. Locate and select a share on any accessible network host.

4. Right-click over the selected share and select **Make Available Offline** from the pop-up menu. This launches the Offline Files Wizard.

5. Click **Next**.

6. Verify that the **Automatically synchronize the Offline Files when I log on and log off my computer** checkbox is selected. Click **Next**.

7. Verify that the **Enable reminders** checkbox is selected and the **Create a shortcut to the Offline Files folder on my desktop** checkbox is not selected. Click **Next**.

8. Select **Yes, make this folder and all its subfolders available offline**, then click **OK**.

9. After the synchronization process, all files that are stored as Offline Files will have a small double arrow image added to their icon to identify it. To disable Offline File support, select an enabled folder, right-click, and select **Make Available Offline**. This will remove the checkbox beside this command and remove the files from local cached storage.

CASE PROJECTS

1. Your organization has decided to allow several employees to work from home. With Windows 2000 Professional on the telecommuters' systems, describe your configuration and setup options, including how you can deal with security and nondedicated connections.

2. After installing a new modem, none of your connection objects will function—even after you've re-created them. Describe the process you would use to troubleshoot this problem.

10

PRINTING

After reading this chapter and completing the exercises, you will be able to:

♦ Understand Windows 2000 print terminology and architecture

♦ Understand the special features of the Windows 2000 print system

♦ Create and manage a printer

♦ Manage printer permissions

♦ Troubleshoot printing

Printing is an integral part of any operating system. Often, people will not believe a concept or layout until they see it on hard copy. In this chapter, you are introduced to some of the concepts associated with Windows 2000 printing, and then you will learn what is involved in installing and configuring printers for Windows 2000. Although this may sound somewhat simplistic, because of the many options that are available when accessing printers in the Windows 2000 environment, this topic is more complex than it may at first appear. For example, it is important to understand the distinction between printers that are directly attached to a computer and those with built-in network interfaces that are attached directly to a networking medium. Finally, you learn how to troubleshoot common printing-related problems on Windows 2000-based networks and systems.

WINDOWS 2000 PRINTING TERMINOLOGY

As is the case in other areas of Windows 2000 system architecture and behavior, Microsoft uses its own unique and specialized terminology to describe and explain how printers interact with the Windows 2000 system, and how its overall printing capabilities work. For the best results with the Microsoft tests, it is important to understand Microsoft's printing subsystem concepts, architecture, and behavior, which is why we begin this chapter with a "vocabulary list" of Microsoft print terminology, before we discuss the key components of the Microsoft print architecture and behavior. For convenience, we present these terms in alphabetical order in the following list:

- *Client application:* An application or service that creates print jobs for output, which may be either end-user-originated or created by a print server (*see also* print client)

- *Connecting to a printer:* The negotiation of a connection to a shared printer through the browser service from a client or service across the network to the machine where the shared printer resides

- *Creating a printer:* Using the Add Printer Wizard in the Printers folder (Start, Settings, Printers) to name and define settings for a print device in a Windows–2000–based network

- *Direct-attached printer:* A print device attached directly to a computer, usually through a parallel port (*see also* network interface printer)

- *Network interface printer:* A print device attached directly to the network medium, usually by means of a built-in network interface integrated within the printer, but sometimes by means of a parallel-attached network printer interface

- *Print client:* A network client machine that transmits print jobs across the network to a printer for spooling and delivery to a designated print device or printer pool

- *Print device:* In everyday language, a piece of equipment that provides output service—in other words, a printer; however, in Microsoft terminology, a printer is a logical service that accepts print jobs and delivers them to some print device for output when that device is ready. Therefore, in Microsoft terminology, a print device is any piece of equipment that can produce output, so this term would also describe a plotter, a fax machine, or a slide printer, as well as a text-oriented output device like an HP LaserJet.

- *Print job:* The contents of a completely or partially interpreted data file that contains text and control characters that will ultimately be delivered to a print device to be printed or otherwise rendered in some tangible form

- *Print resolution:* A measurement of the number of dots per inch (dpi) that describes the output capabilities of a print device; most laser printers usually produce output at 300 or 600 dpi. In general, the larger the dpi rating for a device, the better looking its output will be (but high-resolution devices cost more than low-resolution ones).

- *Print server:* A computer that links print devices to the network and shares those devices with client computers on the network. In the Windows 2000 environment, both Windows 2000 Professional and Windows 2000 Server can function as print servers.

- *Print Server services:* A collection of named software components on a print server that handles incoming print jobs and forwards them to a print spooler for post-processing and delivery to a print device. These components include support for special job handling that can enable a variety of client computers to send print jobs to a print server for processing.

- *Print spooler:* A collection of Windows 2000 dynamic link libraries (DLLs) used to acquire, process, catalog, and dispense print jobs to print devices. The print spooler acts like a holding tank, in that it manages an area on disk called the spool file on a print server, in which pending print jobs are stored until they have been successfully output. The term "despooling" refers to the process of reading and interpreting what is in a spool file for delivery to a print device.

- *Printer (logical printer):* In Microsoft terminology, a printer is not a physical device, but rather a named system object that communicates between the operating system and a print device. The printer handles the printing process for Windows 2000 from the time a print command is issued until a print job has been successfully output. The settings established for a printer in the Add Printer Wizard in the Printers folder (Start, Settings, Printers) indicate which print device (or devices, in the case of a printer pool) will handle print output, and also provide controls over how print jobs will be handled (banner page, special postprocessing, and so forth). Creating a logical printer is detailed in Hands–on Project 10-1. Deleting a printer is covered in Hands–on Project 10-6.

- *Printer driver:* Special-purpose software components that manage communication between the Windows 2000 I/O Manager and a specific print device. Ultimately, printer drivers make it possible for Windows 2000 to despool print jobs, and send them to a print device for output services. Modern printer drivers also allow the printer to communicate with Windows 2000, and to inform it about print job status, error conditions (out of paper, paper jam, and so forth), and print job problems.

- *Printer pool:* A collection of two or more identically configured print devices to which one or more Windows 2000 printers direct their print jobs. Basically, a printer pool permits two or more printers to act in concert to handle high-volume printing needs.

- *Queue (print queue):* A series of files stored in sequential order waiting for delivery from a spool file to a print device

- *Rendering:* Windows 2000 produces output according to the following sequence of steps: (1) A client application or a service sends file information to a software component called the **graphical device interface (GDI)**. (2) The GDI accepts the data, performs any necessary local processing, and then sends the data to a designated printer. (3) If this printer is local, the data is directed to the local print

10

driver; if the printer is remote (located elsewhere on the network), the data is shipped to a print server across the network. (4) Either way, the driver then takes the print job and translates it into the mixture of text and control characters needed to produce output on the designated print device. (5) This file is stored in a spooling file until its turn for output comes up, at which point it is shipped to a print device. (6) The target device accepts the input data and turns it into the proper low-level format for *rendering* on that machine, on a page-by-page basis. (7) As each page image is created, it is sent to the printer's print engine, where it is output on paper (or whatever other medium the print device may use).

- **Spooling**: One of the functions of the print spooler, this is the act of writing the contents of a print job to a file on disk so they will not be lost if the print server is shut down before the job is completed.

Familiarity with these terms is helpful when interpreting questions about Windows 2000 printing on the certification exam, and in selecting the proper answers to such questions. Testing considerations aside, some familiarity with this lexicon makes it much easier to understand Microsoft Help files and documentation on this subject as well.

WINDOWS 2000 PRINT SUBSYSTEM ARCHITECTURE

Given all this specialized terminology, it is essential to put it into context within the Windows 2000 environment, which is why we will describe the architecture of this subsystem next. The Windows 2000 print subsystem architecture consists of several components that turn print data into a printable file, transfer that file to a printer, and manage the way in which multiple print jobs are handled by a printer. These components are:

- GDI
- Printer driver
- Print spooler

We describe each of these elements in the subsections that follow.

Graphical Device Interface (GDI)

The GDI is the portion of Windows 2000 that begins the process of producing visual output, whether that output is to the screen or to the printer—it is the part of Windows 2000 that makes WYSIWYG (What-You-See-Is-What-You-Get) output possible. In the case of screen output, the GDI calls the video driver; in the case of printed output, it calls a printer driver and provides information about the targeted print device and what type of data must be rendered for output.

Printer Driver

A printer driver is a Windows 2000 software component that enables an application to communicate with a printer through the IP Manager in the Executive Services module in the Windows 2000 kernel. A printer driver is composed of three subcomponents that work together as a unit:

- *Printer graphics driver:* Responsible for rendering the GDI commands into **Device Driver Interface (DDI)** commands that can be sent to the printer. Each graphics driver renders a different printer language, for example, Pscript.dll handles PostScript printing requests, Plotter.dll handles the HPGL/2 language used by many plotters, and Rasdd.dll deals with printer languages based on raster images (that is, those based on bitmapped images, which are collections of dots). Rasdd.dll is used by PCL and most dot-matrix printers.

- *Printer interface driver:* You need some means of interacting with the printer, and the role of the printer interface driver is to provide that means; it provides the interface you see when you open the Printers window (Start, Settings, Printers).

- *Characterization data file:* Provides information to the printer interface driver about the make and model of a specific type of print device, including its features, such as double-sided printing, printing at various resolutions, and accepting certain paper sizes

10

Printer drivers are not compatible across hardware platforms, so although several client types (including Windows 2000 Professional and Server, Windows NT 4.0, 3.51, 3.5, and 3.1 Workstation and Server, and Windows 95 and 98) can print to a Windows 2000 print server without first installing a local printer driver—they'll download the driver from the print server—you must make sure that necessary drivers are available for the proper platforms.

Print Spooler

The print spooler (Spoolss.exe) is a collection of DLLs and device drivers that receives, processes, schedules, and distributes print jobs. The spooler is implemented as part of the Spooler service, which is required for printing. By default, the Spooler service is installed as part of the base Windows 2000 installation process (to check its status look at the Spooler entry in the Services Control Panel applet, or look for Spoolss.exe in the list on the Processes tab in the Task Manager). The Spooler includes the following components:

- Print router
- Local and remote print providers
- Print processors
- Print monitor

The print spooler can accept data from the print provider in two main **data types**: enhanced metafile (EMF) or RAW. **Enhanced metafile (EMF)** spool files are device-independent files used in Windows 2000 to reduce the amount of time spent processing a print job—all

GDI calls needed to produce the print job are included in the file. **RAW** spool files are device-dependent output files that have been completely processed (usually by their sending application or service) and are ready for output on the targeted print device. After a spool file has been created, control is restored to the application that created the print job, and other processing can resume in the foreground.

 TIP   EMF spool files are normally smaller than RAW spool files.

RAW spool files are used for local print jobs, for Encapsulated PostScript print jobs, or when specified by the user. Unlike EMF spool files, which still require some rendering once it is determined to which printer they're going, RAW spool files are fully defined when created. The Windows 2000 print processor also recognizes plain ASCII text files, which may be submitted by other clients (especially UNIX machines); the name of this spool file type is TEXT.

Print Router

The **print router** sends print requests from clients to the print server, so the requests can be routed to the appropriate print provider. When a Windows 2000 client computer connects to a Windows 2000 print server, communication takes place in the form of remote procedure calls from the client's print router (Winspool.drv) to the server's print router (Spoolss.dll), at which point the server's print router passes the print request to the appropriate print provider: the local print provider if it's a local job, and either the Windows 2000 or the NetWare print provider if it is sent over the network.

Print Provider

The **print provider** is server-side software that sends a print job to the proper server in the format required by that server. When a client sends a print job to a remote printer, the print router polls the remote print providers on the client computer and passes control of the print job to the first computer that recognizes the name of the specified printer. Windows 2000 uses one of the two following print providers:

- *Windows 2000 print provider (Win32Spl.dll):* Used to transfer print jobs to Windows network print servers
- *NetWare print provider (Nwprovau.dll):* Used to transfer print jobs to NetWare print servers

If the Windows 2000 print provider recognizes the printer name, it sends the print job along in one of two ways, depending on the operating system on the print server. If the print server is running a compatible network operating system (such as Windows NT 3.x, Windows for Workgroups, or LAN Manager), the print job is routed by NetBIOS to the print server. If the print server is running Windows 2000 or Windows NT 4.0, the print provider contacts the spooler service on the print server, which then passes it to the local print provider.

The local print provider writes the contents of the print job to a spool file (which will have the extension .spl) and tracks administration information for that print job. By default, all spool files are stored in the %systemroot%\System32\Spool\Printers directory, although you can change that location if desired (perhaps if you've installed a faster drive) by adjusting the print server settings in the Printers applet in the Control Panel. (You can practice changing the location of the spool file in Hands-on Project 10-4 at the end of the chapter.)

Spool files are normally deleted after the print job to which they apply is completed because they only exist to keep the print job from getting lost in case of a power failure that affects the print server. However, you can configure the spooler to retain all print jobs, even after they are printed. This control is accessed on a per-printer basis on the Advanced tab of the printer's Properties dialog box.

If a NetWare print provider recognizes the printer name, it passes the print job along to the NetWare workstation service, which then passes control of the print job to the NetWare redirector for transfer to the NetWare print server.

 To send print jobs from a Windows 2000 client to a NetWare server, you must have Client Services for NetWare (CSNW) installed on the client computer (see Chapter 8). To route print jobs through a Windows 2000 Server computer to a NetWare print server, the Windows 2000 Server must have the Gateway Services for NetWare (GSNW) installed.

10

Print Processor

A **print processor** works with the printer driver to despool spool files during playback, making any needed changes to the spool file according to its data type. The print processor itself is a PostScript program that understands the format of a document image's file and how to print the file to a specific PostScript printer or class of printers. Windows 2000 Server supports two print processors: one for Windows clients (Winprint.dll) and one for Macintosh clients (Sfmpsprt.dll), which is normally installed only after the Services for Macintosh service is installed. Remember that Services for Macintosh is included only with Windows 2000 Server, which is why this won't be an issue on Windows 2000 Professional machines.

On both Windows 2000 Professional and Server machines, the built-in Windows print processor understands EMF data files, three kinds of RAW data files, and TEXT files. But the Macintosh print processor that's installed on Windows 2000 Server when Services for Macintosh is installed understands only Pstscrpt1, which signifies that the spool file contains PostScript code from a Macintosh client, but that the output is not destined for delivery to a PostScript printer. In actuality, this data type lets the print processor know that a postprocessing job must be performed to translate the PostScript into the equivalent RAW data for output on the target printer before the print job can be spooled to the targeted print device.

Windows 2000 uses a raster image processor to send print jobs from a Macintosh client to a printer. The limitations of this processor mean that print jobs can have a maximum resolution of 300 dpi and must be printed in monochrome, regardless of the capabilities of the targeted printer. However, there are third-party raster image processors available for those who want to use the full capabilities of their printers even when printing via Services for Macintosh.

Print Monitor

The print monitor is the final link in the chain of the printing process. It is actually two monitors: a language monitor and a port monitor. The **language monitor**, created when you install a printer driver if a language monitor is associated with the driver, comes into play only if the print device is bidirectional, meaning that messages about print job status may be sent both to and from the computer. Bidirectional capabilities are necessary to transmit meaningful error messages from the printer to the client. If the language monitor has a role, it sets up the communication with the printer and then passes control to the port monitor. The language monitor supplied with Windows 2000 uses the Printer Job Language. The **Printer Job Language** provides printer control at the print-job level and enables users to change printer default levels such as number of copies, color, and printer languages. If a manufacturer creates a printer that speaks a different language, it would need to define another language monitor, because the computer and print device must speak the same language for communication to work.

The **port monitor** transmits the print job either to the print device or to another server. It controls the flow of information to the I/O port to which the print device is connected (a serial, parallel, network, or SCSI port). The port monitor supplied with Windows 2000 (Localmon.dll) controls parallel and serial ports. If you want to connect a print device to a SCSI port or network port, you must use a port monitor supplied by the vendor. Regardless of type, however, port monitors interface with *ports*, not printers, and are in fact unaware of the type of print devices to which they are connected. The print job is already configured by the print processor before it ever hits the output port.

Windows 2000 supports the following port monitors:

- Local port monitor (Localmon.dll)
- Hewlett-Packard network port monitor (Hpmon.dll)
- Line printer (LPR) port monitor (Lprmon.dll)
- AppleTalk port monitor (Sfmmon.dll)
- DEC network port monitor (Decpsmon.dll)
- LexMark Mark Vision port monitor (Lexmon.dll)
- NetWare port monitor (Nwmon.dll)
- Standard TCP/IP port monitor (SFM)
- Hypertext Transport Protocol (HTTP) port monitor
- PJL monitor (Pjlmon.dll)

> By default, only the local print monitor is installed. To use another monitor, you have to create a new port when configuring a printer from the Printers icon.

At this point, you've now been exposed to the unique Microsoft printing terminology and to the architecture of the Windows 2000 print subsystem. Now, you can learn how to work with printers and to define and configure them.

> In the Windows 2000 world, the focus is on printers, not print devices. As you've seen, in Windows 2000 parlance, printers are logical constructs—named combinations of output ports, a print driver, and configuration settings that may involve one or more print devices, the physical output devices—such as laser, ink-jet, or dot-matrix printers, plotters, fax modems, or slide makers. All the configuring and manipulation you do in Windows 2000 is done to printers, not to the print devices.

PRINTER DRIVER SOFTWARE

The function of a printer driver is to provide an interface between the client and the printer, whether that printer is connected to a print server or directly to the client. In other words, the job of printing software is to insulate applications from having to incorporate the logic and understanding necessary to communicate with a large collection of printers. That's why the functions that take application-specific file data and translate them into formats suitable for printing are included in the printer drivers themselves.

Because selecting a particular printer for output is part of the Windows printing process, it makes perfect sense to put this intelligence into the driver. That's because you must indicate what kind of device to which you want to send a print job as a part of instructing an application to print to a specific printer. Because print devices differ so much from manufacturer to manufacturer, and even from model to model, the right place to bury the details is in the printer driver itself. Not only does this shield application developers from having to write code to drive every kind of print device imaginable, it also puts the task of building the file translation routines on the print device manufacturers because they're the usual source of driver software.

PRINTING ACROSS THE NETWORK

Few organizations can afford to give each user his or her own printer, which explains why printing to a remote printer across the network is by far the most common print scenario on Microsoft networks. (In fact, many experts argue that sharing printers is one of the primary justifications for networking.) Two typical options for printing across the network exist for Microsoft network clients, including Windows 2000 Professional clients:

- You can print to a printer connected to a print server via a parallel or serial port.
- You can print to a printer connected directly to the network.

The main reason to connect a printer directly to the network is for convenience, because the printer doesn't have to be located near the print server. Any Windows 2000-based print server must still provide drivers and print job management.

THE PRINTING PROCESS

Now that you're familiar with the components of the printing process, here is how they fit together when printing from a Windows 2000 Professional client:

1. The user chooses to print from an application, causing the application to call the GDI. The GDI, in turn, calls the printer driver associated with the target print device. Using the document information from the application and the printer information from the printer driver, the GDI renders the print job.

2. The print job is passed to the spooler. The client side of the spooler makes a remote procedure call to the server side, which then calls the print router component of the server.

3. The print router passes the job to the local print provider, which spools the job to disk.

4. The local print provider polls the print processors, passing the job to the processor that recognizes the selected printer. Based on the data type (EMF or RAW) used in the spool file, any necessary changes are made to the spool file to make it printable on the selected print device.

5. If desired, the separator page processor adds a separator page to the print job.

6. The print job is despooled to the print monitor. If the printer device is bidirectional, the language monitor sets up communication. If not, or after the language monitor is done, the job is passed to the port monitor, which handles the job of getting the print job to the port to which the print device is connected.

7. The print job arrives at the print device and is printed.

INSTALLING AND MANAGING PRINTERS

The Printers window is the starting point for all printer installation and management. To reach it, choose Start, Settings, Printers. If there are no printers installed, you see only the Add Printer icon, which you double-click to create a printer (add a local printer definition) or connect to one across the network. After you have created or connected to a printer, it appears in this window with its own icon, as the example in Figure 10-1 shows. To set its properties, right-click the printer and choose Properties from the menu that appears.

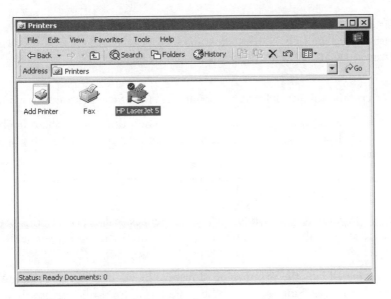

Figure 10-1 The Printers window

Managing Print Jobs

The Printers window comes into play not only when installing and managing printers, but also when managing print queues (see Hands-on Project 10-3). To manage print jobs, open the Printers window and double-click the icon for the printer in question. When you do so, you see a window, similar to the one shown in Figure 10-2, that displays all current print jobs for the selected print device.

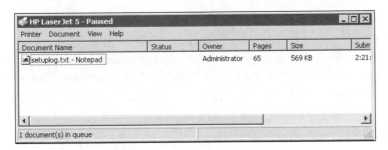

Figure 10-2 A print queue

To manage a print job, select it and then choose the appropriate menu option. For example, to delete a print job, choose Cancel from the Document menu, and the print job is deleted, allowing the next job in the queue to begin. Alternately, you can right-click the print job's list entry, and select Pause or Cancel. If the job has already been partially or completely spooled to the printer, it continues printing until the print device has finished with the spooled data, but no more data will be sent to the printer after you choose to cancel the job.

To delete print jobs, you need Manage Documents or Manage Printers permissions or ownership of the print job. Administrators and Power Users have Print, Manage Printers, and Manage Document permissions over printers by default.

The functions or commands available via the Printer menu of the print queue window are:

- *Connect*—Used to connect to shared printers when the printer share has been dragged-and-dropped into the Printers folder instead of configured using the Add Printer wizard

- *Set As Default Printer*—Sets the system to use this printer as the primary printer choice

- *Printing Preferences*—Opens the Printing Preferences dialog box for this printer. This is the same dialog box reached by pressing the Printing Preferences button on the General tab of the printer's Properties dialog box.

- *Pause Printing*—Halts the printing of all print jobs via this logical printer. When deselected, printing continues from the same point, even mid-print job, where it was paused.

- *Cancel All Documents*—Deletes all print jobs in the queue

- *Sharing*—Opens the printer's Properties dialog box with the Sharing tab selected

- *Use Printer Offline*—Turns a printer queue "off" in much the same way as the offline status of a physical print device

- *Properties*—Opens the Properties dialog box for the printer

- *Close*—Closes the printer window

The options available from the Documents menu are as follows:

- *Pause*—Pauses the print job. If the print job is already in the process of being sent to the printer, no other print jobs will be able to be sent to the printer until it is resumed or canceled. If the print job is still in the queue, other print jobs will bypass it on their way to be printed.

- *Resume*—Resumes printing of a paused print job

- *Restart*—Prints jobs again from the beginning

- *Cancel*—Removes a print job from the print queue

- *Properties*—Opens the Properties dialog box for the selected print job

The Properties dialog box of a print job displays details such as size, pages, data format type, owner, time submitted, layout, and paper tray selection. It also allows you to change the printing priority of the print job and to redefine the schedule. The schedule is the same type of control as a printer's activity time period, meaning that you can set it to either no restriction or define a time within which the print job will be able to be sent to the printer.

Creating a Local Printer

In Windows 2000 jargon, creating a printer means that you're setting up a printer for local use. To do so, double-click the Add Printers icon in the Printers window and answer the questions as prompted, including the following:

- Is the attached printer Plug and Play compatible?
- To which port will the printer be connected?
- What is the make and model of the printer?
- What do you want the printer to be named?
- Do you want the printer to be the default for all print jobs?
- Should the printer be shared with the network?

> If you're not sure whether your printer requires some fine-tuning (such as port configuration), you can create the printer and adjust its properties later.

After you have answered all the questions and supplied the needed files for the installation, you can choose to print a test page to make sure you have set up the printer properly. You can practice creating a printer for local use and sharing it with the network in Hands-on Projects 10-1 and 10-2 at the end of this chapter.

Connecting to a Remote Printer

Connecting to a remote printer is even simpler than creating a printer. Once again, double-click the Add Printer icon in the Printers window, but this time choose to connect to a network printer instead of creating one locally. You are presented with a list of shared printers to which to connect, and have the option of making that printer the default. Select to connect to it, and your work is done. Because Windows 2000 clients download printer drivers from the print server, you don't have to install local drivers.

> Windows 2000 print servers, by default, automatically host and install drivers for Windows 2000 and Windows NT 4.0 (Intel version). They can also host and install drivers for Windows 95/98 if an administrator adds the appropriate drivers.

CONFIGURING A PRINTER

After the printer is created or connected to, configuring it is easy. In the following sections, we explain the options on each tab of the printer Properties dialog box that appears when you right-click a printer in the Printers window and choose Properties.

> **TIP** You can create more than one logical printer for a single print device, so you can set up different configurations for the same print device. Different configurations might include setting up one printer to print high-priority jobs immediately, whereas another might be configured to print low-priority jobs during nonbusiness hours. Just be sure to tell your users to which printer they should connect, so they get the configurations they need.

General Tab

The General tab (see Figure 10-3) in a printer's Properties window contains a variety of controls that you can use to create a text comment that will show up in the Browse list entry for that printer, and to create a separate entry to identify its location. This tab also displays the features and paper sizes currently available for this printer. The Printing Preferences button brings up a window (see Figure 10-4) in which orientation, duplexing, page order, pages per sheet, and paper source tray (Paper/Quality tab) are defined. The Print Test Page button sends a document to the printer.

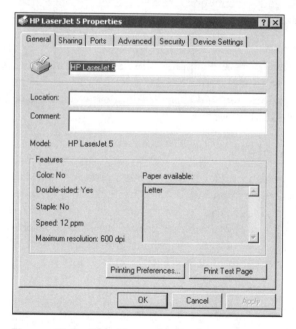

Figure 10-3   The General tab of printer Properties

Sharing Tab

The Sharing tab shown in Figure 10-5 works much like the one for sharing directories. Simply select the "Shared as" radio button and provide a share name for the printer. To install additional drivers for several client types (Windows 2000, Windows NT 4.0, 3.51, 3.5, 3.1, and Windows 95/98) that will be connecting to the printer, click the Additional Drivers button.

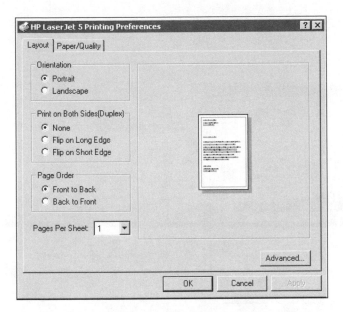

Figure 10-4   Printing Preferences window

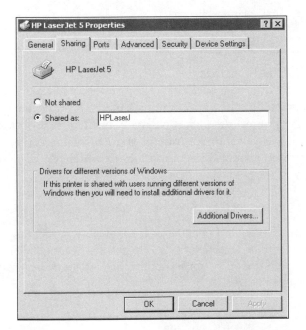

Figure 10-5   The Sharing tab of printer Properties

Ports Tab

On the Ports tab shown in Figure 10-6, you can adjust settings (including interrupts and base I/O addresses) for the ports selected for use with a particular print device. You can also add port monitors by clicking the Add Port button. The bidirectional printing option should be checked for printers that are able to send status information back to the print monitor, where it can provide the basis for user notifications (print job complete, out of paper, paper jam, and so forth).

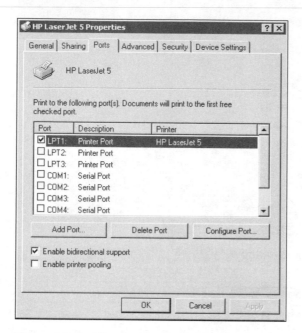

Figure 10-6   The Ports tab of printer Properties

This tab is also used to set up a printer pool, in which more than one print device (the physical printer) is assigned to a single printer (the logical printer construct). This option, which works best with identical print devices, even to the amount of memory installed in each, can reduce waiting time on heavily used printers by sending jobs to whichever print device is least busy.

 Select print devices that are in close physical proximity to each other for pooling. Users will not be able to tell to which pooled print device a print job went, and they're not going to like chasing all over to find their print jobs. Also, pool the fastest printer first, if there's any difference in speed among the pooled printers, because the pooling software will check the first-pooled printer first.

Advanced Tab

Use the Advanced tab shown in Figure 10-7 to set the hours during which the printer is available, set printer priority, and define spooling options. The availability hours are used to enable a printer only within a specified time frame. All print jobs sent to the printer outside this time frame are spooled and printed when the start time is reached. The **printer priority** setting determines which logical printer will be given first access to a printer. This setting is used to grant privileged, faster access to a busy printer for an individual or small group. The higher the number, the higher the priority, ranging from 1 to 99. The default is 1. From this tab, you can also select the printer driver to use or install an updated or alternate driver by clicking the New Driver button.

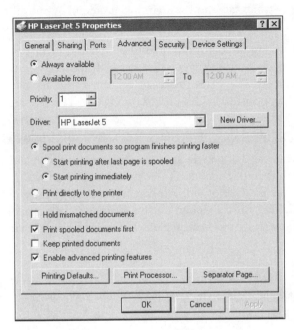

Figure 10-7   The Advanced tab of printer Properties

The spooling options define how print jobs are managed. In most cases, the default options will work well for you, because they'll start the printing process quickly and restore control to the application as rapidly as possible. However, here's what the options mean:

- If you choose to print directly to the printer instead of spooling documents, your application won't regain control until the print job is fully sent to the printer, but it will complete the print job faster.

- Waiting to print until the document has completely spooled to the printer does not hold up the application as printing to the printer does, but it will delay the printing process commensurately with the size of the print job.

- **Mismatched documents** are those for which the page setup and printer setup are incompatible. Holding mismatched documents prevents only those documents from printing, without affecting any others. This setting is useful because it prevents wasted resources, such as printing one character per page, when such documents are sent.

- If you choose to print spooled documents first, the order in which documents spool to the print device will override any print priorities that you have in place. By default, this option is disabled, so printer priority controls the order in which jobs print.

- If you want to be able to print a document again without resubmitting it from the application, choose to keep documents in the spooler after they've printed.

- Enabling advanced printing features activates functions, such as page order, book-let printing, and pages per sheet, that are only available on specific printers (and enabled on the Device Settings tab and the Printing Preferences button on the General tab).

At the bottom of the Advanced tab are three buttons: Printing Defaults, Print Processor, and Separator Page. The Printing Default button accesses the same dialog box as the Printing Preferences button on the General tab. The Print Processor button is used to select an alter-nate printing processor and data type format (RAW, EMF, or TEXT). The selections offered are based on the installed printer drivers and associated printer services. In most cases, you will not change these settings unless specified by a proprietary application or printing procedure.

Separator pages can be handy when several people are using the same printer, and you want to be sure that documents from different users don't get mixed up. Windows 2000 comes with several separator page files: Pcl.sep, Pscript.sep, Sysprint.sep, and Sysprtj.sep, but you can create custom pages in Notepad. Start off the document by putting a character on a line of its own, then use the codes in Table 10-1 to create separator files with the information that you need.

 TIP You can define any character as the lead character for the codes, but in our example, we use the exclamation point (!).

Save the separator page file with a .sep extension in the %systemroot%\System32 directory, and it will be among the options available when you configure the separator page via the Advanced tab.

Security Tab

The Security tab, shown in Figure 10-8, contains options quite similar to those used to set up secure files and directories. Here you can set permissions for printers. The Add and Remove buttons are used to alter the list of users and groups with defined permissions for this printer. The Permissions frame lists the permission types (Print, Manage Printers, and Manage Documents) and offers check boxes to Allow or Deny individual permissions for the selected user or group.

Table 10-1 Separator Page Codes

Code	Function
!B!M	Prints all characters as double-width block characters until the !U code is encountered
!B!S	Prints all characters as single-width block characters until the !U code is encountered
!D	Prints the date the job was printed, using the format in the Regional settings in the Control Panel
!E	Ejects a page from the printer
!F*pathname*	Prints the contents of the file specified in *pathname*, without any formatting
!H*nn*	Prints a printer-specific control sequence, indicated by the hexadecimal number *nn*. Check your printer manual to get the numbers.
!I	Prints the job number (every print job is assigned a number)
!L	Prints all the characters following it until reaching another escape code (!)
!N	Prints the username of the person submitting the job
!*n*	Skips a certain number of lines, where *n* is a number between 0 and 9
!T	Prints the time the job was printed, using the format specified in the Regional Settings in the Control Panel
!U	Turns off block character printing
!W*nn*	Specifies a certain width for the page (counted in characters). The default is 80; the maximum is 256

10

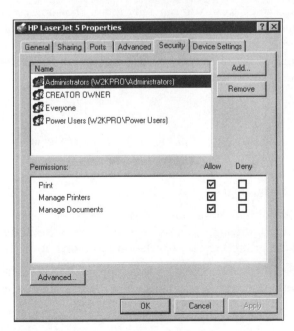

Figure 10-8 The Security tab of printer Properties

The three main permissions for printers, Print, Manage Documents, and Manage Printers, encompass the following capabilities:

- *Print documents*—Print, Manage Documents, Manage Printers

- *Pause, resume, restart, and cancel owned document*—Print, Manage Documents, Manage Printers

- *Connect to a printer*—Print, Manage Documents, Manage Printers

- *Control settings for any print job*—Manage Documents, Manage Printers

- *Pause, resume, restart, and cancel all documents*—Manage Documents, Manage Printers

- *Cancel all documents*—Manage Printers

- *Share a printer*—Manage Printers

- *Delete a printer*—Manage Printers

- *Change permissions*—Manage Printers

The Advanced button reveals another dialog box where more detailed permissions, auditing, and ownership are controlled. On this dialog box (see Figure 10-9), permissions are added on a user or group basis for the detailed permissions of Print, Manage Printers, Manage Documents, Read Permissions, Change Permissions, and Take Ownership. These permission settings can be defined for each user to apply to This printer only, Documents only, or both. The Auditing tab is a control interface similar to the permissions interface where the same types of actions granted via permissions can be set so you can audit them. The audit events created via this object are recorded in the Security Log and viewed through the Event Viewer. The Owner tab is used to take ownership for your user account or one of your groups (of which you are a member). Remember that ownership can only be taken, it cannot be given. Try managing printer permissions in Hands-on Project 10-5.

Device Settings Tab

The final tab in the Properties dialog box (shown in Figure 10-10), the Device Settings tab, is used to make sure that the print device itself is configured properly. Most of these settings shouldn't need to be adjusted if you chose the proper printer driver during setup, but these items may be subject to change as you upgrade your printer:

- *Memory:* Be sure that the amount of memory listed on this tab is equal to that installed in the printer. Too little, and you won't get the good out of it that you should. Too much, and the printer may try to take on more than it can handle.

- *Paper trays and other accessories:* Some printers may be upgraded with particular paper trays. If you install one, or rearrange existing ones, you'll need to update the settings here.

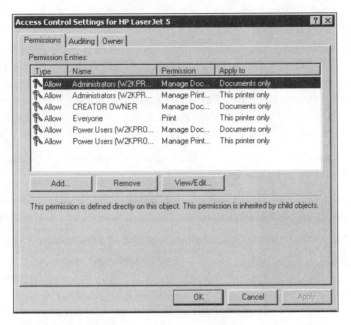

Figure 10-9 Advanced Security dialog box, Permissions tab

10

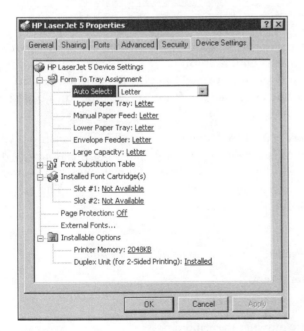

Figure 10-10 The Device Settings tab of printer Properties

There may be other options and functions listed on this tab that are printer model–specific. When these appear, consult the printer's user manual for information on modifying those settings.

PRINTERS AND THE WEB

Windows 2000 has added Web support to its print subsystem, which allows remote users to submit print jobs for printing, view printer queues, and download print drivers. See Hands–on Project 10-8 to configure Windows 2000 Professional to connect to an Internet printer. These features are afforded via the **Internet Printing Protocol (IPP)**. The Web-based features are accessible only when the print server is running Windows 2000 Professional with Peer Web Services or Windows 2000 Server with Internet Information Services (IIS).

IPP offers two main benefits. First, it enables Web-based distribution of printer drivers. Second, it offers Web-based print queue management.

To download a printer driver, simply use a URL as the network path when connecting to a network printer. The URL should be formatted as:

```
http://<printservername>/printers/<printersharename>/.printer
```

To access a print queue via the Web, open a URL with the following formatting: http://<*printservername*>/printers/. Select a printer from the list, then use the Web-based menu to perform print queue management. The operations and commands are the same as those accessed through a normal printer queue window.

MANAGING THE PRINT SERVER

In addition to the configurable properties of each logical printer, the print server itself can be fine-tuned. Opening the Printers window (from either the Start menu or the Control Panel), shows you a list of currently installed printers and the Add Printer Wizard. Selecting Server Properties from the File menu reveals the Print Server Properties dialog box (see Figure 10-11).

The Forms tab of this dialog box is used to define paper sizes. The Ports tab lists all known ports and installed printers on those ports (if any). On this tab, you can add new ports, delete existing ports, or configure individual ports. The Drivers tab lists the installed printer drivers. On this tab, you can add, remove, update, or configure printer drivers. The Advanced tab offers control over the spool file location and several events:

- Log spooler error events
- Log spooler warning events
- Log spooler information events
- Beep on errors of remote documents
- Notify when remote documents are printed
- Notify computer, not user, when remote documents are printed

All of these events, when selected, appear in the System log, viewed through the Event Viewer. The default location for the spool files is %systemroot%\System32\Spool\Printers.

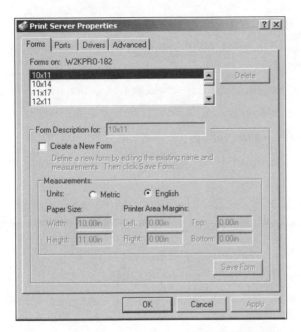

Figure 10-11 The Print Server Properties dialog box, Forms tab

10

TROUBLESHOOTING PRINTING PROBLEMS

Printing from Windows 2000 is usually a trouble-free process, but there's always something that can go wrong. Microsoft recommends following these steps when troubleshooting printing problems:

1. Identify which of the seven components of the printing process is failing (printer creation and configuration, connecting to a shared printer, creating a print job, sending the print job to the spooler, processing the spooled job, sending the processed job to the print device, or printing at the device). To find the correct one:

   a. Analyze the symptoms of the problem.

   b. Change the configuration as applied to that part of the process.

   c. Test the configuration to see if the print job works.

   If the print job now works, you found the right part. If not, then it's time to start over.

2. After you identify the problem, look for documented problem solutions online, in the manuals that ship with Windows 2000 or the printer, or in the Microsoft Knowledge Base (*http://support.microsoft.com/search/*).

3. Implement a short-term solution.

4. Implement a long-term solution, if possible.

Troubleshooting Printing in General

When deciding upon your method of attack for a systematic troubleshooting response to a printing problem, try the following:

- Check the physical aspects of the printer—cable, power, paper, toner, etc.

- Re-create the logical printer on the client.

- Terminate and reshare the printer on the print server.

- Try using a different application, user account, or computer to print to the same printer.

- Check for stalled print jobs.

- Make sure the printer is online (a device setting).

- Reinstall the print driver.

- Start and restart the spooler (discussed later in this chapter).

- Check the free space on the drive where the spooler is directed; at least 75 MB is recommended.

- Try using the Print Troubleshooter by selecting Start, Help, clicking on Troubleshooting, then clicking on Print.

Troubleshooting Network Printing

When troubleshooting network printing problems, add the following steps to your troubleshooting checklist:

1. Verify basic network connectivity, making sure you can see and connect to the print server from your workstation. Try copying a file to or from the server. If you can't do this, the print server itself may be inaccessible.

2. Create a local printer and redirect its port to a network printer. This will determine whether there's a problem copying files from the server to the workstation, as is done when you connect to a shared printer.

3. Print from a DOS-based program using the NET USE command to connect to the printer. If the print job works, this may indicate that the connection to the printer is not persistent and needs to be adjusted.

4. If using TCP/IP printing or connecting to a printer attached directly to the network, try PINGing the printer's IP address (by opening a Command Prompt window and typing *PING* followed by the printer's IP address) to make sure it's functioning. Also, create an LPR port to the printer and connect to that port to allow the computer to act as the printer's queue.

Stopping and Restarting the Print Spooler

The Spooler service is required for printing. Like other services, it's stopped and started—and its startup configured—from the Services tool in Administrative Tools (from the Start, Programs menu or the Control Panel). By default, the Spooler service is set to begin automatically when the system starts. To stop it, select it from the list of services (it's called Print Spooler—see Figure 10-12) and click the Stop button or select Stop from the Action menu. To start it again, select it from the list (it will remain on the list even when stopped) and click Start. Sometimes, stopping and restarting the spooler service can clear up problems that are difficult to troubleshoot.

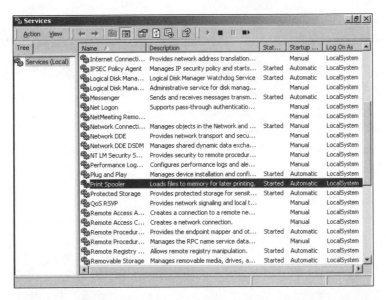

Figure 10-12   Selecting the Print Spooler service from the Services tool

 TIP   For more on troubleshooting printing, see Chapter 16, "Troubleshooting."

FAX SUPPORT

Windows 2000 Professional supports native fax features and operations. The Fax applet in the Control Panel is used to install and configure the fax components of Windows 2000. The Fax applet has four tabs. The first tab, User Information (see Figure 10-13), is used to define information that will be used on your cover pages. The second tab, Cover Pages, is used to define or create cover pages for your outbound faxes. The third tab, Status Monitor, is used to configure notification of fax activities. The fourth tab, Advanced Options, is where you gain access to the Fax Service Management tool. Try Hands-on Project 10-7 to enable fax receiving.

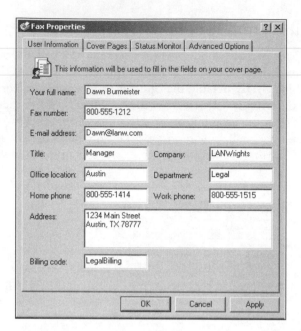

Figure 10-13   The Fax applet, User Information tab

The Fax Service Management tool is used to configure all fax-enabled devices. All fax devices can be set to allow sending and/or receiving of faxes. You can also configure whether to print incoming faxes to a printer, to store them to a folder, or to send them to a local e-mail inbox. The Fax Service Management tool also maintains logs of all inbound and outbound fax activity.

Troubleshooting fax problems is accomplished through a few simple actions. First, check the physical connections of the phone line from the wall to the computer's fax device. Second, verify the driver is properly installed via the Device Manager. Third, check to make sure you have enabled send and/or receive capabilities for that modem. Fourth, check the Receive options to ensure you are handling inbound faxes as you actually intend.

CHAPTER SUMMARY

- ❑ The Windows 2000 print subsystem architecture consists of several components that turn print data into a printable file, transfer that file to a printer, and manage the way in which multiple print jobs are handled by a printer. These components are the GDI, printer driver, and print spooler.

- ❑ Microsoft uses a special vocabulary for printing-related services, software and hardware components, and activities. It is important to grasp this vocabulary to be able to interact with and troubleshoot the Windows 2000 print subsystem.

- ❑ You use the Add Printers Wizard in the Printers folder to create, share, and connect to print devices, whether directly attached to a local machine or shared elsewhere on the network.

❏ You also use the Add Printer Wizard to configure a print device, including the selection of the driver, output configuration, and postprocessing options, and working with two or more identically configured printers to establish a printer pool.

❏ It is important to fine-tune the printing process for various situations, including managing priorities for print jobs, and setting up multiple printers with differing priorities so that multiple-user communities can share a single print device, yet give one community preferential access to the device.

❏ The most common causes of printing problems in the Windows 2000 environment were discussed, along with suggestions for how to isolate and identify their causes, and take the right kinds of corrective actions to resolve them.

❏ You can also add fax support to Windows 2000 Professional through the Fax applet in the Control Panel. Furthermore, fax management is handled through the Fax Service Management tool.

KEY TERMS

characterization data file — The file responsible for rendering the GDI commands into DDI commands that can be sent to the printer. Each graphics driver renders a different printer language.

client application (*see also* print client) — An application or service that creates print jobs for output, which may be either end-user-originated or created by a print server itself.

connecting to a printer — The negotiation of a connection to a shared printer through the browser service from a client or service across the network to the machine where the shared printer resides.

creating a printer — Setting up a printer for local use.

data type — The format in which print jobs are sent to the spooler. Some data types are ready for printing (RAW) and some require further preparation (EMF).

Device Driver Interface (DDI) — A specific code component that handles the translation of generic print commands into device-specific equivalents, immediately prior to delivery of a spool file to a print device.

direct-attached printer — A print device attached directly to a computer, usually through a parallel port (*see also* network interface printer).

enhanced metafile (EMF) — Device-independent spool data used to reduce the amount of time spent processing a print job. Once it's queued, EMF data requires additional processing to prepare it for the printer.

graphical device interface (GDI) — The portion of the Windows 2000 operating system responsible for the first step of preparing all graphical output, whether to be sent to a monitor or to the printer.

Internet Printing Protocol (IPP) — A new Windows 2000 protocol that adds Web support to the print subsystem. IPP allows remote users to submit print jobs for printing, view printer queues, and download print drivers.

10

language monitor — The part of the print monitor that sets up bidirectional messaging between the printer and the computer initiating the print job.

mismatched document — A document with incompatible printer and page settings (that is, the page settings are impossible to produce given the existing printer settings).

network interface printer — A print device attached directly to the network medium, usually by means of a built-in network interface integrated within the printer, but sometimes by means of a parallel-attached network printer interface.

port monitor — The part of the print monitor that transmits the print job to the print device via the specified port. Port monitors are actually unaware of print devices as such, but only know that something's on the other end of the port.

print client — A network client machine that transmits print jobs across the network to a printer for spooling and delivery to a designated print device or printer pool.

print device — In everyday language, a piece of equipment that provides output service—in other words, a printer. However, in Microsoft terminology, a printer is a logical service that accepts print jobs and delivers them to some print device for output when that device is ready. Therefore, in Microsoft terminology, a print device is any piece of equipment that can produce output, so this term would also describe a plotter, a fax machine, or a slide printer, as well as a text-oriented output device such as an HP LaserJet.

print job — The contents of a completely or partially interpreted data file that contains text and control characters that will ultimately be delivered to a print device to be printed, or otherwise rendered in some tangible form.

print processor — Software that works with the printer driver to despool files and make any necessary changes to the data to format it for use with a particular printer. The print processor itself is a PostScript program that understands the format of a document image file and how to print the file to a specific PostScript printer or class of printers.

print provider — The server-side software that sends the print job to the proper server in the format that it requires. Windows 2000 supports both Windows network print providers and NetWare print providers.

print resolution — A measurement of the number of dots per inch (dpi) that describes the output capabilities of a print device; most laser printers usually produce output at 300 or 600 dpi. In general, the larger the dpi rating for a device, the better looking its output will be (but high-resolution devices cost more than low-resolution ones).

print router — The software component in the Windows 2000 print subsystem that directs print jobs from one print server to another, or from a client to a remote printer.

print server — A computer that links print devices to the network and shares those devices with client computers on the network.

Print Server services — A collection of named software components on a print server that handles incoming print jobs and forwards them to a print spooler for postprocessing and delivery to a print device. These components include support for special job handling that can enable a variety of client computers to send print jobs to a print server for processing.

print spooler — A collection of Windows 2000 DLLs used to acquire, process, catalog, and dispense print jobs to print devices. The spooler acts like a holding tank, in that it manages an area on disk called the spool file on a print server, where pending print jobs are stored until they've been successfully output. The term "despooling" refers to the process of reading and interpreting what's in a spool file for delivery to a print device.

printer (logical printer) — In Microsoft terminology, a printer is not a physical device, but rather a named system object that communicates between the operating system and some print device. The printer handles the printing process for Windows 2000 from the time a print command is issued, until a print job has been successfully output. The settings established for a printer in the Add Printer Wizard in the Printers folder (Start, Programs, Printers) indicate which print device (or devices, in the case of a printer pool) will handle print output, and also provide controls over how print jobs will be handled (banner page, special postprocessing, and so forth).

printer driver — Special-purpose software components that manage communications between the I/O Manager and a specific print device. Ultimately, printer drivers make it possible for Windows 2000 to despool print jobs, and send them to a print device for output services. Modern printer drivers also permit the printer to communicate with Windows 2000, and to inform it about print job status, error conditions (out of paper, paper jam, and so forth), and print job problems.

printer graphics driver — The part of the printer driver that renders GDI commands into device driver interface commands that may be sent to the printer.

printer interface driver — The part of the printer driver that provides an interface to the printer settings.

Printer Job Language — A specialized language that provides printer control at the print-job level and enables users to change printer default levels such as number of copies, color, printer languages, and so on.

printer pool — A collection of two or more identically configured print devices to which one or more Windows 2000 printers direct their print jobs. Basically, a printer pool permits two or more printers to act in concert to handle high-volume printing needs.

printer priority — The setting that helps to determine which printer in a pool will get a given print job. The printer with the higher priority is more likely to get the print job.

queue (print queue) — A series of files stored in sequential order waiting for delivery from a spool file to a print device.

RAW — Device-dependent spool data that is fully ready to be printed when rendered.

rendering — Graphically creating a print job.

spooling — One of the functions of the print spooler, this is the act of writing the contents of a print job to a file on disk so they will not be lost if the print server is shut down before the job is completed.

REVIEW QUESTIONS

1. In the Windows 2000 print model, the hardware used to produce printed output is called a _____.

2. What is a print device connected to a computer via a parallel cable known as?

   a. a logical printer

   b. a network-attached printer

   c. a print processor

   d. a direct-attached printer

3. Which of the following is software that enables the operating system to communicate with a printer?

   a. printer driver

   b. print provider

   c. print monitor

   d. print router

4. The _____ service implements the part of the printing software that receives, processes, schedules, and distributes print jobs.

5. Because they're device-independent, EMF spool files are generally smaller than RAW spool files. True or False?

6. Which of the following statements are true about network-attached printers? (Choose all that apply.)

   a. They can be a member of a printer pool.

   b. They can use TCP/IP to receive print jobs.

   c. They can only be serviced by a single logical printer.

   d. They require a print server to operate.

7. Spool files are normally deleted after the print job they prepared is completed. True or False?

8. Which software must you have installed to access a NetWare print server via a Windows 2000 Server machine?

   a. Client Services for NetWare

   b. File and Print Services for NetWare

   c. Internet Printing Protocol

   d. Gateway Services for NetWare

9. Which tool or mechanism is used to grant one user or group faster printing than others?

   a. print resolution

   b. print priority

   c. printer availability

   d. printer pools

10. To delete a print job, you must have Manage Documents permissions. True or False?

11. Auditing can be defined on a permission and user detail level. True or False?

12. What is the function of the .sep files stored in the \System32 directory?

   a. to create custom graphics banner pages for print jobs

   b. to provide templates for separator pages

   c. to provide standard separator pages for immediate use

   d. none of the above

13. When you've got more than one printer set up for the same print device, what is this known as?

   a. print sharing

   b. printer pooling

   c. printer porting

   d. none of the above

14. Ownership of a printer can be assigned to any group. True or False?

15. If you choose to print directly to ports, what will happen?

   a. The job will only be able to print if it can fit all at once into printer memory.

   b. The application will stall until the print job is completed.

   c. The application will stall until the print job is fully spooled to the printer.

   d. Complex pages may not print correctly.

16. Clients connecting to a network over RAS links do not have the ability to print. True or False?

17. What must all logical printers for a single print device have in common?

   a. priority

   b. access time window

   c. driver

   d. paper tray source

   e. none of the above

18. The one restriction on the members of a printer pool is that all printers must be the exact same model. True or False?

10

19. When pages will only print after being fully loaded into printer memory, page protection is _____.

20. The spool files are stored in which location by default?

    a. \Documents and Settings\Printers\Spooler

    b. %systemroot%\System32\Spooler\Printers

    c. %systemroot%\System32\Printers\Spooler

    d. \Temp\Spooler

21. Print queues cannot be managed from a Web browser. True or False?

22. After sending several print jobs to a printer, you discover that they have not printed. You look at the print queue and the only items there are your print jobs. You attempt to delete them but are unable to. What can you do to resolve this?

    a. Make sure the printer is not paused.

    b. Cycle the power on the printer.

    c. Restart the print spooler.

    d. Create a new shared printer on the print server.

23. Which printer permission level has the ability to print documents, connect to a printer, and share a printer?

    a. Print

    b. Manage Documents

    c. Manage Printers

24. What is the first step in troubleshooting network printer problems?

    a. Re-create the local logical printer.

    b. Print from a DOS application.

    c. Change client computers.

    d. Verify that you can see and connect to the print server.

25. Windows 2000 printer settings include both the native internal default controls of the Windows 2000 print system and device-specific proprietary controls of the physical device. True or False?

HANDS-ON PROJECTS

Project 10-1

To create a local printer:

 TIP This hands-on project does not require a physical printer.

1. Open the Printers folder (click **Start**, **Settings**, **Printers**).
2. Double-click the **Add Printer** icon.
3. Click **Next** in the Add Printer Wizard window.
4. Select **Local printer**.
5. Deselect the check box about automatically installing Plug and Play printers if it is selected.
6. Click **Next**.
7. Select **LPT1**.
8. Click **Next**.
9. From the list of manufacturers, locate and select **HP**.
10. From the list of models, locate and select **HP LaserJet 5**.
11. Click **Next**.
12. Provide a name for this printer.
13. Select **Yes** for this printer to be the default.
14. Click **Next**.
15. Select **Do not share this printer** if it is not already selected.
16. Click **Next**.
17. Select **No** to printing a test page if it is not already selected.
18. Click **Next**.
19. Click **Finish**.
20. The newly added printer is displayed in the Printers window (you may need to refresh the display by pressing F5).

10

Project 10-2

To share a printer with the network:

> **TIP** This hands-on project requires that you complete Hands-on Project 10-1.

1. Right-click the printer created in Hands-on Project 10-1, and select **Sharing** from the resulting menu.
2. Click the **Shared as** radio button.
3. Provide a name for the share.
4. Click **OK**.

Project 10-3

To pause a print queue, see documents, delete documents, and restart a print queue:

1. From the **Printers** window, double-click your default printer (the one with the circled check mark).
2. From the **Printer** menu, select **Pause Printing**.
3. Open any application, such as Notepad. Print three documents.
4. Return to the open print queue.
5. Double-click any of the print jobs now appearing in the queue.
6. Explore the information for this document.
7. Click **OK**.
8. Highlight any of the documents in the queue.
9. From the **Document** menu, select **Pause**.
10. Select a different document in the queue.
11. From the **Document** menu, select **Cancel**.
12. Select the paused document in the queue.
13. From the **Document** menu, select **Resume**.
14. From the **Printer** menu, select **Cancel All Documents**.
15. Click **Yes** to confirm the deletion of print jobs if prompted.
16. From the **Printer** menu, select **Pause Printing**.
17. From the **Printer** menu, select **Close**.

Project 10-4

To change the location of the spool files:

1. From the **File** menu, select **Print Server Properties**.

2. Select the **Advanced** tab of the Server Properties dialog box.

3. Change the **Spool** folder field to **g:\temp\spooler** (or something similar that matches an existing folder on your computer).

4. Click **OK**, then click **Yes** to confirm the changes to the spool folder.

Project 10-5

To change printer permissions:

1. Right-click the printer created in Hands-on Project 10-1, and select **Properties** from the resulting menu.

2. Select the **Security** tab from the printer's Properties dialog box.

3. Select the **Power Users** group.

4. Deselect the **Allow** check box for **Manage Printers**.

5. Click **OK**.

Project 10-6

To delete a printer:

1. Select the printer created in Hands-on Project 10-1.

2. From the **File** menu, select **Delete**.

3. Click **Yes** to confirm the deletion.

4. Click **OK** on the warning that the printer has been removed.

5. Close the Printers folder.

Project 10-7

To enable fax receiving:

> **TIP** This hands-on project requires that a fax modem be already present and installed on the system.

1. Open the **Fax** applet by selecting **Start**, **Settings**, **Control Panel**, then double-click **Fax**.

2. Select the **Advanced Options** tab (see Figure 10-14).

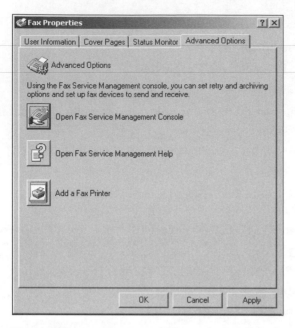

Figure 10-14   The Fax applet, Advanced Options tab

3. Click the **Open Fax Service Management Console** button.

4. Select the **Devices** node in the left pane.

5. Select the listed device in the right pane.

6. From the **Action** menu, select **Properties**.

7. Click to check the **Enable receive** check box if it is not already checked.

8. Set the **Rings before answer** to **1**.

9. Click **OK**.

10. Close the Fax Service Management Console.

Project 10-8

To connect to an Internet printer:

 This hands-on project requires that a Windows 2000 system running IIS/PWS is present and a shared printer is installed on the IIS/PWS host.

1. Open the **Printers** folder by selecting **Start**, **Settings**, **Printers**.

2. Double-click the **Add Printer** icon.

3. Click **Next**.

4. Select **Network Printer**, then click **Next**.

5. Select the **Connect to a printer on the Internet or on your intranet** radio button.

6. Type in the URL to your printer in the form of
http://<*servername*>/printers/<*servername*>/.printer where <*servername*> is the name of the IIS/PWS host/printer server and <*sharedname*> is the name of the printer share.

7. Click **Next**.

8. If prompted for authentication, provide a name and password with access permissions to this printer.

9. Select whether to configure this printer as the default printer for your client. Click **Next**.

10. Click **Finish**.

CASE PROJECTS

1. Your workgroup has a single physical printer. One person in the workgroup generates many memos and other short documents, while another produces very long documents that are (usually) less time-sensitive than the memos. You can't add another printer to the network, and both users must be able to print throughout the workday. How can you make sure that the memos are printed in a timely fashion?

2. Documents sent to your locally attached printer no longer print. Explain the basic troubleshooting steps you would take to resolve the problem.

10

PERFORMANCE TUNING

After reading this chapter and completing the exercises, you will be able to:

♦ Understand the performance and monitoring tools of Windows 2000

♦ Create a Counter log for historical analysis

♦ Create Alert events to warn of performance problems

♦ Create a baseline

♦ Detect and eliminate bottlenecks

Once you have installed and configured Windows 2000 Professional, connected it to the network, and set up printers, you are ready to optimize your computer performance. Windows 2000 includes several tools for monitoring your computer's performance and tuning it for the best output. Tools discussed include the Performance Console, Event Viewer, and Task Manager.

We introduce and describe these tools and discuss specific system objects and counters that are worth monitoring. You learn what combinations of counters can be used to analyze system slowdowns and how to isolate, identify, and correct system bottlenecks. Very few operating systems include the kinds of tools that Windows 2000 offers to help inspect and analyze system performance. In this chapter, you learn how to use these Windows 2000 monitoring tools to good effect.

ESTABLISHING A BASELINE

To recognize when bottlenecks exist, it's first necessary to establish some feeling for what's normal on your system, a **baseline** against which you can measure system behavior. Key elements in a baseline include recorded observations about the characteristics and behavior of the computer system. Baselines can be formed by creating a Counter log for the list of counters you consider important and collecting data for those counters over a period of time at regular intervals. This helps you establish a definition of what a normal load looks like and provides points of comparison for future system behavior.

Of course, you'll want to make sure that your system baseline doesn't itself indicate existing bottlenecks. If you discover unacceptably long queues or evidence of memory problems when you create a baseline, you'll want to address whatever bottlenecks you discover right away. We discuss how you can do this for common Windows 2000 subsystems in the sections that follow.

MONITORING AND PERFORMANCE TUNING

When it comes to system analysis, there are two primary components involved in tackling performance-related issues:

- *Monitoring:* This requires a thorough understanding of system components and their behavior, as well as observation of those components and how they behave on a regular basis.

- *Performance tuning:* This activity consists of changing a system's configuration systematically, and carefully observing performance before and after such changes. Changes that improve performance should be left in place; those that make no difference—or that make things worse—should be reversed. There are many ways to improve Windows 2000 system performance. The more useful of these approaches or configuration changes are covered in this chapter.

In many ways, Windows 2000 does a remarkable job of tuning itself. It is capable of managing both its physical and virtual memory quite well. It also adjusts how it allocates memory dynamically and effectively among a variety of uses, including file caching, virtual memory, system kernel use, and applications use. Because of all of these self-tuning features, Windows 2000 offers a more limited set of tools and utilities to monitor and alter system performance than do older operating systems, such as Windows NT. Changing the Windows 2000 operating system configuration is rarely required. Instead, you learn how to recognize and react to system bottlenecks that can limit a system's overall performance.

Task Manager

Windows Task Manager, shown in Figure 11-1, provides an overview of the current state of a computer. You can access the Task Manager in one of three ways:

- Press Ctrl+Alt+Delete and click the Task Manager button on the Windows Security window.

- Press Ctrl+Shift+Esc.

- Right-click any unoccupied area on the Windows 2000 taskbar and select Task Manager from the menu that appears.

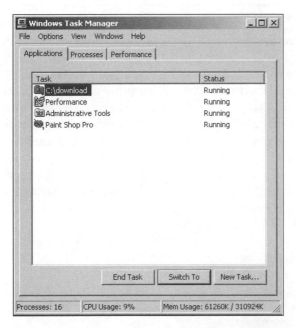

Figure 11-1 Task Manager, Applications tab

The first tab that appears in Task Manager is the Applications tab, which is shown in Figure 11-1. This tab displays all programs currently running on the computer and the status of those programs (usually "Running"). You can use this tab to halt an application by highlighting an entry in the list and clicking the End Task button. To switch to a specific task, highlight an entry and click the Switch To button. To launch a new application, click the New Task button and provide the name of an executable program or command in the Create New Task dialog box that appears.

The Processes tab shows all currently active processes with information about each, including its Process ID number (PID), CPU usage (CPU), CPU time, and Memory Usage. A **process** is an environment that defines the resources available to threads, the executable parts of an application. This display is an excellent instant diagnostic tool to show when ill-behaved applications take up an inordinate amount of CPU time. If this happens at the moment you use Task Manager, you'll see the process's CPU usage spike above 90%. Even if an application is not currently hogging the CPU, the CPU time entry might be high enough (above 80%) to stick out like a sore thumb.

You can change the columns displayed on the Processes tab by choosing Select Columns from the View menu. This tab lists all processes that contribute to the operation of Windows 2000, including Winlogon.exe and Lsass.exe. You can stop any process by selecting it from the list, then clicking the End Process button.

CAUTION

Be wary of ending Windows 2000 processes; you can cripple or disable a system by ending processes that are required for system operation.

The Performance tab, shown in Figure 11-2, provides a graphical representation of cumulative CPU usage and memory usage. The four text windows at the bottom of the screen provide detailed information on the total number of handles, threads, and processes (Totals) active on the system, the amount of memory allocated to application programs or the system (Commit Charge), the amount of physical memory installed on your computer (Physical Memory), and the memory used by the operating system for internal processes (Kernel Memory). A **thread** is the minimal unit of system execution and corresponds roughly to a task within an application, within the Windows 2000 kernel, or within some other major system component, whereas a **handle** is an internal identifier for some kind of system resource, object, or other component that must be accessed by name.

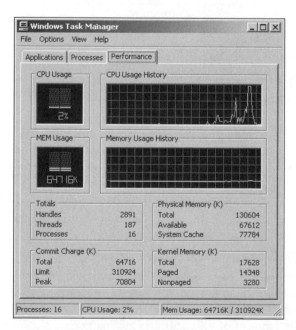

Figure 11-2   Task Manager, Performance tab

You can use the Performance tab in Task Manager to quickly ascertain whether a computer is performing optimally. If the total CPU usage shown in the status bar is consistently high—say over 70%—you can use the Processes tab to identify the process that is monopolizing the CPU, and take corrective action.

System Monitor

The performance monitoring tool included with Windows 2000 can monitor and track many different areas of system performance. Called **System Monitor**, this tool is used to monitor and record the same system measurements that Performance Monitor collected for Windows NT 4.0 systems. As shown in Figure 11-3, System Monitor is a graphical tool that can monitor many different **events** concurrently. By using System Monitor, you can analyze network operations, identify trends and bottlenecks, determine system capacity, notify administrators when thresholds are exceeded, track the performance of individual system devices, and monitor either local or remote computers. To start System Monitor, first open Control Panel via the Start button by selecting Start, Settings, Control Panel. Next, open Administrative Tools by double-clicking its icon. Finally, double-click Performance to launch the Performance Console which contains System Monitor. (Hands-on Project 11-1 shows you how to use System Monitor to monitor memory performance.)

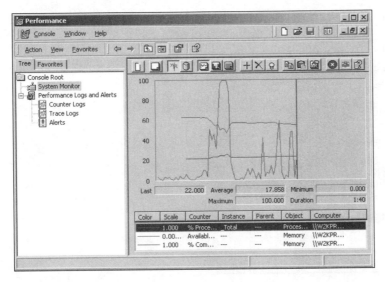

Figure 11-3   System Monitor

System Monitor is capable of a wide range of performance monitoring functions, including real-time monitoring, recording logs for future examination, and generating performance threshold alerts. Through proficient use of these functions, system administrators can effectively monitor their systems for bottlenecks, extract historical trending information, and be notified when abnormal activities occur, all of which are discussed in the following sections.

Realtime Monitoring

Realtime monitoring is the process of viewing the measured data from one or more counters in the System Monitor display area. System Monitor can display realtime (and logged) data in one of three formats: chart (see Figure 11-3), histogram (thermometer bars), or report (text-based instant values). You can select these views, or displays, by clicking the View Chart (default), View Histogram, or View Report buttons on the toolbar.

To begin monitoring a particular counter, click the Add Counters button that looks like a plus sign on the toolbar. You will see the Add Counters dialog box, shown in Figure 11-4. This dialog box reveals the object-oriented architecture of the Windows 2000 system as a whole and of performance monitoring in general. From this dialog box, you select counters based on the following:

- *Local or network accessible computer:* Counters can be read from the local system or any accessible system over a network.

- **Object**: An object is a component of the Windows 2000 system environment; objects range from devices to services to processes.

- **Counter**: Counters are aspects or activities of an object that can provide measurable information.

- **Instance**: An instance is a selection of a specific object when more than one is present on the monitored system; for example, multiple CPUs or hard drives.

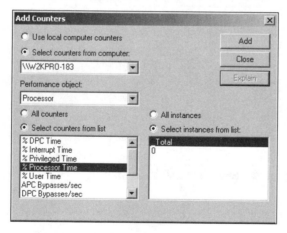

Figure 11-4   Add Counters dialog box

The Add Counters dialog box also allows you to select all counters for a specific object at once or all instances of an object at once. Once you've selected your host computer, object, counter (one or all), and instance (one or all), click the Add button to add the counter(s) and instance(s) to the list. If you need more information on a selected counter, click the Explain button. This reveals a floating window (see Figure 11-5) with additional information about the selected counter. Once you've added all the counters you are interested in monitoring, click Close to return to System Monitor.

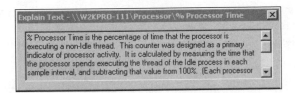

Figure 11-5 The Explain window

As you'll discover if you spend any time with System Monitor, its counters are legion—a plain-vanilla Windows 2000 installation makes it possible to monitor hundreds of such counters. In practice, however, there are only a handful of objects and associated counters that you work with regularly (some more regularly than others). The following list outlines the object and counter pairs that are worth memorizing, as well as several others that you may find useful when evaluating performance on your systems and networks. The list deals with six kinds of objects: LogicalDisk (the divisions of a drive into partitions or dynamic storage units), Memory (RAM), Network, PhysicalDisk (the actual hard disk as a whole), Processor (CPU), and System. For convenience, we present them in alphabetical order, listed in the form *Object: Counter.*

TIP   LogicalDisk and PhysicalDisk objects must first be enabled with the *diskperf* command, which is covered later in this chapter in the "Disk Bottlenecks" section.

11

- *LogicalDisk: Current Disk Queue Length*—If your system includes an older SCSI hard disk or any kind of EIDE or other controller type, measure this counter, which indicates how many system requests are waiting for disk access. If the queue length is greater than 2 for any logical drive, that drive is suffering from congestion. If you can't redistribute the load across multiple logical disks, consider upgrading your disk subsystem. Always check the corresponding PhysicalDisk counter when examining LogicalDisk counters.

- *LogicalDisk: % Disk Time*—This counter measures the percentage of time that a disk is busy handling read or write requests. It's unusual for this percentage to hit 100; it's also unusual for this level to be sustained at levels of 80% or higher. If this occurs, redistribute files to try to spread the load across multiple logical drives. Always check the corresponding PhysicalDisk counter.

- *LogicalDisk: Disk Bytes/Transfer*—This counter measures the average number of bytes transferred between memory and disk during read and write operations. If the value hovers at or near 4 KB (4086 bytes), this can indicate excessive paging activity on that drive. In general, a larger number indicates more efficient transfers than a smaller one, so look for declines against your baseline here.

- *Memory: Available Bytes*—This counter measures the number of bytes of memory available for use on the system at any given moment. Microsoft recommends that this value always be 4096 KB or higher. If values hover at or below this threshold, that's a definite indicator that your system will benefit from additional RAM. You can obtain this number from the Task Manager Performance tab (it's the Available entry in the Physical Memory pane) without having to run System Monitor.

- *Memory: Cache Faults/sec*—This counter measures the number of times that the Windows 2000 cache manager must ask the system to bring a file's page in from disk or locate it elsewhere in memory. Higher values indicate potential performance problems, because a system's performance is best when cache hit rates are high. Establishing a baseline on a lightly loaded system will help you recognize when this counter begins to climb into risky regions (double, or more, the values that appear in the baseline). As with other memory counters, the proper response is to add more memory; in this case, adding more L2 cache is even better than adding main RAM.

- *Memory: Page Faults/sec*—This returns a count of the average number of page faults per second for the current processor instance. A page fault occurs whenever a memory page is referenced that is not already loaded in RAM. When this happens, the Virtual Memory Manager (VMM) must bring that page in from disk and possibly make room for that page by swapping an old page out to disk. This phenomenon helps to explain how memory congestion sometimes manifests itself through excessive disk activity. If this value increases to more than double what you observe in a light-load baseline, it can indicate a need for more RAM.

- *Memory: Pages/sec*—This tracks the number of pages that are written to or read from disk to satisfy requirements of the VMM, and also includes paging traffic for the system cache that occurs to access file data for applications. This is an important counter to watch if paging activity seems high, because it can indicate that paging levels are slowing the system down. If this value increases to more than double what you observe in a light-load baseline (or, in most instances, goes above 20 for a sustained period of time), it strongly indicates a need for additional RAM.

- *Network Interface: Bytes Total/sec*—This counts the total amount of traffic through the computer's network adapter, including all inbound and outbound data (framing characters as well as payload data). This measures the absolute amount of traffic moving through the adapter. When it begins to approach the practical maximum for the type of media in use, trouble lies ahead. It might require a switch to a faster type of network or indicate a need to distribute the machine's load across multiple network segments (and, therefore, multiple adapters).

- *Network Interface: Current Bandwidth*—This measures the current utilization levels of the network medium and provides a background count against which to evaluate the monitored machine's adapter. The same observations about loading and distribution apply to this counter as to the preceding one, except that this counter may indicate the need to partition the network to which this machine is attached, to lower the total traffic on individual cable segments.

- *Network Interface: Output Queue Length*—This measures the number of packets that are queued up for transmission across the network pending access to the medium. As with most other Windows 2000 queues, if this value approaches or exceeds 2, it indicates that network delays are likely and that the bottleneck should be removed, if at all possible.

- *Network Interface: Packets/sec*—This measures the number of packets sent and received across a specific network adapter. Comparison with a baseline indicates when this value is getting out of hand. The observations that apply to the Bytes Total/sec counter apply to this counter as well.

- *PhysicalDisk: Current Disk Queue Length*—PhysicalDisk counters track hard disk activity on a per disk basis and provide much the same kind of information as the LogicalDisk counters. However, calculating pathological queue lengths for physical disks is different than for logical ones: here, the threshold for trouble is between 1.5 and 2 times the number of spindles on the hard drive. For ordinary drives, this is the same as for logical disks. But for RAID arrays (which Windows 2000 treats as a single drive), the number is equal to 1.5 to 2 times the number of drives in the array.

- *PhysicalDisk: % Disk Time*—This counter measures the percentage of time that a hard drive is kept busy handling read or write requests. For Windows 2000 machines, you may see peaks as high as 100%, but the sustained average should not exceed 80%. High sustained averages are not worrisome unless the corresponding queue length numbers are in the danger zone as well.

- *PhysicalDisk: Avg. # Disk Bytes/Transfer*—This counter measures the average number of bytes that read or write requests transfer between the drive and memory. This is a case where smaller values are more worrisome than larger ones, because they can indicate inefficient use of drives and drive space. If this behavior is motivated by applications, try increasing file sizes. If it's motivated by paging activity, an increase in RAM or cache memory is a good idea.

- *Processor: % Processor Time*—This counter measures the percentage of time that the CPU is busy handling nonidle threads—in other words, real work. Sustained values of 80% or higher indicate a heavily loaded machine. Consistent readings of 95% or higher indicate that a machine needs to have its load reduced or its capabilities increased (with a new machine, a motherboard upgrade, or a new CPU). See the section before the summary at the end of this chapter for a discussion of these various performance improvements.

- *Processor: Interrupts/sec*—This counter measures the average number of times per second that some device that requests immediate processing interrupts the CPU. Network traffic and system clock activity establish a kind of background count against which you should compare this number. Pathological increases occur when a malfunctioning device begins to generate false interrupts or when excessive network traffic overwhelms a network adapter. In both cases, this usually creates a count that's five or more times greater than a lightly loaded baseline situation.

- *System: Processor Queue Length*—This counter measures the number of execution threads that are waiting for access to a CPU. If this value increases to more than double the number of CPUs present on a machine (2 for a single-processor system), it indicates a need to distribute this machine's load across other machines, or

11

to increase its capabilities, usually by adding an additional CPU or by upgrading the machine or the motherboard. (Increasing CPU speed does not increase performance as much as you might think, because it does nothing for the machine's cache or its memory and bus transfer capabilities.)

> **TIP** Where we've indicated that more than one counter is worth watching for a particular object (for instance, there are four network-related counters), it's more significant when all counters experience a dramatic change in status simultaneously than when only one or two such counters show an increase. Across-the-board changes are more likely to indicate a bottleneck than are more localized ones (that are more likely to be caused by applications or by shifts in local conditions, traffic levels, and so forth).

You can customize the display of System Monitor through its Properties dialog box. Access the System Monitor Properties dialog box by selecting System Monitor in the left pane, then right-clicking in the right pane and selecting Properties from the resulting menu. The General tab (shown in Figure 11-6) offers the following controls:

- Set the view to Graph, Histogram, or Report (that is, the same function as the toolbar buttons).

- Enable the legend, value bar, and toolbar items.

- Set the report and histogram data to Default, Current, Average, Minimum, or Maximum.

- Set the appearance to 3D or Flat.

- Set the border to None or Fixed Single.

- Set the update/measurement interval in seconds; default is one second.

- Allow duplicate counter instances.

The Source tab (Figure 11-7) is used to set whether the displayed information is pulled from real-time measurements or pulled from a Counter log. (Counter logs are discussed in the "Logging and Using Logged Activity" section later in this chapter.) If a Counter log is used, you must also define the time range.

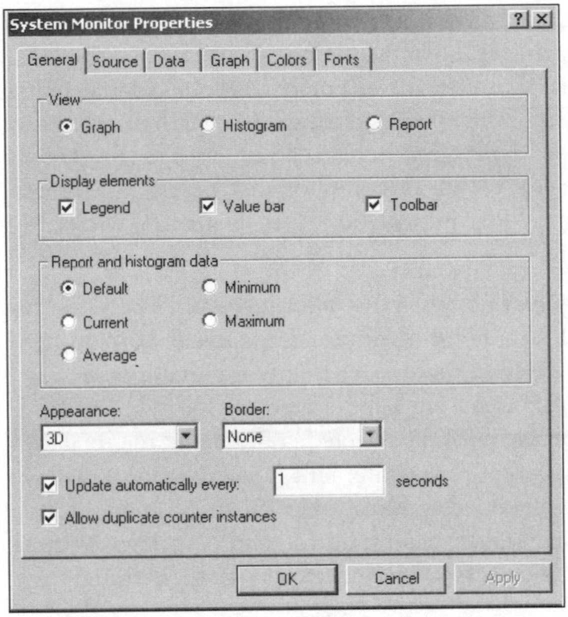

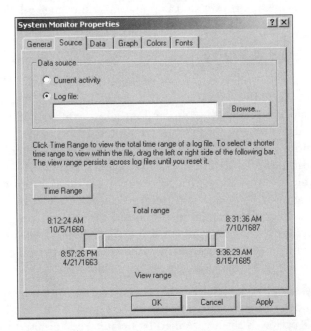

Figure 11-6   System Monitor Properties, General tab

Figure 11-7   System Monitor Properties, Source tab

11

Use the Data tab to add or remove counters, as well as to alter the color, scale, width, and style (all via pull–down lists) of each counter's chart line. The Graph tab defines a title and vertical axis label, enables vertical and horizontal grid lines, indicates whether to display vertical scale numbers, and sets the vertical maximum and minimum scale. Setting the vertical maximum and minimum scale is used to focus or expand the display for the purpose of making displayed counter measurements more informative. For example, if several counters display measurements within .3 deviation of the 80 mark, setting the maximum to 85 and the minimum to 75 expands the displayed information to grant an order of magnitude greater detail. The Colors tab defines the colors for the various components of System Monitor. The Fonts tab defines the font used to display text information. (Try Hands-on Project 11-2 to alter System Monitor display parameters.)

The System Monitor display in Chart (graph) view (refer to Figure 11-3) can show 100 data points from left to right. As each data point is measured, the event horizon line moves one point to the right as the data is added to the display. Below the graph of data in both Chart and Histogram views, five metadata items are listed. These are the value of the last, average, maximum, and minimum measurements of the selected counter and the total duration of the display field (calculated by multiplying the measurement interval by 100). Below these items is the counter legend, which lists all counters displayed in the graph, along with information about color, scale, counter name, instance, parent, object, and computer source. Selecting a counter in the legend causes the five metadata points to change their content.

Report view displays all selected counters grouped by instance, counter, object, and computer in text form. The information displayed in a report is the last measured value when viewing real-time data, or the averaged value over all data points in a time range when viewing logged data.

Logging and Using Logged Activity

The Windows 2000 Performance tool offers two types of logging capabilities. A **Counter log** records measurements on selected counters at regular, defined intervals. A **Trace log** records data only when certain events occur. Counter logs allow you to define exactly which counters are recorded (based on computer, object, counter, and instance). Trace logs record nonconfigurable data from a designated provider (such as the kernel) when an event occurs (such as process creation, thread deletion, disk I/O, and page fault). Trace logs are operating system environment status dumps that are more like a memory dump in the event of a Stop error than a log of performance statistics. You can review Counter log files using System Monitor, but Trace log files require a specialized tool to interpret the data. (Windows 2000 does not include a tool to read Trace log files.) Trace logs differ from counter data logs in that they measure data continually rather than take periodic samples. For more information on working with Trace logs, consult the *Windows 2000 Resource Kit*.

Using Counter logs is fairly simple. First, select the Counter Logs item beneath the Performance Logs and Alerts node of the Performance tool (see Figure 11-8). Notice that a Counter log named System Overview is already defined by default. You can use this predefined Counter log to get a basic look at the performance of the system. It's a basic look because it looks at only three counters—one for memory, one for storage, and one for CPU. Basically, the process requires selecting counters (based on computer, object, counter, and instance), setting the measurement interval, giving file storage information, and setting start and stop times.

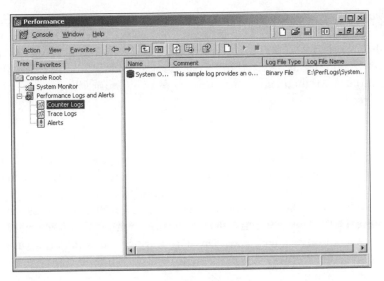

Figure 11-8   Counter Logs node of the Performance tool

 TIP   Counter logs record data by taking measurements at regular intervals. The default interval is 15 seconds, but you can define intervals from 1 second to 999,999 days. All counters in a Counter log are measured at the same interval.

The Properties dialog box for Counter logs has three tabs. The General tab lists all counters included in the log, allows adding and removing counters, and sets the measurement interval. The Log Files tab defines the path and filename (with date stamp) of the log, sets the file type (comma-delimited, tab-delimited, or binary), and sets the maximum file size in KB or available drive space. The Schedule tab defines the start and the termination of a log (either manual or at a specified time). You can terminate a log manually, or set termination to occur after a specified length of time, at a specified time, or when the file is full. Once a log file closes, you can run a command (such as a batch file) or start a new log file (if drive space is available).

Once you define a Counter log, you can either wait for the defined start time or issue the Start command from the Action menu to begin recording data. Once recording, the Counter log will continue to collect data until either you manually stop the recording (by issuing the Stop command from the Action menu) or the defined stop event occurs. The Counter log will record data even when the Performance tool is closed. While a Counter log is recording data, the log icon beside the name will be green. When the recording stops, the icon is red. To learn how to create, start, and stop a Counter log, try Hands-on Project 11-3.

Once you've recorded a log file, it can be used in System Monitor. To do so, open Properties for System Monitor and go to the Source tab (refer to Figure 11-6). Select the Log file radio button, then provide the path to the Counter log file. Next, click the Time Range button to reveal the start and stop time stamps of the recorded data. Using the sliding endpoints, click and drag the view range. Time Range is used to focus the display around important data. Keep in mind that the display area can reveal only 100 measurement points. If you select more than 100 data points, System Monitor will resample the data down to 100 points. For example, if you have 300 points, every three data items will be averaged to produce a single point. System Monitor retains all 300 data points, but only the averaged points are displayed. If fewer than 100 data points are selected in the time range, the data will be displayed without any extrapolation. (You can practice viewing data from a Counter log in System Monitor in Hands-on Project 11-4.)

Alerts

An **alert** is a watchdog that informs you when a counter crosses a defined threshold. Basically, an alert is an automated attendant looking for high or low values. An Alert object can consist of one or more counter/instance-based alert definitions. For example, you can configure an alert to be sent if the CPU goes above 90% usage, which is an indicator of CPU overload (see Figure 11-9). The individual alert definitions within an Alert object share the same sample interval, action triggers, and stop/start settings, but operate as distinct alert events. More than one Alert object can be created to assign different sample rates, action triggers, and stop/start settings.

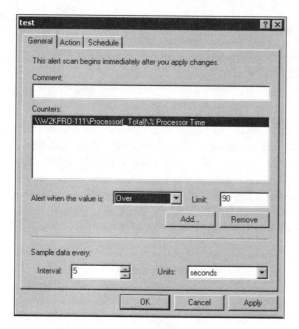

Figure 11-9 Setting an alert

An alert is defined on a counter/instance basis just like counter selection for the Counter log and System Monitor. An alert definition focuses on one or all counters of one or all objects on the local or networked computer. Each alert definition is assigned a threshold and told whether to issue an alert when the measured value is under or over that threshold. An alert event is triggered only when the measured value of the specific counter at the time of alert sampling has crossed the threshold. Counter levels between samplings have no effect on alerts because those levels are unknown to the alert monitoring system. The sampling interval of an Alert object is the same as that of Counter Logs—one second to 999,999 days. (Try Hands-on Project 11-5 to create an Alert object.)

When an alert is triggered, any of four actions can occur. These are enabled and defined on the Action tab of an Alert object's Properties dialog box, as shown for the "test" Alert object in Figure 11-10.

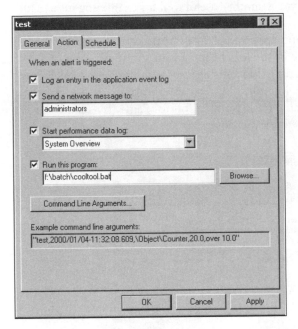

Figure 11-10   The Action tab of an Alert object's Properties dialog box

The possible actions of an alert are as follows:

- *Log an entry into the application event log:* You can view the event detail through Event Viewer.

- *Send a network message:* A single NetBIOS name of a user, group, or computer can be defined. When an alert occurs, a message regarding the alert and the measured counter level is sent.

- *Start performance data log:* Starts the recording of a Counter log.

- *Run this program:* Used to execute a program with command-line options or to launch a batch file. When this action is used, a string of performance-related information can be included at the end of the defined command line in the form. You can choose to have a single argument string with all data points separated with commas, or individual strings with the data elements of date/time, measured value, alert name, counter name, limit value, and a custom text string.

11

The Scheduling tab of an Alert event's Properties dialog box is much the same as that of a Counter log. Use this tab to define a start event that is either manual or at a specified time and a stop event that can be manual, after a length of time, or at a specified time. Similar to Counter logs, Alert events function even when the Performance tool is closed.

Event Viewer

The Windows 2000 **Event Viewer** is another useful tool for examining information about the performance and activities on a system. Event Viewer tracks all events generated by the operating system, as well as security and application events. An event is any activity that causes an event detail to be created in one of the logs of the Event Viewer. Failure of a device to load, an unsuccessful logon, or a corrupt database file can all be recorded by Event Viewer and viewed through one of three log files: System, Application, or Security. Access Event Viewer through the Administrative Tools via the Control Panel (try Hands-on Project 11-6). Figure 11-11 shows a typical Event Viewer displaying the System log.

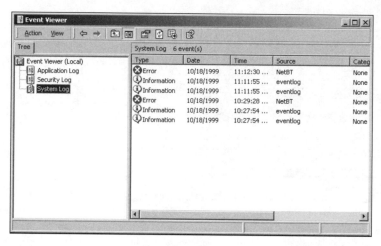

Figure 11-11   Event Viewer, System Log

There are three types of System and Application log events and two types of Security log events that are recorded in Event Viewer. These are listed in Table 11-1.

All Event log entries include the event's date and time, source, category (such as Logon or Logoff), an event number, the name of the account that generated the event, and the name of the computer on which the event occurred. You can use Event Viewer to view logs on other computers. To access log files on other computers, select the Connect to another computer command in the Action menu while Event Viewer (Local) is highlighted.

Each Event Viewer log has customizable properties. Access a log's Properties dialog box by highlighting that log then selecting the Properties command from the Action menu. The Properties dialog box (see Figure 11-12) has two tabs. Use the General tab to set properties such as the displayed name, the maximum file size, action to take when log is full (overwrite as needed, overwrite only events older than a specified number of days, or do not overwrite), and to manually clean out the log. Use the Filter tab to reduce the number of events displayed.

Filter options include sorting by the five event types, source of the event, event category, event ID, user, computer, and date range.

Table 11-1   Event Viewer Event Types

Event Type	Description
Information	Signifies rare but significant events about successful operation of internal services and drivers, indicated by the "i" icon. For example, when a database program loads successfully, it may generate an Information event.
Warning	Signifies potential problems although there is no present danger, indicated by an "!" (exclamation point) icon. For example, if disk space is running low, a Warning event may be logged.
Error	Signifies that significant problems exist that require immediate attention, indicated by a white "x" in a red circle. For example, if a driver fails to load correctly, an Error event is issued.
Success Audit	A Security log event that indicates that an event selected for audit has taken place. For example, when a user successfully logs on to a system, a Success Audit event is logged. A gold key icon represents success audits.
Failure Audit	A Security log event that indicates when an audited event has failed. For example, an unsuccessful attempt to access a network drive is logged as a Failure Audit event. A gold lock icon represents failure audits.

11

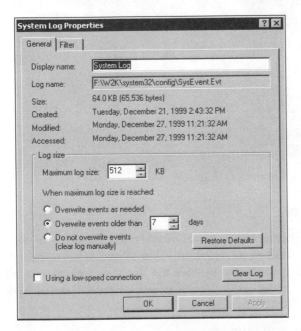

Figure 11-12   The Log Properties dialog box

The System log is the primary log file for most system services, drivers, and processes. Typical System log events occur when device drivers fail to load or load with errors, when system services fail to start, when system service errors or failures occur, or when auditing is enabled and system-related events flagged for auditing occur. The Application log contains event messages that can be generated by Windows 2000 native applications or services. Unlike the System and Application logs, the Security log does not automatically track events. It records audit events such as logon, resource access, and computer restart and shutdown. Auditing must be enabled and configured (for details see Chapter 6).

Performance Options

You use the Performance Options dialog box (see Figure 11-13) to adjust system performance based on applications and virtual memory. Access this dialog box by clicking the Performance Options button on the Advanced tab of the System applet from the Control Panel. You can optimize general system performance by indicating whether the computer is used primarily for user-interactive applications or as a host for network services. The radio button selection of Applications grants foreground processes an additional priority boost, whereas Background services balances the use of processor resources. Use the Change button on the Performance Options dialog box to access the Virtual Memory dialog box, where the size and location(s) of the paging file is defined. See Chapter 3 for more details on optimizing the paging file size.

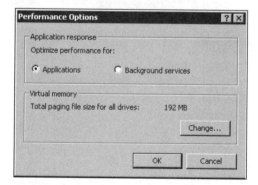

Figure 11-13   The Performance Options dialog box

Setting Application Priority

Windows 2000 uses 32 levels of application priority, numbered 0 to 31. These priority levels are used by Windows 2000 to determine which process should gain access to the CPU at any given moment. Users have only minimal control over the initial startup priority level of any launched task. The following list indicates important ranges and specific priority levels you should be aware of:

- 0–15: User-accessible process priorities

- 16–31: System-accessible process priorities

- 0–6: Low user range

- 4: Low value (as set in Task Manager, or with /low parameter to Start command)

- 5: BelowNormal value (as set in Task Manager)

- 7: Normal (default setting for user processes)

- 8–15: High user range

- 10: AboveNormal value (as set in Task Manager)

- 13: High value (as set in Task Manager, or with /high parameter to Start command)

- 16–24: Realtime values accessible to Administrator-level accounts

- 24: Realtime value (as set in Task Manager, or with /realtime parameter to Start command)

- 25-31: Realtime values accessible to operating system only

There are two techniques available to users and administrators to manipulate process priorities: You can manage already running processes using Task Manager, or use the Start command to launch processes with specific priority settings. One reason you may want to manipulate a process's priority is to give an application that is time-sensitive priority over another application that is not.

To use Task Manager, right-click any unoccupied region of the taskbar and select Task Manager from the menu. On the Processes tab of Task Manager, select the name of the desired process (usually this is the name of an .exe file that corresponds to the process), then right-click that process to produce another menu. From this menu, select the Set Priority item. This is where you can pick one of the predefined priority settings—Low, BelowNormal, Normal, AboveNormal, High, or Realtime. The current setting is the entry marked with a bullet symbol to the left. You must be logged on with Administrator privileges to use the Realtime setting.

You can use the Start command from a command prompt to launch a new application at some priority level other than the default. You can enter this command from either a command prompt or the Run command. The Start command follows this general syntax:

```
start /<priority-level> <program>
```

where /*<priority-level>* must be one of /low, /belownormal, /normal, /abovenormal, /high, or /realtime, and *<program>* is a valid path plus filename for the program you wish to launch at the specified priority level. For more details on the Start command, enter *start /?* from a command prompt.

RECOGNIZING AND HANDLING BOTTLENECKS

A **bottleneck** is a condition in which a limitation in a single component slows down an entire system. The first thing to remember about bottlenecks is that they will always exist in any computer. Applications, hard drives, operating systems, and network interfaces might all act as bottlenecks from time to time, but for any given configuration, it is always possible to identify one component that slows the others down.

11

There is no single bottleneck monitor that can easily identify all possible problems. However, by using the monitoring tools included with Windows 2000, you can identify possible bottlenecks and make adjustments. The goal in performance tuning a workstation is to make bottlenecks unnoticeable for everyday functions. A computer used for CAD requires much greater throughput than a computer used primarily for word processing. Ideally, a computer should be waiting for user input, rather than making users wait for the computer's response. In this ideal case, the user becomes the bottleneck (and because computers cannot do much to speed up humans, this is regarded as an ideal situation).

Although the details will vary from situation to situation, the process of finding and fixing computer system bottlenecks follows a reasonably consistent course, and usually works something like this:

1. Create a baseline for a computer. For Windows 2000, this includes observations of memory usage, disk usage, CPU usage, operating system resource usage and activity, and network utilization, at the barest minimum.

2. The first step in determining potential bottlenecks is to compare baseline observations to current system behavior. In most cases, one or more of the baseline values will have changed for the worse. These changes indicate further areas of investigation.

3. Investigate the more common causes of system problems (some of these for Windows 2000 are documented later in this chapter) to see if any match the symptoms your computer is exhibiting. If you have a match, the causes of bottlenecks are easy to identify and fixes are easy to apply.

4. If the list of "usual suspects" does not produce an obvious culprit, further analysis is required. Part of using System Monitor and other performance tools is knowing how to use them to obtain more detailed statistics on system behavior and being able to analyze their reports and statistics to pinpoint potential bottlenecks. Use the general analytical techniques and combinations of objects and counters described in this chapter to help in isolating and identifying bottlenecks.

5. Once a potential bottleneck is identified, you make changes to the system configuration to correct the situation. Sometimes this involves software configuration changes; other times it can involve adding or replacing specific hardware components or subsystems.

6. Always test the impact of any fix you try on the system. Compile a new set of statistics and compare them to the same system measurements before the fix was applied. Sometimes, the fix does the trick and values return to normal, or at least come closer to acceptable levels. At other times, the fix doesn't make a difference. In that case, further analysis, other fixes, and more testing are required. It's important to keep at the job until something improves the bottleneck conditions.

It's important to understand that bottlenecks can always be fixed, but some fixes are more expensive than others. Remember, you can always replace an overloaded server or workstation with another, bigger, faster system, or you can spread the load of a single overloaded system across multiple systems to reduce the impact on any single machine. These kinds of fixes are a great deal more expensive than tweaking system settings or adding more memory or disk space to a machine. However, in some cases, drastic solutions are necessary. If you do your job of monitoring performance correctly, such radical changes needn't take anyone by surprise.

Common Bottlenecks

In this section, we explain how to use the counters you have chosen to watch, either alone or in combination, to determine what kinds of bottlenecks might be present on a system. We also discuss steps you might consider taking to correct such bottlenecks. We tackle these subjects in the following order:

- Disk bottlenecks
- Memory bottlenecks
- Processor bottlenecks
- Network bottlenecks

Disk Bottlenecks

Disk bottlenecks are the most likely problem when disk-related counters increase more dramatically than other counters, compared to your baseline, or when disk queue lengths become unacceptably long. Windows 2000 collects information about the performance of physical disks (the actual devices) by default. However, to view information about logical disks, you must enable the LogicalDisk object with the *diskperf* command. When you use the *diskperf* command, you must reboot the system for any changes to take effect. The syntax of the *diskperf* command is:

```
diskperf [-y[d|v]] | [-n[d|v]] [\\computername]
```

where:

- –Y enables both PhysicalDisk and LogicalDisk objects.
- –YD enables only the PhysicalDisk object.
- –YV enables only the LogicalDisk object.
- –N disables both the PhysicalDisk and LogicalDisk objects.
- –ND disables only the PhysicalDisk object.
- –NV disables only the LogicalDisk object.
- *computername* performs the object enable/disable on the specified system; this applies to the local system if this item is not included.

You can execute the *diskperf* command from a command prompt or from the Start, Run command. Windows 2000 does not enable the LogicalDisk object by default because measuring that object causes a measurable degradation in storage device performance. You should disable the LogicalDisk object once you have completed your monitoring.

11

If Disk Queue Length and % Disk time values remain consistently high (1.5 or higher and more than 80%, respectively), it's probably time to think about adding more disk controllers or drives or possibly switching existing drives and controllers for newer, faster SCSI equivalents. This costs money, but can provide dramatic performance improvements on systems with disk bottlenecks. Adding a controller for each drive can substantially improve performance, and switching from individual drives to disk (RAID) arrays can also improve performance on such systems. Because high-end disk controllers often include onboard memory that functions as yet another level of system cache, they can confer measurable performance benefits.

Software can also contribute to disk bottlenecks, often because of poor design, configuration settings that affect disk performance, or outdated drivers. Because tweaking an application's source code is beyond the reach of most system administrators, inspect the application to see if you can increase the size of the files it manipulates directly or the size of data transfers it requests.

Memory Bottlenecks

Windows 2000 is subject to several different kinds of **memory bottlenecks**. To begin with, it's important to make sure that the paging file is working as efficiently as possible; that is, its size is two to three times the amount of physical RAM on a machine (see Chapter 3). On machines with more than one drive, Microsoft recommends not situating the paging file on the drive where the Windows 2000 system files reside. If multiple drives are available, it's a good idea to spread the paging file evenly across all such drives (except the drive with the systems files). Better yet is for each drive to have its own disk controller; this allows Windows 2000 to access all drives in parallel.

You can detect excessive paging activity by watching the page-related counters mentioned earlier and by observing the lowest number of Available Bytes over time. (Microsoft recommends that this number never dip below 4 MB or 4096 KB.) Excessive disk time and disk queue lengths can often mask paging problems, so be sure to check paging-related statistics when disk utilization zooms. Adding more memory can fix such problems and improve overall system performance.

Processor Bottlenecks

Processor bottlenecks are indicated when the Processor object's % Processor time counter stays consistently above 80% or when the System object's Processor Queue Length counter remains fixed near a value of 2 or more. In both cases, the CPU is being overworked. However, occasional peaks of 100% for processor time are not unusual (especially when processes are being launched or terminated). The combination of high utilization and overlong queues is more often an indication of trouble than is an occasionally high utilization rate.

Even on machines that support multiple CPUs, it's important to recognize that performance doesn't scale arithmetically as additional CPUs are added. A second CPU gives a more dramatic incremental improvement in performance than a third or fourth; however, two CPUs do not double performance (nor do three, for that matter). You're often better off responding to CPU bottlenecks by redistributing a machine's processing load or by replacing the machine or upgrading its CPU, memory, and motherboard. Simply upgrading or adding another CPU neither increases the amount of cache memory on a system nor improves the system's underlying CPU-to-memory data transfer capabilities, both of which often play a crucial role in improving system performance.

When more than one CPU is present on a system, you can choose to monitor the activity of the CPUs on either an individual basis or as a whole group. To monitor a single CPU, select the individual instance of the CPU. The first CPU is instance 0; the second CPU is instance 1. To monitor the activity of all CPUs as a whole, select the _Total instance.

Network Bottlenecks

Network bottlenecks are not typical on most Windows 2000 machines, because end users seldom load the network sufficiently to experience performance problems. However, it is worth monitoring how much traffic is passing through a workstation's network adapter as compared to the networking medium to which it is attached. Excessive activity can indicate a failing adapter (sometimes called a "jabbering transceiver") or an ill-behaved application. In both cases, the fix is relatively straightforward—replace the NIC or the application, respectively. Occasionally, however, the network itself may be overloaded. This situation is indicated by utilization rates that exceed the recommended maximum for the medium in use. (For example, Ethernet should not be loaded more heavily than 56% utilization; token ring can function adequately at loads as high as 98% utilization.) When this happens, as a network administrator you have two options: divide the network into segments and balance traffic so that no segment is overloaded, or replace the existing network with a faster alternative. Neither of these options is especially fast, cheap, or easy, but the former is cheaper than the latter, and may give your network—and your budget—some breathing room before a wholesale upgrade is warranted.

11

EIGHT WAYS TO IMPROVE WINDOWS 2000 PERFORMANCE

Although there are many things you can do to deal with specific system bottlenecks, there are eight particularly useful changes in system components, elements, approaches, or configuration that are likely to result in improved performance. These are listed in approximate order of their potential value, so always try to hit elements higher in the list first when you are attempting to boost Windows 2000 performance. All elements on this list are worth considering when performance improvements are needed.

- *Buy a faster machine:* It takes only a year or so for a top-of-the-line, heavily loaded PC to become obsolete these days. When you find yourself considering a hardware upgrade to boost performance, compare the price of your planned upgrade to the cost of a new machine. If you're planning on spending more than half the cost of a newer computer (and can afford to double your expenditure), buy the newer, faster machine. Otherwise, you may be facing the same situation again in a few months. The extra cost buys you at least another year before you must go through this exercise again.

- *Upgrade an existing machine:* You might decide to keep a PC's case, power supply, and some of the adapter cards it contains. As long as the price stays below half the cost of a new machine, replacing a PC's motherboard not only gets you a faster CPU, more memory capacity (both cache and main memory), but it can also get you more and faster bus slots for adapter cards. While you're at it, be sure to evaluate the costs of upgrading the disk controller and hard drives, especially if they're more than twice as slow as prevailing access times. (As we write, garden-variety drives offer average access times of around 10 milliseconds, and fast drives offer average access rates of 3 to 4 milliseconds.)

- *Install a faster CPU:* As long as you can at least double the clock speed of your current CPU with a replacement unit, such an upgrade can improve performance for only a modest outlay. Be sure to review your memory configuration (cache and main memory) and your disk drives at the same time. A faster CPU on an otherwise unchanged system can't deliver the same performance boost as a faster CPU with additional memory and faster drives.

- *Add more L2 cache:* Many experts believe that the single most dramatic improvement for an existing Windows 2000 PC comes from adding more L2 cache to a machine (or to buy only machines with the maximum amount of L2 cache installed). The CPU can access L2 cache in two CPU cycles, whereas access to main RAM usually takes 8 to 10 CPU cycles. This accounts for why adding L2 cache to a machine can produce dramatic performance improvements. Although cache chips are quite expensive, they provide the biggest potential boost to a system's performance, short of the more drastic—and expensive—suggestions detailed earlier in this list.

- *Add more RAM:* Windows 2000 is smart about how it uses main memory on a PC. It can handle large amounts of RAM effectively, and it has been widely observed that the more processes that are active on a machine, the more positive the impact of a RAM increase. For moderately loaded workstations (six or fewer applications active at once), 64 MB of RAM is recommended. For heavily loaded workstations, 128 MB or more may improve performance significantly.

 When you add RAM to a Windows 2000 machine, make sure to resize the paging file to properly accommodate the change in physical RAM.

- *Replace the disk subsystem:* Because memory access occurs at nanosecond speeds, and disk access occurs at millisecond speeds, disk subsystem speeds can make a major impact on Windows 2000 performance. This is particularly true in cases where applications or services make frequent accesses to disk, when manipulating large files, or when large amounts of paging activity occur. Because the controller and the drives both influence disk subsystem speeds, we recommend using only Fast Wide SCSI drives and controllers (or the latest of the EIDE drives and controllers) on Windows 2000 machines. However, it's important to recognize that a slow disk controller can limit a fast drive and vice versa. That's why upgrading the entire subsystem is often necessary to realize any measurable performance gains.

■ *Increase paging file size:* Whenever System Monitor indicates that more than 10% of disk subsystem activity is related to paging, check the relationship between the Limit and Peak values in the Commit Charge pane in Task Manager. (Right-click on any empty portion of the taskbar, select Task Manager, then select the Performance tab and check the lower-left corner of the display.) If the Peak is coming any closer than 4096 KB to the limit, it's time to increase the size of this file. We recommend using a figure somewhere between twice and three times the amount of RAM installed in the machine.

■ *Increase application priority:* On machines where a lot of background tasks must be active, you can use the Task Manager's Processes tab to increase the priority of any already running process. Highlight the process entry, then right-click to produce a menu that includes a Set Priority entry. This entry permits you to set the priority to High or Realtime, either of which can improve a foreground application's performance. We recommend that you set only critical applications to Realtime, because they can interfere with the operating system's ability to do its job. To launch an application with an altered priority level, refer to the section, "Setting Application Priority," earlier in this chapter.

CAUTION

Only users with administrator level access to Windows 2000 can run processes at a Realtime priority level. Be aware that raising the priority of a single process causes other background processes to run more slowly. The other performance improvements in this list should improve system performance across the board; this one is limited to those processes whose priorities are increased.

CHAPTER SUMMARY

❑ Windows 2000 Professional provides a number of tools to monitor system performance. By using these tools, it is easy to alleviate the effects of bottlenecks and to improve system response time.

❑ You can use Task Manager to view applications, processes, and overall system performance, or to stop applications and processes, an efficient way to regain control from an application that is experiencing problems. The default configuration of the Processes tab not only displays the names of running processes, but also their process IDs, percentages of CPU and CPU time used, and memory consumption. Other columns, such as Virtual Memory Size and Thread count, can be added to the Processes tab.

❑ The Performance console is an exceptionally useful collection of tools that include System Monitor, log files, and alerts. System Monitor is used to watch real-time performance or review data collected in log files. Log files record performance data for one or more counters over a specified period of time. Alerts inform administrators when specific counters cross defined threshold levels.

❑ The Event Viewer is a less dynamic, but equally important tool that tracks logs generated by the system. Event Viewer monitors three different logs: System, Application, and Security. The System log records system information and errors, such as the failure of device driver to load. The Application log maintains similar information for programs, such as database applications. The Security log monitors system security events and audit activities.

❑ Finally, you should keep an eye on logs and performance counters to isolate any bottlenecks that occur in the system. Once isolated, take the steps necessary to remove the bottleneck and get the system running more smoothly. In addition, try the recommendations listed in this chapter for improving overall system performance.

KEY TERMS

alert — A watchdog that informs you when a counter crosses a defined threshold. An alert is an automated attendant looking for high or low values, and can consist of one or more counter/instance-based alert definitions.

baseline — A definition of what a normal load looks like on a computer system; it provides a point of comparison against which you can measure future system behavior.

bottleneck — A system resource or device that limits a system's performance. Ideally, the user should be the bottleneck on a system, not any hardware or software component.

counter (or **performance counter**) — A named aspect or activity that the Performance tool uses to measure or monitor some aspect of a registered system or application object.

Counter log — A log that records measurements on selected counters at regular, defined intervals. Counter logs allow you to define exactly which counters are recorded (based on computer, object, counter, and instance).

disk bottleneck — A system bottleneck caused by a limitation in a computer's disk subsystem, such as a slow drive or controller, or a heavier load than the system can handle.

event — A system occurrence that is logged to a file.

Event Viewer — A system utility that displays one of three event logs: System, Security, and Application, wherein logged or audited events appear. The Event Viewer is often the first stop when monitoring a system's performance or seeking evidence of problems because it is where all unusual or extraordinary system activities and events are recorded.

handle — A programming term that indicates an internal identifier for some kind of system resource, object, or other component that must be accessed by name (or through a pointer). In Task Manager, the number of handles appears on the Performance tab in the Totals pane. A sudden increase in the number of handles, threads, or processes can indicate that an ill-behaved application is running on a system.

instance — A selection of a specific object when more than one is present on the monitored system; for example, multiple CPUs or hard drives.

memory bottleneck — A system bottleneck caused by a lack of available physical or virtual memory that results in system slowdown or (in extreme cases) an outright system crash.

network bottleneck — A system bottleneck cause by excessive traffic on the network medium to which a computer is attached, or when the computer itself generates excessive amounts of such traffic.

object — A component of the Windows 2000 system environment; objects range from devices to services to processes.

process — An environment that defines the resources available to threads, the executable parts of an application. Processes define memory available, show where the process page directory is stored in physical memory, and other information that the CPU needs to work with a thread. Each process includes its own complete, private 2 GB address space and related virtual memory allocations.

processor bottleneck — A system bottleneck that occurs when demands for CPU cycles from currently active processes and the operating system cannot be met, usually indicated by high utilization levels or processor queue lengths greater than or equal to two.

System Monitor — The utility that tracks registered system or application objects, where each such object has one or more counters that can be tracked for information about system behavior.

thread — In the Windows 2000 run-time environment, a thread is the minimum unit of system execution and corresponds roughly to a task within an application, the Windows 2000 kernel, or within some other major system component. Any task that can execute in the background can be considered a thread (for example, run-time spell checking or grammar checking in newer versions of MS Word), but it's important to recognize that applications must be written to take advantage of threading (just as the operating system itself is).

Trace log — A log that records data when only certain events occur. Trace logs record nonconfigurable data from a designated provider when an event occurs.

11

REVIEW QUESTIONS

1. Monitoring is the act of changing a system's configuration systematically, and carefully observing performance before and after such changes. True or False?

2. In a system that is performing optimally, the user should be the bottleneck. True or False?

3. Which of the following can Task Manager monitor?

   a. application CPU percentage

   b. total CPU percentage

   c. process CPU percentage

   d. all of the above

4. The longer a system is in productive use, the more its performance
   _____.

5. Which of the following are methods to access Task Manager?

   a. Ctrl+Alt+Delete

   b. executing "taskman" from the command prompt

   c. Ctrl+Shift+Esc

   d. Control Panel

6. In System Monitor, the counters are the same for all objects. True or False?

7. A(n) _____ event is issued when a driver fails to load.

8. The _____ provides a detailed description of a counter.

9. To record log files the Performance tool must be open. True or False?

10. A Counter log can include which of the following?

    a. one or more counters

    b. counters from multiple computers

    c. different intervals for each counter

    d. a stop time defined by a length of time

11. A _____ occurs when a system resource limits performance.

12. Which of the following objects cannot be used to obtain measurements of performance by default?

    a. Memory

    b. LogicalDisk

    c. RAS port

    d. System

13. In general, a bottleneck might exist if a queue counter is consistently _____ than the total number of instances of that object.

14. Which one of the following counters is the most likely indicator of a high level of disk activity caused by too little RAM?

    a. Memory: Pages/sec

    b. Memory: Page Faults/sec

    c. Memory: Cache Faults

    d. Memory: Available bytes

15. Which of the following tools can monitor another computer's information?

    a. System Monitor

    b. Task Manager

    c. Event Viewer

16. The _____ on the Source tab is used to select a window of data from a Counter log.

17. The _____ is used to generate system performance reports.

18. What parameter should be used with diskperf to disable only the PhysicalDisk object?

    a. –yd

    b. –yv

    c. –nd

    d. –nv

19. The System Monitor can display only _____ data points.

20. The _____ and _____ event types are available only in the Security log.

21. Of the following commands, which gives the Test.exe application the highest priority level available to ordinary users (not administrators)?

    a. start /abovenormal test.exe

    b. start /normal test.exe

    c. start /high test.exe

    d. start /realtime test.exe

22. Which of the following activities can occur when an alert is triggered?

    a. an alert to a NetBIOS name

    b. shutdown of the system

    c. start the recording of a Counter log

    d. write an event to the Application log

23. The _____ feature of Event Viewer can be used to quickly locate all audit details for a specific user.

24. The Start command can be used to alter the priority of active processes. True or False?

25. What change to a system is most effective in producing a performance improvement?

    a. adding RAM

    b. replacing network cables

    c. adding more processors

    d. updating drivers

HANDS-ON PROJECTS

Project 11-1

To use System Monitor to monitor performance of memory, processor, disks, network, and applications:

1. Open the Control Panel by selecting **Start**, **Settings**, **Control Panel**.

2. Double-click the **Administrative Tools** icon.

3. Double-click the **Performance** icon.

4. Select the **System Monitor** node in the MMC console.

5. Click **Add** on the toolbar (it's the plus sign).

6. Select the **% Processor Time** counter from the **Processor** object, which is selected by default.

7. Use the **Performance** object pull-down list to select the **Memory** object.

8. Select the **Pages/sec** counter.

9. Click **Add**.

10. Click **Explain**. Read the detail about the selected counter.

11. Repeat Steps 7 through 10 to add some or all of the following counters (*Note*: if multiple instances of these objects are present, select one or more instances and/or the _Total instance):

    PhysicalDisk: Current Disk Queue Length
    PhysicalDisk: %Disk Time
    PhysicalDisk: Avg. Disk Bytes/Transfer
    Memory: Available Bytes
    Memory: Cache Faults/sec
    Memory: Page Faults/sec
    Memory: Pages/sec
    Network Interface: Bytes Total/sec
    Network Interface: Current Bandwidth
    Network Interface: Output Queue Length
    Network Interface: Packets/sec
    Processor: Interrupts/sec
    System: Processor Queue Length
    Thread: % Processor Time
    Thread: Priority Current
    Process: % Processor Time
    Process: Elapsed Time
    Process: Page Faults/sec
    Process: Thread Count

12. Click **Close**.

13. Launch and close **Windows Explorer** or any other application several times, read files from disk, access network resources, and so on to cause system activity.

14. Notice how the respective lines of the selected counters change according to system activity.

Project 11-2

To use System Monitor to alter the display parameters:

1. Click the **Properties** button on the toolbar.

2. Change update automatically from every 1 second to **2** seconds.

3. Select the **Data** tab.

4. Select the **Memory: Pages/sec** counter.

5. Change the color, width, and style, using the pull-down lists.

6. Select the **Graph** tab.

7. Select the **Vertical** grid and **Horizontal** grid check boxes.

8. Click **OK** to close the Properties dialog box.

Project 11-3

To create, start, and stop a Counter log:

1. Launch the Performance tool if it is not still open from the previous Hands-on Project.

2. Click the boxed plus sign next to the Performance Logs and Alerts node to expand its contents.

3. Select the **Counter Logs** item.

4. Select **New Log Settings** from the Action menu.

5. Type a name, such as **Set1**. Click **OK**.

6. Click the **Add** button on the General tab.

7. Click the **Add** button on the Select Counters dialog box to add the % Processor Time counter, which is selected by default, to the log.

8. Click **Close**.

9. Change the interval from 15 seconds to **2** seconds.

10. Select the **Log Files** tab. Review its controls, but don't make any changes.

11. Select the **Schedule** tab.

12. If you are prompted that the log file path does not exist but can be created, select **Yes** to create the path.

13. In the Start log area, select the **At** option and change the start time to **3** minutes from the present.

14. In the Stop log area, select the **After** option and change the time to **4** minutes.

15. Click **OK**.

16. Notice the new log appears in the list. Within three minutes, its icon will turn green.

17. After the icon turns green, launch and terminate Windows Explorer several times to cause system activity.

18. After four minutes the icon turns back to red. Do not go on with the next Hands-on Project until the icon is red again.

11

Project 11-4

To view data from a Counter log with System Monitor:

1. Launch the Performance tool if it is not still open from the first Hands-on Project.

2. Select the **System Monitor** node.

3. Right-click the right pane and select **Properties** from the resulting menu.

4. Select the **Source** tab.

5. Select the **Log file** option.

6. Use the **Browse** button to locate and select the Counter log created in Hands-on Project 11-3. Click **Open**.

7. Click **OK** in the System Monitor Properties dialog box.

8. Click the **New Counter Set** button in the toolbar (the blank page with a sparkle on the top-right corner).

9. Click the **Add** button (the plus sign) on the toolbar.

10. Click **Add** to add the % Processor Counter to the System Monitor display. Note the Counter log recorded in the previous Hands-on Project has only this one counter so it is selected by default.

11. Click **Close**.

12. Because the Counter log recorded measurements every 2 seconds for 4 minutes, there are 120 data points that are compressed and averaged to create the display you see. To prevent compression of data, you must select a time range of 100 data points or fewer.

13. Click the **Properties** button on the toolbar.

14. Select the **Source** tab.

15. Click the **Time Range** button to refresh the Counter log data.

16. Click and drag the right slider so that only 198 seconds separate the start and stop ends of the view range.

17. Click **OK**.

18. Notice that now 99 data points are displayed.

Project 11-5

To create an Alert object:

1. Launch the Performance tool if it is not still open.

2. Select the **Alerts** node.

3. Select **New Alert Settings** from the Action menu.

4. Type a name such as **Set1**. Click **OK**.

5. Click **Add**.

6. Click **Add** to add the % Processor Time counter to the alert. Note that this counter is selected by default.

7. Click **Close**.

8. Select **Over** in the "Alert when the value is" pull-down box.

9. Type in **50** in the Limit box.

10. Change the update interval to **1** second.

11. Select the **Action** tab.

12. Select the **Send a network message to** check box.

13. Type in the **username** of the account with which you are currently logged on.

14. Select the **Schedule** tab.

15. Select the **Manually (using the shortcut menu)** option in the Start scan area.

16. Click **OK**.

17. Select the new **Alert object** that appears in the list of alerts.

18. Select the **Start** command from the Action menu. Its icon will be green when active.

19. Launch and terminate Windows Explorer several times to force system activity. When the % Processor Usage crosses the 50 percent threshold, a network message will appear on your screen. Click **OK** to close it.

20. Select the **Delete** command from the Action menu. Click **OK** to confirm the deletion. This deletes the Action object.

Project 11-6

To use Event Viewer to view an event detail:

1. Open the **Control Panel** by clicking the **Start** button, clicking on **Settings**, and then clicking on **Control Panel**.

2. Open the **Administrative Tools** by double-clicking its icon in the Control Panel.

3. Open **Event Viewer** by double-clicking on its icon in the Administrative Tools window.

4. Select the **Application log**.

5. Locate and select an Information detail with a SysmonLog source.

6. Double-click the item to open the event detail.

7. Notice that the Description includes information about the counter and the measured level that caused the alert.

8. Click **OK**.

9. Close the Event Viewer.

11

CASE PROJECTS

1. Performance on a Windows 2000 system used by the accounting department has been slowly degrading. You recently added a 100-Mbps network card, thinking that would correct the problem. To your knowledge, no other hardware has been added to the server, but you suspect someone has been adding software.

   Describe the steps you will use to determine what is causing the system to slow down, including which monitoring applications you will use and on which computer they will be run.

2. You are considering upgrading your Windows 2000 hardware, including memory, hard drive controller, and video card. The only things you are planning to keep are your hard drive, motherboard, and CPU.

   Outline the tools and utilities you will use to measure the performance increase or decrease, as each new component is added. Include information on expected performance changes and actual changes.

12

WINDOWS 2000 APPLICATION SUPPORT

After reading this chapter and completing the exercises, you will be able to:

♦ Understand the run-time environments and application support in Windows 2000

♦ Deploy DOS, Win16, OS/2, and POSIX applications

♦ Fine-tune the application environment for DOS and Win16

In this chapter, you encounter the pieces of the Windows 2000 operating system that endow it with its outstanding power and flexibility. Its numerous run-time environments include support for DOS and 16-bit Windows applications, as well as more modern 32-bit Windows applications, and more limited support for OS/2 (an operating system for PCs developed originally by Microsoft Corporation and IBM, but sold and managed solely by IBM) and POSIX (a portable open systems environment based on UNIX that is mandated in all operating systems that the U.S. government will purchase). You'll have a chance to examine these various subsystems and understand how they work.

WINDOWS 2000 SYSTEM ARCHITECTURE

Fundamentally, the Windows 2000 operating system has three main components: the environment subsystem, Executive Services, and user applications (see Figure 12-1).

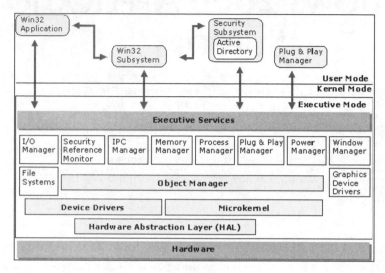

Figure 12-1   Windows 2000 architecture

- **Environment subsystems** offer run-time support for a variety of different kinds of applications under the purview of a single operating system. A **subsystem** is an operating environment that emulates another operating system (such as OS/2 and POSIX) to provide support for applications created for that environment. Just like the applications they support, Windows 2000 environment subsystems run in **user mode**, which means that they must access all system resources through the operating system's **kernel mode**.

- Windows 2000 **Executive Services** and the underlying Windows 2000 **kernel** define the kernel mode of this operating system and its run-time environment. Kernel mode components are permitted to access system objects and resources more or less directly, and provide the many services and access controls that allow multiple users and applications to coexist and interoperate effectively and efficiently.

- User applications provide the functionality and capabilities that make Windows 2000 the most powerful network operating system in use today. All such applications run within the context of an environment subsystem in Windows 2000 user mode. Applications and the subsystems in which they run have a mediated relationship because the client application asks the subsystem to do things for it, and the subsystem complies.

To understand how these components fit together, we need to revisit the concept of processes and threads, building on concepts introduced in Chapter 1.

Kernel Mode Versus User Mode

Before delving further into the architecture of Windows 2000, we'd better make clear the distinction between the Windows 2000 kernel mode and user mode. The main difference between the two modes lies in how memory is used by kernel-mode components and user-mode components.

In user mode, each process perceives the entire 4 GB of virtual memory available to Windows 2000 as its exclusive property—with the condition that the upper 2 GB of addresses are always reserved for system use. This perception remains unaltered, no matter what kind of hardware Windows 2000 may run on. Note also that this address space is entirely virtual, and must operate within the confines of whatever RAM is installed on a machine and the amount of space reserved for the paging file's use. Although the theoretical upper limit for Windows 2000 addresses may be 2 GB (or 4 GB, for system purposes), the real upper limit for Windows 2000 addresses will always be the sum of physical RAM size plus the amount of space in the paging file.

Although processes that operate in user mode may share memory areas with other processes (for fast message passing or sharing information), by default, they don't. This means that one user-mode process cannot crash another, or corrupt its data. This is what creates the appearance that applications run independently, and allows each one to operate as if it had exclusive possession of the operating system and the hardware it controls.

 If a user-mode parent process crashes, it will, of course, take its child processes down with it. (Parent and child processes are discussed later in this chapter.)

 12

Processes running in user mode cannot access hardware or communicate with other processes directly. When code runs in the Windows 2000 kernel mode, on the other hand, it may access all hardware and memory in the computer. Thus, when an application needs to perform tasks that involve hardware, it calls a user-mode function that ultimately calls a kernel-mode function.

Because all kernel-mode operations share the same memory space, one kernel-mode function can corrupt another's data and even cause the operating system to crash. This is the reason why the environment subsystems contain as much of the operating system's capabilities as possible, making the kernel itself less vulnerable. For this reason, some experts voiced concern about the change in the Windows 2000 design that moved graphics handlers to the kernel. But because those graphics components were originally part of the Win32 environment subsystem—which must be available for Windows 2000 to operate properly—a crash in either implementation could bring down the system. That's why this change has had little effect on the reliability or stability of Windows 2000.

 For a review of the user mode and kernel mode architecture of Windows 2000, please refer to Chapter 1.

Processes and Threads

From a user's point of view, the operating system exists to run programs or applications. But from the view of the Windows 2000 operating system itself, the world is made of processes and threads. A **process** defines the operating environment in which an application or any major operating system component runs. Any Windows 2000 process includes its own private memory space, a set of security descriptors, a priority level for execution, processor affinity data (that is, on a multiprocessor system, information that instructs a process to use a particular CPU), and a list of threads associated with that process. A list of currently active processes can be seen on the Processes tab of the Task Manager (see Figure 12-2). You access the Task Manager by pressing Ctrl+Alt+Delete and clicking the Task Manager button.

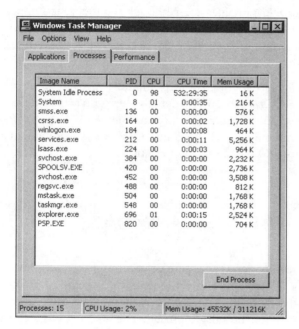

Figure 12-2   The Task Manager Processes tab

The basic executable unit in Windows 2000 is called a **thread**, and every process includes at least one thread. A thread is placeholder information associated with a single use of a program that can handle multiple concurrent users. Within a multithreaded application, each distinct task or any complex operation can be implemented in a separate thread. This explains how Microsoft Word, for instance, can perform spelling and grammar checks in the background while you're entering text in the input window—one thread manages handling input and another performs these checks.

Applications must be explicitly designed to take advantage of threading. Although it's safe to assume that most new 32-bit Windows applications—and the Windows 2000 operating system itself—have been built to use the power and flexibility of threads, older 16-bit Windows and DOS applications are usually single-threaded. Also, it's important to understand that threads are associated with processes and do not exist independently. Processes themselves don't run, they merely describe a shared environment comprising memory, variables, and other system resources; threads represent those parts of any program that actually run.

Processes can create other processes, called **child processes**, and those child processes can inherit some of the characteristics and parameters of the **parent process**. (A child process is a replica of the parent process and shares some of its resources, but cannot exist if the parent is terminated.) This usually works as follows:

- When a user logs on to Windows 2000 successfully, a shell process is created inside the Win32 subsystem within which the logon session operates. The Win32 subsystem is an operating environment that supports 32-bit Windows applications and is required to run Windows 2000. This process is endowed with a security token used to determine if subsequent requests for system objects and resources may be permitted to proceed. This shell process defines the Win32 subsystem as the parent process for that user.

- Each time a user launches an application or starts a system utility, a child process is created within the environment subsystem where that application or utility must run. This child process inherits its security token and associated information from the user account, but is a child of the environment subsystem within which it runs. This "dual parentage" (security information from the user account and, run-time environment from the environment subsystem) explains how Windows 2000 can run multiple kinds of applications, yet maintain consistent control over which system objects and resources any user process is permitted to access.

For example, each of the environment subsystems discussed in the following sections is an executable file—a combination of processes and threads running within the context of those processes (a **context** is the current collection of Registry values and run-time environment variables in which a process or thread runs). When an application runs in a Windows 2000 subsystem, it actually represents a child of the parent process for the environment subsystem, but one that is endowed with the permissions associated with the security token of the account that launches the process. Whenever a parent process halts or is stopped, all child processes stop as well.

Environment Subsystems

Windows 2000 offers support for various application platforms. Although primarily designed for 32-bit Windows applications, Windows 2000 includes support for backward compatibility for 16-bit Windows and DOS applications. To comply with U.S. government purchasing standards, Windows 2000 also includes basic support for OS/2 and POSIX applications.

Windows 2000 support for multiple run-time environments, also known as environment subsystems, confers numerous advantages, including:

- It permits users to run more than one type of application concurrently, including 32-bit Windows, 16-bit Windows, and DOS applications, as well as OS/2 and POSIX applications.

12

- It makes maintaining the operating system easier, because the modularity of this design means that changes to environment subsystems require no changes to the kernel, as long as interfaces remain unchanged.

- Modularity makes it easy to add or enhance Windows 2000—if a new OS is developed in the future, Microsoft could decide to add a subsystem for that OS to Windows 2000 without affecting other environment subsystems.

The catch to using an architecture that supports multiple environment subsystems is in providing mechanisms to permit those subsystems to communicate with one another when necessary. In the Windows 2000 environment, each subsystem runs as a separate user-mode process, so that subsystems cannot interfere with or crash one another. The only exception to this insulation effect occurs in the Win32 subsystem: because all user-mode I/O passes through this subsystem, the Win32 subsystem must be running for Windows 2000 to function. If the Win32 subsystem's process ends, the whole operating system goes down with it. That is *not* true for the POSIX or OS/2 subsystems, which may be shut down without affecting anything but their child processes.

Applications and the subsystems in which they run have a client/server relationship, in that the client application asks the server subsystem to do things for it, and the subsystem complies. For example, if a Win32 client application needs to open a new window (perhaps to create a Save As dialog box), it doesn't create the window itself, but asks the Win32 subsystem to draw the window on its behalf.

The client issues the request via a mechanism known as a **local procedure call (LPC)**. The serving subsystem makes its capabilities available to client applications by linking them to a **dynamic link library (DLL)**. You could think of a DLL as a set of buzzers, where each one is labeled with the capabilities it provides. Pushing a specific buzzer tells the server subsystem to do whatever the label tells it to. This form of messaging is transparent to the client application (as far as it knows, it's simply calling a procedure). When a client pushes one of those buzzers (requests a service), it appears as if the act is handled by the DLL; no explicit communication with a server subsystem is needed. If a service isn't listed in the library, an application can't request it; thus, a word processor running in a command-line environment inside the OS/2 subsystem, for example, can't ask that subsystem to draw a window.

 The inability to provide functions that aren't offered by a subsystem can occasionally present problems. For example, the POSIX subsystem includes no networking capabilities, so POSIX applications can't access the network. Microsoft has no plans to change this arrangement, because doing so would complicate the subsystem design.

Message passing is a fairly time-consuming operation, because any time the focus changes from one process to another, all the information for the calling process must be unloaded and replaced with the information for the called process. In operating system lingo, this change of operation focus from one process to another is called a **context switch**. To permit the operating system to run more efficiently, Windows 2000 avoids making context switches whenever possible. To that end, Windows 2000 includes the following efficiency measures:

- It caches attributes in DLLs to provide an interface to subsystem capabilities, so that (for example) the second time Microsoft Word requests a window to be created, this activity may be completed without switching context to the Win32 subsystem.

- It calls Executive Services (the collection of kernel mode Windows 2000 operating system components that provides basic system services such as I/O, security, object management, and so forth) directly, to perform tasks without requesting help from an underlying environment subsystem. Because the kernel is always active in another process space in Windows 2000, calling for kernel-mode services does *not* require a context switch.

- It batches messages so that when a server process is called, several messages can be passed at once—the number of messages has no impact on performance, but a context switch does. By batching messages, Windows 2000 allows a single context switch to handle multiple messages in sequence, rather than requiring a context switch for each message.

When LPCs must be used, they're handled as efficiently as possible. Likewise, their code is optimized for speed, and special message-passing functions can be used for different situations, depending (for example) on the size of the messages passed, or the circumstances in which they're sent.

So far, we've covered the broad view of how environment subsystems interact with client applications. Now, let's take a closer look at these subsystems.

The Win32 Subsystem

As the only subsystem required for the functioning of the operating system, the **Win32 subsystem** handles all major interface capabilities. In early versions of Windows NT, the Win32 subsystem included graphics, windowing, and messaging support, but since Windows NT 4.0, and in Windows 2000, these have been moved to the kernel and are now part of Executive Services.

In Windows 2000, user mode components of the Win32 subsystem consist of the console (text window support), shutdown, hard-error handling, and some environmental functions to handle such tasks as process creation and deletion. The Win32 subsystem is also the foundation upon which **virtual DOS machines (VDMs)** rest; these permit Windows 2000 to deliver both DOS and Win16 subsystems, so that DOS and Win16 applications can run on Windows 2000 unchanged (we'll talk more about VDMs and the DOS and Win16 subsystems later in this chapter). Try Hands-on Project 13-1 to launch a Win16 application in its own address space.

The OS/2 Subsystem

Unlike the Win32 subsystem, which starts on system startup, the **OS/2 subsystem** only begins when a user launches an application that requires its services, at which point it remains resident in memory until the system is shut down and restarted—logging off and logging back on again will not restart the OS/2 subsystem.

12

The Windows 2000 OS/2 subsystem is limited in several ways. The OS/2 subsystem is limited to OS/2 version 1.x, so, out of the box, this subsystem can run only command-line OS/2 applications.

The POSIX Subsystem

POSIX (Portable Operating System Interface for UNIX) is a set of standards owned by the IEEE (Institute of Electrical and Electronics Engineers) that defines various aspects of an operating system. So far, only one of those standards has been adopted: POSIX.1. The Windows 2000 **POSIX subsystem** (Posix.exe) is POSIX.1-compatible.

POSIX defines only API (application programming interface) calls between applications and the operating system, so in general, any application written for POSIX must rely on other operating systems for functions such as security and networking. Also, any POSIX application that accesses files must have access to an NTFS partition, because NTFS provides functionality that FAT cannot deliver and that POSIX applications need (such as the ability to support multiple names for a single data file). Recently, POSIX.1 and POSIX.2 interfaces were included into a somewhat larger interface known as the X/Open Programming Guide 4.2.

WIN32 APPLICATIONS

So far, we've examined the components of the Windows 2000 operating system kernel. Now, it's time to see how applications run under that operating system.

The Environment Subsystem

As we've mentioned, the Win32 subsystem is the main environment subsystem under Windows 2000, and the only one required for operation. Strictly speaking, even the other environment subsystems (such as OS/2 and POSIX) are Win32 emulation applications that run as child processes to the main Win32 process, although they are full-blown operating systems and not just application environments like the virtual DOS machines (VDMs) that run under Win32 to support DOS applications. (We will explain VDMs and DOS application support in more detail later in this chapter.)

Multithreading

When a program's process contains more than one thread of execution, it's said to be a **multithreaded process**. The main advantage of multithreading is that it provides multiple threads of execution within a single memory space without requiring that messages be passed between processes or that local procedure calls be used, thus simplifying thread communication. Threads are easier to create than processes because they don't require as much context information, nor do they incur the same kind of overhead when switching from one thread to another within a single process.

Some multithreaded applications can even run multiple threads concurrently among multiple processors (assuming a machine has more than one). One more advantage to threading is that it's *much* less complicated to switch operation from thread to thread than to switch from one process to another. That's because every time a new process is scheduled for execution, the system must be updated with all the process's context information. Also, it's often necessary to remove one process to make room for another, which may require writing large amounts of data from RAM to disk for the outgoing process, before copying large amounts of data from disk into RAM to bring in the incoming process.

 TIP As a point of comparison, a thread switch can normally be completed in somewhere between 15 and 25 machine instructions, whereas a process switch can take many thousands of instructions to complete. Because most CPUs are set up to handle one instruction for every clock cycle, this means that switching among threads is hundreds to thousands of times faster than switching among processes.

The big trick with multithreading, of course, is that the chances that one thread could overwrite another are increased with each additional thread, so this introduces the problem of protecting shared areas of memory from intraprocess thread overwrites. Windows 2000 handles this by managing access to memory carefully, and limiting which sections of memory any individual thread can write to by locking them, as you'll see in the next section.

Memory Space

Multithreaded programs must be designed so that threads don't get in each other's way, and they do this by using Windows 2000 **synchronization objects**. A section of code that modifies data structures used by several threads is called a **critical section**. It's very important that a critical section never be overwritten by more than one thread at once. Thus, applications use Windows 2000 synchronization objects to prevent this from happening, creating such objects for each critical section in each process context. When a thread needs access to a critical section, the following occurs:

1. A thread requests a synchronization object. If it is unlocked (not suspended in a thread queue), the request proceeds. Otherwise, go to Step 2.

2. The thread is suspended in a thread queue until the synchronization object is unlocked for its use. As soon as this happens, Windows 2000 releases the thread and locks up the object.

3. The thread accesses the critical section.

4. When the thread is done, it unlocks the synchronization object so that another thread may access the critical object.

Thus, multithreaded applications avoid accessing a single data structure with more than one thread at a time by locking its critical section when it's in use and unlocking it when it's not.

Input Message Queues

One of the roles of the Win32 subsystem is to organize user input and get it to the thread to which that input belongs. It does this by taking user messages from a general input queue, and distributing them to the **input message queues** for the individual processes.

As we'll discuss later in this chapter, Win16 applications normally run within a single process, so they share a message input queue, unlike Win32 or DOS applications with their individual queues.

Base Priorities

When a program is started under Windows 2000, its process is assigned a particular priority class, generally Normal—but there is a range of options (see Figure 12-3). The priority class helps determine the priority at which threads in a process must run, on a scale from 0 (lowest) to 31 (highest). In a process with more than one active thread, each thread may have its own priority, which may be higher or lower than that of the original thread, but that priority is always relative to the priority assigned to the underlying process, which is known as the **base priority**. Managing priorities may be accomplished in one of several ways, and can sometimes provide a useful way to improve application performance. These include Task Manager and the Start command, as discussed in Chapter 11.

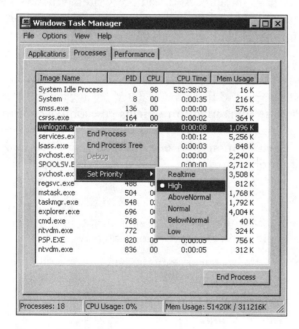

Figure 12-3   The Task Manager Processes tab showing priority options

DOS AND THE VIRTUAL DOS MACHINE

DOS and Win16 applications work somewhat differently from Win32 applications. Rather than each running in the context of its own process, these applications run a virtual DOS machine (VDM), a special environment process that simulates a DOS environment so that non-Win32 Windows applications can run under Windows 2000. In fact, it's reasonable to describe two separate operating environments that can run within a VDM: one supports straightforward DOS emulation and may be called the **DOS operating environment**; the other supports operation of Win16 applications within a VDM, and may be called the **Win16 operating environment**.

The DOS operating environment under Windows 2000 is established by a Win32 process named Ntvdm.exe (see Figure 12-4). In fact, if you look at the Processes tab of the Task Manager when a DOS application is active, you'll see this process. Ntvdm creates the environment where DOS applications execute. Each DOS application that is launched is executed within a separate emulation environment. Thus, if you launch three DOS applications, three instances of Ntvdm will appear in the process list. Once a DOS application terminates, Windows 2000 also shuts down the emulation environment for that application by terminating the associated instance of Ntvdm. This frees the system resources to be used elsewhere and is unlike the behavior of VDMs in Windows NT 4.0.

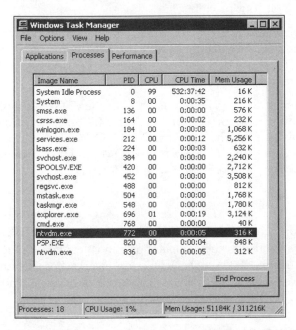

Figure 12-4   The Task Manager Processes tab showing Ntvdm.exe

 The environment created in a VDM is not the same as that available to Win32 applications. Instead, it's equivalent to the environment of Windows 3.x Enhanced mode, in which each DOS application has access to 1 MB of virtual memory, with 1 MB of extended memory and expanded memory if necessary.

By default, all DOS applications run in their own VDM. By default, all Win16 applications share a single VDM (just as they do in "real Windows 3.x" environments).

VDM Components

The VDM runs using the following files:

- *Ntio.sys:* The equivalent of Io.sys on MS-DOS machines, runs in **real mode** (real mode is a mode of operation for x86 CPUs wherein they can address only 1 MB of memory, broken into 16 64–KB segments). It provides "virtual IO" services to the DOS or Win16 applications that run in a VDM.

- *Ntdos.sys:* The equivalent of Msdos.sys, runs in real mode. It provides basic DOS operating system services to the DOS or Win16 applications that run in a VDM.

- *Ntvdm.exe:* A Win32 application that runs in kernel mode. This is the .exe file that provides the run-time environment within which a VDM runs. If you look at the list on the Processes tab of Task Manager, you'll see one such entry for each separate VDM that's running on your machine.

- *Ntvdm.dll:* A Win32 dynamic link library that runs in kernel mode. Ntvdm.dll provides the set of procedure stubs that fool DOS and Win16 programs into thinking they're talking to a real DOS machine with exclusive access to a PC, when in fact they're communicating through a VDM with Windows 2000.

- *Redir.exe:* The virtual device driver (VDD) redirector for the VDM. This software forwards I/O requests from programs within a VDM for I/O services through the Win32 environment subsystem to the Windows 2000 I/O Manager in Executive Services. Whenever a DOS or Win16 program in a VDM thinks it's communicating with hardware, it's really communicating with Redir.exe.

Virtual Device Drivers

DOS applications do not communicate directly with Windows 2000 drivers. Instead, a layer of **virtual device drivers (VDDs)** underlies these applications, and they communicate with Windows 2000 32-bit drivers. Windows 2000 supplies VDDs for mice, keyboards, printers, and communication ports, as well as file system drivers (which include one or more network drivers, each of which is actually implemented as a file system driver).

AUTOEXEC.BAT and CONFIG.SYS

When a DOS application is started, Windows 2000 runs the files specified in the application's program information file (PIF) or in AUTOEXEC.NT (see Figure 12-5) and CONFIG.NT (see Figure 12-6), the two files that replace AUTOEXEC.BAT and CONFIG.SYS for VDMs. AUTOEXEC.NT installs CD-ROM extensions and the network redirector, and can even provide DOS Protected Mode Interface (DPMI) support, to permit DOS and Win16 applications to access more than 1 MB of memory within a virtual (or real) DOS machine. CONFIG.NT loads into an upper memory area for its VDM, and can support HIMEM.SYS to enable extended memory; it also sets the number of files and buffers available to DOS or Win16 programs, and provides necessary details to configure expanded memory. Try Hands-on Project 12-4 to explore AUTOEXEC.NT and CONFIG.NT.

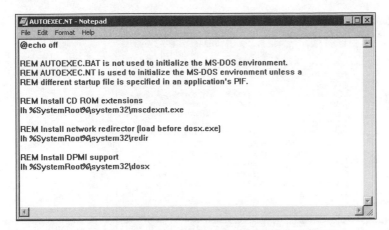

Figure 12-5   AUTOEXEC.NT viewed through Notepad

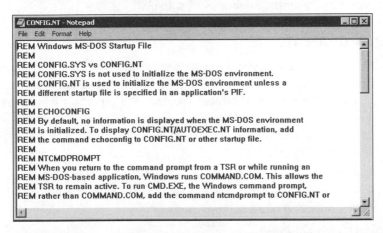

Figure 12-6   CONFIG.NT viewed through Notepad

CONFIG.SYS isn't used at all by Windows 2000, whereas AUTOEXEC.BAT is only used at system startup to set path and environment variables for the Windows 2000 environment. Neither file is consulted when it comes to running applications or initializing drivers; those settings must exist in the system Registry to work at all.

Once read from AUTOEXEC.BAT, path and environment variables are copied to the Registry, to HKEY_LOCAL_MACHINE\SYSTEM\CurrentControlSet\Control\Session Manager\Environment (see Figure 12-7).

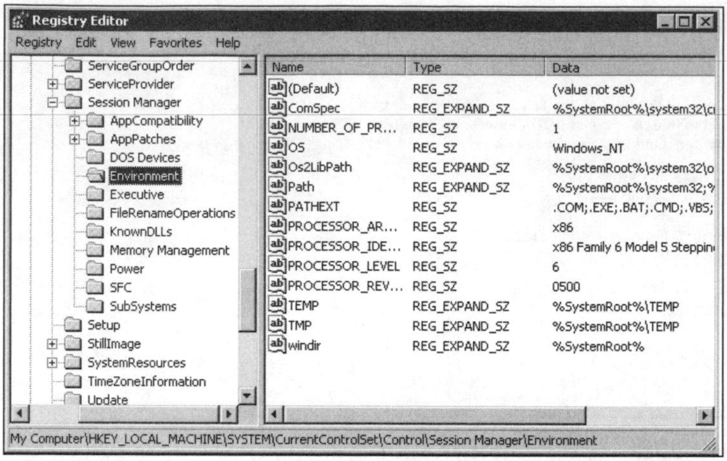

Figure 12-7 Regedit displaying the Environment subkey

Custom DOS Environments

Windows 2000 offers customizable environmental controls for the DOS environment. These controls can be used to fine-tune or simply alter how a DOS application functions. To customize a DOS application's execution parameters, open the Properties dialog box for that executable (.exe or .com) file. This is performed by right-clicking over an executable file and selecting Properties from the resulting menu. Try Hands-on Project 12-2 to explore the properties of a DOS application.

The Properties dialog box for a DOS (FAT 16) executable file has six tabs. The General tab lists the same data items as any other file within the Windows 2000 environment (see Figure 12-8). The Program tab (see Figure 12-9) offers controls over:

- *Filename*—The name of the file

- *Command line*—Used to add command-line parameter syntax

- *Working*—Used to define the working directory, which is the directory from which the application will load files and where it saves files

- *Batch file*—Used to run a batch file before launching the executable file

- *Shortcut key*—Used to define a keystroke that will launch the executable file

- *Run*—Used to define the window size of the DOS environment—normal, maximized, or minimized

- *Close on exit*—Informs the OS to close the DOS window when the application terminates

- *Advanced* button—Allows you to define the path to alternate AUTOEXEC.NT and CONFIG.NT files

- *Change icon* button—Changes the icon displayed for the executable file

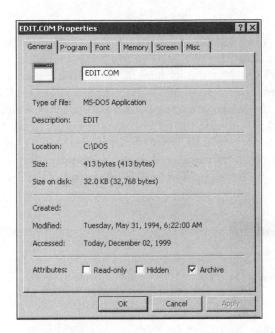

Figure 12-8   EDIT.COM Properties, General tab

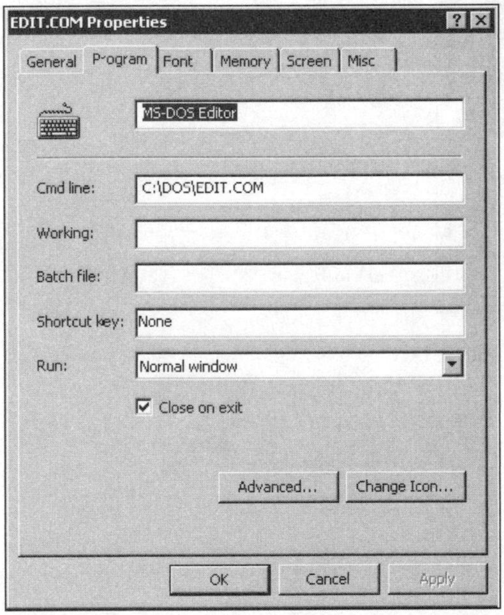

Figure 12-9   EDIT.COM Properties, Program tab

The Font tab is used to define the font used by the DOS application (see Figure 12-10). The Memory tab is used to define the memory parameters of the DOS environment (see Figure 12-11). These controls include settings for conventional memory, expanded memory (EMS), extended memory (XMS), and protected-mode (DBMI) memory. The Screen tab is used to define whether the DOS application loads full-screen or in a window, to emulate fast ROM, and to define whether to allocate dynamic memory (see Figure 12-12). The Misc tab is used to allow a screen saver over the DOS window and to define whether the mouse is used by the DOS application, if the DOS application is suspended when in the background, whether to warn if the DOS application is active when you attempt to close the DOS window, how long the application will wait for I/O before releasing CPU control, whether to use fast pasting (a quick method for pasting information into the application; this doesn't work with some programs, so disable this check box if information does not paste properly), and which Windows shortcut keys will be reserved for use by Windows 2000 instead of the DOS application (see Figure 12-13).

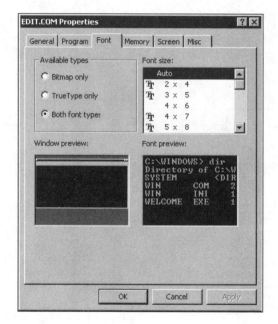

Figure 12-10   EDIT.COM Properties, Font tab

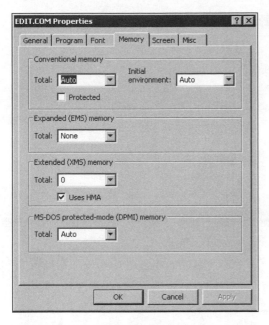

Figure 12-11   EDIT.COM Properties, Memory tab

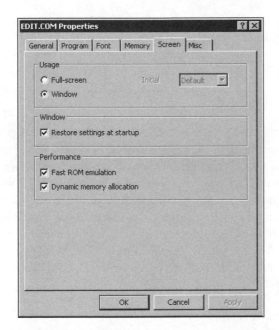

Figure 12-12   EDIT.COM Properties, Screen tab

12

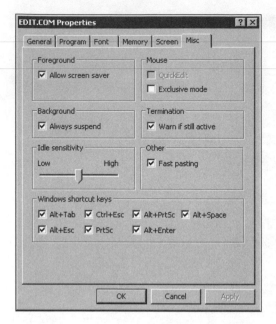

Figure 12-13   EDIT.COM Properties, Misc tab

Once you alter any portion of one of these tabs, a new shortcut for the application is created that will retain these changes. Thus you can reuse and fine-tune your custom DOS environment settings for each application.

WIN16 CONCEPTS AND APPLICATIONS

Like DOS applications, Win16 applications also run in a VDM, although unlike DOS applications, which by default run in their own individual address spaces, all Win16 applications run in the same VDM unless specified otherwise. This permits them to act like Win32 applications, and lets multiple Win16 applications interact with one another in a single VDM. This creates the appearance that multiple applications are active simultaneously. (Usually, only one Win16 application in a VDM can be active at any given moment, but this form of **multitasking**—which Microsoft calls cooperative multitasking—creates a convincing imitation of the more robust and real multitasking available to Win32 applications.) The **Win16-on-Win32 VDM**—usually called **WOW**—runs as a multithreaded application, with each Win16 application being one thread (see Figure 12-14).

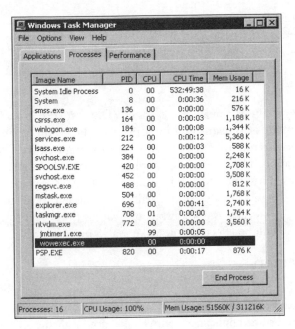

Figure 12-14   The Task Manager Processes tab showing Wowexec.exe

Win16-on-Win32 (WOW) Components

The WOW subsystem has the following components:

- *Wowexec.exe:* Handles the loading of 16-bit Windows-based applications
- *Wow32.dll:* The dynamic link library for the WOW application environment
- *ntvdm.exe*, *ntvdm.dll*, *ntio.sys*, and *redir.exe:* Run the VDM
- *Vdmredir.dll:* The redirector for the WOW environment
- *Krnl386.exe:* Used by WOW on x86-based systems
- *Gdi.exe:* A modified version of Windows 3.10 Gdi.exe
- *User.exe:* A modified version of Windows 3.10 User.exe

Calls made to 16-bit drivers are transferred ("thunked") to the appropriate 32-bit driver, without the application being aware of it. Similarly, if a driver needs to return information to an application, it must be thunked back again. This back and forth translation helps explain why many Win16 applications run more slowly in a VDM on Windows 2000 than they do on other versions of Windows (even Windows 95), where no such translations are required.

Once a WOW environment is created, Windows 2000 will sustain that environment until the system is rebooted or you manually terminate the Wowexec.exe task (such as via the Task Manager Processes tab). Creating new WOW environments each time a Win16 application is launched was deemed more costly in terms of resources and CPU time than maintaining a WOW environment once it has been created throughout a boot session. Thus, if you use

12

Win16 applications often, this function will offer you some benefit. But if you seldom use Win16 applications, you'd be better off terminating the WOW environment after you finish with the hosted application.

Memory Space

By default, all Win16 applications run as threads in a single VDM process (try Hands-on Project 12-5 to explore the number of threads used by a process). However, it might be a good idea not to permit this, because multiple threads running in a single process can affect the performance of each application. This mixture of applications can also make tracking applications more difficult, because most monitoring in Windows 2000 takes place on a per-process basis, not on a per-thread basis. Finally, running all Win16 applications in a single VDM means that if one of those applications goes astray and causes the VDM to freeze or crash, all applications in that VDM will be affected ("just like real Windows 3.x!").

Separate and Shared Memory

The "lose one, lose them all" effect of a single shared VDM explains why you might choose to run Win16 applications in separate VDMs. That way, you'll increase the reliability of those applications as a whole, and one errant application won't take down all the other Win16 applications if it crashes. Likewise, you'll make preemptive multitasking possible (that is, one busy application won't be able to hog the processor), and you'll be able to take advantage of multiple processors if you have them, because all the threads in a single VDM process must execute on the same processor.

The disadvantages of running Win16 applications in separate memory spaces focus on memory usage and interprocess communications: Each additional process running on a machine requires about 2 MB of space in the paging file, and 1 MB of additional working set size, or the amount of data that the application has in memory at any given time. Also, those older Win16 applications that don't support Dynamic Data Exchange (DDE) or object linking and embedding (OLE) won't be able to communicate with each other. Additionally, running Win16 applications as processes instead of threads increases the time it takes to switch from one application to another, because each such switch requires a full context change from one process to another. The best way to observe the impact of this separation is to try it the default way (whereby all Win16 applications share a single VDM), and then set up those Win16 applications in separate VDMs and compare the performance that results from each such scenario.

To launch a Win16 application in a separate memory space, you must first create a shortcut to the executable. Then edit the properties of the shortcut and select the *Run in separate memory space* check box. You can also start 16-bit applications in their own address space via the /separate command line switch. The proper syntax is: start/separate [16-bit program executable name].

 TIP The Run command in Windows 2000 does not have a *Run in separate memory space* check box like Windows NT 4.0; thus, a Win16 application cannot be launched in a separate memory space from the Run command.

Message Queues

As mentioned earlier, the Win32 subsystem is responsible for collecting user input and getting it to those applications that need it. However, unlike Win32 applications, all Win16 applications running in a single process share a message queue. Therefore, if one application becomes unable to accept input, it will block all other Win16 applications in that VDM from accepting further input as well.

Threads

As we mentioned earlier, Win16 threads that run in a VDM do not multitask like threads running in the Win32 subsystem. Instead of being preemptively multitasked, so that one thread can push another aside if its priority is higher, or so that any thread that's been taking up too much CPU time can be preempted, all application threads within a WOW VDM are cooperatively multitasked. This means that any one thread—which corresponds to any Win16 application—can hog the CPU. This is sometimes called the "good guy scheduling" algorithm, because it assumes that all applications will be well behaved and relinquish the CPU whenever they must block for I/O or other system services. The net effect, however, is that WOW VDMs behave as if they have only one execution thread to share among all applications within the VDM.

Using Only Well-Behaved DOS and Win16 Applications

Many DOS applications, as well as numerous older Win16 applications, often take advantage of a prerogative of DOS developers—namely, the ability to access system hardware directly, bypassing any access APIs or drivers that the system might ordinarily put between an application and the underlying hardware. Although such applications will work fine in DOS, Windows 3.x, and even Windows 95, this is not the case with Windows 2000. The division into user mode and kernel mode in Windows 2000 means that any application that attempts to access hardware directly will be shut down with an error message to the effect of "illegal operation attempted."

In Windows 2000 terminology, any application that attempts direct access to hardware is called "ill behaved." Such applications will not run in a VDM. On the other hand, any Win16 or DOS application that uses standard DOS or Windows 3.x APIs instead of attempting direct access to hardware will work in a VDM. Such applications are called well behaved. Unfortunately, there is no list of well-behaved applications available, so the only way to tell the difference is to test the ones you'd like to use with Windows 2000 and see what happens. If an application doesn't perform properly, it shouldn't be deployed on your system. We suggest that you deploy only well-behaved applications for use with Windows 2000, and that you seriously consider replacing any ill-behaved applications you may find in your current collection of programs. Try Hands-on Project 12-3 to explore the effects of VDMs in Windows 2000.

12

THE OS/2 SUBSYSTEM

The Windows 2000 OS/2 subsystem provides a way to run character-mode OS/2 applications on x86 computers. Unlike the VDMs and WOW, the OS/2 subsystem is indeed a separate operating system, albeit one that runs like a Win32 application. It works just as the OS/2 operating system would if it were running independently, although some of its features (such as its ability to share information between processes) are implemented through Windows 2000, not as they would be in OS/2. One thing that *doesn't* work the same as in the original version of OS/2 is the amount of memory available, because the OS/2 subsystem utilizes the 4 GB of memory normally available to Win32 processes, rather than the 16 MB with which OS/2 was designed to work. Because this represents a substantial improvement over the original, this difference has not occasioned too many complaints.

OS/2 Version 1.x

OS/2 1.x doesn't look much like any version of OS/2 you're likely to see, because it's completely character-based and doesn't include the familiar graphical workplace shell. Character-based applications that call the OS/2 Presentation Manager will not run under Windows 2000. This characteristic makes the OS/2 subsystem of limited use in most organizations, because most OS/2 applications require graphical interface support.

OS/2 Components

The OS/2 subsystem has the following components:

- *Os2ss.exe:* The main component of the OS/2 subsystem and the one started when the first OS/2 application is loaded

- *Os2dll.dll:* Shares address space with each OS/2 application and handles the communication between the application and the subsystem, Os2ss.exe

- *Os2.exe:* A Win32 program that passes the name of the OS/2 application and any command-line parameters to Os2srv.exe. This portion of the OS/2 subsystem only starts once, no matter how many OS/2 applications are running.

- *Os2srv.exe:* The component that actually starts each OS2 application for the OS2 subsystem

These components don't start until the first OS/2 application is started, at which point the OS/2 subsystem comes up, and it isn't shut down until the system is rebooted. Logging off and logging back on to a Windows 2000 machine will not reset the OS/2 subsystem; that requires an actual system shutdown or restart.

Bound Applications

Bound applications, or those that can run under either OS/2 or in a VDM, will run in the OS/2 subsystem on an x86 machine if one is available, because they'll run faster. The only way to prevent an application that can go either way from running within the OS/2 subsystem, should you wish to do so (perhaps because that application won't run in OS/2), is to run Forcedos.exe. This utility appears in the \System32 directory, and forces bound applications to run in a VDM instead of in the OS/2 subsystem environment.

OS/2 Configuration

When the OS/2 subsystem starts up for the first time, it checks the Registry for OS/2 setup information. If it doesn't find any, it checks the OS/2 CONFIG.SYS. If CONFIG.SYS does not exist, then the subsystem adds shell initialization information to the Registry.

To update the OS/2 configuration information, you must edit CONFIG.SYS with an OS/2 text editor (Notepad won't do; it must be an OS/2 editor). Open the file, which will be a temporary copy of the configuration information in the Registry. Make the changes and save them, and then those changes will be stored in the Registry and will take effect after you next restart your computer.

When configuring OS/2, you can use the commands shown in Table 12-1. If you use a command not found in this table, it will be ignored.

Table 12-1 OS/2 Subsystem Configuration Commands

Command	Description
protshell	Specifies the command interpreter, although only the Windows 2000 interpreter Cmd.exe is supported
devicename	Specifies a user-defined Windows 2000 device driver used by OS/2 applications
libpath	Specifies the location of the 16-bit OS/2 DLLs
set	Sets environment variables
country	Lets you provide a country code that specifies time, date, and currency conventions
codepage	Specifies the code page the system will use
devinfo=KBD	Specifies the information the keyboard needs to use a particular code page

12

POSIX SUBSYSTEM

As already mentioned, POSIX is a set of APIs intended to permit UNIX applications to run on a variety of operating systems without requiring reimplementation. At this point, only one POSIX standard of the 12 proposed has been formalized: POSIX 1.x. Because POSIX is only an API, the list of what POSIX can't do is as long as the list of what it can do. Because POSIX was designed for use in a very simple operating environment, it supports only local input and output, and does not even support networking (although you can get to network-accessible files via other parts of Windows 2000). Although POSIX technically doesn't support printing, you can pipe information to another Windows 2000 subsystem for output if you connect or redirect a serial or parallel port and access it with the *net use* command from the command prompt.

TIP For expanded POSIX support on Windows 2000, you need to deploy a third-party emulation service. Softway Systems, which has been recently acquired by Microsoft, offers Interix, an expanded POSIX environment emulator and suite of development tools. For more information, see *http://www.interix.com/home.html*.

CHAPTER SUMMARY

❐ Windows 2000 is divided into three main parts: environment subsystems, Executive Services, and user applications. The environment subsystems provide support for applications written for a variety of operating systems, not just for Windows 2000; the Executive Services define the Windows 2000 run-time environment; and user applications provide additional functionality for a variety of services, such as word-processing and e-mail applications.

❐ Three environment subsystems (Win32, OS/2, and POSIX) run under Windows 2000, plus two special-purpose operating environments (VDM and WOW) that provide backward compatibility within the Win32 subsystem for Win16 and DOS applications.

❐ Of these subsystems, only Win32 is crucial to the functioning of Windows 2000 as a whole. The other subsystems only start up as they're needed, but once launched, these subsystems tend to persist until the machine is shut down and restarted.

KEY TERMS

base priority — The lowest priority that a thread may be assigned, based on the priority assigned to its process.

bound application — An application capable of running under the OS/2 subsystem or in a virtual DOS machine. If the OS/2 subsystem is available, it will be used by default.

child process — A process spawned within the context of some Windows 2000 environment subsystems (Win32, OS/2, or POSIX) that inherits operating characteristics from its parent subsystem, and access characteristics from the permissions associated with the account that requested it to be launched.

context — The collection of Registry values and run-time environment variables in which a process or thread is currently running.

context switch — The act of unloading the context information for one process and replacing it with the information for another, when the new process comes to the foreground.

critical section — In operating system terminology, this refers to a section of code that can only be accessed by a single thread at any one time, to prevent uncertain results from occurring when multiple threads attempt to change or access values included in that code at the same time.

DOS operating environment — A general term used to describe the reasonably thorough DOS emulation capabilities provided in a Windows 2000 virtual DOS machine (VDM).

dynamic link library (DLL) — A collection of virtual procedure calls, also called procedure stubs, that provide a well-defined way for applications to call on services or server processes within the Win32 environment. DLLs have been a consistent aspect of Windows since Windows 2.0.

environment subsystem — A mini-operating system running within Windows 2000, providing an interface between applications and the kernel. Windows 2000 has three environment subsystems: Win32, OS/2, and POSIX, but only Win32 is required for Windows 2000 to function.

Executive Services — A set of kernel-mode functions that controls security, system I/O, memory management, and other low-level services.

input message queue — A queue for each process, maintained by the Win32 subsystem, that contains the messages sent to the process from the user, directing its threads to do something.

kernel — The part of Windows 2000 composed of system services that interact directly with applications; it controls all application contact with the computer.

kernel mode — Systems running in kernel mode are operating within a shared memory space and with access to hardware. Windows 2000 Executive Services operates in kernel mode.

local procedure call (LPC) — A technique to permit processes to exchange data in the Windows 2000 run-time environment. LPCs define a rigorous interface to let client programs request services, and to let server programs respond to such requests.

multitasking — Sharing processor time between threads. Multitasking may be preemptive (the operating system may bump one thread if another one really needs access to the processor), or cooperative (one thread will retain control of the processor until its turn to use it is over). Windows 2000 uses preemptive multitasking except in the context of the WOW operating environment, because Windows 3.x applications expect cooperative multitasking.

multithreaded process — A process with more than one thread running at a time.

OS/2 subsystem — The Windows 2000 subsystem used for running OS/2 applications; an emulation of OS/2 version 1.x (character mode only).

parent process — The Windows 2000 environment subsystem that creates a run-time process, and imbues that child process with characteristics associated with that parent's interfaces, capabilities, and run-time requirements.

POSIX subsystem — The Windows 2000 subsystem used for running POSIX applications.

process — An environment in which the executable portion of a program runs, defining its memory usage, which processor to use, its objects, and so forth. All processes have at least one thread. When the last thread is terminated, the process terminates with it. Each user-mode process maintains its own map of the virtual memory area. One process may create another, in which case the creator is the parent process and the created process is the child process.

real mode — A DOS term that describes a mode of operation for x86 CPUs wherein they can address only 1 MB of memory, broken into 16 64-KB segments, where the lower ten such segments are available to applications (the infamous 640 KB), and the upper six segments are available to the operating system or to special application drivers—or, for Windows 2000, to a VDM.

12

subsystem — An operating environment that emulates another operating system (such as OS/2 or POSIX) to provide support for applications created for that environment.

synchronization object — Any of a special class of objects within the Windows 2000 environment that are used to synchronize and control access to shared objects and critical sections of code.

thread — The executable portion of a program, with a priority based on the priority of its process—user threads cannot exist external to a process. All threads in a process share that process's context.

user mode — Systems running in user mode are operating in virtual private memory areas for each process, so that each process is protected from all others. User-mode processes may not manipulate hardware, but must send requests to kernel-mode services to do this manipulation for them.

virtual device driver (VDD) — A device driver used by virtual DOS machines (VDMs) to provide an interface between the application, which expects to interact with a 16-bit device driver, and the 32-bit device drivers that Windows 2000 provides.

virtual DOS machine (VDM) — A Win32 application that emulates a DOS environment for use by DOS and Win16 applications.

Win16 operating environment — The collection of components, interfaces, and capabilities that permits Win16 applications to run within a VDM within the Win32 subsystem on Windows 2000.

Win16-on-Win32 subsystem (WOW) — The formal name for the collection of components, interfaces, and capabilities that permits the Win32 subsystem to provide native support for well-behaved 16-bit Windows applications.

REVIEW QUESTIONS

1. Which of the following is not an environment subsystem? (Choose all correct answers.)

   a. Win32

   b. Win16

   c. OS/2

   d. none of the above

2. If the threads in a process will always run on one processor in a multiprocessor system, that process is said to have a(n) _____ for that processor.

3. Which of the following statements about process termination are true? (Choose all correct answers.)

   a. When a process's last thread is terminated, the process will terminate as well, unless it creates another thread within a certain interval.

   b. When a process terminates, all of its child processes terminate with it.

   c. A process must have at least one thread at all times.

   d. If a parent process terminates, its threads may be taken over by a child process.

4. Which of the following is not a reason to use the environment subsystem/kernel model?

    a. speed

    b. modularity

    c. subsystem protection

    d. ease of communication

5. The _____ subsystem is required for the functioning of the Windows 2000 operating system.

6. Applications and the subsystems in which they run have a _____ relationship, in that the client application asks the server subsystem to do things for it, and the subsystem complies.

7. When an application stops operating in user mode and begins operating in kernel mode, this is called a context switch. True or False?

8. Which of the following is not an attempt to speed up subsystem/user application communications?

    a. LPCs

    b. caching services provided by the subsystem

    c. batching messages

    d. calling kernel services directly

9. Which two parts of the kernel were part of the Win32 subsystem prior to Windows NT 4.0?

    a. GDI

    b. I/O Manager

    c. device drivers

    d. Windows Manager

10. User applications always operate in user mode. True or False?

11. To restart the OS/2 subsystem, you must:

    a. log off and log back on

    b. stop Os2.exe and then start a new OS/2 application

    c. restart the computer

    d. none of the above

12. The Windows 2000 Executive Services define the kernel mode of this operating system and its run-time environment. True or False?

13. POSIX applications must always run on an NTFS partition. True or False?

14. Each time you start a DOS application under Windows 2000, it runs in its own VDM. True or False?

12

15. Which of the following statements are true regarding LPCs, or Local Procedure Calls? (Choose all correct answers.)

    a. used to inform the CPU of I/O

    b. code optimized for speed

    c. supports specialized message passing functions

    d. employed only by the GDI portion of the OS

16. A child process can inherit the security token of its parent, or it can obtain a new security token by querying the Security Accounts Manager. True or False?

17. Windows 16-bit applications rely upon which of the following? (Choose all correct answers.)

    a. NTVDM

    b. POSIX

    c. WOW

    d. Win32

18. Under Windows 2000, what do Win16 applications all share by default? (Choose all correct answers.)

    a. working directory

    b. message queue

    c. address space

    d. NTFS file permissions

19. Which of the following are true statements about Win16? (Choose all correct answers.)

    a. Wowexec.exe functions directly within a Win32 VM.

    b. When Wowexec.exe terminates, its NTVDM host also terminates.

    c. A different kernel driver is used on RISC systems for the WOW environment.

    d. Only a single instance of Wowexec.exe can be launched.

20. Win16 applications can be launched into a separate memory space from the Run command within Windows 2000. True or False?

21. In Windows 2000, DOS applications can be launched into DOS environments with customized memory configurations. True or False?

22. All multithreaded applications running under Windows 2000 could be designed to operate on multiple processors for greater efficiency. True or False?

23. The first 16-bit application always runs in a separate memory space by default, whereas all subsequent 16-bit applications run by default in the same memory space as other applications of their kind. True or False?

24. A section of code that modifies data structures used by several threads is called a
    _____.

25. Neither AUTOEXEC.BAT nor CONFIG.SYS has any role in determining Windows 2000 system configuration. True or False?

HANDS-ON PROJECTS

Project 12-1

To start a Win16 application in its own address space:

1. Open Windows Explorer by selecting **Start**, **Programs**, **Accessories**, **Windows Explorer**.

2. In the left pane, select the drive letter that hosts your Windows 2000 main directory.

3. In the right pane, double-click the Windows 2000 main folder (this is WINNT by default). If necessary, click **Show Files** to see the files in this folder.

4. Scroll down in the right pane to locate Winhelp.exe.

5. Select **Winhelp.exe**.

6. Right-click over **Winhelp.exe** and select **Create Shortcut** from the resulting menu.

7. Select **Shortcut to Winhelp.exe**.

8. Right-click over **Shortcut to Winhelp.exe** and select **Properties** from the resulting menu.

9. Mark the **Run in separate memory space** check box (see Figure 12–15).

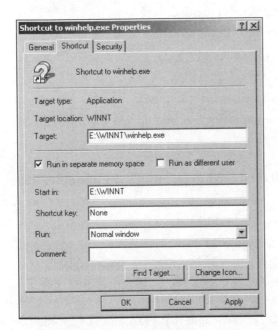

Figure 12-15   Selecting the Run in separate memory space check box

10. Click **OK**.

11. Double-click **Winhelp**.

12. Double-click **Shortcut to Winhelp.exe**.

13. Launch Task Manager by pressing **Ctrl+Shift+Esc**.

14. Select the **Processes** tab.

15. Notice that two WOW environments exist, each hosting an instance of Winhelp.exe

16. Close Task Manager by selecting **File**, **Exit Task Manager**.

17. Close both instances of Winhelp by selecting **File**, **Exit**.

Project 12-2

To explore the Properties configuration for a DOS application:

1. Open Windows Explorer by selecting **Start**, **Programs**, **Accessories**, **Windows Explorer**.

2. Locate the DOS application, **Edit.com**.

3. Right-click **Edit.com** and select **Properties** from the resulting menu.

4. View the details provided on the **General** tab (refer to Figure 12-8).

5. Select the **Program** tab and view the details provided.

6. Click the **Advanced** button and view the details provided.

7. Click **Cancel**.

8. Select the **Font** tab and view the details provided.

9. Select the **Memory** tab and view the details provided.

10. Select the **Screen** tab and view the details provided.

11. Select the **Misc** tab and view the details provided.

12. Explore other tabs, if any, on your Properties dialog box.

13. Click **Cancel** to close the Properties dialog box and discard any mistaken changes.

Project 12-3

To view the effects of various VDM-based applications on Windows 2000:

1. Restart your Windows 2000 system and log on.

2. Launch Task Manager by pressing **Ctrl+shift+esc**.

3. Select the **Processes** tab (refer to Figure 12-2).

4. Launch a DOS application, such as Edit.com, by using the **Run** command. This is performed by clicking the **Start** button then selecting **Run**. Type **c:\WINNT\System32\Edit.com** or a similar path to a DOS application. Click **OK**.

5. Notice in the list of processes via Task Manager that NTVDM has appeared, but the name of the DOS application itself has not.

6. Close the DOS application, using its own commands. For Edit.com this means selecting **File**, **Exit**.

7. Once the application terminates, notice that NTVDM no longer appears in the process list.

8. Launch a Windows 16 bit application, such as Winhelp.exe, by using the Run command. This is performed by clicking the **Start** button then selecting **Run**. Type **c:\winnt\Winhelp.exe** or a similar path to a Win16 application. Click **OK**.

9. Notice in the list of processes via Task Manager that NTVDM appears along with Wowexec.exe and Winhelp.exe as subitems.

10. Close the Win16 application using its own commands. For Winhelp.exe, this means selecting **File**, **Exit**.

11. Notice in the list of processes that NTVDM and WOWEXEC remain.

12. Terminate the WOWEXEC process by selecting it and clicking **End Process**.

13. Click **Yes** to confirm termination.

14. Notice that both NTVDM and WOWEXEC are no longer listed in the processes.

15. Close Task Manager by selecting **File**, **Exit Task Manager**.

Project 12-4

To view the AUTOEXEC.NT and CONFIG.NT files of Windows 2000:

1. Launch Notepad by selecting **Start**, **Programs**, **Accessories**, **Notepad**.

2. Select **File**, **Open**.

3. Change directories to **\WINNT\System32**.

4. Change the **Files of type** to **All Files**.

5. Locate and select **AUTOEXEC.NT**.

6. Click **Open**.

7. View the contents of this file (refer to Figure 12-5).

8. Select **File**, **Open**.

9. Change the **Files of type** to **All Files**.

10. Locate and select **CONFIG.NT**.

11. Click **Open** and view the contents of this file (refer to Figure 12-6).

12. Close Notepad by selecting **File**, **Exit**.

12

Project 12-5

To view the number of threads used by processes under Windows 2000:

1. Launch Task Manager by clicking **ctrl+shift+Esc**.

2. Select the **Processes** tab (refer to Figure 12-2).

3. Select **View**, **Select Columns**.

4. Mark the **Thread Count** check box (see Figure 12-16).

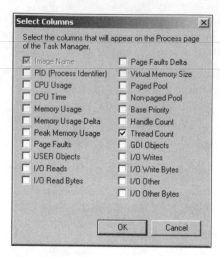

Figure 12-16   Selecting the Thread Count check box

5. Click **OK**.

6. Maximize the Task Manager window.

7. Notice the number of threads for each of the currently active processes.

8. Close Task Manager by selecting **File**, **Exit Task Manager**.

CASE PROJECTS

1. To avoid the need to reimplement old code for your user community, which is in the process of upgrading from Windows 95 to Windows 2000 Professional, you decide to allow your users to run your company's homegrown application, Teller.exe, which is a well-behaved 16-bit Windows application, on their machines. Because this program sometimes hangs for as much as 2 or 3 minutes while computing end-of-day balances, it may cause problems for other 16-bit Windows applications that your users might need to run. What can you do to insulate these other applications from Teller.exe? How might you launch this program to accomplish this goal?

2. At XYZ Corp., the company has decided to switch from its OS/2 machines to Windows 2000 Professional. Your manager informs you that this will be a snap because Windows 2000 includes an OS/2 subsystem that supports the company's homegrown graphical OS/2 applications. What must you tell your manager about his assumptions about Windows 2000 support for OS/2? Why is this a problem?

3. Given a list of DOS and 16-bit Windows applications that you may wish to use on a Windows 2000 machine, what is the proper method to ensure that each of them will (or won't) work with this operating system? What happens if any of these applications is ill behaved?

13

WORKING WITH THE
WINDOWS 2000 REGISTRY

After reading this chapter and completing the exercises, you will be able to:

♦ Understand the function and structure of the Registry

♦ Describe the purpose of each of the five Registry keys

♦ Use the Registry editing tools

♦ Understand the fault-tolerance mechanisms for the Registry

♦ Back up and restore the Registry

Windows 2000 is a complex operating system that relies upon a dynamic data structure to maintain its configuration and operational parameters. This structure is the hierarchical database known as the **Registry**, which contains most of the control and functional settings for Windows 2000 core elements, services, and native applications, as well as many Microsoft and third-party add-on software products. In this chapter, you learn about the Registry, its structure, and tools to edit and manage the Registry, as well as several values you may consider altering to improve or configure system operation.

WINDOWS REGISTRY OVERVIEW

Windows 2000 uses the Registry to provide a database that stores data about a system's configuration in a hierarchical form. The Registry stores information essential to Windows 2000 itself as well as to native applications, added services, and most add-on software products from Microsoft and third-party vendors. The information stored in the Registry is comparable to information stored in initialization (.ini, .dat, .bat, .sys, and so on) files in Windows 3.x or even Windows 95/98. For native Windows 2000 applications, the Registry database takes the place of .ini files, and stores all configuration information. The Registry is not a text file, such as Win.ini or Config.sys from previous operating systems, but rather a multifaceted branch-like grouping of data. Although most Windows 2000 Professional configuration can be performed using the Control Panel applets and the Administration Tools (and in fact, changes made to system configurations through these tools are applied to the Registry database), some settings can be established or changed only by editing the Registry directly, such as the setting for TCPWindowSize, which determines the number of packets transmitted by a system before the receiver will reply with an acknowledgment of receipt. The Registry can be edited by using one of two Registry editors: Regedit and Regedt32, which are discussed in more detail later in the chapter.

CAUTION

Microsoft warns that editing the Registry directly should only be performed when absolutely necessary. If possible, use the Control Panel applets and Administrative Tools to make system modifications rather than manipulating the values in the Registry. Improper editing of the Registry can cause system malfunction or inoperability.

The Registry was designed for programming ease and speed of interaction for processes. This structure, although a bit daunting, is understandable if broken down into its parts. The Registry is divided into keys and subkeys. Each Registry **key** is similar to a bracketed heading in an .ini file, and is the top-level division in the Registry hierarchy. There are five of these highest-level, or root, keys, which start with HKEY to designate their highest-level status. Each key may contain one or more lower-level keys called **subkeys**. Within each subkey, one or more values can exist. A **value entry** is a named parameter or placeholder for a control setting or configuration data. A value entry can hold a single binary digit, a long string of ASCII characters, or a hexadecimal value. The actual data held by a value entry is known as the **value**. Figure 13-1 shows the structure of the Registry contents in Regedit. The left pane shows five root keys, with subkeys displayed for the HKEY_LOCAL_MACHINE key. The right pane shows the value entries for the SYSTEM\ControlSet002\Control subkey.

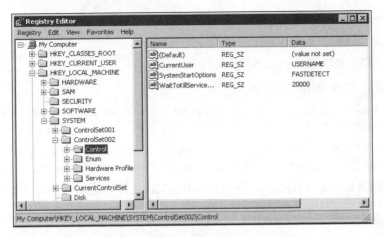

Figure 13-1   View of Registry hierarchy structure

 TIP   A discrete body of Registry keys, subkeys and values stored in a file is also known as a hive.

Value entries within the Registry are composed of three parts: name, type, and data (value). A Registry value entry's name is typically a multiword phrase, without spaces, with title capitalization, such as AutoAdminLogon in Figure 13-2. The data type of a value entry informs the Registry how to store the value. The **data type** defines whether the data is a text string or a number, and gives the numerical base (radix) of that number. Radix types supported by Windows 2000 are decimal (base 10), hexadecimal (base 16), and binary (base 2). All hexadecimal values are listed with the prefix "0x" to identify them clearly (as in 0xF for 15).

13

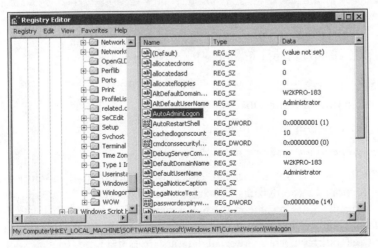

Figure 13-2   AutoAdminLogon value entries

The data types supported by Windows 2000 are:

- **REG_BINARY:** Binary format
- **REG_DWORD:** Binary, hex, or decimal format
- **REG_SZ:** Text-string format
- **REG_MULTI_SZ:** Text-string format that contains multiple human-readable values separated by NULL characters
- **REG_EXPAND_SZ:** Expandable text-string format that contains a variable that is replaced by an application when it is used (%Systemroot%\File.exe)
- **REG_FULL_RESOURCE_DESCRIPTOR:** A resource list for a hardware component or drive, stored as a nested array series (several strings of characters stored in a single value entry)
- **REG_DWORD_LITTLE_ENDIAN:** The same as REG_DWORD, but with a 32-bit number, where the most significant byte is displayed as the leftmost high-order byte
- **REG_DWORD_BIG_ENDIAN:** The same as REG_DWORD, but with a 32-bit number, where the most significant byte is displayed as the rightmost low-order byte
- **REG_LINK:** A symbolic link in the Registry

 The cryptic names of these value types do not provide an easy way to remember their meanings. For example, DWORD stands for data representation, and SZ stands for text string.

 Once a value entry is created and its data type defined, that data type cannot be changed. To alter the data type of a value, you must delete the value entry then re-create it with a new data type.

Important concepts to keep in mind about the Registry are:

- Keys are the top-level, or root, divisions of the Registry
- Keys contain one or more subkeys
- A subkey can contain one or more subkeys
- A subkey can contain one or more value entries

Also note that the Registry is not a complete collection of configuration settings. Instead, it holds only the exceptions to the defaults. Processes within Windows 2000 will operate with their own internal defaults unless a value in the Registry specifically alters that default behavior. This makes working with the Registry difficult, because most often the control you need is not contained in the Registry because internal defaults are being used. To alter such a setting, you'll need to add a new value entry to the Registry. To accomplish this, you must know the exact syntax, spelling, location, and valid values; otherwise, you will be unable to alter the default behavior. Keep in mind that not using the exact syntax, spelling, location, and valid values can result in malfunctions, possibly including an inoperable system. So always edit with extreme care. The *Windows 2000 Resource Kit* includes a help file named Regentry.chm, which lists all of the possible Registry entries and valid values. This is an invaluable tool when attempting to modify existing Registry entries as well as when adding new ones.

Each time Windows 2000 boots, the Registry is loaded into memory from files (see "Registry Storage Files" later this chapter) stored on the hard drive. Each time Windows 2000 shuts down, the Registry is written from memory back to the files. While Windows 2000 is operating, the Registry remains in memory. This makes the Registry easy to access and quick to respond to control queries, and it is the reason why changes to the Registry take effect immediately. Only in extreme cases will Windows 2000 require a reboot to enforce changes in the Registry.

IMPORTANT REGISTRY STRUCTURES AND KEYS

In the following sections, we look at various keys and subkeys of the Registry and explain their functions.

HKEY_LOCAL_MACHINE

The **HKEY_LOCAL_MACHINE** key contains the value entries that control the local computer. These configuration items include information about hardware devices, applications, device drivers, kernel services, and physical settings. This data is used to establish the configuration of the hardware and operating system environment. The content of this key is not dependent on the logged on user or the applications or processes in use; it is dependent only on the physical composition of the hardware and software present on the local computer.

This key has five subkeys (see Figure 13-3): Hardware, SAM, Security, Software, and System, which are detailed in the following sections.

13

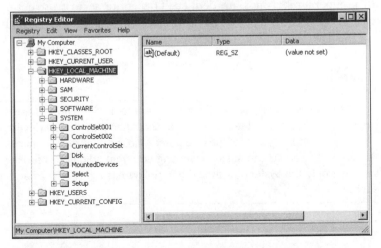

Figure 13-3   HKEY_LOCAL_MACHINE subkeys

HKEY_LOCAL_MACHINE\Hardware

The HKEY_LOCAL_MACHINE\Hardware subkey is the container for data related directly to the installed physical devices of the computer. This subkey stores configuration information, device driver settings, mappings, linkages, relationships between kernel-mode and user-mode hardware calls, and IRQ hooks. This subkey is re-created each time the system boots and is not saved when the system shuts down.

The HKEY_LOCAL_MACHINE\Hardware subkey contains three subkeys: Description, DeviceMap, and ResourceMap. The Description subkey stores data extracted from a device's own firmware or onboard BIOS. The DeviceMap subkey stores information about device driver paths, locations, and filenames. The ResourceMap subkey stores information about the mappings between system resources (I/O ports, I/O memory addresses, interrupts, and direct memory access [DMA] channels) and device drivers. When certain bus types are present in the computer, a fourth subkey named OwnerMap is present. This fourth subkey stores association information about the bus type and device drivers.

> The contents of this subkey should not be manipulated. This key contains data read from the state of the physical devices and associated device drivers. Thus there should be no need or reason to alter the data, because it will be a proper reflection of the state of the system. Second, the data is most often in a binary format; thus deciphering the information will be difficult, if not impossible, for most system users. If you wish to view the data contained in this key, you can do so through the System Information tool within the Computer Management utility in Administrative Tools.

HKEY_LOCAL_MACHINE\SAM

The subkey HKEY_LOCAL_MACHINE\SAM is a hive containing data related to security. The **Security Accounts Manager (SAM)** database is stored in this key and is where user accounts and group memberships are defined. The entire security structure of your Windows 2000 system is stored in this key. In most cases, this data is not accessible from a Registry editor.

> This is another area of the Registry that you should not attempt to modify. Most of the data contained in this subkey is in binary or encrypted format. You should employ the user manager tools (that is, the Local Users and Groups section of the Computer Management tool) to manipulate the data stored in this subkey. Additionally, to aid in preventing you from editing this subkey, it has a security setting such that only the System (or the System utility) has rights to read and alter the contents of this subkey.

HKEY_LOCAL_MACHINE\Security

The subkey HKEY_LOCAL_MACHINE\Security is the container for the local security policy. The local security policy defines control parameters, such as password policy, user rights, account lockout, audit policy, and general security options for the local machine.

CAUTION

This is yet another area of the Registry that you should not attempt to modify. Most of the data contained in this subkey is in binary format or is encrypted. You should employ the Local Security Policy tool to manipulate the data stored in this subkey (see Chapters 5 and 6). Additionally, to prevent you from editing this subkey, it has a security setting such that only the System has rights to read and alter the contents of this subkey.

HKEY_LOCAL_MACHINE\Software

The subkey HKEY_LOCAL_MACHINE\Software is the container for data about installed software and mapped file extensions. These settings apply to all local users. The \Software\Classes subkey contains the same information as the HKEY_CLASSES_ROOT key; in fact the HKEY_CLASSES_ROOT key is created by copying the data from the \Software\Classes subkey.

HKEY_LOCAL_MACHINE\System

The subkey HKEY_LOCAL_MACHINE\System is the container for the information required to boot Windows 2000. This subkey stores data about startup parameters, loading order for device drivers, service startup credentials (settings and parameters), and basic operating system behavior. This key is essential to the boot process of Windows 2000. It contains subkeys called control sets that include complete information about the boot process for the system. This subkey also contains subkeys that host settings for storage devices (such as MountedDevices) and control set boot status (Select), and possibly subkeys left over from upgrading from Windows NT 4.0 (Disk and Setup). The control set keys are named and numbered, for example, ControlSet001 and ControlSet003. In most cases, there will only be two control sets, and those sets will be numbered 001 and 003. These two sets represent the original (001) system configuration set and a backup (003) of the last functioning system configuration set. Thus, there will always be a functioning configuration to allow the operating system to boot (see Chapter 14 for more information on booting). Each control set has four subkeys:

- *Control:* This control set subkey is the container for data related to controlling system startup, boot parameters, computer name, and necessary subsystems to initiate.
- *Enum:* This control set subkey is the container for data regarding required device drivers and their configuration.
- *Hardware Profiles:* This control set subkey is the container for data specific to the hardware profile currently in use.
- *Services:* This control set subkey is the container for data about drivers, services, file systems, applications, and other required hardware components necessary to load all installed and active services during bootup. This subkey also defines the order in which services are called and the way that one service can call or query other services.

13

The value entries under the HKEY_LOCAL_MACHINE\System\Select subkey are used to define how the control sets are employed by Windows 2000. The four value entries are:

- *Default:* Defines which control set will be used during the next bootup

- *Current:* Lists the control set that was used to boot the current session

- *LastKnownGood:* Indicates the control set last used to boot and successfully log on a user (see later in this chapter for more details and its use)

- *Failed:* Lists the control set that was replaced by the control set from the LastKnownGood control set because of a failure to boot

The HKEY_LOCAL_MACHINE\System\CurrentControlSet subkey is a redirector to the actual ControlSet### currently in use rather than a truly distinct subkey. This symbolic link is used to simplify the programming interface of applications and device drivers that need information from the active control set. Because of this redirection, when you need to make modifications to the control set, you should use the CurrentControlSet "subkey" to properly direct your changes to the active control set.

HKEY_CLASSES_ROOT

The **HKEY_CLASSES_ROOT** key is the container for information pertaining to application associations based on file extension and COM object data. The contents of this key are copied from the HKEY_LOCAL_MACHINE\Software\Classes subkey. This key is maintained for backward compatibility with legacy applications and device drivers and is not strictly required by Windows 2000 (see Figure 13-4).

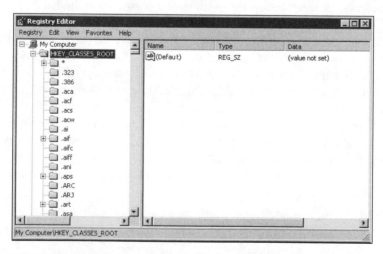

Figure 13-4   HKEY_CLASSES_ROOT

The contents of this key, or the HKEY_LOCAL_MACHINE\Software\Classes subkey, should not be edited directly. Instead, the File Types tab of the Folder Options dialog box should be used. This dialog box is accessed by selecting the Folder Options command from the Tools menu in Windows Explorer or My Computer or by launching the Folder Options applet from the Control Panel.

HKEY_CURRENT_CONFIG

The **HKEY_CURRENT_CONFIG** key is the container for data pertaining to the hardware profile currently in use. This key is just a symbolic link to the HKEY_LOCAL_MACHINE\ System\CurrentControlSet\Hardware Profiles\Current subkey. This key is maintained for backward compatibility with legacy applications and device drivers and is not strictly required by Windows 2000 (see Figure 13-5).

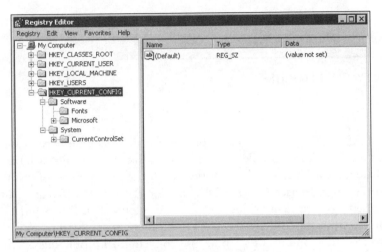

Figure 13-5   HKEY_CURRENT_CONFIG

The contents of this key, and the HKEY_LOCAL_MACHINE\System\CurrentControlSet\ Hardware Profiles\Current subkey, should not be edited directly. Instead, the Hardware Profiles interface and Device Manager should be used. The Hardware Profiles interface is accessed by pressing the Hardware Profiles button on the Hardware tab of the System applet from the Control Panel. The Device Manager is accessed by pressing the Device Manager button on the Hardware tab of the System applet from the Control Panel or by selecting the Device Manager node from the Computer Management utility in Administrative Tools.

HKEY_CURRENT_USER

The **HKEY_CURRENT_USER** key is the container for the profile for the currently logged on user. The contents of this key are built each time a user logs on, by copying the appropriate subkey from the HKEY_USERS key. The contents of this key should not be edited directly; instead, you should modify a user's profile through conventional profile management techniques (see Chapter 5 for more information on profile management). (See Figure 13-6.)

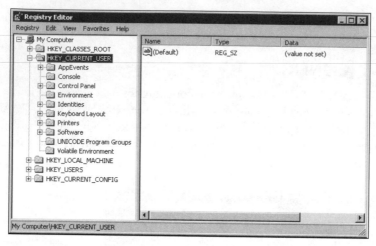

Figure 13-6   HKEY_CURRENT_USER

HKEY_USERS

The **HKEY_USERS** key is the container for profiles for all users who have ever logged on to this system and the default user profile. The contents of this key are built each time the system boots by loading the default file and the locally stored copies of Ntuser.dat or Ntuser.man from user profiles (see Chapter 5). These locally stored copies are found in the \Documents and Settings\<*username*> directory on a Windows 2000 Professional system. To remove a user profile from this key, use the User Profiles tab of the System applet from the Control Panel. To alter the contents of a profile, use conventional profile management techniques (see Chapter 5 for more information on profile management) instead of attempting to edit this key directly (see Figure 13-7).

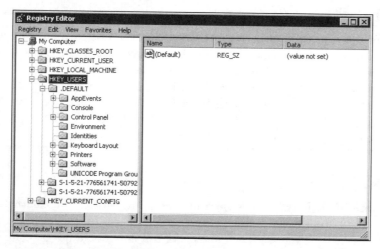

Figure 13-7   HKEY_USERS

THE REGISTRY EDITORS: REGEDIT AND REGEDT32

Because the structure of the Registry is so complex, it requires special tools to operate on directly. In Windows 2000, there are two Registry editors: Regedit and Regedt32. **Regedit** (see Figure 13-8) is a 16-bit application that offers global searching and combines all of the keys into a single display. **Regedt32** (see Figure 13-9) is a 32-bit application that offers access to key and value entry, NTFS-like security, auditing, and ownership, but displays each root key in a separate window (see Hands-on Projects 13-5 and 13-6). Regedt32 also offers a read-only mode so you can explore without the possibility of accidentally altering value entries. Both editors can be used to view keys and values (see Hands-on Project 13-1), perform searches (see Hands-on Project 13-2), add new subkeys and value entries, alter the data in value entries, and import and export keys and subkeys. You'll need to get to know both editors to properly manipulate the Registry.

TIP   If you need to locate a specific key or value, use Regedit. If you need to alter the security settings of a key, use Regedt32.

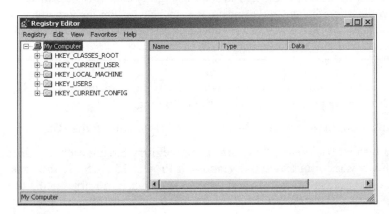

Figure 13-8   Regedit

13

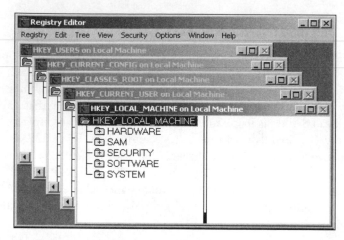

Figure 13-9   Regedt32

As already noted many times in this chapter, editing the Registry directly is a task that should not be undertaken without forethought and planning. It is possible to alter the Registry, whether on purpose or accidentally, in such a way as to render a system completely unrecoverable. If you don't know exactly what you are doing, *don't do it!*

Even when you do think you know exactly what you want to change in the Registry, it is always a good idea to take precautions, such as the following:

- Back up all important data on the computer before editing the Registry.

- Make a distinct backup of all or part of the Registry. Saving each key or subkey individually is recommended (see Hands-on Project 13-3). Store the backup files on local drives, network drives, and floppies or other removable media to ensure access. See the "Backing Up the Registry" section later in this chapter.

- Reboot the machine before editing the Registry.

- Perform only a single Registry modification at a time. Test the results before proceeding.

- Reboot immediately after each change to force full system compliance. This is not strictly necessary, but has often proven a prudent measure.

- Always test changes on a nonproduction system hosting noncritical services before deploying on production systems.

- Use the Regedt32 read-only mode to explore the Registry to ensure that changes are not made accidentally.

REGISTRY SIZE LIMITATIONS

The Registry is stored in active memory so that it is quickly and easily accessible while the operating system is functioning. It resides in the paged pool portion of memory, which means it can be swapped out to disk when not in use. This is unlike the kernel, which resides in a nonpaged pool portion of memory so that it always stays in physical RAM. As your system ages, many changes will accumulate in the Registry, causing the size of the Registry to grow. The initial size of the Registry on a Windows 2000 Professional system is around 10 MB. In order to prevent the Registry from consuming too much memory, Windows 2000 imposes a maximum size for the Registry. This ceiling is set at one-quarter of the current paged pool by default, but can be changed. When the page pool size changes, Windows 2000 will automatically adjust the Registry size ceiling as well. When this value is set to 0, the system automatically creates a maximum Registry size of 33% of the paged pool size. If this value is set to more than 80% of the paged pool size, the system will set the limit to only 80% of the paged pool size.

This value should be changed only when you are prompted to do so by the system. Such a prompt will appear in a message box when the Registry size nears the defined limitation. In most cases, when prompted by the system, increasing the Registry size limitation by 1 or 2 MB is sufficient.

To alter the Registry ceiling, open the Virtual Memory dialog box shown in Figure 13-10 (start from the Control Panel System applet, click the Advanced tab, click the Performance Options button on the Advanced tab, and click Change). Change the value in the number field beside Maximum registry size (MB) within the Registry size area. This value sets only the maximum boundary size for the Registry; it does not allocate paged pool space nor does it guarantee that paged pool space will even be available.

13

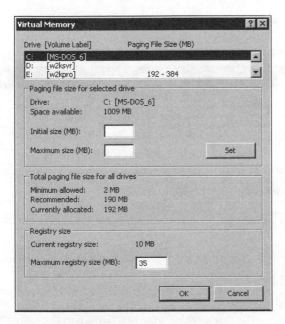

Figure 13-10   Virtual memory dialog box, where the Registry size is defined

REGISTRY STORAGE FILES

The files used to store the Registry are located in the %systemroot%\system32\config and %systemroot%\repair directories of the boot partition (see Figure 13-11). The Registry is not stored in files that match one to one with the top-level keys.

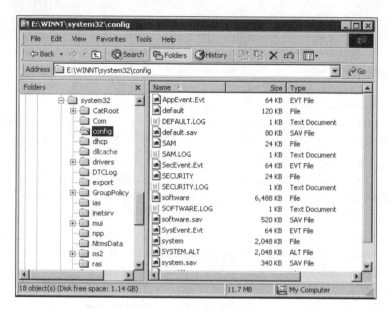

Figure 13-11   The contents of the %systemroot%\system32\config directory

The Registry is stored in various subkey, logging, and backup files, as shown in Table 13-1.

Table 13-1   Registry Storage Files

Registry Key/Subkey	Storage Files
HKEY_LOCAL_MACHINE\SAM	Sam, Sam.log, Sam.sav
HKEY_LOCAL_MACHINE\Security	Security, Security.log, Security.sav
HKEY_LOCAL_MACHINE\Software	Software, Software.log, Software.sav
HKEY_LOCAL_MACHINE\System	System, System.alt, System.log, System.sav
HKEY_USERS\.DEFAULT	Default, Default.log, Default.sav
(Not directly associated with a Registry key)	Userdiff, Userdiff.log
HKEY_CURRENT_USER	Ntuser.dat, Ntuser.dat.log

TIP Note that only four of the HKEY_LOCAL_MACHINE subkeys, the Default subkey of the HKEY_USERS key, and the HKEY_CURRENT_USER key are stored in files. All of the other keys and subkeys are either built "on the fly" at bootup or are copies of a subsection of HKEY_LOCAL_MACHINE.

The HKEY_USERS key is built from the Default file (which represents the default user profile's Ntuser.dat file) and copies of all of the profiles for users who have ever logged on to the computer. These profiles are cached locally in the \Documents and Settings*<username>* directory. A copy of the Ntuser.dat or Ntuser.man file is copied into the repair directory for the currently logged on user.

Notice that four extensions are used by the Registry storage files. These extensions identify the purpose or function of the file:

- *No extension:* The storage file for the subkey

- *.alt:* The backup file of the subkey. Note that only the HKEY_LOCAL_MACHINE\System subkey has a backup file.

- *.log:* A file containing all changes made to a key. This file is used to verify that all modifications to the Registry are properly applied.

- *.sav:* Copies of keys in their original state as created at the end of the text portion of Windows 2000 installation

Under Windows NT 4.0, the Registry files stored in the \Config directory were used to build the emergency repair disk (ERD). Under Windows 2000, these files are no longer copied onto the ERD when it is created. However, you can create your own custom ERD by manually copying the files in the \Config directory to a formatted floppy. You may find having a complete copy of the Registry quite handy when you need to perform a system repair or restore any portion of the Registry because of corruption or human error.

REGISTRY FAULT TOLERANCE

13

If the Registry becomes corrupted or destroyed, Windows 2000 cannot function or even boot. Several mechanisms have been established to prevent the Registry from becoming damaged or to automatically repair minor problems. The fault tolerance of the Registry is sustained by its structure, memory residence, and transaction logs. These mechanisms ensure that all changes or operations performed on the Registry either succeed or fail. This prevents any partially applied alterations that would result in an invalid value entry or entries. This the "all or nothing" guarantee is supported no matter what method of alteration is used, including using a Registry editor or an administration tool, or alterations by an application. If the change action is interrupted (by power failure, too little CPU time, hardware failure, etc.), the Registry will remain intact, even if the desired change was not implemented.

As previously mentioned, when an alteration is made to a value entry in the Registry, that change is made to the Registry in active memory. This means that the change affects the system immediately in most cases. The change to the Registry is only made permanent when the key files are written back to the hard drive. This activity occurs during a flush. A **flush** is a copy procedure to update the files on the hard drive with the new settings stored in the memory-resident version of the Registry. A flush occurs at shutdown, when forced by an application, or just after a Registry alteration.

Transaction logs are files where the system records edits, changes, and alterations to the Registry, similar to a list of orders or commands. When a flush occurs, the transaction log is updated to record all changes currently in memory, which will be stored to the Registry storage files. This log is used by the system to automatically verify that the Registry changes are complete once the flush is concluded.

A flush follows the following sequence of steps:

1. All alterations to a key are appended to that key's transaction log file (.log).

2. The key file is marked as being in transition.

3. The key file is updated with the new data from memory.

4. The key file is marked as complete.

If a system failure occurs between the time the key file is marked as in transition and when it is marked complete, the original state of the key is recovered using the data from the transaction log. If the flush finishes uninterrupted, then the system continues to perform normally.

The flush operation is performed on all keys except the System key. This key contains system-critical data and is a major element in a successful bootup of Windows 2000. For this reason, recovery cannot rely upon transaction logs. Instead, Windows 2000 updates the System key with a different method:

1. The system file is marked as being in transition.

2. The system file is brought up to date with the state of the Registry from memory.

3. The system file is marked as being complete.

4. The System.alt file is marked as being in transition.

5. The System.alt file is brought up to date with the state of the Registry from memory.

6. The System.alt file is marked as being complete.

This dual-file process, with the primary and backup copies of the System key file, ensures that, no matter at which stage the update process might be interrupted, a complete and functional copy of the System key file is available. If the failure occurs within the first three steps, then the nonupdated System.alt file will be used to boot. If the failure occurs within the last three steps, then the updated system file will be used to boot. Once booting is complete after a failure, Windows 2000 will perform the update again to ensure that both copies of the system key are exactly the same. However, if the failure occurred during the first three steps, any changes made to the system will have been lost.

BACKING UP THE REGISTRY

Even though Windows 2000 automatically manages the safety of the Registry via its fault-tolerance mechanisms (.log and .alt files), it is still important for you to take proactive measures to back up the Registry. There are several methods you can employ to create reliable Registry backups:

- Most Windows 2000 backup applications (for example, the built-in Backup tool and third-party products such as Veritas Backup Exec and Stac Replica) include support for full Registry backups. With these products, you can back up the Registry as part of your daily automated backup or as a distinct Registry-only procedure. Backing up the Registry with most of these products consists of selecting a "Back up the Registry" or "System State" (see Figure 13-12) check box when you make file/folder selections before initializing a backup.

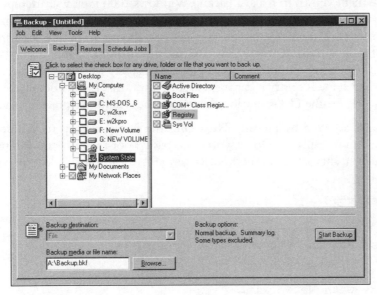

Figure 13-12   Native backup tool showing System State selection

- Regedit or Regedt32 can be used to save all or part of the Registry to distinct files. Both of these tools have an Export or Save command, which is used to save the entire Registry, a single key, or any subportion of a key to a file (try Hands-on Project 13-3).

- Make a copy of the %systemroot%\System32\config and %systemroot%\repair directories manually. Just copy the contents to another location on your local computer, network, or to a floppy disk (if size permits).

- Employ the *Windows 2000 Resource Kit* tools Reg.exe or Regback.exe. Both of these tools offer command-line scripting capabilities. Please explore the *Windows 2000 Resource Kit* for ideas on how to best employ these tools. You can see a syntax parameter listing for these and most command-line tools by issuing a "/?" parameter after the command from a Command Prompt (that is, *reg /?*, or *reg /? | more* if more than one screen's worth of data is displayed).

 No matter what backup method you employ, take the time to make two copies or perform the backup twice. This will provide additional insurance just in case your first backup fails.

RESTORING THE REGISTRY

Obviously, if you are going to take the time to create backups of the Registry, you need to understand how to restore the Registry. You have several options for restoring the Registry, depending on the method used to make a backup. Windows 2000 itself will attempt to maintain a functional Registry, using its own internal automatic fault-tolerance mechanisms. In cases where the automatic restoration process fails, you can first attempt to restore the Last Known Good Configuration. The **Last Known Good Configuration (LKGC)** is the state of the Registry stored in one of the control sets (see earlier this chapter) when the last successful user logon was performed. If the Registry is damaged in such a way that it will not fully boot or will not allow a user to log on, the LKGC option can restore the system to a previous state.

This boot option is accessed by pressing F8 during the initial bootup of Windows 2000 when the boot menu is displayed. Don't worry, the basic boot menu even prompts you to press F8 if you need an alternate boot method. Pressing F8 reveals a new selection menu similar to the following:

```
OS Loader v5.0


Windows 2000 Advanced Options Menu
Please select an option:

Safe Mode
Safe Mode with Networking
Safe Mode with Command Prompt

Enable Boot logging
Enable VGA Mode
Last Known Good Configuration
Directory Services Restore Mode (Windows 2000 domain
controllers only)
Debugging Mode

Boot Normally
Return to OS Choices Menu

Use [up] and [down] to move the highlight to your choice.
Press Enter to choose.
```

Use the arrow keys to highlight the Last Known Good Configuration selection, then press Enter. Keep in mind that any changes made to the system between the time the LKGC was stored and its use to restore the system will be lost. If the LKGC fails to restore the system to a functioning state, then you only have two options:

1. Use your backup software to restore the Registry files. This is only possible if your backup application offers a DOS-based restore mechanism that can bypass NTFS write restrictions. In other words, the backup software must operate without a functional Windows 2000 environment when launched from a bootable floppy. This type of software lets you restore files to the boot and system partitions (such as the Registry) so you can return to a functional OS. Unfortunately, these applications are few. One such product is Replica from Stac (*www.stac.com*).

2. Reinstall Windows 2000, either fully or as an upgrade. An upgrade may replace the section of the Registry that is causing the problems, allowing you to retain most of your configuration, but this is not guaranteed. A full, new installation of Windows 2000 will return the system to a preconfigured state, requiring you to perform all postinstall changes again.

If you are able to boot into the system, but things are not functioning the way they should or services, drivers, or applications are not loading or operating properly, you may need to restore the Registry in part or whole from backup. Simply use the same tool employed to create the backup to restore the Registry. Keep in mind that with some tools, you can restore portions of the Registry instead of the entire database (see Hands-on Project 13-4).

No matter what method you employ to restore the Registry, it's always a good idea to reboot the system to ensure that the restoration completed successfully and that the system is using only the updated (or more correctly reverted to) settings. It's also a good idea to retain the copies of the old Registry until you are confident that the system is functioning normally, and you've had the opportunity to create new backups. In other words, don't throw away the disks, erase the drives, or format the tapes containing the Registry backup; keep a few generations of Registry backups on hand just in case.

13

WINDOWS 2000 RESOURCE KIT REGISTRY TOOLS

The *Windows 2000 Resource Kit* includes several tools that can be used to manipulate the Registry. The *Windows 2000 Resource Kit* is a product release from Microsoft that's separate from the Windows 2000 operating system product. The *Windows 2000 Resource Kit* has additional documentation on Windows 2000, its operations, and its use, as well as a host of useful tools and utilities not included with the shipped software. You can purchase the *Windows 2000 Resource Kit* from Microsoft and most software and book vendors online and off.

Because many of these tools are command-line tools or have significant ancillary materials, we recommend that you peruse the *Windows 2000 Resource Kit* documentation yourself before actually using these tools. Some of the key utilities include:

- *Reg.exe:* Used to perform command line operations on the Registry, ideally suited for batch file operations. Functions include query for value entry data, adding new value entries, changing current values, deleting values or keys, copy keys, back up and restore keys, and load and unload keys. This tool is useful when you need to search for a specific value entry, add new values entries, change an existing value, remove values or keys, create copies of keys, back up or restore keys, and load and unload keys stored in memory.

- *Regdump.exe:* A command-line tool used to dump all or part of the Registry to Stdout. The output of this tool is suitable for the Regini.exe tool. This tool is useful when you need to create scripts based on Registry content by creating a dump of existing settings.

- *Regfind.exe:* A command-line tool used to search for a key, value name, or value data based on keywords. This tool is useful when you need to search for a specific keyword/string in the Registry.

- *Compreg.exe:* A GUI tool used to compare two local or remote Registry keys and highlight all differences. This tool is useful when you need to find the differences between two Registry keys.

- *Regini.exe:* A command-line scripting tool used to add keys into the Registry. This tool is useful when you need to script the amendment of keys to the Registry.

- *Regback.exe:* A command-line tool used to back up keys from the Registry. This tool is useful when you need to create a backup of the Registry via a script.

- *Regrest.exe:* A command-line tool used to restore keys to the Registry. This tool is useful when you need to restore keys to the Registry via a script.

- *Scanreg.exe:* A GUI tool used to search for a key, value name, or value data based on keywords. This tool is useful when you need to search the Registry for a specific keyword or text string.

CHAPTER SUMMARY

- The Windows 2000 Registry is a complex structure consisting of keys, subkeys, values, and value entries.

- The Registry should be manipulated with extreme caution. Unless absolutely necessary, the Registry should not be edited directly; instead, employ the Control Panel applets and Administration Tools to modify system settings.

- Windows 2000 maintains a functional Registry through several fault-tolerant measures, including transaction logs and backup of key files.

❏ The Registry is divided into five main keys. The primary and most important key is HKEY_LOCAL_MACHINE, because it hosts data ranging from system startup information to driver settings to the security database.

❏ Windows 2000 includes two Registry editors, Regedit and Regedt32. The former is useful for global searches, the latter useful for changing security settings on keys and value entries.

❏ As part of your normal system maintenance and administration, you should create copies of the Registry. Backing up the Registry often is the only way to ensure you have a functional Registry to restore in the event of a failure.

KEY TERMS

data type — The setting on a Registry value entry that defines the data format of the stored information.

flush — The activity of forcing the memory-resident copy of the Registry to be written to files stored on the hard drive. A flush occurs at shutdown, when forced by an application, or just after a Registry alteration.

hive — A discrete body of Registry keys, subkeys, and values stored in a file.

HKEY_CLASSES_ROOT — This Registry key contains the value entries that control the relationships between file extensions (and therefore file format types) and applications. This key also supports the data used in object linking and embedding (OLE), COM object data, and file-class association data. This key actually points to another Registry key named HKEY_LOCAL_MACHINE\Software\Classes, and provides multiple points of access to make itself easily accessible to the operating system itself and to applications that need access to the compatibility information already mentioned.

HKEY_CURRENT_CONFIG — This Registry key contains the value entries that control the currently active hardware profile. The contents of this key are built each time the system is booted. This key is derived from data stored in the HKEY_LOCAL_MACHINE\System\CurrentControlSet\HardwareProfiles\Current subkey. This key exists to provide backward-compatibility with Windows 95/98 applications.

HKEY_CURRENT_USER — This Registry key contains the value entries that define the user environment for the currently logged on user. This key is built each time a user logs on to the system. The data in this key is derived from the HKEY_USERS key and the Ntuser.dat and Ntuser.man files of a user's profile.

HKEY_LOCAL_MACHINE — This Registry key contains the value entries that control the local computer. This includes hardware devices, device drivers, and various operating system components. The data stored in this key is not dependent on a logged on user or the applications or processes in use.

HKEY_USERS — This Registry key contains the value entries that define the user environments for all users who have ever logged on to this computer. As a new user logs on to this system, a new subkey is added for that user, which is either built from the default profile stored in this key or from the roaming user profile associated with the domain user account.

13

key — A top-level division of the Registry. There are five keys in a Windows 2000 Registry. A key can contain subkeys.

Last Known Good Configuration (LKGC) — The state of the Registry stored in one of the control sets when the last successful user logon was performed. If the Registry is damaged in such a way that it will not fully boot or will not allow a user to log on, the LKGC option can restore the system to a previous state. Keep in mind that any changes made to the system between the time the LKGC was stored and its use to restore the system will be lost.

REG_BINARY — A Registry value entry data type that stores data in binary format.

REG_DWORD — A Registry value entry data type that stores data in binary, hex, or decimal format.

REG_EXPAND_SZ — A Registry value entry data type that stores data in expandable text-string format that contains a variable that is replaced by an application when it is used (for example, %Systemroot%\File.exe).

REG_MULTI_SZ — A Registry value entry data type that stores data in text-string format that contains multiple human-readable values separated by null characters.

REG_SZ — A Registry value entry data type that stores data in text-string format.

Regedit — The 16-bit Registry editor. Regedit offers global searching and combines all of the keys into a single display. It can be used to perform searches, add new subkeys and value entries, alter the data in value entries, and import and export keys and subkeys.

Regedt32 — The 32-bit Registry editor. Regedt32 offers control over key and value entry security, but displays each root key in a separate window. Regedt32 also offers a read-only mode so you can explore the Registry without the possibility of accidentally altering value entries. It can be used to perform searches, add new subkeys and value entries, alter the data in value entries, and import and export keys and subkeys.

Registry — The hierarchical database of system configuration data, which is essential to the health and operation of a Windows 2000 system.

Security Accounts Manager (SAM) — The database of user accounts, group memberships, and security related settings.

subkey — A division of a Registry key, such as HKEY_LOCAL_MACHINE. A subkey can contain other subkeys and value entries.

transaction log — A file created by Windows 2000 to record Registry changes. These files, with a .log extension, are used to verify that changes to the Registry are made successfully.

value — The actual data stored by a value entry.

value entry — A named Registry variable that stores a specific value or data string. A Registry value entry's name is typically a multiword phrase without spaces and with title capitalization.

REVIEW QUESTIONS

1. The Registry is the primary mechanism for storing data about Windows 2000. Which of the following are configuration files used by other Microsoft operating systems and may still exist on Windows 2000 for backward–compatibility? (Choose all that apply.)

   a. Win.ini

   b. Autoexec.bat

   c. System.ini

   d. Config.sys

2. The Registry is only used to store configuration data for native Windows 2000 applications, services, and drivers. True or False?

3. Which of the following tools are most highly recommended by Microsoft for editing the Registry?

   a. Control Panel applets

   b. Regedit

   c. Reg.exe

   d. Administrative Tools

4. The Registry is an exhaustive collection of system control parameters. True or False?

5. When editing the Registry, especially when attempting to alter the unseen defaults, which of the following pieces of information are important? (Choose all that apply.)

   a. syntax

   b. spelling

   c. subkey location

   d. valid values

   e. time zone

6. Changes made to the Registry never go into effect until the system is rebooted. True or False?

7. The Windows 2000 Registry has how many default keys?

   a. 2

   b. 4

   c. 5

   d. 6

8. Which of the following can host subkeys or value entries?

   a. data type

   b. key

   c. subkey

   d. value data

13

9. Each of the highest-level keys of the Registry is stored in a distinct file on the hard drive. True or False?

10. Which Registry key contains the value entries that control the local computer?

    a. HKEY_LOCAL_MACHINE

    b. HKEY_CLASSES_ROOT

    c. HKEY_CURRENT_CONFIG

    d. HKEY_USERS

11. Which Registry key contains the value entries that define the user environment for the currently logged on user?

    a. HKEY_LOCAL_MACHINE

    b. HKEY_CLASSES_ROOT

    c. HKEY_CURRENT_CONFIG

    d. HKEY_CURRENT_USER

12. Which Registry key contains the value entries that control the relationships between file extensions (and therefore file format types) and applications?

    a. HKEY_LOCAL_MACHINE

    b. HKEY_CLASSES_ROOT

    c. HKEY_CURRENT_CONFIG

    d. HKEY_USERS

13. Which Registry key contains the value entries that control the currently active hardware profile?

    a. HKEY_LOCAL_MACHINE

    b. HKEY_CLASSES_ROOT

    c. HKEY_CURRENT_CONFIG

    d. HKEY_CURRENT_USER

14. From which key can you delete subkeys, using the System applet?

    a. HKEY_LOCAL_MACHINE

    b. HKEY_CLASSES_ROOT

    c. HKEY_CURRENT_CONFIG

    d. HKEY_USERS

15. Some Windows 95 applications require a sixth Registry key. Windows 2000 adds the _____ key to maintain backward compatibility, which is actually a redirector rather than an actual key.

16. After you've created a value entry, you can easily change its data type via the Edit dialog box. True or False?

17. The value entry data type that can store binary, hex, or decimal formatted data is
    _____.

    a. REG_SZ

    b. REG_DWORD

    c. REG_MULTI_SZ

    d. REG_EXPAND_SZ

18. Where are the files used to load the Registry at bootup stored on a Windows 2000 system?

    a. %systemroot%\config

    b. %systemroot%\system32\config

    c. %systemroot%\system\config

    d. %systemroot%\system32\repair

19. Which subkey of HKEY_LOCAL_MACHINE is the only subkey to have a backup file?

    a. SAM

    b. Software

    c. System

    d. Security

20. The process of pushing Registry changes from memory to a hard drive file is known
    as _____.

21. Which type of file (specified by file extension) is used by Windows 2000 to record the
    changes to the Registry for verification purposes?

    a. .alt

    b. .sav

    c. .dat

    d. .log

22. Assume that your system is performing an update to the System subkey. While altering
    the system file, before working on the System.alt file, a system crash occurs. When the
    system reboots, which of the following will occur?

    a. You'll be prompted whether to use the system or System.alt set of configuration
       parameters.

    b. The state of the Registry before changes to the System subkey will be restored.

    c. The state of the Registry after changes to the System subkey will be restored.

    d. The system will fail to boot because of a corrupt system subkey.

23. Which subkey usually cannot be edited with a Registry editor?

    a. Hardware

    b. Software

    c. SAM

    d. CurrentControlSet

13

24. Which ControlSet subkey is the container for data related to controlling system startup, boot parameters, computer name, and necessary subsystems to initiate?

   a. Control

   b. Enum

   c. Hardware Profiles

   d. Services

25. Which subkey of HKEY_LOCAL_MACHINE\System\Select indicates the control set that was last used to boot and successfully log on a user?

   a. Default

   b. Currect

   c. LastKnownGood

   d. Failed

HANDS-ON PROJECTS

Project 13-1

This hands-on project is useful when you want to view the current value of a value entry or to determine if a value entry is even present in the Registry.

To view Registry value entries with Regedit:

1. Click the **Start** menu, then click **Run**.

2. Type **regedit**, then click **OK**. The Registry Editor opens.

3. Double-click **HKEY_LOCAL_MACHINE**.

4. Locate and double-click **SOFTWARE** under HKEY_LOCAL_MACHINE.

5. Locate and double-click **Microsoft** under SOFTWARE.

6. Locate and double-click **Windows NT** under Microsoft.

7. Locate and double-click **CurrentVersion** under Windows NT.

8. Locate and select **Winlogon** under CurrentVersion.

9. In the right pane, locate and select **DefaultUserName**.

10. From the Edit menu, select **Modify**.

11. Notice that the value of this value entry is the name of the user account you are currently using.

12. Click **Cancel**.

13. In the left pane, scroll up until you see HKEY_LOCAL_MACHINE.

14. Double-click **HKEY_LOCAL_MACHINE**. Leave the system as is for the next hands-on project.

Project 13-2

To search for a value entry with Regedit:

 This hands-on project requires that Hands-on Project 13-1 be completed. In this project, you use Regedit to locate a key or value without knowing its path within the Registry. This hands-on project begins at the system status point where the previous hands-on project ended.

1. From the Edit menu, select **Find**.
2. In the Find what field, type **DefaultUserName**.
3. Click **Find Next**. After a few seconds of searching, Regedit will locate the first key, value, or data containing that string.
4. Notice that the first found match is AltDefaultUserName.
5. From the Edit menu, select **Find Next**. The item found now is the actual DefaultUserName value entry that you viewed in Hands-on Project 13-1.
6. In the left pane, scroll up until you see HKEY_LOCAL_MACHINE.
7. Double-click **HKEY_LOCAL_MACHINE**. Leave the system as is for the next hands-on project.

Project 13-3

The ability to make backups of the Registry offers you an additional level of support in the event of a system problem or a human error in regard to the Registry. Plus, backing up the Registry is always a good action to take before beginning any modifications to the Registry, either through the manual tools of Regedit and Regedt32 or through any of the Control Panel or Administrative Tools utilities.

To back up a Registry key:

 This hands-on project begins at the system status point where the previous hands-on project ended.

1. Make sure that the HKEY_USERS key is selected.
2. From the Registry menu, select **Export Registry File**.
3. Select a destination folder (such as c:\Temp) of your choice.
4. Provide a filename, such as **HUsave.reg**.
5. Make sure the **Selected branch** radio button at the bottom of the Export Registry File dialog box is selected and that HKEY_USERS is listed in the text field.
6. Click **Save**.

13

7. The Regedit tool will create a backup file of the selected key. Leave the system as is for the next hands-on project.

 TIP This procedure can be used on larger or smaller portions of the Registry simply by selecting different keys or subkeys. In other words, this process can be used to back up the entire Registry or just a small subset of subkeys.

 ## Project 13-4

If you have made any change to the system or Registry since Hands-on Project 13-3 was performed, you may not want to perform this project because it will discard those changes by restoring the state of the Registry from the saved file.

To restore a Registry key:

 TIP This hands-on project requires that Hands-on Project 13-3 be completed. It begins at the system status point where Hands-on Project 13-3 ended.

1. From the Registry menu, select **Import Registry File**.
2. Locate and select your **HUsave.reg** file.
3. Click **Open**.
4. After a few moments of importing, a message stating whether the import succeeded is displayed; click **OK**.
5. From the Registry menu, select **Exit**.

 TIP This procedure can be used on larger or smaller portions of the Registry simply by selecting different keys or subkeys. In other words, this process can be used to restore the entire Registry or just a small subset of subkeys. However, it does require that the same or the same plus more data be backed up for the material to be restored.

 ## Project 13-5

To use Regedt32:

1. Click the **Start** button, select **Run** to open the Run command dialog box.
2. Type **regedt32**, then click **OK**. The Registry Editor opens.
3. Notice that each key is displayed in a separate window within the Registry editor.
4. Select **HKEY_LOCAL_MACHINE on Local Machine** from the Window menu.
5. From the View menu, select **Find Key**.
6. Type **WinLogon**.

7. Click **Find Next**. Notice that you are back in the same subkey as was viewed in Hands-on Project 13-1.

8. Click **Cancel** in the Find dialog box to close it.

9. From the Options menu, select **Read Only Mode**. Leave the system as is for the next hands-on project.

Project 13-6

To view security with Regedt32:

> **TIP**   This hands-on project requires that Hands-on Project 13-5 be completed.

1. This hands-on project begins at the system status point where the previous hands-on project ended.

2. From the Window menu, select **HKEY_USERS**.

3. From the Security menu, select **Permissions**.

4. A notice may appear stating that you can only view permissions for this key; click **OK**.

5. Notice the Permissions dialog box for the Registry is identical to that used elsewhere in Windows 2000.

6. Click **Cancel**.

7. From the Registry menu, select **Exit**.

13

CASE PROJECTS

1. Describe the actions that you can perform manually or that are performed automatically that provide protection or fault-tolerance mechanisms for the Windows 2000 Registry.

2. You have been asked to perform several Registry modifications to fine-tune an application. You'll be following detailed instructions from the vendor. What steps can you take to ensure that even if the vendor's instructions fail, you'll be able to return to a functioning Windows 2000 system?

14

BOOTING WINDOWS 2000

> **After reading this chapter and completing the exercises, you will be able to:**
>
> ♦ Understand the Windows 2000 boot process
> ♦ Troubleshoot system restoration by using Safe Mode
> ♦ Explain the operation of the key Windows 2000 startup files
> ♦ Understand the boot options offered via the Advanced Options menu
> ♦ Edit the Boot.ini file to manipulate the boot process
> ♦ Understand how multiboot configurations are created and how they function

On the surface, booting a computer seems simple. But in reality, booting is a complex process. In fact, it is important to understand each step of the process by which an inert hunk of metal becomes a computer running Windows 2000. This understanding is essential for the Microsoft certification exam, and for troubleshooting a system that won't boot properly.

In this chapter, you learn the steps that Windows 2000 takes to successfully complete a boot process. The process begins with the initial operation of the hardware, as it finds pointers to the software that ultimately leads to the choice of which operating system to run (and as it goes through the process of loading and starting Windows 2000). The process culminates when a successful user logon occurs. It is only at this point that the Windows 2000 boot process is considered to be complete.

THE BOOT PROCESS

All computers, whether hosting Windows 2000 or another operating system, go through a similar **boot process** when they are turned on. In Windows 2000, this process is broken down into two major phases, the **boot phase** and the **load phase**.

The Windows 2000 boot process is actually a two-part process that includes both the boot phase and the load phase. The boot process takes place when the computer is first powered on, and when you choose Shutdown, Restart from the Shut Down Windows dialog box. This dialog box appears when you select Shut Down from the Windows 2000 Security dialog box that takes over your screen any time you enter the Windows 2000 attention sequence, Ctrl+Alt+Delete. It also appears when you select Restart from the Shut Down Windows dialog box (Start, Shut Down).

WINDOWS 2000 BOOT PHASE

The six steps of the Windows 2000 boot phase are as follows:

1. Power-on self test (POST)

2. Initial startup

3. Boot loader

4. Selecting the operating system

5. Detecting hardware

6. Selecting a configuration

Power-On Self Test (POST)

The **power-on self test (POST)** is the first step in the boot sequence for any computer with an operating system. The POST determines the amount of real memory, and whether or not all necessary hardware components, such as a keyboard, are present. The actual tests can differ, depending on how the BIOS is configured. If the tests are successful, the computer boots itself. If the tests are unsuccessful, the computer reports the error by emitting a series of beeps and possibly displaying an error message and code on the screen. The number of beeps indicates the error, but differs from one BIOS to another. The software for the POST resides in a special, battery-powered chip called the **CMOS (complementary metal-oxide semiconductor)**. This chip can store not only the software necessary to conduct the POST, but also basic configuration information that the POST uses to check the amount of RAM installed in a system, along with other key information. Figure 14-1 shows a typical screen that results from the successful completion of the POST on an Intel PC.

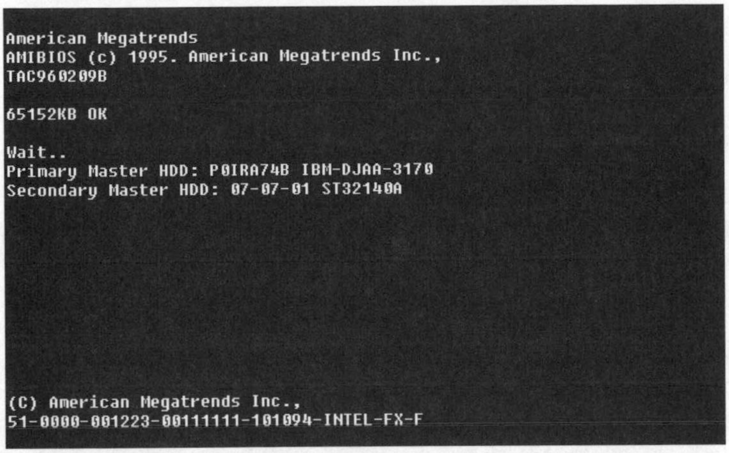

```
American Megatrends
AMIBIOS (c) 1995. American Megatrends Inc.,
TAC960209B

65152KB OK

Wait..
Primary Master HDD: P0IRA74B IBM-DJAA-3170
Secondary Master HDD: 07-07-01 ST32140A




(C) American Megatrends Inc.,
51-0000-001223-00111111-101094-INTEL-FX-F
```

Figure 14-1   The POST display on a PC

After the system POST is completed, each adapter card in the system performs its own self-test. For example, if a computer has a SCSI card in addition to its own built-in adapter cards, it will check its internal configuration and any related devices it sees when it runs its own POST. At the same time, a report on what it finds during this process will appear on the computer monitor in text-only form (because there is no real operating system running at this point, screen output at this stage of the boot process is kept as simple and direct as possible). The screen shown in Figure 14-2 adds the report from an Adaptec 2940 SCSI controller to the information already supplied by the POST routine.

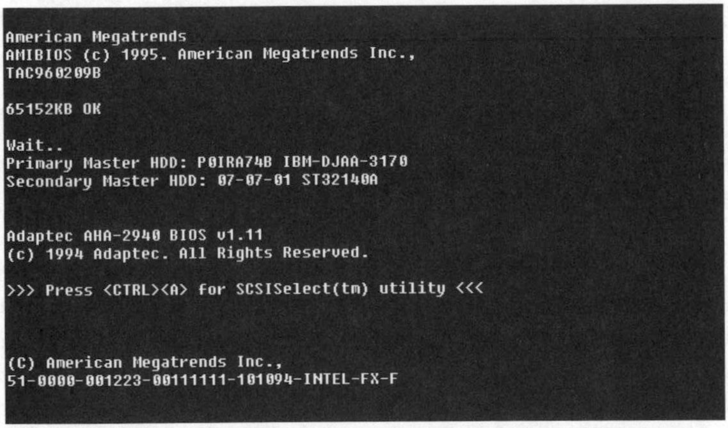

```
American Megatrends
AMIBIOS (c) 1995. American Megatrends Inc.,
TAC960209B

65152KB OK

Wait..
Primary Master HDD: P0IRA74B IBM-DJAA-3170
Secondary Master HDD: 07-07-01 ST32140A


Adaptec AHA-2940 BIOS v1.11
(c) 1994 Adaptec. All Rights Reserved.

>>> Press <CTRL><A> for SCSISelect(tm) utility <<<


(C) American Megatrends Inc.,
51-0000-001223-00111111-101094-INTEL-FX-F
```

Figure 14-2   Output from the BIOS on an Adaptec 2940 SCSI controller

14

Initial Startup

The initial startup sequence involves numerous files and initialization procedures. The first sector of the hard disk contains the Master Boot Record (MBR) and the partition table. The

Master Boot Record (MBR) begins the boot process by looking up the partition table to determine which partition to use for booting. If you are booting from a floppy disk, the first sector contains the **partition boot sector**.

Table 14-1 outlines the startup files for Windows 2000 on Intel (x86) computers.

Table 14-1   Windows 2000 Startup Files

Filename	Location	Explanation
Ntldr	Root of startup disk	Windows 2000 boot loader for PC machines
Boot.ini	Root of startup disk	Windows 2000 PC boot menu information
Bootsect.dos	Root of startup disk	Provides DOS boot information for dual-boot PCs
Ntdetect.com	Root of startup disk	Windows 2000 hardware detection program
Ntbootdd.sys	Root of startup disk	Lets Windows 2000 access SCSI drives on PCs with SCSI controller with onboard BIOS disabled
Ntoskrnl.exe	%systemroot%\System32	Windows 2000 operating system kernel
Hal.dll	%systemroot%\System32	Hardware abstraction layer code (CPU driver for x86 chips)
SYSTEM key	%systemroot%\System32	Key Windows 2000 Registry data
Device drivers	%systemroot%\System32	PC-specific device drivers for Windows 2000 use

When the POST has successfully concluded, the BIOS tries to locate the startup disk. The **BIOS** (basic input/output system) represents a chip-based set of routines that DOS and Windows 95/98 use to drive all system input and output, including access to peripheral devices of all kinds. Windows 2000, on the other hand, uses its own built-in input/output logic and drivers, and ignores whatever BIOS is installed in a computer. By doing this, Windows 2000 is able to manage I/O much more carefully than earlier Windows and DOS operating systems. It also helps to explain why applications that attempt to access drivers or the computer's BIOS or hardware directly are treated as ill behaved in the Windows 2000 environment.

If a floppy disk is in drive A when the BIOS checks that drive, it may decide to use that drive as the startup disk (this decision depends on how the boot sequence has been configured in the PC's CMOS). If there is no floppy disk in that drive, or if the CMOS has been configured to boot from a hard disk, it will use the first hard disk it finds as the boot disk. Of course, if drive A is enabled for booting, and the floppy disk you have inserted in that drive does not have a partition boot sector, you will get a "Non-system disk or disk error: Replace and press any key when ready" message, and the system won't start. This is one of the most common causes of boot failure in the Windows 2000 environment.

 TIP   If you get the "Non-system disk or disk error" message because the system attempted to boot from a non-system floppy, remove the floppy and cycle the power off and on again. It is important to do this (rather than restarting with Ctrl+Alt+Delete) to avoid transferring boot-sector viruses to the computer.

When the BIOS uses the hard disk as its startup disk, it reads the MBR and loads that into memory. The BIOS then transfers system control to the MBR. The MBR scans the partition table to locate the system partition. When the MBR locates the system partition, it loads sector 0 of the partition into memory, and executes it. Sector 0 can contain a diagnostic program, a utility such as a virus scanner, or a partition boot sector that contains the startup code for the operating system. Should the computer boot from a floppy, only the partition boot sector is used.

In general, the MBR is independent of the operating system. For example, the same MBR is used in x86 systems to boot to Windows 95, MS-DOS, Windows NT, Windows 2000, and Windows 3.x.

However, the partition boot sector is completely dependent on the operating system and file system in use. For example, the partition boot sector in a Windows 2000 computer is responsible for a number of operating-system-specific functions. It must understand enough of the file system in use to find **Ntldr**, which is the program that locates and loads the Windows 2000 operating system files in the root folder. On a hard drive with a FAT partition, the partition boot sector is generally one sector long, and points to another location on disk that will ultimately permit the computer to find and launch Ntldr. On an NTFS partition, because the partition boot sector can be as many as 16 sectors long, it can contain all the necessary file system code needed to locate and launch Ntldr, without requiring transfer of control to another area on disk. Thus, the partition boot sector is responsible for loading a boot loader (Ntldr) into memory and initiating boot loader execution.

At this point, the **system partition**, the partition that contains the MBR and partition boot sector, must be on the first physical hard drive in the system. However, the **boot partition**—the partition that contains the Windows 2000 files—can be on the same partition, a different partition on the same drive, or on another drive entirely within the local computer. In other words, you boot Windows 2000 from the system partition, and run the operating system from the boot partition.

14

Because this terminology is counterintuitive (that is, it's the opposite of what you might expect) and because it appears on numerous Windows 2000-related Microsoft exams, it's important to remember this reversal of terminology.

Boot Loader

Boot loader processing and files select an operating system to boot, and load the related operating system files from the boot partition. On PCs, once the boot OS is selected from the Boot.ini menu, Ntldr controls the operating system selection and hardware detection processes before the Windows 2000 kernel is initialized.

Ntldr, Boot.ini, Bootsect.dos, Ntdetect.com, and Ntbootdd.sys may all be present in the root directory of the startup disk (also known as the system partition; see Figure 14-3). Some files may be dimmed because they have the read-only attribute. The partition hosting the boot loader can be formatted with either FAT, FAT32, or NTFS. Of this collection of files, Ntldr, Ntdetect.com, and Boot.ini must always be present for Windows 2000 to boot (the other two are optional, and depend on the configuration of the particular machine in use).

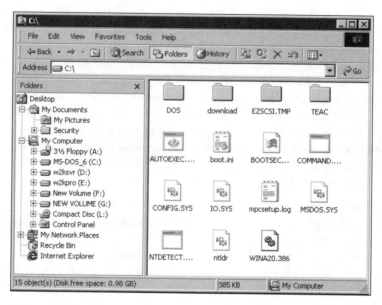

Figure 14-3   The system partition on a typical Windows 2000 system

> **TIP**   Bootsect.dos appears only if the machine has been configured to dual-boot between Windows 2000/Windows NT and DOS, Windows 3.x, or Windows 95. Ntbootdd.sys appears only when a SCSI controller has its built-in BIOS controller disabled; this file supplies the necessary controller driver that the hardware would otherwise provide.

At this point, Ntldr switches the processor into 32-bit flat memory mode. When an x86 computer starts, it is running in real mode, which means it is functioning as an old-fashioned 8088 or 8086 computer. Because Ntldr is a 32-bit program, it must change the processing mode to support the 32-bit flat memory model it uses before it can perform any further processing.

Next, Ntldr starts the appropriate file system. The code to access both FAT and NTFS file systems is programmed into Ntldr so that it can read, access, and copy files on either type of file system.

Next, Ntldr reads the Boot.ini file and displays the operating system selections it contains. The screen that appears at this point is usually called the boot loader screen or the **boot selection menu**, and represents the point at which users may select which operating system they would like to load (or which form of Windows 2000 graphics operation they would like to use).

A typical boot selection menu appears in Figure 14-4. Notice the prompt to access troubleshooting and advanced startup options by pressing F8. These options are discussed in a later section of this chapter.

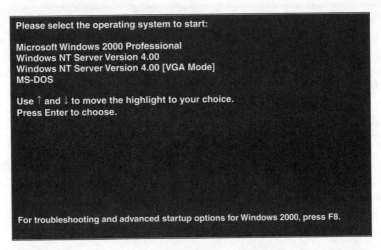

```
Please select the operating system to start:

Microsoft Windows 2000 Professional
Windows NT Server Version 4.00
Windows NT Server Version 4.00 [VGA Mode]
MS-DOS

Use ↑ and ↓ to move the highlight to your choice.
Press Enter to choose.




For troubleshooting and advanced startup options for Windows 2000, press F8.
```

Figure 14-4   A typical Windows 2000 boot selection menu

14

Notice on this particular system, Windows 2000 Professional is present with Windows NT Server 4.0 and MS-DOS. In fact, Windows 2000 will coexist with numerous other operating systems, including those that depend on DOS for their underpinnings.

When you do not manually alter the highlighted selection of the boot menu, a line below the menu displays a counter: "Seconds until highlighted choice will be started automatically: 30". If a selection is not made before the counter reaches zero, the highlighted operating system will start automatically. To change the default operating system to load or the amount of time to wait before automatically loading the highlighted operating system, change the settings in the Boot.ini file, which will be discussed in greater detail later in this chapter.

If the user selects an operating system other than Windows 2000 or Windows NT, the boot loader loads Bootsect.dos and hands over control of the system. The other operating system then starts normally because Bootsect.dos contains the partition boot sector for that operating system. However, if the user selects a version of Windows 2000, the boot loader executes Ntdetect.com to gather hardware information.

The remaining functions of Ntldr (operating system selection, hardware detection, and configuration selection) are discussed later in this section. For now, note that Ntldr maintains control of the computer until it loads Ntoskrnl.exe and passes the hardware information and system control to that program.

Detecting Hardware

Ntdetect.com is executed by the boot loader and is used to collect a list of hardware currently installed in the computer. Ntdetect checks the computer ID, bus/adapter type, video, keyboard, communication ports, parallel ports, floppy disks, and mouse or pointing devices. It creates a system profile that will be compared to Windows 2000 Registry entries that describe the system later during the boot process, at which point the operating system will look for discrepancies or potential problems.

Once hardware is detected, the system needs to select a system configuration, otherwise known as a hardware profile. If only a single hardware profile is defined, this will always be used. If two or more hardware profiles are present, the system will attempt to select a profile based on detected hardware. If the system cannot make an automatic selection, you'll be prompted to manually select a hardware profile.

TROUBLESHOOTING AND ADVANCED STARTUP OPTIONS

Windows 2000 has combined the boot and recovery options of Windows NT and Windows 95/98. The result is a more robust operating system and additional options to restore a malfunctioning system to a functional state. To access the additional startup options, when the boot menu appears, press F8 before the timer expires. Once F8 is pressed, the Advanced Options Menu appears (see Figure 14-5).

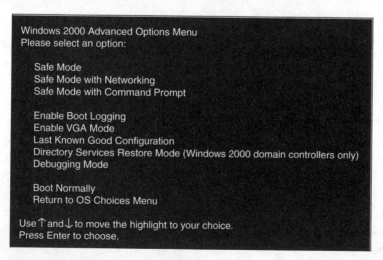

```
Windows 2000 Advanced Options Menu
Please select an option:

    Safe Mode
    Safe Mode with Networking
    Safe Mode with Command Prompt

    Enable Boot Logging
    Enable VGA Mode
    Last Known Good Configuration
    Directory Services Restore Mode (Windows 2000 domain controllers only)
    Debugging Mode

    Boot Normally
    Return to OS Choices Menu

Use ↑ and ↓ to move the highlight to your choice.
Press Enter to choose.
```

Figure 14-5   The Advanced Options Menu

The contents of this menu are somewhat dependent on installed components, such as the Remote Installation Service, but it typically contains the following items:

- *Safe Mode*—Boots Windows 2000 with only the minimum required system files and device drivers. Safe Mode does not load networking components (see Hands-on Project 14-3).

- *Safe Mode with Networking*—Boots Windows 2000 in the same manner as Safe Mode, but adds networking components (see Hands-on Project 14-6).

- *Safe Mode with Command Prompt*—Boots Windows 2000 in the same manner as Safe Mode, but boots to a command prompt instead of to the GUI environment.

- *Enable Boot Logging*—A toggle that enables or disables the boot process and writes details to a log file regarding drivers and services. The log file is located at %systemroot%\Ntbtlog.txt.

- *Enable VGA Mode*—Boots Windows 2000 normally, but uses only the basic VGA video driver (see Hands-on Project 14-5).

- *Last Known Good Configuration*—Boots Windows 2000 with the **Last Known Good Configuration (LKGC)**, the state of the Registry as it was recorded during the last successful user logon (see Hands-on Project 14-4).

- *Directory Services Restore Mode*—Valid only on Windows 2000 domain controllers; used to boot Windows 2000 and restore Active Directory.

- *Debugging Mode*—Boots Windows 2000 normally, but sends debugging information to another system over a serial cable. Details about using this option are included in the *Windows 2000 Resource Kit*.

Advanced Options for booting can be used to recover from a wide variety of system problems or failures. Safe Mode offers the ability to boot into a functioning system even when specific drivers are corrupted or failing. This includes bypassing bad video drivers, network drivers, and even GUI controls by booting into Enable VGA Mode, Safe Mode (without networking support), and/or Safe Mode with Command Prompt, respectively. In most cases, this allows you to replace or remove the problematic driver before rebooting back into normal mode.

14

TIP

If a problem is occurring and you are unable to discern its exact cause or nature, you may want to choose Enable Boot Logging from the Advanced Options menu to record the process of steps performed between the boot menu and the logon prompt. The resultant file, %systemroot%\Ntbtlog.txt, may provide clues as to the driver, system, or procedure that is causing the system malfunction.

If you've recently installed a driver or even an entire software product, or just modified the Registry, and the result is a system that will not fully boot, the Last Known Good Configuration is a great first step in returning the system to a functional state. The LKGC will return the system to the state of the Registry at the time of the last successful logon.

If none of these options provides you a method to restore your system, you do have one final option from the Advanced Options Menu, namely Debugging Mode. This mode is used in conjunction with a second computer connected by a serial cable. Debugging Mode causes the boot process to send detailed information on activities to the companion system. This information can be used to determine at what point in the boot process problems are occurring. The information created by Debugging Mode is rather complex and is typically used only by high-end programmers. If you want more details on the Debugging Mode process and how to interpret the extracted data, please consult the *Windows 2000 Resource Kit*.

BOOT CONFIGURATION AND SELECTING AN OPERATING SYSTEM

The Windows 2000 boot configuration can be controlled through its configuration file, Boot.ini. As mentioned earlier, Boot.ini is located in the root directory of the system partition, and is used by the boot loader to display the list of available operating systems. This file consists of two sections: [boot loader] and [operating systems]. A typical Boot.ini file is shown in Figure 14-6.

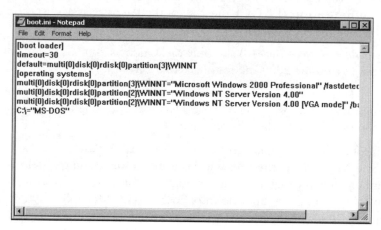

Figure 14-6   Boot.ini viewed through Notepad

[boot loader]

The [boot loader] section of the Boot.ini file contains two items: timeout and default. The *timeout* setting defines the number of seconds the system will wait for the user to select an operating system before loading the default operating system. If timeout is set to zero, Ntldr immediately loads the default operating system without displaying the boot loader screen. To cause the system to wait indefinitely for a selection, set the timeout to –1. This setting, however, can only be altered by using a text editor, because it is an illegal value for the setting from the System icon in the Control Panel. (See the section later in this chapter on editing Boot.ini, which explains how to edit this file, and what kind of text editor to use.) The *default* setting in Boot.ini lists the path to the default operating system.

[operating systems]

The [operating systems] section of Boot.ini lists the available operating systems. Each listing contains the path to the boot partition for the operating system, the text displayed in the boot loader screen, and optional parameters. The text is clipped in the screen capture in Figure 14-6, but here's what it looks like in its entirety:

```
multi(0)disk(0)rdisk(0)partition(3)\WINNT="Microsoft Windows
       2000 Professional" /fastdetect
multi(0)disk(0)rdisk(0)partition(2)\WINNT="Windows NT Server
       Version 4.00"
multi(0)disk(0)rdisk(0)partition(2)\WINNT="Windows NT Server
       Version 4.00 [VGA mode]" /basevideo /sos
C:\="MS-DOS"
```

The following list details some of the switches that can be added to the end of entries in the [operating systems] section of Boot.ini. In most cases, you'll want to employ the F8 Advanced Options menu (see earlier this chapter) to access troubleshooting boot methods. However, you can employ the following switches and switch combinations to mimic the Advanced Options menu selections in your Boot.ini file:

- */BASEVIDEO*—Starts Windows 2000 in standard VGA mode (640 × 480)

- */DEBUG*—Loads the debugger and allows access by a host debugger connected to the computer

- */SOS*—Displays the device driver names when they are loaded

- */SAFEBOOT:MINIMAL*—Boots into Safe Mode

- */SAFEBOOT:NETWORK*—Boots into Safe Mode with Networking

- */SAFEBOOT:MINIMAL(ALTERNATESHELL)*—Boots into Safe Mode with Command Prompt

- */SAFEBOOT:DSREPAIR*—Boots into Directory Services Restore Mode (domain controllers only)

- */BOOTLOG*—Enables boot logging

- */NOGUIBOOT*—Boots without showing the splash screen. Does not determine whether Windows 2000 GUI environment or command prompt is booted

- */FASTDETECT*—Performs a verification of hardware components rather than a full inspection, to speed boot time

TIP   The switches used in the Boot.ini file are not case sensitive.

14

Advanced RISC Computing (ARC) Pathnames

In the Boot.ini file, the path pointing to the \winnt directory is written using the **Advanced RISC Computing (ARC) pathname** naming conventions. These pathnames are described as follows:

- *scsi(n) or multi(n):* This portion of the path indicates the type of the device on which the operating system resides. *scsi* is used if the operating system is on a SCSI hard disk that is connected to a SCSI adapter that has a disabled built-in BIOS. *multi* is used for other hard disks including IDE, EIDE, and SCSI with a built-in BIOS. The *(n)* indicates the hardware adapter from which to boot. It is replaced with a number corresponding to the correct hardware adapter, numbered ordinally (starting with zero).

- *disk(n):* This portion of the path indicates which SCSI bus number should be used. The *(n)* always equals zero when the adapter is a multiadapter (that is, the ARC494 path starts with multi). Otherwise, it is numbered ordinally.

- *rdisk(n):* This portion of the path indicates the SCSI LUN number or selects which of the hard disks attached to the adapter contains the operating system. *(n)* always equals zero when the adapter is SCSI. Otherwise, it is numbered ordinally.

- *partition(n):* This portion of the path selects the disk partition that contains the operating system files. Partition is numbered cardinally (starting with 1).

- *\path:* The final portion of the path indicates the directory on the partition in which the operating system files are found. The default path for Windows 2000 is \Winnt.

EDITING BOOT.INI

To make changes to a Boot.ini file, the user has two options: to use the Control Panel to edit this file indirectly, or to use a text editor to change the file directly.

Using the Control Panel

Using the Control Panel to make changes to Boot.ini is the safest way to proceed (try Hands-on Project 14-1). By opening the System applet in the Control Panel, selecting the Advanced tab, then clicking the Startup and Recovery button (see Figure 14-7), you can make certain changes to your setup. The Startup and Recovery dialog box (shown in Figure 14-8) allows you to choose a default boot selection and to select a delay interval before the boot selection starts automatically. This delay time corresponds to the timeout value set in Boot.ini. These options are depicted in the System startup pane in the Startup and Recovery dialog box. Notice also that the options that control debugging output for system failures appear on this pane as well; this information often comes in handy when severe problems manifest.

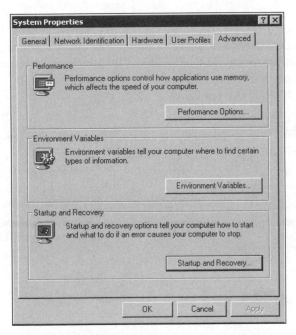

Figure 14-7   The Advanced tab of the System Control Panel applet

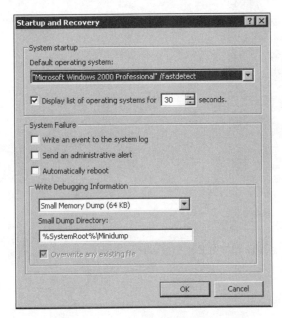

Figure 14-8   Startup and Recovery dialog box

14

Using a Text Editor

You can use Notepad or any other text editor to edit Boot.ini (try Hands-on Project 14–2). As with any initialization file, you should be careful when editing the file. If you configure the file incorrectly, Windows 2000 may not boot. You should always create a backup copy of the file and name it Boot.bak before you make any changes.

TIP If you do decide to edit the Boot.ini file from a text editor, you must first reset the file's attributes to make it editable. By default, this file has the following attributes set: System, Hidden, and Read-only. To edit the file, you must reset it to turn off at least the Read-only attribute (we usually turn off the Hidden attribute as well). To change the file's attributes, locate the file in Windows Explorer, right-click its entry, click Properties, and then uncheck the attribute settings boxes on the General tab that show up by default (see Figure 14-9). After you make these attribute changes, you can edit the file using any simple text editor. (Notepad works fine.)

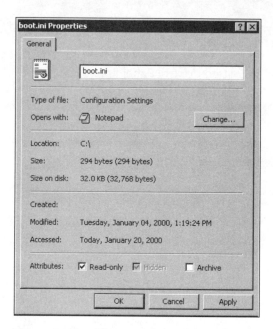

Figure 14-9   The Properties dialog box of the Boot.ini file

WINDOWS 2000 LOAD PHASE

The Windows 2000 load phase begins when the kernel assumes control of the machine. It consists of the following five stages:

- Loading the kernel
- Initializing the kernel

- Services load

- Windows 2000 system start

- Logging on

Loading the Kernel

Once you've selected the option to boot into Windows 2000, a brief "Starting Windows…" text message is displayed before the full Windows 2000 splash screen is shown. This image includes a loading status thermometer bar that gives you a minor indication of progress toward loading. While you are "entertained" by the slow progression of the blue squares, the boot loader loads the Windows 2000 kernel (Ntoskrnl.exe) and the hardware abstraction layer (HAL; file Hal.dll) into memory. However, these programs are not executed at this time. Before executing the programs, the boot loader loads the Registry key HKEY_LOCAL_ MACHINE\SYSTEM from the *%systemroot%*\System32\Config\System directory.

At this point, the boot loader retrieves the configuration you selected from the Registry sub-key HKEY_LOCAL_MACHINE\SYSTEM\Select. Based on the ControlSet00x setting in the subkey, the boot loader knows which ControlSet00x to use. For example, if you chose the Last Known Good Configuration option during the configuration selection process, the **control set** may be ControlSet003 rather than ControlSet001, which is the default config-uration. Notice the values of the Current, Default, Failed, and LastKnownGood value entries in Figure 14-10. (Working with the Registry and the contents of Registry keys are covered in Chapter 13.)

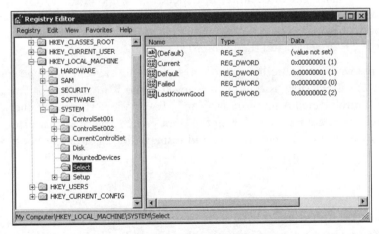

Figure 14-10   The HKEY_LOCAL_MACHINE\SYSTEM\Select subkey

The boot loader then loads the drivers listed in the Registry subkey HKEY_LOCAL_ MACHINE\SYSTEM\CurrentControlSet\Services. These drivers are loaded and/or ini-tialized according to their settings in the Registry.

Initializing the Kernel

After its initialization, the kernel creates the Registry key HKEY_LOCAL_MACHINE\ HARDWARE, using the information received from the boot loader. This key contains the hardware information that is computed when the system is started up, and includes information about components on the system board and the interrupts used by specific hardware devices.

The kernel also creates the CloneControlSet by making a copy of the CurrentControlSet. The Clone set is never modified, because it is intended to be an identical copy of the data used to configure the computer and should not be modified during the startup process.

The kernel then initializes the drivers that were loaded by the boot loader. If drivers experience errors as they load, they send conditions to the kernel that determine how the error is treated. The error levels are as follows:

- *Ignore:* The error is ignored and no message is displayed to the user, if the ignore condition is sent to the kernel.

- *Normal:* The boot process continues, but a message is displayed to the user if the device driver returns the normal error condition.

- *Severe:* The management of this error depends on whether the Last Known Good Configuration is in use or not. If the LKGC is not being used, then the error is displayed to the user, and the boot process restarts using the LKGC. If the LKGC is already in use, then the message is displayed and the boot process continues.

- *Critical:* The management of this error depends on whether the LKGC is in use or not. If not, then the error is displayed to the user, and the boot process restarts using the Last Known Good Configuration. If the LKGC is already in use, then the message is displayed and the boot process fails.

All such events are saved automatically in the System log, and invoke on-screen messages as well. The System log is available as one of the views in the Windows 2000 Event Viewer (Start, Settings, Control Panel, Administrative Tools, Event Viewer), and should always be checked whenever errors are reported during the boot process. Because that process cannot be interrupted, however, it's necessary to wait and inspect the log after the bootup phase is complete.

Services Load

During the services load phase, the kernel starts the Session Manager. The Session Manager reads the entries that are stored in the Registry key: HKEY_LOCAL_MACHINE\SYSTEM\ CurrentControlSet\Control\Session Manager.

It then starts programs that correspond to the key entries under this Registry key: HKEY_LOCAL_MACHINE\SYSTEM\CurrentControlSet\Control\Session Manager\BootExecute.

The default entry for this key is "autocheck autochk *". Autocheck makes sure that the files stored on your hard drive are always consistent. It detects and attempts to repair damaged files and directories. As with any repair utility, it cannot guarantee that all files can be fixed or retrieved.

Once Autocheck is complete, the paging files are set up. These are stored under HKEY_LOCAL_MACHINE\SYSTEM\CurrentControlSet\Control\Session Manager\Memory Management.

The Session Manager then writes the CurrentControlSet and the CloneControlSet to the Registry, and, finally, loads the subsystems that are defined in the Registry.

HKEY_LOCAL_MACHINE\SYSTEM\CurrentControlSet\Control\SessionManager\ Subsystems contains the subsystem information. The Windows (Win32) subsystem is the default subsystem for Windows 2000, and is also the subsystem within which the default user shell always executes.

Windows 2000 System Startup

Once the Windows 2000 services have all started, and the elements in the group of processes that are configured to launch on startup are fired off, the Windows 2000 system may be considered to be fully started. This brief, but meaningful, phase of the process is signaled by the appearance of the Windows 2000 logon screen as the Win32 subsystem starts WinLogon.exe, and that process automatically launches the Local Security Administration (Lsass.exe) process.

Logging On

Unlike Windows NT Workstation 4.0, Windows 2000 Professional does not require the issuing of the Ctrl+Alt+Delete keystroke to initiate the logon dialog box by default. The "Disable Ctrl+Alt+Delete requirement for logon" option in the Security Options section of the Local Security Policy is enabled by default. If you alter this setting, you'll need to issue the keystroke to access the logon dialog box.

Until a user successfully logs on, the boot process is not complete. Once a user logs on, the Clone control set is copied to the Last Known Good control set. This procedure provides the values that will be used the next time the machine is powered up, if the user elects to invoke the Last Known Good Configuration.

14

MULTIPLE-BOOT SYSTEMS

One of the biggest advantages of the Windows 2000 operating system is its ability to peacefully coexist with other operating systems. Each operating system uses one or more file systems to organize the data within the volumes. Some operating systems can use the same file system, whereas others are incompatible. For example, MS-DOS, Windows 95/98, Window NT, and Windows 2000 are able to share files via FAT volumes, and Windows NT and Windows 2000 are able to share files via NTFS volumes. Windows 2000 and UNIX do not have a common file system, although it is possible for Linux to access FAT volumes.

Multiple Windows Operating Systems

Windows 3.1, Windows 3.11, Windows 95/98, and Windows NT can all exist on the same system as Windows 2000. When Windows 2000 is to be installed on a system with another operating system—especially some previous version of Windows—it is important to specify a different partition for installation. Unless you want to upgrade the computer (that is, install Windows 2000 over an existing OS), always define a new main directory and partition, different from the one already in use. Different versions of Windows 2000 may also be installed on the same computer, but, again, each must have a separate partition.

If you plan to use applications from the different versions of Windows you have installed, you must install the application from each operating system. For example, if you intend to use Microsoft Word from both Windows 98 and Windows 2000, you must run the Word setup program while the computer is booted to each operating system.

Multiple Installation Order

When installing multiple operating systems on x86-based computers, the order in which you install the OSs is important. When installing Windows 2000 and MS-DOS, it is best to install MS-DOS first, then Windows 2000. Windows 2000 will see the DOS operating system and leave it intact. The same guideline applies to installing Windows 2000 and Windows 95/98 or Windows NT. At this time, the recommended installation order is: older Windows products first, then Windows 2000. If you plan on running all three operating systems (MS-DOS, Windows 98, and Windows 2000), they should be installed in that order: MS-DOS, then Windows 98, and Windows 2000 last. When installing multiple versions of Windows 2000 or Windows NT onto the same system, it really doesn't matter which one is installed first. As a general rule, install the newest operating system last and the oldest first.

CHAPTER SUMMARY

❑ The Windows 2000 boot process can be daunting, but it is not nearly as mysterious as one first supposes. It follows the same general boot steps as any other operating system, and in fact, "plays well with others." After the POST (power-on self test), the BIOS loads the Master Boot Record (MBR), which then loads the partition boot sector. Then the boot loader takes control of the system and begins the true Windows 2000 boot. The user is presented with options for choosing the operating system to load, and—if he or she chooses Windows 2000, the configuration to use.

❑ When the boot menu appears, you may press F8 to access Advanced Options. The Advanced Options are alternate boot methods that can bypass certain types of drivers or subsystems to aid in troubleshooting. Advanced Options include, among others, Safe Mode, Enable VGA, Enable Boot Logging, and Last Known Good Configuration.

❑ After the boot loader, the kernel is loaded into memory and is granted control of the computer. The kernel loads the operating system files and device drivers before finally allowing the user to log on. When the user successfully logs on to the computer, it is considered a good startup and the configuration is saved to the Registry.

❏ The boot process can be altered by changing the Boot.ini file. This includes information such as the default operating system, its location, and the amount of time to wait before automatically loading the default OS. The type of information displayed and the debugger setting can be changed by adding switches to the configurations in the Boot.ini file.

❏ Windows 3.1, Windows 3.11, Windows 95/98, and Windows NT can all exist on the same system as Windows 2000. You can configure Windows 2000 to offer the choice of booting to other operating systems. In a multiboot system, it's generally best to install in order from older operating systems to newer.

KEY TERMS

Advanced RISC Computing (ARC) pathname — Naming convention used in the Boot.ini file to define the particular hard disk and partition where Windows 2000 operating system files reside.

BIOS (basic input/output system) — A special PC ROM chip that contains sufficient program code to let a computer perform a POST routine, to check its hardware components, and to operate basic input and output routines for keyboard or mouse input, and screen output.

boot partition — In Windows 2000, the disk that contains the Windows 2000 operating system files.

boot phase — Any of a number of stages in the Windows 2000 boot process, starting with the power-on self test (POST), through initial startup activities, to activation of a boot loader program, to selection of the operating system (or version) to boot, to hardware detection (Ntdetect), to selecting a configuration.

boot process — The process of bringing up a completely functional computer, starting from initial power-up (or reboot) through the boot phases and load phases involved in starting the hardware, finding a boot loader, and then loading and initializing an operating system.

boot selection menu — The list of bootable operating systems (or versions) that Boot.ini provides for display at the end of the Windows 2000 boot phase.

CMOS (complementary metal-oxide semiconductor) — A special, battery-powered chip that can store not only the software necessary to conduct the POST, but also the basic, nonvolatile configuration information that POST uses to check the RAM installed in a system, the number and type of hard drives, the type of keyboard and mouse, and so forth.

control set — A special set of Registry values that describes a Windows 2000 machine's startup configuration that is saved each time a Windows machine is shut down (as the current configuration) and each time a user successfully logs on for the first time after bootup (as the Last Known Good Configuration).

Last Known Good Configuration (LKGC) — The control set for Windows 2000 that is automatically saved by the system in a special set of Registry keys the first time a user logs on successfully to a system immediately after it has booted up. This information provides a safe fallback to use when booting the system the next time, if changes made to the Registry in the interim cause problems with booting (or if changes have been introduced that a user does not wish to retain on that system).

14

load phase — The Windows 2000 load phase begins when the kernel assumes control of the machine, and consists of the following five steps: (1) loading the kernel, (2) initializing the kernel, (3) loading services, (4) starting the Windows 2000 system, and (5) logging on. All five steps must be completed successfully for a complete load to occur.

Master Boot Record (MBR) — The partition table for a disk, and the code that permits that partition table to be read. A functioning MBR is required to boot a hard disk.

Ntldr — The Windows 2000 loader program that manages the boot and load phases of Windows 2000 on a PC.

partition boot sector — The partition that contains the information the file system uses to access the volume, including a physical description of the disk, the name and version of the operating system files, the bootstrap code, and an instruction that allows the Master Boot Record to find all this information.

power-on self test (POST) — The system check performed by all computers when they are turned on.

system partition — In Windows 2000, the disk that contains the MBR and partition boot sector.

REVIEW QUESTIONS

1. The _____ contains the files that load the initial components of the operating system.

   a. boot partition

   b. system partition

   c. start partition

   d. kernel partition

2. What program has control of an x86 computer when the user is able to choose which operating system to boot?

   a. Ntldr

   b. Osloader

   c. Boot.ini

   d. Ntbootdd.sys

3. When configuring an x86 computer for multiple operating systems, _____ should always be loaded last.

4. When booting an x86 computer, the boot loader must be installed on a(n) _____ file system. (Choose all that apply.)

   a. NTFS

   b. HPFS

   c. FAT

   d. FAT32

5. The _____ setting in the Boot.ini file defines the operating system that will be automatically loaded.

   a. [operating systems]

   b. [system loader]

   c. [boot loader]

   d. default

6. By default, Windows 2000 Professional requires you to press the Ctrl+Alt+Delete keystroke sequence to access the logon dialog box. True or False?

7. _____ is the primary boot loader for x86-based systems.

   a. Ntldr

   b. Osloader.exe

   c. Bootdd.sys

   d. Bootsect.dos

8. The timeout option is in the _____ section of the Boot.ini file.

9. What portion of a computer system startup is the same on all computers?

   a. POST

   b. initial startup

   c. boot loader

   d. OS selection

10. The Boot.ini file can be changed by one of two methods. What are they?

    a. Control Panel System applet

    b. Control Panel Startup applet

    c. Windows 2000 Configuration Manager

    d. using a plaintext editor

11. The _____ file is only accessed when SCSI disks with onboard BIOS disabled are used.

    a. Multidisk.sys

    b. Scsildr.sys

    c. Rdisk.sys

    d. Ntbootdd.sys

12. Which of the following are selections listed on the Advanced Options menu when you press F8 during the boot menu display? (Choose all that apply.)

    a. Safe Mode with Command Prompt

    b. Enable VGA Mode

    c. NTFS Transfer Mode

    d. Debugging Mode

14

13. Which ARC settings are used only for SCSI controllers without an enabled onboard BIOS? (Choose all that apply.)

    a. multi()

    b. scsi()

    c. rdisk()

    d. disk()

14. The Ntoskrnl.exe file is located in the _____ directory on an x86 system.

15. The Last Known Good Configuration is accessed by pressing the spacebar after the operating system is selected from the boot menu. True or False?

16. You recently installed a new video driver and a new networking interface driver, and now your system will not boot, or at least you never see the logon prompt. Which of the following advanced options should you use to attempt to return to a fully functional system?

    a. Safe Mode

    b. Safe Mode with Networking

    c. Safe Mode with Command Prompt

    d. Enable VGA Mode

    e. Enable Debugging Mode

    f. Enable Boot Logging

17. The Boot.ini parameter switches that mimic the Safe Mode with Networking Advanced Options menu selection are _____?

    a. /SAFEBOOT:MINIMAL(ALTERNATESHELL) /SOS /BOOTLOG / NOGUIBOOT

    b. /SAFEBOOT:DSREPAIR /SOS

    c. /SAFEBOOT:NETWORK /SOS /BOOTLOG /NOGUIBOOT

    d. /BOOTLOG

18. The _____ Boot.ini switch displays the names of the device drivers as they are loaded.

    a. /B

    b. /AT

    c. /SOS

    d. /DRV

19. The Last Known Good Registry key is written or updated after _____.

20. The _____ partition contains the Windows 2000 operating system files.

    a. system

    b. boot

    c. start

    d. kernel

21. If the system and boot partitions are the same and reside on an IDE hard drive, which of the following ARC names would appear in Boot.ini?

    a. scsi(0)disk(0)rdisk(1)partition(1)

    b. multi(0)disk(0)rdisk(0)partition(1)

    c. multi(0)disk(1)rdisk(0)partition(1)

    d. multi(0)disk(0)rdisk(1)partition(1)

22. Windows 2000 uses its own built-in input/output logic and drivers, and ignores whatever BIOS is installed in a computer. True or False?

23. The presence of a floppy in drive A can cause which of the following situations? (Choose all that apply.)

    a. booting from the floppy to whatever OS is installed there

    b. failure to boot due to a missing boot sector on the floppy

    c. "Non-system disk or disk error: Replace and press any key when ready" error message

    d. normal booting from the hard drive

24. The same MBR is found on Windows 95, MS-DOS, Windows NT, Windows 2000, and Windows 3.x systems. True or False?

25. Ntbootdd.sys appears on a system when which of the following operating systems is present in a multiboot configuration with Windows 2000?

    a. MS-DOS

    b. Windows 3.x

    c. Windows 98

    d. none of the above

14

HANDS-ON PROJECTS

Project 14-1

To modify the Boot.ini file by using Control Panel:

1. Open the Control Panel (**Start**, **Settings**, **Control Panel**).

2. Double-click the **System** applet to start it.

3. Select the **Advanced** tab (refer to Figure 14-7).

4. Click the **Startup and Recovery** button. This reveals the Startup and Recovery dialog box (refer to Figure 14-8).

5. Notice that the Startup option defines the default operating system for the computer. Select another operating system from the drop-down list.

6. To modify the amount of time the list appears when the system is booted, change the **Display list of operating systems for** option. Change this setting to **10** seconds by clicking on the down arrow beside the field.

7. The remaining options define what action the kernel will take when a STOP error occurs. In most situations, these should not be changed.

8. To save the configuration to Boot.ini, click **OK**.

9. To see the effect of the changes you made, restart the computer.

10. Repeat this process to restore the original settings.

Project 14-2

To change the Boot.ini settings using a text editor:

1. First create a backup copy of the Boot.ini file: Launch Windows Explorer (**Start, Programs, Accessories, Windows Explorer**); select the root of drive C in the left pane. Right-click drive **c:**, select Folder Options, and make sure that the options for viewing file extensions, hidden files, and protected operating system files are checked. Right-click the **Boot.ini** entry, select the **Copy** entry, then click on the current drive and press **Ctrl+V** (paste). This creates a file named "Copy of boot.ini" in that directory. Rename the file to **Boot.bak**. You may need this if something goes wrong later.

2. Next, the Read-only attribute may have to be removed from the Boot.ini file. To do this, highlight the **Boot.ini** file.

3. Right-click the file and select **Properties**.

4. If the box next to **Read-only** is checked, deselect it. This changes the file's attributes so that it can be altered (refer to Figure 14-9).

5. Click **OK**.

6. Open the Boot.ini file in Notepad: open the **Start** menu, select **Run**, enter **notepad c:\boot.ini** in the box provided, and click **OK**. Notepad opens with the Boot.ini file displayed (refer to Figure 14-6).

7. Restore the timeout to 30 seconds by changing the **timeout=** value to **30**.

8. Save the file by selecting **File, Save**.

9. Exit Notepad by selecting **File, Exit**.

10. Reboot the computer to deploy your changes.

Project 14-3

Rebooting Windows 2000 into Safe Mode:

1. Enter the Windows 2000 attention sequence (**Ctrl+Alt+Delete**) to invoke the Windows 2000 Security dialog box. Click the **Shut Down** button, select **Restart** from the pull-down list, and then click **OK**.

2. As Windows 2000 reboots, watch for the boot selection menu. As soon as it appears, press the **F8** key. This reveals the Advanced Options menu. (Refer to Figure 14-5.)

3. Use the arrow keys on the keyboard to select **Safe Mode** from the list of options.

4. Press the **Enter** key, and allow the boot process to continue to completion.

5. Your system will boot with minimal drivers and without network support.

6. Repeat step 1, and allow your machine to reboot normally.

Project 14-4
Rebooting Windows 2000 with the Last Known Good Configuration:

> **TIP** Performing this project will cause all changes made to the system since the last successful logon to be discarded.

1. Enter the Windows 2000 attention sequence (**Ctrl+Alt+Delete**) to invoke the Windows 2000 Security dialog box. Click the **Shut Down** button, select **Restart** from the pull-down list, and then click **OK**.

2. As Windows 2000 reboots, watch for the boot selection menu. As soon as it appears, press the **F8** key. This reveals the Advanced Options menu (refer to Figure 14-5).

3. Use the arrow keys on the keyboard to select **Last Known Good Configuration** from the list of options.

4. Press the **Enter** key, and allow the boot process to continue to completion.

5. Your system will boot with the state of the Registry recorded at the last successful logon.

Project 14-5
Rebooting Windows 2000 with minimal VGA support:

14

> **TIP** This boot method should be used when a bad video driver is present or incorrect resolution has been set.

1. Enter the Windows 2000 attention sequence (**Ctrl+Alt+Delete**) to invoke the Windows 2000 Security dialog box. Click the **Shut Down** button, select **Restart** from the pull-down list, and then click **OK**.

2. As Windows 2000 reboots, watch for the boot selection menu. As soon as it appears, press the **F8** key. This reveals the Advanced Options menu (refer to Figure 14-5).

3. Use the arrow keys on the keyboard to select **Enable VGA Mode** from the list of options.

4. Press **Enter**, and allow the boot process to continue to completion.

5. Your system will boot normally, but will use the standard VGA video drivers at 640 × 480 with a color depth of 16 or 256 (depending on your video card). This will allow you to correct your display resolution or replace the bad video driver.

Project 14-6

Rebooting Windows 2000 into Safe Mode with Networking:

1. Enter the Windows 2000 attention sequence (**Ctrl+Alt+Delete**) to invoke the Windows 2000 Security dialog box. Click the **Shut Down** button, select **Restart** from the pull-down list, and then click **OK**.

2. As Windows 2000 reboots, watch for the boot selection menu. As soon as it appears, press the **F8** key. This reveals the Advanced Options menu (refer to Figure 14-5).

3. Use the arrow keys on the keyboard to select **Safe Mode with Networking** from the list of options.

4. Press **Enter**, and allow the boot process to continue to completion.

5. Your system will boot with minimal drivers but will include network support. This boot method is useful when attempting to troubleshoot a system that requires network access to tools, data files, or traffic.

CASE PROJECTS

1. The Engineering Department in your company has decided to update their computers to Windows 2000 Professional. They currently have four PCs, two running Windows 3.11 and two running Windows 95. They would like to retain their current configurations and programs. Outline the steps necessary to install Windows 2000 on their systems and explain what configurations will be available after the update is complete.

2. After installing a new graphics controller on a Windows 2000 Professional machine, you start up the system, but when the boot process is complete, you see nothing on the monitor except a small dot of light in the exact center. What boot option can you use to see enough of the screen to try a different driver, or to change display settings in the Display Control Panel applet?

3. By default, the Boot.ini entry for Windows 95 in the boot selection menu reads "MS Windows." How might you edit Boot.ini to change this value to read "Windows 95 Rules!" instead? What part of the Boot.ini file does the appropriate entry reside in, and which entry should you edit?

15

WINDOWS 2000 PROFESSIONAL DISASTER RECOVERY AND PROTECTION

> **After reading this chapter and completing the exercises, you will be able to:**
>
> ♦ Define IntelliMirror technology and describe its key features
> ♦ Back up data and settings on Windows 2000 Professional
> ♦ Recover a Windows 2000 Professional client's applications and data
> ♦ Create and use an Emergency Repair Disk
> ♦ Install and use the Recovery Console
> ♦ Describe remote operating system installation and how it can be used with IntelliMirror to recover an entire PC remotely

Disaster recovery involves minimizing the amount of time a computer is non-functional in the event of a disaster. The causes of a disaster can range from corrupt system files to a hardware failure. Windows 2000 includes several disaster recovery features that can be used in those cases. However, to minimize the chances of such a loss, Microsoft IntelliMirror technologies and built-in backup mechanisms are available. With the use of IntelliMirror, as well as new and enhanced disaster protection and recovery options, Windows 2000 Professional users and system administrators can rest assured that their information and configurations are backed up and ready to be restored at a moment's notice. This chapter discusses IntelliMirror and backup technologies, as well as various disaster recovery methods, including remote OS installation.

MICROSOFT INTELLIMIRROR

IntelliMirror is a term used to describe features of Windows 2000 that help ensure the availability of a user's data and computer configuration. The following list includes its three key elements and explains how each relates to disaster protection and recovery:

- *User data management:* Data backup
- *User settings management:* PC configuration recovery
- *Software installation and maintenance:* Application installation and repair

IntelliMirror greatly reduces the need for and cost of administrative intervention. Therefore, it plays a crucial role in both disaster protection and disaster recovery. If, for any reason, a user loses data or deletes required operating system or application files, that information can be recovered easily, sometimes seamlessly, with minimal or no interaction from an administrator. At the same time, the administrative group also has central administration capabilities so that it can centrally manage users' machines. Therefore, both end users and the administrative team benefit.

Data Backup

As users work at various computers on a network or take their computers home, IntelliMirror can manage their documents and data for them. If users' machines crash, or if they are unexpectedly away from their computer, they will still have access to the information they need. Using the user data management feature of IntelliMirror also means that if a user's data is corrupted on one machine, it can be restored, using the copy of the data on the network.

IntelliMirror technologies in Windows 2000 enable users to easily store and synchronize their data in a specified network location. **Folder redirection** can be done seamlessly via the use of a group policy, or a user can manually set this up. Typically, a user's My Documents folder or other important data folders will be redirected to a share on a Windows 2000 Server on the network. In this case, when a user saves a document to the My Documents folder, it will automatically be saved both on the local machine and on the network share, if the user is on the network. If the user is not on the network, the document will only be saved to the user's hard drive. This process is part of the new offline files feature of Windows 2000, and is discussed in detail in Chapter 9. Then, when the user joins the network again, the local version of the document will automatically synchronize with the network version (see Hands-on Project 15-1). If the network version of the document has also been modified during that time, the user will be prompted as to whether to overwrite the local version, overwrite the network version of the document, or save both copies of the document. Synchronization of data between a local machine and a network share is demonstrated in Figure 15-1. To manually synchronize a file or folder when a user rejoins the network, he or she can highlight the file or folder to be synchronized in Windows Explorer. Then, the user must select Synchronize from the Tools menu, and the synchronization process take place.

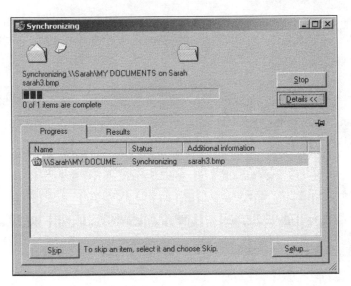

Figure 15-1   Making a file available offline

If one of the copies unexpectedly becomes corrupt or is missing, it will automatically be restored from the existing version of the document. This recovery is transparent to the user.

CAUTION

> Administrators will need to consider the cost of hardware and maintenance of the servers that back up user data. A network's bandwidth could also be affected by the synchronization of users' data; that is, the synchronization process can increase network traffic, thus slowing down the network.

PC Configuration Recovery

As with user profiles in Windows NT 4.0, personalized machine settings can be accessed by Windows 2000 Professional users from whatever machine they use on the network, through the user settings management feature of IntelliMirror. Therefore, if a user's machine crashes or is unavailable, his or her workstation configuration can be easily installed onto a new machine. Personalized settings are customizations of the operating system and applications, including language settings, desktop schemes, and custom dictionaries, and are provided to users when they log on to the system, regardless of which physical computer they use.

Application Installation and Repair

Users may also encounter circumstances in which they need to restore applications they have installed. If users inadvertently remove essential application or system files, or if their systems crash, they can use the software installation and maintenance feature of IntelliMirror to rebuild their machines with the same applications they had previously. By using the **Windows Installer Service (WIS)**, they can reinstall their applications and repair applications seamlessly

15

(see Hands-on Project 15-2 to change or remove an application using WIS via the Control Panel). Restorable applications include software, software upgrades, and even operating system upgrades.

> Windows Installer can also be used to create a software package for end users. Review Windows 2000 Help and the *Windows 2000 Resource Kit* for additional details.

MICROSOFT BACKUP UTILITY

Microsoft IntelliMirror technologies are quite beneficial in the area of backing up user data, applications, and personalized settings, using network shares and policies. However, there are also methods of backing up a PC by using external tools, such as:

- Tape drives
- External hard disks
- Zip or Jaz drives
- Recordable CD-ROM drives
- Logical drives

The **Backup utility** in Windows 2000 provides the easiest method of backing up data onto any one of these media or onto a server on a network (see Hands-on Project 15-3). The Windows 2000 Backup utility can be used for backing up and restoring data and the system configuration. There are three options within Backup:

- Back up programs and files
- Restore programs and files
- Create an **Emergency Repair Disk (ERD)**, a disk that contains configuration information about your PC, which is used to restore a PC if Windows will not start or the system files are corrupt or missing (try Hands-on Project 15-4).

Figure 15-2 shows the initial view of Backup. Using this tool is a good precautionary element in the disaster recovery process. The restore and repair options will be discussed later in this chapter.

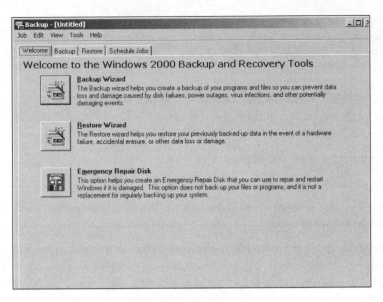

Figure 15-2   Windows 2000 Backup utility

Using the Backup utility, there are two methods you can use to back up your data. You can use the Backup Wizard, or you can click the Backup tab to manually set your backup options (see Figure 15-3). The Wizard takes you, step by step, through the process of defining and scheduling (if necessary) your backups. Hands-on Project 15-5 provides instructions on using the Backup Wizard to schedule a backup.

15

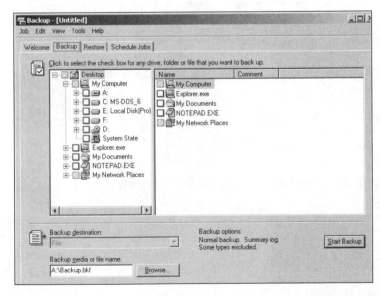

Figure 15-3   The Backup tab of the Windows 2000 Backup utility

TIP You must be an Administrator or a member of the Backup Operators group to back up or restore files using the Backup utility.

To start the Backup utility, choose Start, Programs, Accessories, System Tools, Backup (alternately, you can select Start, Run, and then type *ntbackup* and press Enter). Then, whether you use the wizard or the Backup tab, you will need to choose what to back up:

- Back up everything on the computer

- Back up selected files, drives, or network data

- Only back up the **system state data** (data about the current state and configuration of the operating system)

The first option backs up all the data physically connected to your computer. The second option allows you to choose which directories or drives you want to back up, as shown in Figure 15-4. The third option only backs up the system's boot files, COM settings, and Registry data (see Figure 15-5).

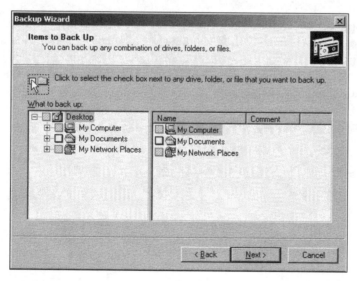

Figure 15-4   List of items to back up, using the Backup utility

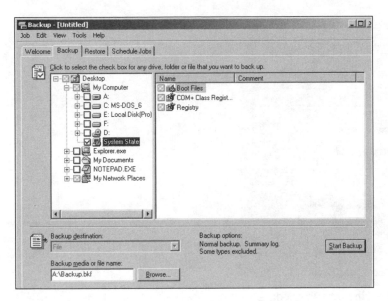

Figure 15-5   Selecting to back up system state data

In addition to choosing what to back up, you can also specify the **backup type**:

- *Copy backup:* Backs up all selected files but does not mark them as being backed up

- *Normal (or full) backup:* Backs up all selected files and marks them as being backed up

- *Daily backup:* Backs up only the selected files that have been created or modified the day that the backup is being performed but does not mark the files as being backed up

- *Differential backup:* Backs up only the selected files that have been created or modified since the last full backup, but does not mark the files as being backed up

- *Incremental backup:* Backs up only the selected files that have been created or modified since the last normal or incremental backup and marks the files as being backed up

TIP   When you use the Backup Wizard and choose either "Back up everything" or "Back up selected files," the backup type defaults to Normal or Incremental, respectively. You can change the backup type from the Completing Backup Wizard screen by clicking the Advanced button.

As previously mentioned, the third option, backing up the system state data, provides a way to back up the Registry, the COM+ Class Registration database, and system boot files. By backing up these files, you can restore your PC's configuration to its original state if neces-sary. Figure 15-6 shows the system state backup process at work.

15

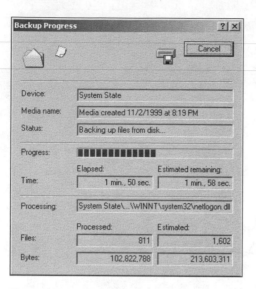

Figure 15-6   Backing up system data

 TIP   When the system state data is backed up, a copy of your Registry files (default, SAM, security, software, and system) is also saved in the \Winnt\Repair\Regback directory. Advanced users can use these files to restore their Registry files manually without restoring the entire system state. (See Chapter 13 for more information on working with the Registry.)

REPAIRING WINDOWS 2000 PROFESSIONAL

Disaster protection is important, but when catastrophe occurs, you'll need to be prepared. If system files become corrupt or are accidentally deleted, or if certain drivers or services are keeping the operating system from loading, you have several options for repairing or restoring your PC:

- Safe Mode (discussed in Chapter 14)
- Recovery Console
- Emergency repair process
- Remote OS installation

These options (except for Safe Mode) are discussed in the following sections.

Recovery Console

Expert users and system administrators may want to utilize the Windows 2000 **Recovery Console** for more precise control over the troubleshooting and repair process (see Hands-on Projects 15-6 and 15-7). If you know which services or drivers may be causing the problem, instead of running the PC in Safe Mode, you can simply use the Recovery Console to disable those specific services or drivers. You can also use the Recovery Console to repair a corrupted Master Boot Record or to copy needed files from a floppy disk, CD-ROM, or a network share to your PC.

You can access the Recovery Console in one of two ways:

- From a command prompt, change directories to your Windows 2000 CD. Run *\i386\winnt32.exe /cmdcons* to install the Recovery Console. When you reboot your machine, you'll notice a new option for starting Windows 2000 Professional with the Recovery Console.

- Use the Windows 2000 CD or startup disks to start your computer. Select the Recovery Console option when you are prompted to choose repair options.

When the Recovery Console opens, you must specify the Windows 2000 client you want to log on to, then you must log on as the Administrator. Table 15-1 lists the commands available from the Recovery Console. To view the command-line parameters and uses for each of these commands, see "Recovery Console commands" in the Windows 2000 Professional online Help.

Table 15-1   Recovery Console Options

Command	Description
attrib	Changes the attributes of a file or directory
batch	Executes the commands specified in a text file
chdir (cd)	Changes directories or displays the current directory name
chkdsk	Checks and reports on the status of the disk
cls	Windows 2000 starts while logging all of the drivers and services that were and were not loaded during the boot process
copy	Copies files
delete (del)	Deletes files
dir	Displays the directory structure
disable	Disables a service or driver
diskpart	Manages partitions
enable	Enables or starts a service or driver
exit	Exits the Recovery Console and restarts the computer
expand	Extracts files from compressed files
fixboot	Writes a new partition boot sector onto the system partition
fixmbr	Repairs the Master Boot Record
format	Formats a disk
help	Displays a list of commands available in the Recovery Console
listsvc	Lists the services available
logon	Logs on to Windows 2000
map	Displays the drive letter mappings

15

Table 15-1   Recovery Console Options (continued)

Command	Description
mkdir (md)	Creates a new folder
more	Displays a text file
rmdir (rd)	Deletes a folder
rename (ren)	Renames a file
set	Displays and sets console environment variables
systemroot	Sets the current folder to the Systemroot folder

Emergency Repair Process

If your problem is caused by corrupt or missing system files, your startup environment, or your partition boot sector, you may want to use the emergency repair process. As with Windows NT 4.0, Windows 2000 lets you create an Emergency Repair Disk (ERD) for repairing your system (see Hands-on Project 15-4). To use the ERD to fully recover your system and return it to its last functional state, you must have created this disk before the system crashed. You can run the emergency repair process without the disk, but all of your personalized settings and updates will most likely need to be reinstalled.

To use the ERD, you will need to reboot your machine with the Windows 2000 Setup disks or the Windows 2000 Professional CD. During Setup, you will be asked if you would like to install Windows 2000. Press Enter to start the installation process. Then you will be prompted as to whether you want to reinstall Windows 2000 or repair an existing version of Windows 2000. Press R to repair Windows 2000. Press R again to repair your system using the emergency repair process. You'll then have two options for repairing Windows 2000:

- *Fast repair:* Requires no user interaction; automatically attempts to repair problems related to the Registry, system files, the boot volume, and your startup environment

- *Manual repair:* Enables the user to choose to repair to the Registry, system files, the boot volume, or startup environment

You can then start the repair process, using the ERD if you have one. If the emergency repair process is successful, the PC will automatically reboot, and everything should be in working order again. As a last resort, if the emergency repair process cannot repair the system, you may want to consider reinstalling Windows 2000. However, this method is time-consuming, and you may need to reinstall many of your applications and upgrades.

Remote OS Installation

Administrators can also enable **remote OS installation**, which can be used along with the Microsoft IntelliMirror technologies to recover an entire PC, including a user's data, individual configurations, and applications. Remote OS installation is a component of the optional Windows 2000 Server **Remote Installation Services (RIS)** (see Chapter 2), which allows a user to remotely rebuild the computer's entire image across the network. No on-site technical support is necessary, so this cuts down on administrative costs and minimizes the downtime of the user's machine.

Client computers that can participate in a remote OS installation must have a **PXE (Pre-boot Execution)** remote boot ROM. Network PCs and computers that comply with an industry-standard hardware guide called PC98 will have this. If the computer does not have the PXE remote boot ROM, then an RIS remote boot disk can be used along with a supported PCI-based network interface card (NIC). These client machines must also use a DHCP (Dynamic Host Configuration Protocol) server on the network.

When a user starts a client with either the PXE remote boot ROM or an RIS remote boot disk, the client can request an installation of Windows 2000 Professional from a remote RIS server. The server will, in turn, provide one of the following types of installations:

- *CD-based:* Similar to installing the OS with a CD, but the source files are on another machine (the RIS server) on the network

- *Remote Installation Preparation (RIPrep) desktop image:* After installing Windows 2000 Professional, installing applications, and making configuration changes on one workstation, an administrator clones the image of that machine and replicates it to an RIS server. The entire **Remote Installation Preparation (RIPrep)** image can then be deployed to other workstations with remote OS installation.

Once the images are on the RIS server, it can be used to install those images to any client that is remote-boot enabled. A user can initiate a network service boot by pressing the F12 key when booting up, at which time the RIS server will install the Client Installation Wizard. This wizard uses Group Policies to give the user a list of available installation options from Active Directory. If the user has only one installation option available, the user will simply be prompted with a confirmation screen, and the installation will begin. Otherwise, the four installation options are:

- *Automatic Setup:* Prompts the user with a list of OS options if there is one, then an unattended installation begins

- *Custom Setup:* Allows the user to specify the computer name and the location where the computer account will reside in Active Directory

- *Restart a Previous Setup Attempt:* Restarts the remote OS installation process if a previous installation attempt failed

- *Maintenance and Troubleshooting:* Provides the user with access to third-party maintenance, pre-OS installation maintenance, and troubleshooting tools

15

CHAPTER SUMMARY

❏ IntelliMirror consists of a set of features within Windows 2000 that utilizes policies, folder redirection, and the Windows Installer Service (WIS) for backing up and restoring users' data, personalized settings, and applications. There are a number of methods for backing up and restoring a client PC by using user and group policies, Windows Installer, and folder redirection.

❏ Windows 2000 includes built-in backup features. You should thoroughly understand the Backup utility and how it can be used to back up and restore a PC.

❏ You can use the emergency repair process to create and use an Emergency Repair Disk (ERD) to repair a system that has failed.

❏ You can install and use the Recovery Console to recover user settings in the event of a system failure.

❏ You can use the Remote Installation Services (RIS) for a complete remote system restoration.

KEY TERMS

backup type — A backup configuration that determines how often data is backed up and the way old and new files should be handled. The types of backups are copy, daily, differential, incremental, and normal.

Backup utility — A tool that enables users to back up and restore their data and system configurations in case of a hardware or software failure.

copy backup — A method of backing up all selected files without marking them as being backed up.

daily backup — A method of backing up only the selected files that have been created or modified on the day that the backup is being performed. They are not marked as being backed up.

differential backup — A method of backing up selected files that have been created or modified since the last full backup. They are not marked as being backed up.

Emergency Repair Disk (ERD) — A disk that contains configuration information about your PC. It can be used to restore a PC if Windows will not start or the system files are corrupt or missing.

folder redirection — A component of IntelliMirror technologies that uses group policies to place specified user folders on a share on the network.

incremental backup — A method of backing up selected files that have been created or modified since the last normal or incremental backup. These files are marked as being backed up.

IntelliMirror — A set of features within Windows 2000 that utilizes policies, folder redirection, and the Windows Installer Service (WIS) for backing up and restoring users' data, personalized settings, and applications.

normal (or full) backup — A method of backing up all selected files and marking them as being backed up.

PXE (Pre-boot Execution) — A standard environment in PC98-compliant computers and network computers that can be used for a remote OS installation.

Recovery Console — A command-line interface that provides administrative tools useful for recovering a system that is not booting correctly.

remote OS installation — A component of Remote Installation Services (RIS) that can install Windows 2000 Professional on remote-boot-enabled PCs across a network.

Remote Installation Services (RIS) — An optional service in Windows 2000 Server that works with various other services to enable remote installations, including a remote operating system installation.

Remote Installation Preparation (RIPrep) — A type of installation used with remote OS installation whereby an administrator can take an entire image of one Windows 2000 Professional machine and install that image onto other workstations.

system state data — A collection of system-specific data that can be backed up and restored using the Windows 2000 Backup utility.

Windows Installer Service (WIS) — A Windows 2000 component that manages the installation and removal of applications by applying a set of centrally defined setup rules during the installation process.

REVIEW QUESTIONS

1. Which of the following types of media can be used to back up a user's data? (Choose all that apply.)

   a. tape drives

   b. external hard drives

   c. logical drives

   d. network shares

2. The Recovery Console can be used to stop and start services. True or False?

3. Which of the following could *not* participate in remote OS installation?

   a. a network computer with no RIS remote boot disk

   b. a PC with a PXE-based remote boot ROM, but with no RIS remote boot disk

   c. a PC with an RIS remote boot disk, but with no PXE-based remote boot ROM

   d. an undocked laptop with an RIS remote boot disk

4. Which of the following backup types backs up only the selected files that have been created or modified since the last normal or incremental backup? (Choose all that apply.)

   a. normal

   b. daily

   c. differential

   d. incremental

15

5. Which of the following tools can you use to create an Emergency Repair Disk?

   a. Add/Remove Programs applet in the Control Panel

   b. Backup utility

   c. Disk Manager

   d. Disk Cleanup

6. Which of the following boot options is used to send debugging information from one computer to another computer on the network?

   a. Last Known Good Configuration

   b. Safe Mode with networking

   c. Enable boot logging

   d. Debugging Mode

7. John has offline folders set up to synchronize with his machine, and he is currently not connected to the network. John is working on a file that he will need to synchronize with the network version when he logs on to the network. Unknown to him, Libby has just updated the network version of that same document. When John logs on to the network, what will happen when he tries to synchronize his local files with the network version of the files?

   a. John's file will overwrite Libby's version.

   b. Libby's version will overwrite John's version.

   c. John will be prompted as to whether he wants to update the network version or his local version.

   d. John's version and Libby's version will merge into a combined document.

8. Which of the following IntelliMirror technologies is associated with recovering a user's personal desktop settings?

   a. user data management

   b. software installation

   c. user setting management

   d. user desktop management

9. Which of the following items are backed up when backing up the system state data, using the Backup utility? (Choose all that apply.)

   a. COM+ Class Registration database

   b. Registry files

   c. system boot files

   d. the \Winnt\System32 directory

10. Folder redirection is set up using the Synchronization Manager. True or False?

11. When the _____ repair option is run, the system automatically attempts to repair problems related to the Registry, system files, the boot volume, and the startup environment.

12. Which of the following backup types marks backed up files as being backed up? (Choose all that apply.)

    a. copy

    b. daily

    c. differential

    d. incremental

    e. normal

13. Which of the following users can use the Backup utility to back up secured files on a Windows 2000 Professional computer? (Choose all that apply.)

    a. a member of the Administrators group

    b. a member of the Backup Operators group

    c. any user that has Log On Locally rights

    d. a member of the Backup utility group

14. When the system state data is backed up, a copy of the Registry files is copied into the _____ directory.

15. A Windows 2000 ERD is used in which of the following?

    a. Recovery Console

    b. emergency repair process, Fast Repair

    c. full backup

    d. Registry restore process using Regedit

16. You can install the Recovery Console by using the Winnt32.exe program on the Windows 2000 CD with the _____ switch.

17. If you wanted to use the Emergency Repair Disk (ERD), which of the following could you use to boot your machine? (Choose all that apply.)

    a. Windows 2000 CD

    b. Windows 2000 Setup disks

    c. an Emergency Repair Disk

    d. a system boot disk

18. You can use the Recovery Console to create an Emergency Repair Disk. True or False?

19. _____ can be used along with IntelliMirror technologies to recover an entire PC's image.

20. You need to create an Emergency Repair Disk to perform the emergency repair process. True or False?

21. In order to use the Remote Installation Services (RIS), a machine must be a DHCP client. True or False?

15

22. Which of the following are types of installations that an RIS server can offer a client?

    a. client-based

    b. RIPrep desktop image

    c. CD-based

    d. network-based

23. A user can initiate a network service boot by pressing the _____ key when booting up.

24. Which of the following tools does an RIS server install first on a client PC that is requesting a remote OS installation?

    a. Recovery Console

    b. Client Installation Wizard

    c. Windows 2000 Professional

    d. PXE Remote Boot ROM

25. Which of the following setup options can an RIS server provide for a remote OS installation via the Client Installation Wizard? (Choose all that apply.)

    a. Automatic Setup

    b. Custom Setup

    c. Restart a Previous Setup Attempt

    d. Maintenance and Troubleshooting

HANDS-ON PROJECTS

Project 15-1

To enable your files to be synchronized with the network's copy of your files when you log off:

1. Open Synchronization Manager (**Start, Programs, Accessories, Windows Explorer, Tools, Synchronize**).

2. Click **Setup**, then click the **Logon/Logoff** tab (see Figure 15-7).

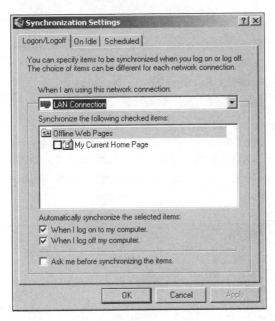

Figure 15-7   Synchronization Manager Setup, Logon/Logoff tab

3. In the **When I am using this network connection** list, select the network connection you want to use.

4. In the **Synchronize the following checked items** list, select the files or folders you want to synchronize when you log on to and log off the network.

5. Under **Automatically synchronize the selected items**, select both **When I log on to my computer** and **When I log off my computer**.

6. Click **OK** to close the Synchronization Settings dialog box.

Project 15-2

To install packages using the Windows Installer packages:

1. Open the **Control Panel** (**Start**, **Settings**, **Control Panel**).

2. Double-click **Add/Remove Programs**.

3. Depending on whether you want to change an application or remove it, click the **Change** or **Remove** button.

4. Follow the prompts to make the necessary changes.

5. Close any open dialog boxes or windows and the Add/Remove Programs applet. You may also need to restart your computer if prompted.

Project 15-3

To back up the contents of your My Documents folder using the Windows Backup utility:

1. Choose **Start**, **Programs**, **Accessories**, **System Tools**, **Backup**.

2. Click the **Backup** tab.

3. Check the box next to **My Documents**. Notice that a gray check box automatically appears next to the drive containing My Documents and that the check boxes next to each of the subdirectories under My Documents are automatically checked.

4. In the bottom-left corner, change path in the **Backup media or file name** field to **c:\backup.bkf** (see Figure 15-8).

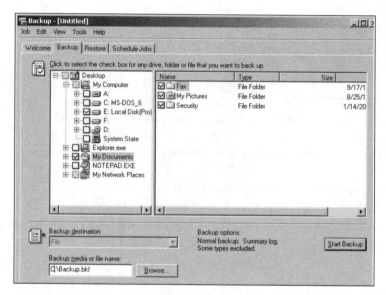

Figure 15-8   Backing up My Documents and specifying the backup location

5. Look over your options, then click **Start Backup**.

6. When the backup is complete, close the Backup utility.

Project 15-4

To create an Emergency Repair Disk:

1. Open the Backup utility (**Start**, **Programs**, **Accessories**, **System Tools**, **Backup**).

2. Click **Emergency Repair Disk**.

3. You will be prompted to insert a floppy disk into drive A. Check the box to also back up the Registry (see Figure 15-9). Then insert a blank formatted disk into drive A. Click **OK**.

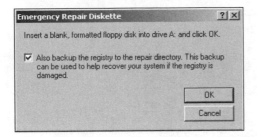

Figure 15-9   Creating an Emergency Repair Disk

4. When the files are finished copying, click **OK**.
5. Close the Backup utility.

Project 15-5

To schedule a backup of your My Documents folder, using the Windows Backup utility:

1. Choose **Start**, **Programs**, **Accessories**, **System Tools**, **Backup**.
2. Click the **Backup Wizard** button.
3. Windows will display a Welcome screen. Click **Next**.
4. At the next screen, select the **Back up selected files, drives, or network data** radio button (see Figure 15-10). Click **Next**.

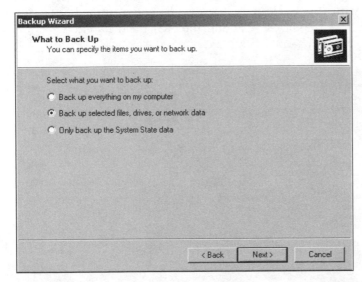

Figure 15-10   Backing up selected files, drives, or network data

5. Select the items to be backed up (refer to Figure 15-4). Click **Next**.
6. In the **Backup media or file name** field, change the path to **c:\backup.bkf**. Click **Next**.

7. On the Completing the Backup Wizard page, click the **Advanced** button, and select **Incremental** from the list (see Figure 15-11). Click **Next**.

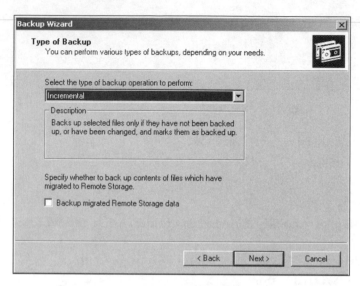

Figure 15-11   Selecting Incremental backups

8. Read through your verification and compression options, then click **Next**.

9. Under **If the archive media already contains backups**, select **Replace the data on the media with this backup**. Notice that the option at the bottom is no longer dimmed. Check the check box so that only the owner and administrators can access the backups (see Figure 15-12). Click **Next**.

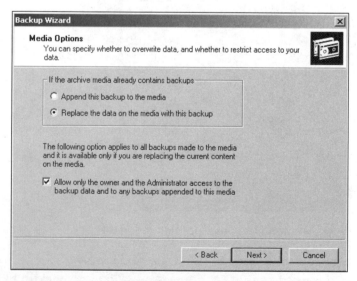

Figure 15-12   Selecting media options

10. Accept the default labels. Click **Next**.

11. In the **When to Back Up** dialog box, choose **Later**. When prompted for your account information, enter a username and password of an Administrator or Backup Operator. Click **OK**.

12. In the **Job name** field, type **Daily Backup of My Documents**. Then click **Set Schedule**.

13. Under **Schedule Task**, choose **Daily** from the drop-down list and set the start time (see Figure 15-13).

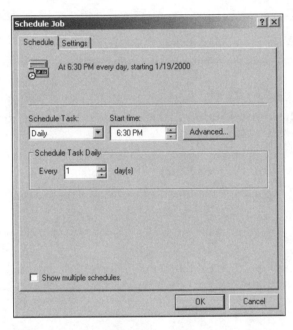

Figure 15-13   Scheduling a backup

15

14. Click the **Settings** tab to review your options, but accept the defaults. Click **OK** to continue. Then click **Next**.

15. Review your settings, and click **Finish** to schedule the backup.

16. Close the Backup utility.

Project 15-6

To install the Recovery Console:

1. From a Command Prompt (**Start**, **Programs**, **Accessories**, **Command Prompt**), browse to the i386 folder of a Windows 2000 Professional CD.

2. Run **winnt32 /cmdcons**.

3. You will be prompted by a Windows 2000 Setup dialog box explaining how to use the Recovery Console (see Figure 15-14). Click **Yes** to install it.

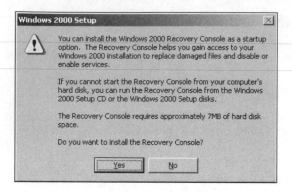

Figure 15-14   Setting up the Windows 2000 Recovery Console

4. The necessary files will be copied to your system. When finished, click **OK**.

5. Choose **Start**, **Shutdown**. Choose **Restart** from the menu, and click **OK**.

6. When prompted, choose **Microsoft Windows 2000 Recovery Console** from the list of available operating systems.

7. You will be prompted for which operating system you'd like to log on to. Type the number for your operating system, and press **Enter**.

8. You will then be prompted for the local administrator password. Type that in, and press **Enter**.

9. Type **help** at the command prompt for a list of commands that you can use in the Recovery Console.

10. Type **exit** at the command prompt to exit and restart Windows. This time, choose your Windows 2000 operating system to boot up.

Project 15-7

To uninstall the Recovery Console:

1. Double-click **My Computer**. Choose **Tools**, **Folder Options**. Then click the **View** tab.

2. Click **Show hidden files and folders**, and then clear the **Hide protected operating system files check box** (see Figure 15-15). Click **OK**.

3. Browse to the root directory, and delete the **\Cmdcons** folder and the file called **Cmldr**.

4. On your computer's boot disk, locate the **Boot.ini** file, right-click it, select **Properties**, and deselect the **Read-only** check box and click **OK**.

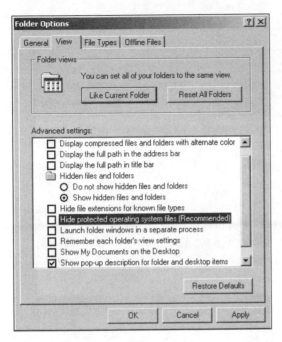

Figure 15-15 Setting advanced file and folder settings

Before continuing, copy your Boot.ini file and rename the copy Boot.bak. You can use this file later if the Boot.ini file should become damaged. Be extra careful with the next step to make sure that you delete only the line for the Recovery Console. An incorrect Boot.ini file could keep your computer from restarting.

5. Using Notepad (**Start**, **Programs**, **Accessories**, **Notepad**), open the **Boot.ini** file in the root directory. Remove the entry for the Recovery Console. For example, you would need to delete the last line in the following sample Boot.ini file:

```
[boot loader]
timeout=10
default=multi(0)disk(0)rdisk(0)partition(1)\WINNT
[operating systems]
C:\="Microsoft Windows"
multi(0)disk(0)rdisk(0)partition(1)\WINNT="Microsoft Windows
  2000 Professional" /fastdetect
C:\CMDCONS\BOOTSECT.DAT="Microsoft Windows 2000 Recovery
  Console" /cmdcons
```

6. Save the file and close it.

7. Close any open windows.

15

CASE PROJECTS

1. You're in charge of backing up all of your organization's data stored on Windows 2000 Professional machines. Your organization consists of 2500 users, and 500 of those users usually dial in from home. All of your users use Windows 2000 Professional. Which of the following backup methods will you use across your organization? Choose all that apply, and justify your choice(s).

   a. tape backups

   b. Zip drives

   c. folder redirection

   d. remote OS installation

2. Describe the three key features of IntelliMirror, and describe a scenario for each feature that explains how that feature reduces the total cost of ownership (TCO).

3. Describe a situation in which it would make more sense to use the Recovery Console than the emergency repair process.

16

TROUBLESHOOTING
WINDOWS 2000

After reading this chapter and completing the exercises, you will be able to:

♦ Collect documentation about your systems to aid in troubleshooting and preventing problems

♦ Review common-sense approaches to troubleshooting

♦ Troubleshoot general problems with Windows 2000

♦ Use some of the troubleshooting tools of Windows 2000

Windows 2000 troubleshooting is an important and vast area. In this chapter, you learn how to detect, isolate, and eliminate problems with installation, printing, remote access, the network, disks, and other aspects of a Windows 2000 system.

In addition to the techniques discussed in this chapter, important troubleshooting options and features of Windows 2000 have been covered in earlier chapters. The Registry is a common location in which problems occur as well as a source for implementing solutions. Working with the Registry is discussed in Chapter 13. The Windows 2000 boot process is often a source of problems. These problems and their respective solutions are discussed in Chapter 14. Catastrophic events, virus infections, or simple hardware failure can leave you without a functioning system. Disaster recovery and backups are discussed in Chapter 15. Keep the troubleshooting advice provided in the previous three chapters in mind when attempting to prevent and resolve problems involving Windows 2000.

GENERAL PRINCIPLES OF TROUBLESHOOTING

When trouble arises in Windows 2000, you need to take action to resolve the issue as quickly as possible. Troubleshooting is the art and science of systematically eliminating problems in a computer system. Although troubleshooting may sound exciting, in reality it is usually a fairly tedious process. In the following sections, we outline some procedures and common-sense guidelines that should improve your troubleshooting skills and help you keep downtime to a minimum.

Collecting Information

The first rule of troubleshooting is that you can never have too much information. In fact, information is your best weapon, not just for resolving problems, but also for preventing them in the first place. Useful information typically falls into three areas: details about your system (hardware and software), details about previous troubleshooting, maintenance, and configuration activities, and details about the current problem.

Collecting information about your system's hardware and software is a preventive mainte-nance task. It requires that you gather all pertinent information and keep it in an accessible form and location. We call this collection a **computer information file (CIF)**. A good CIF provides a detailed collection of all information related to the hardware and software prod-ucts that compose your computer (and even your entire network). A CIF is not just a single file, but an ever-expanding accumulation of data sheets sorted into related groupings. Your CIF should be stored in a protected area (such as a safe or fireproof vault) that can be accessed in the event of an emergency (a bank's safety deposit box won't allow you to get at the infor-mation at three o'clock in the morning). Obviously, constructing a CIF from scratch is a lengthy process, but one that will be rewarded with averted problems, easy reconfigurations, or simplified replacement of failed components.

Some of the important items to include in your CIF are:

- Platform, type, brand, and model number of each component
- Complete manufacturer specifications
- Configuration settings, including jumpers and DIP switches, plus what each set-ting means, including IRQs, DMA addresses, memory base addresses, and port assignments
- Manuals, users' guides, or configuration sheets
- Version of BIOS, driver software, patches, fixes, etc., with floppy copies
- Printed and floppy copies of all parameter and initialization files
- Detailed directory structure printout
- Name and version of all software
- Network-assigned names, locations, and addresses

- Status of empty ports, upgrade options, or expansion capabilities

- System requirements, such as the manufacturer's listed minimum requirements for its operating system, driver, applications, and hardware

- Warranty information, such as service phone numbers and e-mail addresses

- Complete technical support contact information, including support Web site URLs

- Error log with detailed and dated entries of problems and solutions

- Date and location of last complete backup, and other backup items

- Network layout and cabling map

- Copies of all software, operating system, and driver installation or source CDs and/or diskettes

Each of these items should be dated and initialed. However, your CIF is not complete with only hardware and software details. You should also include the nonphysical characteristics of your system, such as:

- Information services present, such as Web, FTP, e-mail, newsgroups, and message boards

- Important productivity services, such as productivity suites (Microsoft Office), collaboration utilities, whiteboard applications, and video conferencing products

- Plans for future service deployment

- A mapping or listing of related hardware and software for each service or application present on the system

- Structure of authorized access and security measures

- Training schedule

- Maintenance schedule

- Backup schedule

- Contact information for all system administrators

- Personnel organization or management hierarchy

- Workgroup arrangements

- Online data storage locations

- In-house content and delivery conventions

- Authorship rights and restrictions

- Troubleshooting procedures

Neither of these lists is exhaustive. As you operate and maintain your systems you'll discover other important items to add to the CIF.

16

Remember, if you don't document it, then you won't be able to find it when you really need it. A good way to keep the CIF current is to add, remove, or modify its contents each time you make a system modification. Performing a quarterly or semiannual audit of the CIF is not a bad idea, either.

It is essential that the content of the CIF be thorough and up to date. Without thorough, specific, and accurate information about the products, configuration, setup, and problems associated with your network, the CIF will be useless. Keep in mind that the time you spend organizing your CIF will reduce the time required to locate information when you really need it. It is wise to create a correlation system so that you can easily associate items in the CIF with the actual component, using, for example, an alphanumeric labeling system. For instructions on how to create a CIF, see Hands-on Project 16-2.

 We recommend maintaining both a printed/written version and an electronic version of the CIF. Every time a change, update, or correction occurs, it should be documented in the electronic version, and a printout made and stored. Murphy's Law guarantees that the moment you need your electronic data most is when your system will not function.

Common-Sense Troubleshooting Guidelines

When problems occur, you would like to be at your sharpest. However, by a corollary to Murphy's Law, you'll probably find that problems tend to occur when you are stressed, when you are short on time, or when it is just generally inconvenient. If you take the time to keep your CIF up to date and keep the following common-sense guidelines in mind, you'll take some of the headache out of troubleshooting, and be better prepared to resolve problems quickly.

- *Be patient:* Anger, frustration, hostility, and frantic impatience usually cause problems to intensify rather than dissipate.

- *Be familiar with your system's hardware and software:* If you don't know what the normal baselines for your system are, you may not know when a problem is solved or when new problems surface. (See Chapter 11 for information on creating baselines.)

- *Attempt to isolate the problem:* When possible, eliminate segments or components that are functioning properly, thus narrowing the range of suspected problem sources.

- *Divide and conquer:* Disconnect, one at a time, as many nonessential devices as possible, to narrow down the investigation.

- *Eliminate suspects:* Move suspect components, such as printers, monitors, mice, or keyboards, to a known good computer to see if they work in the new location.

- *Undo the most recent change:* If you have recently made a change to your system, the simplest fix may be to undo the most recent alteration, upgrade, or change.

- *Investigate the most common points of failure:* The most active or sensitive components are the most common points of failure—these include hard drives, cables, and connectors.

- *Recheck items that have caused problems before:* As the old axiom goes, "history repeats itself" (and usually right in your own backyard).

- *Try the easy and quick fix first:* Try the easy fixes before moving on to the more time-consuming, difficult, or even destructive measures.

- *Let the fault guide you:* The adage, "Where there is smoke, there is fire" applies to computer problems as well as to life in general. Investigate components and system areas associated with the suspected fault.

- *Make changes one at a time:* A step-by-step process enables you to clearly distinguish the solution when you stumble upon it.

- *Repeat the failure:* Often, being able to repeat an error is the only way to locate it. Transient and inconsistent faults are difficult to find due to their "now you see it, now you don't" nature.

- *Keep a detailed log of errors and attempted solutions:* Keep track of everything you do (both successful and failed attempts). This will prove an invaluable resource when an error occurs again on the same or a different system, or when the same system experiences a related problem.

- *Learn from mistakes (your own and others'):* Studying the mistakes of others can save you from making the same mistakes; a wise person looks at failures as aids to finding a better solution.

- *Experiment:* Try similar tasks to see if a pattern develops.

There is probably not much in this list of common-sense items that you don't already know. The hardest part is remembering them when you are in the heat of a crisis.

TROUBLESHOOTING TOOLS

16

Becoming familiar with the repair and troubleshooting tools native to Windows 2000 can save you countless hours in troubleshooting. In the next sections, we detail how to use the Event Viewer and the Computer Management tools.

Event Viewer

The **Event Viewer** is used to view system messages regarding the failure or success of various key occurrences within the Windows 2000 environment (see Figure 16-1). The items recorded in the Event Viewer logs inform you of system drivers or service failures as well as security problems or ill-behaved applications (see Hands-on Project 16-1).

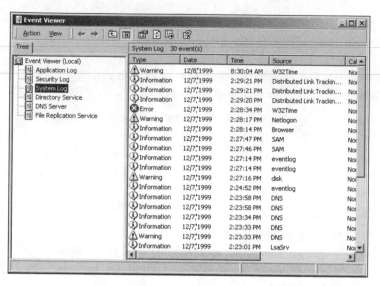

Figure 16-1 Event Viewer with System Log selected

Located in the Administrative Tools section of the Control Panel and Start menu, the Event Viewer is used to view the logs created automatically by Windows 2000. These logs are:

- **System log:** The System log records information and alerts related to the Windows 2000 internal processes, including hardware and operating system errors, warnings, and general information messages.

- **Security log:** The Security log records security-related events, including audit events of failed logons, user-right alterations, and attempted object access without sufficient permission.

- **Application log:** The Application log records application events, alerts, and system messages.

Each log records a different type of event, but all the logs collect the same metainformation about each event: date, time, source, category, event, user ID, and computer. Each logged event (Figure 16-2 shows the properties of a logged event) includes some level of detail about the error, ranging from an error code number to a detailed description with a memory HEX buffer capture. For example, Figure 16-2 shows an event detail involving a time problem from a domain controller; it states how to rectify the problem with a command, and includes the HEX result that caused the problem (however, the HEX information listed is of no help to you for this specific problem). Most system errors, including Stop errors that result in the blue screen, are recorded in the System log. This allows you to review the time and circumstances of a system failure. The details in the Event Viewer can often be used as evidence in your search for the cause of a problem. However, the event details offer little information on how to actually resolve a problem.

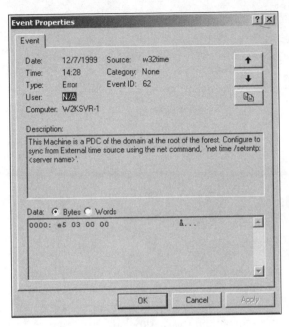

Figure 16-2 Event Viewer event detail

Computer Management Tool

Windows 2000 combines the robustness of Windows NT with the ease of configuration of Windows 98 Plug and Play. An added advancement in hardware support, and a useful side effect of Plug and Play, is the simplicity of the troubleshooting tools for nearly every aspect of Windows 2000. Most of these tools are collected into a single interface called the Computer Management tool (see Figure 16-3), found in the Administrative Tools section of the Control Panel and Start menu.

16

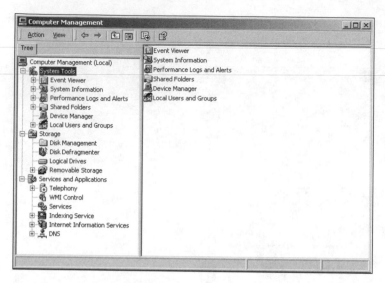

Figure 16-3 Computer Management

The Computer Management tool includes many tools similar to those in Windows NT and Windows 98, as well as several new utilities. Grouping all of these utilities in a single interface makes locating and resolving problems on key system components easier (see Hands-on Project 16-3). The Computer Management console is divided into three sections: System Tools, Storage, and Services and Applications. The System Tools section contains six tools:

- *Event Viewer:* Used to view system messages regarding the failure and/or success of various key occurrences within the Windows 2000 environment. Details about system errors, security issues, and application activities are recorded in the logs viewed through the Event Viewer. See the description of the Event Viewer earlier in this chapter. Hands-on Project 16-1 shows you how to use the Event Viewer.

- *System Information:* Used to gain configuration information and status summaries for the computer and operating system environment. You can quickly discover information such as system model numbers, free IRQs, sharing conflicts, and component configurations. This tool is invaluable when attempting to add new hardware into your system. Hands-on Project 16-2 shows you one way to use this tool.

- *Performance Logs and Alerts:* Another means to access the performance monitoring tool of Windows 2000 (see Chapter 11 for examples and hands-on projects involving this tool).

- *Shared Folders:* Used to view the shared folders on the local system. This interface shows hidden shares, current sessions, and open files. This tool allows you to view and alter the share configuration settings for user limit, caching, and permissions.

- *Device Manager:* Used to view and alter current hardware configurations of all local devices. Details on how to use the Device Manager, examples, and hands-on projects for this tool are located in Chapter 3.

- *Local Users and Groups:* Used to create and manage local user accounts and groups. (This tool is disabled when Active Directory is present.) Details on how to use this tool, examples, and hands-on projects are located in Chapter 5.

The Storage section of Computer Management has four tools used to simplify storage device administration. Details on how to use the Storage tools, examples, and hands-on projects are located in Chapter 4.

- *Disk Management:* Used to view and alter the partitioning and volume configuration of hard drives.

- *Disk Defragmenter:* Improves the layout of stored data on drives by reassembling fragmented files and aggregating unused space.

- *Logical Drives:* Used to gain information about logical drives (that is, those which you've formatted and assigned drive letters to).

- *Removable Storage:* Used to manage removable media such as floppy disks, tapes, and Zip drives.

The Services and Applications section contains management controls for various installed and active services and applications. The actual contents of this section depend on what is installed on your system. Some of the common controls are:

- *Services:* For stopping and starting services as well as configuring the startup parameters for services (such as whether to launch when the system starts and if to employ a user account security context to launch the service). Hands-on Project 16-8 shows you one way to use this tool.

- *Indexing Service:* For defining the collection of documents indexed for searching by the Indexing Service. For information on using this tool, consult the *Windows 2000 Resource Kit.*

- *Internet Information Services:* For managing Internet services. For information on using this tool, consult the *Windows 2000 Resource Kit.*

- *DNS:* For managing the Domain Name Service. For information on using this tool, consult Chapter 7 and the *Windows 2000 Resource Kit.*

16

TROUBLESHOOTING INSTALLATION PROBLEMS

Unfortunately, the installation process of Windows 2000 is susceptible to several types of errors: media errors, domain controller communication difficulties, Stop message errors or being hung up on a blue screen, hardware problems, and dependency failures. The following list contains a short synopsis of each error type and possible solutions:

- *Media errors:* Media errors are problems with the distribution CD-ROM itself, the copy of the distribution files on a network drive, or the communications link between the installation and the distribution files. The only regularly successful solution to media errors is to switch media, for example, copying the files to a network drive, linking to a server's CD-ROM, or installing a CD-ROM on the workstation. If media errors are encountered, always restart the installation process from the beginning.

- *Domain controller communication difficulties:* Communication with the domain controller is crucial to some installations, especially when attempting to join a domain. Most often this problem is related to mistyping a name, password, domain name, etc., but network failures and offline domain controllers can be causes as well. Verify the viability of the domain controller directly and from other workstations (if applicable), and then check that there are no mistyped entries in the installation process.

- *Stop message errors or halting on the blue screen:* Using an incompatible or damaged driver controller is the most common cause of Stop messages and halting on the blue screen during installation. If any information is presented to you about an error, try to determine if the proper driver is being used. Otherwise, double-check that your hardware has the drivers required to operate under Windows 2000.

- *Hardware problems:* If you failed to verify your hardware with the HCL (hardware compatibility list), or if a physical defect has occurred in a previously operational device, very strange errors can surface. In such cases, replacing the device is the only viable solution. Before you go to that expense, however, double-check the installation and configuration of all devices within the computer.

- *Dependency failures:* The failure of a service or driver due to the failure of a foundation or prior service or driver is a dependency failure. An example of a dependency failure is the Server and Workstation services failing (see Hands-on Project 16-8) because the NIC fails to initialize properly. Often Windows 2000 will boot in spite of these errors, so check the Event log (see Hands-on Project 16-1) for more details (see Figure 16-4).

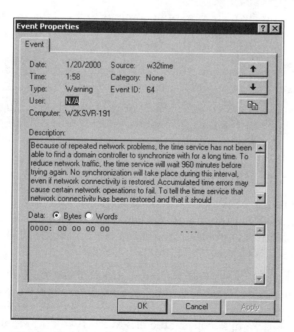

Figure 16-4   A dependency failure event detail from the System log of the Event Viewer

Just knowing about these installation problems can help you avoid them. Unfortunately, successfully installing Windows 2000 does not eliminate the possibility of further complications. Fortunately, Microsoft has included several troubleshooting tools that can help locate and eliminate most system failures (see the "Troubleshooting Tools" section earlier in this chapter).

TROUBLESHOOTING PRINTER PROBLEMS

Problems with network printers can often bring normal productive activity to a halt. Printer problems can occur anywhere from the power cable of the printer to the application attempting to print. Systematic elimination of possible points of failure is the only reliable method of eliminating printing errors. Here are some common and useful tips for troubleshooting printer problems:

- Check that the physical aspects of the printer—cable, power, paper, toner, and so on—are functional.

- Make sure the printer is plugged in and online. There is typically a light or an LCD message to indicate this. You may need to press the Reset button or the Online button to set or cycle the printer into online mode.

- Make sure the printer server for the printer is booted.

- Check the logical printer on both the client and server. Verify that they exist. Check their configuration parameters and settings. For details on logical printers and their multitude of controls, see Chapter 10.

- Check the print queue for stalled jobs (see Figure 16-5, which shows a stalled print job). If a print job does not otherwise have a status listing—such as waiting, paused, or printing—you can assume that it is stalled. The print queue is accessed by clicking the Start menu, selecting Settings, selecting Printers, then double-clicking on the icon for the printer.

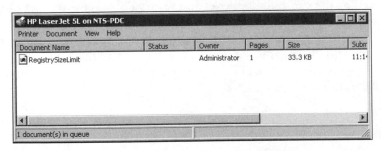

Figure 16-5 A printer queue

- Reinstall or update the printer driver to correct for a corrupt or incorrect print driver.

- Attempt to print from a different application or a different client.

- Attempt to print using Administrator access.

16

- Stop and restart the Print Spooler service, using the Services tool found via Computer Management (try Hands-on Project 16-4).

- Check the status and CPU usage of the Spoolsv.exe file, using the Task Manager (see Figure 16-6). If the spooler seems to be stalled by not receiving CPU time or is consuming most of the CPU, you should stop and restart the Spooler service.

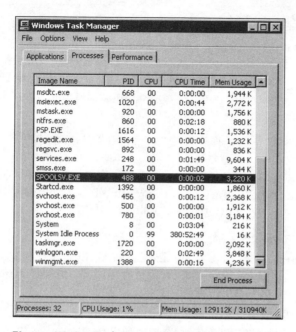

Figure 16-6 Task Manager viewing the CPU usage of SPOOLSV

- Check the free space on the drive hosting the spooler file, and change its destination (see Figure 16-7). The amount of free space needed for the spooler file is determined by the size and number of your print jobs and the settings of the logical printer; typically, 100 MB is sufficient. You should change the spool file host drive if there is insufficient space or if you suspect that the drive is not performing fast enough. This change is made on the Advanced tab of the Server Properties dialog box, accessed from the File menu of the Printers folder. See Chapter 10 for more information.

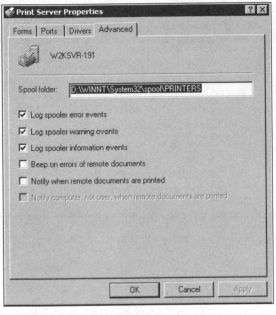

Figure 16-7   The Advanced tab of the Printer Server Properties dialog box, showing the spool folder

Table 16-1 summarizes some common network printing problems and their solutions.

Table 16-1   Printer Troubleshooting

Network Printing Problem	Solutions
Pages print, but only a single character appears on each page. —or— Pages print but they include the control codes in the document. —or— Pages print, but they show random characters instead of the desired document.	1. If the print job has not completed printing, delete it from the print queue to prevent wasting more paper. 2. Configure the printer to "Hold mismatched documents" (printer Properties dialog box, Advanced tab). 3. Remove and reinstall the logical printer and/or the printer driver on the client (if only a single workstation experiences the problem) or on the server (if all workstations experience the problem). 4. Verify that the data type set in the logical printer is correct for the application used, printer driver installed, and capabilities of the physical print device. 5. Stop and restart the Print Spooler service.

16

Table 16-1   Printer Troubleshooting (continued)

Network Printing Problem	Solutions
An access denied or no access available message is displayed when a print job is submitted.	This is typically caused by improper permissions defined on the printer share. Double-check the permission settings. You may also need to review the group memberships of the affected users if you are employing any Deny permissions on the printer share.
A network-attached printer shows an error light on the network interface.	A network communication or identification error has occurred. Cycling the power on the printer may resolve the problem. If not, try disconnecting then reconnecting the network media while the printer is powered off.
No documents are being created by the physical print device, but the print queue shows that the print job is printing.	1. View the print queue to see if a print job is stalled or paused. If so, delete or resume the print job. 2. If no other print job is present, delete the current print job and resubmit it from the original application. 3. Stop and restart the Print Spooler service.
The printer share is not visible from a client (that is, it does not appear in Network Neighborhood or My Network Places).	1. The client system may not be properly connected to the network. Shut down the client, check all physical network connections, and reboot. Test to see if you can access any other network resources. 2. Check the installed protocol and its settings, especially if TCP/IP is being used. 3. Check the domain/workgroup membership of the client.
On larger print jobs, pages from the end of the print job are missing from the printed document.	This can occur when insufficient space is available on the drive hosting the spooler file. Either free up space on the host drive or move the spooler file to a drive with more available space.

This section covers most of the more common print-related problems. To start step-by-step printer troubleshooting, try Hands-on Project 16-4. For more tips on printer troubleshooting, consult the *Windows 2000 Resource Kit*.

TROUBLESHOOTING RAS PROBLEMS

Remote Access Service (RAS) is another area with numerous possible points of failure—from the configuration of the computers on both ends, to the modem settings, to the condition of the communications line. Unfortunately, there is no ultimate RAS troubleshooting guide, but here are some solid steps in the right direction:

- Check all physical connections.

- Check the communications line itself, with a phone if appropriate.

- Verify the RAS configuration and the modem setup. To verify these items, attempt to establish a connection to another server or delete and re-create the connection object. For detailed examples and hands-on projects for this subject, see Chapter 9.

- Check that the client and the server dial-up configurations match, including speed, protocol, and security (see Figure 16-8 for an example of the security settings for a dial-up connection. You'll need to view the other tabs to compare and confirm speed, protocol, and other connection settings).

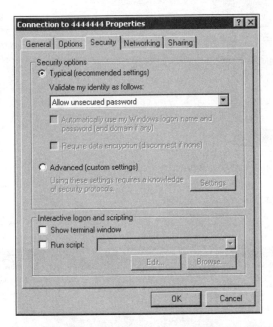

Figure 16-8   The Security tab of the Properties dialog box of a Connection object

- Verify that the user account has RAS privileges.

- Inspect the RAS-related logs: Device.log and Modemlog.txt. Look for errors involving failure to connect, failure to dial, failure to authenticate, failure to negotiate encryption, failure to establish a common protocol, and link termination.

- Remember that Multilink and callback will not work together. You must select one or the other. Figure 16-9 shows a configuration setting on a connection object that allows the caller to define the callback number.

- Autodial and persistent connections may cause the computer to attempt RAS connection at logon.

16

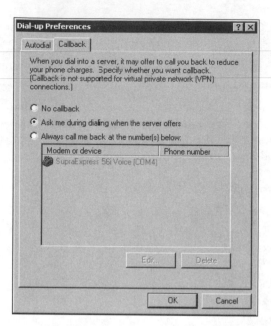

Figure 16-9   The Callback tab of the Dial-up Preferences dialog box

Table 16-2 outlines common RAS problems and solutions.

Table 16-2   RAS Troubleshooting

RAS Problem	Solutions
The connection object fails to establish a network link with the remote server.	1. Check the username, password, and phone number. 2. Verify that the modem device is powered on and properly connected to the computer and the phone line. You should also check the installed driver and update it if necessary. 3. Verify that the security settings match those required by the remote server. 4. Verify that the protocol settings match those required by the remote server.
The client has Multilink enabled and has three identical modems for the connection, but only a single modem establishes a network link with the remote server.	1. Verify that the remote server supports Multilink and that it has Multilink connections enabled. 2. Verify that you need to dial the same, or different, phone numbers when establishing a Multilink connection. 3. Cycle the power on the modems. Verify that they are properly attached to the computer and the telephone line.

Table 16-2   RAS Troubleshooting (continued)

RAS Problem	Solutions
A network link is broken during a remote session after a successful link is established.	1. Your phone line probably has call waiting, and another call came in. Disable call waiting via the connection object. 2. Your telephone line quality is poor, as is the case when old wiring is present, when phone lines pass by electrical interference, or when the weather is bad. You may need to upgrade your internal wiring, request a service upgrade from the telephone company, reroute wiring to avoid interference, or wait until the weather clears. 3. Remote systems can disconnect you for a variety of reasons, most beyond your control and knowledge. In most cases, simply try to reestablish the connection.

TIP Most RAS problems are related to misconfiguration. For more details on RAS, refer to Chapter 9 or the *Windows 2000 Resource Kit*.

TROUBLESHOOTING NETWORK PROBLEMS

Network problems can range from faults in the network cables or hardware, to misconfigured protocols, to workstation or server errors. As with other troubleshooting, attempt to eliminate the obvious and easy possibilities (such as physical connections and permissions) before moving on to more drastic, complex, or unreliable measures (IP configuration, routing, and domain structure). Cabling, connections, and hardware devices are just as suspect as the software components of networking. Verifying hardware functionality involves more than just looking at it; you may need to perform some electrical tests, change physical settings, or update drivers/ROM BIOS.

Some common-sense first steps you can take include:

- Check to see if other clients, servers, or subnets are experiencing the same problem.

- Check physical network connections, including the NIC, media cables, terminators, and logically proximate network devices (such as hubs, repeaters, and routers).

- Check protocol settings.

- Reboot the system.

- Verify that the NIC drivers are properly installed. Use the self-test or diagnostic tools or software for the NIC if available.

- Verify the domain/workgroup membership of the client.

16

Table 16-3 shows some common connectivity problems and their solutions.

Table 16-3   Network Connection Troubleshooting

Connectivity Problem	Solutions
The client does not seem to connect to the network (that is, no objects are visible in the Network Neighborhood). —or— The client is unable to be authenticated by the domain.	1. Use the Event Viewer to look for errors in the System log. Resolve any issues discovered. 2. Check the physical network connections, including the NIC, media, and local network devices. 3. Check the NIC driver, and update or replace it, if necessary. 4. Check the installed protocol and its configuration settings. 5. Check the domain/workgroup membership. 6. Reboot the client.
A system disconnects from the network randomly or when other computers boot onto the network.	1. Check to see that you are not violating the length, segments, or nodes per segment limitations on the network media in use. 2. Verify that all systems have unique address assignments and system computer names. 3. Check for breaks in the network media or the proximity of electrical or magnetic interference.
Shared network resources, such as folders and printers, cannot be accessed from a client.	1. Check the assigned permissions on the share itself and on the object (if applicable). 2. Check group memberships, if any Deny permissions are used. 3. Attempt to access the resources by using a different user account or client. 4. Check that the computer is connecting to the network.

TROUBLESHOOTING DISK PROBLEMS

The component on your computer that experiences the most activity is the hard drive, even more so than your keyboard and mouse. It should not be surprising that hard drive failures are common. Windows 2000 is natively equipped to maintain the file system (see Chapter 4), but even a well-tuned system is subject to hardware glitches. Most partition, boot sector, and drive configuration faults can be corrected or recovered from by using the Disk Management tool from the Computer Management utility of Administrative Tools (see Figure 16-10). However, the only reliable means of protecting data on storage devices is to maintain an accurate and timely backup, as discussed in Chapter 15. For detailed examples and information on using the Disk Management tool and troubleshooting disk problems, see Chapter 4.

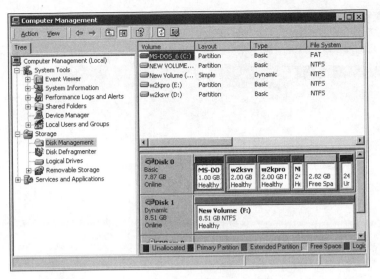

Figure 16-10   Disk Management tool from the Computer Management interface

MISCELLANEOUS TROUBLESHOOTING ISSUES

There are several troubleshooting tips that don't fit into the other categories described in this chapter. They are included here.

Permission Problems

Permission problems (problems with accessing or managing system resources such as folders, files, or printers) usually occur when a user is a member of groups with conflicting permissions or when permissions are managed on a per-account basis. To test for faulty permission settings, attempt the same actions and activities with Administrator privileges (try Hands-on Project 16-5). Double-check a user's group memberships to verify that there are no Deny access settings causing the problem. This means examining the access control lists (ACLs) of the objects and the share, if applicable (see Figure 16-11).

16

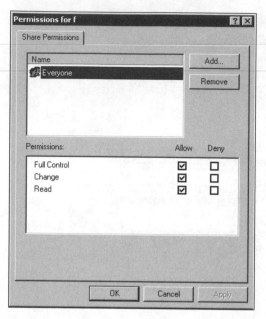

Figure 16-11   The Permissions dialog box for a share

 TIP   It is important to remember that any changes to the access permissions of individual users or groups will not affect those users until the next time they log on. The access token used by the security system is rebuilt each time a user logs on.

Master Boot Record Problems

As you learned in Chapter 14, the master boot record (MBR) is the area of a hard drive that contains the data structure that initiates the boot process. If the MBR fails, the Emergency Repair Disk (ERD) cannot be used to repair it. Instead, you'll need to use a DOS 6.0+ bootable floppy disk and execute *FDISK /MBR* from the command prompt. This will re-create the drive's MBR and restore the system correctly. If you don't have access to DOS FDISK, you'll have to perform a complete install/upgrade of Windows 2000 to allow the setup routine to re-create the MBR. It may also be possible to use the Recovery Console fixmbr command to repair a corrupt master boot record.

Using the Dr. Watson Debugger

Windows 2000 has an application error debugger called **Dr. Watson**. This diagnostic tool detects application failures and logs diagnostic details. Data captured by Dr. Watson is stored in the Drwtsn32.log file. Dr. Watson can also be configured to save a memory dump of the application's address space for further investigation. However, the information extracted and stored by Dr. Watson is really only useful to a Microsoft technical professional who is well versed in the cryptic logging syntax used.

Windows 2000 automatically launches Dr. Watson when an application error occurs. To configure Dr. Watson, however, you'll need to launch it from the Start, Run command with *DRWTSN32*. Figure 16-12 shows the configuration dialog box for Dr. Watson.

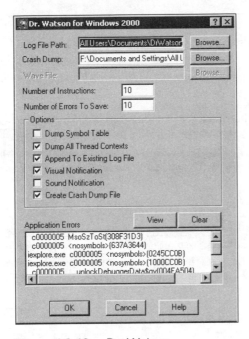

Figure 16-12   Dr. Watson

As you can see, this dialog box lists the configuration items for the following:

- The log file path, which is where the Dr. Watson log file is stored

- The crash dump, which provides the dump location for an application's virtual machine's address space

- The number of instructions and errors to record in log file

- Options for what to include in the log file and the way to notify the user of an application fault

- A list of previous application errors, with access to the log file details

APPLYING SERVICE PACKS AND HOT FIXES

A **service pack** is a collection of code replacements, patches, error corrections, new applications, version improvements, and/or service-specific configuration settings from Microsoft that correct, replace, or hide the deficiencies of the original product or preceding service packs or hot fixes. A **hot fix** is similar to a service pack, except that it addresses only a single problem, or a small number of problems, and may not be fully tested.

16

You should apply a hot fix only if you are experiencing the problem it was created to fix, otherwise the hot fix may cause other problems.

Service packs are cumulative. For example, Service Pack 3 (SP3) for Windows NT 4.0 contains SP2 plus all post-SP2 hot fixes. Thus, the latest service pack is all you need to install. For instructions on installing and removing service packs, try Hands-on Projects 16-6 and 16-7.

At this writing, Microsoft has announced that it will release the first service pack for Windows 2000 by summer 2000. We crafted this section based on prerelease documentation and our experience with Windows NT service packs. Take the time to review the documentation included with the service pack once it is available.

It is a common practice among production networks to wait one to three months after the release of a new service pack before deploying it. This gives the installed community time to test and provide feedback about the patch. The track record of initial reliability of service packs is varied, so it's best to wait and verify reliability.

A few important points to remember about patches such as service packs and hot fixes include:

- Always make a backup of your system before applying any type of patch; this will give you a way to restore your system if the fix damages the OS.

- Be sure to retrieve a patch for the correct CPU type and language version.

- Always read the readme and Knowledge Base documents for each patch before installing it.

- Update your Emergency Repair Disk (ERD) both before and after applying a patch.

- Make a complete backup of the Registry, using the Registry Editor or the Regback utility from the *Windows 2000 Resource Kit.*

- Export the disk configuration data from Disk Administrator.

- Because service packs rewrite many system-level files, you must disconnect all current users, exit all applications, and temporarily stop all unneeded services before installing any service pack or patch.

To locate Microsoft Knowledge Base documents, visit or use one of these resources:

- Web site: *http://support.microsoft.com/*

- TechNet CD

- Microsoft Network

- CompuServe: GO MICROSOFT

- Resource Kit documentation (online help file)

Service packs and hot fixes can be retrieved from:

- Microsoft FTP site: *ftp://ftp.microsoft.com/bussys/winnt/winnt-public/fixes/usa/*

- The Microsoft Windows Web site: *http://www.microsoft.com/windows/* (look for the download link)

To determine what service packs have been applied to your system, you can use one of the following techniques:

- Enter *WINVER* from a command prompt to view an About The System dialog box.

- Select Help, About Windows 2000 from the menu bar of any native tool such as Windows Explorer.

- Use the Registry Editor to view the *CSD Version* value in the HKEY_LOCAL_MACHINE\SOFTWARE\Microsoft\WindowsNT\ CurrentVersion subkey.

USING MICROSOFT REFERENCES FOR TROUBLESHOOTING

Several Microsoft resources are available to aid you in troubleshooting and working with Windows 2000:

- *Microsoft Web site: http://www.microsoft.com/windows/*

- *The Knowledge Base:* The predecessor to and a resource for the TechNet CD is the online Knowledge Base. This resource can be accessed by several means, which we detailed earlier in this chapter.

- *TechNet:* The best periodic publication from Microsoft is *TechNet*. This multi-CD collection is an invaluable resource for white papers, FAQs, troubleshooting documents, book excerpts, articles, and other written materials, plus utilities, patches, fixes, upgrades, drivers, and demonstration software. At only $300 per year (as of this writing), it is well worth the cost. It is also available online in a limited form at *http://www.microsoft.com/technet/*.

- *Resource Kits:* The Resource Kits (RKs) are useful information sources. These are available in electronic form through TechNet as a whole and through the online services in portions. RKs document material outside that contained in the manuals, and often include add-on software utilities to enhance product use.

16

CHAPTER SUMMARY

❏ Information is the most valuable tool for troubleshooting. Maintain a Computer Information File (CIF) and a detailed history log of troubleshooting activities.

❏ No matter what problems or errors are discovered on your computer system, there are several common-sense principles of troubleshooting that you should always follow. These include performing one task at a time, remaining calm, isolating the problem, and performing the simplest fixes first.

❏ The Windows 2000 tools most often used for troubleshooting are Event Viewer and the Computer Management tool.

❏ There are five common installation problems: media errors, domain controller communication difficulties. Stop message errors or halting on blue screen, hardware problems, and dependency failures.

❏ Printer problems are most often associated with physical configuration or spooling problems.

❏ RAS and network problems are caused by several types of problems, but the most common is misconfiguration.

❏ Service packs and hot fixes are used to repair portions of Windows 2000 after its release.

❏ Microsoft has provided several avenues to gain access to information about the operation and management of Windows 2000, including a substantial collection of troubleshooting documentation.

KEY TERMS

Application log — A log automatically created by Windows 2000 that records application events, alerts, and system messages.

computer information file (CIF) — A detailed collection of all information related to the hardware and software products that compose your computer (and even your entire intranet).

Dr. Watson — An application error debugger. This diagnostic tool detects application failures and logs diagnostic details.

Event Viewer — The utility used to view the three logs automatically created by Windows 2000: the System log, Application log, and Security log.

hot fix — Similar to a service pack, except that a hot fix addresses only a single problem, or a small number of problems, and may not be fully tested.

Security log — A log automatically created by Windows 2000 that records security-related events.

service pack — A collection of code replacements, patches, error corrections, new applications, version improvements, or service-specific configuration settings from Microsoft that correct, replace, or hide the deficiencies of the original product or preceding service packs or hot fixes.

System log — A log automatically created by Windows 2000 that records information and alerts about the Windows 2000 internal processes.

REVIEW QUESTIONS

1. When approaching a computer problem, which of the following should you keep in mind? (Choose all that apply.)

   a. how the problem was last solved

   b. what changes were recently made to the system

   c. information about the configuration state of the system

   d. the ability to repeat the failure

2. If a media error occurs during installation, which of the following are steps you should take to eliminate the problem? (Choose all that apply.)

   a. Attempt to recopy or reaccess the file that caused the failure.

   b. Switch media sources or types.

   c. Open the Control Panel and reinstall the appropriate drivers.

   d. Restart the installation from the beginning.

3. Which of the following Windows 2000 repair tools can be used to gain information about drivers or services that failed to load?

   a. Event Viewer

   b. Registry

   c. System applet

   d. Dr. Watson

4. In addition to the Event Viewer and the System Information tool, which of the following are useful tools in troubleshooting? (Choose all that apply.)

   a. Advanced Options Boot Menu

   b. Registry editors

   c. backup software

   d. Time/Date applet

5. Your best tool in troubleshooting is:

   a. a protocol analyzer

   b. information

   c. administrative access

   d. redundant devices

6. Which of the following are possible troubleshooting techniques for eliminating printer problems? (Choose all that apply.)

   a. Check the physical aspects of the printer—cable, power, paper, toner, and so on.

   b. Check the print queue for stalled jobs.

   c. Attempt to print from a different application or a different client.

   d. Stop and restart the spooler, using the Services tool.

16

7. What is the most common cause of RAS problems?

   a. telco service failures

   b. misconfiguration

   c. user error

   d. communications device failure

8. A user's ability to access a resource is controlled by access permissions. If you suspect a problem with a user's permission settings, what actions can you take? (Choose all that apply.)

   a. Attempt the same actions and activities with the Administrator account.

   b. Delete the user's account and create a new one from scratch.

   c. Double-check group memberships to verify that no Deny access settings are causing the problem.

   d. Grant the user Full Access to the object directly.

9. What application automatically loads to handle application failures?

   a. Event Viewer

   b. System applet

   c. Computer Management

   d. Dr. Watson

10. If you are going to create a CIF, which of the following is the most important?

    a. Include the vendor's mailing address.

    b. Keep everything in electronic form.

    c. Update the contents often.

    d. Use nonremovable labels on all components.

11. Which of the following are important actions to perform before installing a service pack or a hot fix? (Choose all that apply.)

    a. Make a backup of your system.

    b. Read the readme and Knowledge Base documents.

    c. Make a complete backup of the Registry.

12. What are some common-sense approaches to troubleshooting? (Choose all that apply.)

    a. Understand TCP/IP routing table configuration.

    b. Know your system.

    c. Undo the last alteration to the system.

    d. Replace all server hardware when one device fails.

    e. Let the fault guide you.

13. You can often resolve problems or avoid them altogether if you take the time to write out a history or log of problems and both failed and successful solution attempts. True or False?

14. When installing a new Windows 2000 domain controller into an existing domain, you can experience communication problems with the current domain controller. After you've verified that the current domain controller is online and properly connected to the network, what other items should be considered as possible points of failure? (Choose all that apply.)

    a. administrative account name

    b. subnet mask

    c. password

    d. domain name

15. Blue screen or Stop errors often occur on a system containing one or more devices that are not found on the HCL. True or False?

16. If the driver for your network interface card fails, which other components of your system are most likely to fail due to dependency issues? (Choose all that apply.)

    a. network protocol

    b. Client Services for NetWare

    c. video driver

    d. WinLogon

17. Errors involving internal processes, such as hardware and operating system errors, warnings, and general information messages, are recorded in the Application log of the Event Viewer. True or False?

18. The best way to resolve a hardware problem during installation is to:

    a. Restart the installation from scratch without any other modifications.

    b. Press and hold the Ctrl key during the installation.

    c. Remove or replace the non-HCL hardware.

    d. Recopy the distribution files.

19. An event detail viewed from the Event Viewer's logs provides specific information on the time, location, user, service, and resolution for all encountered errors. True or False?

20. The Computer Management tool offers links to several important administrative and management utilities including: (Choose all that apply.)

    a. Control Panel

    b. Event Viewer

    c. Performance Monitor

    d. Local Security Policy

    e. Local Users and Groups

21. The Storage section of the Computer Management tool offers utilities to perform what types of operations? (Choose all that apply.)

    a. defragmentation

    b. partitioning

16

c. managing removable storage

d. compressing floppies

22. When a printer fails to output your documents, which of the following is a possible troubleshooting first step?

a. replacing the printer

b. restarting the spooler

c. reinstalling the operating system

d. deleting and re-creating the shared printer

23. Both printers and RAS connections can suffer from the most common problem: physical connection interruptions. True or False?

24. When a user complains about being unable to access a resource that other users of similar job descriptions are able to access, what should you consider when attempting to troubleshoot this issue? (Choose all that apply.)

a. group memberships

b. ACL on the object

c. domain membership

d. speed of network connection

25. When you alter the group memberships of a user, you need to perform what operation to ensure that the changes are taking effect?

a. reboot the server

b. enable auditing on file objects

c. restart the messaging and alert services

d. log the user account off, then have the user log back on

HANDS-ON PROJECTS

Project 16-1

To use the Event Viewer:

1. Open the Event Viewer from the Start menu (click **Start**, point to **Programs**, point to **Administrative Tools**, click **Event Viewer**).

2. Select the **System Log** from the list of available logs in the left pane.

3. Notice the various types of events that appear in the right pane.

4. Select an event in the right pane.

5. Select the **Action** menu, then **Properties**.

6. Review the information presented by the event detail. Try to determine on your own what types of errors, warnings, or information are presented in the detail and why the detail was created.

7. Click the up and/or down arrows to view other event details.

8. Click **OK** to close the event detail.

9. Close Event Viewer.

Project 16-2

To extract information for a CIF:

 This hands-on project suggests a method to obtain some information about your system for a CIF; it does not constitute a complete or exhaustive collection of data. This activity is only one part of the task of creating a CIF.

1. Open the Control Panel (click **Start**, point to **Settings**, click **Control Panel**).

2. Double-click **Administrative Tools**.

3. Double-click **Computer Management**.

4. In the left pane, select **System Information** (see Figure 16-13) from within the Computer Management portion of the list.

5. Expand the **System Information** entry by clicking the boxed plus sign to the left of the node.

6. Take the time to expand and select each item within the System Information node hierarchy. As you view each page of data, consider the value of this data for future troubleshooting and decide whether to print or save the information.

7. To print a page, click the **Print** button in the toolbar.

8. To save a page, click on the **Save System Information File** or **Save Text Report** button in the toolbar.

9. When you have finished examining the System Information tool, close the Computer Management utility.

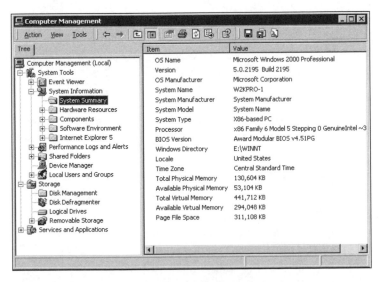

Figure 16-13   The System Information tool

Project 16-3

To explore the Computer Management utility:

1. Open the **Control Panel** (click **Start**, point to **Settings**, click **Control Panel**).

2. Double-click **Administrative Tools**.

3. Double-click **Computer Management**.

4. Notice that the left pane has three divisions: System Tools, Storage, and Services and Applications.

5. If necessary, expand the **System Tools** entry by clicking the boxed plus sign located to the left of the node name.

6. Explore the contents of the Event Viewer, System Information, Performance Logs and Alerts, Shared Folders, Device Manager, and Local Users and Groups sections by expanding them one at a time. To view the contents of any item, select it in the left pane so that its contents will be displayed in the right pane.

7. Once you've viewed the contents of the System Tools section, view the contents of the Storage section. This section includes Disk Management, Disk Defragmenter, Logical Drives, and Removable Storage.

8. Once you've viewed the contents of the Storage section, view the contents of the Services and Applications section. The items in this section vary based on installed applications and services but can include Telephony, WMI Control, Services, and Indexing Service.

9. Once you've viewed the contents of the Services and Applications section, close the Computer Management utility.

Project 16-4

To troubleshoot a printer problem:

 This hands-on project is not an exhaustive process for printer troubleshooting; it includes some of the actions that may be required to resolve a printer problem.

1. First, check that the printer is online and has power, paper, and toner. Check the printer's own error-reporting center (often a light or an LCD) for any possible hardware errors.

2. Open the Printers applet (click **Start**, point to **Settings**, click **Printers**).

3. To display the printer queue window, double-click the installed printer that you suspect is having a problem.

4. If any documents appear in the printer queue window, select the topmost document, then select **Document**, **Restart**.

5. If the printer still fails to function, go to the Control Panel (click **Start**, point to **Settings**, click **Control Panel**).

6. Double-click the **Administrative Tools** icon.

7. Double-click **Computer Management**.

8. Drill down in the hierarchy in the left pane to locate and select the Services tool (**Computer Management**, **Services and Applications**, **Services**).

9. Locate and select the **Print Spooler** service (see Figure 16-14).

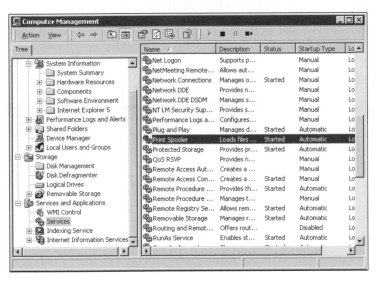

Figure 16-14   The Print Spooler service as seen through the Services tool

10. Select **Action**, **Stop**.

11. Select **Action**, **Start**.

12. Close the Computer Management utility.

13. Close the Control Panel.

14. If the printer still fails to function, return to the Printer queue window that was left open.

15. Select the topmost document in the printer queue.

16. Click the **Document** menu, then select the **Cancel** command to remove the print job from the queue.

17. If this was the only print job in the queue, print another document. If this was not the only print job in the queue, wait to see if the remaining print jobs print.

18. Close the Printer queue.

16

TIP   Consult Chapter 10 for more details on managing and troubleshooting printing.

Project 16-5

To troubleshoot permission problems:

>
> This hands-on project is not an exhaustive process for permission troubleshooting; it includes only some of the actions that may be required to resolve permission problems.

1. If a user cannot access a resource to which they should have access, first reboot their system (**Start**, **Shutdown**). Select **Restart** from the drop-down menu, then click **OK**.

2. After rebooting, log back on as the user. Test to see if you can access the resource.

3. If the resource is still not accessible, log off and log back on as an administrator. Press **Ctrl+Alt+Delete** at the logon prompt, provide the user account name for the administrator and the associated password, and click **OK**.

4. Once logged on as the administrator, attempt to access the resource. If the resource can be accessed, the problem is with the assigned permissions for the user account. Most likely the user account is not a member of the proper group or is a member of a group that has Deny access set for that resource.

5. If the resource cannot be accessed by the administrator, the problem may lie with the system. This could include network communications, domain membership, or corrupted system drivers and files. You will need to troubleshoot these other possible causes of the problem.

6. If you discover that group membership is the problem, make the appropriate group membership changes, then force the user to log off, then log back on (changes do not take effect until the next logon).

Project 16-6

To apply a service pack:

1. Move or copy the service pack (SP) file into an empty directory as follows: from within Windows Explorer, create a new directory on a volume with at least 100 MB of free space (more may be required depending on the size of the service pack). Move or copy the SP into the new empty directory.

2. Close all applications, especially debugging tools, virus scanners, and any other non-Microsoft or third-party tools.

3. Locate and execute **Update.exe** with the **Start**, **Run** command.

4. Follow any prompts that appear. If you want the ability to uninstall the service pack, be sure to select the option to store uninstall information. It's generally a good idea to select this option.

5. When instructed, reboot your system.

6. After rebooting, you can delete the service pack files and the temporary directory from your hard drive (refer to Step 1).

Project 16-7

To uninstall a service pack:

> You must have selected the "save uninstall information" option during the initial application of the service pack in order to uninstall it.

1. Extract the original SP archive into an empty directory. If you retained the SP archive and temporary directory from the installation procedure, you do not need to repeat this activity.
2. Locate and execute **Update.exe**.
3. Follow the prompts that appear.
4. Click the **Uninstall a previously installed service pack** button.
5. Follow the prompts.
6. Reboot.

Project 16-8

To verify that the Workstation and Server services are started after bootup:

1. Open the **Control Panel** (click **Start**, point to **Settings**, click **Control Panel**).
2. Double-click **Administrative Tools**.
3. Double-click **Computer Management**.
4. Expand the **Services and Applications** section by clicking on the boxed plus sign next to the node name, if it is not already expanded.
5. Select the **Services** object.
6. Scroll down in the right pane to locate the Workstation service.
7. Notice the item in the Status column. If it says "Started," then you can skip to Step 9.
8. If the Status column is blank for the Workstation service, it failed to launch at startup. You can attempt to launch the service by selecting it, then clicking the Action menu, then clicking on Start.
9. Scroll down in the right pane to locate the Server service.
10. Notice the item in the Status column. If it says "Started," then you can skip to Step 12.
11. If the Status column is blank for the Server service, it failed to launch at startup. You can attempt to launch the service by selecting it, then clicking the Action menu, then clicking on Start.
12. Close the Computer Management console.

16

CASE PROJECTS

1. After installing a new drive controller and a video card, along with their associated drivers, Windows 2000 refuses to boot, and booting with the Last Known Good Configuration (LKGC) option does not result in an operational system.

   Required result:

   ❐ Return the system to a bootable and operational state.

   Optional desired results:

   ❐ Retain the Security ID.

   ❐ Retain most, if not all, of the system's configuration.

   Proposed solution:

   Perform a complete reinstallation of Windows 2000.

   Indicate which of the following occurs, and explain why.

   a. The proposed solution produces the desired result and produces both of the optional desired results.

   b. The proposed solution produces the desired result, but only one of the optional desired results.

   c. The proposed solution produces the desired result, but neither of the optional desired results.

   d. The proposed solution does not produce the desired result.

2. After installing a new drive controller and a video card, along with their associated drivers, Windows 2000 refuses to boot and the LKGC does not result in an operational system.

   Required result:

   ❐ Return the system to a bootable and operational state.

   Optional desired results:

   ❐ Retain the Security ID.

   ❐ Retain most, if not all, of the system's configuration.

   Proposed solution:

   Perform an upgrade reinstallation of Windows 2000.

   Indicate which of the following occurs, and explain why.

   a. The proposed solution produces the desired result and produces both of the optional desired results.

   b. The proposed solution produces the desired result, but only one of the optional desired results.

   c. The proposed solution produces the desired result, but neither of the optional desired results.

   d. The proposed solution does not produce the desired result.

3. Describe the common problems associated with installing Windows 2000 and the steps to take to either avoid these problems or resolve them.

Exam Objectives Tracking for MCSE Certification Exam # 70-210:

Installing, Configuring, and Administering

Microsoft Windows 2000 Professional

Installing Windows 2000 Professional

Objective	Chapter: Section
Perform an attended installation of Windows 2000 Professional	Chapter 2: Planning the Installation, Beginning the Windows 2000 Professional Installation, Windows 2000 Professional Setup: Step by Step
Perform an unattended installation of Windows 2000 Professional ♦ Install Windows 2000 Professional by using Windows 2000 Server Remote Installation Services (RIS) ♦ Install Windows 2000 Professional by using the System Preparation Tool ♦ Create unattended answer files by using Setup Manager to automate the installation of Windows 2000 Professional	Chapter 2: Unattended Installations, Alternate Automation Options, Creating the UDF
Upgrade from a previous version of Windows to Windows 2000 Professional ♦ Apply update packs to installed software applications ♦ Prepare a computer to meet upgrade requirements	Chapter 1: Windows 2000 Professional Hardware Requirements Chapter 2: Upgrading versus Installing Chapter 16: Applying Service Pack Updates
Deploy service packs	Chapter 16: Applying Service Pack Updates
Troubleshoot failed installations	Chapter 16: Troubleshooting Installation Problems

Implementing and Conducting Administration of Resources

Objective	Chapter: Section
Monitor, manage, and troubleshoot access to files and folders ♦ Configure, manage, and troubleshoot file compression ♦ Control access to files and folders by using permissions ♦ Optimize access to files and folders	Chapter 4: File System Object Level Properties, Managing NTFS Permissions, Managing Shared Folders, Troubleshooting Access Problems
Manage and troubleshoot access to shared folders ♦ Create and remove shared folders ♦ Control access to shared folders by using permissions ♦ Manage and troubleshoot Web server resources	Chapter 4: Managing Shared Folders, Troubleshooting Permissions Problems Chapter 9: Peer Web Services

A

Objective	Chapter: Section
Connect to local and network print devices ♦ Manage printers and print jobs ♦ Control access to printers by using permissions ♦ Connect to an Internet printer ♦ Connect to a local print device	Chapter 10: Printing Across the Network, Creating a Local Printer, Connecting to a Remote Printer, Installing and Managing Printers, Managing Print Jobs, Managing the Printer Server, Security Tab, Printers and the Web
Configure and manage file systems ♦ Convert from one file system to another file system ♦ Configure file systems by using NTFS, FAT32, or FAT	Chapter 4: File Storage Basics, File Systems, File System Object Level Controls

Implementing, Managing, and Troubleshooting Hardware Devices and Drivers

Objective	Chapter: Section
Implement, manage, and troubleshoot disk devices ♦ Install, configure, and manage DVD and CD-ROM devices ♦ Monitor and configure disks ♦ Monitor, configure, and troubleshoot volumes ♦ Monitor and configure removable media, such as tape devices	Chapter 3: Add/Remove Hardware, Sounds and Multimedia, Installing Hardware Chapter 4: Disk Management Actions, Drive Configurations Chapter 11: Performance Monitor, Disk Bottlenecks Chapter 16: Computer Management, Troubleshooting Disk Problems
Implement, manage, and troubleshoot display devices ♦ Configure multiple-display support ♦ Install, configure, and troubleshoot a video adapter	Chapter 3: Add/Remove Hardware, Display, Video
Implement, manage, and troubleshoot mobile computer hardware ♦ Configure Advanced Power Management (APM) ♦ Configure and manage card services	Chapter 3: Installing Hardware, Add/Remove Hardware, Hardware Profiles, Power Options, PCMCIA or PC Cards

Objective	Chapter: Section
Implement, manage, and troubleshoot input and output (I/O) devices ♦ Monitor, configure, and troubleshoot I/O devices, such as printers, scanners, multimedia devices, mouse, keyboard, and smart card reader ♦ Monitor, configure, and troubleshoot multimedia hardware, such as cameras ♦ Install, configure, and manage modems ♦ Install, configure, and manage Infrared Data Association (IrDA) devices ♦ Install, configure, and manage wireless devices ♦ Install, configure, and manage USB devices	Chapter 3: Installing Hardware, Add/Remove Hardware, Fax, Game Controllers, Keyboard and Mouse, Printers, Scanners and Cameras, Sounds and Multimedia, Modems, Installing RAS Hardware, Phone and Modem Options Chapter 10: Troubleshooting Printing Problems Chapter 11: Performance Monitor Chapter 16: Computer Management
Update drivers	Chapter 3: Installing Hardware, Add/Remove Hardware
Monitor and configure multiple processing units	Chapter 1: Microsoft Network Family, Multithreading Chapter 2: Planning the Installation Chapter 11: Performance Monitor, Processor Bottlenecks
Install, configure, and troubleshoot network adapters	Chapter 3: Installing Hardware, Add/Remove Hardware Chapter 7: Networking Under Windows 2000

Monitoring and Optimizing System Performance and Reliability

Objective	Chapter: Section
Manage and troubleshoot driver signing	Chapter 3: System
Configure, manage, and troubleshoot the Task Scheduler	Chapter 3: The Windows 2000 Task Manager
Manage and troubleshoot the use and synchronization of offline files	Chapter 9: Using Offline Files
Optimize and troubleshoot performance of the Windows 2000 Professional desktop ♦ Optimize and troubleshoot memory performance ♦ Optimize and troubleshoot processor utilization ♦ Optimize and troubleshoot disk performance ♦ Optimize and troubleshoot network performance ♦ Optimize and troubleshoot application performance	Chapter 11: Task Manager, Performance Monitor, Performance Options for Windows 2000, Memory Bottlenecks, Disk Bottlenecks, Eight Ways to Improve Windows 2000 Performance Chapter 12: Windows 2000 Application Support

A

Objective	Chapter: Section
Manage hardware profiles	Chapter 3: Hardware Profiles
Recover systems and user data ♦ Recover systems and user data by using Windows Backup ♦ Troubleshoot system restoration by using Safe Mode ♦ Recover systems and user data by using the Recovery Console	Chapter 14: Troubleshooting and Advanced Startup Options Chapter 15: Recovery Console, Data Backup, Microsoft Backup Utility

Configuring and Troubleshooting the Desktop Environment

Objective	Chapter: Section
Configure and manage user profiles	Chapter 5: Users, User Profiles
Configure support for multiple languages or multiple locations ♦ Enable multiple-language support ♦ Configure multiple-language support for users ♦ Configure local settings ♦ Configure Windows 2000 Professional for multiple locations	Chapter 3: Regional Settings Chapter 9: Phone and Modem Options
Install applications by using Windows Installer packages.	Chapter 15: Application Installation and Repair
Configure and troubleshoot desktop settings	Chapter 3: The Control Panel
Configure and troubleshoot fax support	Chapter 3: Fax
Configure and troubleshoot accessibility services	Chapter 3: Accessibility Options

Implementing, Managing, and Troubleshooting Network Protocols and Services

Objective	Chapter: Section
Configure and troubleshoot the TCP/IP protocol	Chapter 7: TCP/IP, TCP/IP Architecture, TCP/IP Configuration
Connect to computers by using dial-up networking ♦ Connect to computers by using a virtual private network (VPN) connection ♦ Create a dial-up connection to connect to a remote access server ♦ Connect to the Internet by using dial-up networking ♦ Configure and troubleshoot Internet Connection Sharing	Chapter 9: Remote Access Service, Dial-up to Private Network, Point-to-Point Tunneling Protocol, Layer Two Tunneling Protocol, Connect to a Private Network Through the Internet, Dial-up to the Internet
Connect to shared resources on a Microsoft network	Chapter 7: Server Service Chapter 9: Remote Access Service

Implementing, Monitoring, and Troubleshooting Security

Objective	Chapter: Section
Encrypt data on a hard disk by using Encrypting File System (EFS)	Chapter 6: Encrypting File System (EFS)
Implement, configure, manage, and trouble-shoot local Group Policy	Chapter 5: Local Security Policy Chapter 6: Windows 2000 Security and Access Controls
Implement, configure, manage, and trouble-shoot local user accounts ♦ Implement, configure, manage, and troubleshoot auditing ♦ Implement, configure, manage, and troubleshoot account settings ♦ Implement, configure, manage, and troubleshoot account policy ♦ Create and manage local users and groups ♦ Implement, configure, manage, and troubleshoot user rights	Chapter 5: Windows 2000 Professional User Accounts, Managing User Accounts, Audit Policies, Local Security Policy, Local Users and Groups MMC Snap-in Chapter 6: Auditing, Windows 2000 Security and Access Controls
Implement, configure, manage, and trouble-shoot local user authentication ♦ Configure and troubleshoot local user accounts ♦ Configure and troubleshoot domain user accounts	Chapter 5: Logging On to Windows 2000 Professional, Windows 2000 Professional User Accounts, Managing User Accounts Chapter 6: Logon Authentication, Customizing the Logon Process
Implement, configure, manage, and trouble-shoot a security configuration	Chapter 5: Local Security Policy Chapter 6: Windows 2000 Security and Access Controls

B

ACTIVE DIRECTORY OVERVIEW

Active Directory is a service included with Windows 2000 Server. It stores information about network objects, and makes that information available to Active Directory clients, which can include Windows 2000 Professional as well as Windows 95 or Windows 98 clients. This appendix serves only as an introduction to this topic. To fully understand all the nuances of this service, refer to the Windows 2000 Server documentation and online Help.

In common usage, a **directory** is an information source used to store information about useful, manageable **objects**. For example, a telephone directory stores information about telephone subscribers. In a distributed computing system or a computer network, there are many objects, such as printers, fax servers, applications, databases, and other users. Users want to find and use these objects; administrators want to manage how these objects are used. There is a common need to have usable objects that can be accessed and managed.

In this appendix, the terms directory and directory service refer to the directories found in public and private networks. A **directory service** differs from a directory in that it is defined as both the directory information source (that is, the database of system objects), and the services, such as **LDAP (Lightweight Directory Access Protocol)**, that make the information available to and usable by users and administrators.

What Is Active Directory?

Active Directory is the directory service included with Windows 2000 Server. It extends the features of previous Windows-based directory services and adds entirely new features. Active Directory is secure, distributed, partitioned, and replicated (each of these features is discussed in more detail later in this appendix). It is designed to work well in any size installation, from a single server with a few hundred objects to thousands of servers and millions of objects. Active Directory has many features that make it easy to navigate and manage large amounts of information, generating time savings for both administrators and end users.

Active Directory and the X.500 Standard

Active Directory is based on (but exceeds) the **X.500** standards for directory services. X.500 is a series of International Telecommunications Union (ITU) protocol recommendations that specify a model for connecting local directory services to form one distributed global directory. Following the strict interpretation of the recommendation, local databases hold and maintain a part of the global database, and make directory information available through a local server called a directory service. The user perceives the entire directory to be accessible from the local server.

X.500 also supports data management functions such as the addition, modification, and deletion of entries. Within Active Directory, each directory stores entries in an X.500-like naming scheme, but each directory duplicates the information held by other directories. This duplication provides an implementation that is both faster and more fault-tolerant in a large distributed enterprise.

Active Directory Management

All objects in Active Directory are protected by access control lists (ACLs). ACLs determine who can access the object and what actions each user can perform on the object. The existence of an object is never revealed to a user who is not allowed to access it.

An ACL is a list of access control entries (ACEs) stored with the object it protects. In Windows 2000, an ACL is stored as a binary value called a Security Descriptor. Each ACE contains a security identifier (SID), which identifies the **principal** (user or group) to whom the ACE applies and information on what type of access the ACE grants or denies.

ACLs on directory objects contain ACEs that apply to the object as a whole and ACEs that apply to the individual attributes of the object. This information allows an administrator to control not only which users can access an object, but also what properties those users can see. For example, all users might be granted read access to the e-mail and telephone number attributes for all other users, but security properties of users might be denied to all but members of a special security administrators group. Individual users might be granted write access to personal attributes, such as the telephone and mailing addresses, on their own user objects.

B

Delegation

Delegation is an important security feature of Active Directory. Delegation allows a higher administrative authority to grant specific administrative rights for **containers** and subtrees to individuals and groups. (See Chapter 5 for more general information on users and groups.) This eliminates the need for domain administrators with sweeping authority over large segments of the user population. For example, there could be a separate administrator for a Corporate Accounting organizational unit.

ACEs can grant specific administrative rights on the objects in a container to a user or group. Rights are granted for specific operations on specific object classes via ACEs in the container's ACL. Specific information on the ACL is covered in Chapter 6. For example, to allow user James Smith to be an administrator of the Corporate Accounting organizational unit, you would add ACEs to the ACL on "Corporate Accounting" as follows:

```
"James Smith";Grant ;Create, Modify, Delete;Object-Class User
"James Smith";Grant ;Create, Modify, Delete;Object-Class Group
"James Smith";Grant ;Write;Object-Class User; Attribute Password
```

Now James Smith can create new users and groups in Corporate Accounting and set the passwords on existing users, but he cannot create any other object classes and he cannot affect users in any other containers (unless, of course, ACEs grant him that access on the other containers).

Inheritance

Inheritance lets a given ACE propagate from the container where it was applied to all children of that container. Inheritance can be combined with delegation to grant administrative rights to a whole subtree of the directory in a single operation. For more information on inheritance, see Chapter 4.

Groups

Windows 2000 introduces the following new group features:

- Groups can be treated as distribution lists (a list of accounts to send e-mail to) if the next major release of Microsoft Exchange (version at this writing is 5.5) is installed.

- Groups can contain nonsecurity members (this is important when the group is used for both security and distribution list purposes).

- Administrators can disable security usage of groups (this is important when the group is solely used as a distribution list).

- Groups can be nested.

- A new group type, the universal group, is introduced.

A universal group is the simplest form of group, i.e., logical components used to associate user objects. Universal groups can appear in ACLs anywhere in the forest, and can contain other universal groups, global groups, and users. Small installations can use universal groups exclusively and not concern themselves with global and local groups. Additional information about groups is provided in Chapter 5.

A global group can appear in ACLs anywhere in the forest. A global group can contain users and other global groups from its own domain.

A domain local group can be used in ACLs only it its own domain. A domain local group can contain users and global groups from any domain in the forest, universal groups, and other domain local groups in its own domain.

The three group types provide a rich and flexible access control environment, while reducing **replication** traffic to the global catalog (GC) caused by group membership changes. A universal group appears in the GC, but will contain primarily global groups from domains in the forest. Once the global groups are established, the membership in the universal group will change infrequently. Global groups appear in the GC, but their members don't. Membership changes in global groups are not replicated outside of the domain where they are defined. Domain local groups are valid only in the domain where they are defined and do not appear in the GC at all.

Transitive Bidirectional Trust

When a domain is joined to a Windows 2000 domain tree, a **transitive bidirectional trust** relationship is automatically established between the joined-from domain and its parent in the tree. The **trust** is transitive (that is, when a domain joins an existing forest, a trust is automatically established) and bidirectional (that is, the trust exists both ways between the domains, no additional trust relationships are required among tree members). The trust hierarchy is stored as part of the directory metadata in the configuration container (an object that can logically contain configuration information about other objects—for example, a folder is an object that contains file objects).

Active Directory Replication

Active Directory provides **multi-master replication**. Multi-master replication means that all replicas of a given partition are writeable. This allows updates to be applied to any replica of a given partition. The Active Directory replication system propagates the changes from a given replica to all other replicas. Replication is automatic and transparent.

Server Affinity

Windows 2000 uses site information to locate an Active Directory server close to the user to speed communication between the user and the server. A **site** is an area of the network where connectivity among machines is assumed to be very good. Windows 2000 defines a site as one or more IP **subnets**. This is based on the assumption that computers with the same subnet address are connected to the same network segment, typically a LAN or other high-bandwidth environment such as Frame Relay, ATM, or others.

When a user workstation connects to the network, it receives a TCP/IP address from a Dynamic Host Configuration Protocol (DHCP) server, which also identifies the subnet to which the workstation is attached. Workstations that have statically configured IP addresses also have statically configured subnet information. In either case, the Windows 2000 domain controller (DC) locator will attempt to locate an Active Directory server located on the same subnet as the user, based on the subnet information known to the workstation.

Sites and Replication

The Windows 2000 replication system automatically generates a ring topology for replication among Active Directory servers in a given site. Within a site, directory replication is performed via remote procedure call (RPC). Between sites, replication can be selectively configured to use RPC or messaging. Windows 2000 provides simple Simple Mail Transfer Protocol (SMTP) messaging as a standard feature. If Microsoft Exchange is available, intersite replication can be carried via Exchange, using any of the many mail transports supported by Exchange (this includes SMTP, X.400, and others).

Publishing Objects

Publishing in Active Directory is the act of creating objects in the directory that either directly contain the information you want to make available or provide a reference to the information you want to make available. For example, a published user object might contain useful information about users, such as their telephone numbers and e-mail addresses, whereas a published volume object might contain a reference to a shared file system volume.

When to Publish

Information should be published in Active Directory when it is useful or interesting to a large part of the user community and when it needs to be highly accessible.

Information published in Active Directory has two major characteristics:

- It is relatively static and changes infrequently. Telephone numbers and e-mail addresses are examples of relatively static information suitable for publishing; the user's currently selected e-mail message is an example of highly volatile information.

- It is structured and can be represented as a set of discrete attributes. A user's business address is an example of structured information suitable for Active Directory publishing; an audio clip of a user's voice is an example of unstructured information better suited to sharing via the network.

Operational information used by applications is an excellent candidate for publishing in Active Directory. This includes global configuration information that applies to all instances of a given application. For example, a relational database product could store the default configuration for database servers as an object in Active Directory. New installations of that product would collect the default configuration from the object, simplifying the installation process and enhancing the consistency of installations in an enterprise.

Applications can also publish their connection points (network location) in the directory. Connection points are used for a client/server rendezvous. Active Directory defines an architecture for integrated service administration, using Service Administration Point (SAP) objects, and provides standard connection points for RPC, WinSock, and COM applications. Applications that do not use the RPC or WinSock interfaces for publishing their connection points can explicitly publish Service Connection Point objects in the directory.

Application data can also be published in the directory, using application-specific objects. Application-specific data should meet the criteria discussed previously. That is, data should be globally interesting, relatively nonvolatile, and structured.

How to Publish

Publishing contents to Active Directory must be handled from Windows 2000 Server. The publishing process is managed by Microsoft Management Console (MMC) snap-ins and other administrative tools that are not included for use with Windows 2000 Professional. From a Windows 2000 server, the means of publishing information varies according to the application or service:

- *RPC:* RPC (remote procedure call) applications use the RpcNs family of APIs to publish their connection points in the directory and to query for the connection points of services that have published theirs.

- *Windows Sockets:* Windows Sockets applications use the Registration and Resolution family of APIs available in WinSock 2.0 to publish their connection points and query for the connection points of services that have published theirs.

- *DCOM:* DCOM (distributed component object model) services publish their connection points via the DCOM Class Store, which resides in Active Directory.

ACCESSING ACTIVE DIRECTORY

Active Directory supports clients running Windows 2000 Server and Windows 2000 Professional, as well as Windows 95 and 98 clients that have Active Directory add-on software installed. A client discovers its site by presenting its subnet to the first Active Directory server contacted. The workstation determines the subnet by applying its subnet mask to its IP address. The subnet mask and IP address can be assigned by DHCP or statically configured. The first server contacted uses the presented subnet to locate the Site object for the site where the workstation is located. If the current server is not in that site, the server notifies the workstation of a better server to use.

How Does a Workstation Find a Directory Server?

A workstation finds a directory server by querying the Domain Network System (DNS). Directory servers for a given domain publish Service Resource Records (SRVs) in DNS with names in the following form:

```
_LDAP._TCP.<domain name>
```

Thus, a workstation logging on to *Microsoft.com* might query DNS for SRV records for _LDAP._TCP.killfear.com. A server will be selected from the list and contacted. The contacted server will use the subnet information presented by the workstation to determine the best server, as described in answer to the previous query.

How Do Users Log On?

A user can use a variety of names in a variety of formats to log on to Windows 2000 Professional as part of Active Directory. These include the name formats supported by the Win32 application programming interface **DsCrackNames**, which are used to convert these name forms as necessary.

Domain NetBIOS Name and SAM Account Name

This is the Windows NT 4.0-style logon name. The domain NetBIOS name is the name the domain had prior to migration. The Security Accounts Manager (SAM) account name is the account name the user had prior to migration.

User Principal Name (UPN)

This is in the format *<friendly name>@<dotted-dns-domain-name>*. If the name is not unique, the logon attempt will fail with an Unknown User error.

ACTIVE DIRECTORY AND WINDOWS 2000 PROFESSIONAL

As part of an Active Directory, Windows 2000 Professional provides mobile users with the same work environment whether online or offline. As a result, users can work in the same files, folders, or Web sites whether they are connected or disconnected, and easily synchronize those resources. Consistent access to network-based resources helps users stay more productive, whether on an airplane or working at a remote site.

Accessing Files and Folders When Offline

The Offline Files and Folders feature (discussed in Chapter 9) allows mobile users to easily take any combination of files, folders, or entire **mapped drives** with them offline. Instead of using a separate tool, such as the Briefcase, users simply right-click any network-based file or folder and select Make Available Offline from the resulting menu.

When the computer is offline, the files and folders appear in the same directory as they did online—as if they still resided in the same location on the network. This makes them easy to find. Plus, files and folders are visually tagged for offline use by the "roundtrip" arrows in their bottom-left corner.

Synchronization Manager

Using the new Synchronization Manager tool in Windows 2000 Professional, users can synchronize all network resources, including files, folders, e-mail, and databases, in a single location. For details on using Synchronization Manager, see Chapter 15. Users can set the Synchronization Manager to automatically synchronize some or all of their resources. For example, users can set certain files and folders to be synchronized every time they log on or off the network. The Synchronization Manager quickly scans the system for any changes, and if it detects changes, the resources are automatically updated. Only resources that have changed are updated—vastly speeding up the **synchronization** process.

Users can also determine whether files are synchronized when the system is idle, or schedule synchronization for specific time increments, such as every evening. As a result, mobile users always have the most up-to-date information, such as pricing, inventory, or sales data, to communicate to partners and clients—even when traveling.

Synchronization Manager users can also synchronize resources according to their connection types. For example, a user can save time by specifying that large database files only be synchronized when the computer is using a high-speed connection and that all personal documents stored in a specific file are synchronized every time they are connected to the corporate LAN.

Although Synchronization Manager is designed primarily to synchronize documents, it also includes the ability to resolve version conflicts in the event that multiple people edit the same document.

KEY TERMS

Active Directory — A directory and a directory service. The directory is modeled after the X.500 recommendation. In addition, the services component is modeled after the Lightweight Directory Access Protocol (LDAP). Combining these two methods also allows Active Directory to leverage the globally recognized host name resolution protocol DNS (Domain Name System).

container — A logical component used for delegation. Containers contain objects such as "user" type or "computer" type objects.h

delegation — The process of assigning groups or individuals access to manage objects. In Active Directory, delegation allows a domain to be segmented into various logical components. Permissions to manage these logical segments can also be delegated.

directory — An information source used to store information about useful, manageable objects.

directory service — A service that differs from a directory in that it is defined as both the directory information source (that is, the database) and the services (that is, LDAP) that make information available to and usable by the users and administrators.

DSCrackNames — A specific Windows 2000 NTDS API (NT Directory Services Application Programming Interface) that accepts a name and then outputs the desired result. As an example, you could offer DsCrackNames a Windows NT 4 style name "DOMAIN\USER" and request a User Principal Name (UPN). Your result would be *user@domain.com*.

inheritance — A process that lets a given ACE propagate from the container where it was applied to all children of the container.

Lightweight Directory Access Protocol (LDAP) — An X.500-based protocol used to access information directories.

mapped drive — A share on Windows 2000 or NT servers that has been linked to drive letters on the client.

multi-master replication — A replication model that is different from other models because any domain controller can accept and replicate directory changes.

objects — The basis for all things managed in a directory. The "directory dictionary," also known as the schema, defines objects. Objects exist in the form of "user" type, "computer" type. Using these base objects, Active Directory creates an object that can be managed, such as a user "joshuak."

principal — A security object in Kerberos. In Active Directory the Security Principals include Users, Computers, and Groups.

replication (directory replication) — The process of two systems in a homogenous system sharing directory information over the directory services interface. The directory services interface could be based on LDAP or the X.500 DRA (Directory Replication Agent).

sites — The logical definitions in Active Directory that relate to the IP physical substructure of a company. Sites are defined as one or more IP subnets. This in turn relates to your network topology.

subnet — A logical network defined by specifying bits, using the IP addressing and subneting algorithms (bit anding)

synchronization (directory synchronization) — A process in which two systems in a heterogeneous system share directory information, using an interim agent. The agent contains mapping tables and protocol support for both directories.

transitive bidirectional trust — A standard trust relationship that occurs when a domain joins an existing tree. All domains in the tree have two-way trusts established automatically.

trusts — The administrative links that allow user and group object security information to pass between secure boundaries (domains) in Active Directory.

X.500 — A series of International Telecommunications Union (ITU) protocol recommendations that specify a model for connecting local directory services to form one distributed global directory.

GLOSSARY

access control list (ACL) — A list of security identifiers that are contained by a resource object. Only those processes with the appropriate access token can activate the services of that object.

access token — Objects containing the security identifier of an active process. These tokens determine the security context of the process.

account lockout policy — Defines the conditions that result in a user account being locked out.

Active Directory — A centralized resource and security management, administration, and control mechanism used to support and maintain a Windows 2000 domain. The Active Directory is hosted by domain controllers, and contains information about a domain's user accounts, group memberships, group policies, and access controls for resources.

active partition — The partition that the computer uses to boot.

Address Resolution Protocol (ARP) — The IP protocol used to resolve numeric IP addresses into their MAC layer physical address equivalents.

Administrator — The Windows 2000 account designed to perform a full array of management functions.

Advanced RISC Computing (ARC) pathname — Naming convention used in the Boot.ini file to define the particular hard disk and partition where Windows 2000 operating system files reside.

alert — A watchdog that informs you when a counter crosses a defined threshold. An alert is an automated attendant looking for high or low values, and can consist of one or more counter/instance-based alert definitions.

answer file — A text file that contains a complete set of instructions for installing Windows 2000.

AppleTalk — The network protocol stack used predominantly in Apple Macintosh networks; this protocol is bundled with Windows 2000.

applet — A tool or utility found in the Control Panel that typically has a single focused purpose or function.

Application log — A log automatically created by Windows 2000 that records application events, alerts, and system messages.

application programming interface (API) — A set of software routines referenced by an application to access underlying application services.

architecture — The layout of operating system components and their relationships to one another.

Asynchronous Transfer Mode (ATM) — A cell-oriented, fiber- and copper-based networking technology that supports data rates from 25 Mbps to as high as 2.4 Gbps.

audit policy — Defines the events that are recorded in the Security log of the Event Viewer.

auditing — The recording of the occurrence of a defined event or action.

authentication — The process of validating a user's credentials to allow access to certain resources.

author mode — The condition of a console that allows users to add and remove snap-ins, create new windows, view the entire console tree, and save new versions of the console.

backup type — A backup configuration that determines how often data is backed up and the way old and new files should be handled. The types of backups are copy, daily, differential, incremental, and normal.

Backup utility — A tool that enables users to back up and restore their data and system configurations in case of a hardware or software failure.

base priority — The lowest priority that a thread may be assigned, based on the priority assigned to its process.

baseline — A definition of what a normal load looks like on a computer system; it provides a point of comparison against which you can measure future system behavior.

basic storage — The drive division method that employs partitions.

bindery — The database used by versions of NetWare before 4.0 to store network resource configuration information.

binding — The process of developing a stack by linking network services and protocols. The binding facility allows users to define exactly how network services operate in order to optimize the network performance.

BIOS (basic input/output system) — A special PC ROM chip that contains sufficient program code to let a computer perform a POST routine, to check its hardware components, and to operate basic input and output routines for keyboard or mouse input, and screen output.

boot loader — The software that shows all operating systems currently available and, via a menu, permits the user to choose which one should be booted.

boot partition — The partition that hosts the main Windows 2000 system files and is the initial default location for the paging file. The boot partition can be the same partition as the system partition, or it can be any other partition (or logical drive in an extended partition) on any drive hosted by the computer.

boot phase — Any of a number of stages in the Windows 2000 boot process, starting with the power-on self test (POST), through initial startup activities, to activation of a boot loader program, to selection of the operating system (or version) to boot, to hardware detection (Ntdetect), to selecting a configuration.

boot process — The process of bringing up a completely functional computer, starting from initial power-up (or reboot) through the boot phases and load phases involved in starting the hardware, finding a boot loader, and then loading and initializing an operating system.

boot selection menu — The list of bootable operating systems (or versions) that Boot.ini provides for display at the end of the Windows 2000 boot phase.

Boot.ini — The text file that creates the Windows 2000 boot loader's menu.

bottleneck — A system resource or device that limits a system's performance. Ideally, the user should be the bottleneck on a system, not any hardware or software component.

bound application — An application capable of running under the OS/2 subsystem or in a virtual DOS machine. If the OS/2 subsystem is available, it will be used by default.

boundary layer — Microsoft term for an interface that separates two classes of network or other system components. Boundary layers make it simpler for developers to build general-purpose applications without requiring them to manage all the details involved in network communications.

certificate — An electronic identity verification mechanism. Certificates are assigned to a client or server by a certificate authority. When communication begins, each side of the transmission can decide to either trust the other party based on its certificate and continue with the communication or not to trust the other party and terminate communication.

characterization data file — The file responsible for rendering the GDI commands into DDI commands that can be sent to the printer. Each graphics driver renders a different printer language.

child process — A process spawned within the context of some Windows 2000 environment subsystems (Win32, OS/2, or POSIX) that inherits operating characteristics from its parent subsystem, and access characteristics from the permissions associated with the account that requested it to be launched.

clean installation — *See* fresh installation.

client — A computer used to access network resources.

client application (*see also* print client) — An application or service that creates print jobs for output, which may be either end-user-originated or created by a print server itself.

Client Service for NetWare (CSNW) — Service included with Windows 2000 Professional that provides easy connection to NetWare servers.

cluster — One or more sectors grouped into a single non-divisible unit.

CMOS (complementary metal-oxide semiconductor) — A special, battery-powered chip that can store not only the software necessary to conduct the POST, but also the basic, nonvolatile configuration information that POST uses to check the RAM installed in a system, the number and type of hard drives, the type of keyboard and mouse, and so forth.

computer information file (CIF) — A detailed collection of all information related to the hardware and software products that compose your computer (and even your entire intranet).

connecting to a printer — The negotiation of a connection to a shared printer through the browser service from a client or service across the network to the machine where the shared printer resides.

connection-oriented — A class of network transport protocols that includes guaranteed delivery, explicit acknowledgment of data receipt, and a variety of data integrity checks to ensure reliable transmission and reception of data across a network. Although reliable, connection-oriented protocols can be slow because of the overhead and extra communication.

connectionless — A class of network transport protocols that makes only a "best effort" attempt at delivery, and that includes no explicit mechanisms to guarantee delivery or data integrity. Because such protocols need not be particularly reliable, they are often much faster and require less overhead than connection-oriented protocols.

console — The collection of snap-ins and extensions saved as an .msc file loaded into the MMC that offers administrative controls.

container — A logical component used for delegation. Containers contain objects such as "user" type or "computer" type objects.

context — (1) The collection of Registry values and run-time environment variables in which a process or thread is currently running. (2) The location of an NDS object in the NDS tree.

context switch — The act of unloading the context information for one process and replacing it with the information for another, when the new process comes to the foreground.

Control Panel — The collection or organization of tools and utilities, called applets, within Windows 2000 (and Windows 95, 98, and Windows NT) where most system- and hardware-level installation and configuration take place.

control set — A special set of Registry values that describes a Windows 2000 machine's startup configuration that is saved each time a Windows machine is shut down (as the current configuration) and each time a user successfully logs on for the first time after bootup (as the Last Known Good Configuration).

cooperative multitasking — A computing environment in which the individual application maintains control over the duration that its threads use operating time on the CPU.

copy backup — A method of backing up all selected files without marking them as being backed up.

counter (or performance counter) — A named aspect or activity that the Performance tool uses to measure or monitor some aspect of a registered system or application object.

Counter log — A log that records measurements on selected counters at regular, defined intervals. Counter logs allow you to define exactly which counters are recorded (based on computer, object, counter, and instance).

creating a printer — Setting up a printer for local use.

critical section — In operating system terminology, this refers to a section of code that can only be accessed by a single thread at any one time, to prevent uncertain results from occurring when multiple threads attempt to change or access values included in that code at the same time.

daily backup — A method of backing up only the selected files that have been created or modified on the day that the backup is being performed. They are not marked as being backed up.

Data Link Control (DLC) — A low-level network protocol designed for mainframe connectivity, remote booting, and network printing.

data type — (1) The format in which print jobs are sent to the spooler. Some data types are ready for printing (RAW) and some require further preparation (EMF). (2) The setting on a Registry value entry that defines the data format of the stored information.

defragmentation — The process of reorganizing files so they are stored contiguously and no gaps are left between files.

delegation — The process of assigning groups or individuals access to manage objects. In Active Directory, delegation allows a domain to be segmented into various logical components. Permissions to manage these logical segments can also be delegated.

demand paging — The act of requesting free pages of memory from RAM for an active application.

device — A physical component either internal or external to the computer that is used to perform a specific function. Devices include hard drives, video cards, network interface cards, and printers.

Device Driver Interface (DDI) — A specific code component that handles the translation of generic print commands into device-specific equivalents, immediately prior to delivery of a spool file to a print device.

differential backup — A method of backing up selected files that have been created or modified since the last full backup. They are not marked as being backed up.

direct-attached printer — A print device attached directly to a computer, usually through a parallel port (*see also* network interface printer).

directory — An information source used to store information about useful, manageable objects.

directory service — A service that differs from a directory in that it is defined as both the directory information source (that is, the database) and the services (that is, LDAP) that make information available to and usable by the users and administrators.

disabled — The state of a user account which is retained on the system but cannot be used to log on.

disk bottleneck — A system bottleneck caused by a limitation in a computer's disk subsystem, such as a slow drive or controller, or a heavier load than the system can handle.

Disk Management — The Microsoft Management Console (MMC) snap-in used to manage drives.

disk quota — A limitation on the amount of disk space that can be consumed by a user.

Distributed File System (DFS) — A Windows 2000 Server hosted service used to manipulate and manage shared resources from various locations throughout a network in a single hierarchical system.

DMA (direct memory access) — A channel used by a hardware device to access memory directly, bypassing the CPU. Windows 2000 supports eight DMA channels, numbered 0 through 7.

docking station — An expansion device for notebook computers that allows additional peripherals to be used by the portable computer. Typically, a docking station is used to add a full-sized monitor, keyboard, mouse, CD-ROM drive, tape backup, or printer to a notebook computer.

domain — An organizational unit used to centralize network users and resources.

domain controller (DC) — A computer that maintains the domain's Active Directory, which stores all information and relationships about users, groups, policies, computers, and resources.

domain model — The networking setup in which there is centralized administrative and security control. One or more servers are dedicated to the task of controlling the domain, providing access and authentication for shared domain resources to member computers.

Domain Name Service (DNS) — TCP/IP service that is used to resolve names to IP addresses.

domain security — The control of user accounts, group memberships, and resource access for all members of a network instead of for only a single computer.

domain user account — A user account that can be used throughout a domain.

DOS operating environment — A general term used to describe the reasonably thorough DOS emulation capabilities provided in a Windows 2000 virtual DOS machine (VDM).

Dr. Watson — An application error debugger. This diagnostic tool detects application failures and logs diagnostic details.

drive letter — One of two methods of accessing file system resources on formatted volumes under Windows 2000. A drive letter can be assigned to a partition or volume or a drive configuration of multiple components.

driver — A software element that is used by an operating system to control a device. Drivers are usually device-specific.

DSCrackNames — A specific Windows 2000 NTDS API (NT Directory Services application programming interface) that accepts a name and then outputs the desired result. As an example, you could offer DsCrackNames a Windows NT 4 style name "DOMAIN\USER" and request a User Principal Name (UPN). Your result would be *user@domain.com.*

dual-boot system — A multiboot system with only two operating systems.

Dynamic Data Exchange (DDE) — A method of interprocess communication within the Windows operating system.

Dynamic Host Configuration Protocol (DHCP) — An IP-based address management service that permits clients to obtain IP addresses from a DHCP server. This allows network administrators to control and manage IP addresses centrally, rather than on a per-machine basis.

dynamic link library (DLL) — A Microsoft Windows executable code module that is loaded on demand. Each DLL performs a unique function or small set of functions requested by applications.

dynamic storage — The drive division method that employs volumes. It is a new standard supported only by Windows 2000.

effective policy — The cumulative result of the priority application of group policies.

Emergency Repair Disk (ERD) — A disk that contains configuration information about your PC. It can be used to restore a PC if Windows will not start or the system files are corrupt or missing.

encrypting file system (EFS) — A security feature of NTFS under Windows 2000 that allows files, folders, or entire drives to be encrypted. Once encrypted, only the user account that enabled the encryption has the proper private key to decrypt and access the secured objects.

enhanced metafile (EMF) — Device-independent spool data used to reduce the amount of time spent processing a print job. Once it's queued, EMF data requires additional processing to prepare it for the printer.

environment subsystem — A mini-operating system running within Windows 2000, providing an interface between applications and the kernel. Windows 2000 has three environment subsystems: Win32, OS/2, and POSIX, but only Win32 is required for Windows 2000 to function.

Ethernet II — An older version of Ethernet that preceded the 802.3 specification, offering the same 10 Mbps as standard Ethernet, but using a different frame format.

event — Any significant occurrence in the system or in an application that requires users to be notified or a log entry to be added. Types of events include audits, driver failures, user logons, process launchings, and system shutdowns.

Event Viewer — A system utility that displays one of three event logs: System, Security, and Application, wherein logged or audited events appear. The Event Viewer is often the first stop when monitoring a system's performance or seeking evidence of problems because it is where all unusual or extraordinary system activities and events are recorded.

Executive Services — The collection of kernel mode components designed for operating system management.

extended partition — A type of partition on a basic disk that can be divided into logical drives. Only a single extended partition can exist on a physical disk, and when present only three primary partitions can exist.

extension — A component that adds additional functions to a snap-in.

FAT (file allocation table) or **FAT16** — The file system used in versions of MS-DOS. Supported in Windows 2000 in its VFAT form, which adds long filenames and 4 GB file and volume sizes.

FAT32 — The 32-bit FAT file system. As supported under Windows 2000, it can be used to format partitions or volumes up to 32 GB.

FDISK — A DOS utility used to partition a hard disk. The DOS FDISK tool can only recognize and manipulate primary NTFS partitions; it cannot even view logical drives in an extended partition formatted with NTFS.

Fiber Distributed Data Interface (FDDI) — A 100 Mbps fiber-based networking technology.

file system — The method used to arrange files on disk and read and write them. Windows 2000 supports NTFS, FAT, and FAT32 disk file systems.

File Transfer Protocol (FTP) — The protocol and service that provides TCP/IP-based file transfer to and from remote hosts and confers the ability to navigate and operate within remote file systems.

flush — The activity of forcing the memory-resident copy of the Registry to be written to files stored on the hard drive. A flush occurs at shutdown, when forced by an application, or just after a Registry alteration.

folder redirection — A component of IntelliMirror technologies that uses group policies to place specified user folders on a share on the network.

format — Rewriting the track and sector information on a disk. This process removes all data previously on the disk.

fragmentation — The division of a file into two or more parts where each part is stored in a different location on the hard drive. As the level of fragmentation on a drive increases, the longer it takes for read and write operations to occur.

frame type — One of four available packet structures supported by IPX/SPX and NWLink. The four frame types supported are Ethernet 802.2, Ethernet 802.3, Ethernet II, and Ethernet SNAP.

fresh installation — The installation method in which an operating system is installed without regard to preexisting operating systems. In other words, all settings and configurations are set to the OS's defaults.

gateway — A computer that serves as a router, a format translator, or a security filter for an entire network.

global group — A group which exists throughout a domain. A global group can be created only on a Windows 2000 Server system.

graphical device interface (GDI) — The portion of the Windows 2000 operating system responsible for the first step of preparing all graphical output, whether to be sent to a monitor or to the printer.

group policy — An MMC snap-in that is used to specify desktop settings for group members.

groups — Named collections of users to which you assign permissions. For example, the Administrators group contains all users who require administrative access to network resources and user accounts.

handle — A programming term that indicates an internal identifier for some kind of system resource, object, or other component that must be accessed by name (or through a pointer). In Task Manager, the number of handles appears on the Performance tab in the Totals pane. A sudden increase in the number of handles, threads, or processes can indicate that an ill-behaved application is running on a system.

hardware abstraction layer (HAL) — One of the few components of the Windows 2000 architecture that is written in hardware-dependent code. It is designed to protect hardware resources.

hardware compatibility list (HCL) — Microsoft's updated list of supported hardware for Windows 2000.

hardware profile — A collection of custom device settings used on computers with changing physical components.

hive — A discrete body of Registry keys, subkeys, and values stored in a file.

HKEY_CLASSES_ROOT — This Registry key contains the value entries that control the relationships between file extensions (and therefore file format types) and applications. This key also supports the data used in object linking and embedding (OLE), COM object data, and file-class association data. This key actually points to another Registry key named HKEY_LOCAL_MACHINE\ Software\Classes, and provides multiple points of access to make itself easily accessible to the operating system itself and to applications that need access to the compatibility information already mentioned.

HKEY_CURRENT_CONFIG — This Registry key contains the value entries that control the currently active hardware profile. The contents of this key are built each time the system is booted. This key is derived from data stored in the HKEY_LOCAL_MACHINE\ System\ CurrentControlSet\ HardwareProfiles\Current subkey. This key exists to provide backward-compatibility with Windows 95/98 applications.

HKEY_CURRENT_USER — This Registry key contains the value entries that define the user environment for the currently logged on user. This key is built each time a user logs on to the system. The data in this key is derived from the HKEY_USERS key and the Ntuser.dat and Ntuser.man files of a user's profile.

HKEY_LOCAL_MACHINE — This Registry key contains the value entries that control the local computer. This includes hardware devices, device drivers, and various operating system components. The data stored in this key is not dependent on a logged on user or the applications or processes in use.

HKEY_USERS — This Registry key contains the value entries that define the user environments for all users who have ever logged on to this computer. As a new user logs on to this system, a new subkey is added for that user, which is either built from the default profile stored in this key or from the roaming user profile associated with the domain user account.

HOSTS — A static file placed on members of a network to provide name resolution between hosts and IP addresses.

hot fix — Similar to a service pack, except that a hot fix addresses only a single problem, or a small number of problems, and may not be fully tested.

I/O port — The section of memory used by the hardware to communicate with the operating system. When an IRQ is used, the system checks the I/O port memory area for additional information about what function is needed by the device. The I/O port is represented by a hexadecimal number.

identification — The process of establishing a valid account identity on a Windows 2000 machine by supplying a correct and working domain name (if necessary) and an account name at logon.

idle disconnect — A feature that breaks off a RAS connection after a specified period of time has gone by with no activity. This feature reduces the costs of remote access, helps you troubleshoot by closing dead connections, and frees up inactive RAS ports.

imported user account — A local account created by duplicating the name and password of an existing domain account. An imported account can be used only when the Windows 2000 Professional system is able to communicate with the domain of the original account.

incremental backup — A method of backing up selected files that have been created or modified since the last normal or incremental backup. These files are marked as being backed up.

inheritance — A process that lets a given ACE propagate from the container where it was applied to all children of the container.

input message queue — A queue for each process, maintained by the Win32 subsystem, that contains the messages sent to the process from the user, directing its threads to do something.

instance — A selection of a specific object when more than one is present on the monitored system; for example, multiple CPUs or hard drives.

Integrated Services Digital Network (ISDN) — A direct, digital, dial-up Public Switched Telephone Network (PSTN) Data Link layer connection that operates at 64 KB per channel over regular twisted-pair cable between a subscriber site and a PSTN central office.

IntelliMirror — A set of features within Windows 2000 that utilizes policies, folder redirection, and the Windows Installer Service (WIS) for backing up and restoring users' data, personalized settings, and applications.

Internet Control Message Protocol (ICMP) — The protocol in the TCP/IP suite that handles communication between devices about network traffic, quality of service, and requests for specific acknowledgments (such as those used in the PING utility).

Internet Printing Protocol (IPP) — A new Windows 2000 protocol that adds Web support to the print subsystem. IPP allows remote users to submit print jobs for printing, view printer queues, and download print drivers.

Internet Protocol (IP) — The protocol that handles routing and addressing information for the TCP/IP protocol suite. IP provides a simple connectionless transmission that relies on higher-layer protocols to establish reliability.

Internet Protocol Security (IPSec) — A security protocol that secures data at the packet level.

Internetwork Packet Exchange (IPX) — The protocol developed by Novell for its NetWare product. IPX is a routable, connection-oriented protocol similar to TCP/IP but much easier to manage, and with lower communication overhead.

interprocess communication (IPC) — The mechanism that defines a way for internal Windows processes to exchange information.

IPX/SPX — The protocol suite consisting of IPX and SPX. *See* IPX and SPX for more information.

IRQ (interrupt request) — The interrupt request level that is used to halt CPU operation in favor of the device. Windows 2000 supports 16 interrupts, namely IRQ 0 through 15.

Kerberos — An encryption authentication scheme employed by Windows 2000 to verify the identity of a server and a client before actual data is transferred.

kernel — The part of Windows 2000 composed of system services that interact directly with applications; it controls all application contact with the computer.

kernel mode — Systems running in kernel mode are operating within a shared memory space and with access to hardware. Windows 2000 Executive Services operates in kernel mode.

key — A top-level division of the Registry. There are five keys in a Windows 2000 Registry. A key can contain subkeys.

language monitor — The part of the print monitor that sets up bidirectional messaging between the printer and the computer initiating the print job.

Last Known Good Configuration (LKGC) — The control set for Windows 2000 that is automatically saved by the system in a special set of Registry keys the first time a user logs on successfully to a system immediately after it has booted up. This information provides a safe fallback to use when booting the system the next time, if changes made to the Registry in the interim cause problems with booting (or if changes have been introduced that a user does not wish to retain on that system).

Layer 2 Tunneling Protocol (L2TP) — A VPN (virtual private network) protocol developed by Cisco to improve security over Internet links by integrating with IPSec (IP Security).

Lightweight Directory Access Protocol (LDAP) — An X.500-based protocol used to access information directories.

LMHOSTS — File used in Microsoft networks to provide NetBIOS name-to-address resolution.

load phase — The Windows 2000 load phase begins when the kernel assumes control of the machine, and consists of the following five steps: (1) loading the kernel, (2) initializing the kernel, (3) loading services, (4) starting the Windows 2000 system, and (5) logging on. All five steps must be completed successfully for a complete load to occur.

local computer policy — A Windows 2000 security control feature used to define and regulate security-related features and functions.

local computer security — The control of user accounts, group memberships, and resource access for a single computer.

local group — A group which exists only on the computer where it was created. A local group can have users and global groups as members.

local procedure call (LPC) — A technique to permit processes to exchange data in the Windows 2000 run-time environment. LPCs define a rigorous interface to let client programs request services, and to let server programs respond to such requests.

local profile — A set of specifications and preferences for an individual user stored on a local machine.

Local Security Policy — The centralized control mechanism which governs password, account lockout, audit, user rights, security options, public key, and IP security.

local user account — A user account that exists on a single computer.

locked out — The state of a user account that is disabled because of repeated failed logon attempts.

logon authentication — The requirement to provide a name and password to gain access to the computer.

logon script — A code script that can map drive letters, launch applications, or perform other command-line operations each time the system boots.

long filenames (LFNs) — Filenames up to 256 characters in length, supported by all file systems under Windows 2000.

mandatory profile — A user profile which does not retain changes after the user logs out. Mandatory profiles are used to maintain a common desktop environment for users.

mapped drive — A share on Windows 2000 or NT servers that has been linked to drive letters on the client.

master boot record (MBR) — The first sector on a hard disk, which contains executable code and a partition table, which stores information about the disk's primary and extended partitions. A functioning MBR is required to boot a hard disk.

memory bottleneck — A system bottleneck caused by a lack of available physical or virtual memory that results in system slowdown or (in extreme cases) an outright system crash.

memory page — *See* page.

Microsoft Management Console (MMC) — The standardized interface into which consoles, snap-ins, and extensions are loaded to perform administrative tasks.

mirrored volume — A drive configuration of a single volume is duplicated onto another volume on a different hard drive and provides fault tolerance. In Windows NT, a mirror onto a drive hosted by a different drive controller was called duplexing, but this distinction is no longer used in Windows 2000 (Windows 2000 Server only).

mismatched document — A document with incompatible printer and page settings (that is, the page settings are impossible to produce given the existing printer settings).

mode — A programming and operational separation of components, functions, and services.

mount point or **mounted volume** — A new drive access technique that maps a volume or partition to an empty directory on an NTFS volume or partition.

MS-DOS — One of the most popular character-based operating systems for personal computers. Many DOS concepts are still in use by modern operating systems.

multiboot system — A computer that hosts two or more operating systems that can be booted by selecting one from a boot menu or boot manager during each power on.

Multilink PPP — The ability of RAS to aggregate multiple data streams into one network connection for the purpose of using more than one modem or ISDN channel in a single connection.

Multiple Universal Naming Convention Provider (MUP) — A Windows 2000 software component that allows two or more UNC providers (for example, Microsoft networks and NetWare networks) to exist simultaneously. The MUP determines which UNC provider will handle a particular UNC request and forwards the request to that provider.

multiple-user system — An operating system which maintains separate and distinct user accounts for each person.

multiprocessing — The ability to distribute threads among multiple CPUs on the same system.

multitasking — Sharing processor time between threads. Multitasking may be preemptive (one thread may bump another one if the thread really needs the processor), or cooperative (one thread will retain control of the processor until its turn to use it is over). Windows 2000 uses preemptive multitasking except in the context of the WOW operating environment, because Windows 3.x applications expect cooperative multitasking.

multithreaded process — A process with more than one thread running at a time.

multithreading — The ability of an operating system and hardware to execute multiple pieces of code (or threads) from a single application simultaneously.

multi-master replication — A replication model that is different from other models because any domain controller can accept and replicate directory changes.

Multi-Provider Router (MPR) — A file system service that can designate the proper redirector to handle a resource request that does not use UNC naming. The MPR lets applications written to older Microsoft specifications behave as if they used UNC naming. The MPR is able to recognize those UNCs that correspond to defined drive mappings.

naming convention — A standardized regular method of creating names for objects, users, computers, groups, etc.

NDS tree — The hierarchical representation of the Novell Directory Services database on NetWare 4.0 and higher networks.

NetBIOS Enhanced User Interface (NetBEUI) — A simple transport program developed to support NetBIOS installations. NetBEUI is not routable, so it is not appropriate for larger networks.

NetBIOS gateway — A service provided by RAS that allows NetBIOS requests to be forwarded independently of transport protocol. For example, NetBEUI can be sent over the network via NWLink.

NetWare Core Protocol (NCP) — The protocol used by CSNW to make file and print services requests of NetWare servers.

network adapter — Another name for network interface card (NIC), the piece of hardware that enables communication between the computer and the network.

network authentication — Part of the act of connecting to or accessing resources from some other member of the domain network. Network authentication is used to prove that you are a valid member of the domain, that your user account is properly authenticated, and that you have access permissions to perform the requested action.

Network Basic Input/Output System (NetBIOS) — A client/server interprocess communication service developed by IBM in 1985. NetBIOS presents a relatively primitive mechanism for communication in client/server applications, but allows an easy implementation across various Microsoft Windows computers.

Network Basic Input/Output System (NetBIOS) — The method used by LANManager for network naming and transport functions.

network bottleneck — A system bottleneck cause by excessive traffic on the network medium to which a computer is attached, or when the computer itself generates excessive amounts of such traffic.

Network Driver Interface Specification (NDIS) — Microsoft specification that defines parameters for loading more than one protocol on a network adapter.

Network Dynamic Data Exchange (NetDDE) — An interprocess communication mechanism developed by Microsoft to support the distribution of DDE applications over a network.

Network File System (NFS) — A UDP-based networked file system originally developed by Sun Microsystems and widely used on many TCP/IP networks. (Windows 2000 does not include built-in NFS support, but numerous third-party options are available.)

network interface printer — A print device attached directly to the network medium, usually by means of a built-in network interface integrated within the printer, but sometimes by means of a parallel-attached network printer interface.

network number — The specific network identifier used by IPX for internal and network communication.

normal (or full) backup — A method of backing up all selected files and marking them as being backed up.

Novell Directory Services (NDS) — The hierarchical database used by NetWare 4.0 and higher servers to store network resource object configuration information.

NTFS (New Technology File System) — The preferred file system of Windows 2000. Supports file level security, encryption, compression, auditing, and more. Supports volumes up to 2 TB.

Ntldr — The Windows 2000 loader program that manages the boot and load phases of Windows 2000 on a PC, as soon as the MBR passes control to that program, through the loading of Ntoskrnl.exe (the Windows 2000 kernel program), which completes the loading of the operating system itself.

NTLM (NT LAN Manager) authentication — The authentication mechanism used on Windows NT that is retained by Windows 2000 for backward compatibility.

NWLink — Microsoft's implementation of Novell's IPX/SPX protocol suite.

object — Everything within the Windows 2000 operating environment is an object. Objects include files, folders, shares, printers, and processes.

Open Datalink Interface (ODI) — A part of the Novell protocol suite that provides the ability to bind more than one protocol to an adapter.

operating system — Software designed to work directly with hardware to provide a computing environment within which production and entertainment software can execute, and which creates a user interface to allow human interaction with the computer.

organizational unit (OU) — A container object that is an administrative partition of the Active Directory. OUs can contain users, groups, resources, and other OUs. OUs enable the delegation of administration to distinct subtrees of the directory.

OS/2 — An operating system developed by IBM. Windows 2000 offers some OS/2 application support.

OS/2 subsystem — The Windows 2000 subsystem used for running OS/2 applications; an emulation of OS/2 version 1.x (character mode only).

Packet Internet Groper (PING) — An IP-based utility that can be used to check network connectivity or to verify whether a specific host elsewhere on the network can be reached.

page — A 4 KB chunk of data, which is the smallest unit managed by the Virtual Memory Manager. Pages are moved around physical RAM and to and from the paging file.

paging file — A file stored on a hard drive, employed by the Virtual Memory Manager as a temporary storage container for inactive memory pages. Its name is Pagefile.sys.

parent process — The Windows 2000 environment subsystem that creates a run-time process, and imbues that child process with characteristics associated with that parent's interfaces, capabilities, and run-time requirements.

partition — A space set aside on a disk and assigned a drive letter. A partition may take up all or part of the space on a disk. You create partitions when installing an operating system or when adding new drives.

partition boot sector — The partition that contains the information the file system uses to access the volume, including a physical description of the disk, the name and version of the operating system files, the bootstrap code, and an instruction that allows the Master Boot Record to find all this information.

password — A unique string of characters that must be provided before a logon or an access is authorized. Passwords are a security measure used to restrict initial access to Windows 2000 resources.

password policy — Defines the restrictions on passwords.

PC Cards — The modern name of the PCMCIA technology. PC Cards are credit card-sized devices typically used to expand the functionality of notebook or portable computers.

PCMCIA (Personal Computer Memory Card International Association) Cards — The older name for the technology now labeled PC Cards. PCMCIA Cards are credit card-sized devices typically used to expand the functionality of notebook or portable computers.

peer-to-peer — A type of networking in which each computer can be a client to other computers, and act as a server as well.

Plug and Play — A technology that allows an operating system to inspect a device, determine exactly what the device is, install the correct driver, and enable the device—all without user interaction. Plug and play simplifies the addition and removal of hardware and can often offer on-the-fly reconfiguration of devices without rebooting.

Point-to-Point Protocol (PPP) — A Network layer transport protocol that provides connectivity over serial or modem lines. PPP can negotiate any transport protocol used by both systems involved in the link and can automatically assign IP, DNS, and gateway addresses when used with TCP/IP.

Point-to-Point Tunneling Protocol (PPTP) — A network protocol that allows users to create secure connections to corporate networks over the Internet, using virtual private networks (VPNs), which use encryption to transport private data across public links.

policy — A set of configuration options that defines aspects of Windows 2000 security.

port — Any physical communications channel to which a modem, direct cable, or other device can be connected to enable a link between two computers.

port monitor — The part of the print monitor that transmits the print job to the print device via the specified port. Port monitors are actually unaware of print devices as such, but only know that something's on the other end of the port.

POSIX (Portable Operating System Interface for Computing Environments) — A set of standards drafted by the Institute of Electrical and Electronic Engineers (IEEE) that defines various aspects of an operating system, including topics such as programming interface, security, networking, and graphical interface.

POSIX subsystem — The Windows 2000 subsystem used for running POSIX applications.

power-on self test (POST) — The system check performed by all computers when they are turned on.

preemptive multitasking — A computing environment in which the operating system maintains control over the duration of operating time any thread (a single process of an application) is granted on the CPU.

primary partition — A type of partition on a basic disk that can be marked active. Up to four primary partitions can exist on a physical disk, but only one partition can be active.

principal — A security object in Kerberos. In Active Directory the Security Principals include Users, Computers, and Groups.

print client — A network client machine that transmits print jobs across the network to a printer for spooling and delivery to a designated print device or printer pool.

print device — In everyday language, a piece of equipment that provides output service—in other words, a printer. However, in Microsoft terminology, a printer is a logical service that accepts print jobs and delivers them to some print device for output when that device is ready. Therefore, in Microsoft terminology, a print device is any piece of equipment that can produce output, so this term would also describe a plotter, a fax machine, or a slide printer, as well as a text-oriented output device such as an HP LaserJet.

print job — The contents of a completely or partially interpreted data file that contains text and control characters that will ultimately be delivered to a print device to be printed, or otherwise rendered in some tangible form.

print processor — Software that works with the printer driver to despool files and make any necessary changes to the data to format it for use with a particular printer. The print processor itself is a PostScript program that understands the format of a document image file and how to print the file to a specific PostScript printer or class of printers.

print provider — The server-side software that sends the print job to the proper server in the format that it requires. Windows 2000 supports both Windows network print providers and NetWare print providers.

print resolution — A measurement of the number of dots per inch (dpi) that describes the output capabilities of a print device; most laser printers usually produce output at 300 or 600 dpi. In general, the larger the dpi rating for a device, the better looking its output will be (but high-resolution devices cost more than low-resolution ones).

print router — The software component in the Windows 2000 print subsystem that directs print jobs from one print server to another, or from a client to a remote printer.

print server — A computer that links print devices to the network and shares those devices with client computers on the network.

Print Server services — A collection of named software components on a print server that handles incoming print jobs and forwards them to a print spooler for postprocessing and delivery to a print device. These components include support for special job handling that can enable a variety of client computers to send print jobs to a print server for processing.

print spooler — A collection of Windows 2000 DLLs used to acquire, process, catalog, and dispense print jobs to print devices. The spooler acts like a holding tank, in that it manages an area on disk called the spool file on a print server, where pending print jobs are stored until they've been successfully output. The term "despooling" refers to the process of reading and interpreting what's in a spool file for delivery to a print device.

printer (logical printer) — In Microsoft terminology, a printer is not a physical device, but rather a named system object that communicates between the operating system and some print device. The printer handles the printing process for Windows 2000 from the time a print command is issued, until a print job has been successfully output. The settings established for a printer in the Add Printer Wizard in the Printers folder (Start, Programs, Printers) indicate which print device (or devices, in the case of a printer pool) will handle print output, and also provide controls over how print jobs will be handled (banner page, special postprocessing, and so forth).

printer driver — Special-purpose software components that manage communications between the I/O Manager and a specific print device. Ultimately, printer drivers make it possible for Windows 2000 to despool print jobs, and send them to a print device for output services. Modern printer drivers also permit the printer to communicate with Windows 2000, and to inform it about print job status, error conditions (out of paper, paper jam, and so forth), and print job problems.

printer graphics driver — The part of the printer driver that renders GDI commands into device driver interface commands that may be sent to the printer.

printer interface driver — The part of the printer driver that provides an interface to the printer settings.

Printer Job Language — A specialized language that provides printer control at the print-job level and enables users to change printer default levels such as number of copies, color, printer languages, and so on.

printer pool — A collection of two or more identically configured print devices to which one or more Windows 2000 printers direct their print jobs. Basically, a printer pool permits two or more printers to act in concert to handle high-volume printing needs.

printer priority — The setting that helps to determine which printer in a pool will get a given print job. The printer with the higher priority is more likely to get the print job.

process — The primary unit of execution in the Windows 2000 operating system environment, a process may contain one or more execution threads, all associated with a named user account, SID, and access token. Processes essentially define the container within which individual applications and commands execute under Windows 2000.

processor bottleneck — A system bottleneck that occurs when demands for CPU cycles from currently active processes and the operating system cannot be met, usually indicated by high utilization levels or processor queue lengths greater than or equal to two.

profile — *See* user profile.

proxy server — Software that sits between network users and the Internet, providing a layer of security to reduce the risk of network break-ins from the Internet.

public key policy — A security control of Windows 2000 whereby recovery agents for EFS and domain-wide and trusted certificate authorities are defined and configured. These policies can be enforced on a user-by-user basis.

PXE (Pre-boot Execution) — A standard environment in PC98-compliant computers and network computers that can be used for a remote OS installation.

queue (print queue) — A series of files stored in sequential order waiting for delivery from a spool file to a print device.

RAID 5 volume — A drive configuration of three or more (up to 32) parts of one or more drives or three or more (up to 32) entire drives. Data is written to all drives in equal amounts to spread the workload. Parity information is added to the written data to allow for drive failure recovery. Provides fault tolerance. If one partition or drive fails in the set, the other members can re-create the missing data on the fly. When the failed member is replaced or repaired, the data on that drive can be rebuilt and restored. This is also known as disk striping with parity (Windows 2000 Server only).

RAW — Device-dependent spool data that is fully ready to be printed when rendered.

real mode — A DOS term that describes a mode of operation for x86 CPUs wherein they can address only 1 MB of memory, broken into 16 64-KB segments, where the lower ten such segments are available to applications (the infamous 640 KB), and the upper six segments are available to the operating system or to special application drivers—or, for Windows 2000, to a VDM.

Recovery Console — A command-line interface that provides administrative tools useful for recovering a system that is not booting correctly.

redirector — Software that examines all requests for system resources and decides whether such requests are local or remote.

REG_BINARY — A Registry value entry data type that stores data in binary format.

REG_DWORD — A Registry value entry data type that stores data in binary, hex, or decimal format.

REG_EXPAND_SZ — A Registry value entry data type that stores data in expandable text-string format that contains a variable that is replaced by an application when it is used (for example, %Systemroot%\File.exe).

REG_MULTI_SZ — A Registry value entry data type that stores data in text-string format that contains multiple human-readable values separated by null characters.

REG_SZ — A Registry value entry data type that stores data in text-string format.

Regedit — The 16-bit Registry editor. Regedit offers global searching and combines all of the keys into a single display. It can be used to perform searches, add new subkeys and value entries, alter the data in value entries, and import and export keys and subkeys.

Regedt32 — The 32-bit Registry editor. Regedt32 offers control over key and value entry security, but displays each root key in a separate window. Regedt32 also offers a read-only mode so you can explore the Registry without the possibility of accidentally altering value entries. It can be used to perform searches, add new subkeys and value entries, alter the data in value entries, and import and export keys and subkeys.

Registry — The hierarchical database of system configuration data, which is essential to the health and operation of a Windows 2000 system.

Remote Access Service (RAS) — The service in Windows 2000 that allows users to log on to the system remotely over phone lines.

Remote Installation Preparation (RIPrep) — A type of installation used with remote OS installation whereby an administrator can take an entire image of one Windows 2000 Professional machine and install that image onto other workstations.

Remote Installation Services (RIS) — An optional service in Windows 2000 Server that works with various other services to enable remote installations, including a remote operating system installation.

remote execution (rexec) — The IP-based utility that permits a user on one machine to execute a program on another machine elsewhere on the network.

remote OS installation — A component of Remote Installation Services (RIS) that can install Windows 2000 Professional on remote-boot-enabled PCs across a network.

remote shell (rsh) — The IP-based utility that permits a user on one machine to enter a shell command on another machine on the network.

removable storage device — Any type of floppy, cartridge, or drive that can be either removed between reboots or as a hot swappable device.

rendering — Graphically creating a print job.

replication (directory replication) — The process of two systems in a homogenous system sharing directory information over the directory services interface. The directory services interface could be based on LDAP or the X.500 DRA (Directory Replication Agent).

resources — Any useful service or object on a network. This includes printers, shared directories, and software applications. A resource can be accessible by everyone across the network or by only one person on a single machine, and at any level in between.

restartable file copy — A RAS feature that automatically retransmits file transfers that are incomplete because of a RAS connectivity interruption.

Reverse Address Resolution Protocol (RARP) — Used to map from a MAC-layer address to a numeric IP address.

roaming profile — A profile that resides on a network server to make it broadly accessible. When a user whose profile is designated as roaming logs on to any Windows 2000 system on the network, that profile is automatically downloaded when the user logs on.

sector — The smallest division (512 bytes) of a drive's surface.

Secure Sockets Layer/Transport Layer Security (SSL/TLS) — A mechanism used primarily over HTTP communications to create an encrypted session link through the exchange of certificates and public encryption keys.

Security Accounts Manager (SAM) — The database of user accounts, group memberships, and security related settings.

security ID (SID) — A unique name that identifies a logged-on user to the security system. SIDs can identify one user or a group of users.

Security log — A log automatically created by Windows 2000 that records security-related events.

security options — Define and control various security features, functions, and controls of the Windows 2000 environment.

Sequenced Packet Exchange (SPX) — Novell's connection-oriented, reliable network communications protocol.

Serial Line Internet Protocol (SLIP) — An implementation of the IP protocol over serial lines. SLIP has been made obsolete by PPP.

server — The networked computer that responds to client requests for network resources.

Server Message Block (SMB) — The protocol used by Microsoft clients to request file and print services from Microsoft servers such as Windows 2000 Advanced Server.

Server service — The Windows 2000 component that handles the creation and management of shared resources and performs security checks against requests for such resources, including directories and printers. The Server service allows a Windows 2000 computer to act as a server on a client/server network, up to the maximum number of licensed clients.

service — A software element used by the operating system to perform a function. Services include offering resources over the network, accessing resources over the network, print spooling, etc.

service pack — A collection of code replacements, patches, error corrections, new applications, version improvements, or service-specific configuration settings from Microsoft that correct, replace, or hide the deficiencies of the original product or preceding service packs or hot fixes.

setup boot disks (or floppies) — The four disks used by Windows 2000 to initiate the installation process on computer systems that do not have an existing OS, do not have a CD-ROM that supports bootable CDs, or that do not have network access to a Windows 2000 distribution file share. These disks can be created by running the Makeboot file from the Bootdisk directory on the distribution CD.

Setup Manager — The Windows 2000 tool that provides you with a GUI interface for creating an answer file.

share — A resource, such as an application, file, printer, or other device, that can be accessed over the network.

shell — The default user process that is launched when a valid account name and password combination is authenticated by the WinLogon process for Windows 2000. The default shell of Windows 2000 is Windows Explorer. The default shell process manages the desktop, Start menu, taskbar, and other interface controls. The shell process defines a logged-on user's run-time environment from the point of authentication forward, and supplies all spawned processes or commands with its access token to define their access permissions, until that account logs out.

Simple Mail Transfer Protocol (SMTP) — The IP-based messaging protocol and service that supports most Internet e-mail.

Simple Network Management Protocol (SNMP) — The IP-based network management protocol and service that makes it possible for management applications to poll network devices and permits devices to report on error or alert conditions to such applications.

simple volume — A drive configuration of all or part of a single drive. Does not provide any fault tolerance. NTFS volumes can be extended; FAT and FAT32 volumes cannot be extended.

sites — The logical definitions in Active Directory that relate to the IP physical substructure of a company. Sites are defined as one or more IP subnets. This in turn relates to your network topology.

snap-in — A component that adds control mechanisms to a console for a specific service or object.

spanned volume — A drive configuration of two or more (up to 32) parts of one or more drives or two or more entire drives; the elements of the spanned volume do not have to be equal in size.

spooling — One of the functions of the print spooler, this is the act of writing the contents of a print job to a file on disk so they will not be lost if the print server is shut down before the job is completed.

striped volume — A drive configuration of two or more (up to 32) parts of one or more drives or two or more (up to 32) entire drives. Data is written to all drives in equal amounts (in 64 KB units) to spread the workload and improve performance.

subkey — A division of a Registry key, such as HKEY_LOCAL_MACHINE. A subkey can contain other subkeys and value entries.

subnet — A portion of a network that might or might not be a physically separate network. A subnet shares a network address with other parts of the network but is distinguished by a subnet number.

subnet mask — The number used to define which part of a computer's IP address denotes the host and which part denotes the network.

subsystem — An operating environment that emulates another operating system (such as OS/2 or POSIX) to provide support for applications created for that environment.

synchronization (directory synchronization) — A process in which two systems in a heterogeneous system share directory information, using an interim agent. The agent contains mapping tables and protocol support for both directories.

synchronization object — Any of a special class of objects within the Windows 2000 environment that are used to synchronize and control access to shared objects and critical sections of code.

Sysdiff — The Windows 2000 utility used to take a snapshot of a basic installation and, after changes have been made, record the changes and then apply them to another installation.

System log — A log automatically created by Windows 2000 that records information and alerts about the Windows 2000 internal processes.

System Monitor — The utility that tracks registered system or application objects, where each such object has one or more counters that can be tracked for information about system behavior.

system partition — In Windows 2000, the disk that contains the MBR and partition boot sector.; the active partition where the boot files required to display the boot menu and initiate the booting of Windows 2000 are stored.

System Preparation tool (Sysprep) — A tool used to duplicate an entire hard drive. This tool is useful when installing Windows 2000 onto multiple identical systems that require identical configurations.

system state data — A collection of system-specific data that can be backed up and restored using the Windows 2000 Backup utility.

Task Scheduler — The component of Windows 2000 used to automate the execution or launch of programs and batch files on the basis of time and system conditions.

Telephony Application Programming Interface (TAPI) — A Windows feature that supplies a uniform way of accessing fax, data, and voice. TAPI is part of the Windows Open System Architecture (WOSA) developed to aid third-party vendors in designing powerful, integrated telephony applications.

Telnet — The TCP/IP-based terminal emulation protocol used on IP-based networks to permit clients on one machine to attach to and operate on another machine on the network as if the other machines were terminals locally attached to a remote host.

thread — In the Windows 2000 run-time environment, a thread is the minimum unit of system execution and corresponds roughly to a task within an application, the Windows 2000 kernel, or within some other major system component. Any task that can execute in the background can be considered a thread (for example, run-time spell checking or grammar checking in newer versions of MS Word), but it's important to recognize that applications must be written to take advantage of threading (just as the operating system itself is).

Trace log — A log that records data when only certain events occur. Trace logs record nonconfigurable data from a designated provider when an event occurs.

transaction log — A file created by Windows 2000 to record Registry changes. These files, with a .log extension, are used to verify that changes to the Registry are made successfully.

transitive bidirectional trust — A standard trust relationship that occurs when a domain joins an existing tree. All domains in the Active Directory tree have two-way trusts established automatically.

Transmission Control Protocol (TCP) — The reliable, connection-oriented, IP-based transport protocol that supports many of the most important IP services, including HTTP, SMTP, and FTP.

Transmission Control Protocol/Internet Protocol (TCP/IP) — A suite of Internet protocols upon which the global Internet is based. TCP/IP is the default protocol for Windows 2000.

Transport Driver Interface (TDI) — The specification to which all Windows transport protocols must be written to be used by higher-layer services, such as programming interfaces, file systems, and interprocess communication mechanisms.

Trivial File Transfer Protocol (TFTP) — A lightweight alternative to FTP that uses UDP to provide only simple get-and-put capabilities for file transfer on IP-based networks.

trusts — The administrative links that allow user and group object security information to pass between secure boundaries (domains) in Active Directory.

unattended installation — A Windows 2000 installation that uses a previously made script to install from. Such an installation method does not require user interaction.

uniqueness database file (UDF) — A text file that contains a partial set of instructions for installing Windows 2000, to specify settings for individual users. Used to supplement an answer file, when only minor changes are needed that don't require a new answer file.

Universal Naming Convention (UNC) — A multivendor, multiplatform convention for identifying shared resources on a network.

upgrade installation — The installation method in which data and configuration settings from the previous operating systems remain intact. The level or amount of retained data varies according to the existing operating system's type.

user account — A named security element used by a computer system to identify individuals and to record activity, control access, and retain settings.

User Datagram Protocol (UDP) — A lightweight, connectionless transport protocol used as an alternative to TCP in IP-based environments to supply faster, lower overhead access, primarily (but not exclusively) to local resources.

user mode — (1) Systems running in user mode are operating in virtual private memory areas for each process, so that each process is protected from all others. User-mode processes may not manipulate hardware, but must send requests to kernel-mode services to do this manipulation for them. (2) The condition of a console that prevents adding or removing snap-ins or resaving the console file.

user profile — A collection of user-specific settings that retain the state of the desktop, start menu, color scheme, and other environmental aspects across logons. By default, user profiles are stored in \Document\Settings\ *<username>*, where *username* is the name of the user to whom the profile applies.

User Rights Policy — Defines which groups or users can perform the specific privileged action.

value — The actual data stored by a value entry.

value entry — A named Registry variable that stores a specific value or data string. A Registry value entry's name is typically a multiword phrase without spaces and with title capitalization.

virtual device driver (VDD) — A device driver used by virtual DOS machines (VDMs) to provide an interface between the application, which expects to interact with a 16-bit device driver, and the 32-bit device drivers that Windows 2000 provides.

virtual DOS machine (VDM) — A Win32 application that emulates a DOS environment for use by DOS and Win16 applications.

virtual memory — A Windows 2000 kernel service that stores memory pages that are not currently in use by the system in a paging file. This frees up memory for other uses. Virtual memory also hides the swapping of memory from applications and higher-level services.

Virtual Memory Manager (VMM) — The part of the operating system that handles process priority and scheduling, providing the ability to preempt executing processes and schedule new processes.

virtual private networks (VPNs) — Network connections that use encryption to transport private data across public links.

volume — (1) In basic storage, a collection of 2 to 32 partitions into a single logical structure. (2) In dynamic storage, any division of a physical drive or collection of divisions into a drive configuration.

volume set — A collection of disk partitions that are treated as a logical drive. A volume set may be expanded after it has already been created. To make a volume set smaller, however, you must back up all the data, delete the volume set, define a new (smaller) volume set, and restore the data to that set. If you lose one drive in a volume set, you lose all the data in the entire set, because it offers no fault tolerance.

Win16 operating environment — The collection of components, interfaces, and capabilities that permits Win16 applications to run within a VDM within the Win32 subsystem on Windows 2000.

Win16-on-Win32 subsystem (WOW) — The formal name for the collection of components, interfaces, and capabilities that permits the Win32 subsystem to provide native support for well-behaved 16-bit Windows applications.

Win32 — The main 32-bit subsystem used by Win32 applications and other application subsystems.

Windows 2000 Advanced Server — The new Microsoft network operating system (NOS) version designed to function as a high-end resource on a network.

Windows 2000 Datacenter Server — An enhanced version of Windows 2000 Server developed to host high-end applications, as well as support data warehousing, real-time transaction processing, and enterprise Web site hosting.

Windows 2000 Professional — The new Microsoft NOS version designed to function as a client/workstation on a network.

Windows 2000 Server — The new Microsoft NOS version designed to function as a resource host on a network.

Windows 3.x — An older, 16-bit version of Windows. Windows 2000 supports backward compatibility with most Windows 3.x applications.

Windows 95 — The 32-bit version of Windows that can operate as a standalone system or in a networked environment.

Windows 98 — An updated version of Windows 95 with improved Internet and network connectivity.

Windows for Workgroups — A version of Windows 3.x that includes minimal network support to allow the software to act as a network client.

Windows Installer Service (WIS) — A component of Windows 2000 that manages the installation and removal of applications by applying a set of centrally defined setup rules during the installation process.

Windows Internet Naming Service (WINS) — A service that provides NetBIOS name-to-IP-address resolution.

Windows NT — The Microsoft network operating system that was the predecessor to Windows 2000.

WinLogon — The process used by Windows 2000 to control user authentication and manage the logon process. WinLogon produces the logon dialog box where username, password, and domain are selected, and it controls automated logon, warning text, the display of the shutdown button, and the display of the last user to log onto the system.

Winnt — The 16-bit Windows 2000 installation program.

Winnt32 — The 32-bit Windows 2000 installation program.

wizard — A tool or utility that has an interactive step-by-step guide to walk you through a complex or detailed configuration process.

workgroup — A networking scheme in which resources, administration, and security are distributed throughout the network.

workgroup model — The networking setup in which users are managed jointly through the use of workgroups to which users are assigned.

Workstation service — The Windows component that supports client access to network resources and handles functions such as logging on, connecting to network shares (directories and printers), and creating links using the Windows 2000 IPC options.

X.25 — An ITU standard for packet-switched networking; common outside of the United States where its robust handling makes it a good match for substandard telephone networks.

X.500 — A series of International Telecommunications Union (ITU) protocol recommendations that specify a model for connecting local directory services to form one distributed global directory.

x86 — The chip architecture used by Intel and others to create 386 and later CPUs (including the Pentium).

INDEX

MCSE CoursePrep ExamGuide/StudyGuide Exam #70-210

Installing, Configuring, and Administering Microsoft Windows 2000 Professional

TABLE OF CONTENTS

PREFACE

The *CoursePrep ExamGuide for MCSE Exam 70-210* and *CoursePrep StudyGuide for MCSE Exam 70-210* are the very best tools to prepare for exam day. *CoursePrep ExamGuide* and *CoursePrep StudyGuide* provide you ample opportunity to practice, drill, and rehearse for the exam!

COURSEPREP EXAMGUIDE

The *CoursePrep ExamGuide for MCSE Exam 70-210*, included with this book, provides the essential information you need to master each exam objective. The *ExamGuide* devotes an entire two-page spread to each certification objective for the exam, helping you understand the objective and giving you the bottom line information—what you really need to know. Memorize these facts and bulleted points before heading into the exam. In addition, there are several practice test questions for each objective on the right-hand page. That's hundreds of questions to help you practice for the exam! *CoursePrep ExamGuide* provides the exam fundamentals and gets you up to speed quickly. If you are seeking even more opportunity to practice and prepare, we recommend that you consider our total solution, *CoursePrep StudyGuide*, which is described below.

COURSEPREP STUDYGUIDE

For those really serious about certification, we offer an even more robust solution—the *CoursePrep StudyGuide for MCSE Exam 70-210*, ISBN 0-619-01511-X. This offering includes all of the same quality material you get with the *CoursePrep ExamGuide*, including the unique two-page spread, the bulleted memorization points, and the practice questions. In addition, you'll receive a password valid for six months of practice on CoursePrep, a dynamic test preparation tool. The password is found in an envelope in the back cover of the *CoursePrep StudyGuide*. CoursePrep is a Web-based pool of hundreds of sample test questions. CoursePrep exam-simulation software mimics the exact exam environment. The CoursePrep software is flexible and allows you to practice in several ways as you master the material. Choose from Certification Mode to experience actual exam-day conditions or Study Mode to request answers and explanations of practice questions. Custom Mode lets you set the options for the practice test, including number of questions, content coverage, and ability to request answers and explanations. Follow the instructions on the inside back cover of the book to access the exam simulation software. To see a demo of this dynamic test preparation tool, go to *www.courseprep.com*.

FEATURES

The *CoursePrep ExamGuide for MCSE Exam 70-210* and *CoursePrep StudyGuide for MCSE Exam 70-210* include the following features:

Detailed coverage of the certification objectives in a unique two-page spread Study strategically by really focusing in on the MCSE certification objectives. To enable you to do this, a two-page spread is devoted to each certification objective. The left-hand page provides the critical facts you need, while the right-hand page features practice questions relating to that objective. You'll find the certification objective(s) and sub-objectives(s) clearly listed in the upper left-hand corner of each spread.

An overview of the objective is provided in the ***Understanding the Objective*** section. Next, ***What you Really Need to Know*** lists bulleted, succinct core facts, skills, and concepts about the objective. Memorizing these facts will be important for your success when taking the exam. ***Objectives on the Job*** places the objective in an industry perspective, and tells you how you can expect to incorporate the objective on the job. This section also provides troubleshooting information.

Practice Test Questions on each right-hand page help you prepare for the exam by testing your skills, identifying your strengths and weaknesses, and demonstrating the subject matter and format you will face on the exams. Written in a similar fashion to actual MCSE exam questions, these questions test your knowledge of the objectives that are described on the left-hand page and in the *MCSE Guide to Microsoft Windows 2000 Professional* on pages 1–575 of this book. Answers to the practice test questions are found at the back of this guide.

Acronym Glossary The world of networking, perhaps more than any other computer-related discipline, uses a language all its own, which is comprised largely of acronyms. You will find a complete list of all acronyms used in this Guide, along with their meanings, at the back of the book.

Section 1

Installing Windows 2000 Professional

1.1 Perform an attended installation of Windows 2000 Professional

ATTENDED INSTALLATION

UNDERSTANDING THE OBJECTIVE

Windows 2000 supports two basic methods of installation—attended or unattended—the difference being whether the questions encountered during the installation are answered manually by the user performing the installation or automatically. Automatic, or unattended, installations are discussed in Objective 1.2.

WHAT YOU REALLY NEED TO KNOW

◆ Both attended and unattended installations support two methods for locating the installation files: over the network or from CD-ROM.

◆ The Windows 2000 Professional CD-ROM comes with four boot floppies that are used for installation. If they're not available, re-create them with the tools in the \Bootdisk folder on the CD-ROM.

◆ Floppyless installations are possible if you are upgrading a system that has an existing operating system or if the CD-ROM drive is bootable.

◆ You can install across the network by accessing the installation files on a shared network folder (that is, the \I386 folder on the CD-ROM).

◆ Choose the file system and partition size before you begin the installation. Windows 2000 supports three file systems: **FAT**, **FAT32**, and **NTFS**.

◆ FAT and FAT32 are nearly the same and provide almost no security. The NTFS file system was designed for Windows NT and has advanced security options.

OBJECTIVES ON THE JOB

Those familiar with installing other Windows operating systems, particularly Windows NT 4.0, will be familiar with the steps involved in performing an attended installation of Windows 2000 Professional. Whether booting from the installation boot floppies or from the CD-ROM itself, upgrading an existing system via CD-ROM or across the network, once the installation begins, the steps are the same. However, when using the boot floppies or booting from the CD-ROM, the first few steps are performed in "text only" mode; you then proceed to **GUI** mode.

PRACTICE TEST QUESTIONS

1. **When installing from CD-ROM, which of the following installations starts in GUI mode?**
   a. Upgrade
   b. Bootable CD
   c. Boot floppy
   d. None of the above

2. **Which of the following file systems provides the highest level of security?**
   a. FAT
   b. FAT32
   c. NTFS

3. **Jamie is asked to upgrade a number of Intel-based Windows 98 systems at her office to Windows 2000 Professional. Rather than carry the Windows 2000 Professional CD-ROMs from computer to computer, she would like to perform the installation over the network. Which of the following statements accurately describes the steps Jamie can take to perform the installations over the network? (Choose all that apply.)**
   a. Copy the entire Windows 2000 Professional CD-ROM to a directory on the server.
   b. Copy the \I386 folder from the Windows 2000 Professional CD-ROM to a shared directory on the server.
   c. Share the \I386 folder directly from the Windows 2000 Professional CD-ROM.
   d. Jamie's out of luck; she'll have to carry the CDs with her.

4. **Which of the following accurately describes a method by which Windows 2000 can be installed if the original boot floppies are unavailable? (Choose all that apply.)**
   a. Re-create the boot floppies using WINNT32 /b.
   b. Perform a floppyless installation across a network.
   c. Boot directly from the Windows 2000 Professional CD-ROM.
   d. Re-create the boot floppies using the programs in the \Bootdisk folder on the Windows 2000 Professional CD-ROM.

5. **When a shared folder on the network is used to store the installation files for Windows 2000 Professional, which of the following permissions must be assigned for the Everyone group?**
   a. Full Control
   b. Modify
   c. Read
   d. Read Only

1.2 Perform an unattended installation of Windows 2000 Professional

UNATTENDED INSTALLATION • SWITCHES • UDF

UNDERSTANDING THE OBJECTIVE

Windows 2000 Professional can be installed with little or no user intervention through an unattended installation. During an unattended installation, the installation program refers to an answer file for questions asked during installation, such as whether the system is a member of a domain. Working with unattended installations takes time and practice, but can save significant time if Windows 2000 needs to be installed on many systems.

WHAT YOU REALLY NEED TO KNOW

- ◆ To perform an unattended installation, use WINNT with the /U and /S switches, or WINNT32 with /UNATTEND and /S. You must use the /S switch if you are performing an unattended installation.

- ◆ The /U and /UNATTEND options allow you to specify the name of the answer file to be used; the /S option indicates the location of the Windows 2000 installation source files.

- ◆ A sample answer file, called UNATTEND.TXT, is included with Windows 2000 Professional in the \I386 folder.

- ◆ Using the unattended installation options indicates that you have read, understand, and agree to the license agreement.

- ◆ Answer files are used in conjunction with **UDFs**. UDF files can be used to provide the system's computer name, user name, workgroup, and so forth.

- ◆ To use a UDF file in conjunction with an answer file, specify the /UDF:id option for WINNT or WINNT32.

- ◆ Both answer files and UDFs are plain-text files that can be edited using programs such as Notepad.

OBJECTIVES ON THE JOB

Using Windows 2000 Professional answer files and UDFs for unattended installations greatly reduces the time it takes to install Windows 2000 on multiple systems. Although answer files are handy, the greatest benefit is realized when they are combined with UDFs. For example, one UDF file can be created for each department deploying Windows 2000. This approach limits the number of files to be created, while making each file easy to manage: a file containing too many entries is difficult to use. A detailed description of all possible answer file and UDF entries is located on the Windows 2000 Professional CD-ROM in the \Support\Tools directory. This folder includes a number of tools that aid in Windows 2000 setup and management, including the file DEPLOY.CAB. The description file is called UNATTEND.DOC and is located in DEPLOY.CAB.

PRACTICE TEST QUESTIONS

As the network administrator for a manufacturing company, it is your responsibility to upgrade the computers connected to your network to Windows 2000 Professional. You work through the pilot test for the implementation, identify potential problems, and are ready to roll out the operating system to the remaining 650 workstations on your network. Fortunately, your company owns three large buildings, and all of the systems are located relatively close together. Not surprisingly, you do not relish the idea of manually installing Windows 2000 Professional 650 times. Computer names are assigned based on the department in which they are used (for example, ACCOUNTING12 and MARKETING15). The Engineering department runs its own peer-to-peer network, rather than attaching to the company-wide domain.

1. **Which of the following describes an effective way to install Windows 2000 on all systems?**
   - a. Use an answer file.
   - b. Use an answer file and a UDF for each department.
   - c. Use an answer file and a UDF for each building.
   - d. Manually install Windows 2000 Professional.

2. **The /UNATTEND switch can be used independently to perform an unattended installation with WINNT32.**
   - a. True
   - b. False

3. **Which of the following statements can be used in a UDF for the Engineering department?**
   - a. JoinWorkgroup="BuildingA"
   - b. JoinDomain="Engineering"
   - c. JoinDomain="BadCompany"
   - d. JoinWorkgroup="Engineering"

4. **Because all systems are located in the same geographic area, which of the following entries need not be included in the UDF files?**
   - a. TimeZone
   - b. Building
   - c. ComputerName
   - d. TargetPath

5. **Review the UDF segment below.**

   [UniqueIDs] UserB=UserData, GuiUnattended, Identification

   [UserB:UserData] FullName="Michele Rush" ComputerName="HelpMe"

   Which of the following switches should be used when installing the operating system on Michele's system?
   - a. /UDFid:UserB
   - b. /UDF:Michele
   - c. /UDF: "Help Me"
   - d. /UDF:UserB

1.3 Install Windows 2000 Professional by using Windows 2000 Server Remote Installation Services (RIS)

REMOTE INSTALLATION SERVICES

UNDERSTANDING THE OBJECTIVE

In Windows 2000, Microsoft introduced a set of services designed to ease implementation. One of those services, **RIS**, provides a method for administrators to set up a workstation, including applications; make an image of the system; and duplicate the system any number of times.

WHAT YOU REALLY NEED TO KNOW

- ◆ RIS must be used to duplicate systems, because each Microsoft-based computer must have a unique **SID**.
- ◆ RIS can be used to install only Windows 2000 Professional images; other versions of Windows or non-Windows operating systems cannot be installed with RIS.
- ◆ RIS can be used only on client systems with a limited choice of network interface cards.
- ◆ The RIS diskette includes drivers for only 25 **PCI** network cards—not PC, **ISA**, or other PCI cards.
- ◆ RIS is limited to imaging the C: drive on the target system.
- ◆ When the image is applied to the target system, it provides an exact duplicate, including the size and file system of the partition.

OBJECTIVES ON THE JOB

To perform duplication services, RIS requires a Windows 2000 Server or group of servers to store the RIS images and provide RIS services. One benefit of RIS is that it supports multiple images on the RIS server. The RIS server must also be configured in Active Directory as a **DHCP** server. Remote boot disks must be created from the RIS server using the RBFG.EXE program. The workstation from which the image is created is the prototype system. First, prepare the prototype system and ensure that it has all desired software and is running well. Next, create the image using the Remote Installation Services Preparation Wizard (RIPRep). RIPRep is located on the RIS server within the REMIST\Admin\I386 folder. After finishing the initial wizard, reboot the prototype system. When it restarts, the RIPRep executes the Mini-Setup, which removes the machine-specific information, including the SID, from the image. To install the image on the target system, insert the RBFG boot disk and reboot.

PRACTICE TEST QUESTIONS

1. The partition size created on the target system is exactly the same size and exactly the same file system as the partition on the prototype system.
   a. True
   b. False

2. Which of the following configurations can be duplicated and installed using RIS?
   a. Windows 98 only
   b. Windows 2000 Professional with Office 2000 Professional
   c. Windows 2000 Server with Office 2000 Professional
   d. Windows NT 4.0 Workstation only

3. Which of the following must be unique for each system using a Microsoft operating system?
   a. IP address
   b. Computer name
   c. SID
   d. User name

4. Which of the following are limitations placed on the image storage drive on the RIS server?
   a. It can store a maximum of three system images.
   b. It cannot reside on the same drive as the server's operating system.
   c. It cannot be the boot drive for the server.
   d. It cannot be used to store IIS Web server files.

5. Which of the following programs is used to create boot disks for use with RIS?
   a. RIPRep
   b. REMINST
   c. RISDisk
   d. RBFG

6. Which of the following systems can use RIS to install Windows 2000 Professional?
   a. A portable system using a PCI-based docking station
   b. A portable system using a PC card to connect to the network
   c. A desktop system using an ISA network interface card
   d. A desktop system using a PCI network interface card

7. Geoffrey is planning to use RIS to duplicate a Windows 2000 Professional installation to multiple systems. He configured a Windows 2000 Server as the RIS server and is ready to begin the process. Before continuing, which of the following services must Geoffrey ensure is installed and functioning? (Choose all that apply.)
   a. DHCP
   b. Active Directory
   c. TFTP
   d. DNS

1.4 Install Windows 2000 Professional by using the System Preparation Tool

SYSPREP

UNDERSTANDING THE OBJECTIVE

The System Preparation Tool (SYSPREP.EXE) automates Windows 2000 installations. Sysprep prepares a system's operating system and application for disk imaging duplication. However, Sysprep is merely a preparation tool, designed for use with third-party drive duplication tools such as Symantec's Ghost or PowerQuest's Drive Image Pro.

WHAT YOU REALLY NEED TO KNOW

- ◆ Sysprep removes the system-specific information and prepares the system to redetect all Plug and Play devices upon start-up.
- ◆ Unlike RIS, Sysprep is not limited to Windows 2000 Professional; it can be used to prepare Windows 2000 Server systems as well.
- ◆ Once the source system, or a system created from an image of the source system, is restarted, a new SID is assigned and the Setup Wizard is launched.
- ◆ The Setup Wizard runs the Mini-Setup Wizard and prompts only for system-specific information like the computer name, product ID, and user name.
- ◆ The information required by Mini-Setup can be automated with an answer file.
- ◆ The system then completes the setup process, including a complete detection of Plug and Play devices.

OBJECTIVES ON THE JOB

When setting up the computer that will act as the source of the image, do not join a domain and do not assign an Administrator password. If the Administrator password is not blank, it cannot be changed when Setup runs upon reboot. After installing Windows 2000, configure the computer with additional software, local user accounts, and so forth, then test the system and ensure that everything is working properly. To run Sysprep, you need both the SYSPREP.EXE and SETUPCL.EXE files, which are located in the \Support\Tools/Deploy.cab file. Run Sysprep to ready the system for duplication. After Sysprep executes, it either shuts down automatically or lets you know that it is safe to shut the system down. At this point, use a third-party disk duplication utility to create an image of the system. The next time the system starts, Setupcl runs, Plug and Play devices are detected, and the Mini-Setup Wizard runs. Mini-Setup checks for an answer file called SYSPREP.INF. If it is present, the wizard uses the information in the answer file to automatically provide feedback to Setup. SYSPREP.INF uses the same syntax and parameters as the standard answer file UNATTEND.TXT. Two options are used only in SYSPREP.INF: InstallFilesPath and KeepPageFile. These keys are described, with all other answer file options, in the UNATTEND.DOC file in the DEPLOY.CAB file on the Windows 2000 CD-ROM.

PRACTICE TEST QUESTIONS

1. **Which of the following can be prepared for duplication using Sysprep?**
   a. Windows 98 only
   b. Windows 2000 Professional with Office 2000 Professional
   c. Windows 2000 Server with Office 2000 Professional
   d. Windows NT 4.0 Workstation only

2. **When can configurations be duplicated and installed using RIS?**
   a. After Sysprep executes during the boot process
   b. After the Mini-Setup Wizard begins
   c. Before the source system is shut down
   d. After DEPLOY.CAB is executed during the boot process

3. **Which of the following must you remember when preparing the source system for duplication? (Choose all that apply.)**
   a. Ensure that the system is working properly before proceeding.
   b. Do not join a domain.
   c. Do not install software other than the operating system before duplication.
   d. Leave the Administrator password blank.

4. **Each system created from the source image will have the same SID as the source system.**
   a. True
   b. False

5. **Which of the following are located in the DEPLOY.CAB archive file?**
   a. UNATTEND.DOC
   b. UNATTEND.TXT
   c. RSYSPREP.EXE
   d. SETUPCL.EXE

6. **Which of the following Sysprep switches instructs the program to operate without intervention from the user?**
   a. /nouser
   b. /nosidgen/
   c. /noinput
   d. /quiet

7. **Which of the following answer file entries is recognized only by the Sysprep application?**
   a. KeepPageFile
   b. NetAdapters
   c. SysprepLocation
   d. NewSID

1.5 Create unattended answer files by using Setup Manager to automate the installation of Windows 2000 Professional

SETUP MANAGER • ANSWER FILES

UNDERSTANDING THE OBJECTIVE

The answer files used by Windows 2000 for unattended installations are plain-text files that can be modified using a standard editor, such as Notepad. To make them even easier to use, Microsoft included a utility to create and modify answer files. Setup Manager is included on the Windows 2000 CD-ROM as part of the DEPLOY.CAB file.

WHAT YOU REALLY NEED TO KNOW

- ◆ Unattended answer files such as UNATTEND.TXT and SYSPREP.INF are used to automate the Windows 2000 installation process.
- ◆ Setup Manager is a Microsoft utility that is used to create unattended answer files.
- ◆ Setup Manager is included as part of the support tools included with Windows 2000 and is located in the DEPLOY.CAB file in the \Support\Tools folder on the CD-ROM.
- ◆ The Setup Manager Wizard can be used to duplicate the current system's configuration in an answer file, edit an existing answer file, or create a new answer file.

OBJECTIVES ON THE JOB

Regardless of the method chosen to create or modify the answer file, the Setup Manager walks you through the configuration options. The Setup Manager included with Windows 2000 Professional can create answer files for Windows 2000 Server and Professional. Through this utility, the Administrator can specify the required level of user interaction during installation, default user information (organization or user name), a predefined or automatically generated computer name, a standard Administrator password, permission for the user to specify the Administrator password, default display settings, time zone and regional settings, telephony (modem) settings, default network settings, IE 5 settings (proxy server, configuration scripts, and so on), and commands to be run when the system is started or after setup. When the Setup Manager Wizard concludes, three files are created with the filename specified and the extensions .txt, .udf, and .bat. Many variations are available through this process. It is recommended that you first make an answer file based on the configuration of the current system, then review the files created, and expand from there. More information on the exact options available through the Setup Manager is available in the UNATTEND.DOC file.

PRACTICE TEST QUESTIONS

1. **For which of the following Microsoft operating systems installations can answer files be created using Setup Manager? (Choose all that apply.)**
   - a. Windows NT Server 4.0
   - b. Windows NT Workstation 4.0
   - c. Windows 2000 Professional
   - d. Windows 2000 Server

2. **Which of the following is not an option for the level of user interaction available through an automated answer file?**
   - a. No user interaction
   - b. Hide pages
   - c. Provide defaults
   - d. Read only

3. **You are prompted through the Setup Manager Wizard to specify the domain to which the system will belong.**
   - a. True
   - b. False

4. **In addition to Setup Manager, which of the following can be used to modify an existing answer file?**
   - a. Wordpad
   - b. Edit
   - c. Notepad
   - d. All of the above

5. **Match the following Sysprep switches with the appropriate description.**

Provide Defaults	a. The program does not allow the user to view provided answers if all settings are specified by the script.
Fully Automated	b. The script provides answers only to the text portion of the Setup.
Hide Pages	c. The user is able to accept the answers provided by the script or make adjustments as necessary.
Read Only	d. The user is unable to view or change settings during installation.
GUI Attended	e. The user is able to view the provided settings but unable to make any adjustments.

6. **After using Setup Manager, which of the following can be used to utilize the new answer file? (Choose all that apply.)**
   - a. WINNT
   - b. The newly created .bat file
   - c. The newly created .txt file
   - d. WINNT32

1.6 Upgrade from a previous version of Windows to Windows 2000 Professional

UPGRADING • FAT, FAT32, NTFS • WINNT.EXE, WINNT32.EXE

UNDERSTANDING THE OBJECTIVE

For the most part, Windows 2000 Professional is implemented on existing computers, rather than purchasing new computers with Windows 2000 Professional already installed. For this reason, it is important to understand the process for upgrading from a previous version of Windows.

WHAT YOU REALLY NEED TO KNOW

- ◆ Like Windows NT 4.0, Windows 2000 Professional allows for dual-boot systems.
- ◆ Most often, the operating system is upgraded or replaced entirely.
- ◆ You must determine whether to upgrade or replace the operating system before the installation process begins.
- ◆ You should replace the operating system unless there is a reason to retain a system's network configuration or desktop settings.
- ◆ Windows 2000 Professional supports a dual-boot configuration with Windows 95/98, Windows NT 3.51, or Windows NT 4.0 without using a third-party boot manager, such as Partition Magic.
- ◆ If implemented with a third-party boot manager, Windows 2000 can be installed with other operating systems such as Linux.

OBJECTIVES ON THE JOB

Upgrading to Windows 2000 Professional from an existing Windows installation is a straightforward process. First, insert the Windows 2000 Professional CD-ROM. If Autorun is enabled, the Microsoft Windows 2000 CD Wizard starts. If Autorun is not enabled on the system, open Windows Explorer, select the CD-ROM drive, and open the \I386 folder. Depending on the current operating system installed, open either WINNT.EXE or WINNT32.EXE. Windows 2000 Professional supports three file systems: FAT, FAT32, and NTFS. Depending on the existing operating system, you may be presented with the option of upgrading the file system on the computer during the installations. Windows 95 and 98 systems support FAT and FAT32, whereas Windows NT systems have the ability to use NTFS. Note that the NTFS implementation for Windows 2000 is version 5, which is upgraded from that used with Windows NT. To access an NTFS partition in a dual-boot NT/2000 scenario, the NT version must have the updated NTFS drivers, which are part of Service Pack 4.

PRACTICE TEST QUESTIONS

Four systems at LuxOMatic Enterprises must be upgraded to Windows 2000 Professional to support a new distributed application. The network administrator for LuxOMatic performed an inventory of the systems and determined that everything is ready for the upgrade. All systems are currently used by other networking staff, but one of the systems (Workstation V) has experienced problems with its network adapter since a new software package was installed. Because one of the network technicians uses a network monitoring application that is currently not supported by Windows 2000, Workstation IX must be able to dual-boot between Windows NT 4.0 Workstation and Windows 2000 Professional. The LuxOMatic systems currently use the following operating systems:

Workstation III—Windows 98 using FAT

Workstation V—Windows 98 using FAT32

Workstation VII—Windows NT Workstation 4.0 with Service Pack 4 using NTFS

Workstation IX—Windows NT Workstation 4.0 with Service Pack 2 using NTFS

1. **Which of the following changes must be made to Workstation IX to support a dual-boot configuration with Windows 2000 Professional?**
   a. Apply Service Pack 4.
   b. Install Partition Magic or another boot manager.
   c. Install updated drivers for NTFS.
   d. No changes must be made to allow a dual-boot configuration.

2. **Which of the following programs upgrades Workstation III to Windows 2000?**
   a. WINNT.EXE
   b. CONVERT.EXE
   c. WINNT32.EXE
   d. UPGRADE.EXE

3. **For which of the systems described in the scenario is an upgrade most appropriate? (Choose all that apply.)**
   a. Workstation III
   b. Workstation V
   c. Workstation VII
   d. Workstation IX

4. **Which of the following accurately describes the steps that can be taken when upgrading the file system for Workstation III? (Choose all that apply.)**
   a. The file system can remain intact as FAT.
   b. The file system must be upgraded to FAT32.
   c. The file system must be upgraded to NTFS.
   d. The file system can be upgraded to NTFS32.

OBJECTIVES

1.7 Apply update packs to installed software applications

UPDATE PACKS

UNDERSTANDING THE OBJECTIVE

Microsoft and other software companies provide incremental updates to their software, similar to the service packs discussed later in this section. Obtaining and installing application update packs is briefly covered on the exam.

WHAT YOU REALLY NEED TO KNOW

- ◆ Microsoft operating systems, beginning with Windows 98, have dedicated Web sites that include update downloads. The Windows 2000 site is *www.microsoft.com/windows2000/downloads/*.

- ◆ Microsoft applications also operate under the same process. Check out *www.microsoft.com/office/downloads.htm*.

- ◆ The Internet Explorer update site is located at *www.microsoft.com/windows/ie/ download/default.htm*.

- ◆ Other applications, such as Norton Antivirus, support periodic updates and utilize their own methods for obtaining and installing the software.

- ◆ Periodically check the update Web sites for the applications installed on your system to ensure that the most up-to-date files are installed.

OBJECTIVES ON THE JOB

Updates to Microsoft products are available from the Microsoft Web site. Navigate the Web site or directly enter one of the URLs listed above. After locating the appropriate update, click the link to begin the download. Microsoft provides detailed descriptions of each download, including information on exactly which issues are addressed by the update. Many updates are available that may not be necessary for your particular configuration. Microsoft classifies the updates into various categories including Critical Updates, Other Downloads, and categories specific to the application being updated. For example, the Internet Explorer site currently includes a Preview category that includes beta versions of the software. Before proceeding with the installation, carefully read the description of the update to be sure that it is necessary for your situation. Critical Updates most often deal with essential application components, such as security. In fact, the majority of the Critical Updates on the Internet Explorer Web site today are security fixes or enhancements. Recommended Updates are more configuration-specific and are not required for all users. For example, the Windows 2000 Recommended Update section includes the 128-bit encryption download and AOL Image Support Update. Installing the software update is usually as simple as launching the downloaded file to start an installation wizard. Specific instructions are included as part of the wizard and may require restarting the system after installation.

PRACTICE TEST QUESTIONS

1. **Which of the following application updates is not available to customers in all countries outside the United States?**
    a. Windows 2000 Cluster Server
    b. AOL Image Support Update
    c. 128-bit encryption update
    d. Internet Explorer 5.5

2. **Which of the following updates should you consider installing first?**
    a. Windows 2000 Security Update (Critical Update)
    b. Active Directory Client Extensions (Management Tools Update)
    c. Windows 2000 Resource Kit Tools (Other Download)
    d. Terminal Service Advanced Client (Recommended Update)

3. **It is always a good idea to install all available application updates.**
    a. True
    b. False

4. **Which of the following methods would you use to easily access the Windows 2000 Update Web site?**
    a. Open Internet Explorer and enter the URL.
    b. Click the Windows Update utility in the Control Panel.
    c. Click the Windows Update utility in the Start menu.
    d. Access the Windows Update FTP site using an FTP client.

5. **In which of the following categories would an update for a specific hardware configuration most likely be found?**
    a. Critical Updates
    b. Recommended Updates
    c. Product Enhancements
    d. Other Updates

6. **Which of the following accurately describes how often an Administrator should check for and apply application updates?**
    a. Applications' update availability should be reviewed weekly.
    b. Applications' update availability should be reviewed quarterly.
    c. Applications' update availability should be reviewed only if problems are encountered.
    d. Applications' update availability should be reviewed on a case-by-case basis (for example, virus-scanning applications more often than office applications.)

1.8 Prepare a computer to meet upgrade requirements

HARDWARE REQUIREMENTS • HCL

UNDERSTANDING THE OBJECTIVE

Even more so than previous versions of Windows or Windows NT, Windows 2000 supports a very specific set of hardware. To successfully answer the questions for this objective, you must know what the minimum requirements for Windows 2000 Professional are, how to determine if an existing computer meets those requirements, and how to determine whether a specific piece of hardware meets the requirements.

WHAT YOU REALLY NEED TO KNOW

◆ Windows 2000 Professional has the following minimum hardware requirements: 133 MHz Pentium, 64 MB of RAM, VGA or higher video adapter and monitor, 2 GB hard disk drive with 650 MB available, keyboard, pointing device (mouse), a CD-ROM drive, 3.5-inch floppy disk drive (if necessary to install), and a network interface card.

◆ The components in the system to be upgraded must comply with the **HCL**. If a device is installed in a Windows 2000 system and is not on the HCL, Microsoft will not support the installation.

◆ The most accurate information regarding hardware compatibility for Windows 2000 is on the HCL Web site *www.microsoft.com/hcl/default.asp*.

◆ The Microsoft Logo program defines the level of compatibility with the operating system and is divided into three levels: Beta, Compatible, and Logo.

◆ To access the Compatible Hardware Devices site, go to *www.microsoft.com/ windows2000/*, click Upgrading to Windows 2000, click Check Hardware and Software Compatibility, and then click the Hardware Devices link.

OBJECTIVES ON THE JOB

In most cases, you will expend more resources in upgrading existing systems than in purchasing new systems that meet the Windows 2000 Professional requirements. The most important aspect of this process is an accurate inventory of the equipment to be upgraded, including the make and model of each device in each system. If such an inventory does not already exist, it is imperative that you review each system and create a detailed list of the connected devices. Using this inventory, ensure that all systems currently meet the minimum requirements for Windows 2000 Professional. If they do not, upgrade the systems with components listed on the HCL. If they meet the requirements, compare the components list to the information on the HCL. Microsoft does not provide support for components that are not on the HCL.

PRACTICE TEST QUESTIONS

Stan is a help desk manager for a securities company in Chicago. He has six systems to be used for a Windows 2000 implementation pilot. Because hardware is at a premium, Stan was given older machines for the pilot. The system configurations are:

TestSystem1 and **TestSystem2**: 350 MHz AMD K6-2s, 64 MB RAM, 2.4 GB SCSI drives (1 GB free), Diamond Multimedia Speedstar video cards, and 3Com NICs

TestSystem3 and **TestSystem4**: 133 MHz Intel Pentiums, 32 MB RAM, 1.0 GB IDE drives (250 MB free), Diamond Speedstars, and 3Com NICS

TestSystem5 and **TestSystem6**: 233 MHz Intel Pentium IIs, 128 MB RAM, 6.4 GB IDE drives (2.2 GB free), nVidia Riva TNT2 video cards, and 3Com NICs

1. **When Stan starts the pilot, his Internet connection is down and he is unable to access the Web. Without access to the Internet, how can Stan begin the upgrade preparation process?**
    a. Because all systems are currently running Windows NT 3.51, Stan can assume everything is compatible and proceed.
    b. Stan can research the systems' components on the HCL located on the Windows 2000 Professional CD-ROM.
    c. Stan can research the systems' components using the information in the February 2000 issue of *Windows* magazine.
    d. There is nothing Stan can do until he has access to the Internet.

2. **Based on the minimum requirements for Windows 2000, which of the following changes must be made to TestSystem3 and TestSystem4 before installing Windows 2000? (Choose all that apply.)**
    a. Upgrade their processors to at least 266 MHz.
    b. Upgrade their memory to at least 64 MB.
    c. Upgrade their hard drives to at least 2.0 GB.
    d. Upgrade their network cards.

3. **Based on the excerpt from the Windows 2000 CD-ROM HCL below, the display adapters in TestSystem1 through TestSystem4 are compatible with Windows 2000.**

Display Adapter:
Diamond Multimedia Speedstar 64 Graphics 2200XI (PCI)
Diamond Multimedia Speedstar 64 PCI (PCI)

    a. True
    b. False

4. **TestSystem1 and TestSystem2 have Adaptec 2742W SCSI controllers. Stan is not able to find the controllers listed on the CD-ROM HCL or on the Compatible Hardware Device Web site. On the HCL Web site, he finds that the controllers are rated Compatible with Windows NT 4.0 What is the best option for Windows 2000 compatibility?**
    a. Search the Adaptec Web site for updated drivers.
    b. Search the Windows Update Web site for updated drivers.
    c. Replace the SCSI controllers with devices that appear on the HCL.
    d. Nothing is necessary because compatible Windows NT 4.0 devices always work with Windows 2000.

1.9 Deploy service packs

SERVICE PACKS • BACKUPS

UNDERSTANDING THE OBJECTIVE

Microsoft periodically updates its operating systems through patches and updates called service packs. Applying a service pack is as easy as installing an application. You should, however, proceed with caution when deploying a service pack as they do not always fix problems and sometimes even create new ones.

WHAT YOU REALLY NEED TO KNOW

◆ Service packs address specific issues with the operating system, and each service pack comes with a list of those issues.

◆ Enhancements required for specific environments are sometimes available only through the service packs (for example, Windows NT 4. supports NTFS 5 only after Service Pack 4 is installed).

◆ Service packs are cumulative, meaning that everything in Service Pack 1 is contained in Service Pack 2, and Service Pack 4 contains the updates from Service Packs 1, 2, and 3.

◆ Service packs can be ordered from Microsoft or downloaded from its Web site at *www.microsoft.com/windows2000/servicepacks* or *www.microsoft.com/windows2000/ downloads.*

◆ Determine whether a service pack is installed and which version is present by either typing WINVER at a command prompt, selecting Help, About in Explorer, or referencing the Registry key CSD Version in the HKEY_LOCAL_MACHINE\ SOFTWARE\Microsoft\WindowsNT\CurrentVersion.

OBJECTIVES ON THE JOB

The first service pack for Windows 2000 (SP1) was introduced in July 2000 and includes updates related to Windows Setup, the reliability of the operating system, and security. Microsoft makes it very clear that it may not be necessary for everyone to install SP1, however, and recommends that you review the documentation before taking this step. This holds true for all service packs and should be considered a hard and fast rule. In addition, keep the following in mind when dealing with updates to the operating system: Read all available documentation on the service pack before upgrading the system. Make sure you completely understand how the service pack is installed and uninstalled. Make a complete backup of your system to guard against problems that may result from the upgrade. Make a separate backup of the Registry using the Registry Editor. Ensure that the correct version of the service pack is used for the upgrade. Disable all antivirus programs and other nonessential utilities before running the update.

PRACTICE TEST QUESTIONS

1. **In which of the following service packs would you find an update that was initially introduced in July 2000?**
    a. Service Pack 1 dated July 2000
    b. Service Pack 4 dated February 2001
    c. Service Pack 7 dated April 2002
    d. All of the above

2. **Which of the following is not a method by which you can obtain a Windows 2000 service pack?**
    a. The Microsoft FTP site
    b. The Microsoft Web site
    c. Order directly from Microsoft
    d. None of the above

3. **Which of the following is not necessary before installing a service pack?**
    a. Create an image of the system.
    b. Create a backup of the Registry.
    c. Disable antivirus programs.
    d. Review all available documentation.

4. **Which of the following is located in the DEPLOY.CAB archive file?**
    a. SYSCONFIG
    b. WINVER
    c. IPCONFIG
    d. SYSVER

5. **Which of the following technologies is included with Windows 2000 to apply service pack updates to a set of installation files, thereby ensuring that all subsequent installations include the service pack's updates?**
    a. Quick updating
    b. Install updating
    c. Slipstreaming
    d. Upgrading

6. **Which of the following is true of service packs applied to Windows 2000 computers?**
    a. After adding or removing a service, the service pack must be reapplied.
    b. After adding or removing a service, the service pack is reapplied automatically.
    c. Before adding or removing a service, the service pack must be removed.
    d. Changes to existing services do not affect service packs.

1.10 Troubleshoot failed installations

MEDIA ERRORS • INSUFFICIENT DISK SPACE • STOP MESSAGES • DOMAIN CONTROLLER COMMUNICATIONS FAILURES • DEPENDENCY FAILURES • HARDWARE PROBLEMS

UNDERSTANDING THE OBJECTIVE

Although installation of Windows 2000 is successful a large percentage of the time, there is always a chance that an installation may fail. Installation failures fall into one of six categories: media errors, insufficient disk space, stop message or blue screen errors, domain controller communication issues, dependency failures, and hardware problems.

WHAT YOU REALLY NEED TO KNOW

- ◆ Media errors—Media errors are problems with the Windows 2000 distribution media—that is, the CD-ROM. The only solution is to switch installation media.

- ◆ Insufficient disk space—This error is generated when the minimum amount of free space is not available on the destination partition. Solutions include moving or deleting existing files, formatting the partition, or deleting and re-creating the destination partition.

- ◆ Stop message or blue screen errors—These errors occur when an incompatible or damaged hard drive controller is used.

- ◆ Domain controller communication failures—If you choose to join a domain during installation and are unable to communicate with the controller for the specified domain, the installation cannot continue. This error usually occurs when the domain name, user name, or password is mistyped. There may also be a problem with the network configuration of the workstation. Try connecting to the domain from other workstations to assist in identifying the problem.

- ◆ Dependency failures—A dependency is the reliance of one driver or service on another for successful operation. A dependency failure occurs when the lower-level process fails. To identify the failure and possible solutions, use Event Viewer and Computer Manager.

- ◆ Hardware problems—Hardware issues occur when hardware actually fails or when the target system uses unsupported hardware. Verify that all system components are included in the HCL and that all drivers are updated according to the tested level. If the installation is still unsuccessful, a component may be suspect and should be tested or replaced.

OBJECTIVES ON THE JOB

If an installation fails, the reason is most likely one of those found in the list above. Being familiar with potential problems helps avoid them during installation. In addition to the information provided in this objective, you can consult the Event Viewer and the Computer Management Tool.

PRACTICE TEST QUESTIONS

1. **For which of the following errors should you expect to restart the installation from the beginning? (Choose all that apply.)**
   a. Stop messages
   b. Hardware failures
   c. Insufficient disk space
   d. Media errors

2. **Which of the following errors may be generated if the installed equipment is not listed in the HCL? (Choose all that apply.)**
   a. Hardware failures
   b. Media errors
   c. Stop messages
   d. Domain controller failures

3. **Which of the following accurately describes a media error?**
   a. Inability to write to the destination partition
   b. Inability to install the necessary drivers for the CD-ROM
   c. Inability to read the installation files
   d. Inability to create the destination partition

4. **Which of the following tools is used to identify the point of a dependency failure? (Choose all that apply.)**
   a. Network Manager
   b. Event Viewer
   c. System Manager
   d. Computer Manager

5. **Domain controller failures are logged in which of the following files?**
   a. NETSETUP.LOG
   b. NETERROR.LOG
   c. SETUPERR.LOG
   d. COMSETUP.LOG

6. **Which of the following best describes the action log?**
   a. A detailed account of the steps taken by the user during installation
   b. A detailed account of the actions Setup performs during installation
   c. An account of all errors encountered during the installation
   d. An account of all errors encountered with multimedia devices

Section 2

Implementing and Conducting Administration of Resources

2.1 Monitor, manage, and troubleshoot access to files and folders

SECURITY • PERMISSIONS

UNDERSTANDING THE OBJECTIVE

Windows 2000 includes extensive security features that allow you to closely control which users have access to particular files and folders, and the functions users can perform on those files and folders. The level of security available depends on the partition's file system.

WHAT YOU REALLY NEED TO KNOW

◆ While Windows 2000 supports the FAT and FAT32 file systems, they provide only limited security features at the folder level.

◆ FAT and FAT32 permissions are limited to granting or denying users the Full Control, Change, or Read permissions to the folder.

◆ NTFS provides more extensive and dynamic security down to the individual file level.

◆ NTFS file objects support five basic permissions, folders support six basic permissions, and both support 13 advanced permissions.

◆ To monitor permissions' success or failure, Microsoft provides NTFS auditing. Auditing can be enabled or disabled for individual files or folders.

◆ Troubleshooting access errors can be tedious unless you have a firm grasp of how the permissions were established and the rules that apply. Begin with the level of access the user should have and work back from the file or folder level, bearing in mind that group memberships can affect permissions.

OBJECTIVES ON THE JOB

Because FAT and FAT32 partitions can secure folders but not files, provide no auditing ability, and must be shared to secure a folder on a FAT partition, NTFS is the recommended file system for Windows 2000. If you must maintain a FAT partition, you are only able to grant or deny Full Control, Change, or Read permissions to users and groups. NTFS, on the other hand, can secure both files and folders and allows multiple security levels. On NTFS, the file or folder does not need to be shared before permissions can be assigned. Auditing can also be enabled through the object's Advanced properties. Auditing allows the Administrator to monitor a user's or group's success or failure in accessing a resource. With auditing enabled, a message is written to the Event Log when the audit criteria are met. For example, an Administrator can configure the system to record a message when a user tries to access a file but is denied access. This feature can be a useful tool when diagnosing access problems.

PRACTICE TEST QUESTIONS

1. **Attempts to access which of the following objects can be logged by Windows 2000?**
   a. The file USERINFO.DBS on a FAT32 partition
   b. The folder Users on a FAT partition
   c. The file USERINFO.DBS on an NTFS partition
   d. The folder Userdata on a FAT32 partition

2. **Which of the following permissions are available for both NTFS and FAT32 objects? (Choose all that apply.)**
   a. Write
   b. Full Control
   c. Read
   d. Create

3. **Through the Advanced configuration tab, which of the following permissions can be assigned to a FAT32 object?**
   a. Read
   b. Change
   c. Full Control
   d. None of the above

4. **By default, the group Everyone is granted Full Control to all objects.**
   a. True
   b. False

5. **Which of the following object settings must be taken, rather than assigned?**
   a. Full Control
   b. Owner
   c. Read Only
   d. Create

6. **It comes to your attention that an application accessed by many users was deleted from the system. Going back through your configuration logs, you note that access to the individual files in the folder was explicitly limited to Read Only. However, two groups required Full Control access to the folder. You find that a user in one of these groups deleted the folder. Which of the following describes the change that must be made to the folder's permissions to ensure that this problem does not happen again?**
   a. For both groups, clear Write Extended Attributes permission to the folder.
   b. For both groups, clear Change Permissions permission to the folder.
   c. For both groups, clear Delete Subfolders and Files permission to the folder.
   d. For both groups, clear Take Ownership permission to the folder.

7. **Which of the following groups is maintained by the system and includes only a single user or group?**
   a. Authenticated Users
   b. Network
   c. Interactive
   d. Creator Owner

2.2 Configure, manage, and troubleshoot file compression

FILE COMPRESSION • COMPACT

UNDERSTANDING THE OBJECTIVE

To better utilize available disk space, Windows 2000 provides the ability to automatically compress files on NTFS partitions. This feature compresses entire volumes, folders, or individual files. Each object is controlled independently to provide the greatest flexibility.

WHAT YOU REALLY NEED TO KNOW

◆ Compression is possible only on NTFS volumes.

◆ Windows 2000 manages file compression and decompression automatically. When a compressed file is accessed, the system decompresses the file for use without intervention.

◆ Compression is an attribute that can be set for each NTFS object.

◆ Files and folders can also be compressed using a command-line utility called Compact.

◆ Special rules apply to moving and copying files. The compression state of the file may change when it is moved or copied.

OBJECTIVES ON THE JOB

By utilizing Windows 2000 file compression, an administrator can provide more efficient file storage and possibly reduce the amount of money spent on disks. The first opportunity you have to enable compression is when the volume is formatted with NTFS. Even if compression is enabled on the volume, individual files or folders can be designated to remain uncompressed. In addition to changing an object's compression status through its properties, the Compact utility can be used from a command prompt to compress specific files. Compact is generally employed in one of two instances: as part of a batch script or to force compression caused by a system failure. Keeping track of the compression state for a particular file can prove somewhat difficult. When an uncompressed file is moved on an NTFS volume, it remains uncompressed, regardless of the compression state of the folder to which it is moved. The same holds true for moving a compressed file. When you copy a file on an NTFS volume, however, it takes on the compression attribute of the destination folder. In other words, copying a compressed file to an uncompressed folder results in an uncompressed copy of the file. Remember, though, that moving or copying any file to a FAT volume means that the file will be uncompressed in its new location. Because Windows 2000 handles the compression automatically, failures occur only if an issue arises during compression or decompression. To address compression issues, try forcing a change in the compression state using Compact or the object's properties.

PRACTICE TEST QUESTIONS

1. **Which of the following is best suited to compress 15 individual files in different folders?**
   a. Each file's properties
   b. Each folder's properties
   c. Compact
   d. Compression enabled on the entire volume

2. **If you experience problems in accessing a compressed file, what is the first step you should take?**
   a. Recover the file from backup
   b. Force the compression or decompression
   c. Reboot and allow the compression algorithm time to operate
   d. Change the compression status of the file's folder

3. **Which of the following describes the compression rule used when copying files in NTFS volumes?**
   a. The destination file maintains its compression state, regardless of the folder's compression state.
   b. The destination folder adjusts to the compression state of the file.
   c. The destination file is compressed during the copy process, regardless of its original state.
   d. The destination file takes on the compression state of the destination folder.

4. **Which of the following describes the compression rule used when moving files from an NTFS volume to a FAT32 volume?**
   a. The destination file is written uncompressed.
   b. The destination file takes on the compression state of the destination folder.
   c. The file maintains its compression state.
   d. The destination folder is compressed if the file is compressed.

5. **Which of the following can be configured to help easily identify the compression states of files and folders?**
   a. Display compressed file and folder names in italics
   b. Display compressed file and folder names in bold
   c. Display compressed file and folder names in a new font
   d. Display compressed file and folder names in a different color

6. **As a rule, which of the following files should not be compressed by Windows 2000 Professional because resources are wasted?**
   a. Operating system files
   b. Files compressed with utilities such as PKZIP
   c. Database files
   d. Image files

2.3 Control access to files and folders by using permissions

FAT/FAT32 AND NTFS PERMISSIONS

UNDERSTANDING THE OBJECTIVE

The Windows 2000 security system was designed to give administrators the opportunity and flexibility to configure their environment to be as secure as possible without limiting user productivity. The security level available on a particular system depends on the partition's file system. FAT and FAT32 provide only basic security for shared folders (discussed in Objective 2.7), but offer no control over local user access. NTFS provides a much more robust security model that can be used to grant or deny a local user access to files and folders.

WHAT YOU REALLY NEED TO KNOW

◆ FAT and FAT32 permissions cannot be assigned to local folders unless they are shared. It is not possible to secure a FAT folder that is not shared first.

◆ FAT supports three permission levels: Full Control, Change, and Read.

◆ NTFS permissions can be assigned to both files and folders, which do not have to be shared. Permissions are assigned through the Security tab of the object's Properties dialog box.

◆ NTFS file objects have five basic permission levels: Read, Write, Read & Execute, Modify, and Full Control. Folder objects have the same five basic permissions, plus List Folder Contents. Both have 13 advanced permission levels.

◆ An NTFS object's permissions are inherited from the object's container, unless they are specifically modified by the Administrator.

◆ NTFS permission application rules apply to requests for any NTFS object.

OBJECTIVES ON THE JOB

The available FAT permissions are straightforward and easy to remember. The NTFS basic permissions and their results follow: Read allows users to view and access the contents of the folder or file; Write allows users to create new folders, overwrite the file, or change its attributes; List Folder Contents gives users visibility to the names of the files in the folder; Read & Execute allows users to run program files from the folder and to view and access the contents of the folder; Modify allows users to delete folder and list contents and to delete or change the file; Full Control provides complete and unrestricted access to the file or folder. By default, the group Everyone is granted Full Control to all new objects. NTFS utilizes a strict set of permissions rules when granting or denying access to a resource. NTFS permissions apply to all access requests, regardless of whether the requesting user is local or remote. NTFS permissions are cumulative; that is, user-level permissions are combined with group-level permissions to arrive at the granted access level. NTFS file permissions take precedence over contradictory folder permissions. In addition, Denied access takes precedence over contradictory Allow permissions. Inherited NTFS permissions can be disabled for an object, at which point the permissions must be specified.

PRACTICE TEST QUESTIONS

1. Which of the following is used to describe the process by which a file obtains its permissions settings from its container folder?
   a. Transference
   b. Update
   c. Inheritance
   d. Conversion

2. Specified NTFS file permissions are superseded by container folder permissions.
   a. True
   b. False

3. Which of the following permission settings applies to both NTFS file and folder objects? (Choose all that apply.)
   a. Read
   b. Change
   c. Read and Execute
   d. Full Control

4. Frank is in the Accounting department and is a member of both the Accounts Payable and Accounts Receivable network groups. Frank worked on an application and database for use by the Accounts Receivable group and is ready to share the file with his co-workers. Frank granted Read and Execute access to the file for the AR group, and denied access to the folder for the AP group. In its current configuration, does the Accounts Receivable group have sufficient access to work with the database?
   a. Yes
   b. No

5. Given the scenario in Question 4, does Linda, a member of both the AR and AP groups, have access to the database files?
   a. Yes
   b. No

6. Which of the following file system components contains a list of all user and group accounts granted access to a specific file or folder?
   a. UNC
   b. ACL
   c. NTFS
   d. ACE

2.4 Optimize access to files and folders

AUTHENTICATED USERS GROUP • DISTRIBUTED FILE SYSTEM

UNDERSTANDING THE OBJECTIVE

Because Windows 2000 was designed around providing access to resources, it quickly responds to requests for resources. Sometimes, however, it may be necessary to modify the way in which a system operates to provide more efficient access to files and folders.

WHAT YOU REALLY NEED TO KNOW

- ◆ Two steps can be taken to optimize file and folder access: utilize the Authenticated Users group and/or work with a new Windows 2000 Distributed File System.
- ◆ The system automatically generates the Authenticated Users group, which includes all currently authorized users.
- ◆ Because its configuration is always kept in memory, granting Authenticated Users permissions to files or folders speeds up the process of accessing resources.
- ◆ The **Dfs** is a Windows 2000 Server service used to organize and manage shared network resources.
- ◆ Utilizing Dfs makes it easier for users to locate and access shared resources.

OBJECTIVES ON THE JOB

Windows 2000 automatically manages the Authenticated Users group, which includes all users who are currently logged in and have legitimate access to the system. Although the system automatically manages it, the Authenticated Users group can be treated just like any other group. To speed up access to specific files or folders, Administrators can grant access to the Authenticated Users group. Note, however, that this group is accessible only through the object's Security tab—not through the Users and Groups option in the Computer Management application. If you decide to use this group, you should carefully plan and test your permissions design before implementation. The Dfs used in conjunction with a Windows 2000 Server provides an easily navigated representation of available resources. The Dfs server Administrator organizes available resources into a single hierarchical system called the Dfs tree, which presents the end user with a single access point for all network resources. Resources shared by Windows 2000 Professional systems can be included in the Dfs design in the same manner as Windows 2000 Server resources are.

PRACTICE TEST QUESTIONS

1. **Which of the following Dfs components hierarchically represents the available shared resources on the network?**
   a. Dfs root
   b. Dfs server
   c. Dfs tree
   d. Dfs path

2. **Which user is responsible for monitoring and updating the Authenticated Users group?**
   a. Administrator
   b. SuperUser
   c. LANMan
   d. None

3. **Which of the following reasons provides an incentive to grant access to the Authenticated Users group, rather than a different group?**
   a. The Authenticated Users group's configuration is always kept in memory on the system.
   b. Everyone who logs on is part of the group.
   c. The group has Administrator-level access.
   d. The system queries the Authenticated Users group first.

4. **Once configured, the Dfs structure can include, in the same manner as Windows 2000 Professional, which of the following?**
   a. The local file system
   b. A shared network resource
   c. A CD-ROM
   d. An object in the Active Directory

5. **Which of the following Windows 2000 utilities provides more efficient access to files and folders on the hard disk?**
   a. Backup
   b. Compact
   c. Share
   d. Disk Defragmenter

6. **Which of the following groups is managed by Windows 2000 Professional and can provide more efficient access to specific groups of users? (Choose all that apply.)**
   a. Interactive
   b. Everyone
   c. Dialup
   d. Network

2.5 Manage and troubleshoot access to shared folders

MANAGING SHARED FOLDERS

UNDERSTANDING THE OBJECTIVE

One of the primary driving factors in establishing computer networks is the desire to allow users to share resources. In the Windows 2000 Professional environment, local folders can be shared, thereby permitting access by users from other systems on the network.

WHAT YOU REALLY NEED TO KNOW

◆ Folders on Windows 2000 computers can be shared without regard for the file system, because share permissions control resource access across the network.

◆ Regardless of the system's configuration, the default permission for the group Everyone is Full Control of the shared folder.

◆ After the user is granted access to the resource by the share, the NTFS permissions (if applicable) are applied and the most restrictive permission level dictates the level of access that the user actually receives.

◆ Troubleshooting shared resource issues often boils down to access permissions, either to the share or to the object.

OBJECTIVES ON THE JOB

After sharing the folder, an Administrator can use one of two configuration methods to manage access to the shared resources. Through the Sharing tab, the Administrator can click the Permissions button to make adjustments to the current restrictions. The same options are available through Computer Management by selecting the share, choosing Properties from the Action menu, and selecting the Share Permissions tab. Through these configuration methods, an Administrator can specify the number of concurrent users who are able to access a share and indicate whether the files in the share are cached locally when accessed remotely. Similar rules apply to accessing shared resources as apply to NTFS permissions. Multiple share permissions are cumulative, and the most restrictive is applied. Explicit Deny always takes precedence over Allow. If a folder is moved, it does not retain the shared information. Share permissions restrict only network users, not local users. Connecting to a shared resource can be performed by any number of methods, including Windows Explorer, My Computer, and My Network Places.

PRACTICE TEST QUESTIONS

1. **When creating a share through Computer Management, you are asked to select the access level for users. Which of the following access levels is unique to this share creation method?**
   a. All users have Full Control.
   b. Administrators have Full Control; other users have Read Only access.
   c. Administrators have Full Control; other users have no access.
   d. None of the above.

2. **While researching an access problem on a shared folder, Jamie discovers that one of the users was granted Full Control to the NTFS object and Read permission to the share. Which of the following best describes the user's true access level?**
   a. The user cannot access the share over the network.
   b. The user can see the contents of the share, but is not able to save any changes or modify the files on the share.
   c. The user can attach to the share, but cannot access the files within the share.
   d. The user can perform any function, including deleting or modifying the contents of the share

3. **Share permission levels are applied to both local and remote users.**
   a. True
   b. False

4. **Which of the following entries must be provided before a share can be created?**
   a. Name of the share
   b. Description of the share
   c. Default user access
   d. Share administrator

5. **Which of the following objects cannot be shared?**
   a. An entire volume
   b. A program's folder
   c. An individual file
   d. None of the above; they can all be shared

6. **Which of the following symbols is used to identify a share automatically created by Windows 2000 for administrative purposes?**
   a. %
   b. $
   c. &
   d. #

7. **A new employee joined the company and connects to the network via dial-up from his home. After only a few days' work, he calls to complain that accessing files on the network is too slow. Which of the following settings can speed up access to files for this remote user?**
   a. Enable caching for offline access
   b. Upgrade the user's connection speed
   c. Limit the user's access time to late evening and early morning
   d. Limit other users' available bandwidth

2.6 Create and remove shared files

CREATING SHARED FOLDERS • REMOVING SHARED FOLDERS

UNDERSTANDING THE OBJECTIVE

As with many things in Windows 2000, you can create and share a folder in multiple ways, and you can remove a shared folder. Beyond Windows Explorer, however, additional methods for creating shared folders exist.

WHAT YOU REALLY NEED TO KNOW

◆ Creating a folder in Windows Explorer is simple and can be done in any number of ways.

◆ Using Computer Management, you can create a folder at the same time that you create a new share.

◆ If necessary, you can share a folder and monitor the status of all shares from a command prompt. To share a folder, type NET SHARE <sharename>=path.

◆ To stop sharing a resource, you can use any of these utilities.

OBJECTIVES ON THE JOB

The method used for creating and removing shared folders is, at best, a personal preference. Try each approach to determine which is best for you. For the purpose of the exam, be aware that there are always many ways to skin the Windows cat.

PRACTICE TEST QUESTIONS

1. **Which of the following utilities restricts you when sharing an existing folder? (Choose all that apply.)**
   - a. NET SHARE
   - b. Network Management
   - c. Computer Management
   - d. Folder Properties

2. **In addition to monitoring resources being shared on the network, which of the following fall under the Shared Folders service? (Choose all that apply.)**
   - a. NTFS Permissions
   - b. Shared Files
   - c. Open Files
   - d. Sessions

3. **Which of the discussed share management techniques provides the highest level of security?**
   - a. Computer Manager
   - b. Folder Properties
   - c. NET SHARE
   - d. None is any more secure than the other

4. **If a folder has been shared more than once, which option is used to delete one share but continue sharing the folder?**
   - a. Do Not Share This Folder
   - b. Remove Share
   - c. Delete Share
   - d. Stop Share

5. **Which of the following file system objects can be configured to be cached?**
   - a. Individual file
   - b. Unshared folder
   - c. Shared folder
   - d. All of the above

6. **Suzanne is installing a new application accessed from a shared folder on a server. Because the folder resides on a FAT32 volume, the security assigned to the share must be complete. Which of the following actions should Suzanne take to ensure effective use of the application? (Choose all that apply.)**
   - a. Change Everyone's access from Full Control to Read access
   - b. Assign the Administrators group Full Control access
   - c. Assign the Connected Users group Read access
   - d. Create a group for users who edit the data files and assign the new group Change access

2.7 Control access to shared folders by using permissions

SECURITY SETTINGS • PERMISSIONS

UNDERSTANDING THE OBJECTIVE

Although you often provide shared folders for the benefit of many users, some circumstances require limiting access to the shared resources. For example, a folder containing sensitive Human Resources data may be accessed by members of the HR department, but should not be available to other users on the network. This restriction is applied by assigning share permissions granting or denying specific users and groups access to the folder. In fact, this security structure is the only method of restricting user access to data on FAT and FAT32 partitions.

WHAT YOU REALLY NEED TO KNOW

◆ By default, the Everyone group is granted Full Control permission to all new shares. If NTFS is used, the NTFS folder or file permissions will be applied.

◆ Share-level permissions are the only method for improving security on systems with FAT partitions.

◆ Users and groups are either granted or denied access to each permission level through the share's properties.

◆ Full Control grants users unrestricted access to the shared folders and their contents.

◆ Change grants users the ability to access, execute, and open the folder's contents; modify or delete existing objects; and create new objects within the folder.

◆ Read grants users the ability to access, open, and execute the share's contents.

◆ Share permissions influence only users' ability to access the resources remotely; they cannot control local access to the folder.

◆ Multiple share and NTFS permissions are cumulative, and the most restrictive permission set is applied.

◆ If user permissions and group permissions contradict each other, denied permission overrides allowed permission to the share.

OBJECTIVES ON THE JOB

You can modify a share's security settings through a number of methods, including the folder's Properties dialog box's Sharing tab and the Shared Folders section of the Computer Management utility. Note that allowing Change permission automatically gives Read permission. Also, allowing or denying Full Control automatically allows or denies the other selections. When other permissions are used in conjunction with NTFS permissions, changing the default access for Everyone is not necessary because NTFS permissions are more dynamic and the cumulative, most restrictive access level is assigned to the user.

PRACTICE TEST QUESTIONS

1. **Which of the following utilities cannot be used to modify a share's permissions on a FAT32 volume?**
   a. Computer Management
   b. The share's Properties dialog box's Sharing tab
   c. Net Share Permissions
   d. None of the above

2. **Which of the following applies to both NTFS folder permissions and share permissions? (Choose all that apply.)**
   a. The Read permission allows users to view, access, and execute programs in the folder.
   b. Permissions are cumulative, and the most restrictive is used to determine a user's access level.
   c. Denied access overrides allowed access when user and group permissions conflict with each other.
   d. The Full Control permission provides users with unrestricted access to the folder and its contents.

3. **Allowing the Change share permission automatically applies the Full Control permission.**
   a. True
   b. False

4. **Which of the following applies when a shared folder is moved to new NTFS volume?**
   a. The folder's configuration is maintained, including its share information.
   b. The folder's NTFS configuration is maintained, but its share information is lost.
   c. The folder's share information is maintained, but its NTFS information is lost.
   d. Neither the folder's NTFS configuration nor its share information is maintained.

5. **Tim is sharing a folder on his system so that his co-workers can access its contents. The four other supervisors in his department should be able to change the contents of the folder, but most of the users should be allowed only to read it contents. Which of the following assignments should Tim make to ensure secure access to the share? (Choose all that apply.)**
   a. Grant Everyone Read
   b. Deny Everyone Full Control
   c. Grant each Supervisor Full Control
   d. Grant Supervisors Change

6. **To manage applications that allow only a specific number of users concurrent access, which share setting should you use?**
   a. Caching
   b. Share Settings
   c. Permissions
   d. User Limit

2.8 Manage and troubleshoot Web server resources

IIS

UNDERSTANDING THE OBJECTIVE

Windows 2000 includes software that makes it possible to share Internet documents with other users. You can install **IIS** through the Add/Remove Windows Components section of the Add/Remove Programs Wizard.

WHAT YOU REALLY NEED TO KNOW

◆ IIS version 5.0, which is included with Windows 2000 Professional, replaces Peer Web Services, which was used with Windows NT Workstation 4.0.

◆ Windows 2000 Professional users can use IIS to provide Web and FTP service to a small number of users on the Internet or on an intranet.

◆ IIS on Windows 2000 Professional is limited to 10 concurrent users.

◆ Although it is installed automatically during the Windows 2000 Server Setup, IIS on Windows 2000 Professional must be selected as an option during installation or installed at a later time. IIS can be installed through the Add/Remove Windows Components utility.

◆ Because only 10 users can be connected at the same time, IIS on Windows 2000 Professional systems are typically used for testing or for providing very limited access to workgroup Web sites.

◆ Except for the user limitation, the version of IIS included with Windows 2000 Professional is identical to that included with Windows 2000 Server.

OBJECTIVES ON THE JOB

IIS installs components that either service requests from remote users or are used to manage the services: **FTP**, **NNTP**, **SMTP**, World Wide Web Service (which distributes **HTML** documents), FrontPage 2000 Server Extensions, the Internet Information Services **MMC** snap-in, and two versions of the Internet Services Manager. IIS provides support for multiple, independent Web sites by assigning multiple IP addresses to a single computer or by using **HTTP** 1.1 custom headers. Each Web site is configured in IIS through either the Installation Service Manager or the Services and Applications section of the Computer Management utility. Many Web sites do not require the user to provide a logon name and password. This statement does not mean that the user is not authenticated. By default, Web sites allow anonymous logons and browsers automatically provide the information. IIS lets Administrators disable anonymous logons and specify an authentication method. Because IIS resources are essentially shares for Internet or intranet users, they are subject to the same rules as are other shared folders. Troubleshooting Web resource issues should focus on the permissions granted to the user and communication with the IIS system.

PRACTICE TEST QUESTIONS

1. **Which of the following features is not available for Windows 2000 Professional IIS implementations?**
   a. NNTP
   b. Multiple Web sites
   c. Unlimited users
   d. Anonymous logon

2. **In which of the following scenarios is IIS installed automatically when upgrading from Windows NT Workstation 4.0 to Windows 2000 Professional?**
   a. PWS was installed before the upgrade.
   b. IIS was installed before the upgrade.
   c. Service Pack 6 was applied before the upgrade.
   d. IIS is never installed automatically.

3. **Which of the following IIS utilities includes an HTML interface for remote management?**
   a. FrontPage 2000 Server Extensions
   b. Internet Services Manager
   c. MMC
   d. IIS Manager

4. **If a Web site managed through IIS resides on an NTFS volume, to which of the following groups should NTFS permissions be allowed for anonymous access?**
   a. Everyone
   b. Interactive
   c. Online
   d. IIS

5. **Which of the following Control Panel utilities can you use to determine the cause of a Web resource access problem?**
   a. Administrative Tools, Computer Management
   b. Internet Options
   c. Services
   d. Network and Dial-up Connections

6. **Which of the following IIS applications provides file management services to clients?**
   a. NNTP
   b. FTP
   c. DHCP
   d. SMTP

2.9 Connect to local and network print devices

PRINTER • PRINTER DRIVER • PRINT SERVER • PRINT JOB

UNDERSTANDING THE OBJECTIVE

Although we are quickly moving to a purely electronic age, paper remains an important part of our lives, and hard copies of documents are often preferred. Like nearly all operating systems before it, Windows 2000 provides support for printing hard copies or files. In addition to supporting two traditional print devices (locally connected printers and network printers), Windows 2000 includes a new feature—printing to Internet-connected printers.

WHAT YOU REALLY NEED TO KNOW

◆ Microsoft uses unique terminology to refer to the Windows printing process. Knowing the definitions of the terms is important to correctly address printing issues and questions as they arise.

◆ A print device is the physical device from which the hard copy is generated. In normal parlance, it is a printer. Microsoft defines printers another way, however.

◆ In Microsoft terminology, a printer is a named system object that manages communication between the operating system and a print device. In some cases, a printer represents a specific print device. It could also comprise a group of printers (printer pool) or a fax modem.

◆ A print job is the information to be passed to the print device for output.

◆ A print server is a computer that links print devices to the network and shares the devices with the network. Windows 2000 Professional and Server computers can operate as print devices.

OBJECTIVES ON THE JOB

The printing process follows these basic steps:

The user indicates that he or she would like a hard copy of the current document. An internal Windows process called the **GDI** begins communication with the printer driver and print device and creates the print job.

The print job is passed to the spooler, which calls the print server for the device and passes the job to the print router.

The print router on the server accepts the job and temporarily writes the data to the hard disk so that it is not lost. The print router then passes the job to the print server's local print provider.

The local print provider identifies the print processor for the indicated device and passes the job to the processor.

The print processor retrieves the spooled file from the hard disk and passes the job to the print monitor.

The print job reaches the print device.

PRACTICE TEST QUESTIONS

1. **Windows 2000 Professional is capable of producing hard copy only on devices directly connected to the system.**
    a. True
    b. False

2. **Which of the following most accurately describes the process of spooling?**
    a. The printer identifies the print router to which the print job should be sent.
    b. The print device performs a system check to ensure that the paper feeder is working correctly.
    c. The print job is encrypted for transmission over a network.
    d. The print job is written to the hard disk for storage until the hard copy is produced.

3. **Which of the following terms describes the software component used to facilitate communication with the print device?**
    a. Printer driver
    b. Printer router
    c. Printer
    d. Print job

4. **Which of the following print process components links print devices to the network and shares those devices?**
    a. Print monitor
    b. Print server
    c. Printer driver
    d. Print router

5. **Which of the following indicates a print device physically connected to a system?**
    a. Network interface print device
    b. Internet printer
    c. Direct-attached printer
    d. Local printer

6. **Which of the following Printer Wizard options is used to connect to a printer at a specified IP address?**
    a. Select COM1 from the port list.
    b. Create a new port and select Direct IP from the list.
    c. Create a new port and select Standard TCP/IP port.
    d. Select LPT1 from the port list.

7. **Which of the following systems can be used as a print server that hosts both Macintosh and Microsoft print jobs?**
    a. Windows 2000 Server
    b. Windows 98
    c. Windows 2000 Professional
    d. Windows NT Workstation 4.0

2.10 Manage printers and print jobs

PRINTER SETTINGS: GENERAL, SHARING, PORTS, ADVANCED, SECURITY, AND DEVICE

UNDERSTANDING THE OBJECTIVE

The Windows 2000 print process allows for a high degree of management of both printers and print jobs. Part of managing printers involves knowing the steps necessary to create the local system object. Once it is created, you can manage how the printer handles all print jobs. Once a print job has been created, you can individually manage how the job is processed.

WHAT YOU REALLY NEED TO KNOW

♦ Before a printer can be used, it must be defined in the operating system. Referred to as creating the printer, this step is done through the Printers applet (Start, Settings, Printers).

♦ Create a local printer definition by double-clicking the Add Printer icon. Specify whether it is a local or network printer, the make and model of the printer, and its name.

♦ Right-click the printer icon and select Properties from the menu to configure the printer's options.

♦ To change how a print job is processed, double-click the printer icon, right-click the specific print job, and select Properties from the menu.

OBJECTIVES ON THE JOB

Regardless of whether the print device is directly connected to the system or resides somewhere on the network, a local system object (the printer) must be created. This creation is accomplished through the Printers applet, the Add Printer utility. For a network printer, you must specify the printer name or browse the network and select from a list of available printers. Next, indicate whether the new printer should be the default printer for Windows. If the printer driver is not already loaded, you will be asked to select the make and model of the printer.

Once the printer has been created, you can configure its operation by selecting its icon and choosing Properties from the File menu in the Printers window. The specific tabs that appear depend on the print device, but some are standard across all devices: General, Sharing, Ports, Advanced, Security, and Device Settings. The information on the General tab identifies the printer. The Sharing tab allows you to share the printer on the network. The Ports tab allows you to indicate the physical port to which the print device is connected. The Advanced tab allows you to change settings such as the hours during which the printer is available. The Security tab is used to configure the user's rights to the printer. The Device Settings tab displays information on the print device's configuration.

Basic print job management allows you to pause, cancel, or restart a print job. To further manage a print job, select the job and choose Properties from the File menu in the print device window. A dialog box then allows you to adjust how the print job is managed, including its priority in the queue.

PRACTICE TEST QUESTIONS

1. **Which of the following is not requested when creating a network printer?**
   a. Whether the printer is Plug and Play
   b. The name of the printer
   c. The make and model of the printer
   d. Whether to make the printer become the default for Windows

2. **On which of the following printer configuration tabs can you specify who is able to access and manage the printer?**
   a. Sharing
   b. Security
   c. Device Settings
   d. General

3. **What steps reassign the default printer?**
   a. Right-click the printer's icon and select "Set as default printer".
   b. Select the printer and choose "Set as default printer" from the File menu.
   c. Double-click the printer's icon and select "Set as default printer" from the Printer menu.
   d. All of the above

4. **On which of the standard printer properties tabs would you find the amount of memory installed in the printer?**
   a. Security
   b. General
   c. Device Settings
   d. Ports

5. **Which of the following print job functions cannot be performed through the menu that appears when you right-click the job?**
   a. Cancel the job
   b. Pause the job
   c. Restart the job
   d. Change the job's priority

6. **Gina is setting up a new group of printers for the accounting department. Rather than reconfiguring many of the systems to utilize individual printers, she wants to configure the printers as a group. In this configuration, a group of users can print to one printer, and the print devices operate more efficiently. What is the term used to describe the environment Gina is creating?**
   a. Print Server
   b. Printer Group
   c. Printer Pool
   d. Print Mass

7. **In the example given in Question 6, Gina wants to ensure that the print jobs sent by the manager are printed first. How can this goal be accomplished?**
   a. Set a higher priority level on the printer used by the manager.
   b. Set a lower priority level on the printer used by the manager.
   c. Set a higher priority level on the group Everyone.
   d. Set a lower priority level on the group Everyone.

2.11 Control access to printers by using permissions

PRINTER PERMISSIONS

UNDERSTANDING THE OBJECTIVE

Like many Windows 2000 objects, printers are tightly integrated with the security subsystem. This relationship provides Administrators with a method for controlling which users have access to printers and what those users are allowed to do when managing the printers and print jobs.

WHAT YOU REALLY NEED TO KNOW

- ◆ Permissions for printers relate to three basic functions: Print, Manage Documents, and Manage Printers.

- ◆ Like other Windows 2000 permissions, printer permissions can be assigned to users and groups, depending on the need.

- ◆ Unlike other permissions, however, the default setting for Everyone is not full access (Manage Printers), but rather Print only.

- ◆ The Print permission allows users to print documents; pause, resume, restart, and cancel their own documents; and connect to a printer.

- ◆ The Manage Documents permission allows everything allowed by Print permission, plus the ability to cancel, resume, restart, and cancel other users' documents.

- ◆ The Manage Printers permission allows everything in Manage Documents permission, plus the ability to share a printer, delete a printer, and change the printer's permissions.

- ◆ You can access additional permissions settings for printer ownership and auditing by clicking the Advanced button.

OBJECTIVES ON THE JOB

Controlling how a printer is managed is achieved through the printer's permissions settings. These settings are accessed through the Security tab of the printer's Properties dialog box. The default settings allow all users to connect to the printer, print documents, and manage their own print jobs. In large organizations, decentralized printer administration is achieved by granting some users permission to manage the documents sent to the printer. The highest permission level allows users to fully manage the printer.

PRACTICE TEST QUESTIONS

Joan is responsible for the printers found in a large call center in Tampa, Florida. In this role, she manages 130 printers on a Windows 2000 network. The call center's 750 employees are split into 25 teams, each of which has a pair of team supervisors. To ease administration, Joan created a group for each team and added the users accordingly.

1. **To provide the most efficient print management, what is Joan's best option to assign printer permissions?**
   a. Assign Everyone—Manage Documents access to the printers.
   b. Assign the team supervisors Manage Documents access to their printers.
   c. Assign the team supervisors Manage Printers access to their printers.
   d. Assign Everyone—Manage Printers access to the printers.

2. **Where would Joan change the printer's configuration to let her know when someone attempted a permission violation?**
   a. Owner tab of the printer's Properties dialog box
   b. Auditing tab of the printer's Properties dialog box
   c. Permissions tab of the printer's Advanced Properties dialog box
   d. Auditing tab of the printer's Advanced Properties dialog box

3. **By default, what are all users on Joan's network allowed to do?**
   a. Change the printer's port configuration
   b. Manage their own print jobs
   c. Cancel other users' print jobs
   d. Change the printer's share settings

4. **If Joan assigns the team supervisors Manage Documents access to their printers, which of the following will have the ability to share the printers?**
   a. All users
   b. The team supervisors
   c. Joan
   d. None of the above

5. **Some of the users on Joan's network use Windows NT 3.51 on their desktops. Where would Joan configure the printers to provide the drivers for these users?**
   a. The printer's Properties Sharing tab
   b. The printer's Properties Device Settings tab
   c. The System utility for the print server
   d. Joan must manually supply the drivers each time she configures an older workstation.

6. **Joan hires an assistant. During the assistant's probation period, Joan cannot grant him full access to the printers. Which of the following settings allows Joan's assistant to have the highest level of security without granting full control?**
   a. Print
   b. Advanced
   c. Manage Printers
   d. Manage Documents

OBJECTIVES

2.12 Connect to an Internet printer

UNDERSTANDING THE OBJECTIVE

Beginning with Windows 2000, Microsoft has included support for printing directly to Internet-connected printers. This is achieved through the use of the **IPP**. IPP is supported on Windows 2000 Professional systems running **PWS** or on Windows 2000 Server systems running **IIS**.

WHAT YOU REALLY NEED TO KNOW

◆ Connecting to an Internet printer involves the same process as connecting to a network printer. When asked for the location of the printer, select "Internet printer" and enter its **URL**.

◆ The Internet printing feature also allows users the ability to download the print driver for a printer to which they are connecting.

◆ PWS must be installed before Windows 2000 Professional can connect to Internet printers.

◆ When connecting to an Internet printer, it is possible to be granted the same printer management permissions as those granted on the local printer.

◆ When managing an Internet printer, or print jobs sent to an Internet printer, the operations and commands are the same as those used with the local printer.

OBJECTIVES ON THE JOB

The majority of the configuration to support Internet printing occurs on the server side. The most important thing to remember when configuring a Windows 2000 Professional system to utilize IPP is that PWS must be installed. In addition, you must know the URL for the printer or print server before creating the printer. Beyond that, connecting to an Internet printer is much the same as connecting to a network printer.

PRACTICE TEST QUESTIONS

1. **Which of the following configurations support Internet printing? (Choose all that apply.)**
   - a. Windows 2000 Server with PWS
   - b. Windows 2000 Professional with PWS
   - c. Windows NT Workstation 4.0 with IIS
   - d. Windows 2000 Server with IIS

2. **When sending a print job to an Internet printer, what level of visibility does a user have?**
   - a. None; once the job is sent, the user must assume that the print job was successful.
   - b. The print job information available is the same as that available when printing to a local printer.
   - c. The print job information is limited to whether the job is in the queue.
   - d. Print job information is returned via e-mail message.

3. **Which Internet printing feature enhances remote users' ability to utilize Internet printing?**
   - a. Mobile printer access
   - b. Download access to the printer driver
   - c. Multiple user printer management
   - d. Encrypted print job transmission

4. **Jason works with a new user who requested access to an Internet-based printer. Because it's been a while since Jason connected to a printer on the server that the user requested, he is unsure of the exact name of the printer share. Which of the following could Jason use to obtain a list of printers connected to an Internet server?**
   - a. *http://server_name/listprinters*
   - b. *http://server_name/showprinters*
   - c. *http://server_name/printers*
   - d. *http://server_name/printershare*

5. **Which of the following protocols is required for printing to an Internet printer?**
   - a. TCP/IP
   - b. DNS
   - c. IPP
   - d. DHCP

2.13 Connect to a local print device

LOCAL PRINT DEVICE • LPT PORT • COM PORT • USB

UNDERSTANDING THE OBJECTIVE

Windows 2000 Professional supports a number of methods for directly connecting a print device to a system. In addition to the more traditional **LPT** and **COM** port connections, Windows 2000 Professional supports **USB** and infrared connections, as well as direct printer communication using **TCP/IP**.

WHAT YOU REALLY NEED TO KNOW

◆ Local printers are, by definition, physically connected to a port on the print server.

◆ Connecting to a local print device usually involves only making the physical connection.

◆ Many printers today are Plug and Play compatible and are automatically configured when connected to a Windows 2000 Professional computer.

◆ Printers connected to COM and USB ports are detected automatically. Printers connected to LPT ports must be discovered through the Add New Hardware Wizard or upon rebooting.

◆ To set up a printer, use the Add New Printer utility in the Printers window (Start, Settings, Printers).

OBJECTIVES ON THE JOB

Connecting to a local printer is achieved through the Printers utility, accessed via the Start menu, Settings option. Double-click the Add New Printer icon to start the Add New Printer Wizard. To add a new local printer to your system's configuration, you should know the answers to the following questions: To which physical port is the printer connected? Is the new printer Plug and Play compatible? Which vendor manufactured the printer? What model is the printer? What will the printer be called? Will the new printer be the default for all Windows print jobs? Will the new printer be shared with other users on the network?

If the printer is not Plug and Play compatible, you must choose the printer manufacturer and model from a list of drivers included with Windows 2000. If the printer you are installing includes a set of drivers, select the Have Disk option, indicate the location of the drivers, and choose the printer accordingly. If the system to which you are connecting the printer includes a USB or infrared (IrDA) port, either of these ports can be used to communicate with the printer. In addition, Windows 2000 allows users to connect to network interface print devices as if they were directly attached. To do so, the port selected must be compatible with standard TCP/IP, and you must provide the address of the printer. From that point, the local system will use the printer as if it were directly attached.

PRACTICE TEST QUESTIONS

1. **For a local print device, where is the print spool located?**
   a. A local shared folder
   b. The local Temp folder
   c. A remote Temp folder
   d. Directly on the printer

2. **Which of the following printers does Windows 2000 Professional recognize immediately upon connection and start the Add New Printer Wizard? (Choose all that apply.)**
   a. A Hewlett-Packard DeskJet connected to USB1
   b. A Hewlett-Packard LaserJet connect to TCP/IP port 192.168.56.2
   c. A Lexmark Laser connected to LPT1
   d. An Epson Stylus connected to COM1

3. **When setting up a new local printer, are drivers for different operating systems made available to other users?**
   a. Yes, additional drivers are always copied.
   b. Yes, but they are available only for Windows 98.
   c. No, the printer must be shared for this option.
   d. No, additional drivers are never copied.

4. **Which of the following Windows 2000 printing functions helps users identify print jobs when completed?**
   a. Separator Page
   b. Print Processor
   c. Print Spooler
   d. Header Page

5. **Through which configuration area can Windows 2000 Professional be configured to restrict local users' access to a local printer?**
   a. Sharing
   b. Device Settings
   c. Services
   d. Security

6. **After configuring a new local printer, what is the first step in verifying the installation?**
   a. Reboot the system to ensure that the new printer is recognized.
   b. Print a test page through the printer's properties.
   c. Print a sample document from Word.
   d. Review the device settings through the printer's properties.

7. **When a local printer is shared, what role is the Windows 2000 Professional system fulfilling?**
   a. Print Manager
   b. Print Monitor
   c. Print Server
   d. Printer Pool

2.14 Configure and manage file systems

FAT • FAT32 • NTFS • CLUSTER • PARTITION • VOLUME

UNDERSTANDING THE OBJECTIVE

A file system defines the method by which data is organized on disks and the way in which that data is read from and written to the disk. Windows 2000 Professional supports three file systems: FAT, FAT32, and NTFS. Full understanding of the capabilities and limitations of each file system is a necessity.

WHAT YOU REALLY NEED TO KNOW

- ◆ Windows 2000 Professional supports FAT, FAT32, and NTFS. FAT partitions are limited to 4 GB, FAT32 partitions are limited to 32 GB, and NTFS partitions are limited to 2 TB.

- ◆ The system partition is the active partition on which the boot files reside. The boot partition contains the Windows 2000 system files.

- ◆ Hard disks and volumes are managed through the Storage portion of the Computer Management tool, which is accessed as follows: Start, Settings, Control Panel, Administrative Tools.

- ◆ FAT and FAT32 are more efficient than NTFS on volumes smaller than 256 MB. The root directory can include only 512 entries. No file-level compression or security is supported.

- ◆ The NTFS root directory has no limitations. File-level compression, security, and encryption are supported. NTFS also includes POSIX support for IEEE compatibility.

- ◆ A cluster is a group of sectors on a hard drive that are organized into a single unit. File system limitations dictate the number of clusters that can be accessed. FAT and FAT32 partitions automatically determine the default cluster size based on the size of the partition. NTFS supports clusters as large as 4 KB.

OBJECTIVES ON THE JOB

After the operating system is installed, disks, partitions, and volumes are managed through the Computer Management Storage utility. You can configure and format a new partition through this utility as well. Right-click the drive or partition to be managed, and select Properties to change an object's settings. By default, the operating system automatically assigns drive letters during the boot process. Alternatively, you can specify the drive letter assigned to each device by selecting Change Drive Letter and Path after right-clicking the object.

PRACTICE TEST QUESTIONS

1. **Which of the following Microsoft operating systems support FAT32? (Choose all that apply.)**
   a. Windows 98
   b. Windows NT 4.0 Workstation
   c. Windows 95 (OSR2)
   d. Windows NT 3.51

2. **Which of the following is not supported on NTFS partitions with cluster sizes larger than 4 KB?**
   a. File-level security
   b. File-level compression
   c. File-level encryption
   d. Disk quotas

3. **Which file system supported by Windows 2000 can handle the largest partitions?**
   a. FAT
   b. POSIX
   c. FAT32
   d. NTFS

4. **Match the following file system components with their descriptions.**

   spanned volume amounts   a. Object on which data is written to all drives in equal amounts

   boot partition   b. Object containing the Windows 2000 system files

   striped volume   c. Object containing boot files

   system partition   d. Object on which data is written from one drive to the next in order

5. **Which of the following Windows 2000 drive configurations provides fault tolerance? (Choose all that apply.)**
   a. Mirroring
   b. RAID 5
   c. Duplexing
   d. Disk striping

6. **Which of the following Windows 2000 components is not limited to one physical hard drive?**
   a. Partition
   b. Volume
   c. Cluster
   d. Sector

7. **The _____ file system supports LFNs, while storing a list of equivalent 8.3 names for use by applications that do not support LFNs.**
   a. NTFS
   b. FAT
   c. POSIX
   d. MAC

2.15 Convert from one file system to another file system

FAT • NTFS • CONVERT.EXE

UNDERSTANDING THE OBJECTIVE

During formatting of a partition, a file system is specified. At some point, it may become necessary to change the file system on the partition. If the file system is currently NTFS, the partition must be reformatted. If the file system is currently FAT or FAT32, it can be converted to NTFS.

WHAT YOU REALLY NEED TO KNOW

◆ In some instances, the existing partition must be converted to another file system. For example, a system upgraded from Windows 98 may require the enhanced security settings available with NTFS.

◆ Conversion from NTFS to FAT is not possible. To achieve this change, the data must be backed up, the partition formatted, and the data restored.

◆ Use the Convert utility to convert a partition from FAT to NTFS.

◆ Before proceeding with a conversion, be certain to have a valid backup of the data on the partition. If errors are encountered during conversion, data may be lost.

◆ Once the conversion occurs, it cannot be reversed. File system conversion is final.

◆ CONVERT.EXE is the command used to convert a file system from FAT to NTFS. If the operating system cannot obtain exclusive access to the partition, the conversion process commences when the system is restarted.

OBJECTIVES ON THE JOB

Because NTFS provides a significantly higher level of security—file-level compression, file-level encryption—and more efficient operation, it is recommended that Windows 2000 be installed on NTFS whenever possible. Generally, only systems that dual-boot with Windows 95 or 98 require a FAT partition. Not every system will be completely ready for the switch to Windows 2000 and NTFS immediately. Sometimes, the existing file system must remain intact for a period of time, and then be converted. When this time arrives, you can use the Convert utility to convert a FAT partition to an NTFS partition. Convert is a command-line utility that uses the following syntax:

convert VOLUME /fs:NTFS /V

Here, VOLUME indicates the partition to be converted and is represented as the drive letter, followed by a colon (for example, E:). Although Convert supports only the conversion from FAT to NTFS, the new file system must still be specified. /V indicates that the conversion should take place in verbose mode, providing detailed information at each step along the way.

PRACTICE TEST QUESTIONS

1. **Which of the following is not supported by FAT? (Choose all that apply.)**
   a. File-level compression
   b. Partitions as large as 4 GB
   c. File-level encryption
   d. Share-level security

2. **A cluster is best described as a group of _____ that function as one unit.**
   a. sectors
   b. users
   c. servers
   d. volumes

3. **Which of the following is a GUI tool used to convert file systems?**
   a. Convert
   b. Disk Manager
   c. Computer Manager
   d. None of the above

4. **Which version of NTFS is supported by Windows NT 4.0 systems that have been updated with Service Pack 3?**
   a. NTFS 3.0
   b. NTFS 4.0
   c. NTFS 5.0
   d. NTFS 2000

5. **Which of the following utilities is used to convert an NTFS partition to a FAT32 partition?**
   a. Disk Manager
   b. Computer Manager
   c. Convert
   d. None of the above

6. **After executing Convert from the command line, under what circumstances will the conversion not take place until the system is rebooted?**
   a. The partition is configured for compression.
   b. The partition is smaller than 4 GB.
   c. The partition cannot be exclusively controlled.
   d. The conversion never takes place before the system restarts.

2.16 Configure file systems by using NTFS, FAT32, or FAT

COMPRESSION • ENCRYPTION • DISK UTILITIES

UNDERSTANDING THE OBJECTIVE

Few configuration options are specifically centered on the file systems and their performance. In fact, all utilities are designed to work with the NTFS file system. Some tools can, however, prove especially beneficial when working with file systems.

WHAT YOU REALLY NEED TO KNOW

◆ NTFS supports file-level security, compression, and encryption. You configure each of these attributes through the Properties dialog box of the file or folder.

◆ You can enhance system performance by using Windows 2000 disk utilities such as Disk Cleanup, ScanDisk, and Disk Defragmenter.

◆ Access the Disk Cleanup tool through any disk object's Properties dialog box, or through Start, Programs, Accessories, or System Tools. This utility reviews the current status of the partition and makes suggestions for cleaning up the drive.

◆ ScanDisk verifies the integrity of the partition and is accessed through the System Tools menu. It looks at the state of the physical media and marks suspect sectors.

◆ Disk Defragmenter decreases the time it takes to retrieve files from the hard disk by moving files so that they occupy contiguous space on the disk.

◆ Additional performance improvements can be achieved by updating specific Registry settings that manage disk performance.

OBJECTIVES ON THE JOB

To utilize or configure NTFS security, compression, or encryption, right-click a file or folder and then select Properties. To configure encryption and compression, click the Advanced button. To configure security, select the Security tab. Disk Cleanup scans the partition for files that can most likely be deleted, then provides you with the opportunity to remove them. For example, Disk Cleanup looks for temporary Internet files and allows you to delete them immediately. When files are written to a drive, they are written to the first available cluster, regardless of the number of contiguous clusters. If files are moved around the drive until they occupy contiguous space, the drive's read heads must move to only one place to retrieve the entire file. NTFS provides enhanced performance and security, but at the price of some memory and processor overhead. To limit the overhead required of the system, you can change Registry settings such as ntfsDisable8dot3NameCreation, which instructs the system to not maintain a list of equivalent 8.3 names. More information is available online.

PRACTICE TEST QUESTIONS

1. **Which of the following utilities generally executes if Windows is not properly shut down?**
   a. Disk Defragmenter
   b. ScanDisk
   c. Compress
   d. Disk Cleanup

2. **Which of the following NTFS features configures stored files to use as little space as possible?**
   a. Encryption
   b. Security
   c. Compression
   d. Impression

3. **Why does NTFS create a list of equivalent 8.3 file names?**
   a. Compatibility with the FAT32 file system
   b. Compatibility with Macintosh computers
   c. Compatibility with legacy applications
   d. Compatibility with Internet utilities

4. **How would a user recover files that were deleted using Disk Cleanup?**
   a. Through Recycle Bin
   b. Through Windows Explorer
   c. Through Computer Manager
   d. Files deleted with Disk Cleanup cannot be restored.

5. **Which of the following files are not optimized using Disk Defragmenter? (Choose all that apply.)**
   a. Read-only files
   b. Applications
   c. The page file
   d. System files

6. **Which file does ScanDisk create when it finds orphaned file fragments?**
   a. FRAGMENT .001
   b. SCANDISK .001
   c. FILEFIND .001
   d. FILE0001

Section 3

Implementing, Managing, and Troubleshooting Hardware Devices and Drivers

3.1 Implement, manage, and troubleshoot disk devices

BASIC STORAGE • DYNAMIC STORAGE • VOLUME • SPANNING • STRIPED

UNDERSTANDING THE OBJECTIVE

Storage solutions for Windows 2000 Professional fall into one of two categories: basic and dynamic. Basic storage refers to the traditional method of segmenting drives into partitions and working within the confines of the partition. Dynamic storage uses volumes to represent an entire disk and can be expanded in real time, without resetting the system.

WHAT YOU REALLY NEED TO KNOW

- ◆ A physical disk can be configured for either basic storage or dynamic storage, but not both. You can, however have both types of disks in one system.

- ◆ Dynamic storage is available only with Windows 2000. It views a disk as a single partition encompassing the entire disk.

- ◆ A disk configured for basic storage is called a basic disk. A disk configured for dynamic storage is called a dynamic disk.

- ◆ Dynamic storage is not as limited as basic storage. For example, you can expand a dynamic disk or volume without losing data or restarting the system.

- ◆ You manage both basic and dynamic disks through the Disk Manager tool, which is accessed through Start, Settings, Control Panel, Administrative Tools, Computer Management or Storage.

- ◆ Troubleshooting disk errors is accomplished through a number of utilities, including CHKDSK, virus scanners, and FDISK.

- ◆ For the most part, the best defense against disk error or failures is having a good backup.

OBJECTIVES ON THE JOB

Basic disks are divided into two types of partitions: primary and extended. A disk can contain as many as four partitions, but only one extended partition. That is, it can be divided into at most four primary partitions, or three primary partitions and one extended partition. The active partition contains the files required to boot up the system. Only one active partition can be designated per disk, and only primary partitions can be marked as active. Basic disks can be upgraded to dynamic disks, then used within a Windows 2000 volume. Windows 2000 supports three types of volumes: simple, spanned, and striped. The majority of problems experienced at the disk level are caused by viruses, so maintaining a current virus-scanning program reduces this risk significantly. Of course, hardware does eventually fail. If you are experiencing problems with disks in your system, run CHKDSK /R to scan the physical disk for corruption.

PRACTICE TEST QUESTIONS

1. **Which of the following does not accurately describe a limitation on an extended partition?**
    a. The extended partition can be designated as active.
    b. A disk can contain only one extended partition.
    c. An extended partition cannot be the Windows 2000 system partition.
    d. Extended partitions are divided into segments.

2. **How many partitions are allowed on a single disk?**
    a. 2
    b. 3
    c. 4
    d. 6

3. **Which of the following fault-tolerance features is available only when using basic storage?**
    a. Mirror set
    b. RAID 5
    c. Disk sharing
    d. Striped volume

4. **Which of the following partitions are available on removable media such as CD-ROMs?**
    a. Enhanced
    b. Primary
    c. Extended
    d. Simple

5. **When working in a dual-boot environment with Windows 2000 and Windows 98, which of the following is true?**
    a. The extended partition must be formatted with FAT32.
    b. The extended partition must be formatted with NTFS.
    c. The primary partition must be formatted with NTFS.
    d. The primary partition must be formatted with FAT32.

6. **Which of these Microsoft storage technologies is supported only by Windows 2000?**
    a. Striped volumes
    b. Dynamic storage
    c. Basic storage
    d. Extended partitions

3.2 Install, configure, and manage DVD and CD-ROM devices

UDF • CD-ROM • DVD

UNDERSTANDING THE OBJECTIVE

Windows 2000 supports **CD-ROM** and **DVD** devices for both storage and multimedia. From a storage perspective, these devices are considered removable storage media. To utilize them as multimedia devices, Windows 2000 includes drivers and utilities such as the Windows Media Player.

WHAT YOU REALLY NEED TO KNOW

- ◆ Prior to the advent of Windows 2000, CD-ROM drives were mounted using their own file system, **CDFS**. Today, the industry standard, UDF, is supported by Windows 2000.

- ◆ UDF is used to read many optical media, including CD-ROMs, DVDs, and magneto-optical devices.

- ◆ Windows 2000 includes a virtual CD player so that you can listen to CD-audio discs. All necessary audio decoders are included.

- ◆ Windows 2000 also includes a DVD player to view DVD movies. You must install, a software or hardware DVD decoder before you can view DVD movies on the system.

- ◆ Windows 2000 supports three DVD formats: DVD-Video, **DVD-ROM**, and **DVD-RAM**.

- ◆ Data can be written to **CD-R** and **DVD-WO** formats only once, whereas the **CD-RW** and **DVD-RAM** formats support multiple recording.

- ◆ Third-party software is required with CD-R, CD-RW, DVD-WO, and DVD-RAM disks.

- ◆ CD-ROM and DVD devices can be shared and secured using share-level security.

OBJECTIVES ON THE JOB

Disks created to the UDF standard can be used in systems running many operating systems, including Windows 2000. Windows 2000 supports UDF version 1.5 for a variety of removable media, including DVDs, CDs, and magneto-optical devices.

CD drives can be used to read audio and data disks immediately after installation, with no additional configuration. Writing to a CD-R or CD-RW disk requires third-party software.

DVD drives can read data immediately, but a decoder must be installed in the system before multimedia disks can be accessed. DVD decoders consist of either hardware devices or software utilities. Many software decoders include applications for viewing DVD movies. If a hardware decoder is installed, the Windows 2000 DVD player (DVDPLAY.EXE) can be used instead. Writing to a DVD-WO or DVD-RAM drive requires third-party software.

Optical devices (or folders) are shared by accessing the object's properties and selecting the Sharing tab. Both CD and DVD devices support share-level security.

PRACTICE TEST QUESTIONS

1. **As part of his college semester project, Kyle designed a searchable archive containing Audubon's images. In addition to installing IIS to share the archive on the Internet, Kyle would like to provide a CD-ROM version. When all is said and done, the program and its data require 7 GB of drive space. Which of the following is the best method for Kyle to distribute his program?**
   a. A set of 11 CD-ROMs
   b. A set of 15 CD-RWs
   c. One DVD-ROM
   d. Three DVD-RAMs

2. **Which of the following optical file systems is not supported by operating systems from other companies?**
   a. CDFS
   b. NTFS
   c. DVFS
   d. UDF

3. **Which of the following share permissions is not necessary for files written to CD-R disks?**
   a. Modify
   b. Change
   c. Read
   d. Full Control

4. **In her new role as training coordinator, Karen learned that copies of the training material must be available to all users. Many users are connected to the network, but approximately 15% of the trainees work at remote locations. Which of the following methods could Karen use to ensure that all users are able to review the training material? (Choose all that apply.)**
   a. Burn the training material onto a CD-R, creating one copy for each user.
   b. Burn the training material onto a CD-R, creating a copy for each remote user.
   c. Share the training material folder on the server's volume.
   d. Share the training material on a CD-ROM drive.

5. **For Christmas this year, Stan received a DVD drive and movies from his grandmother, who lives in England. After installing the drive in his system, Stan attempts to play a movie, but is unsuccessful. The DVD drive included a decoder card, which Stan installed, and there are no problems detected on the hardware. What step should Stan take?**
   a. Verify his computer's time zone settings.
   b. Verify that the movies are in English.
   c. Verify that the DVD is correctly connected to the system.
   d. Verify the DVD Player's Region settings.

3.3 Monitor and configure disks

PHYSICAL DISK • LOGICAL DISK • DISK MANAGEMENT • PERFORMANCE

UNDERSTANDING THE OBJECTIVE

Windows 2000 provides Administrators with the ability to manage and configure disk drives on local and remote systems through the Storage section of the Computer Management utility. The System Monitor, which is part of the Performance tool, tracks the performance of system objects such as disks, processors, and memory.

WHAT YOU REALLY NEED TO KNOW

- ◆ Use the Storage section of the Computer Management utility to configure disk devices.
- ◆ The computer's physical and logical disks are managed and configured through the Disk Management plug-in. Configuration options include changing the object's assigned letter and path, and enabling or disabling compression on the disk.
- ◆ The Performance utility's System Monitor traces object counters and displays their values in a graphical format.
- ◆ Object counters monitor system components such as disks, memory, processors, and network interface cards. Each object offers a unique set of counters to monitor performance.
- ◆ Windows 2000 includes separate sets of object counters for physical and logical disks. By default, the physical disk counters are enabled during installation of the operating system. The logical disk counters must be enabled manually.
- ◆ Disk performance is affected by file system configuration and performance.

OBJECTIVES ON THE JOB

Windows 2000 provides the highest level of configuration of any Microsoft operating system to date. You use the Disk Management tool to administer the system's physical and logical disks and volumes. To adjust a device's settings, right-click the object and select Properties. Windows 2000 automatically assigns drive letters based on the order in which they are addressed to the system. For example, a system with four IDE devices will assign C: to device 0 on channel 0, D: to device 1 on channel 0, E: to device 0 on channel 1, and F: to device 1 on channel 1. You can change these settings by right-clicking the object and selecting Change Drive Letter and Path.

The System Monitor displays object counter values in a graphical format. Counters monitor specific areas of an object's performance, such as the percentage of free space on a logical disk or the number of packets sent per second through the NIC. The physical disk counters are enabled during installation of Windows 2000, whereas the logical disk counters are not. Use the DISKPERF command to change the settings for the disk counters.

PRACTICE TEST QUESTIONS

1. **To facilitate network printing, you configured a Windows 2000 Professional computer to act as a print server. Because the demands on the system are light, you installed the bare minimum hardware configuration, including memory, processor, and hard drive. Recently, employees in the accounting department have complained that their end-of-month reports do not print upon completion. You suspect that the print server may be running out of space, but you have not been able to confirm your suspicions because the job runs automatically at 3:00 a.m. How can you use the Windows 2000 System Monitor to pinpoint the problem?**
   a. Configure Performance logging to regularly record the chart's image to a file.
   b. Configure an Alert through System Monitor that logs an error and sends an e-mail when the percentage of free space on the logical drive is less than 1 MB.
   c. Configure Auditing to notify you when the printer fails.
   d. Assign a network technician to the task of monitoring Performance when the accounting report is printed.

2. **Which of the following is used to disable logical disk monitoring?**
   a. diskperf –nl
   b. diskperf –np
   c. diskperf –nv
   d. diskperf –nd

3. **A system that originally included one hard disk and one CD-ROM was upgraded to include a new hard disk. Two of the currently installed applications require that the data CD be located on the D: drive. The drives are recognized by Windows 2000 as follows: C:=HDD on IDE00, D:=HDD on IDE01, E:=CD-ROM on IDE 11. Which of the following is the most efficient method for ensuring that all applications are functional?**
   a. Disconnect drives D: and E: and physically switch their connections.
   b. Use Disk Management to change the drive letter assignment first for IDE01, then for IDE11.
   c. Remove and reinstall the applications that require the CD-ROM found on drive D:.
   d. Open the disks' properties through Explorer and change their drive letter assignments.

4. **Which of the following counters is available only for the Physical Disk object?**
   a. % Free Disk Space
   b. Average Disk Queue Length
   c. % Disk Time
   d. None of the above

3.4 Monitor, configure, and troubleshoot volumes

SIMPLE VOLUME • SPANNED VOLUME • STRIPED VOLUME

UNDERSTANDING THE OBJECTIVE

The Windows 2000 dynamic storage feature lets Administrators configure a system's storage structure to provide the most efficient use of available space. A volume consists of at least one portion of a dynamic disk. It can also include a number of portions on the same disk or parts of many dynamic disks.

WHAT YOU REALLY NEED TO KNOW

- ◆ Dynamic disks are required for volumes. Basic disks cannot be included in volumes.

- ◆ You can upgrade a basic disk to a dynamic disk without any loss of data. In that case, existing partitions and logical drives will become simple volumes. A dynamic disk cannot be turned into a basic disk without data loss.

- ◆ A simple volume consists of a single disk. A spanned volume can include as many as 32 disks, and its space is used sequentially (drive 1 is filled before drive 2 is used). A striped volume includes a maximum of 32 disks, and the space is used across all disks at the same rate.

- ◆ Striped volumes are more efficient than spanned volumes, because all disks work at the same time. All disks in the striped volume should be about the same size to provide the greatest efficiency.

- ◆ No Windows 2000 Professional volume configuration is fault-tolerant. Fault-tolerant systems are only part of Windows 2000 Server.

- ◆ You can create dynamic disks on drives formatted with any Windows 2000 file system. Conversely, a volume that includes FAT or FAT32 drives cannot be extended.

- ◆ Volumes are monitored via the System Monitor utility through physical and logical disk objects and counters.

- ◆ Troubleshooting volumes follows the same guidelines as troubleshooting drive shares.

OBJECTIVES ON THE JOB

Using volumes gives you the ability to use a system's available drive space more efficiently. Because volumes are identified as single logical objects, they can also prove easier to use than basic disk partition configurations. For example, a system with three 20 GB SCSI hard drives can be configured with one volume, making C: hold 60 GB! Because volumes created on NTFS partitions can be expanded after they are created, NTFS is the preferred file system. Whenever a disk is added to a system, select Rescan Disks from the Action menu in Disk Management. Once the new disk is recognized, it can be added to an existing volume by right-clicking its icon and selecting Add Disk.

PRACTICE TEST QUESTIONS

1. **It is the end of the Windows 2000 pilot, and the system you have been using for testing purposes is being dismantled. The six 20 GB SCSI drives were configured as a single spanned volume. Which of the following systems will be able to view the data contained on the drives? (Choose all that apply.)**
   a. Windows Millennium Edition
   b. Windows 2000 Professional
   c. Windows 2000 Server
   d. Windows NT 4.0 Workstation

2. **Which of the following is limited to a single hard drive?**
   a. A simple volume
   b. A spanned volume
   c. A dynamic disk
   d. A striped volume

3. **Which of the following changes in volume structure results in loss of data? (Choose all that apply.)**
   a. Removing a disk from a spanned volume
   b. Removing a disk from a striped volume
   c. Reverting from a dynamic disk to a basic disk
   d. Inserting a disk from a different system

4. **Which of the following is a limitation placed on spanned volumes?**
   a. They cannot exceed 16 drives.
   b. They can include only FAT32 partitions.
   c. They must be contained on a single hard drive.
   d. They cannot be part of a striped volume.

5. **Which of the following provides the best combination of performance and efficiency?**
   a. FAT32 striped volume
   b. NTFS striped volume
   c. NTFS basic volume
   d. FAT32 spanned volume

3.5 Monitor and configure removable media, such as tape devices

REMOVABLE STORAGE • MEDIA • MEDIA POOL • BACKUP TYPES

UNDERSTANDING THE OBJECTIVE

Windows 2000 Professional includes a utility that manages removable media and their devices. Part of the Storage section of Computer Management, this utility is called Removable Storage and manages all levels of use—from the tape drive in your desktop system to a fully automated, robotic, tape library system.

WHAT YOU REALLY NEED TO KNOW

♦ To Windows 2000, removable media include CDs, DVDs, magnetic disks (Zip disks), magneto-optical, 8mm tape, DAT, and many others. All of these media are managed through Removable Storage.

♦ Media is defined as the physical objects on which the data is stored (for example, a CD-ROM). The term "cartridge" is also used to describe media, generally when discussing tape drive media. Floppy diskettes and other small-capacity media are considered too small to be managed as removable media.

♦ The primary role of Removable Storage is to prepare and organize media and control access to the cartridges. For the most part, Windows 2000 Professional systems do not require Removable Storage management.

♦ Windows Backup works in conjunction with Removable Storage to track cartridge use and availability. It is not strictly necessary to work with Removable Storage before using Backup.

♦ Backup is a full-featured data backup utility that is geared toward using tape media for backups. It does not support writing to CD-R or CD-RW devices.

♦ Removable media devices such as tape and CD drives are monitored through the Physical Disk and Logical Disk counters in System Monitor.

OBJECTIVES ON THE JOB

Windows 2000 Professional supports myriad removable media devices, including tape, CD, and DVD drives. The Removable Storage utility is used to organize media into logical groups called media pools. A major advantage of using Removable Storage to manage your media pools relates to its security. Each media pool can be configured to grant or deny access to specific groups or users. This feature is especially useful in a large enterprise environment, where workgroup administrators need to perform backups but should not be able to see the data. Media pool security options include Use, Modify, and Control. Of course, share and file system permissions apply to the data being backed up, which provides yet another level of security. You use Windows Backup to create a copy of a user's system or files to ensure against catastrophic data loss. Backup allows you to select the destination device or opt to back up to a file. Files can then be stored on media not supported by Backup (CD-RW, for example).

PRACTICE TEST QUESTIONS

1. **Match the backup types below with their description.**

   Differential   a. Copies all selected files and marks them as archived

   Normal   b. Copies the selected files modified on the day on which the backup was performed

   Daily   c. Copies the files that have changed since the last update and does not mark them as archived

   Incremental   d. Copies the files that have changed since the last update and marks them as archived

2. **When a backup device such as a Travan tape drive is added to a Windows 2000 Professional computer, which of the following groups is not granted the ability to control the device?**
   a. Power Users
   b. Administrators
   c. Backup Operators
   d. Users

3. **Which of the following media library terms describes the device used to move cartridges from their storage location to the drive and back again?**
   a. Transport
   b. Bar Code Reader
   c. Slot
   d. Mail slot

4. **A CD-ROM drive on a desktop computer is considered a _____ library.**
   a. complete
   b. stand-alone
   c. robotic
   d. offline

5. **Wayne was charged with testing the backup process for his organization. To perform this task, he ran a Normal backup on a Windows 2000 system that is currently using Removable Storage to manage its cartridges. To ensure that everything worked properly, Wayne used a blank tape, added it to the Backup library, and then performed the backup. Now the system is no longer accessible, and Wayne wants to restore the data on his Windows 2000 Professional system. If Windows can identify the cartridge format, into which pool will the cartridge automatically be placed on his system?**
   a. System Pool
   b. Import Pool
   c. Unrecognized Pool
   d. Free Pool

3.6 Implement, manage, and troubleshoot display devices

MULTIPLE DISPLAY SUPPORT • VIDEO ADAPTER • DISPLAY DEVICE

UNDERSTANDING THE OBJECTIVE

Windows 2000 Professional supports a multitude of methods for displaying its information, including various monitors and video adapters. Windows 2000 continues Microsoft's support for viewing via two or more monitors attached to a system.

WHAT YOU REALLY NEED TO KNOW

- ◆ Windows 2000 Professional supports ISA, PCI, and **AGP** video adapters. A variety of display devices are also supported, including standard **CRT** monitors, flat-panel displays, and projectors.

- ◆ The maximum resolution and color depth supported by Windows 2000 on a particular system are dictated by the limitations of the hardware.

- ◆ Color depth is the number of bits per pixel (**BPP**). Windows 2000 supports color depths ranging from 1 BPP to 32 BPP, or from 1 color (monochrome) to 1.7 million colors.

- ◆ All components of the system's display are configured through the Display utility in the Control Panel. You set the resolution and color depth through the Settings tab.

- ◆ Windows 2000 Professional supports connecting more than one monitor to the system, which allows the user to view the desktop over multiple displays. A maximum of 10 monitors can be configured for simultaneous use with Windows 2000.

- ◆ The video adapters are key considerations when supporting multiple monitors. Both video adapters must be either PCI or AGP devices. The primary display is specified by the BIOS and cannot be stopped. If the system uses an onboard video adapter, it serves as the secondary adapter.

OBJECTIVES ON THE JOB

Windows 2000 uses a variety of devices to display its output. At a minimum, it requires a VGA-compatible video adapter and monitor, which supports 16 colors with a resolution of 640 by 480 pixels. To configure the display settings, you use the Control Panel Display utility. Basic settings are established through the Background, Screen Saver, and Appearance tabs. The Settings tab is used to set the resolution and color depth, to access the Advanced configuration options, and to launch the Troubleshooter.

Windows 2000 must be set up before you can install a second video adapter and configure multiple monitor support. Once the system is operational, you install the secondary adapter and let Windows 2000 load the drivers and configure the card. To view the desktop over the secondary monitor, select the monitor, and then check the Extend My Windows Desktop Onto This Monitor check box. Troubleshooting a single display entails verifying the connections, drivers, and compatibility with Windows 2000. For secondary adapters, you should also verify that the Extend My Desktop check box is selected, and that Windows 2000 recognizes the adapter.

PRACTICE TEST QUESTIONS

1. After installing three display adapters in his system, Jeremy opened the Display utility to configure multiple monitor support. Because one of the new cards is ISA, it does not support Plug and Play. Jeremy manually loaded the drivers for this card. Which of the settings on the ISA card must be configured to support multiple monitors?
   a. Enable Multiple Monitor Support
   b. Extend My Desktop Onto This Monitor
   c. Enable Desktop Display On This Monitor
   d. None of the above

2. Which of the following is not true for the Windows 2000 multiple monitor implementation?
   a. All display devices must have the same color settings.
   b. Windows can be stretched across both monitors.
   c. Devices must appear on the HCL.
   d. Onboard video adapters can be used as secondary devices.

3. Which of the following must be checked before you can change the settings for a secondary device?
   a. Enable Multiple Monitor Support
   b. Extend My Desktop Onto This Monitor
   c. Allow Windows 2000 Access To This Monitor
   d. Change This Monitor's Settings

4. After months of scrimping and saving, Amanda finally purchases her dream system. She wants the best and fastest of everything and can't wait to try out some of the new 3-D games. Which of the following video adapters should Amanda buy to get the best performance from her new system?
   a. 2X AGP adapter
   b. PCI adapter
   c. 4X AGP adapter
   d. ISA adapter

5. Which of the following Control Panel settings allows you to change the video adapter's performance?
   a. Software Acceleration
   b. Hardware Acceleration
   c. Optimal Performance
   d. Color Depth

6. With Windows 2000 Professional, it is necessary to restart the system after changing the display resolution.
   a. True
   b. False

3.7 Implement, manage, and troubleshoot mobile computer hardware

APM • ACPI • PC CARD • CARDBUS

UNDERSTANDING THE OBJECTIVE

Users who primarily rely on portable computers have a unique set of requirements and challenges. Windows 2000 Professional makes their lives just a bit easier by providing special programs and utilities, including offline file storage, power management, mobile user profiles, and card services. Offline file storage and profiles are discussed later in this book.

WHAT YOU REALLY NEED TO KNOW

- ◆ Windows 2000 Plug and Play support works with **ACPI** to support hot docking and undocking of mobile computers, hot swapping devices, docked and undocked hardware profiles, and dynamic PC Card and CardBus device configuration.

- ◆ Power management features reduce the electricity used when the system is idle. Windows 2000 supports the APM and ACPI standards.

- ◆ **APM** is supported in Windows 2000 only for older portable computers. Most new systems are compatible with ACPI.

- ◆ If the computer is APM-compatible, power management is not automatically enabled. ACPI is automatically enabled on compatible systems.

- ◆ On mobile computers, the Power Options utility includes the Alarms and Power Meter tabs, as well as separate options used when the computer is plugged in and when it is running on batteries.

- ◆ ACPI includes a new power management level, Hibernate, that saves more power than when the system goes into Standby mode.

- ◆ Troubleshoot power management issues by changing the configuration and verifying that all devices being managed are ACPI- or APM-compatible.

- ◆ CardBus is a 32-bit version of PC Card, which is comparable to PCI. Plug and Play-compatible PC Card and CardBus devices are automatically recognized and configured by Windows 2000.

OBJECTIVES ON THE JOB

Many advanced features of Windows 2000 require ACPI support, including expanded power management options, hot docking, hot swapping, and dynamic device configuration. Verify that the system is ACPI-compatible before you install Windows 2000. If the BIOS on a system running Windows 2000 is upgraded to become ACPI-compliant, Windows 2000 must be reinstalled before the features will be recognized.

Windows 2000 includes six preconfigured power schemes to manage the system's power settings. You can change these schemes or create new schemes as necessary.

To determine whether a system is running in APM mode, check the Shutdown dialog box for the Standby option. To find out whether a system is running in ACPI mode, check the Device Manager, System devices for the Microsoft ACPI-compliant system device.

PRACTICE TEST QUESTIONS

1. Martin uses his laptop continuously when he travels, but had some problems recently. While working on an airplane, he fell asleep and lost the file on which he was working when his battery ran out. Martin has heard of the advanced power settings available through Windows 2000 and decides to investigate them. Which of the following actions should Martin take to ensure that his data remains safe?
    a. Activate the Critical alarm and play a sound when it is used.
    b. Activate the Critical alarm and hibernate when it is used.
    c. Activate the low battery alarm and display a message when it is used.
    d. Activate the low battery alarm and run the Shutdown program when it is used.

2. Which of the following power schemes provides the most aggressive power management options?
    a. Max Battery
    b. Portable/Laptop
    c. Minimal Power Management
    d. Presentation

3. When discussing device swapping and docking systems, what does the term "hot" mean?
    a. The system is in Standby or Hibernate mode.
    b. The system is running above normal temperature.
    c. The system is running normally.
    d. The system has been shut down.

4. Which of the following device types must be used to support high-throughput applications such as streaming video?
    a. PC Card
    b. ACPI
    c. CardBus
    d. Plug and Play

5. When Windows 2000 is installed on a portable computer, which of the following hardware profiles is automatically created? (Choose all that apply.)
    a. Mobile
    b. Docked
    c. Undocked
    d. Detached

6. Which of the following utilities is used to specify the event that will wake the system from Standby mode?
    a. Power Options
    b. Device Manager
    c. Computer Management
    d. Task Scheduler

3.8 Implement, manage, and troubleshoot input and output (I/O) devices

I/O DEVICE • HID • MULTIFUNCTION PERIPHERAL

UNDERSTANDING THE OBJECTIVE

Windows 2000 can accept input from and direct output to any number of devices. For example, keyboards, mice, scanners, and digital cameras are possible input devices, and printers and sound cards are potential output devices. All of these components are grouped into the category of **I/O** devices.

WHAT YOU REALLY NEED TO KNOW

◆ The complete list of Windows 2000 I/O devices is too lengthy to itemize. Virtually any device connected to the computer falls into this category, including smart card readers, joysticks, video capture devices, and alternative pointing devices such as digitizing tablets.

◆ Windows 2000 supports hardware developed to the **HID** specification. Although it was originally developed for USB, Windows 2000 supports HID devices through other connections.

◆ You configure and manage I/O devices through the Device Manager and individual utilities in the Control Panel.

◆ Smart cards are a highly secure method for authenticating a user and controlling access to the system.

◆ Scanners and digital cameras are both managed through the same Control Panel utility (Scanners and Cameras).

◆ **MFP** devices fall into more than one I/O category. For example, devices such as the Hewlett-Packard OfficeJet can print, scan, and fax, and they should be included in each configuration utility.

OBJECTIVES ON THE JOB

The majority of the I/O devices attached to a Windows 2000 computer are automatically detected and configured. Some of a device's advanced features may not be supported by the default Windows 2000 driver, however. For example, wheel mice may require updated drivers to fully utilize their features. Troubleshoot I/O devices by checking their physical connections and verifying that the newest drivers are installed. If all MFP functions are not recognized, restart the computer or use the Hardware Wizard.

PRACTICE TEST QUESTIONS

1. Stan is upgrading his Windows 2000 computer and installed a Creative Labs SoundBlaster Live audio card. After installing the card, however, his joystick no longer works. Through which of the following utilities would Stan check the status of the joystick?
   a. Device Manager
   b. Multimedia
   c. Game Controllers
   d. I/O Manager

2. Windows 2000 provides a number of configuration options designed to facilitate access by disabled users. Which of the following is used to adjust the length of time that the system waits before repeating a character when a key is held down?
   a. Keyboard utility, Speed tab
   b. Accessibility utility, Keyboard tab
   c. Accessibility utility, StickyKeys option
   d. Device Manager, Keyboards option

3. Which of the following standards is applied to Windows 2000 support of specialized I/O devices such as virtual reality gloves and helmets?
   a. ACPI
   b. ANSI
   c. HID
   d. MFP

4. Windows 2000 supports the IEEE 1394 standard for high-speed serial data transmission. Which of the following devices is most likely to utilize this capability? (Choose all that apply.)
   a. Digital video adapter
   b. Digital video disk drive
   c. Digital audio editing hardware
   d. Digital camcorder

5. Jason needs to replace the sound card in his Windows 2000 system. Until he can purchase a new card, he wants to use an old SoundBlaster Pro that he already has. Jason installs this card and reboots the computer. When the system has finished booting, he still has no sound. Why?
   a. The SoundBlaster Pro is damaged and will not work.
   b. The SoundBlaster Pro must be installed in Slot 2 to be recognized.
   c. The SoundBlaster Pro is not Plug and Play-compatible and must be configured manually.
   d. The SoundBlaster Pro is not on the HCL and is not supported by Windows 2000.

6. Firewire is a common name for which of the following specifications?
   a. USB
   b. IEEE 1394
   c. Plug and Play
   d. IEEE 1297

3.9 Install, configure, and manage modems, Infrared Data Association (IrDA), wireless, and USB devices

MODEM • USB • IRDA • WIRELESS

UNDERSTANDING THE OBJECTIVE

Windows 2000 supports a number of methods for communicating with devices or other computers—analog signaling via modem, infrared links using **IrDA** standards, other wireless methods such as **RF**, and **USB** connections.

WHAT YOU REALLY NEED TO KNOW

◆ Installing devices that support any of these communication methods is much the same as installing any other device. The major exception involves modems, which require a COM port for communication.

◆ Windows 2000 automatically recognizes and configures Plug and Play devices. A Plug and Play modem's COM port settings are also automatically assigned. The default COM port and I/O addresses are COM1 at 3F8, COM2 at 2F8, COM3 at 3E8, and COM4 at 2E8.

◆ The USB specification provides Plug and Play support for external devices. USB devices are automatically recognized and configured and can be attached or removed while the system is running, called hot plugging.

◆ USB supports many types of devices, including keyboards, mice, CD-ROMs, disk drives, network adapters, scanners, monitors, and digital cameras.

◆ Devices are managed and configured through Control Panel utilities, modems through Phone and Modem Options, and IrDA and wireless devices through Wireless Link. USB-attached devices are managed according to their type.

◆ IrDA connections are used to communicate with many devices, including printers, **PDA**s, digital cameras, and other computers.

◆ Other wireless links are established using technologies such as RF communication. Generally, non-IrDA wireless devices are used in networking, but RF mice and keyboards are also available.

OBJECTIVES ON THE JOB

As with all devices, installing and configuring communication devices, such as modems, is easiest when you are dealing with Plug and Play-compatible hardware. If you are installing a non-Plug and Play modem, you must configure its COM port either through the Install New Modem Wizard or the Add/Remove Hardware Wizard. Launch the Install New Modem Wizard by double-clicking the Phone and Modem Options utility. Although IrDA hardware is built into many laptops, few desktop systems include it. If an IrDA transceiver is connected to a serial port, you must configure it through the Add/Remove Hardware Wizard.

PRACTICE TEST QUESTIONS

1. **Which of the following technologies ensures that no resource conflicts will cause a device to fail?**
    a. IrDA
    b. Firewire
    c. USB
    d. IEEE 1394

2. **Samson is installing a new modem in his Windows 2000 Professional system. Unfortunately, this modem is not Plug and Play-compatible. Samson currently has a scanner connected to serial port 1 and a printer connected to parallel port 1. Assuming that no other devices are connected to the system, which of the following should Samson use for his modem settings?**
    a. COM3 at 3E8
    b. COM2 at 3E8
    c. COM4 at 2E8
    d. COM2 at 2F8

3. **Which of the following accurately describes an infrared link? (Choose all that apply.)**
    a. The IR system tray icon changes to indicate that an infrared device is in range.
    b. Infrared links do not require line-of-sight connections.
    c. More than one program can use an established link.
    d. Once the link is established, data transfer is initiated automatically.

4. **To install a non-Plug and Play modem in a system that has previously not included a modem, which utility would you use?**
    a. Add/Remove Hardware
    b. Device Manager
    c. Network and Dialup Connections
    d. Phone and Modem Options

5. **How many devices can be connected to a system via USB?**
    a. 56
    b. 127
    c. 24
    d. 218

6. **You can connect multiple USB devices to a computer by using USB hubs. The system itself is considered the root or root hub. You would like to connect a USB printer to your system. A number of devices are already attached to your system, and you connected five USB hubs in a chain (that is, Hub1 is connected to your computer, Hub2 is connected to Hub1, Hub3 to Hub2, and so on). Will the printer be able to communicate with your system and, if not, why?**
    a. Yes, the printer will communicate with the system.
    b. No, too many devices are attached to the USB chain.
    c. No, too many hubs appear between the printer and the system.
    d. No, the printer is more than 25 feet away from the system.

OBJECTIVES

3.10 Update drivers

WINDOWS UPDATE • DEVICE MANAGER

UNDERSTANDING THE OBJECTIVE

Periodically, Microsoft and hardware manufacturers may provide new hardware drivers for Windows 2000. You should check for updated drivers if you are experiencing problems with a device at regular intervals (once per quarter, for example).

WHAT YOU REALLY NEED TO KNOW

◆ The Windows Update Web site includes the most recent versions of signed drivers for all versions of Windows 2000.

◆ Only signed drivers that exactly match the installed hardware are available through Windows Update.

◆ Windows Update allows you to update many drivers at the same time. Device drivers can also be updated individually through the devices' configuration utilities or the Device Manager.

◆ In the Update Device Driver Wizard, you can have the system to search for a new driver or display a list of all drivers. If searching is selected, you have the options of searching floppy disk drives, searching CD-ROM drives, specifying another location, or accessing the Microsoft Windows Update Web site.

◆ You can also obtain drivers from the hardware manufacturer. In such a case, verify that the driver is signed by Microsoft and approved for Windows 2000.

OBJECTIVES ON THE JOB

When you connect to the Windows Update Web site, an ActiveX utility compares the drivers installed in your system with the latest updates available. Microsoft's policy and download information states that no information is sent to Microsoft during this process. Once the ActiveX utility is complete, the Windows Update site displays a unique list of new drivers in the Device Drivers section. Launching the Update Device Driver Wizard is accomplished through different steps for each device. For example, to launch the Update Device Driver Wizard for a video adapter through the Display Control Panel utility, click the Settings tab, the Advanced button, the Adapter tab, the Properties button, the Driver tab, and then the Update Driver button. If you obtain a new driver from the hardware manufacturer's Web site, download the driver to the local hard drive in a temporary folder and then specify that folder in the wizard.

PRACTICE TEST QUESTIONS

1. **Maria is experiencing problems with an SCSI adapter in her Windows 2000 Professional system. The adapter appeared to be working for two months, but inexplicably, began malfunctioning. Suspecting an outdated driver, Maria connects to the Windows Update Web site. In the Device Drivers section of the Web site, however, nothing is listed. What is her next step?**
   a. Replace the SCSI adapter with one that is Windows 2000-compliant.
   b. Search the Windows 2000 CD-ROM for similar drivers.
   c. Contact the adapter manufacturer to obtain an updated driver.
   d. Continue troubleshooting because the problem is not the SCSI adapter.

2. **The network administrator for your work site dropped by your desk yesterday, handed you a floppy disk, and told you to update the drivers for your network interface card. You open Device Manager, double-click Network Adapters, and double-click the icon for your adapter. You select the Driver tab, Update Driver, Search for a suitable driver, Floppy disk drives, and then click Next. The wizard returns a message indicating that no suitable drivers were located. Why?**
   a. The network administrator gave you a floppy disk with the wrong drivers.
   b. The network adapter already has the best driver installed.
   c. The driver on the floppy is older than the installed driver.
   d. Your system did not recognize the floppy disk.

3. **In addition to the specified locations, where does the Update Device Driver Wizard search for drivers?**
   a. The Windows folder on the local hard drive
   b. The hardware manufacturer's Web site
   c. The Windows 2000 Professional CD-ROM
   d. The Temp folder on the local hard drive

4. **If you opt to display a list of known drivers in the Update Device Driver Wizard, which of the following can you specify as the location for the driver? (Choose all that apply.)**
   a. The floppy disk drive
   b. The Windows Update Web site
   c. The local hard drive
   d. A shared folder on the network

5. **It has come to your attention that a new security standard has been adopted that requires you to install new drivers for all communications devices. Your Windows 2000 Professional system includes a network adapter, a modem, and an IrDA interface. What is the best method to update these drivers?**
   a. Device Manager
   b. Control Panel
   c. Each device's Properties dialog box
   d. The Windows Update Web site

3.11 Monitor and configure multiple processing units

TASK MANAGER • SYSTEM MONITOR • OBJECT COUNTER

UNDERSTANDING THE OBJECTIVE

Windows 2000 Professional supports systems with a maximum of two microprocessors (also called processors or CPUs). To efficiently use both processors, Windows 2000 employs a technique called symmetric multiprocessing (**SMP**).

WHAT YOU REALLY NEED TO KNOW

◆ Windows 2000 Professional can be installed on systems with two processors. To support more than two processors, you must install Windows 2000 Server.

◆ APM does not work on multiprocessor systems.

◆ SMP runs application threads on any available processor. This approach significantly reduces the time needed to perform a function and increases the system's overall processing capacity.

◆ The Task Manager Performance tab displays four graphs (CPU Usage, Memory Usage, CPU Usage History, and Memory Usage History) and four text boxes (Totals, Commit Charge, Physical Memory, and Kernel Memory).

◆ To specify whether the CPU History area should show one graph for each CPU or one graph with all CPUs, select CPU History from the View menu in Task Manager.

◆ Key System Monitor processor performance-monitoring counters deal with processor time, processor queue length, interrupts, threads, and context switches.

◆ Some System Monitor objects can monitor multiple components. Each component is represented as an instance within the counter.

◆ Thread partitioning, software interrupt partitioning, and hardware interrupt partitioning can all affect SMP performance.

OBJECTIVES ON THE JOB

While it is normal for CPU usage to spike sometimes as the system is used, each processor should not maintain a high usage percentage under normal circumstances. The processor queue length counter reports the number of threads that are assigned to the processors, but waiting for execution. For some systems, the queue may be as high as 10 or 12, but this level should not be maintained over time. Context switches occur whenever a new thread runs. Because they require system resources, having a large number of context switches can reduce overall system performance. Partitioning threads, software interrupts, and hardware interrupts all assign individual functions to specific processors, thereby ensuring dedicated processor time and leading to fewer context switches.

PRACTICE TEST QUESTIONS

1. **The System Monitor groups counters into categories called objects. Which of the following objects includes counters important to monitoring processor performance? (Choose all that apply.)**
   a. Processor
   b. System
   c. I/O
   d. Thread

2. **Which of the following Windows 2000 Professional utilities would you use to set an application's affinity?**
   a. System Monitor
   b. Device Manager
   c. Task Manager
   d. System Manager

3. **Which of the following System Monitor counters includes instances for each processor?**
   a. Processor object, % processor time
   b. System object, processor queue length
   c. Process object, % processor time
   d. Thread object, context switches / sec

4. **Which of the following Task Manager settings is enabled to display the percentage of processor time being used by Kernel Mode processes?**
   a. Options menu, Display kernel usage
   b. View menu, Display kernel usage
   c. Options menu, Show kernel times
   d. View menu, Show kernel times

5. **In addition to graphically displaying the system's CPU and memory utilization, what functions does the Task Manager perform? (Choose all that apply.)**
   a. Monitor hard disk performance
   b. Stop and start system processes
   c. Optimize memory utilization
   d. Stop and start applications

6. **Which of the following is another term for deferred procedure calls (DPCs)?**
   a. Hardware interrupts
   b. Context switches
   c. Thread partitions
   d. Software interrupts

3.12 Install, configure, and troubleshoot network adapters

DEVICE MANAGER • NETWORK AND DIAL-UP CONNECTIONS • NETDIAG

UNDERSTANDING THE OBJECTIVE

To communicate across a network, a computer must have a network adapter, also called a network interface card (NIC). Windows 2000 supports many brands and types of network adapters. The configuration options available depend on the type of adapter and the network architecture.

WHAT YOU REALLY NEED TO KNOW

- ◆ Like other devices, Plug and Play network adapters are automatically identified and configured by Windows 2000. Legacy adapters are also supported with the correct drivers.

- ◆ Devices other than typical network adapters (Ethernet or token ring cards) are sometimes considered network adapters and are displayed in the Network adapters section of Device Manager.

- ◆ You use the Network and Dial-up Connections utility to manage network connections.

- ◆ When a network adapter is installed, Windows 2000 automatically creates the local area connection.

- ◆ **WAN** devices such as Frame Relay or ATM adapters are included as network adapters. Although they are used to connect to a WAN, the Network and Dial-up Connections utility handles WAN connections as **LAN** connections.

- ◆ Network adapter settings are configured through one of two methods—Network and Dial-up Connections or Device Manager.

- ◆ The General tab of the network adapter's Properties dialog box includes a button to launch the Windows 2000 Hardware Troubleshooter. This utility poses questions to help you pinpoint problems and presents possible solutions.

- ◆ The Device Manager and NETDIAG utilities provide additional troubleshooting help.

OBJECTIVES ON THE JOB

When configuring a network adapter, the choice of settings depends on the type of adapter involved. For example, a Fast Ethernet adapter can be configured to operate at 10 Mbps or 100 Mbps or to automatically select the transmission rate. You configure these settings through the Advanced tab of the adapter's Properties dialog box. NETDIAG is a command-line utility that provides very detailed information about the network's status by running a series of tests on the system. The tests can be run individually or as a complete set. The results of the tests can be logged to a file by using the /1 option.

PRACTICE TEST QUESTIONS

1. You have decided to create a home network for sharing files and printers among the computers in your house. Your primary system is a Windows 2000 Professional powerhouse that is connected to the Internet via a cable modem. At this time, none of the other systems in the house needs access to the Internet. Consequently, you decide to create a separate network for the home systems and put a second network adapter in your main system. You have learned that Windows 2000 automatically creates a network connection for each adapter and assigns unique names, such as local area connection 1 and local area connection 2. How can you avoid any confusion about which network is which?

   a. During the network adapter installation process, assign a unique name to the new network connection.
   b. Before installing the new adapter, rename the existing connection "Internet Access" through the connection's Properties.
   c. After installing the new adapter, note the new connection's location in the Network and Dial-up Connections utility.
   d. There's nothing to be done—hope for the best.

2. A user on your network just informed you that "the network is down." Knowing that no major issues are affecting network performance at this time, you proceed to the user's desk to troubleshoot the system. When you arrive, you open the Network and Dial-up Connections utility and see that the local area connection icon has a red X across it. How can you locate the problem?

   a. Check the network adapter's configuration through Device Manager.
   b. Check the connection's configuration through Network and Dial-up Connections.
   c. Verify that the user's departmental hub is on and functioning.
   d. Verify that the cable connecting the computer to the hub is attached and undamaged.

3. A connection using which of the following devices is not shown as a local area connection in Network and Dial-up Connections? (Choose all that apply.)

   a. X.25
   b. Serial cabling
   c. FDDI
   d. Cable modem

4. Which of the following switch groups provides the most thorough test and the most detailed output?

   a. netdiag /q/1
   b. netdiag /test:Autonet
   c. netdiag /v /d /1
   d. netdiag /debug /1

Section 4

Monitoring and Optimizing System Performance and Reliability

4.1 Manage and troubleshoot driver signing

DRIVER SIGNING • WHQL • FILE SIGNATURE VERIFICATION TOOL

UNDERSTANDING THE OBJECTIVE

In an effort to provide users with the most accurate information regarding a device's compatibility with their operating systems, Microsoft created the **WHQL**. The WHQL puts hardware and drivers through a rigorous series of tests to certify that the devices are compatible. When a device/driver combination passes the tests, Microsoft digitally signs the driver, signifying that it is supported and recognized natively by Windows 2000.

WHAT YOU REALLY NEED TO KNOW

◆ WHQL signed drivers for distribution with Windows 2000 in the following categories: keyboard, mouse, hard disk controller, video display, multimedia device, network adapter, SCSI adapter, printer, modem, and smart card reader.

◆ Windows 2000 Professional checks for signed drivers when a new device is installed and can be configured to warn the user when an unsigned driver is to be installed. In addition, the installation of unsigned drivers can be systematically prevented.

◆ In addition to the checks performed automatically by Windows 2000, you can check a driver's signature status by using the File Signature Verification tool, SIGVERIF.EXE.

◆ Windows 2000 signature verification has three configuration levels: Block, which prevents the installation of any driver whose signature check fails; Warn, which informs the user of the driver's signature status and lets the user decide whether to proceed or cancel; and Ignore, which installs all drivers, regardless of their signature status.

◆ The File Signature Verification tool not only gives you the ability to check a driver's signature status, but also determines whether the driver has been changed since it was certified by Microsoft.

OBJECTIVES ON THE JOB

Because hardware connected to Windows 2000 systems must pass such a rigorous battery of tests before Microsoft will verify its compatibility, Windows 2000 is more stable than other operating systems. All drivers included on the Windows 2000 Professional distribution CD were certified by Microsoft before the operating system's release. By default, Windows 2000 warns the user if an unsigned driver is being installed. It is recommended that, at a minimum, this option be used for all hardware. When possible, you should block the installation of drivers that are not certified by Microsoft. As with the HCL, the chances are good that Microsoft does not support an installation using unsigned drivers. SIGVERIF.EXE can scan the entire system and verify the status of all drivers, or you can configure it through the Advanced button to check only specific files or folders.

PRACTICE TEST QUESTIONS

1. **After running a standard check using the File Signature Verification tool, which of the following contains detailed results of the scan?**
   - a. SIGSCAN.TXT
   - b. SIGNATUR.TXT
   - c. SIGVERIF.TXT
   - d. FILESCAN.TXT

2. **Which of the following files is used to verify a driver's digital signature? (Choose all that apply.)**
   - a. INF file associated with the driver
   - b. SIG file associated with the driver
   - c. CAT file associated with the driver
   - d. PST file associated with the driver

3. **At the time Windows 2000 was released, which of the following driver classes were not being tested by the WHQL? (Choose all that apply.)**
   - a. CD-ROM drive
   - b. SCSI adapter
   - c. Floppy drive
   - d. Hard drive

4. **Devices that appear on the HCL are automatically certified by WHQL, and vice versa.**
   - a. True
   - b. False

5. **Windows 2000 is not the first Microsoft operating system to apply driver signing to its operation. For which of the following Microsoft operating systems are drivers also certified?**
   - a. Windows NT 4.0 Professional
   - b. Windows Me
   - c. Windows 95
   - d. Windows NT 3.51 Server

6. **You recently upgraded your system from Windows NT Workstation to Windows 2000 Professional. The SCSI controller in your system is a bit old and an updated driver was not included on the distribution media. After scanning for unsigned drivers, you decide to bring the system into compliance. What is your next step?**
   - a. Contact the hardware vendor to obtain an updated driver.
   - b. Contact Microsoft to obtain an updated driver.
   - c. Visit the WHQL Web site to obtain an updated driver.
   - d. Buy a new SCSI card.

4.2 Configure, manage, and troubleshoot the Task Scheduler

TASK SCHEDULER • AT COMMAND • SCHEDULED TASKS

UNDERSTANDING THE OBJECTIVE

One of the system automation utilities included with Windows 2000 is the Task Scheduler. Task Scheduler allows users to schedule scripts, programs, or commands to run once at a specified time, regularly at specified intervals, or whenever a particular system event occurs.

WHAT YOU REALLY NEED TO KNOW

◆ The Task Scheduler is a service that runs automatically when the computer starts.

◆ You add new tasks to the schedule through the Scheduled Task Wizard or by using the AT command line utility.

◆ You can manage and view commands added through AT from the command line. Commands added through AT can also be viewed and managed through the Scheduled Tasks folder. If a task's properties are modified from within Scheduled Tasks, however, it is no longer visible to AT.

◆ The Scheduled Tasks folder is automatically shared on a Windows 2000 computer. A task's configuration can be copied to another Windows 2000 computer on the network by dragging the item to the Scheduled Tasks folder on the other computer.

◆ Like all Windows 2000 tools, Task Scheduler supports extensive security and auditing features.

OBJECTIVES ON THE JOB

Creating and managing scheduled events in Task Scheduler is very straightforward. To take full advantage of Task Scheduler, you must enable its advanced features. For example, in the Scheduled Tasks folder's Advanced menu, you can choose to be notified whether a task is missed and which account is used by tasks entered through AT. Because Windows 2000 was designed with multiple users in mind, scheduled tasks include security settings. If a user other than the job's creator attempts to modify a task, he or she must provide the job creator's user name and password, unless the job's permissions have been modified via the Security tab. You can specify any of five permissions to users or groups: Write, Read, Read & Execute, Modify, and Full Control.

PRACTICE TEST QUESTIONS

1. **How can you specify the password for the account to be used for a task created through the Schedule Task Wizard? (Choose all that apply.)**
   a. Open the task's properties, select the Task tab, and click Set password.
   b. Select Open advanced properties for this task when I click Finish, select Task tab, and click Set password.
   c. Use the Schedule Task Wizard.
   d. Open the task's properties, select the Security tab, and click Set password.

2. **You're working with a user and trying to troubleshoot a problem with a scheduled task. When you open the Scheduled Tasks folder in the Control Panel, the only information displayed for each job is its icon. How can you obtain more information for all jobs in the task list?**
   a. Select Details from the Advanced menu.
   b. Select Folder Options from the Tools menu.
   c. Select Folder Properties from the File menu.
   d. Select Details from the View menu.

3. **Charles is working on a Windows 2000 Professional computer that was upgraded from Windows NT 4.0 Workstation. Under Windows NT, the system automatically updated a set of files on the computers in the office, and Charles created a batch file to schedule the jobs. Now that Windows 2000 is installed, Charles wants to use the same batch file to establish the task list. The process copies the files to each of the computers in the office in the following order: ACCSYS1, DEVSYS1, PROGSYS1, ACCSYS2, DEVSY2. Assuming that Charles runs the batch file before adding other jobs to the task list, which of the following indicates the copy process for PROGSYS1 in the Scheduled Tasks folder?**
   a. Copy PROGSYS1
   b. Copy3
   c. AT3
   d. PROGSYS1

4. **In the scenario cited in Question 3, Charles is experiencing problems copying files to one of the systems on the list. For an unknown reason, the copy to the ACCSYS2 system fails. A new user was assigned to the system, and she assured Charles that no changes have been made. Which of the following is a possible cause for the failure?**
   a. The folder to which the files were being copied no longer exists.
   b. The processes are set to log on as Administrator on all systems, and the new user changed the Administrator password.
   c. The system has no free space available on the drive.
   d. The Task Scheduler is occupied with another task at the time when the ACCSYS2 process is supposed to run.

4.3 Manage and troubleshoot the use and synchronization of offline files

OFFLINE FILE • CACHING • SYNCHRONIZATION • PINNING

UNDERSTANDING THE OBJECTIVE

As many mobile users know, ensuring that your computer has the most up-to-date versions of files can be frustrating. With this in mind, Microsoft designed a Windows 2000 system to synchronize files between servers and mobile workstations.

WHAT YOU REALLY NEED TO KNOW

- ◆ On the network share, the folder's caching options are set to either Automatic Caching for Documents, Automatic Caching for Programs, or Manual Caching for Documents (the default setting). You cannot set caching for individual files.

- ◆ On the client computer, offline file and folder access must be enabled.

- ◆ From the perspective of the application on the mobile computer, the file is located on a network share. In reality, the files are stored locally in a hidden folder that is viewed by clicking View Files on the Offline Files tab.

- ◆ If the client accesses a folder whose settings indicate automatic caching, the files are copied to the local drive without user interaction. These files can be deleted automatically by the system if the cache becomes full.

- ◆ If the manual caching option is specified, the files must be marked to be available offline. To do so, access the server from the client computer, highlight the file or folder, and select Make Available Offline from the file menu. This process is called "pinning" the document. Pinned documents are not automatically deleted.

- ◆ A file or folder's synchronization status is visible through the Offline Files folder.

OBJECTIVES ON THE JOB

The Windows 2000 offline files system is most often used on mobile computers such as laptops, although it can also be used on systems in remote offices with less-than-reliable connections to the main office. Through the Synchronization utility, you can specify how and when each offline folder is synchronized with the server: automatically at logon, automatically at logoff, when the system is idle, at a specific date and time, or manually. Use care when deleting synchronized files. If you delete a cached file improperly, it will be restored the next time the systems are synchronized.

PRACTICE TEST QUESTIONS

1. **With which of the following systems is a Windows 2000 Professional computer able to synchronize offline files?**
   a. Windows NT 4.0 Server
   b. Linux Workstation
   c. Windows 98 desktop computer
   d. All of the above

2. **Which of the following synchronization options allows you to specify whether to connect if you are not already connected?**
   a. Automatically at logon
   b. Scheduled
   c. Manually
   d. Automatically at logoff

3. **By default, which of the following files cannot be cached? (Choose all that apply.)**
   a. *.dbf
   b. *.mpg
   c. *.pst
   d. *.pdf

4. **Through which configuration option do you modify the list of file types that cannot be cached?**
   a. Folder Options
   b. File Options
   c. Synchronization
   d. Group Policy

5. **You developed a Microsoft Access database of client information that needs to be shared with local and remote users. The Springfield, Illinois, office must be able to connect to the database, but all users dial into the Chicago office for their connection. Without special configuration changes, will users in the Springfield office have the ability to access your database?**
   a. Yes, but only after synchronization
   b. No, a dial-up line is too slow
   c. No, MDB files are not synchronized by default
   d. Yes, under all circumstances

6. **Which of the following is true if the file on the client computer and the file on the server have both been changed since the last synchronization?**
   a. The file from the server overwrites the client file by default.
   b. The Resolve file conflicts dialog box opens, allowing you to correct the problem.
   c. The file from the client computer overwrites the server file by default.
   d. Both files are copied to the Exception folder on the network share.

OBJECTIVES

4.4 Optimize and troubleshoot performance of the Windows 2000 Professional desktop

SYSTEM MONITOR • OBJECT • COUNTER

UNDERSTANDING THE OBJECTIVE

Windows 2000 Professional includes a group of tools and utilities for monitoring and tuning system performance. These tools, which include System Monitor, provide a detailed picture of the system's operation and issues affecting performance.

WHAT YOU REALLY NEED TO KNOW

- ◆ System Monitor reports counter values for system objects such as hard drives and processors.

- ◆ You access System Monitor through the Control Panel, Administrative Tools folder. You can add a counter to the chart to track an object's performance.

- ◆ You can track memory performance by charting the Memory object's Available Bytes and Pages/sec counters, as well as the Process object's Working Set counter.

- ◆ You can track processor performance with the Processor object's %Processor Time counter and the System object's Processor Queue Length counter.

- ◆ To enable hard disk drive performance tracking run DISKPERF. Track disk performance with the Logical Disk and Physical Disk objects' Current Disk Queue Length, Avg. Disk Queue Length, Disk Bytes/sec, and %Disk Time counters.

- ◆ You can monitor network performance through the Network Interface object's Bytes total/sec and Packets total/sec counters, as well as the transmission counters for the individual protocols being used.

- ◆ Application performance is governed by a combination of the objects listed above. Identify application-driven performance bottlenecks by using Task Manager to monitor a specific process. If one application dominates the processor's time, consider moving that application to another system or running the application during off-hours.

OBJECTIVES ON THE JOB

Fine-tuning a Windows 2000 installation for optimum performance is a never-ending process. Ideally, the slowest parts of computer systems will be the users themselves. That is seldom the case, however, as a system device is often the cause of the bottleneck. Take the time to review the counters available through System Monitor; these counters are key to identifying system bottlenecks, but by no means make up the entire list of counters. In general, utilization percentages should be low; queue lengths, on average should also be low. Throughput per second (that is, Disk Bytes/sec or Network Interface Packets/sec) should be high, but not at the maximum. Throughput at the maximum possible levels indicates an excess of data to be processed.

PRACTICE TEST QUESTIONS

1. **Which of the following describes a standard of normal operation against which future tests are measured?**
   - a. Origin
   - b. Baseline
   - c. Goal line
   - d. Performance level

2. **Which of the following is an example of a monitoring instance?**
   - a. The combination of all threads in a process
   - b. The only network card in a system
   - c. The first of two processors in the system
   - d. The number of system calls per second

3. **Which of the following counters, in conjunction with the physical memory counter, measures the system's utilization of virtual memory?**
   - a. Paging File
   - b. Distributed Transaction Coordination
   - c. Cache
   - d. System

4. **Which of the following memory bottlenecks also affects physical disk performance?**
   - a. Soft Page Fault
   - b. Context Switch
   - c. Hard Page Fault
   - d. Pool Fault

5. **Which of the following System Monitor views displays the data for the current time slice as a percentage?**
   - a. Chart
   - b. Report
   - c. Logs and Alerts
   - d. Histogram

6. **Which of the following can you use to obtain detailed data about a specific counter or object?**
   - a. Explain button in the Add Counter dialog box
   - b. MS Help Feature
   - c. Microsoft Technical Reference Library
   - d. HCL

4.5 Manage hardware profiles

HARDWARE PROFILE • SYSTEM

UNDERSTANDING THE OBJECTIVE

Hardware profiles give users the ability to configure different physical system configurations, which are automatically recognized by Windows 2000. Hardware profiles are especially useful for users with mobile computers or users who frequently add or remove hardware, such as hot swappable CD-ROM drives.

WHAT YOU REALLY NEED TO KNOW

◆ The default profile's name depends on the type of system being installed. On most systems, it is called profile 1. However, on portable computers, the first profile is either Docked or Undocked, depending on the system's state at installation.

◆ By default, every device in the system is enabled when the operating system is installed.

◆ Hardware profiles are managed through the Control Panel System utility.

◆ Create, modify, or copy the system's hardware profiles list through the Hardware Profiles dialog box.

◆ If the system has multiple hardware profiles, the user is asked to choose one when the system starts. The default profile is listed first in the dialog box and can be changed by moving a new profile to the top of the list.

◆ TC configure general profile options, you select the profile and click Properties. Hardware-specific configurations (such as whether to enable the modem in a configuration) are managed through the device's properties.

OBJECTIVES ON THE JOB

Windows 2000 support for hardware profiles provides the biggest benefit to users with portable computers. For example, many laptop computers include an optional docking station that supports PCI or ISA adapters. When the laptop is installed in the docking station (docked), devices such as additional hard drives, high-speed network adapters, and multifunction print devices can be attached to it. When the laptop is removed from the docking station (undocked), the only device connected may be a PC Card modem. Because all of these devices use different drivers and configurations, Docked and Undocked profiles are ideal for managing them. When the system is started in the docking station, Windows 2000 recognizes that fact and selects the Docked profile. Another benefit from hardware profiles arises when conflicts between legacy devices occur. For example, if a system included a SCSI adapter and a modem, both of which required IRQ3, one hardware profile can be created with the modem configured and another with the SCSI adapter configured.

PRACTICE TEST QUESTIONS

1. Susan is configuring hardware profiles for a user on her network. She has finished creating the actual profile. Through which of the following utilities can Susan configure the profile's specific configuration?
    a. Device Manager
    b. Hardware Profiles dialog box
    c. Computer Management
    d. System Manager

2. Which of the following options do you use to instruct the system to wait indefinitely until a profile is selected?
    a. Automatically select the first profile in: 00 seconds
    b. Select the first profile listed if I don't select a profile in: 999 seconds
    c. Do not automatically select the first profile
    d. Wait until I select a hardware profile

3. Which of the following dictates the order in which profiles are presented at start-up and the way in which Windows 2000 selects a profile?
    a. Profiles are displayed in the order in which they were created.
    b. Profiles are adjusted by the user, with the preferred profile appearing at the bottom of the list.
    c. Profiles are adjusted by the user and assigned ID numbers dictating their order in the list.
    d. Profiles are placed in order by the user, with the preferred profile appearing at the top of the list.

4. By default, all devices in the system are enabled for all profiles.
    a. True
    b. False

5. Which of these devices cannot be disabled for a particular hardware profile? (Choose all that apply.)
    a. Primary network adapter
    b. Primary video adapter
    c. Primary floppy disk controller
    d. Primary mouse

6. Which of the following Windows 2000 features does the system use to determine the makeup of the Docked and Undocked profiles for mobile users?
    a. USB
    b. PC Card Services
    c. Plug and Play
    d. ACPI

4.6 Recover system state data and user data using Windows Backup, safe mode, and the Recovery Console

BACKUP • SAFE MODE • RECOVERY CONSOLE • ERD

UNDERSTANDING THE OBJECTIVE

Windows 2000 has a number of methods for restoring user and system state data. Note, however, that a restoration is only as successful as the previous backup. You should regularly back up user and system state data, and test the process to ensure that you are prepared for the worst.

WHAT YOU REALLY NEED TO KNOW

♦ User data consists of all files on the system's disk drives. System state data consists of the Registry and protected system files. Because they are protected, system state data files are not backed up like user data files.

♦ Safe mode is a mode of limited operation that is used to troubleshoot system problems. When booting into basic safe mode, Windows 2000 loads only the basic files and drivers without network support. Another option is to boot into safe mode with network support.

♦ The **ERD** is created during installation and should be updated regularly. It is not the recommended method for restoring the Registry.

♦ The Recovery Console is a command-line option that allows you to change the Windows 2000 system.

♦ Be very careful when recovering system state data, and particularly the Registry! There's always the chance you'll leave the system worse than when you started.

OBJECTIVES ON THE JOB

We all live in the real world and understand that bad things sometimes happen; hardware fails and data is lost. To minimize the damage when disaster strikes, you should implement a solid backup strategy. Test your backups to ensure that they can be accessed before you need them.

PRACTICE TEST QUESTIONS

1. **Which of the following disaster recovery processes must be accessed during the boot process? (Choose all that apply.)**
   a. Windows Backup
   b. Safe mode
   c. Regback
   d. Recovery Console

2. **Which of the following includes an option to check and verify the Windows 2000 System files before performing a repair?**
   a. Restoration via Recovery Console
   b. Restoration via Windows Backup
   c. Restoration via Emergency Repair Disk
   d. Restoration while in safe mode

3. **You have recently installed a new video adapter and drivers. Since the installation, the system boots but nothing appears on the screen. Which of the troubleshooting methods discussed should you use to work on the system?**
   a. Safe mode
   b. Safe mode with network support
   c. Recover Console
   d. Windows Backup

4. **In addition to the Registry, which of the following Windows 2000 components is considered system state data? (Choose all that apply.)**
   a. Performance counter configuration information
   b. Files protected by Windows File Protection
   c. Files in the My Documents folder
   d. Network configuration files

5. **Of the recovery methods discussed, which should be used whenever possible to restore the Registry?**
   a. Windows Restore
   b. Recovery Console
   c. Windows Backup
   d. ERD

6. **Which of the following Windows 2000 system files is not backed up by default and should not be restored?**
   a. WINNT32.EXE
   b. PAGEFILE.SYS
   c. OUTLOOK.PST
   d. BACKUP.EXE

Section 5

Configuring and Troubleshooting the Desktop Environment

5.1 Configure and manage user profiles

USER PROFILE • ROAMING • LOCAL • MANDATORY

UNDERSTANDING THE OBJECTIVE

Individual users' application and desktop settings are maintained by the system such that their environment is the same, regardless of whether many users share the same system. The group of folders and configuration information makes up the user profile.

WHAT YOU REALLY NEED TO KNOW

◆ User profiles maintain the user's current desktop configuration, Start menu settings, network connections, and application configurations. A user profile contains the My Documents folder, which is the recommended storage location for a user's files.

◆ The first time that a user logs on to a computer, his or her local user profile is created and stored on the system.

◆ User profiles are managed through two utilities: the Computer Management utility, Users and Groups section, and the Control Panel System utility.

◆ Through the System utility's User Profiles tab, you can copy, edit, or delete a user profile. In addition, you can change the user profile type from the default (local) to roaming or mandatory.

◆ A user profile on a Windows 2000 system connected to a domain can be configured so that the user's settings remain the same regardless of which computer the user logs on. This type of user profile is called a roaming profile.

◆ A mandatory profile is a read-only roaming profile, meaning that any changes made to the user's configuration become lost when the user logs off. Both roaming and mandatory user profiles require interaction with a Windows 2000 Server and a domain.

◆ Roaming user profiles should be created only for roaming desktop users or portable users whose primary connection is to the network.

◆ User-specific profile configuration options are available through the Users and Groups section of Computer Management.

◆ A home folder is similar to My Documents, but can be configured on a network share, rather than the local hard drive.

OBJECTIVES ON THE JOB

For the most part, unless the computer is used by multiple end users, all of whom must start with the same settings, user profiles operate automatically without intervention. If the system is connected to a domain with many users logging on different computers, user profiles are a perfect fit. The same is true when a stand-alone system has many different users who need to maintain individual environment settings.

PRACTICE TEST QUESTIONS

1. **Recently, Marcus's company hired more staff than it has desks. This setup generally works very well because not everyone is at work at the same time. Rather than assigning one desk to two or three phone representatives, the company decided to move to a "hoteling" model. To ensure that the phone representatives' configurations are available no matter when or where they work, which of the following should Marcus implement?**
   a. Roaming profiles
   b. Home folders
   c. Mandatory profiles
   d. My Documents

2. **For the following list, specify whether the setting is managed through the System utility or the Users and Groups utility.**
   a. Profile path settings
   b. Home folder
   c. Roaming profile
   d. Copy profile
   e. Login script path

3. **To create their local user profiles, end users must do which of the following?**
   a. Copy another user's profile through the System utility.
   b. Complete the profile questionnaire in Control Panel.
   c. Restart the system and log on as Administrator.
   d. Log on to the system for the first time.

4. **Which of the following limitations applies to mandatory user profiles?**
   a. Attempted changes are rejected with an error.
   b. Attempted changes are discarded when the user logs off.
   c. Changes are accepted and applied to all users' subsequent logons.
   d. Changes are accepted and are maintained until the next logon.

5. **What would happen if a user accidentally deleted all of the user profiles on a system?**
   a. Users would be automatically logged off.
   b. Users would be denied access to the system.
   c. The profiles would be recreated automatically the next time the users logged on.
   d. Nothing; you cannot delete all profiles from a system.

6. **Why should all applications be closed before you copy a local user profile from one user to another?**
   a. The new profile's SID cannot be written if applications are open on the system.
   b. User profiles include application information that cannot be copied if the program is open.
   c. Local user profiles are accessed from many systems.
   d. If the profile is copied while applications are open, the new profile will include the required passwords for the applications that were open.

5.2 Configure support for multiple languages or multiple locations

MULTILANGUAGE VERSION • LOCALE

UNDERSTANDING THE OBJECTIVE

Windows 2000 Professional allows you to install more than one language group on any given system. As a result, you can use the system with information displayed in a variety of languages and compose documents in a language other than the default.

WHAT YOU REALLY NEED TO KNOW

◆ The English version of Windows 2000 Professional allows you to view, print, and enter information in any of 60-plus languages.

◆ Windows 2000 Professional is also available in translated versions in 24 languages. With these versions, you can view the user interface in the translated language and view, print, and enter information in any of the languages.

◆ To fully utilize the multilanguage features of Windows 2000 Professional, you must obtain the Multilanguage version.

◆ Windows 2000 Professional English version can be upgraded to the Multilanguage version. Translated versions cannot be upgraded.

◆ An input locale (or simply a locale), controls the way in which programs display numbers, dates, times, and currency. To adjust for country-specific variances in a language, the locale used often corresponds to the computer's geographic location. For example, a computer in Trinidad would use the input locale English (Trinidad).

◆ When more than one input locale is available, you can easily switch between locales by pressing Left Alt+Shift. You can also configure a keystroke sequence to switch to the English locale, even though one is not set by default.

◆ When adding a new input locale, you must specify the geographic locale—such as English (Australian) or French (Belgium)—and the keyboard layout.

OBJECTIVES ON THE JOB

In today's global economy, chances are good that you will travel to another country or help a user who is visiting from abroad. In addition, many companies cross international borders and documents must be shared among their employees in different countries. For the majority of Windows 2000 Professional users, the individual language groups are sufficient. Using the Multilanguage version, however, gives Administrators the opportunity to establish a single system configuration that can be implemented anywhere in the world.

PRACTICE TEST QUESTIONS

1. **Which of the following language groups must be obtained from the Microsoft Web site, rather than the installation CD-ROM?**
   a. Cyrillic
   b. Japanese
   c. Hebrew
   d. All of the above

2. **Through which of the following utilities can you manage and configure the system's input locales? (Choose all that apply.)**
   a. Keyboard
   b. Date/Time
   c. Regional Settings
   d. System

3. **If you obtained a system that originally had a translated version of Windows 2000 Professional installed, what would you have to do to use the Multilanguage version?**
   a. Upgrade the system.
   b. Install the MultiLanguage group.
   c. Format the drive and reinstall the operating system.
   d. Install the English version patch.

4. **Stan recently acquired a pen pal in Switzerland. The two agreed to write letters in Microsoft Works and send them via e-mail. To practice, Stan agreed to write in German and his pen pal in English. Stan is running Windows 2000 Professional English version, and his correspondent is using the French version. Which of the following must be true before they can proceed? (Choose all that apply.)**
   a. Stan must have the French language files.
   b. The pen pal must have the English language files.
   c. Stan must have the German language files.
   d. They must both upgrade to the Multilanguage version.

5. **Which of the following is the designation for a "normal" keyboard?**
   a. Dvorak
   b. English
   c. QWERTY
   d. American Standard

6. **With the English version of Windows 2000 Professional installed, are additional files copied when a new input locale using the English (Ireland) designation is added?**
   a. Yes
   b. No

5.3 Manage applications by using Windows Installer packages

INSTALLER PACKAGE • PRODUCT • FEATURE • COMPONENT

UNDERSTANDING THE OBJECTIVE

With Windows 2000, Microsoft introduced the Windows Installer service. This service ensures that all applications adhere to the same standards for installation. In addition, Administrators use it to update a group of systems to the same configuration.

WHAT YOU REALLY NEED TO KNOW

◆ An Installer package file is a database that contains the information on the application's installed state. It uses the .msi extension.

◆ Windows Installer is an operating system-based service that is part of Windows 2000 and is available in service packs for other Windows operating systems.

◆ Windows Installer hierarchically organizes applications into products, features, components, and resources.

◆ Windows Installer products are complete applications, such as Microsoft Office.

◆ Features are the individual pieces of an application, which can be configured during installation to one of the following settings: Installed on Hard Disk, Installed to Run from Source, Advertised, or Not Installed. Within Microsoft Office, for example, Excel, Works, PowerPoint, and Access are features.

◆ Components are the pieces that make up the application's features. For example, Word's components include the core programs, spelling checker, and so on.

◆ Resources are objects such as files, Registry settings, and shortcuts that are delivered via Windows Installer.

◆ Applications installed using the Windows Installer can be self-repairing. If the installation is missing or becomes damaged, this service attempts to reload the files the next time the user attempts to access them.

OBJECTIVES ON THE JOB

Because Windows Installer provides greater flexibility than do other installation methods, this service gives users and Administrators more options for using applications in a networked environment. For example, if the majority of workstations on your network have very little disk space available, you can set the standard for applications to be run from their source location, which could be a shared directory on the network. The Windows Installer service natively supports patches and upgrades. Administrators can easily use, Windows Installer packages to apply patches to network applications during installation, which are then rolled out to client computers. The Administrator can also modify an installer package to adjust the installation process.

PRACTICE TEST QUESTIONS

1. **Which of the following is assigned to a Windows Installer component to identify the component and prevent interference from other components?**
   a. GUID
   b. Keypath
   c. Component code
   d. Component ID

2. **Which of the following pieces of the installer process identifies the default method for installing application features?**
   a. Installer program
   b. Installer path
   c. Installer package
   d. Installer component

3. **Many features of Microsoft Office 2000 are not necessarily helpful to all users. These functions are accessible through the menus in the same manner as standard features like Spelling and Grammar. Which of the following installation settings is assigned to these features in the Windows Installer package?**
   a. Not Installed
   b. Advertised
   c. Installed to Run from Source
   d. Installed on Local Hard Disk

4. **Which of the following file types is used to modify an Installer package?**
   a. Customizations (*.cmt)
   b. Modifications (*.msm)
   c. Adjustments (*.msa)
   d. Transforms (*.mst)

5. **Which of the following Microsoft operating systems does not natively support the Windows Installer service? (Choose all that apply.)**
   a. Windows 2000 Professional
   b. Windows NT 4.0 Workstation
   c. Windows 98
   d. Windows 2000 Advanced Server

6. **Which of the following Windows 2000 Professional components is used to create Windows Installer package files for distribution?**
   a. WinInstall LE
   b. WinPackage
   c. Windows Installer
   d. None of the above

5.4 Configure and troubleshoot desktop settings

ACTIVE DESKTOP • DISPLAY SETTINGS • GROUP POLICIES

UNDERSTANDING THE OBJECTIVE

The Windows 2000 desktop encompasses the entire work area, and its settings control the look and feel of the interface. Although many configuration options are available, the desktop remains one of the most basic Windows components and is the most familiar to users.

WHAT YOU REALLY NEED TO KNOW

♦ You can configure the Start menu so that your most frequently used applications, folders, and Web sites are easily accessible.

♦ Items in the Programs menu are configured through the same method as the Start menu.

♦ Active Desktop is a feature that displays Internet content on the desktop instead of wallpaper.

♦ You use the Display Settings utility to specify the desktop's background and appearance, the screen saver settings, the display effects used, and the video device's advanced settings.

♦ Group policies can be configured to control how the Windows 2000 desktop is displayed and managed. By using group policies, you can prevent users from changing the Start and Program menus, hide some or all icons on the desktop, and secure the Active Desktop.

♦ Problems with the desktop are rare and typically relate to the Active Desktop or group policies. If a computer using Active Desktop to display a Web page is unable to reach the Web site, the desktop background color will be white.

OBJECTIVES ON THE JOB

Generally, the Windows desktop settings are unique for each user who logs on to a system. With group policies, however, desktop settings can be standardized to maintain a consistent look and feel. Group policies can also be used to secure the desktop configuration, ensuring that users do not change some or all of the settings. For example, all systems in a call center may be required to have the same background and color settings to provide continuity, no matter which user is logged on to the system.

PRACTICE TEST QUESTIONS

1. **Which of the following icons can be configured individually to be displayed on the desktop? (Choose all that apply.)**
   a. My Computer
   b. My Network Places
   c. Internet Explorer
   d. My Documents

2. **How do you list the items in the Programs menu alphabetically?**
   a. Manually drag them into position.
   b. Choose Alphabetize from the Taskbar and Start Menu utility.
   c. Right-click the menu and select Sort by Name.
   d. Select Sort Alphabetically from the Display utility.

3. **Which of the following commands is used to update the information displayed in Active Desktop?**
   a. Compare
   b. Update
   c. Search
   d. Synchronize

4. **To eliminate some confusion, the default Windows 2000 configuration hides which of the following effects?**
   a. Keyboard navigation indicators
   b. Large icons
   c. Dynamic screen fonts
   d. Transition effects

5. **Which of the following terms describes a group of font and color settings?**
   a. Appearance group
   b. Background item
   c. Appearance scheme
   d. Effects scheme

6. **Which of the following folders contains the desktop settings for all users?**
   a. Winnt\Settings\All Users
   b. Documents and Settings\All Users
   c. My Documents\All Users
   d. Program Files\Settings\All Users

7. **Expanded versions of Printers, Network and Dial-up Connections, and My Documents can be displayed automatically through the Start menu. How are these items configured?**
   a. Through the Start menu's Control Panel utility
   b. Through the Taskbar and Start menu utility's Advanced tab
   c. By dragging them to the Start menu from Explorer
   d. By right-clicking them in Explorer and selecting Add to Start menu

5.5 Configure and troubleshoot fax support

FAX DEVICE • FAX PRINTER • COVER SHEET • FAX SERVICE

UNDERSTANDING THE OBJECTIVE

The Windows 2000 Telephony subsystem provides full support for fax-capable modems. Fax processing is also supported through multifunction devices. Fax management is accomplished through the Fax service.

WHAT YOU REALLY NEED TO KNOW

◆ Although fax modems are telephony devices, faxing is actually grouped with printing. To add a new fax device, you use the Add Printer Wizard.

◆ When the system detects a fax device, Windows automatically installs the Fax service and a fax printer. You manage fax device properties through the Fax utility.

◆ When the Fax service is installed, the Fax group is added to the Start menu under Programs, Accessories, Communications. The options in this group include Fax Queue, Fax Service Management, Help, My Faxes, and Send Cover Page Fax.

◆ You use Fax Queue to manage fax jobs, including viewing fax job status and pausing, canceling, or restarting a fax. You can also access it by double-clicking the Fax printer icon in the Printers utility.

◆ You use the Fax Service Management utility to configure the fax device to receive faxes, set the number of rings before the fax device answers, specify the number of retries when sending a fax, and configure the security settings for the Fax service.

◆ Although fax printers cannot be shared, Windows 2000 Professional provides full security support for local users and groups for fax printers and the Fax service.

OBJECTIVES ON THE JOB

The first time you fax a document, you are prompted to fill in the user information in the Fax Control Panel utility. You can choose to enter the information at a later time. To do so, open the Fax utility and populate the fields in the User Information tab. From the Fax utility, you can also manage personal cover pages (four default cover pages are included), configure the Status Monitor, open the Fax Service Management Console, open Help, and add a fax printer. Regardless of how it is initiated, the Send Fax Wizard controls the transmission of the fax. In this wizard, you indicate the recipient, the fax number, the cover page, the subject line, and the schedule for sending the fax. You can also use dialing rules when sending a fax. To receive a fax, configure the fax device through the Fax Service Management Console.

PRACTICE TEST QUESTIONS

1. **Which of the following Fax service security settings is not allowed for the group Everyone by default?**
   a. View fax jobs
   b. Manage documents
   c. Manage fax jobs
   d. Submit fax jobs

2. **Jessica configured her network's printing architecture to utilize departmental printer managers. She wants to establish the same structure for her fax devices on the network. Which step should Jessica take to accomplish this goal?**
   a. Configure the fax printer so that the Fax Managers group is granted Full Control.
   b. Assign the Allow setting to the Departmental Managers for the Manage fax jobs, Manage fax service, and Manage fax devices permissions.
   c. Make the departmental managers become members of the Print Managers group.
   d. Because fax printers can't be shared, the structure cannot be the same.

3. **Which of the following must be manually configured before faxes can be received?**
   a. Set Enable Receive on the fax device's properties.
   b. Set the fax printer to Receive mode.
   c. Configure the User Settings for the fax device.
   d. Set the dialing properties for the fax device.

4. **Which of the following extensions is used to signify a fax cover page?**
   a. .fcp
   b. .fax
   c. .cov
   d. .doc

5. **Ken decides to install a Windows 2000 Professional system dedicated to sending and receiving faxes. His company frequently sends faxes to all of its clients, informing them of new products and special deals. To save money, Ken configured the fax service to send faxes only overnight, when long-distance rates are lower. Rather than hang around to monitor the fax system, which of the following can Ken use to automatically receive notification that faxes were sent successfully?**
   a. E-mail notification through the Printing Preferences option
   b. Windows message notification via the Fax Service Management Console
   c. Pager notification through the fax device's properties
   d. Exception reports through the Event Viewer

6. **Which of the following is not a default cover page included with the Fax service?**
   a. FYI
   b. From the desk of…
   c. Confidential
   d. Urgent

5.6 Configure and troubleshoot accessibility services

ACCESSIBILITY WIZARD • NARRATOR • MAGNIFIER • UTILITY MANAGER

UNDERSTANDING THE OBJECTIVE

Windows 2000 Professional includes a set of enhanced accessibility features that make computers easier to use for people with various disabilities. Specifically, you can customize the **UI** to assist users with vision, hearing, physical, or cognitive disabilities.

WHAT YOU REALLY NEED TO KNOW

◆ Customization of the UI is not limited to the desktop display. Rather, it includes alternative input methods such as speech recognition, alternative output methods such as voice synthesis, and better representation of screen elements.

◆ Use the Accessibility Wizard to configure Windows 2000 Professional's accessibility settings.

◆ To facilitate configuring a computer's accessibility settings, Windows 2000 groups the settings by the type of disability.

◆ The Windows 2000 Accessibility features include Utility Manager, Narrator, Magnifier, On-Screen Keyboard, SoundSentry, AutoComplete, MouseKeys, SerialKeys, BounceKeys or FilterKeys, StickyKeys, ToggleKeys, and the Dvorak keyboard layout.

◆ Users with cognitive disabilities such as Down syndrome or dyslexia most often benefit from using AutoComplete, AutoCorrect, and FilterKeys.

◆ Users with hearing difficulties may find features such as ShowSounds, SoundSentry, and modified sound schemes helpful when working on the system.

◆ Users who find it difficult to use the mouse or keyboard due to physical impairments often use the Keys features and On-Screen Keyboard.

◆ Visually impaired users, such as those with low vision or color blindness, often use Narrator, Magnifier, and the font and color settings to improve their computer access.

OBJECTIVES ON THE JOB

In addition to the accessibility features built into Windows 2000 Professional, other products and services are available to users with disabilities. Using these products, make sure that they have been tested and are supported by Windows 2000 Professional as well as Windows 2000 Server. One exception is the automatic logon feature, which is not supported by Windows 2000 Server. On Windows 2000 Professional systems, this feature can eliminate the need for the user to press Ctrl+Alt+Del to log on. Bear in mind that enabling this feature always logs the same user on to the computer. SerialKeys differs from the other features in that it is used to allow alternative pointing devices to access the system via the computer's COM port.

PRACTICE TEST QUESTIONS

1. **Which of the following accessibility features can be enabled by pressing the Shift key five times?**
   a. BounceKeys
   b. FilterKeys
   c. StickyKeys
   d. MouseKeys

2. **Which of the following accurately describes the role of the Utility Manager?**
   a. It groups all of the computer management utilities (Control Panel, System Monitor, and so on) into a single location.
   b. It displays the status of accessibility features and allows you to configure them.
   c. It monitors the myriad keyboard features and reports their status.
   d. It verifies that devices attached to the computer's COM port are responding.

3. **Christine experiences problems with arthritis and has difficulty moving the mouse. She wants to continue her research on the Internet, but is discouraged that she must use the mouse to move the cursor around the desktop. Which of the following features can Christine use to move the cursor via the keyboard?**
   a. MouseKeys
   b. FilterKeys
   c. SerialKeys
   d. On-Screen Keyboard

4. **Match each of the following accessibility components with its description.**

BounceKeys	a. Plays a sound when Caps Lock or Num Lock is pressed
StickyKeys	b. Displays closed-captioning information when available
ToggleKeys	c. Displays a visual cue when a sound is played
SoundSentry	d. Ignores repeated keystrokes and slows down the repeat rate
ShowSound	e. Allows users who cannot press multiple keys simultaneously to press keys one at a time

5. **Although it is useful for many people with visual impairments, which of the following may not be sufficient for users with very low vision capabilities?**
   a. Magnifier
   b. Large fonts
   c. High-contrast color schemes
   d. On-Screen Keyboard

Section 6

Implementing, Managing, and Troubleshooting Network Protocols and Services

6.1 Configure and troubleshoot the TCP/IP protocol

TCP/IP • IP ADDRESS • SUBNET MASK • DEFAULT GATEWAY • DNS • DHCP

UNDERSTANDING THE OBJECTIVE

TCP/IP is the primary protocol used on the Internet and the native protocol for Windows 2000. It is used to transport Windows 2000 network traffic as well as provide access to industry-standard Internet and intranet resources. TCP/IP is an extensive protocol suite that is covered in detail on the Network Infrastructure (70-216) exam.

WHAT YOU REALLY NEED TO KNOW

- ◆ Windows 2000 installs TCP/IP automatically during installation if a network device is present, or during configuration when a new network device is installed.

- ◆ The Windows 2000 TCP/IP implementation supports a number of features that were not available in earlier operating systems. These include **IPSec**, **APIPA**, **QoS**, and dynamic name resolution.

- ◆ Addressing in TCP/IP is handled by **IP**. IP addresses are 32 bits long and are written in dotted-decimal format.

- ◆ IP addresses are assigned automatically, using services such as DHCP and APIPA, or manually by the Administrator. You should dynamically assign addresses to Windows 2000 Professional systems that do not require a static IP address.

- ◆ IP addresses are divided into two sections: the host ID and the subnet ID. The subnet mask indicates which bits represent the subnet ID. Devices on the same subnetwork must have the same subnet ID.

- ◆ Most IP devices can initially communicate only with other devices on the same network.

- ◆ Multihomed systems are configured with more than one network adapter and are able to route traffic between networks.

- ◆ Because the Windows network architecture relies on computer names for identification, name resolution is very important. Associating a computer's name with its IP address is handled by **DNS** and **WINS**.

OBJECTIVES ON THE JOB

Whenever possible, use automatic address assignment. When properly configured by the Administrator, automatic address assignment ensures that all computers are correctly configured and no duplication exists. Many utilities and programs are available to troubleshoot TCP/IP configuration, including **IPCONFIG**, **NSLOOKUP**, System Monitor, and **PING**.

PRACTICE TEST QUESTIONS

1. **Which of the following is not a valid IP address?**
    a. 253.19.112.1
    b. 265.254.1.33
    c. 192.1.33.39
    d. 99.99.99.99

2. **Which of the following subnet masks allows for at least 65,000 devices per network?**
    a. 255.0.0.0
    b. 255.255.0.0
    c. 255.255.255.0
    d. 255.255.199.0

3. **Which of the following TCP/IP protocols is used to dynamically update a router's information tables? (Choose all that apply.)**
    a. RIP
    b. ICMP
    c. POP
    d. OSPF

4. **Group the following binary values with its decimal representation.**
    11101001   a. 39
    10110000   b. 176
    00100111   c. 204
    11111011   d. 86
    01010110   e. 233
    11001100   f. 251

5. **Kevin just installed a new Windows 2000 computer and manually assigned its IP address. After doing so, he is able to communicate with other computers on the same network, but not with computers on a different network. Which of the following settings is most likely wrong?**
    a. IP address
    b. Subnet mask
    c. Default gateway
    d. DNS server

6. **Which of the following addresses is reserved for loopback testing?**
    a. 156.24.88.02
    b. 255.255.255.0
    c. 192.156.0.0
    d. 127.0.0.1

OBJECTIVES

6.2 Connect to computers by using a virtual private network (VPN) connection

VPN • PPTP • L2TP

UNDERSTANDING THE OBJECTIVE

A **VPN** is created by making an encrypted connection between private networks over a public network such as the Internet. It provides all the security of a direct connection to a private network while taking advantage of the flexibility of the Internet.

WHAT YOU REALLY NEED TO KNOW

◆ VPN connections are created on Windows 2000 systems in the same manner as other connections, through the Network and Dial-Up Connections utility.

◆ VPN connections are created by encapsulating normal TCP/IP traffic within an encrypted transport protocol. This process is called tunneling.

◆ Windows 2000 Professional supports two protocols for VPN connections: **PPTP** and **L2TP**.

◆ PPTP is supported by many different operating systems and configurations, including Windows NT 4.0 Workstation and Windows 98.

◆ L2TP, a new protocol supported by only Windows 2000, is an enhancement to PPTP that uses **L2F** technology with PPTP to provide efficient, secure VPN connections. When attaching across a VPN, Windows 2000 automatically senses which protocol is being used.

◆ When you create a VPN connection, you are asked to specify the host name or IP address of the computer or network to which you are connecting, to state whether the connection is available to all users or just the current user, and to decide whether to enable **ICS** on the connection.

◆ If a VPN is established over a dial-up connection, you can specify that the dial-up connection be established before attempting the VPN connection.

◆ Because only certain users should be allowed access to the network from the Internet, many levels of authentication can be mandated for a VPN connection.

◆ To accept connections via VPN or other methods, you must create and configure a different connection type: an incoming connection.

OBJECTIVES ON THE JOB

To create an incoming connection, launch the Network Connection Wizard, choose Accept incoming connections, and then specify the connection over which incoming connections are allowed. You must then choose whether to allow incoming VPN connections. Next, select the list of users or groups to be allowed through the incoming connection as well as the networking components to enable for incoming connections. Finally, name the connection and click Finish.

PRACTICE TEST QUESTIONS

1. **By default, which of the following authentication protocols is enabled over VPN connections?**
   - a. MS-CHAP
   - b. PPTP
   - c. PAP
   - d. SPAP

2. **Through which of the following Labs in the Virtual Private Connection Properties dialog do you manually configure a connection for PPTP?**
   - a. Security
   - b. Sharing
   - c. Options
   - d. Networking
   - e. General

3. **You are in the process of configuring a VPN connection to your out-of-state headquarters. The system to which you are connecting is a Windows 2000 Advanced Server that supports 250 remote users worldwide. Which of the following tunneling protocols should you use for this connection?**
   - a. L2F
   - b. L2TP
   - c. PPTP
   - d. PPP

4. **To ensure the security of your VPN connection, which of the following encryption requirements should you use?**
   - a. No encryption allowed
   - b. Optional encryption
   - c. Require encryption

5. **Frances is a member of the Power Users and Backup Operators groups on a Windows 2000 Professional system. She was granted access to an incoming connection, but the groups of which she is a member did not receive such access. Can Frances access the computer across the incoming connection?**
   - a. Yes
   - b. No

6. **Which of the following tunneling technologies was developed by Cisco Systems?**
   - a. PPTP
   - b. L2F
   - c. L2TP
   - d. PPP

6.3 Create a dial-up connection to connect to a remote access server

RAS • RRAS • MS-CHAP • EAP • EAP-TLS • CHAP • SPAP

UNDERSTANDING THE OBJECTIVE

RAS is Microsoft's dial-in server offering. Available for Windows NT 4.0 and Windows 2000 as part of **RRAS**, it is used to configure and manage direct dial-in connections. The RRAS features also support advanced features like VPN.

WHAT YOU REALLY NEED TO KNOW

◆ RRAS is largely a server-based service. Therefore, the majority of the configuration steps are performed on the server.

◆ You can connect to a RAS server from a Windows 2000 Professional system by creating and configuring a dial-up connection.

◆ RAS supports many different authentication and encryption protocols, each providing a different level of security and efficiency.

◆ Secure user authentication validates the remote user's access through an encrypted user credential exchange. This authentication method is supported by RAS via the **EA**, **MS-CHAP** (v.1 and v.2), **CHAP**, and **SPAP** protocols. If the client cannot provide authentication, access is denied.

◆ Mutual authentication validates both ends of the connection by exchanging encrypted user credentials. Only the **EAP-TLS** and MS-CHAP v.2 protocols support mutual authentication. If neither party can perform authentication, the connection is terminated.

◆ Once the connection is created, you can configure the authentication and security settings through the connection's properties. Three basic security settings exist: Allow unsecured password, Require secured password, and Use smart card. When a secure password is required, you can use the Advanced settings to specify that your Windows logon identity and password be used by the connection.

◆ RAS uses TCP/IP-based protocols for transport and authentication, but it can also encapsulate other protocols such as **NWLink** and **NetBEUI**. As a consequence, RAS can be used to connect non-IP remote networks. These protocols are configured through the Network tab on the connection's properties sheet.

OBJECTIVES ON THE JOB

To securely and successfully use Windows 2000 Professional to attach to a RAS server, both systems must support enhanced authentication protocols. If the RAS server uses an operating system other than Windows 2000, consider upgrading the server. Always use the most secure authentication method available.

PRACTICE TEST QUESTIONS

1. Which of the following security settings ensures that the remote user is connecting from a specific location? (Choose all that apply.)
   a. Data encryption
   b. Callback
   c. Remote access lockout
   d. Caller ID

2. Which of the following methods do the CHAP protocols use for authentication of clients and servers?
   a. Unencrypted plain text
   b. Encrypted tunneling
   c. Challenge–response one-way encryption
   d. 128-bit two-way encryption

3. Which of the following mutual authentication protocols operates at the Transport level?
   a. EAP-TLS
   b. EAP
   c. MS-CHAP v.2
   d. MS-CHAP v.1

4. Which of the following authentication protocols is an enhancement to PPP?
   a. PPTP
   b. CHAP
   c. NLSP
   d. EAP

5. For which of these connections does the Windows 2000 RAS provide the underlying support?
   a. Incoming connections
   b. Local area connections
   c. Virtual private network connections
   d. Dial-up connections

6. The RAS settings on a Windows 2000 Professional computer can be standardized for all users by using which of the following system components?
   a. Group policies
   b. Users and Group Permissions
   c. Connection Security settings
   d. Protocol settings

6.4 Connect to the Internet by using Dial-Up Networking

DUN • PPP • SLIP • CSLIP • NETWORK AND DIAL-UP CONNECTIONS

UNDERSTANDING THE OBJECTIVE

Today, the vast majority of computers connect to the Internet at one time or another. Establishing a connection with the Internet is accomplished through the connections utilities.

WHAT YOU REALLY NEED TO KNOW

◆ **DUN** is a legacy service used since Windows 95 to connect client computers to RAS servers, other dial-up services, and the Internet. The services provided by DUN were merged with the networking services to create the Network and Dial-Up Connections service.

◆ Creating a connection for Internet access is most easily accomplished by running the Internet Connection Wizard.

◆ If you already have an **ISP**, it is far simpler to create a connection for the Internet through the Make New Connection Wizard in Network and Dial-Up Connections.

◆ By default, Internet connections are configured to use PPP with no intervention in the logon process. If your ISP indicates that settings other than these are needed, click the Advanced button before proceeding.

OBJECTIVES ON THE JOB

Most of today's ISPs use PPP as the default protocol for transport and do not require manual logins. Sometimes, however, you may need to change the settings. In addition to PPP, **SLIP** and **CSLIP** are supported. SLIP and CSLIP are used mostly to connect to UNIX systems and may be required by some ISPs. If your ISP assigns a static IP address to each user, rather than dynamically assigning addresses as needed, use the Advanced settings option in the Internet Connection Wizard or the Networking tab in the connection's properties sheet to change the settings.

PRACTICE TEST QUESTIONS

1. **Which of the following remote connection protocols supports compression beyond that of the original standard?**
   a. SLIP
   b. PPP
   c. CSLIP
   d. PPTP

2. **Link Control Protocol extensions must be enabled to support which of the following security features?**
   a. Caller ID
   b. Secure authentication
   c. Callback
   d. Mutual authentication

3. **To create an Internet connection that uses an ISDN modem and line, which type of connection should you choose in the Make New Connection Wizard?**
   a. Dial-Up Connection
   b. Local Area Connection
   c. Virtual Private Network Connection
   d. Incoming Connection

4. **Jonathan has used the same ISP for many years, and his computer is configured to use a static IP address and DNS server. Recently he received a message indicating that he needed to change his IP settings. As yet, Jonathan hasn't had time to make the changes. He has started experiencing sporadic failures when trying to reach some Web sites. Which of the following could be causing Jonathan's recent spate of connection problems? (Choose all that apply.)**
   a. The IP address assigned to his system has been automatically assigned to another user, and both are attempting to access the Internet.
   b. The ISP added a DNS server of which Jonathan's system is not aware.
   c. Jonathan's ISP did not complete its upgrade and some features are not yet available.
   d. Jonathan did not update the version of PPP used by his system.

5. **Through which of the following settings can you easily monitor activity on a connection, regardless of type?**
   a. System Monitor, "Network and Dial-Up Connections" counter
   b. Network and Dial-Up Connections, "Monitor all connections"
   c. Internet Connection Wizard, "Monitor Internet Connections"
   d. Connection properties, "Show icon on task bar when connected"

6.5 Configure and troubleshoot Internet Connection Sharing (ICS)

ICS • DNS • DHCP

UNDERSTANDING THE OBJECTIVE

ICS is a feature that was first introduced with Windows 98 Second Edition. Now supported by Windows 2000, it allows a computer with two connections to act as a gateway to the Internet for other computers on the network.

WHAT YOU REALLY NEED TO KNOW

◆ ICS is supported only on computers with two or more connections—that is, a network adapter and a modem, or two network adapters. One adapter connects to the local network, the other to the Internet.

◆ ICS is designed on the premise that the Windows 2000 computer manages the network configuration and Internet connection. The ICS computer is intended to be the only connection from the local network to the Internet.

◆ ICS will not work if the local network includes DNS or DHCP servers.

◆ ICS performs IP address assignment, network address translation, and name resolution for the local computers accessing the Internet. In fact, the ICS computer actually fulfills the role of DHCP server for the local network.

◆ Although ICS can be configured to use a dial-up line, the transmission rate would render this connection virtually useless.

◆ Be certain that you enable ICS on the adapter connecting to the Internet. Otherwise, the ICS system might respond to IP address requests from computers on the Internet, wreaking havoc with your ISP.

◆ If the Internet connection is a dial-up connection, you also have the option of enabling on-demand dialing. The ICS system can then establish a connection to the Internet if one of the client computers requests access.

◆ Configuring the local client computers to use the ICS system as their Internet gateway is easily accomplished. To do so, set the TCP/IP configurations to automatically obtain an IP address and DNS server addresses.

OBJECTIVES ON THE JOB

Many households today have more than one computer, and the number of multiple-computer homes is growing. ICS can be used to connect a home network to the Internet over a broadband line such as DSL or a cable modem. Small businesses often use ICS if all of the office's computers will access the Internet via a single Windows 2000 Professional ICS machine. To simplify the configuration process, rename the connections on the ICS computer before enabling Internet Connection Sharing. For example, a dial-up connection to MSN can be named "MSN Internet Connection," rather than "Dial-Up Connection."

PRACTICE TEST QUESTIONS

1. **When accessing the Internet through a Windows 2000 Professional system running ICS, which of the following computer configurations is supported?**
   - a. Macintosh G3
   - b. Windows 98 PC
   - c. Linux PC
   - d. Windows NT 4.0 Workstation PC
   - e. Windows 95 PC
   - f. All of the above

2. **By default, ICS configures the local area network with a Class C subnet mask. Which of the following represents the default subnet mask?**
   - a. 0.0.255.255
   - b. 255.255.255.0
   - c. 255.0.0.0
   - d. 0.255.255.255

3. **In the default configuration, how many computers, other than the ICS system, can be connected to the local network?**
   - a. 255
   - b. 254
   - c. 253
   - d. 252

4. **Chris configured ICS on his Windows 2000 Professional system and is sharing a dial-up connection to the Internet with his Windows 95 computer. After school one day, Chris came home, logged on to the Windows 95 system, and attempted to connect to the Internet. His attempt was unsuccessful. Which of the following is the most likely reason that Chris could not reach the Internet?**
   - a. On-demand dialing was not enabled on the shared connection.
   - b. The Windows 95 system's address conflicts with the ICS system.
   - c. Chris enabled Internet connection sharing on the network adapter.
   - d. The modem suffered a power surge and must be replaced.

5. **You've configured ICS and enjoyed some success in accessing the Internet from client computers on the local network. One system is having problems accessing specific Web sites, however. When you enter the URL, you are unable to connect to the site; if you enter the IP address, you are able to make a connection. What is the problem?**
   - a. The ICS computer is not properly resolving the name request.
   - b. The DNS configuration on the client computer is not set to automatic.
   - c. The DHCP configuration on the client computer is not set to automatic.
   - d. The WINS server at the ISP is not functioning properly.

6.6 Connect to shared resources on a Microsoft network

SHARE • UNC • MY NETWORK PLACES

UNDERSTANDING THE OBJECTIVE

Microsoft created a networking environment that is both user-friendly and secure. Connecting to shared resources on a network can be a straightforward, almost seamless process.

WHAT YOU REALLY NEED TO KNOW

- ◆ Perhaps the simplest method for accessing a shared resource is to directly connect to a resource that has already been configured. For example, a user's profile may be configured to assign drive letter M: to a shared folder on the network.

- ◆ Another method to access a shared resource on the network is to browse the network with Windows Explorer. Unless you know, or have a good idea of, the name of the server and share, this method can be tedious on a large network.

- ◆ If you know the exact name of the server and share, you can access the resource directly by entering the share's **UNC** path in any number of applications: My Computer, Windows Explorer, even the Run option in the Start menu.

- ◆ When you use the UNC to access a shared printer, the printer object opens. If you access a shared folder using its UNC, the folder opens in Windows Explorer but no folder list appears in the left pane.

- ◆ The UNC provides a method of identifying shared resources and servers on a network. All UNC addresses start with two backslashes (\\), followed by the server name, then the share name (for example, \\SERVERB\CDRIVE).

- ◆ When accessing a shared folder, the UNC path can be extended to include subdirectories and files within the folder. For example, to directly launch an Excel file called BUDGET, you can enter the following UNC: \\ACCTSERVER\ADMINFILES\FY00\BUDGET.XLS.

- ◆ Many Microsoft applications also give you the opportunity to access network resources. For example, the Office programs can browse the network through My Network Places or accept a UNC path for a share file.

OBJECTIVES ON THE JOB

Many methods for accessing shared resources exist. If problems arise when you attempt to access resources, first check that the resource is available. Next, try accessing the resource from another computer on the network. Also, verify that the user has sufficient permissions to access the resource in question.

PRACTICE TEST QUESTIONS

1. **Frank attempts to access a shared file on a server across the WAN in Houston. He has accessed this file a number of times in the past without incident. Now, when he enters the file's UNC in Microsoft Excel, he receives a message indicating that the device is not ready. What is causing this error?**
   a. The network connection to the server is down.
   b. The file is located on a shared CD-ROM and the disk is not in the drive.
   c. The Administrator has changed Frank's access permissions to the drive.
   d. Frank has mistyped the UNC path for the file.

2. **Brenda is asked to cover for another user while he is on vacation. She is granted access to the shared folder and can see its contents, but is unable to run the program located in the folder. Which of the following is the reason Brenda is experiencing difficulties?**
   a. She was not granted Full Control to the share.
   b. She was not made a member of the Everyone group.
   c. She was not granted the Read & Execute NTFS permission.
   d. She was not provided with the password needed to access the share.

3. **Kurt's network administrator asked him to configure his entire local D: drive to be shared on the network. When Kurt opens the drive's properties and accesses the Sharing tab, he sees that a share named D$ exists. Kurt assumes that the administrator has already done the work for him. Can other users on the network access his D: drive? Why or why not?**
   a. Yes, the existing share is sufficient.
   b. No, Kurt must set the permissions for the share.
   c. No, the existing share is an administrative share and cannot be accessed by remote users.
   d. No, Kurt does not have sufficient rights to assign new permissions to the share.

4. **As administrator for a small network, you recently implemented a much stricter security plan. A major issue was that the Everyone group was able to access Human Resources documents on the Human Resources Director's hard drive. No one complained when you mentioned restricting access to the folder, but you suspect that one of the technicians likes to snoop around. How can you monitor attempted access to the shared folder?**
   a. Configure alarms through the Shared Folders section of Computer Management.
   b. Configure e-mail alerts through the share's properties.
   c. Configure auditing through the share's properties.
   d. Configure tracing on the suspected snoop's system.

Section 7

Implementing, Monitoring, and Troubleshooting Security

7.1 Encrypt data on a hard disk by using Encrypting File System (EFS)

EFS • RECOVERY AGENT • RECOVERY POLICY

UNDERSTANDING THE OBJECTIVE

EFS is a new extension to NTFS. It uses symmetric key encryption and public key technology to protect sensitive files from unauthorized access. Only the file's owner can open and work with a protected file. Recovery agents can also be assigned to recover EFS objects in the event that data becomes lost.

WHAT YOU REALLY NEED TO KNOW

◆ EFS provides the highest level of security available with Windows 2000 Professional. It ensures that access is granted only to the file's or folder's owner. If the owner's encryption key becomes lost or damaged, then the file cannot be accessed normally.

◆ To facilitate recovery of encrypted data, Windows 2000 uses a recovery agent. This agent is automatically assigned a special certificate and private key that allows it to recover data based on the object's recovery policy.

◆ By default, the recovery agent is the local administrator on a stand-alone system, and the domain administrator on a system connected to a Windows 2000 Server-based network.

◆ Only Windows 2000 supports EFS.

◆ EFS cannot be used on compressed files or folders. To encrypt a file or folder that is currently compressed, you must first decompress the file and then encrypt it.

◆ Files or folders secured with EFS cannot be shared.

◆ Because EFS is part of NTFS, it cannot be implemented on FAT partitions. EFS-encrypted files or folders that are copied or moved from an NTFS partition to a FAT partition lose their encryption.

◆ In addition to encrypting files on the local computer, users can secure files with EFS on servers configured to support remote encryption.

◆ The recovery agent uses the cipher command to decrypt files whose encryption keys have been damaged or are unavailable.

◆ The recovery agent uses the Export command in Certificate Manager to back up the file encryption certificates and keys.

OBJECTIVES ON THE JOB

To facilitate administrative duties, encrypt a single folder on the local system and place all sensitive files in that folder. This approach is preferable to encrypting a single file, because temp files created by applications are not encrypted by default, even if the original file is encrypted. Cut and paste files into the folder; pasted files are automatically encrypted, whereas dropped files are not.

PRACTICE TEST QUESTIONS

1. **Which of the following users can delete an encrypted file or folder?**
   a. All users
   b. Any user with delete permission
   c. Only the recovery agent
   d. Only the owner

2. **To track unsuccessful attempts to access encrypted files, which of the following auditing options should you enable?**
   a. Read Data Failure through the object's Auditing tab
   b. Enable Auditing through the Certificate Manger
   c. Read Access Denied through the Event Viewer
   d. Track access attempts through Performance Monitor

3. **Which of the following must be in place to make a user (other than the default) become a recovery agent?**
   a. The computer must be configured as a stand-alone Windows 2000 Professional system.
   b. The user must be a member of the local Administrators group.
   c. The computer must be part of an Active Directory domain, and Certificate Services must be installed.
   d. Nothing; Windows 2000 Professional supports alternative recovery agents by default.

4. **Which of the following is used to disable EFS for a set of computers, users, or groups?**
   a. A blank data recovery agent policy
   b. Deselect Enable EFS through Computer Management Storage
   c. In each object's properties, select Disable EFS
   d. Specify the Administrator as the data recovery agent

5. **Which of the following steps is used to encrypt a file or folder on a Windows 2000 Professional system?**
   a. Through Windows Explorer, select the object and choose Encrypt from the File menu
   b. Through System, highlight the object, click Advanced, and then select Encrypt folder contents
   c. Through Computer Management, select the object and click Encrypt
   d. Through the object's properties, click Advanced, and then select Encrypt contents to secure data

6. **Through which of the following policies are recovery agents identified?**
   a. Private Key Policies, Agents—Data Recovery
   b. System Public Policies, Data Recovery Users
   c. Local Policies, Recovery Agents
   d. Public Key Policies, Encrypted Data Recovery Agents

7.2 Implement, configure, manage, and troubleshoot local security policy

POLICY • LOCAL SECURITY SETTINGS

UNDERSTANDING THE OBJECTIVE

A security policy is a group of permissions that specifies the security settings for a computer, desktop, or domain. On a Windows 2000 Professional system not connected to a domain, the local security policy controls the computer environment. On a computer connected to a domain, the domain's security policy overrides the local security policy.

WHAT YOU REALLY NEED TO KNOW

♦ The relationship between a computer and a security policy is similar to the relationship between a user and a group. In a domain environment, the same security settings can be applied to multiple computers through a security policy in the same way that groups apply security settings to many users.

♦ A security policy is applied when the system starts and can be refreshed without restarting the system if changes are made.

♦ Four security setting categories exist: Account Policies, Local Policies, Public Key Policies, and IP Security Policies on Local Machine.

♦ Account Policies include two groups of settings: Password Policy and Account Lockout Policy.

♦ Three Local Policies exist: Audit Policy, User Rights Assignment, and Security Options.

♦ Public Key Policies include only the Encrypted Data Recovery Agent policy.

♦ IP Security Policies on Local Machine does not include a subcategory. Policies in this category control IPSec communications.

♦ If the computer is connected to a domain and multiple policies are set for a user, group, or computer, then the most restrictive policy applies.

OBJECTIVES ON THE JOB

The extent of the security policy feature is not fully realized until the computer is connected to a Windows 2000 domain. When it is connected to a domain, the various settings can be applied to groups and computers within the domain, rather than to all users on the local computer. When a computer is configured as a stand-alone system, settings apply to all users that access the system locally. Review the available policies in each category to ensure that you have a complete picture of the local security policy on your system.

PRACTICE TEST QUESTIONS

1. **Through which of the following policy groups would you establish the list of users who can access the computer across the network?**
   a. User Rights Assignment
   b. Audit
   c. Password
   d. Security Options

2. **Which of the following policies is available on domain computers, but not on stand-alone Windows 2000 Professional computers?**
   a. Password
   b. Account Lockout
   c. Kerberos Authentication
   d. IP Security

3. **By default, which of the following settings is not configured?**
   a. Log on locally
   b. Reset account lock after
   c. Act as part of the operating system
   d. Disable Ctrl+Alt+Delete requirement for logon

4. **Virginia is concerned that the default Windows 2000 users are well known by hackers; she wants to ensure that these defaults are not used to access her computer. Which of the following policy settings can she use to protect against hacker attacks? (Choose all that apply.)**
   a. Rename the Administrator account
   b. Disable the Administrator account
   c. Rename the Guest account
   d. Access the computer from the network
   e. Enforce the password history
   f. Rename the Backup Users group

5. **By default, unless the Password never expires option is checked for a particular user, how many days can a user keep a password?**
   a. 30
   b. 36
   c. 42
   d. 49

6. **Which of the following policy group settings consists of only user and group lists?**
   a. Auditing Policies
   b. Group Policies
   c. Users Rights Assignment
   d. Security Options

7.3 Implement, configure, manage, and troubleshoot local user and group accounts

COMPUTER MANAGEMENT • LOCAL USERS AND GROUPS

UNDERSTANDING THE OBJECTIVE

User accounts are required to gain access to all Windows computers, whether those machines are part of a domain or operate by themselves as stand-alone systems. Local user accounts allow the user to directly log on to a computer and access its resources. Domain user accounts authenticate the user within the domain. The Windows 2000 Professional exam focuses on creating and managing local user accounts.

WHAT YOU REALLY NEED TO KNOW

◆ A local user account is required to access resources on the local computer. When a local user is created, his or her security settings are stored in a local security database, which is not shared with other computers on the network.

◆ A group of interconnected computers configured with local user and group accounts is called a peer-to-peer network. If a user must access a computer across such a network, a local user account must be created on that computer. Windows 2000 Professional computers that are domain members do not support local accounts.

◆ Two local user accounts are created automatically when the operating system is installed: Administrator and Guest. By default, the Guest user is disabled. You can rename these accounts, but you cannot delete them.

◆ During installation, you can also specify a new name for the Administrator user. This renaming does not prevent the creation of the Administrator user; it simply creates a new user with the same settings.

◆ Six local group accounts are created automatically during installation: Users, Replicators, Power Users, Guests, Backup Operators, and Administrators.

OBJECTIVES ON THE JOB

In a peer-to-peer environment, user accounts must be established for each person accessing the computers. For example, if Charles needs access to SYSA, SYSC, and SYSD, the Administrator must create a user account for him on each system. Use groups to logically organize the users on the system, and assign permissions and rights to groups rather than users. Establish and follow naming and password standards to provide for consistency and easy administration of the system. Recommended standards include always requiring a password (no blank passwords), user names that are at least five characters long, mixed-case passwords, and so on.

PRACTICE TEST QUESTIONS

1. **In addition to Computer Management, which of the following utilities allows you to perform limited user account management?**
   a. System
   b. Users and Passwords
   c. Control Panel
   d. Add/Remove Users

2. **Which of the following configuration options is available only through the Computer Management Local Users and Groups option?**
   a. Change Password
   b. Group Membership
   c. Profile
   d. User Name

3. **When establishing a naming convention for your users, which of the following should you take into consideration?**
   a. Users with the same name
   b. Identification of users by department as well as by name
   c. Permissions to be assigned to the users
   d. Invalid user name characters

4. **Tim and his family are adding a new Windows 2000 Professional computer to their peer-to-peer network. At this time, anyone in the family can sit down at any computer and access files on any other system. Tim would like to add the new system into the mix with minimal configuration, but the same functionality. Which of the following describes the steps that Tim must take when configuring his new system?**
   a. None; the network will recognize the new system and automatically load the user account information.
   b. If the Administrator password is the same on the new system as on the other computers, Tim must initiate the user data transfer.
   c. He must include the new system in the Domain Computers group on the other computers.
   d. He must create a user account for each family member on the new system.

5. **During the Windows 2000 Professional installation, you specified an alternative user name for the Administrator. Which of the following users was then automatically disabled?**
   a. Administrator
   b. Guest
   c. The user specified
   d. None of the above

OBJECTIVES

7.4 Implement, configure, manage, and troubleshoot auditing

AUDITING • LOGS

UNDERSTANDING THE OBJECTIVE

Through the Windows 2000 auditing feature, you can track the success or failure of attempts to access the computer's files, folders, printers, and other resources and events. To audit resources and events on a Windows 2000 Professional computer, you must create an audit policy and specify which events to audit.

WHAT YOU REALLY NEED TO KNOW

- ◆ Windows 2000 uses three logs—Application, System, and Security—to record information about use of the system. You can see these logs with Event Viewer.

- ◆ The Application and System Logs are automatically enabled. Windows 2000 uses them to report non-user-related events.

- ◆ To use the Security Log, you enable auditing for specific events through an audit policy.

- ◆ Configuring the audit policy allows you to track the following event types: Account Logon Events, Account Management, Directory Service Access, Logon Events, Object Access, Policy Change, Privilege Use, Process Tracking, and System Events.

- ◆ It is important to plan your audit policy before you enable any auditing features. Recording too many events will strain the system and render the data unusable because of its sheer volume.

- ◆ After establishing the audit policy, you must configure auditing for specific resources.

- ◆ Auditing for files and folders is available only on NTFS partitions.

- ◆ Logs are written on the computer on which the events occur. You can use Event Viewer to review logs on other systems.

OBJECTIVES ON THE JOB

After enabling auditing through Local Security Settings, you must configure auditing for each resource that will be monitored. For example, to record each time a user successfully accesses a color laser printer, you would go into the printer's properties sheet, access the Security tab, click Advanced, and select Auditing. You would then choose the Add the user or group to audit option, and select a level of auditing. With printers, you can track the success or failure of the following: Print, Manage Printers, Manage Documents, Read Permissions, Change Permissions, and Take Ownership.

PRACTICE TEST QUESTIONS

1. **Which of the following events requires two configuration steps for auditing? (Choose all that apply.)**
   a. Successful logon to the system
   b. Unsuccessful access to a printer
   c. Unsuccessful attempt to change the system's time
   d. Successful access to a shared folder

2. **Which of the following audit events is applicable only to Windows 2000 Professional computers that are part of a domain?**
   a. Logon Events
   b. Account Management
   c. Account Logon Events
   d. Privilege Use

3. **Pam is trying to identify a user who continues to attempt to access a file to which he or she does not have permission. Within Local Security Settings, she has enabled tracking for failed Privilege Use and has configured file auditing for failed Read Data and Write Data events. Will Pam successfully log the failed attempts to access the file?**
   a. No, she must track failed Object Access, not Privilege Use.
   b. No, she must track failed Read Attributes, not Read Data or Write Data.
   c. No, she has not configured Event Viewer for this function.
   d. Yes, she will log the failed attempts.

4. **To audit changes made to a printer's settings, which event would you use?**
   a. Change Permissions
   b. Read Permissions
   c. Manage Documents
   d. Manage Printers

5. **By default, what is the size of each Windows 2000 audit log?**
   a. 1024 KB
   b. 64 KB
   c. 128 KB
   d. 512 KB

6. **Which of the following Event Viewer settings ensures that no log data will be lost?**
   a. Overwrite Events Older Than X Days
   b. Allow Unlimited Log Size
   c. Do Not Overwrite Events
   d. Overwrite Events as Needed

7.5 Implement, configure, manage, and troubleshoot account settings

LOCAL USERS AND GROUPS • USERS AND PASSWORDS

UNDERSTANDING THE OBJECTIVE

Windows 2000 Professional user accounts offer a variety of configuration settings, which allow Administrators to control the user's interaction with the system to a greater degree.

WHAT YOU REALLY NEED TO KNOW

◆ The only field that is absolutely required when setting up a new user is the User name. Many of the other settings are recommended (for example, require a password), however.

◆ You can configure some user account settings through the Control Panel Users and Passwords utility. This utility does not provide all configuration options for a user account, however.

◆ The Users and Passwords utility has two tabs: Users and Advanced.

◆ When they are accessed through Users and Passwords, the user's properties are controlled through two tabs: General and Group Membership. When they are accessed through Local Users and Groups, the user's properties are managed through three tabs: a more extensive General tab, the Member Of tab, and the Profile tab.

◆ The Group Membership tab is a wizard-style dialog that presents three options: Standard User (which makes the user a member of the Power Users group), Restricted User (which makes the user a member of the Users group), and Other (which includes a drop-down list of all groups on the system).

◆ The Member Of tab lists the groups to which the user belongs.

◆ Once a user account has been created, any setting for it can be changed, including the user name.

OBJECTIVES ON THE JOB

The Users and Passwords utility is designed for less-experienced users. If you are comfortable with the process of creating user accounts and adjusting account settings, you will probably prefer to work with the Local Users and Groups utility. Unless you are using the computer in a secure environment or at home, you should not use the Password never expires option; it leaves the system open to repeated attempts at guessing the password.

PRACTICE TEST QUESTIONS

1. **Which of the following options is not available through Users and Passwords?**
   a. User cannot change password
   b. User name
   c. Description
   d. Full name

2. **Which of the following describes the utility for creating a new user through Local Users and Groups?**
   a. A wizard asks you to provide the user name and password on the first screen.
   b. A wizard asks you to provide the user name, full name, and description on the first screen.
   c. A dialog allows you to verify previously entered information.
   d. A dialog provides all possible options in one window.

3. **On the Profiles tab, which of the following settings identifies a list of commands to be run after the user is authenticated?**
   a. Home Folder
   b. Logon Script
   c. Authentication Commands
   d. Profile Path

4. **By default, new users are members of which of the following local groups?**
   a. Administrators
   b. Power Users
   c. Users
   d. Backup Operators

5. **Gail's weekly job responsibilities call for her to add new users to the systems' configurations. As her company has grown, Gail's job has become increasingly more time-consuming. This week, Gail has 13 people to add before 5:00 on Friday. Which of the following would be the most efficient method for Gail to add these new users?**
   a. Computer Management
   b. Domain Users and Groups
   c. Local Users and Groups
   d. Users and Passwords

6. **Which of the following accurately describes the method for accessing one user configuration utility from the other?**
   a. Users and Passwords, General tab, User Properties
   b. Users and Passwords, Advanced tab, Advanced button
   c. Local Users and Groups, Advanced tab, User Properties
   d. Local Users and Groups, General tab, Advanced button

OBJECTIVES

7.6 Implement, configure, manage, and troubleshoot account policy

MMC • GROUP POLICY

UNDERSTANDING THE OBJECTIVE

Windows 2000 Professional policies establish guidelines for system operation. From the minimum length of a user's password to the requirement for pressing Ctrl+Alt+Delete to log on, all aspects of the system are governed by policies. Working in conjunction with the local security policy, the account policies control many system settings.

WHAT YOU REALLY NEED TO KNOW

◆ You manage the group policy through the MMC Group Policy snap-in.

◆ Two account policy categories exist: Password Policies and Account Lockout Policies.

◆ The Password Policy options are as follows: Enforce password history; Maximum password age; Minimum password age; Minimum password length; Passwords must meet complexity requirements; and Store password using reversible encryption for all users in the domain.

◆ The Account Lockout Policy options are as follows: Account lockout duration; Account lockout threshold; and Reset account lockout counter after.

◆ Only the Store password using reversible encryption for all users in the domain option must be explained. This option is enabled only when end users connect to a Windows 2000 network with Macintosh computers.

OBJECTIVES ON THE JOB

To provide greater protection against outside attack, it is a good idea to enable and configure the account policy settings. Enforcing password history ensures that users cannot switch between two passwords (DENNIS1 and DENNIS2, for example). Password complexity requirements force users to adhere to the minimum password length and history settings, while also ensuring that passwords include capital letters, numbers, or special characters and do not contain the user's user name or full name. The Account Lockout Policy is invoked if a user fails to log on to a system for a consecutive number of attempts. The Account lockout duration setting specifies the length of time during which the user will be locked out of the system.

PRACTICE TEST QUESTIONS

1. **What is the default setting for the minimum password length?**
    - a. 4
    - b. 5
    - c. 3
    - d. 6

2. **If the maximum password age is 45, the password history setting is 6, and a user changes her password on January 1, when can she use the same password again?**
    - a. November 12 of the same year
    - b. September 28 of the same year
    - c. February 15 of the next year
    - d. January 15 of the next year

3. **What is the maximum password length supported by Windows 2000?**
    - a. 10
    - b. 12
    - c. 8
    - d. 14

4. **Kerry believes that a disgruntled employee is trying to access her boss's files after hours. So far, the employee has not been able to guess the boss's password, but that failure may end soon. Because she has no proof, Kerry does not want to confront the employee's boss at this time. How can she reduce the chance that the user will gain access without disturbing her boss?**
    - a. Set the minimum password age to 3
    - b. Set the account lockout threshold to 15
    - c. Set the lockout duration to 4 hours so that it will be reset by the time the boss comes in
    - d. Enable password history tracking

5. **With password complexity enabled, which of the following is not a valid password?**
    - a. Jazz1
    - b. austin
    - c. 32skadoo
    - d. BIGtime

7.7 Implement, configure, manage, and troubleshoot user rights

LOCAL SECURITY POLICY • USER RIGHTS

UNDERSTANDING THE OBJECTIVE

User rights are assigned to specific users or groups by the Administrator and are actually implemented as part of the local security policy. These security settings let users perform specific tasks (such as backing up files and directories). Rights should not be confused with permissions: Rights are associated with specific users and groups, whereas permissions are associated with specific objects.

WHAT YOU REALLY NEED TO KNOW

◆ User rights are classified into two categories: logon rights and privileges.

◆ Logon rights for local users control how those users access the system. Examples of logon rights include Log on locally and Deny access to this computer from the network.

◆ Privileges grant users the ability to interact with the system more closely. Examples of privileges include Create a pagefile and Lock pages in memory.

◆ You manage user rights through the Local Security Policy utility.

◆ You can configure 32 rights for a specific group or user account. These rights are displayed in a list that includes the local setting (a list of users configured for the right) and the effective setting (a list of users granted the right).

◆ Once a user has been added to the list and granted the right, he or she cannot be removed from the list.

◆ User rights are cumulative. If a user belongs to more than one group, all of the groups' rights are granted. For example, if a user is granted the ability to back up files through one group membership and the ability to change the system time through another membership, he or she can perform both tasks.

◆ In some cases, user rights override the permissions set for specific objects. For example, members of the Backup Operators group are granted the ability to read and back up all files on the system, even if permissions deny them access to those files.

OBJECTIVES ON THE JOB

When modifying the user rights for a system, you should use a number of groups rather than granting the rights to individual users. This approach simplifies administration. To disable a specific user's right, remove the user from the group with that right. You can also manage local user rights through the MMC Group Policy snap-in, which should be used in a Windows 2000 domain environment. For stand-alone systems, a local security policy is preferred.

PRACTICE TEST QUESTIONS

1. **By default, which of the following logon rights is not assigned to the Administrators group? (Choose all that apply.)**
   a. Log on locally
   b. Log on as batch job
   c. Access this computer from the network
   d. Log on as a service
   e. Deny logon as a batch job

2. **Which of the following groups is automatically granted the rights to back up and restore files? (Choose all that apply.)**
   a. Power Users
   b. Backup Operators
   c. Users
   d. Administrators
   e. Everyone
   f. Interactive

3. **Match each user right below with its description.**
   Bypass traverse checking
   Increase scheduling priority
   Profile a single process
   Modify firmware environment variables
   Lock pages in memory

   a. Lets the user monitor nonsystem processes through System Monitor
   b. Lets the user manage process execution through Task Manager
   c. Lets the user modify system variables via System Properties
   d. Lets the user prevent the system from paging data to virtual memory
   e. Lets the user navigate through directories he or she would not normally be able to access

4. **Which of the following user rights has the potential to allow users to grant themselves anonymous access to the system, thereby bypassing security settings?**
   a. Log on locally
   b. Create a pagefile
   c. Act as part of the operating system
   d. Load and unload device drivers

5. **Which of the following user rights are granted to members of the Power Users group, but not to members of the Users group?**
   a. Change the system time
   b. Log on locally
   c. Back up files and directories
   d. Generate security audits

7.8 Implement, configure, manage, and troubleshoot local user authentication

SAM • KERBEROS • KDC • NTLM

UNDERSTANDING THE OBJECTIVE

Before a user can be granted access to a Windows 2000 system, his or her identity must be authenticated. For stand-alone or workgroup Windows 2000 Professional systems, authentication occurs locally, by comparing the information provided by the user with the credentials in the **SAM** database.

WHAT YOU REALLY NEED TO KNOW

◆ Unlike the interaction that takes place with a domain-connected computer, user authentication on a stand-alone or workgroup Windows 2000 Professional system occurs locally. This authentication method is known as interactive logon.

◆ The Windows 2000 system stores local user and security information in a SAM database. Users authenticated in this manner are granted access only to local resources.

◆ With Windows 2000, the Kerberos v.5 authentication protocol is used as the primary method of local and remote authentication.

◆ Kerberos is an industry-standard, IP-based authentication. **NTLM** is the legacy authentication method supported by Windows NT 4.0.

◆ Even if the Windows 2000 Professional system is configured for autologon, authentication is still taking place. The system merely uses a predetermined user name and password for authentication.

OBJECTIVES ON THE JOB

In everyday application, local user authentication on a Windows 2000 Professional system takes place almost seamlessly. The authentication process occurs transparently, and failures are almost entirely user-related. If you experience problems when logging on to a Windows 2000 computer as a local user, first verify that the user name is permitted access and that the password is correct. User names are not case-sensitive, but passwords are. Try logging on to the system with another user name, preferably the user name of a member of the Administrators group. If you succeed in accessing the system with another user name, verify the policy and permissions settings for the computer before attempting another logon. If it is configured, review the Security Log to help pinpoint the reason for the failure. For this exercise to be effective, you must have auditing enabled and configured to record failed logon events.

PRACTICE TEST QUESTIONS

1. **Which of the following illustrates the difference in the authentication procedures for workgroup computers and stand-alone computers?**
   a. Workgroup authentication is performed on a remote system.
   b. Stand-alone authentication provides access only to local resources.
   c. Workgroup authentication is performed with the SAM database.
   d. No differences exist between workgroup and stand-alone authentication.

2. **Which of the following network configurations can utilize the Kerberos authentication method?**
   a. A Windows NT 4.0 Workstation accessing a Windows NT 4.0 Server
   b. A Windows 2000 Professional system accessing a Windows NT 4.0 Server
   c. A Windows NT 4.0 Server connecting to a Windows 2000 Server
   d. A Windows 2000 Professional system accessing a Windows 2000 Server

3. **Which of the following authentication methods is employed on systems that do not use interactive logon?**
   a. Passive logon
   b. Network authentication
   c. Remote authentication
   d. Domain logon

4. **Which of the following system components defines file system and share permissions?**
   a. ACLs
   b. KDCs
   c. TCPs
   d. SAMs

5. **Which authentication protocol utilizes a challenge–response architecture?**
   a. Kerberos v.4
   b. TCP/IP
   c. NTLM
   d. Kerberos v.5

6. **Which of the following most accurately describes authentication on peer-to-peer networks?**
   a. Centralized
   b. Decentralized
   c. Mobile
   d. Diverse

7.9 Configure and troubleshoot domain user accounts

ACTIVE DIRECTORY • USERS AND COMPUTERS

UNDERSTANDING THE OBJECTIVE

Typically, a Windows 2000 Professional system will be connected to a domain-based network. On this type of network, authentication occurs on the domain controller. Domain user groups are managed by Domain Administrators, and their settings are configured on the domain controllers.

WHAT YOU REALLY NEED TO KNOW

- ◆ Windows 2000 has moved away from the classic domain model and toward Active Directory. Nevertheless, Windows 2000 computers remain able to participate in a legacy domain configuration.

- ◆ A member of the Domain Administrators group must configure domain users and groups. Prior to the introduction of Windows 2000, user maintenance took place on the domain controller system itself. That approach is no longer necessary with Windows 2000 Active Directory system; the MMC snap-in can be launched from any domain-connected Windows 2000 computer.

- ◆ User objects in the Active Directory structure include many more configuration options. The user object's properties include the following tabs: General, Address, Account, Profile, Telephones, Organization, Remote Control, Terminal Services Profile, Member Of, Dial-in Environment, and Sessions.

- ◆ Active Directory is designed to function as a repository for user and group information. It can serve as the central database for storing phone numbers, e-mail addresses, and more. Many of the configuration options are applicable for information purposes only and are not required for the user to be granted access.

- ◆ Another feature available with Active Directory that is not available to local users and groups is the ability to copy a user. This feature offers many benefits, such as eliminating the need to duplicate a known-good user's configuration.

OBJECTIVES ON THE JOB

If your Windows 2000 Professional system is part of a domain, plan to take advantage of the many domain-related features available, particularly if the computer has a Windows 2000 Server-based Active Directory configuration. For example, you can utilize the informational fields provided in the user properties sheet. In a networking environment, having too much information is better than having too little. Similar to the situation with locally authenticated users and groups, domain user access and authentication occur transparently to the user. If problems arise, you should first verify that the user name and password are correct and that the appropriate password case is being used. If the domain controller is not available to authenticate a user, check whether other users are experiencing difficulties, and verify permissions and policies for both the user and the groups to which that user belongs.

PRACTICE TEST QUESTIONS

1. **Which of the following user properties is concerned solely with Terminal Services?**
   a. Environment
   b. Account
   c. Remote Control
   d. Address

2. **For a domain user, on which of the following tabs would you change the user name?**
   a. General
   b. Address
   c. Account
   d. Profile

3. **When accessing a Windows 2000 Active Directory domain from a Windows 95 computer, the user and/or computer must be a member of which of the following groups?**
   a. Legacy Access Support
   b. Power Users
   c. Compatibility Support Users
   d. Pre-Windows 2000 Compatible Access

4. **Which of the following policy areas is available only for domain computers and controllers?**
   a. Public Key Policies
   b. Kerberos Policies
   c. Scripts
   d. Audit Policy

5. **Which of the following utilities is disabled on domain controllers?**
   a. Event Viewer
   b. Local Users and Groups
   c. Shared Folders
   d. Disk Management

6. **Which of the following utilities brings many of the Server utilities together within a single interface?**
   a. Computer Manager
   b. System Manager
   c. Configure Your Server
   d. Control Panel

7.10 Implement, configure, manage, and troubleshoot a security configuration

SECURITY TEMPLATES • SECURITY AND CONFIGURATION ANALYSIS

UNDERSTANDING THE OBJECTIVE

Windows 2000 includes a new set of tools designed to facilitate security standardization, implementation, and analysis. The Security Configuration Tool Set ties the various security-related utilities into a single, centralized interface. In addition, the security tools let you copy one computer's security configuration, including policies, file system settings, and Registry options, to another computer.

WHAT YOU REALLY NEED TO KNOW

◆ The Windows 2000 Security Configuration Tool Set includes two MMC snap-ins (the Security Templates snap-in and the Security Configuration and Analysis snap-in), an extension to the Group Policy utility (the Security Settings extension), and a command-line utility (SECEDIT.EXE).

◆ The Security Templates snap-in allows you to create plain-text security files that can be used as the basis for the security configuration of another system. These template files contain the settings for all security areas on a system.

◆ The Security Configuration and Analysis snap-in enables you to configure all security settings from a single interface. Also included in this snap-in are utilities for analyzing the system's current security configuration and comparing it to a template so as to identify any differences.

◆ The Security Settings extension lets Administrators configure both local and domain security policies.

◆ SECEDIT is a command-line version of Security Configuration and Analysis.

◆ Windows 2000 includes a set of templates that are geared toward various configurations. For example, BASICWK.INF is designed for Windows 2000 Professional systems.

◆ Before you can analyze your system's security configuration, you must create a security setting database.

OBJECTIVES ON THE JOB

Proceed with caution when using the security-related tools. Before configuring the system with a new security setting, for example, back up the current settings by using the Export command in Security Configuration and Analysis. You can then reapply the old configuration if a failure should occur.

PRACTICE TEST QUESTIONS

1. **Which of the following Security Configuration and Analysis settings ensures that members of the default Windows 2000 groups are strictly controlled?**
   a. Restricted Groups
   b. Managed Groups
   c. System Services
   d. Group Services

2. **Through the System Services configuration tree, which settings are available?**
   a. Enabled or Disabled
   b. Automatic Startup
   c. Permission Level
   d. Allowed Groups

3. **After analyzing your system's security settings, how can you tell which settings do not match the database? (Choose all that apply.)**
   a. Review the log file for mismatch messages
   b. Check the template for incorrect settings
   c. Check the rights list for icons marked with a red X
   d. Review the database configuration file

4. **Which SECEDIT switch would you use to work only with the User Rights security-setting group?**
   a. /settings=USER_RIGHTS
   b. /USER_RIGHTS
   c. /config=USER_RIGHTS
   d. /area USER_RIGHTS

5. **Which of the following security areas is used to configure security settings for a dual-boot FAT32 partition?**
   a. File System
   b. System Services
   c. Registry
   d. None of the above

6. **Which of the following predefined security templates is designed to update specific settings but exclude settings that are not being modified? (Choose all that apply.)**
   a. HISECWS.INF
   b. OCFILESW.INF
   c. BASICSV.INF
   d. COMPATWS.INF

ANSWER KEY

Section 1.0

Objective 1.1

Practice Questions:

1. a
2. c
3. b, c
4. b, c, d
5. c

Objective 1.2

Practice Questions:

1. b
2. b
3. d
4. a
5. d

Objective 1.3

Practice Questions:

1. a
2. b
3. c
4. c
5. d
6. d
7. a, b, d

Objective 1.4

Practice Questions:

1. b, c
2. b
3. a, b, d
4. b
5. a, c, d
6. d
7. a

Objective 1.5

Practice Questions:

1. c, d
2. d
3. a
4. d
5. Provide Defaults(c), Fully Automated(d), Hide Pages(a), Read Only(e), GUI Attended(b)
6. a, b, d

Objective 1.6
Practice Questions:
1. a
2. b
3. a, c
4. c

Objective 1.7
Practice Questions:
1. c
2. a
3. b
4. c
5. b
6. d

Objective 1.8
Practice Questions:
1. b
2. b, c
3. a
4. c

Objective 1.9
Practice Questions:
1. d
2. a
3. a
4. b
5. c
6. b

Objective 1.10
Practice Questions:
1. a, d
2. a, c
3. c
4. b, d
5. a
6. b

Section 2.0

Objective 2.1
Practice Questions:
1. c
2. a
3. d
4. a
5. b
6. c
7. d

Objective 2.2
Practice Questions:
1. c
2. b
3. d
4. a
5. d
6. b

Objective 2.3
Practice Questions:
1. c
2. b
3. a, b, d
4. a
5. b
6. b

Objective 2.4
Practice Questions:
1. c
2. d
3. a
4. b
5. d
6. a, c, d

Objective 2.5
Practice Questions:
1. c
2. b
3. b
4. a
5. c
6. b
7. a

Objective 2.6
Practice Questions:
1. a, c
2. c, d
3. d
4. b
5. c
6. a, b, d

Objective 2.7
Practice Questions:
1. c,
2. b, c, d
3. a
4. d
5. a, d
6. d

Objective 2.8
Practice Questions:
1. c
2. a
3. b
4. b
5. c
6. b

Objective 2.9
Practice Questions:
1. b
2. d
3. a
4. b
5. d
6. c
7. a

Objective 2.10
Practice Questions:
1. a
2. b
3. d
4. c
5. d
6. c
7. a

Objective 2.11

Practice Questions:
1. b
2. b
3. b
4. c
5. a
6. c

Objective 2.12

Practice Questions:
1. b, d
2. b
3. b
4. c
5. c

Objective 2.13

Practice Questions:
1. b
2. a, b, d
3. c
4. a
5. d
6. b
7. c

Objective 2.14

Practice Questions:
1. a, c
2. b
3. d
4. spanned volume(d), boot partition(b), striped volume(a), system partition(c)
5. a, b, c
6. b
7. a

Objective 2.15

Practice Questions:
1. a, c
2. a
3. d
4. b
5. d
6. c
7. c

Objective 2.16

Practice Questions:

1. b
2. c
3. c
4. d
5. a, c
6. d

Section 3.0

Objective 3.1

Practice Questions:

1 a
2. c
3. a
4. b
5. b
6. d

Objective 3.2

Practice Questions:

1. c
2. a
3. b
4. b, c, d
5. d

Objective 3.3

Practice Questions:

1. b
2. c
3. b
4. d

Objective 3.4

Practice Questions:

1. b, c
2. a
3. a, c
4. d
5. b

Objective 3.5

Practice Questions:
1. Differential (c), Normal (a), Daily (b), Incremental (d)
2. c
3. a
4. b
5. b

Objective 3.6

Practice Questions:
1. d
2. a
3. b
4. c
5. b
6. b

Objective 3.7

Practice Questions:
1. b
2. a
3. c
4. c
5. b, c
6. d

Objective 3.8

Practice Questions:
1. c
2. b
3. c
4. a, c, d
5. c
6. b

Objective 3.9

Practice Questions:
1. c
2. d
3. a, c
4. d
5. b
6. c

Objective 3.10

Practice Questions:
1. c
2. a
3. a
4. a, c, d
5. d

Objective 3.11

Practice Questions:
1. a, b, d
2. c
3. a
4. d
5. b, d
6. d

Objective 3.12

Practice Questions:
1. b
2. d
3. a, b
4. d

Section 4.0

Objective 4.1

Practice Questions:
1. c
2. a, c
3. b
4. b
5. b
6. a

Objective 4.2

Practice Questions:
1. a, b, c
2. d
3. c
4. b

Objective 4.3

Practice Questions:
1. d
2. b
3. a, c
4. d
5. c
6. b

Objective 4.4

Practice Questions:
1. b
2. c
3. a
4. c
5. d
6. a

Objective 4.5

Practice Questions:
1. a
2. d
3. d
4. a
5. b, d
6. c

Objective 4.6

Practice Questions:
1. b, d
2. c
3. a
4. a, b
5. c
6. b

Section 5.0

Objective 5.1

Practice Questions:
1. a
2. a=Users and Groups, b=Users and Groups, c=System, d=System, e=Users and Groups
3. d
4. b
5. d
6. b

Objective 5.2
Practice Questions:
1. a
2. a, c
3. c
4. b, c
5. c
6. b

Objective 5.3
Practice Questions:
1. c
2. c
3. b
4. d
5. b, c
6. d

Objective 5.4
Practice Questions:
1. b, c, d
2. c
3. d
4. a
5. c
6. b
7. b

Objective 5.5
Practice Questions:
1. c
2. d
3. a
4. c
5. a
6. b

Objective 5.6
Practice Questions:
1. c
2. b
3. a
4. ToggleKeys(a), ShowSound(b), SoundSentry(c), BounceKeys(d), StickyKeys(e)
5. a

Section 6.0

Objective 6.1

Practice Questions:
1. b
2. b
3. a, d
4. 11101001=233 (e), 10110000=176 (b), 00100111=39 (a), 11111011=251 (f), 01010110=86 (d), 11001100=204 (c)
5. c
6. d

Objective 6.2

Practice Questions:
1. a
2. d
3. b
4. c
5. a
6. b

Objective 6.3

Practice Questions:
1. b, d
2. c
3. a
4. d
5. c
6. a

Objective 6.4

Practice Questions:
1. c
2. c
3. a
4. a, b
5. d

Objective 6.5

Practice Questions:
1. f
2. b
3. c
4. a
5. b

Objective 6.6
Practice Questions:
1. b
2. c
3. b
4. c

Section 7.0

Objective 7.1
Practice Questions:
1. b
2. a
3. c
4. a
5. d
6. d

Objective 7.2
Practice Questions:
1. a
2. c
3. b
4. a, c
5. c
6. c

Objective 7.3
Practice Questions:
1. b
2. c
3. a, b, d
4. d
5. b

Objective 7.4
Practice Questions:
1. b, d
2. c
3. a
4. d
5. d
6. c

Objective 7.5

Practice Questions:

1. a
2. d
3. b
4. c
5. c
6. b

Objective 7.6

Practice Questions:

1. c
2. a
3. d
4. c
5. b

Objective 7.7

Practice Questions:

1. b, d, e
2. b, d
3. Bypass traverse checking (e), Increase scheduling priority (b), Profile a single process (a), Modify firmware environment variables (c), Lock pgs in memory (d)
4. c
5. a

Objective 7.8

Practice Questions:

1. a, c
2. c
3. d
4. b
5. b
6. c

Objective 7.9

Practice Questions:

1. d
2. d
3. b
4. a
5. c
6. b

Objective 7.10

Practice Questions:

1. a
2. b
3. a, c
4. d
5. d
6. a, b, d

GLOSSARY OF ACRONYMS AND ABBREVIATIONS

A

ACPI – Advanced Configuration and Power Interface
AGP – Accelerated Graphics Port
APIPA – Automatic Private IP Addressing
APM – Advanced Power Management

B

BPP – Bits Per Pixel

C

CDFS – Compact Disk File System
CD-R – Compact Disk-Recordable
CD-RW – Compact Disk -Rewritable
CD-ROM – Compact Disk-Read Only Memory
CHAP – Challenge Handshake Authentication Protocol
CRT – Cathode Ray Tube
CSLIP – Compressed Serial Line Internet Protocol

D

Dfs – Distributed File System
DHCP – Dynamic Host Configuration Protocol
DNS – Domain Name Service
DUN – Dial-Up Networking
DVD – Digital Versatile Disk
DVD-WO – Digital Versatile Disk- Write Once
DVD-ROM – Digital Versatile Disk-Read Only Memory
DVD-RAM – Digital Versatile Disk-Random Access Memory

E

EAP – Extensible Authentication Protocol
EAP-TLS – Extensible Authentication Protocol, Transaction-level Security
EFS – Encrypting File System
ERD – Emergency Repair Disk

F

FAT – File Allocation Table
FTP – File Transfer Protocol

G

GDI – Graphics Device Interface
GUI – Graphical User Interface

H

HCL – Hardware Compatibility List
HID – Human Interface Device
HTML – Hypertext Markup Language
HTTP – Hypertext Transport Protocol

I

ICS – Internet Connection Sharing
IIS – Internet Information Services
I/O – Input/Output
IP – Internet Protocol
IPCONFIG – IP Configuration
IPP – Internet Printing Protocol
IPSec – IP Security
IrDA – Infrared Data Association
ISA – Industry Standard Architecture
ISP – Internet Service Provider

L

L2F – Layer Two Forwarding
L2TP – Layer Two Tunneling Protocol
LAN – Local Area Network
LPT – Line Printer

M

MMC – Microsoft Management Console
MFP – Multifunction Peripheral
MS-CHAP – Microsoft Challenge Handshake Authentication Protocol

N

NetBEUI – NetBIOS Enhanced User Interface
NNTP – Network News Transport Protocol
NSLOOKUP – Name Server Lookup
NTFS – New Technology File System
NTLM – Windows NT LAN Manager
NWLink – NetWare link

P

PCI – Peripheral Computer Interface
PDA – Personal Digital Assistant
PING – Packet Internet Groper
PPTP – Point-to-Point Tunneling Protocol
PWS – Peer Web Services

Q

QoS – Quality of Service

R

RAS – Remote Access Services
RF – Radio Frequency
RIS – Remote Installation Services
RRAS – Routing and Remote Access Service

S

SAM – Security Accounts Manager
SID – Security ID
SLIP – Serial Line Internet Protocol
SMP – Symmetric Multiprocessing
SMTP – Simple Mail Transfer Protocol
SPAP – Shiva Password Authentication Protocol

T

TCP/IP – Transmission Control Protocol/Internet Protocol

U

UDF – Universal Disk Format
UI – User Interface
UNC – Universal Naming Convention
URL – Uniform Resource Locator
USB – Universal Serial Bus

V

VPN – Virtual Private Network

W

WAN – Wide Area Network
WHQL – Windows Hardware Quality Lab